Sociology Explained

ANDY BARNARD AND TERRY BURGESS

CAMBRIDGE
UNIVERSITY PRESS

Published by the Press Syndicate of the University of Cambridge
The Pitt Building, Trumpington Street, Cambridge CB2 1RP
40 West 20th Street, New York, NY 10011-4211, USA
10 Stamford Road, Oakleigh, Melbourne 3166, Australia

© Cambridge University Press 1996

First published 1996

Printed in Great Britain at the University Press, Cambridge

A catalogue record for this book is available from the British Library

ISBN 0 521 42671 5 paperback

Cover illustration by Elaine Cox
Line illustrations by Gerry Ball (4, 8, 13); map by Jeff Edwards (355)

Acknowledgements

Many people have helped in the completion of this book. In particular the author would
like to thank Spencer Phelan and Suzanne Quinney, who wrote some of the sections; Pam
Robinson, who typed the manuscript; the staff at CUP; and Richard Croucher, Spencer
and Jo, who kick-started him into teaching and writing.

The author and publisher are grateful to the following for permission to reproduce illustra-
tions: 95, Graham Turner/*Guardian*; 105, Laurie Sparham/Network; 168, Hulton Deutsch
Collection; 186, Ford Motor Company Photographic Service; 230, United Artists (The
Kobal Collection); 248 Steve Bell; 285, Stephanie Henry/Format Pictures; 373, Eason/
Hulton/© Steve Eason; 451, Popperfoto

The extract from *Animal Farm* (8–9) is copyright © The estate of the late Sonia Brownell
Orwell and Martin Secker and Warburg Ltd; Tables 3.3, 3.4 and 9.3 are reproduced by permission of Oxford University Press; and all tables from *Social Trends* and the *Labour Force Survey*,
as well as Tables 4.3, 6.3, 10.3 and 10.4, are Crown copyright and are reproduced with the
permission of the Controller of HMSO.

Every effort has been made to reach copyright holders; the publishers would like to hear
from anyone whose rights they have unwittingly infringed, in particular Carl Uytterhaegen
(121), whom we have been unable to locate.

Contents

ANDY BARNARD

Midway through the writing of this book, Andy was admitted to hospital with what was later diagnosed as heart disease. He died after a short illness in November 1993. He was 37.

This book is for Linda, Natalie, Erika, Stefan and Daniel.

1 Theory and methods

Schools of sociology are an invention of the writers of textbooks.

Ronald Fletcher, Comte Memorial Lecture, 1966

INTRODUCTION

In this chapter you will examine a variety of sociological perspectives. The discussion focuses on functionalism and Marxism as examples of the structural viewpoint and then goes on to look at Max Weber and phenomenology. You will then look at the question of whether sociology can be scientific in its approach. Values and their place in sociology are then examined. The range of methods used in sociology and how they relate to the perspectives discussed earlier, as well as the relationship between sociology and social policy, are also discussed.

Perspectives and 'perspectivitis'

Most sociology textbooks, this one included, present sociology as a divided discipline, with a marked cleavage between two philosophical traditions. Figure 1.1 reflects the commonly accepted structure of sociological perspectives.

Figure 1.1

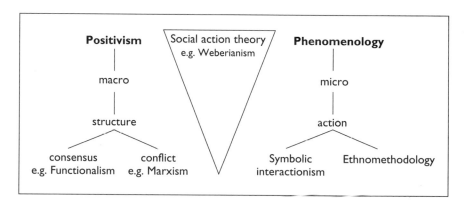

Positivism and phenomenology

Positivism and phenomenology are the philosophical roots or traditions from which the main perspectives in sociology have evolved. Positivism, a term first brought into use by Auguste Comte (1798–1857), holds that all knowledge can be based on science and scientific thought, and that all behaviour, whether of objects or of people, is subject to general laws. The possibility of identifying these laws inspired a generation of mid-to-late nineteenth-century theorists in many areas of knowledge, although the extent of its influence on writers such as Marx and Durkheim remains under dispute.

The term phenomenology is most closely associated with Edmund Husserl (1859–1938), and in sociology with Alfred Schutz (1899–1959). In this tradition the belief is that positivism's search for social causes is illusory, falling into the trap of determinism. Phenomenology denies that social behaviour, like the movement of atoms and molecules, is determined by external forces which are beyond human control. All that can realistically be achieved is an understanding of how people, individually and collectively, interpret, understand and place meaning on their social reality. Phenomenologists assert that people possess a greater degree of free will than positivist sociologists are willing to admit.

Structure and action

The debate between the two camps of sociology can also be seen as one between the concepts of structure and action. For the structuralists, sociology should be the study of the effects of the structure of society on social life – the macro or large-scale view. Patterns created by structures such as religion, the family, organisations or, for Marxists, capitalist relations of production, are seen to be the starting point in explaining anything in society. The analysis begins at a structural level. Hence some may argue that an increase in unemployment can lead to an increase in the crime rate, or that social disintegration is the cause of suicide. 'Social facts' exist as definite realities.

Other sociologists, taking the micro or small-scale view, doubt the validity of this position. The idea of a social structure is an abstract one, assuming a world 'out there' for us to investigate. The truth is that we are already in that world, with each of us having very different assumptions of what it looks like. They argue that the search for structural clues to social causes and effects should be abandoned in favour of piecing together the way individuals and groups make sense of the world they live in. This involves the analysis of social action, not the intangible structures they are thought to inhabit. 'Social facts' do not exist but are created and constructed in the process of social interaction.

These two approaches can be compared to a telescope. One end will show everything in enlarged form and in great detail (the microview), the other will display a world that is small and distant (the macroview). Both are 'true' pictures of the same thing. In sociology, there is no agreement about which approach is best or how the two can be made compatible.

Marxism and functionalism

Marxism and functionalism are seen as two perspectives both of which look at how the structure of society determines behaviour.

Symbolic interactionism and ethnomethodology

Symbolic interactionism and ethnomethodology are presented as perspectives emphasising small-scale understanding of how groups and individuals structure their perception of action and meaning in society. Somewhere in between the two is the tradition emanating from Max Weber, which explores the possibility of uniting theories of structure and action in society.

This view of sociology is certainly taken by the dominant examining board at A-level, the Associated Examining Board (AEB), where a typical exam question, implicitly or explicitly, amounts to 'Compare and contrast Marxist and interactionist views of sociology', and most textbooks are written to cater for this demand.

Whether intended or not, the end result is an intellectual condition known as 'perspectivitis', whose main symptoms are the obsessive need to label a piece of sociological research positivist or phenomenological, Marxist, functionalist or Weberian, interactionist or ethnomethodological. The truth is, however, that such simplistic labelling can be misleading.

'Good' sociology

While it is certainly true to say that clearly discernible sociological traditions of thought do exist, very few writers begin their sociological research solely in order to contribute to the body of knowledge of a given perspective. What they are principally trying to create is 'good' sociology, attempting to answer the question: 'How much can we reliably and validly know about human societies?' If they find that the best way to do this is by drawing on the theoretical assumptions and methodological techniques of the dominant sociological traditions, then so be it. There is no reason, as Paul Willis (1977) found, why someone using observation techniques, typical of the interactionist perspective, should not come to conclusions informed by Marxism. Similarly, feminism draws from all perspectives, while at the same time being both critical and sceptical of the inherent male bias in sociological theory and research to date.

The Chief Examiners' view

So what is 'good' sociology? Two sociology lecturers put exactly this question to all the Chief Examiners of the main A-level boards, and found, in particular, that the examiners are concerned by students' persistence in presenting sociological issues in a compartmentalised and fragmentary manner, one that can overemphasise division within the subject, or even imply dispute where none exists' (Moores and Breslin, 1991). Or, as one of the Chief Examiners quoted by Moores and Breslin states: 'Bad sociology is sociology which presents the subject as a series of divisions which are irreconcilable e.g. macro vs. micro / functionalist vs. conflict / modernisation vs. dependency / qualifiable vs. quantifiable … kids seem to feel that they have to be either Positivist or ANTI-positivist.' What should be encouraged is the view that a range of studies can be complementary, although 'some have more value in certain contexts than others'.

Finally, the Chief Examiners' view of what all sociologists – from GCSE to post-doctoral research – should be striving for emerges: 'students should aim to display a consciousness of the intellectual development of the discipline as a whole, some conception of theories and approaches popular at different points in time, the reasons for their popularity and their status today in light of more recent developments'.

QUESTIONS

1 **You have looked at a discussion of sociological perspectives. Now try to define the following terms:**

   (a) a sociological perspective
   (b) positivism
   (c) phenomenology

2 **What is meant by 'structure' and 'action' in sociology?**

Functionalism

Emile Durkheim (1858–1917)
French sociologist who did much to establish sociology as a discipline, particularly with works such as Suicide (1897). He emphasised the importance of examining society as a whole and the role of the 'collective conscience'. He strongly influenced the work of Talcott Parsons and the development of American structural functionalism.

No one has ever seen a society. All they can ever see is small parts at work at different times in different places. The nearest anyone could come would be to observe a small community, preferably with what seems to be a simple way of going about their everyday life. It should then be possible to work out what the importance of the things these people do is to the way their community works. Some anthropologists, who themselves come from industrial societies, have undertaken studies of pre-industrial societies still in existence. Among the best known is A.R. Radcliffe-Brown (1881–1955). A central part of the way he observed these pre-industrial societies was his belief that social activity, if it was recurrent, must be functional to the working of that community. In other words, an observable pattern of group activity must help maintain the life of that community: it must have a function. If, for example, a group of people are regularly observed sitting around smoking pipes communally, this activity may function to bind together or integrate the group as a community and reinforce the values of friendliness and co-operation. If the men taking part in this activity are elderly then it may be one way of maintaining their social power, and a respect for age.

In this way, a wider picture of how society works can be built up. Like many sociologists before him, Radcliffe-Brown made great use of what is called the organic analogy in his examination of the way societies work, though this idea really comes from Herbert Spencer (1820–1903) and was also used by Emile Durkheim.

The organic analogy

The idea behind the organic analogy is that societies can be compared to the way a biological organism works. Someone who had no idea how the body works might find, from slicing a human apart, that there were various organs inside that make humans work. The heart functions to pump blood around the veins and arteries, the kidneys clean the blood, the intestines are involved in digestion and so on. Each organ has a function which contributes to the working of the greater whole. So too with society, where the organs might be the family, education, the system of religion, work, etc. Any examination of these institutions should begin by asking the question: 'What does it do to help the wider society function?' Homeostasis is the term applied to the way in which an organism regulates itself to cope with changes in internal and external conditions. For example, after exercise, the heated-up body sweats to help the body temperature to stay stable. When this concept is used to understand how equilibrium is maintained in society, then the organic analogy becomes more effective.

The analogy also has many limits, however. It is difficult, for example, to compare the way organisms grow to the way societies grow and change. Is there a social equivalent to DNA, the genetic programme present in every species? Does a society really have a series of complementary institutions which work together to make the whole function smoothly to the mutual benefit of all? In the same way that the skin holds a human body together, so too do norms and values bind society together. But does this help us understand who determines the norms and values by which we live and how the wider society is organised?

Another way of looking at society is to compare it to a mechanism in the way it works, where all the small parts, such as in a clockwork watch, function together to achieve the aim of demonstrating the time of day. Similarly, when people pull together in society, they can achieve collectively held goals such as improvement in the overall standard of living.

Parsonian functionalism

This is close to Talcott Parsons' (1902–1979) view of the way society functions, and in the 1950s and 1960s Parsonian functionalism was virtually the dominant paradigm in sociology. The model of society he put forward has been subsequently heavily criticised, but it is important to understand how his model of society worked in order to understand the criticisms. What is taught at GCSE is effectively functionalist sociology.

> **Talcott Parsons (1902–79)**
> *American sociological theorist and leader of the functionalist school that dominated American sociology from the 1940s to the 1960s. In his famous work* The Social System *(1951) Parsons tried to show how consensus based on shared values is essential to social order. The stratification system is crucial in maintaining consensus in society.*

Parsons argues that any society has four functional needs or pre-requisites that need to be met for it to survive: these are adaptation, goal attainment, integration and latency (AGIL). It is hard to believe now that sociologists were excited by the bland and fruitless way that Parsons went about examining society, but many US college students went into their exams with the four letters AGIL stuck in their heads (or on the palms of their hands).

They then would have given Parsons' view that, firstly, all societies must have ways of adapting to change, whatever that change might be (A); they must have social aims that everyone wants which help the society determine the direction it's going in (G); they must have ways of binding their members together to identify with and realise these collective goals whether through religion or newspapers or marriage or whatever (I); and there must be a way in which a society's way of living can survive through generations of people (L). This scheme can be found detailed in works of his such as *The Social System* (1951). People born within this system are socialised into it and come to take on the roles the system demands: the whole is greater than the sum of its parts.

Manifest and latent functions

One of the key additions to Parsons' structural-functionalism has been made by his American contemporary, Robert Merton (born 1910). This is the distinction between manifest and latent functions. A manifest function is evident when an institution achieves the goal it clearly intended, for example the way a family socialises its young. A latent function would be an unintended consequence of an aspect in society. No one commits a crime with the deliberate intention of revealing the boundaries of normative behaviour to the rest of society! Nevertheless, a latent function of their criminal behaviour is to demonstrate the limits of socially acceptable behaviour.

Criticisms of functionalism

One of the most frequent criticisms of the functionalist perspective is of a logical problem it embraces: if something in society is recurrent, functionalists say that it must be meeting a need. But how do we know that this need exists? Because of the phenomenon that we observe! It exists because it exists; it is because it is. In philosophy, this type of going-nowhere argument is known as a tautology.

Secondly, because it focuses on the way in which different members of society integrate and work in harmony around a value consensus, functionalism lacks any real power to explain social change. One concept that attempts to overcome this is Merton's use of the concept of dysfunction: the way in which some aspects of society work against its overall harmony and consensus. Functionalism leans heavily towards describing society in a stable condition, and seems to emphasise the status quo: inequality is inevitable; poverty is inevitable; the media reflect all views; women are domestically orientated; marriages are happy. Functionalists such as Parsons and Merton appear to be using their own middle-class, middle-American view of the world and saying this is what society is like.

Functionalism should not be dismissed too quickly, however. Functionalists argue that advanced industrial societies are stable: people do seem to have faith in their political system in a democracy; industrial conflict is diminishing; and the major political parties are competing for the same middle ground. It is not difficult even now to make a strong case for arguing that a value consensus exists in advanced societies.

QUESTION **You have now looked at an introduction to functionalism. Try to define the following terms:**

> **(a) the organic analogy**
> **(b) functional needs**
> **(c) the mechanical analogy**
> **(d) a manifest function**
> **(e) dysfunction**

Marxism

At first sight, Marxism seems difficult to understand. It seems to use more new words and phrases than any other perspective in sociology. This is not because Marx was being awkward, but because of the richly creative nature of his thought. He needed a number of new terms to describe his ideas.

Marx's historical materialism

Marx did not want to simply analyse the world; he wanted to play a part in changing it. His life's work was devoted to understanding the way in which modern industrial societies change. Marx's theory is sometimes described as 'historical materialism'. The term materialism is often used to describe the acquisition of consumer goods (consumerism) but in Marx's time materialism meant the opposite of idealism, the belief that the physical world is created by ideas, particularly religious ideas. Marx argued instead that ideas themselves are products of the material struggle for existence in the economic base of society. Historical materialism sees change in society emerging from this struggle.

There are, according to Marx, three main periods of change that have occurred in the way human societies are organised. These periods he calls epochs, which are characterised by the way in which produc-

Karl Marx (1818–83)
German-born economist, sociologist, philosopher and revolutionary. Spent most of his life in poverty in London, financed by his friend, Friedrich Engels. Developed the theory of historical progression to communism through class struggle (historical materialism). His best-known works are The Communist Manifesto *(1848) and* Capital *(1867).*

tion happens – the mode of production. The three main epochs are the classical societies of ancient Rome and Greece, the feudal societies of the Middle Ages, and the one in which he lived (and which interested him most) – capitalist society.

What distinguishes each epoch are the different relations of production, determined by who owns the means of production – the method of producing the things we need to survive. In a classical society, the relations of production were between slave owner and slave; in feudal times they were between the landowner and his serf. In the development from land-based production to factory production, the key relationship became the one between the bourgeoisie, who owned the means of production (usually in the form of a factory), and the people hired by the (bourgeois) capitalists – the new landless working class or proletariat. According to Marx, it is conflict about ownership of the means of production, that is the class struggle, that causes change in society. In his various writings, Marx projected that this cause of conflict would only come to an end when there was no separate ownership of the means of production. He believed that the new industrial working class would be the class that brought about this change, taking over the means of production from the bourgeoisie. No new classes would be formed in their wake, so the result would eventually be a classless (or communist) society.

The labour theory of value

The bulk of Marx's work in the period from writing *The Communist Manifesto* (1848) to his death was devoted to showing how this transition to communism would come about. The bourgeoisie, he says, is an immensely dynamic and creative class. They were the driving force behind the Industrial Revolution, it was with their capital that mines were dug, roads were built, canals constructed, ships riveted together and steel foundries opened. But the bourgeoisie were only part of the story. Who actually hammered the rivets into the ships, took the pickaxe to the coal-face and shovelled out the earth to make the road? Not the bourgeoisie, but the people who have only their ability to work – labour power – which they sell to the bourgeoisie to make a living – the proletariat. And, Marx asks, what do they get in return? This point is perhaps best put by Orwell in *Animal Farm* (1945).

> 'Now, comrades, what is the nature of this life of ours? Let us face it: our lives are miserable, laborious, and short. We are born, we are given just so much food as will keep the breath in our bodies, and those of us who are capable of it are forced to work to the last atom of our strength; and the very instant that our usefulness has come to an end we are slaughtered with hideous cruelty. No animal in England knows the meaning of happiness or leisure after he is a year old. No animal in England is free. The life of an animal is misery and slavery: that is the plain truth.

'But is this simply part of the order of nature? Is it because this land of ours is so poor that it cannot afford a decent life to those who dwell upon it? No, comrades, a thousand times no! The soil of England is fertile, its climate is good, it is capable of affording food in abundance to an enormously greater number of animals than now inhabit it. This single farm of ours would support a dozen horses, twenty cows, hundreds of sheep — and all of them living in a comfort and a dignity that are now almost beyond our imagining. Why then do we continue in this miserable condition? Because nearly the whole of the produce of our labour is stolen from us by human beings. There, comrades, is the answer to all our problems. It is summed up in a single word — Man. Man is the only real enemy we have. Remove Man from the scene, and the root cause of hunger and overwork is abolished for ever.

'Man is the only creature that consumes without producing. He does not give milk, he does not lay eggs, he is too weak to pull the plough, he cannot run fast enough to catch rabbits. Yet he is lord of all the animals. He sets them to work, he gives back to them the bare minimum that will prevent them from starving, and the rest he keeps for himself. Our labour tills the soil, our dung fertilizes it, and yet there is not one of us that owns more than his bare skin. You cows that I see before me, how many thousands of gallons of milk have you given during the last year? And what has happened to that milk which should have been breeding up sturdy calves? Every drop of it has gone down the throats of our enemies. And you hens, how many eggs have you laid this year, and how many of those eggs ever hatched into chickens?'

Major's speech from Animal Farm by George Orwell.

Profit and surplus value

The owner of capital wants to invest this money in order to make more capital. This is done by first buying the raw materials, machines and tools necessary for the manufacture of goods. Let us say that the capitalist believes that wooden chairs will be a good source of potential profit. They therefore buy the necessary wood, lathe machines, chisels etc. for their chair factory. Labour is taken

Figure 1.2 The cycle of capital

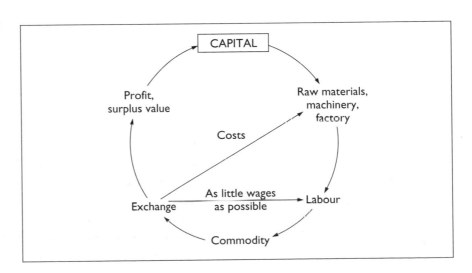

on for the production of the commodity (anything which is bought and sold), in this case chairs. Once the chairs are sold the capitalist has a lot of money but now needs to pay for the machinery, raw materials and any other overheads, principally wages. How much should the proletariat be paid? The capitalist is only in business for one reason – to make as much profit (which Marx calls surplus value) as possible. The workers will therefore be paid as little as the capitalist can get away with. But who actually turned the raw materials into saleable commodities? The labour of the proletariat is added to the raw material to turn it into a marketable commodity; in return they receive as little payment as possible. It is this difference that Marx calls exploitation. When the true nature of this exploitation becomes realised – when they achieve class consciousness – the proletariat will become revolutionary and overthrow the exploitative bourgeoisie. Another way of understanding the Marxist concept of exploitation is to consider the situation of builders who spend their lives building houses but may never be able to own one themselves.

Although the meaning of the terms 'profit' and 'surplus value' is close, Marx does not use them interchangeably. When workers add value to things and turn them into commodities, what they are adding is their labour-time. The amount of labour-time – 'necessary labour' – put in to earn their wages is not the same as their total output. The labour-time remaining is called 'surplus labour', in which time the worker will create 'surplus value'. It is in this time that the worker will be reproducing capital for the capitalist. 'What appears as surplus value on capital's side appears identically on the workers' side as surplus labour in excess of his requirements as a worker, hence in excess of his immediate requirements for keeping himself alive' (Karl Marx, *Outlines of Political Economy*, 1857/8, more commonly known as the *Grundrisse*). Without surplus value produced in this way by extra unpaid labour-time there can be no profit. The rate of profit is not the same as the rate of surplus value, because the concept of profit involves variables such as the total amount of all possible capital used, or the amount of raw materials. The rate of profit is always lower than the narrower concept of the rate of surplus value. This difference was an important element in Marx's view of the labour process in relation to work, automation and unemployment.

Class consciousness

Why the proletariat never achieves revolutionary class consciousness is the central question asked of Marxism, though its supporters point to the closing years of the First and Second World Wars, and the British General Strike of 1926 as examples of heightened class awareness. One answer is because the structure of bourgeois society works continuously in favour of the bourgeoisie. Because they control the most important aspect of society – the means of production – they are able to decisively influence the structure of everything else. This is what is meant by the economic base determining the superstructure, which is composed of the other vital aspects of society – the family, religion and the political, educational and judicial systems. As we describe in later chapters, for Marxists all of these institutions serve, in a capitalist society, to maintain bourgeois control.

Marxism after Marx

In the twentieth century, particularly from the 1950s on (when Marxist sociology began to witness a revival in the West), many people have argued that, given the obvious failings of the former Soviet Union, 'Marxism doesn't work.' This point of view was considerably strengthened by the spectacular collapse of communist regimes in Eastern Europe at the end of the 1980s and the break-up of the Soviet Union in 1991. So is Marxism dead?

Stalinism and the Soviet bloc

There are a number of points to be made here. Firstly, Marx would not have identified the Eastern Bloc countries of 1917–91 as lying beyond capitalism. These societies were, from 1930 on, Stalinist, not Marxist, and many non-Soviet Marxist studies have highlighted this crucial difference.

Although Stalin's Soviet Union claimed to be Marxist, Stalin's own ideas and the unique historical and political situation were much more influential than the political and economic theories of Marx. Marx had envisaged a socialist revolution based on class struggle between a rising proletariat and a decadent bourgeoisie in advanced capitalist countries, particularly Germany. This was definitely not the situation in pre-revolutionary Russia, which was a largely peasant-based society, not dissimilar to some of today's Third World countries. The perceived need to ruthlessly accelerate the economies of what became the Eastern Bloc in order to catch up with and overtake the more developed West meant that Stalinism superseded Marxism. After the Soviet invasion of Hungary in 1956, many Western Marxists finally broke with what they then saw as a grotesque misrepresentation of Marx's ideas in the Soviet Union. This led to the emergence of the 'New Left' and eventually 'Eurocommunism'.

One of the main criticisms levelled at Marxists since the death of Marx is that it has become a complex and sophisticated excuse for the lack of socialist revolution in advanced industrial nations, as Marx had predicted. Most revolutions carried out in his name have occurred in countries with mainly agricultural economies, such as China, Cuba, Nicaragua and even Ethiopia.

Neo-Marxism is concerned with explaining the reasons for this non-revolution, and concentrates on analysing the use of ideological means of control by the ruling class. Working-class consciousness has been prevented from crystallising in any decisive way by ideological State apparatuses such as the media, politics and education.

Marxism has been used by sociologists as a tool of analysis of capitalist societies in the post-war period and has produced remarkably fruitful studies. For these Marxists, nothing has essentially changed the nature of Western capitalism to make these societies less amenable to Marxist analysis; the class structure may have changed slightly, but capital and the bourgeoisie are as much in control as ever (see chapter 3).

QUESTIONS

1 **You will now be aware of the basic principles of the Marxist perspective. Now try to define the following terms:**

   (a) mode of production
   (b) forces of production
   (c) relations of production
   (d) capitalism
   (e) class consciousness

2 **How does a Marxist explanation of the way a society works differ from the functionalist explanation?**

Weberianism

Max Weber (1864–1920) is one of the most difficult, but also one of the most important, theorists to come to terms with in sociology. In attempts to 'pigeon-hole' him, no one quite knows where to put him. He was aware that social structures exist and are important, but he was also aware that these structures are, at the same time, made up of individuals, with their own understanding of the meaning of their actions.

Weber and Marx

One of the standard sociological clichés is to say that Weber's work amounts to a 'debate with the ghost of Marx'. This is a phrase which is meant to highlight the similarities as well as differences between the two. Weber was, in part of his work, pointing out an alternative theory to Marx's materialism, but much of his output was concerned with completely different areas of sociology.

One reason for this was that, while Marx was concerned to develop a revolutionary theory for the proletariat and their allies, Weber, as a co-founder of the German Sociological Association, was more interested in establishing sociology as an academic discipline. If Weber's

Max Weber (1864–1920)
Highly influential German sociologist and founder of the German Sociological Association. He made important contributions to most areas of sociology including religion (e.g. in The Protestant Ethic and the Spirit of Capitalism, *1904–5), organisations and theory. His criticisms of the limitations of social science are particularly important.*

ideas seem hard to grasp it is because Weber was a complex and profound thinker – because his ideas *are* difficult and, sometimes, even contradictory and the subject of continuing debate. Weber's analysis of Marx's ideas is an important aspect of his work but, rather than being involved in a debate with Marx, he actually took account of Marx's economic theories and to a certain extent encompassed them within his own larger argument. He agreed with much of the economic theory which Marx put forward, but he attempted to describe a more complex system of stratified inequality in capitalist societies. Weber saw his version of the social structure as running alongside that of Marx and believed that there was a need for as many alternative explanations as possible in order to arrive at some sort of understanding. He stressed that the researcher should consider as many aspects of each social structure as possible, and not focus on the economic level alone.

To study each society, the sociologist must study its history, its economy, and its culture, and attempt to understand that culture. According to Weber, each society is unique. History was important to Weber but he did not see it as just the history of class struggle. Like Marx, Weber saw that conflict is of great consequence in the analysis of human actions. Economic class, he believed, is often a source of conflict, particularly in capitalism, but economic relations are not the only source of conflict in society.

Rationalisation

Weber considered that the growth of 'rational' thinking – a scientific way of understanding – was taking over from previous, supernatural, sacred ways of looking at the world. The concept of rationalisation of thought plays an important part in his theories. The industrialisation of societies and the growth of complex social structures required a cultural outlook which could cope with rapid change. It was no longer enough to put it all down to God or the devil; humans needed more satisfying explanations to help them take control of their lives.

This is clear from what is perhaps Weber's best-known work, *The Protestant Ethic and the Spirit of Capitalism* (see also chapter 11). Here, Weber also outlines his views on social change. He is concerned with the simultaneous emergence of a particular type of Protestantism (Calvinism) and the capitalist mode of production, though he is quick to point out that there is not a causal relationship. One did not cause or invent the other, rather they happened to arise at the same time and complemented each other. He calls this an 'elective affinity'. It is a good example of the need to understand all the aspects of a culture that make society work. Calvinism preached that only a chosen few could get to heaven. Its followers did not know who was among the chosen, so the best bet was to be honest, hard working, thrifty and live decent, sober lifestyles. These attributes happened to fit in well with the 'spirit' of capitalism, being a more rational approach to economic organisation. Looking to the East and discerning slow or non-existent industrial growth, he wondered if the nature of eastern religions was incompatible with the sort of organisation that makes capitalism possible. His later religious studies centred on this.

However, Weber also saw the growth of rationalisation as the downfall of industrial societies. With the State ruling through what he called 'rational-legal' authority, an overwhelming system of bureaucracy would arise. Although he saw bureaucracies as the most rational and efficient way of pursuing organisational goals, red tape would proliferate and bureaucratic regulations would begin to function purely for their own sake. The white-collar class would expand to become the largest group in society, a group to deal with and create more rules. The individual would eventually be swamped and life in these societies would become stifled by an 'iron cage' of bureaucracy. Life would become aimless and purposeless unless strong political control was exercised over the bureaucrats by politicians. His predictions of the future, then, took a very different path from those of Marx. Where one saw a vision of true communism and people leading fulfilled lives, the other envisaged a bureaucratic nightmare.

Ideal types A major concept that Weber introduced is that of the 'ideal type' – a model idea which is used to help the researcher when studying an area of society. This 'ideal' can never be a reality but it is used as a perfect hypothetical example against which reality – such as the organisation of the church, market competition or bureaucracies – can be compared. For Weber, any theory in society was an ideal type.

As well as making important contributions to the sociology of organisations, religion and stratification – in fact most areas of sociological theory – Weber also initiated and developed some of the central methodological debates that persist today, particularly the issues of value freedom (discussed later in this chapter) and the importance of interpretation.

It is another of the clichés of sociology to say that Weber is 'the father of interpretive sociology', though this perhaps overstates the case. In a number of texts Weber highlighted the need for sociology and social science to move away from seeing human behaviour as a response to external stimuli and, instead, to develop an understanding of what he called 'social action'. By this he meant human activity in a social context that is conscious, meaningful and purposive, not reactive. It is necessary to understand human action as being both rational and as existing in a social context. Weber used the German word *verstehen* to convey this. This takes sociology away from its positivistic roots and in a new direction where human values and beliefs matter.

However, in saying this, Weber remained unwilling to depart from a structural analysis of social causes, as the phenomenologists were later to do, though the extent that he wanted sociology to move in this direction continues to be debated. Weber has a foot in both camps. He is widely seen as having opened the door to interpretive sociology, although he did not describe in detail what lay beyond that door.

Weber, then, was more concerned with the practical and theoretical considerations of sociological research than Marx, and he was as concerned to debate methodology with the positivists as he was to take issue with Marx's economics. His overall contribution to sociology is massive, and only now are the effects becoming apparent. With his method of using structure and interpretation in the study of society, he opened up the possibility of a sociology which takes account of history, social structure and the richness and complexity of everyday life.

QUESTIONS

1 **Try to define the following terms associated with the sociology of Max Weber:**

   (a) **ideal type**
   (b) **social action**
   (c) **bureaucracy**
   (d) **rational-legal authority**

2 **How does the sociology of Max Weber differ from that of Marx?**

Symbolic interactionism

The founder of symbolic interactionism, George Herbert Mead (1863–1931), was more interested in psychology than sociology, and some critics say his theory reflects this. Symbolic interactionism is essentially a theory of socialisation. Becoming a human is not just a matter of being born. It's all about becoming a social being, which happens through interactions between the child and those around it.

Language and socialisation

According to Mead the inner 'I' has to be converted into the social 'me' – an individual with a social identity and understanding of the world based upon the shared experiences of interacting with others. Mead goes into great detail on how this comes about, comparing the evolution of the species with the creation of the social self. Humans have evolved beyond other animals, due to the complexity of human consciousness linked to the intricate system of symbols which we use to communicate with each other. This symbolic system is called language, and it is through using these shared meanings to communicate that humans come to be aware of themselves. Self-conscious beings learn to understand that if they wish to take part in social interactions, they will have to recognise that they have a role to play, and the way they play this role will affect other people. They must learn to try and gauge the effect they are having on other people – to see themselves as others see them. Mead calls this 'taking on the attitude of the other'.

Primary socialisation

The human infant learns that far from being 'at one' with its mother, as it had been up to birth, it is a separate being, an individual. Psychologists use the rouge test to prove this. At about eight months the child begins to recognise a mirror image as itself, and will, for example, remove a smudge of red make-up from its nose. This is a crucial stage in the development of a social self. The child will then go on to see its own actions in terms of the effects they have on specific others in its life – parents or caregivers. Writing on the wallpaper, for example, produces anger. The child also 'tries on' the role of others by dressing up in parents' clothes, wearing lipstick or giving the teddy bears and dolls a hard time for being naughty. To see yourself and the consequences of your behaviour as others might see them is the first step on the road to becoming a social being.

Secondary socialisation

The next stage is to move beyond the world of the family and primary socialisation into the wider society and secondary socialisation. This is called the 'game stage' by Mead, who compares it to playing as a team member. To do this successfully it is not enough to judge the effects of your performance on the reactions of a specific other; the individual must gauge the response of a whole group of people. When you learn to operate as a member of a wider group you are taking the attitude of the generalised other in Mead's terms. Your behaviour will be noted not just by those nearest to you but by the rest of your social group. What you have done is to develop an inner moral conscience, making you the guardian of your own behaviour. Talcott Parsons calls it internalisation of norms and values. Marx calls it taking on the ideology of the ruling class. Mead's contribution is to provide an in-depth interactionist account of how this actually happens.

Labelling and self-fulfilling prophecies

The taking on of the attitudes of others has a clear relationship to a central premise of interactionist theory – labelling. By accepting the judgements of others in this way, we are socialised into accepting the prophecies which others make about us. This is why they become self-fulfilling (see also chapters 5 and 14). However, Mead points out that the process is not just one way. There is conflict, and the inner 'I' is never totally blotted out. The individual is capable of acting upon these social situations, of influencing interactions. Therefore, the social world is never entirely taken for granted, but is the result of social constructions through symbolic interactions. Ethnomethodology takes the construction of social reality a lot further.

QUESTIONS

1 **Define the following in terms that are associated with symbolic interactionism:**
    (a) the social self
    (b) socialisation
    (c) the 'I' and the 'me'

2 **When does a human being become a social being?**

3 **What is meant by 'self-fulfilling prophecy'?**

Ethnomethodology

Harold Garfinkel

The theory which stands at the opposite end of sociology to the most extreme forms of positivist, so-called scientific research, is ethnomethodology. This is about the way all people try to make sense of what other people do and say. It is usually associated with Harold Garfinkel, an American who studied sociology under the leading functionalist of the 1950s, Talcott Parsons. Garfinkel's perspective could be seen as a reaction to Parsons' middle-class, right-wing theories. The essence of Garfinkel's approach is that there is no such thing as society, so there is no point in arguing about which theory you use to investigate social behaviour. We all attempt to make sense of social experiences by formulating theories in our everyday lives to interpret and explain what is happening to us. Sociological explanations may be more precisely stated, but that does not make them any better than individual theories of social behaviour.

Ethnomethodology and social reality

Positivists claim that social reality exists in the form of social facts, for example crime rates and suicide rates. The symbolic interactionists see social reality in the shared use of symbols in the process of social interactions. However, according to ethnomethodology, it is something which is never actually there. Small-scale analyses of social situations reveal that the best we can do is to arrive at some sort of shared reality during the course of one encounter with another human being. This shared reality breaks down quite easily under certain types of pressure. Conversational analysis shows the fragility of interactions such as these:

> *'Hello, how are you?'*
> *'Hello, I'm fine. How are you?'*
> *'Very well, thank you.'*

All very well on the surface, but does it actually mean anything? Garfinkel's method of studying such social encounters would be to get an experimenter to work at undermining this shared reality:

> *'Hello, how are you?'*
> *'How am I what?'*
> *'Well, how are you doing?'*
> *'How am I doing what?'*

This would continue until the interaction breaks down in embarrassment or anger. The other participant would usually attempt to ignore these inconsistencies, trying desperately to retrieve some sense of social reality from the situation. Eventually, however, they would break off blaming you for the failure of communication.

Garfinkel's students were encouraged to undermine social reality at every opportunity. When family and friends realised that their strange behaviour was associated with sociological studies, this was grasped at with relief as an explanation. What they were investigating was the nature of social reality, and how it depends upon each individual attempting to make sense of the situations they become involved in.

There is no guarantee that all of the people in any one situation will hold the same interpretation as to what is going on. For example, the police often find eye-witness accounts of the same event vary widely. When people discuss a film or television programme they have seen they may find they have different explanations of the plot, motive or outcome. Look around at people in a lecture or a lesson. Some are listening, some are daydreaming, others are just asleep. When they all leave that room, do they carry the same social reality, the same experience? Or, as the positivists would argue, does the register – the official statistical record of who attended that class on that day – hold the only reality?

Atkinson (1978) worked in coroner's courts and examined the interpretative processes by which suicide verdicts were arrived at. He concluded that the ways in which coroners work, their concepts and interpretations, lead to the 'official' suicide rates. He said that there is no 'real' suicide rate because the official statistics are produced after the process of interpretation.

If you have been sitting in your sociology class planning what to do at the weekend, that has been your reality. The official story has it that you were studying sociology for a specified amount of time on a certain day in a particular room.

Is ethnomethodology a social science? The positivists and structuralists would say that ethnomethodological investigations tell us little of sociological significance. Garfinkel encourages people to pick up the phone when it rings and say nothing. The caller is supposedly confused, because they have no cues for the interaction. Undoubtedly true, but what does it reveal? Ethnomethodology ignores the impact of the social structure upon these situations. Class, culture, socio-economic status can all provide explanations which could help us to understand everyday interactions. Ethnomethodology is more like social psychology than sociology, but it does play an important role in the debate between micro and macro perspectives, and highlights the problems of accepting 'social facts' as reality.

QUESTIONS

1 **How does ethnomethodology undermine belief in 'social facts'?**

2 **How do ethnomethodologists interpret the phrase 'social reality'?**

Feminism

In the past few decades, a new approach has emerged which challenges the way that sociologists have looked at the society they study. Feminism criticises sociology for uncritically adopting a male perspective and marginalising the roles of females in society. Feminists believe that this failure both reflects and contributes to the undervaluing of women. Why has sociology had so little to say about women's lives and experiences?

'Malestream' sociology

Prior to the 1960s, there was undoubtedly a strong case for arguing that sociology could be seen as male ideology. Women did not figure in studies of social mobility; little was written about women and deviance; their 'natural' domestic role went largely unquestioned; studies of work were largely about men. Feminists argue that the consequence of this 'malestream' research is that women have been ignored, distorted and marginalised in sociology.

Feminist responses

Following the realisation that sociology has looked at society only from a male perspective, feminists have responded by trying to create a sociology that explores and attempts to explain women's subordination and places women at the centre of the sociological study. It has not been a unified response, but one which has taken three directions: integrationalist, separatist and reconceptualist. The integrationalist approach argues that sexism in sociology can be overcome by making every attempt to take the role of women into account when looking at work, leisure, crime, education and so on, grafting them on to the existing body of knowledge. The separatist approach argues that women should be studied separately from men, on the grounds that all women's experience is qualitatively different from men's. The most important division in society, separatist feminists argue, is based on gender. (This point of view is examined further in chapter 3.) The reconceptualist approach argues that it is not possible to make up for the imbalance in sociology by simply including women in existing research, or by constructing a sociology of women only. Instead, sociology and sociological priorities must be reconceptualised: sociological theory must be rethought and rewritten, and the basic assumptions of malestream sociology fundamentally challenged. This third view implies a revolution in the way sociology is practised, breaking down the traditional categories of sociology and emphasising new priorities, especially the private sphere of the home and domestic relationships.

Feminism: a new perspective?

Are we then entitled to add feminism to the list of existing perspectives in sociology (functionalism, Marxism, Weberianism, ethnomethodology and symbolic interactionism)? Abbott and Wallace (1990) argue that the answer is no 'because there are a number of distinct feminist perspectives, not just one'. Feminist sociologists may embrace other perspectives: 'what they have in common is a commitment to looking at the world through the female prism'.

The debate regarding the status of feminism within sociology continues, and is a necessary part of the development of sociological theory. The impact of feminism upon sociology is undisputed, and has broadened and deepened the analysis of society. Why 'malestream' sociology emerged in the first place is now the subject of much feminist analysis, and is a good example of the way sociology continually examines and criticises itself.

QUESTIONS

1 **What are the main issues that concern feminist sociologists?**

2 **Why has it been necessary to develop a feminist viewpoint in an attempt to understand society?**

Sociology and science

In the early nineteenth century the French mathematician, Auguste Comte (1798–1857), impressed by the achievements being made in natural sciences such as physics, chemistry and geology, argued that there were three discernible stages in the evolution of human thought. The first stage, which he called the 'theological' or 'fictitious' stage, explained events as God's work, for example thunder occurring when God is angry, or famines being the result of not worshipping him enough. The second stage was characteristic of the middle ages with explanations involving subtle emissions from the divine and mystic influences. He called this the 'metaphysical' stage. The third stage was based on the evidence of the previous two hundred years which appeared to demonstrate that the natural world is subject to the rule of definite laws that can be observed through experiment and the collection of 'positive facts'.

His boldest assertion was to take this one stage further and state that the systematic collection of facts and the search for laws should not be limited to the natural world. Everything, even human society, obeys laws of behaviour. He foresaw a new science of society which would discover these laws and become the 'queen' of all science. In anticipation he called this as yet unresearched science 'sociology'. When all human thought was based on science then the positive stage would be complete.

Many sociologists are unhappy with the idea that the work of writers such as Marx and Durkheim can be called positivist in any meaningful way. They point to studies such as Durkheim's *Suicide*, which argues that the real cause of suicide is not religion, the family or the contemporary political situation but something unmeasurable – the extent of integration and moral regulation in society. Strictly speaking, then, positivism in sociology corresponds to the narrow definition of science as quantifiable, generalisable and concerned to identify clearly observable causes and correlations. Theorists such as Marx and Durkheim were working towards a broader view of this scientific project.

Positivist and structural sociology

Positivism is one of the key concepts in social science. Unhelpfully, it is used differently in subjects such as law ('positive' law), economics ('positive' economics) and sociology. In sociology, positivist sociology and structural (or 'realist') sociology are often thought of as the same thing.

Positivist sociology is similar to the concept of empiricism, mainly interested in pursuing a research programme that is parallel to that

SCIENTIFIC RESEARCH METHODS

Many scientists would argue that good science proceeds through the following stages:

*1 **Observation** All scientific activity depends on systematic observation, recording and description of its subject matter.*

*2 **Conjecture** In order to explain any given observation scientists must think up a plausible reason for its occurrence.*

*3 **Hypothesis formation** The conjecture must be 'operationalised', in other words it must be put in a form which will allow the scientists to determine how well it explains the occurrence of the observation. At this stage, an attempt is made to predict the result of a test.*

*4 **Testing** The hypothesis must be rigorously tested under controlled conditions through an experiment to show whether it can be proved wrong or not.*

*5 **Generalisation** If the hypothesis has not been proved wrong by the test, it shows that the conjecture explains the occurrence of the observation. It can then be generalised, either into a law-like statement (for example, light rays bend at an angle dependent on the density of the medium they enter) or a probabilistic statement (for example, there is a 70 per cent probability that x will occur when y is also present under conditions z).*

*6 **Theory formation** A number of generalisations are ordered into a coherent model or theory, which explains a given range of phenomena.*

***Objectivity** The researcher must be totally neutral at all times, and in no way allow their own views or prejudices to colour any aspect of the research programme. If they don't remain objective but become subjective, then their work ceases to be scientific and becomes propaganda.*

of the natural sciences, seeking to discover patterned and regular events in the social world whose occurrence is either caused by another event, or is strongly correlated with that event. A social mechanism may be clearly identified and measured, for example the relation between attendance at parents' evenings and the educational attainment of the children.

Structural sociology is thought to be concerned with the cause of events at such a deep level that they may not be observable in a simple way so that it is not possible to say that one event causes another to happen. Causes exist in the structure of power and social relations. Society is not a simple series of mechanisms like a grandiose Heath-Robinson device. Empirical research therefore becomes much more difficult.

However, the idea of formulating a science of society was attractive to many, and by the mid nineteenth century writers were beginning to claim this status for their social theories. Marx, for example, in outlining historical materialism, describes 'the material transformation of the economic conditions of production which can be determined with the precision of natural science'. He contrasted his own view of how socialism would emerge from capitalism with that of others, claiming that his view was scientific and theirs merely utopian. They might wish it to happen, but he could identify how it was written into the laws of historical development. By the turn of the century Durkheim could show that suicide in society could be understood through the collection of 'social facts' and the identification of external variables determining human behaviour. His contemporary, Weber, though, had profound reservations about the search for general social laws, believing each society to be a unique formation. He also wrestled with the problem of determinism, suggesting instead that humans have some control over their lives.

Although a 'positivist' sociology clearly now exists, scepticism exists both inside and outside sociology as to how successful and valid it is. Social science has not achieved anything like the degree of unanimity, certainty or ability to predict of the natural sciences. Its methods are nothing like as rigorous. It cannot, for example, use laboratory experiments in the same way to derive its data. Aside from the ethical problems of placing people in artificial situations, it only makes sense to study people's behaviour in an existing social setting. The closest sociologists can get to orthodox scientific methods is to use field experiments – for example gauging reactions by posing as old when you're young, or black when you're white – or by making comparisons between different groups, societies and cultures (the comparative method). These, of course, are difficult to repeat or have other researchers verify. With these limitations, social scientists have far greater difficulty in establishing the cause or causes of events. At best, all that can be established are strong correlations. It lacks the precision of natural science.

Sociologists have responded to these criticisms in a number of ways. From a positivist point of view, while many of the above criticisms are accepted, the argument remains that what most sociologists do is, nevertheless, scientific in that sociology constitutes a body of organised knowledge developed through systematic enquiry, using techniques that approximate to those of natural science, yielding data of similar reliability and validity.

The realist approach

An altogether different view of science has emerged from what has been termed the 'realist' school. This argues that it is misleading to typify science as being based on experiment and that, outside the laboratory, scientists are faced with as many uncontrollable variables as social scientists. Although men have landed on the moon with great scientific precision, meteorologists, with banks of technical equipment, cannot tell you with certainty whether it will rain or not in a month or even a day's time, or for how long. Nor is it the case that scientists work solely on the basis of observation. They cannot see viruses spreading from human to human or continents drifting apart, but they are able to surmise these facts from the evidence of epidemics striking people down, or from earthquakes and volcanic eruptions. The real causes are often knowable only by their effects. This, the realists claim, allows social scientists to claim that they, too, are engaged in the same scientific project where many and complex variables are at work.

The phenomenological approach

Phenomenologists regard the question of the relationship between sociology and science with great scepticism. Whatever the claims of natural science, there is a crucial difference between people and inanimate objects in that humans think for themselves and have reasons for their behaviour. This, in turn, enables them to make active sense of their world. Sociologists should be concerned with interpreting this view. Whether social causation exists or not is irrelevant.

Scientists themselves, from the phenomenological point of view, are as involved in interpreting reality as any other group in society. All knowledge is simply the product of interaction between human beings. It is more valid – as well as more interesting – to analyse science as a set of subjectively held meanings. Events are not passively observed. To understand anything, whether tribal life in the South Pacific or the messages across VDUs sent by radio telescopes, a theoretical framework has to be imposed on what is observed. Forming this framework is a creative process, derived from ideas of what is thought to be already there. All knowledge is socially constructed.

There are at least three positions, then, on the debate about the scientific status of science. Positivist sociologists claim that the methods they use, while not identical to those of the natural sciences, approximate closely enough to them. Social science can be like natural science. The realists claim that in both branches of science, similar problems are faced in postulating the influence of unseeable structures and forces. For phenomenologists, the search for causes and laws is dismissed and science itself is studied as a social construct.

QUESTIONS

1 **What differences are there between natural and social science?**

2 **What is the realist view of science?**

3 **What does it mean to say that knowledge is socially constructed?**

Is science scientific?

While there has been considerable pressure on sociologists to consider what they mean by their use of the word 'science', the use of this word by natural scientists has also come under the microscope. What does it mean to call their work scientific? Are they any more objective, rigorous or closer to 'the truth' than social scientists? Even if objectivity is possible, should these scientists want to claim detachment from the objects they study?

At first sight, it seems easy enough to assume that what natural scientists do is to systematically record observations of the patterns of behaviour and movement of matter, without preconceptions of what they might find. As many philosophers of science have pointed out though, the process is more complex – and less objective – than it first appears.

Popper The very idea of deriving conclusions from the process of making observations is itself problematic. Although 999 white swans may have been observed floating past a point on a river, it is a logical mistake to assume that the next swan to swim past will also be white. This is what Karl Popper (1963) identifies as the problem of induction. It cannot be assumed that what has always happened in the past will always happen in the future. It follows, for Popper, that collecting more and more data about an event will not prove a proposition to be true, as there is no reason why past events should predict the future. The black swan of scientific data may well be around the corner, waiting to drift into view.

Instead, Popper argues that scientists should proceed by looking, not for the proof of their hypotheses, but for their disproof. Although it cannot be proved that something is true – only that something has always happened that way in the past – the best evidence will be that it has not yet been disproved or 'falsified'. Science must abandon the inductive method of attempting to make theories fit facts and adopt a deductive method where facts are only admitted into a theory through the process of falsification.

Kuhn In one of the most important books on this subject, Thomas Kuhn (1962) asks whether scientists do indeed allow the possibility of their theories being falsified, and examines how new scientific theories emerge. According to Kuhn, scientists work not as individuals but as part of a community. Within this scientific community a consensus exists about the nature of the world they are investigating. Kuhn calls the theoretical framework that results from this consensus a paradigm. For long periods of time the scientific community engages in activity designed to bear out the validity of this paradigm. Kuhn calls this a time of 'normal science'. Eventually, though, individuals or groups working outside the dominant paradigm will put forward alternative theories that can be supported by equally valid evidence. They will have to be outside of the dominant paradigm to do this. There then follows a period of revolutionary or 'multi-paradigmatic' science where the rival paradigms struggle for supremacy, and advocates of alternative theoretical frameworks are overthrown or beaten off.

An example of what Kuhn had in mind would be the challenge mounted against Newtonian physics by Albert Einstein in the early part of this century, where intense battles were unsuccessfully waged by the 'normal' scientists to maintain scientific orthodoxy. If long-standing paradigms can be overthrown, then the defeated scientists have to admit that the theories they were working with were not so much 'true' as merely 'very useful' in helping them make sense of the data they had gathered.

It is not the case, then, that those who are working within paradigms of normal science approach what they examine with open minds, or are prepared to look anew each time at what they are observing. Some commentators have argued that the problem is more deep-set than this, in that all scientists, by definition, start off with the unfalsifiable assumption that every event has a cause. Furthermore, from the realist point of view, not every event – or every possible cause – is observable or knowable. The study of plate tectonics and earthquakes by geologists, for example, requires a series of guesses to be made about what is probably happening in the earth's structure. The problem of causation, of identifying specific causes, is as much of a problem for natural scientists as it is for social scientists.

In the same vein, it is no less true to say that, although the subject of natural scientific study may be inanimate or non-human, scientists themselves are human beings who have to impose a structure on what they see in order to make sense of it and they have to select some facts from others to put a theory together. In this way, scientists are as prone to imposing their own subjective views of the world as any other humans. That they need to choose to prioritise some data means that they are making value judgements about which data is most helpful to test their hypothesis. When they start making choices about the status of facts, then they have, strictly speaking, ceased to be objective. Facts have become values.

Questions have been asked not only about the methodology of the natural sciences but also their ethics. Radical and feminist critics have brought into the debate not only the methodology of science but the knowledge the application of this methodology produces.

'Big' science Sociologists have argued that scientific knowledge in the natural world arises from an objective and independent search for truth and also from the priorities and values of those who have funded the research. For Sklair (1973), what most people think of as scientific knowledge is better thought of as 'big' science – research undertaken to further the control and interests of the military-industrial state over its people. Examples of this would include research into space and weapons technology, or business-led research into systems whose sole aim is profit-maximisation. The resulting popular image is of scientists as men in white coats, developing large-scale and impersonal structures on multi-billion pound projects without regard for how their creations will be used. Their technology is thought to be part of an objective science because of the power and prestige of the funders behind them. Their concerns are thought to be our concerns.

Feminism For feminists, science is a male world from which women have always been excluded. Scientific achievements and scientific knowledge reveal only male priorities in which nature, always characterised as female, has to be brought under control. Areas of traditionally female knowledge of previous centuries such as healing and midwifery have become the brutal male domains of medicine and obstetrics. For Hilary Rose (1982), it is male science that has brought about 'the mechanisation of childbirth through routine induction, massive pollution of the environment and the ultimate terror of nuclear holocaust', as well as forms of contraception based on controlling women's – rather than men's – fertility.

Male science is not objective if objectivity is thought only to concern how scientific research is done, and not the reason why that research came into existence, or what the social consequences are. Sandra Harding (1987) states that 'Defining what is in need of scientific explanation only from the perspective of bourgeois, white men's experiences leads to partial and even perverse understandings ... an androcentric [male-centred] picture of nature and social life emerges from the testing by men of hypotheses generated by what men find problematic in the world around them.' It was, after all, this very same male-centred science that claimed to have 'proved' that women were biologically and socially inferior to men. Furthermore, it is men alone who have produced the technology to make chemical and nuclear weapons.

If women are to enter the exclusive world of male science then, feminists have argued, science must be reconceptualised and made more humane. Scientists themselves have to become accountable for their actions. Technology will be seen not as 'value-free' but assessed in terms of the impact it has in bringing about meaningful change in social relations. Men, as well as women, would be seen as capable of reproduction. Given that scientific advance has relied as much on inspired guesses as its own methodology, a feminist perspective would reintroduce and relegitimise the intuitive approach. In this way science will become a means of enhancing human freedom rather than being a threat to survival as at present. What has been a defensive and conservative discipline will become healthy and liberatory.

It can be argued, then, that there are a number of ways in which the supposed objectivity of science can be questioned, to such an extent that belief in objectivity in science – within and without the scientific world – is now crumbling. If this is the case, then it begs the question of the status of sociology as a social science, conceived specifically to emulate the achievements and aspirations of natural science.

QUESTIONS

1 **What does Kuhn mean by 'paradigms' in science?**

2 **How do feminists view science?**

3 **What is the 'inductive method'?**

Values and sociologists

One of Max Weber's main aims in setting up the German Society for Sociology was to establish sociology as a discipline free from value judgements. What he meant by this was clear from the society's statute, which demanded the advancement of sociology as a science, giving equal space to all directions and methods in sociology, without at the same time advancing any specific religious, political or ethical goals.

Weber In this aim he has been frequently misunderstood and misinterpreted. He did not mean that sociologists could not be politically active, that they should not hold opinions about the worth or relevance of their work or that they should not be interested in the values and opinions of the people they studied. What he really wanted was for sociologists to recognise that facts and values are separate phenomena. 'These two things are logically different and to deal with them as though they were the same represents a confusion of entirely heterogeneous problems.' Weber believed that sociologists should propagate facts, not values, although he knew it was not easy to recognise where the line between the two should be drawn.

Nevertheless, Weber argued that values in sociology are important in that they help guide sociologists towards relevant areas of research. These will be decided by what are seen as the dominant cultural problems of the age, and will change over time. In this, he anticipates the possibility of paradigmatic change in all forms of science. Value freedom, however, is not the same as objectivity. Values concern the choice of subjects studied; objectivity refers to the collection of data without bias or prejudice. Yet objectivity is only possible within a framework of values.

Sociologists need to recognise that the choice of studying ethnic minorities in education rather than girls in education; working-class rather than middle-class deviance; or dependence on the Welfare State rather than the distribution of wealth is an evaluative one. Clearly, some choices are affected by the researcher's own values. What Weber was concerned with was that these values should be recognised and clearly stated. Only then can data be gathered and conclusions reached in an objective way. If values still influence the process then the researcher is guilty of making 'value judgements' and the status of the resulting research must be called into question. Often the 'facts' which a sociologist unearths are picked out because they suit his or her values, while other, perhaps equally relevant, 'facts' are ignored. Facts are often established because they fit in with an underpinning theory.

Functionalism For Alvin Gouldner (1970), the functionalism of Parsons and Merton is a good example of misunderstanding Weber. What these writers have done is claim a value-free status for their work, projecting an image of political and ideological neutrality. They saw their work as above politics and non-partisan and, to that extent, as value-free. This can be construed as a form of intellectual dishonesty: the truth is that it is a conservative ideology presented as social science, believing in the inherent harmony and stability of the status quo. Hiding this confuses objectivity with value freedom.

At the other extreme are the openly partisan sociologists, for example Howard Becker and many Marxists and feminists. In Becker's work (1967 and 1973), values dominate the choice of which social phenomena are studied. Scientific and moral questions are inseparable. Some people may want to disguise their morals as science, because it gives their moral stance greater weight. Instead he suggests that those opposed to the status quo 'whose sympathies I share, should attack injustice and oppression directly and openly, rather than pretend that the judgement that such things are evil is somehow deducible from sociological first principles, or warranted by empirical findings alone … we sometimes begin with the actions we want to take and the people we want to help, as a basis for choosing problems and methods'. This does not necessarily mean to say that how something is studied is lacking in objectivity, even if values determine which social phenomena are studied.

An example given by Becker is the disproportionate amount of research into juvenile behaviour and crime which is conducted. According to Becker, most researchers begin by asking 'what is wrong with the kids of today?' This shows an immediate bias towards the status quo, reflecting the views of the police, parents and social workers. Resulting explanations, if allowed to masquerade as value-free science, take on the status of 'truth'. This could be to the detriment of those involved, particularly the young. Openly partisan, Becker sympathises with the underdog, suggesting that it would be equally valid to ask the question 'what is wrong with the parents of today?'

Marxism A similar campaigning thrust exists among Marxists, taking their cue from Marx's statement (1845): 'The philosophers have only interpreted the world in different ways; the point is to change it.' Marxism is openly value-laden in its examination of social dynamics, being anti-capitalist and pro-communist, although Marxists nevertheless believe that their depiction of reality is objective and scientific: the progression from capitalism to communism is inevitable.

Feminism Likewise with feminism, which criticises existing sociology for reflecting male values and male methods. Explicitly feminist knowledge, it has been claimed (Harding, 1987), 'emerges for the oppressed only through the struggles they wage against their oppressors. It is through feminist struggles against male domination that women's experience can be made to yield up a truer (or less false) image of a social reality than that available only from the perspective of the social experience of the ruling class races. Thus a feminist standpoint is not something anyone can have by claiming it, but an achievement. (A standpoint differs in this respect from a perspective).'

Ann Oakley (1981) argues that feminism demands a particular rationale of research, which breaks down patriarchal approaches by seeing respondents as equals, to whom information is divulged by the researcher as willingly as it is given by the respondent. Feminist theory therefore has a built-in inclination towards qualitative methods.

The problem of objectivity and value freedom is unlikely to be easily solved. Because sociology is the study of humans by other humans, the problem of consciousness and selective perception will always be present. Whether this jeopardises the possibility of a 'scientific' status for sociology depends on how both sociology and science are defined.

QUESTIONS
1 You have read the section on sociology and values. Now try to define the following terms:

   (a) objectivity
   (b) subjectivity
   (c) value freedom
   (d) ideology
   (e) patriarchy

2 Are sociological perspectives value free or should they be viewed as ideologies?

The link between theory and methods

The link between theory and research methods is considered to be at the heart of the understanding of sociology. Sociologists emphasise the importance of this link, a concern which can be really frustrating for students who want to get to grips with some actual explanations for the things which happen in society. The whole point about this so-called 'science' of society is that the arguments about the explanations are as important (if not more so) as the explanations themselves.

Sociology is a set of disagreements, firstly about the type of explanatory framework to use – theoretical disagreements – and secondly about the actual explanations which you provide. So if you're a Marxist you look for conflict, if you're a functionalist you look for consensus, and interactionists just look! A theory is a frame through which we can look at society and see a particular view. Once you have chosen your frame you find out that along with the set of ideas which link together to provide an explanation of society – theoretical concepts – comes a set of ways in which to apply these concepts in research – research methods.

Positivist and interactionist methods

The relationship between theory and methods is actually quite straightforward. If you take the positivist viewpoint, that the structure of society is the place where explanations for social behaviour can be found, you will not be concerned with the feelings, emotions and experiences of human individuals. To the positivists these are not important – they are simply a product of the workings of the larger society. To study society means to study the social structure in order to understand what makes it work. The logical, scientific analysis of numerical data, gathered using such sources as official statistics, questionnaires and structured interviews, provides the raw material which can then be examined and explained by the scientific sociologist. However, from the interactionist viewpoint the reality of social behaviour is to be found when human individuals interact and create their own social experiences. To understand these, the sociologist must attempt to probe into the meanings and beliefs of individuals acting together in groups. Numerical data is itself a product of human interactions, and therefore not to be taken at face value. Instead of researching in the files and statistical tables the interactionists would actually observe these figures being constructed. They would not consult the statistics on bullying in the playground, but rather disguise themselves as a climbing frame and watch it happening. This data deals with the 'quality' of human experience, not in the 'quantities' which record some aspects of it.

Quantitative and qualitative methods

If you are a structural, positivist sociologist, you believe that individuals are determined, shaped and moulded by the larger society, and to understand that moulding process, you must analyse the 'quantitative data'. Large-scale 'macro' analysis will provide a knowledge which is on a par with natural science. If you are an interpretive, interactionist sociologist, you believe that individuals create society through their joint activities. To explain social behaviour, you need to understand individual interpretations, the meanings which individuals themselves give to that behaviour. This data, supposedly rich in 'quality' and depth of meaning, is 'qualitative data'. These two very different types of data, qualitative and quantitative, are related to the type of sociological theory you use. They are collected using completely different methods. In the minds of the sociologists who use them, their own methods and data are the only approach to the study of society. It is obvious, then, that the 'two sociologies' are in complete disagreement. Each one thinks that the theory and methods of the opposing side are worthless. Are they both right?

The positivist view

From the positivist view, the starting point of interactionism is wrong. To provide explanations based only upon the in-depth analysis of individual meanings or processes uncovered by observing group interactions is just a descriptive exercise. The quality of data is equal to that given by a journalist or novelist, interesting to read but telling us nothing about the causes of behaviour. These 'causal relationships' can only be discovered by analysing the social structure in which behaviour takes place. The scientific method which positivists are so keen on is all about discerning patterns in the data collected, and locating the reasons for these patterns within the wider framework of society. Positivists wish to rise above the merely subjective, descriptive data which interactionist sociology provides, to identify patterns and their underlying senses and therefore establish general laws which can be used to predict (and perhaps manipulate!) future behaviour. Positivists look for 'structural switches' which turn the lights of society on and off. They claim that they deal in 'hard facts', whereas interactionists gather more wool than hard data. Objective, social facts are taken as evidence to back up theoretical assumptions. Subjective reports of experience and meaning are discarded as interesting but irrelevant. Positivists believe that it is pointless to rely on reported experiences, because the people involved are not aware of the extent to which their lives and actions are influenced by constraining factors within the social structure.

The interactionist view

On the other hand, the interactionists are critical of the positivist stress upon 'social facts'. To base all of your explanations upon official statistics or questionnaires, the interactionists say, is to ignore the ways in which this type of data is constructed, that is by human beings who bring their interpretations and meaning systems to bear upon the very construction of the so-called facts. If this 'hard evidence' is created by humans who use their own experiences and feelings in the process, then the starting point for analysis has to be in that process. To ignore the human factor is to provide false explanations. The classic example here is inevitably suicide. Durkheim's (1897) analysis of the official statistics is regarded by positivists as a masterpiece of sociological enquiry (see also chapter 14). Durkheim argues that rigorous analysis and comparison of the official suicide statistics provide 'social facts'. But according to interactionism they are social facts compiled by humans – doctors, coroners, the police and the families and friends of the dead person – who all have an axe to grind. Taking these official statistics at face value, they argue, is to ignore the interactive processes which contribute to their creation.

Positivists claim that examining human interactions in 'micro' detail is not 'proof' in the scientific sense. Each study is merely descriptive because the sample is small and unrepresentative; no generalisations can be made and therefore no laws established. According to interactionists, positivist methods, which attempt to apply science to the study of society, are inappropriate because people do not react like substances in the natural sciences. People react, reflect on their own behaviour, have awareness and consciousness of their existence, and therefore explanations for the patterns of their lives can never be found using the cold objective approach of the scientists.

QUESTIONS

1 **What are the main criticisms that positivists make of the interactionist approach?**

2 **What are the main criticisms that interactionists make of the positivist approach?**

3 **How are theoretical approaches linked to sociological research methods?**

Generating data in sociology

Primary and secondary data

Sociologists have two sources of data available to them: data and information they have generated themselves (primary data); or already existing data created for non-sociological purposes (secondary data). Primary data can result from, for example, the employment of questionnaires; structured, semi-structured and unstructured interviews; and observation techniques.

Secondary data can be more or less anything else: statistics produced by the State (for example from the decennial census) and by private companies, letters, diaries, newspapers, books, television (where the study of the mass media is called content analysis) and so on. Secondary data have the great advantage of being cheaply, quickly and easily obtained but have the serious disadvantage of not having been produced by sociologists. They are therefore unlikely to match sociologists' requirements exactly. Sociologists are wary, for example, of using uncritically statistics produced by civil servants.

Quantitative and qualitative data

This data can also be described as quantitative or qualitative. Quantitative data is usually presented in numeric form and derives from large-scale survey methods. Data from the various social mobility studies (see chapter 3), showing how many people have or have not changed their class in their lifetime (but not what it is like to experience this change), are a good example of this type of data.

Qualitative data deals directly with people's experiences, as well as their feelings about and interpretations of the situations they find themselves in. This data is generated through in-depth contact with sociologists, whether by in-depth (or unstructured) interviews or through observation, and will normally appear in prose form or as transcripts of conversations. Sociologists working from within the positivist tradition often use quantitative data whereas sociologists working within the interactionist tradition may use qualitative data.

Sampling

Structural sociologists, particularly those from a positivist background, try to show how, by 'dipping' into a part of society, their findings and results can be broadened (or generalised) to reveal wider social patterns and trends. This dipping is called sampling.

Sampling techniques fall into two different categories: probability and non-probability samples. At their most basic, probability samples can be simple random samples, where anyone in the population to be studied – the sampling frame – has an equal chance of being studied. Respondents are chosen randomly. A systematic sample would take people evenly from the sampling frame, for example every tenth person. A stratified random sample will divide the population into strata, on the grounds of class, age, sex and so on, and a simple random sample will be taken from each strata. In all these ways, generalisations can be made from the sample. This is exactly how opinion polls work in the study of voting intentions and behaviour.

Non-probability sampling does not attempt to allow for an equal probability of any individuals being selected. Quota sampling, for example, deliberately selects specific individuals from a stratum or group. Snowball sampling takes place when contacts are built up from a particular group understudy, for example from a criminal group, as with Polsky's (1969) study.

Pilot studies

When a research technique and choice of sample have been decided upon, the researcher may choose to undertake a pilot study. This is an attempt to test the appropriateness of the chosen method by trying it out on a small sample to see if the project itself is feasible either in principle or in the precise form chosen. Changes to the method are then made, if necessary, before the full-blown study is undertaken.

A case study is an in-depth study of a particular group or phenomenon. Such a study makes no claims to be representative; instead it seeks to typologise a social phenomenon. By its very nature, it is impossible to generalise from such a study as it is a study of one group at one time in one place. Paul Willis's (1977) study of twelve youths in 'Hammertown' (see chapter 5) is a good example of this technique.

Longitudinal studies take place over time, looking at one group or phenomenon, usually over a period of years. The best-known such study is Independent Television's *Seven Up*, which has looked at the lives and fortunes of a group of people every seven years from the age of seven, beginning in the early 1960s. These studies can be quantitative, looking at the same issues over and over again, or qualitative, seeing how people change in the course of a lengthy study.

Official statistics

Official statistics are a favourite source of data for the scientific school of sociology. The official records of such 'social facts' as rates of suicide, marriage, divorce, crime, exam passes, household size, voting patterns, birth, death, health, wealth and poverty can be collected, analysed and compared. These are not tailor-made by the sociologist – manufactured facts, shaped to fit a theory – but are seen as neutral, objective statistical evidence, untainted by values and subjective interpretations. Such statistics are usually accessible, reasonably quick and cheap to obtain (important methodological considerations) and are therefore a major source of data for the number-crunching, scientific sociologists. But are they external, objective records of society's activities, as the positivists would claim, or observed examples of the human experience, as the interactionists would assert? The interactionist criticism is obvious. It is human beings who produce official statistics. They interpret and analyse, categorise and codify in accordance with their views of reality. Behind these apparent 'facts' is a whole hidden agenda of interpretations and cover-ups as well as political and economic considerations. Anyone who uses published data uncritically ignores the 'reality' behind them.

Questionnaires and structured interviews

Questionnaires and structured interviews (the same as a questionnaire, but conducted verbally) are also much loved by the positivists and the structuralists. Postal questionnaires containing 'closed' questions, that is questions requiring a yes or no answer, are ideal for scientific purposes. They are quick and cheap. The sample can be controlled to ensure representation, it covers a large number of people,

Reliability and validity

The concepts of 'reliability' and 'validity' are important in the evaluation of any research. If the findings of one piece of work can be replicated by another research group, or the same research group on a later occasion, and it produces the same result or results, then it is deemed to be reliable. A good example is the varied results deriving from studies of work satisfaction (see chapter 6). Total reliability is difficult to achieve in any social research, and is almost impossible in any qualitative research, given that this research may typically take the form of a single individual observing a group over several years.

'Validity' concerns whether a research method successfully achieves what it claims to have set out to do. Is, for example, the Registrar-General's scale – or 'Standard Occupational Classification' – an effective way of measuring social class? Is John Goldthorpe's classification (see pp. 76–77) better, or, as Marxists and others argue, are they both equally invalid because they fail to show the real dynamics of class relations? The most valid research will result from the successful employment of the most appropriate research methods.

is easily collated and can be analysed with statistical ease. There is no ambiguity in the results and therefore it is more straightforward to draw conclusions. On the negative side, there is a low response rate, the questions predetermine the type of information which comes in, they restrict the respondent to clear-cut statements, and people may lie through boredom, destructiveness or just carelessness. There is no in-depth research and the picture produced is cold and static, a one-sided image, the tip of the social iceberg. The structured interview, a kind of questionnaire with human involvement, is hardly any better according to interactionists. The weaknesses of the questionnaire are all there, plus the added problem of interviewer bias which might influence the respondent. For positivists the structured interview has the advantage that the interviewer can clarify the questions.

Interactionist research is not restricted by the rigid use of natural science methods. The whole focus is upon the elements of society which can be observed and uncovered by taking part, to a greater or lesser degree, in everyday human activities. These events are then described and analysed and a 'micro' view of social life presented. By observing and extracting the meanings which people give to their day-to-day experiences, interactionists attempt to show how 'reality' is socially constructed in the human exchanges which define and form 'society'.

It is here that one of the main differences between positivists and interactionists becomes clear. The positivists believe that individuals are created and controlled by the social structure. Their existence is 'determined' by society. They are born into an existing structure, internalise its norms and values, and become units within the larger framework. Individual thought, meaning and action are of little importance. Greater forces are at work, and these need to be studied using objective and value-free scientific methods.

Interactionists see the individual as a social agent, an autonomous, self-directing actor who, either alone or with others, influences, changes and participates in the creation of society. Individuals are not the slavish automatons visualised by positivism, but are said to have 'free will', taking decisions and creating their own social circumstances. Although interactionists often do acknowledge the influence of aspects of the social structure, for example the effect of class on educational chances, they analyse these from the context of the individual's experience of them, and the decisions and choices made in the particular situation. Rather than study the statistical aspects of the structure of society, interactionists acknowledge that, because they have self-awareness, people cannot be studied like microbes in a test tube; on the contrary they can act upon and influence the test and the researchers.

Observational methods

Observational methods do not result in a formal hypothesis but in a set of preliminary aims, which can be modified, retained or thrown out completely as research proceeds and unexpected and interesting material presents itself. Observation ranges from mere eavesdropping or staring to participating in the activities of the people involved. *Overt* participant observation means that those being studied are aware of the true reason for the sociologist's presence. This has the considerable disadvantage of ensuring that the subjects do not behave as they normally would. Tales abound in sociology of factory workers who double productivity (the Hawthorne effect; see chapter 6) and gangs who put on extravagant displays to impress their willing audience. The answer is to conduct under-cover or *covert* research which is supposed to reveal the real nitty-gritty of human experience.

In interactionist terms, the purpose of research is to get as close as possible to the realities underlying human interactions. All forms of observation could be said to do that, to a greater or lesser degree, and they all provide more depth than scientific methods. The time spent observing is an important element, as more and more aspects of a situation will become apparent over a long period. This is expensive. However, critics argue that observers run the risk of getting so close to their subjects that they fail to see aspects of a process which they are a part of. The covert researcher also runs the risk of being discovered – an element of personal danger which tends to lend this research its glamorous character.

Observation and ethics

A more serious academic criticism is an ethical one. Is it fair, is it morally correct, to study people by befriending them, winning their confidence, and then ultimately betraying their trust by 'informing' on them, even if it is only to a limited audience of sociologists? The defenders of the practice claim that the end justifies the means. If this is the only way to find out about the topic in question, then it is worth the possible breach of ethics.

Humphreys' (1970) famous study of homosexual behaviour in public toilets, or 'tearooms' as they were known, is a case in point. Humphreys was able to participate in the clandestine sexual activities of these men by taking on the role of voyeur. His presence was tolerated and apparently welcomed. Humphreys was criticised on ethical grounds, but pointed out that had his subjects been aware of his real identity and purpose, they would not have behaved naturally. Clearly, this question of ethics is dependent to a certain extent upon what is being studied. Another major criticism is that the data gathered by such observational methods is useless because no matter how well the situation is described, the sample is so small in scale as to be unrepresentative and therefore of no value in generalising and formulating laws.

Unstructured interviews

The unstructured interview – a second important method pioneered by interactionists – is a method designed to allow the interviewee to 'open up', giving an in-depth picture of their world and allowing the important feelings and understandings of the individual to emerge. The questions are completely open-ended. A list of general areas acts as a guideline, but the subject may provide a line of thought not anticipated by the questioner. The relaxed, informal setting allows this line of thinking to be followed, and thus fresh and interesting ideas can be developed. The techniques of interviewing are to establish a rapport and to encourage intimate disclosures. The interview is taped and subsequently transcribed and analysed by the interviewer. As with observation, the risk is that the researcher and subject get to be too close, and the researcher then becomes a part of the process being studied. Also, the interviewer is more likely to bias the responses, as the subject, having formed a cosy relationship, does not wish to displease the interviewer, and will try to give responses which gain approval. This method, designed to avoid false, superficial pictures in order to get at the truth, could end up being the cause of yet another false picture being painted. Another fault is that the researcher, as well as 'leading' the interview into the areas desired, is free, during the analysis and discussion, to select what they think are the most important factors in the interview.

The whole area of interactionist research, concerned as it is with the subjective, value-laden side of social behaviour, stands accused by positivism as being itself subjective and value-laden. Interactionist methods all entail close, in-depth study of individuals and small groups, such as conversational analysis, where the micro details of spoken conversations are scrutinised, or studies which, for example, plot the friendships of schoolchildren. These, and associated methods, all provide the kind of close-up view which allows a depth and quality of insight into the motivations, emotions and experiences of individuals. For interactionists, these areas are the focal point of social analysis, because this is where society is created, where social reality exists. Methods which only collect numerical data miss the point. Interactionist theory and method are therefore bound together. These methods are used by interactionist sociologists because they allow them to uncover the only kind of data they are interested in – qualitative data.

Interactionism has become a growing trend in sociology since it first became popular in the mid 1960s. Structuralists of the old school dismiss the latest interactionist accounts of greeting behaviours

TABLE 1.1   **Main sociological research methods**

METHOD	STRENGTHS	WEAKNESSES	USED BY	COMMENTS
Official statistics	Quick. Easily obtained. Often seen as valid and reliable. Cheap.	Can be misleading e.g. 'dark figure'[1] of crime, 'real' suicide rate.	Durkheim, *Suicide: A Study in Sociology*, 1897.	Secondary data – not originated by sociologists.
Questionnaires	Reaches many respondents. Quick. High reliability.	'Leading' questions. Same questions may be interpreted differently.	Townsend, *Poverty in the UK*, 1979.	Questions can be 'open' or 'closed'. Also postal.
Structured interviews	Misinterpretations can be clarified. High response rate.	'Interviewer bias'. Respondents may lie.	Goldthorpe *et al.*, *The Affluent Worker in the Class Structure*, 1969.	Very similar to questionnaires. Quantitative data.
Unstructured interviews	In-depth questioning. Meanings, reasons and motives can be explored.	Time-consuming. Interviewers may still 'lead' respondents. Too close to conversation.	Barker, *The Making of a Moonie*, 1984. Oakley, *The Sociology of Housework*, 1974b.	Qualitative data.
Observation – participant and non-participant	Close to 'real' situation. Change may be observed over time.	Difficult to generalise. Low reliability. 'Hawthorne effect'.	Patrick, *A Glasgow Gang Observed*, 1973. Whyte, *Street Corner Society*, 1955.	May be covert or overt. Sometimes called 'ethnography'.

[1]*The 'dark figure' of crime is the difference between reported and unreported crime.*

among street traders in Puerto Rico as social psychology and not sociology. Some sociologists attempt to combine a variety of approaches and methods, discussed in the next section.

QUESTIONS

1 **Give some examples of sociological methods that fit in the following categories:**

(a) **quantitative sociological methods**
(b) **qualitative sociological methods**

2 **Give some reasons why positivist sociologists prefer quantitative methods.**

3 **What are the strengths and weaknesses of the following?**

(a) **questionnaires**
(b) **unstructured interviews**
(c) **participant observation**

4 **Give some reasons why ethical considerations are important in conducting sociological research.**

5 **Apart from their theoretical position, what other factors could affect a sociologist's choice of methods?**

Methodological pluralism and methodological purism

So far in this book we have suggested that there is a strong relationship between positivism and quantitative methods on the one hand and interactionism and qualitative methods on the other. This division is real in sociology, marking a real debate, as Martyn Hammersley acknowledges: 'While positivist social scientists have themselves varied somewhat in their interpretations of science, in general they have taken quantitative measurement and the experimental or statistical manipulation of variables as its key elements. And it is against this conception of scientific methods that anti-positivists in the social sciences have rebelled most strongly, often advocating instead the use of qualitative methods' (Hammersley, 1993).

Behind this statement lies the argument that the use of a particular method or methods aligns the researcher with a particular view of what the world is like, and how the study of society should be carried out, given the researcher's real aim of generating theory.

Triangulation Increasingly, as we have argued at the beginning of this chapter, sociologists are prepared to drop this division in favour of simply 'doing' sociology, using whatever methods are appropriate, whether quantitative or qualitative. At the same time, they do not seek to call themselves positivists or interactionists but simply sociologists. This approach is called methodological pluralism or sometimes, using Denzin's (1970) term, triangulation. Thus sociologists are willing to use a range of methods while at the same time refusing to have themselves simplistically pigeonholed as belonging to one or other of the perspectives in sociology.

As early as 1957, Trow argued that we should 'be done with the arguments of participant observation versus interviewing … and get on with the business of attacking our problems with the widest array of conceptual and methodological tools that we possess and they demand'.

A good example of a response to such a challenge of methodological pluralism was provided by Howard Gans in *The Levittowners* (1967), where his main method was participant observation achieved by buying a house in Levittown, USA (see also chapter 13). He also, however, sent out 3,100 questionnaires to people about to move to Levittown, and conducted structured interviews with a smaller sample of Levittown residents, repeated after two years. Gans was thus prepared to use a range of methods in order to discover what it was like to move to, and live in, Levittown.

Disciplinary ethnocentrism

Researchers such as Gans had few qualms about combining quantitative and qualitative data, believing that there would be no corresponding loss of theoretical rigour and coherence. For this to continue, what Warwick (1983) calls 'disciplinary ethnocentrism' will have to come to an end. 'Many quantitative social scientists,' he argues, 'fancy themselves as "hard heads" – true scientists whose propensity for numbers betokens a deep and undying commitment to truth. Those who do not share this faith are "soft heads" who do not deserve the name of science. For their part social scientists of a qualitative persuasion often portray their approach as humane, sensitive, intuitive and comprehensive … Quantitative researchers, by contrast, are methodologically gross, insensitive to contexts and more often than not wrong in their assessment of community dynamics.'

At the heart of this debate concerning the reliability and validity of types of data in sociology is the question of the status of the sociology produced through the employment of these methods. 'Purist' sociologists at either end of the spectrum will remain convinced that their unadulterated perspective will produce either the most reliable or valid information about the nature of human organisation. Positivists will continue to see their work as a contribution to scientific knowledge. Given Durkheim's aim of developing a science of society, it is hard, for example, to see him using anything other than quantitative methods in his study of suicide (see chapter 14). Phenomenologists will continue to make fundamental objections to the way such data seems to fail to describe people and the societies they live in. The danger of methodological pluralism may well be the creation of a generation of sociologists who are competent in everything and proficient in nothing.

QUESTIONS

1 **What are the strengths and weaknesses of 'methodological pluralism'?**

2 **In what ways would Durkheim's study of suicide have changed if he had gathered qualitative data?**

3 **Is disciplinary ethnocentrism simply a form of arrogance?**

Sociology and social policy

Social problems

All social problems turn out finally to be problems of social control.

R. E. Park and E. Burgess, 1921

Before going on to examine the relationship between sociological theory and social policy it is necessary to examine the nature of social problems. The following may be considered to be social problems:

poor housing and homelessness	misuse of drugs and alcohol
poverty	immigration
crime	poor health
gender inequalities	vandalism
unemployment	ethnic inequalities
divorce	Aids
public safety	sexual abuse
football hooliganism	home repossessions
suicide	industrial conflict
scroungers	profits
mugging	delinquency
care of the elderly	the family
the care system	riots

It is questionable whether there is a general consensus about what are the most important social problems, but the important questions for sociologists to consider are:

- What is considered a social problem?
- Why is it a social problem?
- Who says it is a social problem?
- Why is this issue being considered to the exclusion of others?
- What are the policies proposed and who will benefit from them?

Subjective and objective elements

Social problems tend to have a subjective and an objective element, with interactionists emphasising the former while structuralists emphasise the latter. During the nineteenth and early twentieth centuries the origin of social problems was located in individuals. To some extent this perspective re-emerged in the 1980s. Individuals may experience a problem subjectively – it is their problem and they are suffering from it. It may cause anxiety, tension, stress or depression. Such subjective feelings may be caused by poverty or unemployment, for example. At the same time unemployment is an 'objective' reality in that it transcends the individual and has structural causes. Its solution lies in collective action and relatively large amounts of investment and spending.

The concept of a social problem is relative. What constitutes a social problem in one society may not be regarded as such in another. Poverty is an example of this. Even within a particular society social problems can be and often are viewed differently. For example, some groups in our society may regard immigration as a problem while others may regard racism as a problem.

Voluntary and involuntary problems

Some social problems are 'voluntary', for example divorce and vandalism. Other social problems are 'involuntary' such as being elderly or black. This distinction between the voluntary and the involuntary may be criticised as many social problems are a mixture of the two. Behaviour is patterned, follows social trends and is influenced by structural forces. To what extent therefore is divorce or unemployment voluntary? Equally it is not so much the involuntary growing old or being black that matters so much as society's 'voluntary' attitudes and response to these phenomena.

Power

It is important to discover where the power lies in the process of identifying and dealing with social problems. This emphasis on power is made largely by Marxists but is accepted by interactionists. The role of the media in developing our 'awareness' of certain social problems to the exclusion of others should not be underestimated and has been highlighted in the work of the Glasgow Media Group, Stan Cohen's work on mods and rockers (1972) and others (see chapter 15).

The poorest in our society and those marginalised within it have great difficulty in getting their definitions of the situation accepted by the wider society and the agenda setters. This could be due to lack of economic resources or to ideological subjugation and exclusion from the media and seats of power.

Social policies

The existence of social problems suggests that not all members of society are equal beneficiaries of its wealth and institutions. Some may be regarded as victims of society or trouble-makers within it. What may be at stake is a conflict of ideologies and interests. In the formulation of social policy there are many possible means to achieve a given end. The means chosen depend largely on the ideology of those with the power to determine social policy. In order to reduce poverty, some policies (particularly those on the left) advocate a redistribution of wealth, a minimum wage and a minimum income. Others argue that in order to reduce poverty we must encourage economic growth; this may lead to increasing inequality but the wealth will trickle down and everyone will benefit. Social policies may have unintended side effects: some right-wingers argue that a minimum wage will have the unintended effect of increasing unemployment and poverty by increasing industry's costs. On the other hand, increasing wealth and income at the top may result in lower productivity due to a lack of incentive to work. It may also result in the creation of an underclass with no vested interest in the social and economic system and which therefore poses a threat to social stability.

The list of questions and policy options is endless. Consider the following:

- Is crime best reduced by 'short sharp shocks' or by the creation of more alternatives to custody schemes?

- Do we need more police in patrol cars or more bobbies on the street?

- Are the interests of the elderly or mentally ill best served by the process of deinstitutionalisation? There is much evidence, for example, that such a process places a great burden on the family and particularly women in the family. This may be regarded as an unintentional consequence or it may be regarded as the result of patriarchal attitudes by those in positions to make decisions. It is also necessary to note that the process of deinstitutionalisation – community care – arose due to economic pressure on the Welfare State and the problems associated with institutions.

- Should welfare be provided by the State or by the private sector?

- Should welfare benefits be universal or should they be targeted at those who most need them?

Historical development

The relationship between sociology and social policy is not particularly clear from a reading of the writers who laid the foundations of sociological thought. For Comte, sociology was the new religion, the scientific humanism that would unravel the laws of human society and lead to rational social planning. Yet Comte's sociology was profoundly conservative in nature and advocated a 'wise resignation to the facts'. Such social facts were not open to reason. Comte's sociology was therefore unlikely to give rise to a social policy that played a radical or reforming role, despite his wish that sociology should influence rational social planning.

Some sociologists of the late nineteenth century and early twentieth century, such as Rowntree and Booth, adopted a much more empirical approach in their sociological investigation of a particular social problem. Even here, though, the relationship between sociology and social policy is quite crude – the main method employed by these sociologists in their demonstration of poverty at the turn of the century in England was that of the exposé.

Importantly, the period 1930–1960 is marked by the increasing attempt by sociology to be accepted as a discipline into the academic world. As part of this (largely successful) process the scientific nature of the discipline was stressed. This included a need to detach the subject from its perceived link with the identification of social problems and consequent social reform.

The concept of values has been discussed earlier in this chapter. Nevertheless, it will be useful to highlight some aspects of this issue here. There is a great deal of controversy within sociology as to whether sociologists should have any direct input into the study of particular social problems or should be involved in espousing particular social policies. This is due to the desire on the part of some sociologists to produce value-free sociology and themselves remain neutral. Such a desire is linked to conceptions of what constitutes science and indeed what constitutes social science or sociology. It is also linked to a desire to be accepted into the academic establishment, to secure adequate funding and to get one's research actually used.

Weber   Writing in the early part of this century, Max Weber (1904–5) was at pains to clarify the role of sociology in social research. He makes a clear distinction between research and researcher when he states that 'To apply the results of [sociological] analysis in the making of decisions … is not a task which science can undertake; it is rather the task of the acting, willing person: he weighs and chooses from among the values involved according to his own conscience and his personal view of the world. Science can make him realise that all action and naturally, according to the circumstances, inaction imply in their consequences the espousal of certain values and … the rejection of certain others.'

Weber accepted that it is within the role of a sociologist to choose the social problems they wish to consider but emphasised that the actual research must be strictly objective. He also wished to distinguish sharply between sociology and social policy which he saw as two different 'worlds', both of which are valuable but whose distinctions and ways of working should be made clear. In discussing Weber on this subject, James Coleman (1979) draws on the analogy of the two worlds of discipline and action, with sociology being in the world of discipline and social policy being in the world of action. The term 'discipline' in this context means an area of academic study. The world of discipline is pure and value-free; the world of action is impure, laden with conflicting interest groups, may be secretive and is not value-free. The sociologist treads a wary line between the two worlds.

Weber's conception of the relationship between sociology and social policy is that sociology provides the technical information from which policy makers decide social policy. In this respect Weber is a technician. Much of American empirical sociology since the Second World War has been of this technical nature. Clearly not all sociologists take this view. Marx said that 'Philosophers have interpreted the world. The point is to change it'. So Marx himself did not share the same concern about being value-free and on the contrary wished to join in the world of action.

Other sociologists see a place for values in sociology and a place for the sociologist in the making of social policy. Robert S. Lynd (1939) does not quite go this far but he does argue that values are relevant in the choosing of an important social problem and in the guiding of policy makers on the likely outcome of their decisions. C. Wright Mills (1959), too, against the trend of contemporary American sociologists, took an anti-technician stance and argued for the place of values in sociological research. Howard Becker, the interactionist (1967), argues not only for the place of values in sociology but for a particular set of values which promote a favourable outcome in social policy terms for disadvantaged members of society. This position is one shared by many European left-wing sociologists such as Peter Townsend, Stuart Hall and Jeremy Seabrook.

Undertaking research   Of course the underdogs in society are not in much of a position to initiate social policy research themselves. Indeed much social policy research is carried out for various interested parties. These include:

- government – both national and local, who may want to test the water before applying new social policies;

- government – both national and local, who wish to assess the impact of existing social policy;

- business interests – wishing to develop market research into present and future lifestyles;

- business interests – wishing to develop raw data which support a particular lobbying position that promotes their interests, e.g. Adam Smith Institute;

- promotional interest groups – wishing to influence government, public opinion, or gain media time, e.g. Friends of the Earth;

- sectional interest groups – establishing the effects of current or future social policy on a particular social group, e.g. trade union support of the Low Pay Unit or Child Poverty Action Group;

- independent researchers – rarely.

Results   One argument that seems to present itself here is that social policy research does not necessarily reduce conflict between interested parties and produce social laws as Comte might have hoped, but such research may make the conflicting interest groups better informed – if the information is freely available.

Hostility to social policy   In April 1979, the incoming Conservative government, for example, appeared to have little interest in social policy research. It abolished the Royal Commission on the Distribution of Wealth and Income almost immediately, leaving the Inland Revenue as the main source of this type of data for sociologists. In April 1980, the authors of an inquiry commissioned by the previous Labour government into inequalities in health – *The Black Report* (see chapter 10) – submitted their findings to the Secretary of State for Health and Social Security. This was eventually released in the form of 260 duplicated typescript copies and a statement to the press issued on the Friday before the August bank holiday. In his preface to the Report, the Secretary of State, Patrick Jenkin, made it clear that the 'additional expenditure which could result from the Report's recommendations – the amount involved could be upwards of £2 billion a year – is quite unrealistic in present or any foreseeable economic circumstances, quite apart from any judgement that may be formed of the effectiveness of such expenditure in dealing with the problems identified. I cannot, therefore, endorse the Group's recommendations.' Seven years later, the publication of the Health Education Council's *The Health Divide* met with a similar response when government officials were widely suspected of cancelling press conferences concerning its release.

In the early 1980s, the main funding body for social policy research, the Social Science Research Council, was renamed the Economic and Social Research Council, dropping the word 'Science' from its title. Needless to say, sociology is not a prescribed subject on the National Curriculum. From this time, there has been an increased emphasis, both inside and outside sociology, on cultural factors rather than structural factors when investigating problems.

On the relationship between social policy research and power there are of course different positions. Some sociologists have argued that the increased knowledge gained will enable those with power to strengthen their hold by manipulating their subjects. The increased information may help those in power to respond to public wishes and remain in power. Alternatively policy research may undermine those in authority by revealing the gap between their claims and the actual outcome of their policies. However, in order for this to be the case such policy results would have to be placed in a context where they could be published and utilised by alternative decision makers.

Social policy has different and competing goals. There are also different means of achieving the same policy goal. Sociology has had an uneasy relationship with social policy. This was seen in Comte's conservatism, the attempt to disassociate sociology from social problems and the controversy over values. Conflicting interests sponsor research. The effects of research on those in authority is uncertain, as are the uses to which research is put.

QUESTIONS

1 **What is meant by the term 'social policy'?**

2 **What are the differences between sociology and social policy?**

3 **Is there likely to be a link between the findings and recommendations of a piece of research and the agency funding it?**

FURTHER READING

This book concentrates on the 'knowledge' aspect of sociology. It does not attempt to deal with the interpretive and evaluative skills required by many exam and validating boards. There are, however, many books and packs available that deal with this aspect of sociology and would be helpful to anyone taking a coursework option.

For example:

V. Bailey, G. Benrose, S. Goddard, R. Imprey, E. Joslyn, J. Mackness, *Essential Research Skills*, Collins Educational, 1995

D. Barratt and T. Cole, *Sociology Projects: A Students' Guide*, Routledge and Kegan Paul, 1991

J. Bell, *Doing Your Research Project*, Open University Press, 1987

R. Burgess, *Research Methods*, Nelson, 1993

H. Chignell, *Data in Sociology*, Causeway Press, 1990

A. Dunsmuir and L. Williams, *How to do Social Research*, Collins Educational, 1991

N. Howe, *Advanced Practical Sociology*, Nelson, 1994

M. Kirby, F. Koubel and N. Madry, *Sociology: Developing Skills through Structured Questions*, Collins Educational, 1993

P. Langley and P. Corrigan: *Managing Sociology Coursework*, Connect Publications, 1993

A. Lawson, *Sociology for A-level: A Skills-based Approach*, Collins Educational, 1993

P. McNeill, *Research Methods*, Routledge, 1990

2 Culture and identity

Culture is one of the two or three most complicated words in the English language:.

Raymond Williams

INTRODUCTION

In this chapter you will start by looking at the part played by norms, values, roles and status in society. The next section examines the way individuals develop a 'self', the part played by socialisation in this process, and the role of culture. The final section looks at how sociologists have analysed the concept of culture, focusing specifically on the work of élite theorists and Marxists such as the Frankfurt School and the Centre for Contemporary Cultural Studies.

Norms, values, roles and status

In a book that emphasises the disagreements between sociologists, it is perhaps most helpful to start by considering what they do agree on. Sociologists agree that sociology is about understanding what humans do, not through studying the biological or individual psychological make-up of individuals, but by examining the way that the society in which they live influences and shapes what they do. In the debate about whether humans behave 'naturally' or are 'nurtured', sociologists are firmly on the side of nurture. This is the central argument of sociology.

Socialisation Societies work or function because each individual member of that society plays particular roles and that each role carries a status and norms which are informed by the values and beliefs of the culture of that society. The process of learning these roles and the norms and values appropriate to them from those around us is called socialisation. It takes place because people learn that social sanctions exist to encourage behaviour appropriate to their roles and to discourage inappropriate behaviour. These sanctions may be negative or positive. Negative sanctions operate at a number of levels. Gender roles, for example, can be maintained informally by calling people names, such as 'tomboy' for girls and 'cissy' for boys. Persistent offenders may be ridiculed or even excluded by those around them. Positive sanctions can include praise for appropriate behaviour, remarking on a girl's pretty dress or a boy's toughness and determination. The most intensive period of socialisation occurs within the family and is called primary socialisation. It is in the family that, by imitation, babies learn to walk and talk, to act like mummy and daddy, and in the process take on the gender roles of those they identify with. In this way, we learn to be human.

That this is not an automatic process is evident from the examples of 'wild' children such as Amala and Kamala, the Indian 'wolf-children' discovered earlier this century, who took on wolf-like behaviour, not sleeping at night, howling, gnawing at bones and crawling rather than walking. Although they were thought to be about two and eight years old when they were discovered, there was nothing 'human' about their behaviour.

Roles The values of the culture in which we live define the roles that we play and the pattern of behaviour that goes with those roles. Roles can be defined as a set of normative expectations. We all play many roles in the course of our life, sometimes even in the same day. Other people see us not as the unique individuals we perceive ourselves to be but by the particular roles we are playing at that time. The relationships we form as a direct result of having a role are called a role set. Unhappiness with or consciousness of playing this role is described as role distance. Social order is only possible because we understand that others are playing certain roles. Some roles are replicated throughout institutions, for example teacher and student. On occasion, individuals may find themselves playing two contradictory roles at the same time, such as employee and mother, or they may define their role differently to the way others expect them to. Such situations involve role conflict.

Norms Norms are defined as expected patterns of behaviour, and are defined by the wider values of a society's culture. The normative activity of attending a place of worship, for example, may be influenced by the cultural value placed on piety. Norms surrounding what we eat and how we eat it may be influenced by the values and beliefs surrounding ideas of hygiene and health. In some societies, choosing a mate may be a practical and economic decision, unaffected by ideas of romantic love. Even the number of husbands and wives men and women may marry at any one time may be the product of cultural rather than individual influences. Different cultural values produce different cultural norms.

Status The term status refers to the level of social honour or prestige given to someone by others, either as a result of the formal role they are playing in their social position, or for the individual skills and talents they display. Different occupations are associated with different levels of status, although differences of status also exist within an occupation – a status hierarchy. Some statuses are given to us or ascribed, such as mother, father, daughter or son. Others may be chosen, or achieved, such as employment roles – being a firefighter or a judge. The status accorded a role is defined by the culture in which you live. The elderly as a status group, for example, carry a lower status in Western than other societies. Taking on a new role that carries higher status than the previous role may lead to status dissonance if individuals find it difficult to play that role.

In industrial societies, the primary stage of socialisation is further extended when children enter the education system. This is called secondary socialisation. At school they learn wider values of society outside their experience of the family, and are treated not as particular individuals but as members of a larger community. When they leave school socialisation continues as they prepare to enter adulthood and when they become parents the cycle begins all over again. Socialisation is a continuous, never-ending process.

Criticisms This somewhat mechanical picture becomes far more complicated when attempts are made to operationalise these concepts, that is, to make them work in a meaningful way in the process of research. Over time, these terms have come to be hotly contested in such a way that the simple and one-dimensional definitions given above are no longer agreed upon by sociologists.

The link between norms and values, for example, may not be as strong as first supposed. Some people may share a cultural desire to become close to God, and this may be their sole reason for attending a place of worship. Others may go to please their family and friends, or to maintain their social status. Just because people behave in the same way it does not mean that their motives are the same. This may mean that it is not possible for sociologists to make generalisations about the motives behind behaviour.

Further questions have to be asked: do people have a choice in playing their various roles? Exactly how does socialisation happen? Can it be resisted? What are sociologists referring to when they describe the culture of a society? Does everyone really share the same values of the culture they live within? It may be the case, if we look carefully, that there is as much evidence of conflict around these values, as there is consensus.

The clear implication of these questions is that there can be no one single view of culture and socialisation; rather there are many. Taken to its extreme, there could be as many views as to what constitutes a culture as there are individuals living in that culture, as we cannot assume that everyone perceives the world around them in the same way. Sociologists can choose to don many different pairs of spectacles in their efforts to 'see' something as complex as a society. As with other academic disciplines, there are many perspectives in sociology. The most important of these are outlined in chapter 1.

QUESTIONS

1 **Define the following terms which were discussed in the previous section:**

   (a) **norms**
   (b) **values**
   (c) **role set**
   (d) **status**

2 **Describe the values of schools or colleges with which you are familiar.**

3 **What are the norms involved in classroom behaviour?**

4 **What are the differences between the roles played by teachers and the roles played by students?**

5 **List the roles that you may play in any one day of your life.**

Self, identity, socialisation and culture

Different conceptions of what is meant by the term socialisation, and of how this process takes place, tell us much about the wider philosophical positions taken in sociology and outlined in the previous chapter. In particular this debate concerns the question of whether a social identity is something that can be chosen and interpreted by individual actors or whether an individual's identity is in reality more analogous to an actor playing a role in a stage play where their lives and lines have already been written for them.

Durkheim

From one point of view, socialisation is seen as a one-way process in which society, through agencies such as the family, the education system and peer groups, inculcates individuals into the roles already prescribed for them by those agencies. This view is strongly put by one of the 'founding fathers' of sociology, Emile Durkheim: 'Certainly society is greater than, and goes beyond, us, for it is infinitely more vast than our individual being; but at the same time it enters into every part of us. It is outside us and envelopes us, but it is in us and is everywhere an aspect of our nature. We are fused with it. Just as our physical organism gets nourishment outside itself, so our mental organism feeds on ideas, sentiments, and practices that come to us from society' (Durkheim, 1902–6). Society can be seen as a system of moral norms in which individuals are essentially passive, responding without choice to imposed rewards and punishments. Socialisation then comes to mean virtually the same as training, or even taming, where each individual becomes a microcosm of a society's values. As the emphasis is on the lack of choice open to an individual in taking on their social roles, this is also sometimes described as the 'totalitarian' view of socialisation.

Parsons

This view is less stridently present in the systems theory of Talcott Parsons (see chapter 1, section on functionalism). Here, the focus is on how society as a social system maintains order, where a system is defined as 'two or more interacting units which are at the same time actors and social objects to each other' (Parsons, 1951). Social order is maintained by individuals learning to desire what the culture of a society provides, and in doing so their personalities become structured by the social roles they internalise, i.e. these social roles become part of them. The end result is conformity. Deviant behaviour – behaviour that goes against social norms – can therefore be explained as the consequence of inadequate socialisation. The consequences of this particular argument and much of what follows below are explored in much greater detail in the sociology of crime and deviance (see chapter 14).

Mead

From another perspective, built on the theories of G.H. Mead outlined in chapter 1 in the section on symbolic interactionism, the focus is on how an individual passes through a series of stages in taking on their social identity. From birth, children are confronted with a number of ready-made roles which, as they pass through the various stages of socialisation, they consult in the same way that a map can be read. In doing so, they become socially competent, taking on the social skills and knowledge necessary to interact with others. Individuals are portrayed as active in the acquisition and negotiation of their social identities or selfhood. This is a continuous process throughout their lives, sometimes referred to as a 'biography'.

> ### G.H. Mead (1868–1931)
> American social psychologist and a founder of symbolic interactionism. Mead's social psychology revolved around the theory of the way the mind worked, the concept of 'self', the origin of communication and the social act. In sociology his ideas were built upon by Blumer as a basis for symbolic interactionism.

> ### C.H. Cooley (1864–1929)
> Early American sociologist. Trained as an engineer, he moved away from science and turned to sociology. He advocated that sociologists should try to use the sociological imagination to imagine the imagination of actors. He came up with some major concepts: the looking-glass self and the idea that there is a distinction between primary groups, characterised by face-to-face interaction and co-operation, and secondary groups.

It is through the family that the child's identity is formed, a process identified by C.H. Cooley as primary socialisation. Even here there is opportunity for reciprocity and negotiation in that parents learn their roles as parents (defined with the birth of the first child) at the same time as the child learns its role. A child may be said to have become self-conscious when it realises that it can talk not only to others but can be reflexive and talk to itself. It can objectify itself when it realises that it exists as an independent entity. It becomes a self-conscious individual only through interaction with others: its 'I' becomes the socialised 'me', where the socialised part of the self is seen as its identity, and socialisation is equated with the acquisition of language.

Secondary socialisation

H. Blumer (1900–86)
American sociologist. He is credited with developing the term symbolic interactionism. He advocated the small-scale study of social interaction against the claims of large-scale, abstract theorising.

Goffman

Erving Goffman (1922–82)
American sociologist and major contributor to the interactionist perspective, particularly in works such as Asylums *(1961) and* The Presentation of Self in Everyday Life *(1959). The study of small encounters and interaction in everyday life is of particular interest to Goffman.*

Later in life, at the stage of secondary socialisation, it will choose from the roles of the generalised other – which at its widest is society. By taking on the role of the generalised other, the self becomes fully social. Primary socialisation may not be a lasting or determining influence on this stage. Does the school, for example, simply take over from the family? Some symbolic interactionists employ the concept of a career here, though they stress that in these careers, there is no necessary, laid-down path for people to follow in their identity transformations. This is particularly true in the notion of 'deviant careers', for example becoming a drug user or an alcoholic. At this stage, in responding to 'situations', there are a great many opportunities for the negotiation and interpretation of identities. H. Blumer emphasises the choices facing individuals: 'the acting unit necessarily has to identify the things that it has to take into account – tasks, opportunities, obstacles, means, demands, discomforts, dangers, and the like; it has to assess them in some fashion and it has to make decisions on the basis of the assessment' (Blumer, 1969).

For Erving Goffman, roles are best seen as played, performed or dramatised within the rules surrounding social rituals (for example, getting dressed up to 'go out'), where what we do in private is seen as backstage activities, and possessions are seen as props. Of particular interest to Goffman is what happens when these props are removed, for example on entering an asylum, when 'existence is cut to the bone' and the individual undergoes what Goffman calls 'mortification of the self'. In the asylum studied by Goffman, patients' personal possessions were taken away from them, the patients were cleaned and issued with clothing by the asylum. All this entails a loss of their former sense of self. An individual's sense of self is recovered by a range of modes of adjustment, for example bending the rules of the institutions: 'Our status is backed by the solid buildings of the world, while our sense of personal identity often resides in the cracks.' He therefore moves beyond Mead's view of the self as a constant entity by distinguishing 'person' from self: 'Person and self are portraits of the same individual, the first encoded in the actions of others, the second in the actions of the subject himself' (Goffman, 1971).

Although two different perspectives on socialisation are being presented here, one emphasising the action of society on individuals, the other emphasising the individual's interpretation of social roles, neither are uncritically accepted, either inside or outside sociology. Other sociologists have been critical of the lack of attention paid to economic and political forces, arguing that being born into a rich or poor family, for example, influences the form taken by primary socialisation. Psychologists, following Freud, question whether sociologists, in denying the importance of nature, limit their view of a process as complex as the acquisition of a human social identity.

Wrong and oversocialisation

In what has become an important and influential essay, Dennis Wrong (1961) takes issue with what he believes has become the 'oversocialised concept of man in modern sociology'. In using the term 'oversocialisation' Wrong is highlighting what he believes is sociology's inability to take into account the emotional or affective aspect of people's lives. Socialised individuals cannot be seen simply as 'roles in system'. The internalisation of norms is not analogous to the programming of a computer, with humans dehumanised into an input/output model. There is no necessary reason to suppose that individuals will automatically play the roles assigned to them, or will internalise them to the same degree. They can become overburdened by the weight of role prescriptions. Wrong holds that psychology, Freudian psychology in particular, has important lessons for sociology.

Freud

> ### Sigmund Freud (1856–1939)
> Practising physician, specialist in the treatment of nervous diseases, and founder of psychoanalysis. Freud developed the concept of the unconscious. According to this, motives and ideas, unavailable to the conscious mind, originating in childhood, play a major part in the life of the adult.

Psychology has been much concerned with the problems of innate behaviour in its debates about the relative importance of 'nature' and 'nurture'. Freud was less concerned with innate behaviour, but he did aim to analyse forms of unconscious conditioning. Freud chose to use the German word 'Trieb' rather than 'Instinkt' to denote what he saw as psychological drives and desires rather than biological instincts. Freud saw an individual's psyche as being in a state of conflict between their ego (the conscious reality-testing self), their id (instincts and unconscious, perhaps repressed life) and their super-ego (the values internalised from parents and the wider society). What we know of someone is only their ego. Internalisation of values is not synonymous with conformity. Hence, as Wrong states, 'To Freud, it is precisely the man with the strictest superego, he who has most thoroughly internalised and conformed to the norms of his society, who is most wracked with guilt and anxiety.' Such a person, rather than being the 'best' socialised, may suffer psychological illnesses and be unable at times to function well in society.

> ### Harold Garfinkel (1917–)
> He is most strongly associated with ethnomethodology, examining how people make sense of everyday life. His work was of most interest in the 1970s; there is less enthusiasm for it now.

It would also be a mistake to believe that because an individual has taken on a role they have therefore been socialised into it – that they have internalised the role. It is important to distinguish between socialisation and social control, where the latter refers to situations where individuals have no choice but to play their role. The ethnomethodologist Harold Garfinkel criticises ways of looking at people as 'cultural dopes', as if they simply play roles given to them. The interactive process of socialisation is missing, as is the possibility of people individually or collectively rejecting their roles. As Blumer argues, 'The common repetitive behaviour of people in such situations should not mislead the student into believing that no process of interpretation is in play.' Furthermore, this type of sociological thought 'rarely recognises or treats human societies as composed of individuals who have selves … These typical conceptions ignore or blot out a view of group life or of group action as consisting of the collective or concerted actions of individuals seeking to meet their life situations' (Blumer, 1969). This moves the emphasis away from seeing people as harmoniously socialised into the world.

Both Mead and Parsons were aware of the implications of Freud's work for their own theories and chose to reject or incorporate parts of his work. Parsons, for example, admits that there are many aspects of personality that cannot be explained by 'role obligation' and he describes these aspects as an individual's 'autonomy'. Indeed, he says, without this autonomy, creativity and personal morality would not be possible (Parsons and Shils (eds.), 1951). In order to understand how individuals come to develop the 'need dispositions' that enable the social system to function, Parsons employed Freud's concept of the super-ego. This concept, he argues, is equivalent to Durkheim's notion of the constraining role of moral norms. The similarity between these two ideas, he says, 'from two quite distinct and independent starting points, deserves to be ranked as one of the truly fundamental landmarks of the development of modern social science' (Parsons, 1952), although the problem of conflict within an individual's psyche is left unresolved.

Gerth and Mills

Problems with Mead's account of secondary socialisation and the 'generalised other' were taken up by Hans Gerth and C. Wright Mills (1954). For Mead 'generalised other' refers to the general values and moral rules of the culture in which a child develops. But does this culture mean the whole society or only part of it? Mead gives no clear definition of what he means by the term 'society' – 'the great co-operative community process', seeing it in places as synonymous with 'the generalised other'. For Gerth and Mills, the generalised other of any given person or persons, however, does not necessarily represent the 'entire community' or 'the society', but only those who have been or who are significant to them. From this point of view, it is difficult to know what Mead means by the term society in any detail if all individuals one comes into contact with are significant others, representatives of the generalised other.

Gerth and Mills' own attempts to integrate Freud's theories with Mead's are only partially achieved. They reject any notion of instinct and choose instead to employ neo-Freudian notions of the self as plastic or malleable. Freud's 'drives' or unconscious motives are seen simply as 'unverbalised areas of feeling and conduct' which may be obstacles to self-realisation. In doing so, they claim that 'Various philosophical assumptions that had crept into Freud's theory have been torn out with little or no damage to what remains as usable heritage.'

On the central question of socialisation, some writers have argued that a synthesis of Parsons' and Mead's positions can be achieved if it is accepted that Parsons starts with society and ends with the individual and Mead simply does the opposite. This conclusion has been vigorously resisted by Mead's defenders, particularly Herbert Blumer, who argues that, in reality, there is no opportunity for individual choice in Parsons' theory, and therefore he is incompatible with Mead: 'The gap between Mead and Parsons is profound' (Blumer, 1975). Moreover, 'Structural features such as "culture", "social systems", "social stratification" or "social roles", set conditions for … action but do not determine action.' Attempts to fully incorporate Freud's model of the self have also largely been resisted although Marxist sociologists such as Marcuse, Habermas and Althusser and non-Marxists such as Parsons and Philip Rieff have used other aspects of his theories. What we are left with is an unresolved debate concerning the problem of the self, identity, socialisation and oversocialisation. This debate reproduces itself in all other areas of sociology.

QUESTIONS

1 **What is the difference between primary and secondary socialisation?**

2 **What is meant by oversocialisation? Have sociologists successfully countered its implications?**

3 **How important is language in socialisation?**

Culture

Culture

Culture has frequently been used by sociologists to denote the way of life of a society. This concept has itself been adapted from social anthropology, where in the late nineteenth century E.B. Tylor used it to describe 'that complex whole which includes knowledge, belief, arts, morals, law, customs and any other capabilities acquired by man as a member of society' (Tylor, 1871). If society is composed of social institutions and activities, then culture defines the values and beliefs that underly those institutions, activities and the form that they take, whether they are the family, education, religion, or even what is acceptable to eat and the way it is eaten. The focus is on shared meanings. This way of looking at culture is sometimes described as the culturalist view, where the stress is on interpreting the meanings of a culture that is lived.

> **Claude Lévi-Strauss (1908–)**
> *An anthropologist and the founder of structural analysis in this discipline. This looks at how the analysis of concepts can reveal the working of the human mind by reference to myths, totems and language. His work has strongly influenced writers such as Barthes, Foucault and Lacan.*

The investigation of the nature and dynamic of these shared meanings has come to be a central concern for sociology. However, a second definition of 'culture' has also been used by sociologists, and this originates in social anthropology and the work of Claude Lévi-Strauss. This sees culture as a social practice where communication is the central activity. This communication can take many forms, for example verbally in the form of language, but principally takes the form of the signs and symbols which create shared meanings. From this point of view, culture is a set of signifying practices – an example of which could be the way that authority is symbolised. All of these produce meaning, according to the structure by which they are arranged. These symbolic forms, which can be any cultural artefact, are described as texts. As such, they can be read or 'decoded' by sociologists. This approach is often described as a structuralist approach, where the focus is on the analysis of the production of meaning, although the term structuralism is also used to emphasise the influence of society as a whole.

It is a short step from Lévi-Strauss's concept of structuralism to the more modern discipline of semiotics (see also chapter 15). Here, the emphasis is on the communication between signifier, signified and sign. The sign can be anything – the clothes you wear, the commodities you buy, the newspapers you read. These signs are said to denote in representing particular cultural values, they also connote by engendering particular feelings. It is this interpretation of culture that has been of particular value in the study of youth cultures (see also chapter 3).

In attempting to answer the question of whose meanings are being shared, and where they have originated from, many writers have distinguished not one culture within the structure of Western societies but many. Most are agreed that something that could be described as a separate culture exists among a minority at the apex of society, though opinion is divided as to how to describe this minority, whether as an élite or as a ruling class.

High culture

This culture, usually described as 'high culture', is frequently mistaken as constituting the sole culture of a society, to the extent that high culture and high society have been read as *the* culture and *the* society. This stems partly from claims it makes for itself, as Q.D. Leavis (1932) made clear: there exists 'a select, cultured element of the community that sets the standards of behaviour and judgement, in direct opposition to the common people'. For her, and many other members of a disparate group described as the 'élite' or 'mass society' school, this culture is clearly superior to any other form of culture, being the location of virtue, reason and human excellence –

'the best that has been thought and said in the world', in Matthew Arnold's phrase. Those outside of this culture are seen as the folk, the people or, following the growth of mass education, universal suffrage and the mass media at the end of the nineteenth century, the masses.

Edward Shils (1971) has described not two but three distinct levels of culture in industrial societies: the highbrow (superior and refined), middlebrow (mediocre) and lowbrow (brutal), where, in the latter, 'the depth of penetration is almost always negligible, subtlety is almost entirely lacking, and a general grossness of sensitivity and perception is a common feature'.

Elite theory

As the pre-industrial folk culture of the people gave way to mass culture and 'mass man', many writers, such as Vilfredo Pareto, Friedrich Nietzsche, Dwight Macdonald, T. S. Eliot and F. R. Leavis (with differing emphases) gave great attention to the question of how high culture could be kept separate and preserved. Little good could be found in the culture of the masses, who, as Giner remarks, were 'seen as powerless when well ruled, and ephemerally powerful when its riotous crowds are allowed to get out of control … This mass is basically amoral, superstitious and ignorant … mass man … is not really a member of civil society: he is manipulated, unfree and alienated' (Giner, 1976). In the view of mass society theorists what lay beyond high culture was moral disorder, the disintegration of traditional society ties that bound individuals to the community, and anarchy.

One of the main forces in the creation of this mass culture was the mass media, originally the press and cinema, which substituted a 'pulp' culture for folk culture. 'Mass' man ceased to be directed by inner feelings and traditions and instead became 'other directed' – easy to manipulate by those who control the mass media. The implications of this argument are explored further in chapter 15.

Criticisms of élite theory

Most of the claims of the élite or mass society theorists have been contested. Doubts have been raised about their romanticisation of folk culture; the argument that high culture is superior to, rather than different from, other cultures; and the simple division of society into an élite and the mass. Edward Shils, for example, argues against 'the utterly erroneous idea that the twentieth century is a period of severe intellectual deterioration and that this alleged deterioration is a product of a mass culture … Indeed, it would be far more correct to assert that mass culture is now less damaging to the lower classes than the dismal and harsh existence of earlier centuries

59

had ever been.' Other writers have argued that the high/mass culture distinction is better described as bourgeois and working class or popular culture. Finally, the idea of a single mass culture has been queried.

The Frankfurt School

Some of the élite theorists' fears about mass culture were shared – albeit for different reasons – by a theoretical school formed in Germany in the 1920s. The writers of the Frankfurt-based Institut für Sozialforschung (Institute for Social Research) considered the question of culture from a broadly Marxist perspective. They were concerned to explain the failure of the Russian Revolution of 1917 to spread across the industrial world as Marxists expected it would. Class conflict appeared to be dying out. For these writers, particularly Theodor Adorno, Max Horkheimer and Herbert Marcuse, the emergence of mass culture did not promise social improvement but rather the opposite and could substantially help explain the apparent absence of class conflict, and even the rise of fascism in the inter-war period. For these writers, who came to be called critical theorists, 'all mass culture is identical'. Mass culture produced not anarchy but uniformity, standardisation, conformity and predictability and was a major prop to maintaining the status quo. Mass culture was directed and controlled by a capitalist culture industry, served up like any other commodity. Consciousness of the need for, and possibility of, social change was being eliminated by cultural practices that contained and defused conflict between social classes. The working classes were being depoliticised. At the same time, the suffocating spread of bureaucracy and 'technical reason' (the unfeeling logic of a technologically based society) had also carried into the intellectual world in the form of rationalism, positivism and value-neutrality.

Marcuse

Herbert Marcuse (1895–1979)
An important member of the Frankfurt School, influenced by Marx, Freud and phenomenology, he attempted to explain how capitalism produces false consciousness in the working class.

For Marcuse, capitalism would always deliver the goods, which had become ends in themselves, symbolising all that was good in capitalism: 'The products indoctrinate and manipulate; they promote a false consciousness ... it becomes a way of life. It is a good way of life – much better than before – and as a good way of life it militates against qualitative change. Thus emerges a pattern of one-dimensional thought and behaviour' (Marcuse, 1964). Knowledge of any other possibility of social and cultural organisation becomes impossible as society falls under the hypnotic spell of a capitalist mass culture. The massification of high culture removes its key quality – its separateness and its critical quality, even its capacity to subvert the existing status quo – and it ceases to be two-dimensional. It loses its 'authenticity'. Marcuse and others of the Frankfurt School aimed to develop critical theory, which could 'transform the will itself, so that people no longer want what they now want'.

Criticisms of the Frankfurt School

Although the Frankfurt School theorists have been influential critics within cultural studies, they have been criticised by other Marxists for being insufficiently orthodox in their Marxism. In particular, it has been argued that they overemphasised the importance of the 'superstructure' of society and downplayed the social 'base'. In Marxism the base refers to the economic conditions of production, and the superstructure refers to the social and political forms. This is made clear by Marx in one of his most quoted passages: 'The mode of production of material life determines the general character of the social, political and spiritual processes of life. It is not the consciousness of men that determines their being, but, on the contrary, their social being determines their consciousness' (Marx, 1859). In this reading, what we have been calling 'culture' cannot be studied in isolation but has to be understood as the product of the specific mode of production and social relationships in operation at the time. Capitalism is an economic system in which a small social class, the bourgeoisie, owns the capital and a large social class, the working class, has only its labour to sell. The culture of a capitalist society is everywhere affected by these basic social relationships.

Marxism and ideology

For Marxists, the concept of culture overlaps, although not exactly, with the concept of ideology. As Stuart Hall remarked: 'Something is left over when one says "ideology", and something is not present when one says "culture". "Culture" … operates along certain dimensions which "ideology" does not, while "ideology", in its turn, brings into play a set of meanings which are not present in the concept of "culture"' (Hall, 1978). The concept of ideology adds a political dimension to the concept of culture. Marx himself had no doubt where the leading ideas in society originate: 'The ideas of the ruling class are in every epoch the ruling ideas, that is, the class which is the ruling material force of the society is at the same time its ruling intellectual force' (Marx, 1845–6). This formulation explicitly relates economics, politics and culture in a way which cultural theory does not.

Many Marxists, however, have tried to develop a more subtle understanding of the relationship between the base of society and the superstructure, arguing that Marx can also be read in such a way as to show a two-way interaction between the two.

Althusser

This interpretation is present in the writings of the French Marxist, Louis Althusser, although his style of writing was itself far from straightforward and is itself the subject of many competing interpretations. This is particularly true of the way he uses the term 'ideology'. In one formulation he uses it to describe how ideology blinds people to the real nature of their social relationships, making them see imaginary relationships, not real ones. Ideology is 'profoundly

Louis Althusser (1918–89)
A French communist intellectual and Marxist philosopher. He argues that social formations consist of distinct areas – economic, political and ideological – each of which has a level of independence from the others. The economic area determines the shape of a society, in the last instance, but not without the influence of the other areas.

unconscious'. Furthermore, it is through ideology that social relations are reproduced through what he calls 'ideological State apparatuses', for example the family, education, religion, politics and the culture industry. These are not neutral institutions but are filled throughout with ideological assumptions (for example, the way 'knowledge' is presented in a school – see chapter 5).

In turn, however, Althusser has been criticised for seeing ideology as all-pervasive, and capitalism as all-powerful. There seem to be no chinks in the armoury of capitalist ideology. If it cannot be resisted or challenged then the dominance of the bourgeoisie is permanent. It is for this reason that the concept of hegemony, developed by the Italian Marxist Antonio Gramsci, has in recent decades been built into the way ideology is understood.

Hegemony

Hegemony refers not to ideological dominance but to ideological leadership, and does not presuppose that the ruling class will be the leading intellectual or moral force, or that the subordinate class or 'masses' are passive and quiescent. The hegemony of one group over another is never total but has to be continually won, maintained and reproduced in the form of consent. This was, after all, how the bourgeoisie came to be the leading class as it won social and political power from the aristocracy in the formation of the capitalist mode of production. Importantly, if hegemony can be won then it can also be lost. In the resulting 'crisis of hegemony', when consent is being lost, order can only be maintained through the coercive power of 'repressive state apparatuses', such as the army, the police and the prisons. This fact was of particular relevance to Gramsci, who spent much of his adult life in prison under Mussolini's fascist government.

Antonio Gramsci (1891–1937)
Italian Marxist imprisoned for ten years by Mussolini. Best known for the concept of hegemony, he argued that ideas are not produced in the economic base alone. He also identified the importance of civil society as an arena for struggle.

Hegemony is never fully achieved as it ultimately always relies on consent. Gramsci describes this as a 'moving equilibrium'. It is the possibility of punching holes in the canopy of hegemony that has allowed many writers to argue that what has traditionally been seen as 'mass culture' is better described as 'popular culture', where cultural activity that has traditionally been seen as being imposed from above becomes seen as working-class people gaining 'cultural space' for themselves, and transforming ideas and artefacts for their own purposes. This has also been construed as the beginnings of proletarian resistance.

Popular culture

As with all of the terms we have discussed in this section, 'popular culture' has been variously defined. In this case, what matters is what it is being contrasted with. In some usages it describes everything that is left over when high culture has been taken into consideration, or it is used as a synonym for 'mass culture'. In these usages, popular culture is compared unfavourably with a pre-industrial folk culture and, as we have seen, is thought to have little intrinsic value or worth.

The concept of hegemony, however, allows for a different interpretation, in that popular culture can be seen as the cultural activity that emerges from 'the people', in all their various guises, including resisting their position as a subordinate group or challenging their consensual role as recipients of an imposed culture. It is in this light that many writers (particularly those at the Centre for Contemporary Cultural Studies at the University of Birmingham) have examined a wide variety of groups such as youth, ethnic minorities, women's groups and many aspects of working-class culture.

Mods, skinheads and punks, for example, have been examined, not simply as examples of popular culture but as groups taking everyday items provided for them (such as boots, scooters and bin liners) and reappropriating them in their attempts to gain 'cultural space'. This challenge is seen not ahistorically but in the context of a break-down in hegemony. How successful they are in achieving this, and how they are reincorporated, is of great importance to the usefulness of hegemony as an analytical concept. The authenticity of groups such as rastafarians or punks has to be questioned if the oppositional content can be defused, for this is what defines them as 'popular culture' in this definition, and they can be easily incorporated and become a source of profit for record companies and merchandisers and, in the process, it seems, become part of mass culture. It is for this reason that popular culture in general is seen not simply as the culture of resistance, but as an area of negotiation and transaction, of exchange, between a culture imposed from above and its active consumption by popular forces. This process of resistance, challenge and incorporation recurs throughout in the study of sociology.

QUESTIONS

1 **How can high culture be distinguished from mass or popular culture?**

2 **Is it true to say that high culture is superior to mass or popular culture?**

3 **How does culture differ from ideology?**

4 **In what ways can popular culture be seen as a culture of resistance?**

FURTHER READING

S. Aronowitz, **The Politics of Identity**, Routledge, 1992

R. Billington *et. al.*, **Culture and Society: The Sociology of Culture**, Macmillan, 1991

D. Hebdige, **Subculture: The Meaning of Style**, Methuen, 1979

C. Jencks, **Culture**, Routledge, 1993

H. Marcuse, **One Dimensional Man**, Routledge and Kegan Paul, 1964

D. Strinati, **An Introduction to Theories of Popular Culture**, Routledge, 1995

R. Williams, **Keywords**, Fontana, 1976

3 Stratification and differentiation

This chapter begins by looking at what is meant by stratification. You will then examine functionalist, Marxist and Weberian conceptions of social stratification. The chapter goes on to look at the difficulties encountered by sociologists in measuring levels of social mobility in society. Later there is a discussion of the idea that the working class are adopting middle-class norms and values and this is contrasted to the opposite theory of proletarianisation. You will then examine the notion of the underclass. The section closes with a discussion of different forms of stratification: gender, ethnicity, age and disability.

Dimensions of inequality

Social stratification is the term used by sociologists to describe the patterned structures of inequality that are present in all societies. The lines of four important social divisions are clearly identifiable to most sociologists: those of class, gender, ethnicity and age. These are the four keys that are used to unlock any social analysis. Together and separately they can be used to define and measure the strata that exist within society. As with most terminology used by sociologists, however, there is no precise agreement on what these terms mean, or how they should be used.

Many people, when discovering the way that sociology operates, are unwilling to accept the validity of these concepts of stratification in the first place. From their point of view, structured inequalities only exist because sociologists perceive them to exist – they are simply an invention of sociologists. There are no class divisions, nor is there a systematic bar in operation against women or ethnic minorities. Age does not matter. Society is made up of unique individuals who fail or succeed, are powerful or weak, not as a consequence of stratification but because of their individual biographies.

Class Against this, there is a wealth of evidence which strongly suggests that social divisions are real and tangible. Figures demonstrating the distribution of wealth and income quickly show that substantial financial resources are held by very few in our society. If the Standard Occupational Classification is used (formerly the Registrar-General's Scale – see below), the statistics show that the higher class a person is in then the more likely they are to survive the first year of their life, to do well in school examinations, to get into higher education, to live longer, and even have their natural teeth into old age. As we shall see, many sociologists have argued that different classes display different norms and values, have different lifestyles and perceptions of society, in short that distinct class cultures exist. For them, the real debate is about where the line between these classes should be drawn, a consideration that has occupied much of sociology's time and thought in the twentieth century.

Gender

It is only in recent decades that gender has been considered as a dimension of stratification, yet this inequality is evident in all walks of life. Although there are more women than men in the United Kingdom, they have much less social, economic, political and domestic power than men. Occupationally, they are under-represented in the boardrooms and senior management positions of the largest companies. On average, they earn less than men (see chapter 6). They are vastly outnumbered in the House of Commons, where men make decisions on the availability of contraception, abortion, pornography and divorce. When a woman becomes a cabinet minister it is still a rare enough event for it to provoke great interest.

Ethnicity

It is a similar picture for members of ethnic minorities, though here it is important to be specific about which ethnic minority is being considered. Careful study has revealed distinct differences in the social and economic position and experience of groups classed as either 'West Indian' or 'Indian', for example, reflecting their different cultural histories. Different patterns of integration are evident, and sociologists have had to learn to be careful to make these distinctions.

Age

The need for careful distinctions is generally true of all studies of stratification. The fact of age stratification is obvious, with the young and old being the least powerful, in a society where age determines many life events, whether it is starting school, finishing school or retiring from employment. The problems begin when age is seen to be the only important or determinant aspect of a group or individual's existence. The experiences of middle-class teenagers may be very different from those of working-class teenagers. The financial situation, health and social integration of retired middle-class men tend to be much more favourable than for retired working-class men. The life experiences of black working-class people and white working-class people may be very different. Although age stratification is very important and helps us to explain and understand a great deal about people's experiences, other ways of stratifying may cut across those based on age.

Sociologists of stratification attempt to explore and explain the reasons for divisions in society and also to analyse how society holds together under such strains. The models constructed by sociologists are, in Weber's terms, 'ideal types' which need refining on the evidence of research. What sociologists have found is that class, ethnicity, gender and age are all complexly interrelated dimensions of stratification. How much weight should be given to each remains debatable. Marxists assert that class is most important. Some feminists see gender divisions as being more significant. Youth cultures may be viewed as expressions of age, gender, class or ethnic identities – or all of them.

Class

If Britain is a classless society, then why don't we all eat the same type of food? It is not just about money; it is about taste. What do Class I professionals eat? What do the aristocracy eat? What do Class V unskilled workers eat? Why the differences? One idea which emerges from sociology is that of class culture – the set of beliefs, attitudes and customs which act as a guide to living. It affects your choice of food, clothes, your accent, the way you live and behave at home, the work you do and your leisure time. Class culture permeates all of an individual's life.

Leisure The use of leisure is a good example of the variation in class. Some people dine out as a way of passing the evening, whereas others eat at home, then go to the pub, club or bingo hall and have a few drinks. They may not know how to behave in unaccustomed environments. The doctor and his wife might go to the local pub for a pie and a pint, but it's very unlikely that they would then go to the bingo hall. Social activities are varied – golf, squash, dog racing, pigeon fancying, drinking, theatre- or cinema-going, watching videos and so on. There are economic barriers but these are not the only barriers. There are a thousand social rules and regulations attached to social activities and these can only be fully understood through class culture. Not knowing which cutlery to start with at an ornately laid table is a clichéd example, but it pinpoints the differences. Why do some know and others not? More importantly, why should it matter so much? It matters because of class culture.

Attitudes to work   Class culture is reflected in the labour market. The sons and daughters of the middle classes by and large go on to middle-class occupations. They have absorbed the attitudes and hopes of their parents. They work hard at school, value and accept the teachers' definition of knowledge and success. They defer gratification of their desires until they are established in a career. They see life as a series of upward moves, ending up with a good pension and their own home. The working classes revere practical skills, reject middle-class educationalists' ideas of knowledge, live for today and accept their fate cheerfully. They work to live, not live to work, and they spend their disposable income rather than saving it buying, for example, cars, technology and holidays.

The Registrar-General's classification   It is difficult to discuss class culture without using stereotypes, such as those above. Before turning to the models of class that sociologists have attempted to construct, we can briefly consider the official view of class, and the reasons that sociologists find it inadequate. This is the classification created by the Registrar-General of the Office of Population and Census Surveys in the late nineteenth century. In order to yield more fruitful data from the ten-yearly census, the Registrar-General has grouped the working population into six occupational classifications. By the time of the 1991 census, this was described as a classification of 'Social class based on occupation', and is shown in *Table 3.1*.

Limitations of official data   For most of the twentieth century, this method of measuring class has been used to yield data on almost every aspect of life, from infant mortality to life expectancy, from educational achievement and dietary habits to how many hours of television each group watches and the data produced have become a useful source of secondary data for some sociologists. They are not used without reservations, however. Such models can hide as much as they reveal. They tell us little about those who are without occupations, such as the unemployed, students, or 'housewives' and 'househusbands'. The scale shows class as static, without any notion of class as a power relationship. It ignores the question of ownership of property – are professionals really in the same class as the large-scale owners of the means of production who have the power to hire and fire them? It assumes that occupation is the most important dimension of class. It is for these reasons that sociologists have attempted to devise their own models of stratification in society.

TABLE 3.1   **Social class based on occupation (%)**

			ALL	MEN	WOMEN
I		Professional occupations	6	8	3
II		Managerial and technical occupations	27	27	26
III	N	Skilled non-manual occupations	24	12	38
III	M	Skilled manual occupations	22	34	8
IV		Partly-skilled occupations	15	14	16
V		Unskilled occupations	6	4	7

Source: Labour Force Survey, *1990 and 1991*

QUESTIONS

1 What is meant by the term 'class culture'?

2 Give some examples of class-based norms and values.

3 Offer some criticisms of the Registrar-General's classification.

4 What criteria does the Registrar-General use to grade occupations?

Theories of class

In sociology, three main theories exist which attempt to explain the nature and prevalence of stratification. These derive from Marx, Weber and functionalism. The contrast between Marxism and functionalism is noticeably at its sharpest in this area, exposing the weakest area in functionalist theory, and the strongest area in Marxism.

Functionalist theories of stratification

Functionalism is weak on the concept of stratification partly because so little has been written from this perspective. Stratification is certainly discussed by early functionalists such as Herbert Spencer and Emile Durkheim, but neither saw it as the focus of their study. Durkheim evidently saw social inequality as a necessary and universal feature of society because functionally more important roles should have higher status and rewards. Unlike Marx, he did not see social inequality as a key source of social conflict, and in any case believed that inequality could be mitigated by the prevalence of social mobility – movement of people from one stratum to another.

Davis and Moore

These points were taken up and enlarged upon by the authors of what has become one of the main statements of the functionalist view of stratification. Davis and Moore's (1945) view is that some positions in society become more functionally important than others, because of the organisational demands necessary for any society to function. Some roles can only be taken by certain individuals. Only they possess the necessary scarce skills and initiative. In order to entice them into these positions, they have to be rewarded with greater status and rewards than others. Systems of stratification exist to ensure that the most appropriate people are selected for these roles. Moreover, because stratification is functional, it follows that it must be a permanent, inevitable and necessary fact of the way any society is constructed. Attempts to alter or do away with social inequality are at best misguided. Similar points are made by Talcott Parsons (1953).

Criticisms of the functionalist view

In putting this view forward, these post-war American functionalists have been heavily criticised for the assumptions they have made about the existence of a meritocratic society, i.e. a society where everyone has an equal chance of achieving high social status and reward. Such a benign view of the role and effects of stratification only works if many other features of society are ignored or even distorted. Firstly, as Tumin (1953) asks, why are some social positions assumed to be functionally more important than others? Who decides and how? Is it functionally more important to be the director of a company making products that are not necessary than to nurse people, dig coal or clean streets?

Meritocracy

The functionalist view also assumes the existence of a meritocratic society, where everyone has an equal opportunity to rise to the top. It can be equally forcibly argued that the system of stratification prevents as many people – if not more – from rising to the top as it allows through (see pp. 75–80). From this latter perspective, at best a genuinely meritocratic society lies far into the future, at worst it is a naive view. In a deeply unequal society such as that in Britain the existence of private schools, for example, allows social status to be bought, regardless of any innate talent.

The functionalist view of how power and status are gained and maintained is also a serious weakness in the theory. Does the wealthiest man in Britain, Gerald Grosvenor, Duke of Westminster, own 138,000 of the world's most expensive acres because he possesses the scarce skills needed to perform a functionally important role in society, for which he should be rewarded with high status and privilege? Perhaps a more realistic view is that the Grosvenor family wealth exists because, many centuries ago, a distant ancestor of his received Mayfair as a wedding dowry when it was still farmland. His status was not achieved by him but was rather ascribed to him at birth.

Class power

This opens up a wider consideration of class power. Writing from a Marxist perspective, Westergaard and Resler (1976) point out that the more property an owner has, the more immune he or she is from the need to render any service of social substance at all. The wealthier you become, the less socially significant your contribution. Little research of any real value has ensued from the functionalist view of stratification, and it is difficult to square the perception of the nature of stratification put forward by writers such as Davis and Moore with any empirically based study. Too much contradictory data exist surrounding studies of social mobility, education and wealth and income for it to have any real currency. Instead, some writers, for example Frank Parkin (1971), have suggested that the functionalist view is little more than an ideological justification of inequality in society that is intended to make inequality acceptable. More searching explanations and insights are required.

The Marxist view

Class is the most important concept in Marxism. As Marx (1848) wrote: 'The history of all hitherto existing societies is the history of class struggles.' His view was that when these struggles come to an end, with the emergence of a classless society, then the first stage of history – what will be seen as prehistory – will be over. Humans will at last be able to live in a world where they are not prevented from realising their full potential by the constraints of class societies.

The collapse of capitalism

What excited Marx was that he believed that, in his age – the nineteenth century it was possible to witness the emergence of the preconditions necessary for the transition to a classless, or communist society. Two great classes – the bourgeoisie and the proletariat (see chapter 1) were assuming formations that would lead to the disappearance of one and the victory of the other. For Marx, the bourgeoisie was doomed, unable to control socio-economic forces beyond its grasp, prone to greater and greater crises in profitability, accumulation and production. The details of this emerging crisis were elaborated in his book, *Capital* (1867).

Since the publication of *Capital*, Marxists have sought to identify signs of this historical dynamic in motion, most clearly in connection with the First World War (1914–18) but also at several other junctures in the twentieth century, for example the General Strike of 1926 in Britain, or the events in France in May 1968 when the Gaullist government came close to being overthrown by sections of the working class. The central idea that modern Western societies are composed of two antagonistic classes, one of which benefits at the direct expense of the other, has led to rich fields of research in all areas of sociology, particularly the family, education, stratification, power, work and poverty. It is when attempts are made to operationalise the key concepts in Marxist theory that disputes have emerged.

What did Marx mean by class?

The concept of class itself is highly problematic in Marxism. At first sight it is clear what Marx meant by this term – the bourgeoisie rule by virtue of their ownership of the means of production and therefore constitute a class. In the mid nineteenth century, when Marx was writing, only those with titles or property were able to participate in political activity. This political power was manifestly derived from economic power. Those who had only their labour to sell were the proletariat, the source of the bourgeoisie's wealth. They too constituted a class. The difference between the two classes lay in the level of self-realisation. The bourgeoisie were conscious of their own existence as a class, both in itself and for itself. The proletariat had yet to realise their existence as a powerful and ultimately victorious class. This, future Marxists were to decide, was the task of Marxist socialists, leaders of the working class.

Leaving aside the important question of whether there remains a clear link between economic and political power (see chapter 8), a further question to face is whether anything as tangible as a working class, in Marx's sense of being potentially class-conscious and revolutionary, any longer exists. In recent decades there has been little real evidence (apart from in Eastern Europe) to suggest this development is still possible.

The proletariat

In Britain the people whom Marxists describe as 'the proletariat' rarely act as one. They do not vote uniformly for the largest working-class party – the Labour Party – nor are they interested in the many neo-Marxist parties in existence. Trade-union membership is in long-term decline, and the traditional working class, built on the Victorian staple industries of iron and steel, coal, shipbuilding, textiles and engineering, underwent a major transformation in the 1980s. The industries themselves shrank rapidly, while many of those people still in work, far from having nothing to lose, found their houses, cars, foreign holidays and videos threatened by loss of employment. In the Western world (and increasingly in Eastern Europe) the power of capital has never looked stronger, and proletarian revolution less likely.

While Marxism has not been abandoned as a tool of analysis, and though it is still very easy to demonstrate, objectively, that capitalist societies are highly divided on class lines, the paradigm Marxism puts forward of a polarised class society looks implausible at a subjective level. A more fruitful analysis has, therefore, been sought by sociologists to accommodate the shortfalls of Marxist analysis.

QUESTIONS

1 **Why do functionalists think stratification is inevitable and necessary?**

2 **What is meritocracy from the functionalist perspective?**

3 **Can functionalism be accused of being an ideological justification for inequality?**

4 **From the Marxist perspective, what is the relationship between class struggle and history?**

5 **Why don't the proletariat act as a class?**

6 **How did Marx see the downfall of capitalism coming about?**

7 **What criticisms would a functionalist make of the Marxist concept of class?**

The Weberian view

Although Marx recognised the existence of other classes – the petty bourgeoisie (or small-scale owners, for example shopowners) and the lumpenproletariat (the unemployed, vagrants etc.) – the underlying dynamic at work in his view of class conflict means that economic forces – primarily the centralisation of capital – would bring the two great classes in history into direct conflict.

Aware of this view, and provoked by it, Max Weber produced his own conflict-based theory of stratification. While owing something to Marx, it made considerable and important refinements, playing down the importance of class, adding a further dimension to its meaning, and introducing other, separate factors that he believed contributed to stratification in societies. Weber's theory has opened up new areas of insight within sociology, and comes closest to explaining the dynamics of stratification in modern societies. Like Marx, he recognised the importance of ownership of property, and the existence of conflict between owners and workers. Unlike Marx, he anticipated a greater proliferation of classes, with a new class of white-collar employees, administrators, technicians and civil servants, growing in number and importance. He highlights the importance not of property relations but market position and marketability as decisive in determining an individual's class position. He rejected Marx's view that workers (or employees) have nothing but their labour to sell to the highest bidder. What they possessed, in greater or lesser quantity, were skills, the distribution of which could be controlled to be kept scarce and increase their marketability. This was particularly true of white-collar workers – those who are involved in non-manual work.

Status and party

For Weber, class was not the only factor determining social status. It could be mitigated by two other aspects of individual or group positions, neither of which necessarily depended on class. These he called 'party' – access to political power – and 'status' – the amount of honour or prestige accorded to someone (Weber, 1922–3). By separating politics from class he was clearly distinguishing himself from Marx in his belief that political power and activity were not simply expressions of the economic base. Many groups could possess effective political power without direct economic leverage, for example the military or trade unions through political parties. Social inequality could exist because some were more politically powerful than others.

So too with status, one of Weber's most slippery concepts. He recognised, and believed to be important, the observation that people could be of the same class but have different social statuses. Equally, they could have the same status but occupy different class positions. The use of the concept of status is Weber's recognition that life chances are determined by more than class. The concept of status has a wide meaning, embracing all the ways that individuals and groups are regarded by others in recognising your social standing. If you are newly rich, you may find it harder to be accepted – to gain status – by the established rich, even though objectively you are of the same class. If you are born an untouchable in India, no matter how wealthy you become abroad, you will remain an untouchable within the Indian caste system. Weber was aware of this example of ascribed status. In his concept of status, Weber used terms of reference other than property qualifications or market position. This definition has been used in recent decades by neo-Weberians to understand the position in stratification systems of many groups, for example ethnic minorities. They may occupy the same class position as some white groups in Britain, but they do not command the same political or social status. The life chances of a black doctor or manual worker are different to those of white ones.

Marx and Weber

Because Marx and Weber contested the same terrain, it is worth contrasting the differences in their approach to stratification in society. Where Marx believed that relationship to the means of production was all-important, Weber focused more on the market position of those in employment. Where Marx saw a progression towards increasing polarity between classes and revolution, Weber saw the growth of a large white-collar class that would mitigate against the collapse of capitalism. Where Marx believed that class was an all-embracing fact of life, Weber allowed for separate political and status factors to come into play. We can therefore say that, despite similarities in the natures of the societies they perceived, they came to different understandings of other, more important, forces they saw at work in capitalist societies.

QUESTIONS

1 What are the differences between the Marxist and Weberian concepts of class?

2 What does Weber mean by the terms 'status' and 'party'?

Social mobility

Intra- and intergenerational mobility

Much of the functionalist case in the sociology of stratification rests on the argument that in industrial societies there is a more open system of stratification than in closed, pre-industrial societies. This argument is also at the heart of Talcott Parsons' theory of the changing nature of the family (see chapter 4). The key change for this view is that from ascribed status, which supposedly characterises pre-industrial societies, to achieved status, which supposedly characterises modern industrial societies. Ascribed status refers to social positions that are fixed through life, as with a caste system. An achieved status is one where individuals take up a social position according to their own talent and ability. It should therefore follow that any systematic investigation into the amount of movement by individuals up and down the class structure – social mobility – should reveal high rates of mobility as a feature of industrial societies. To examine this hypothesis, the first question must be: how can social mobility be measured? As all models of stratification have so far been based in some way on occupation, this is generally the measure used. Intragenerational mobility measures occupational mobility during someone's working life. Intergenerational mobility measures the difference between an individual's occupation and that of their parents, almost always their father. Most studies of social mobility are based on intergenerational mobility data.

David Glass

There have been two major studies of social mobility in Great Britain. The first was carried out by David Glass's research team in 1949 (published 1954). In order to analyse both the system of stratification in Britain and movement within it, Glass used a more sophisticated version of the Registrar-General's scale – the Hall–Jones scale. This has seven levels:

The Hall–Jones scale

1 Professional and high administrative
2 Managerial and executive
3 Inspectional, supervisory and other non-manual (higher grade)
4 Inspectional, supervisory and other non-manual (lower grade)
5 Skilled manual and routine grades of non-manual
6 Semi-skilled manual
7 Unskilled manual

Glass obtained his results by comparing the occupational position of 3,497 men with that of their fathers (*see Table* 3.2). Reading the table

TABLE 3.2   Social mobility (%) – Glass

FATHER'S STATUS CATEGORY	SON'S STATUS CATEGORY						
	1	2	3	4	5	6	7
1	39	15	20	6	14	5	2
2	11	27	23	12	21	5	2
3	4	10	19	19	36	7	6
4	2	4	11	21	43	12	6
5	1	2	8	12	47	17	13
6	0	1	4	9	39	31	16
7	0	1	4	8	36	24	27

from left to right, it shows that, for example, 39 per cent of sons whose fathers were in status category 1 are themselves in status category 1, while only 2 per cent of them are in status category 7. Similarly, 27 per cent of those whose fathers were in status category 7 have remained in that category, while none of them have moved to status category 1. The main finding of Glass's study is that although social mobility exists – a third experienced upward mobility and a third downward mobility – most of it was short-range, or across only one or two bands. There was very little long-range mobility, where individuals have moved from one end of the scale to the other. For example, only 13 per cent of the sample had moved from category 7 to above category 5, and no one from this band had moved into the top band. This pattern is almost identical in category 6. Most mobility for the working class was therefore within the working class itself.

The Oxford Mobility Study

In a similar but more widely based study of 8,575 men, a research team of sociologists at Nuffield College, Oxford University, undertook a second intergenerational study with 1972 as the base year. This is frequently referred to as the Oxford Mobility Study, whose findings were written up by John Goldthorpe (1980). The stated intention of this study was not only to update Glass's work, but to examine the reality of three theories of social mobility and class formation. These were that there is social closure at the top of the class structure; that there is a buffer zone around the manual/non-manual boundary beyond which it is difficult to progress; and that education is the main means of social mobility. The Oxford study used a seven-point scale which was similar but not identical to the Hall–Jones model (*see Table* 3.3).

The scale used here is not directly comparable to that used by Glass, but is as follows:

1 Higher professionals, higher-grade administrators, managers in large industrial concerns and large proprietors

TABLE 3.3 **Social mobility (%) – The Oxford Mobility Study**

FATHER'S CLASS	SON'S CLASS						
	1	2	3	4	5	6	7
1	46	19	12	7	5	5	6
2	29	23	12	6	10	11	9
3	19	16	13	7	13	16	16
4	14	14	9	21	10	15	16
5	14	14	10	8	16	21	17
6	8	9	8	6	12	31	26
7	7	9	9	6	13	25	32

2 Lower professionals, higher-grade technicians, lower-grade administrators, managers in small businesses and supervisors of non-manual employees
3 Routine non-manual workers
4 Small proprietors and self-employed artisans
5 Lower-grade technicians and supervisors of manual workers
6 Skilled manual workers
7 Semi-skilled and unskilled manual workers

The chief difference between the two scales is that, where the Hall–Jones scale used by Glass emphasises occupational prestige, the Oxford scale emphasises concepts of market rewards. In the first table, the manual working class embrace three bands; in the second only two.

The Oxford Mobility Study clearly identifies greater long-range mobility than that discovered by Glass. More, for example, have moved intergenerationally from the top to the bottom and vice-versa. As many as 7 per cent of those whose fathers were in class 7 have moved to class 1, and 6 per cent of those born in class 1 have now moved to class 7. Those who experience this long-range down-ward mobility are sometimes called 'skidders'. But, on the other hand, 46 per cent of those who began life in class 1 have managed to remain in it. This is called 'élite self-recruitment'.

Service, intermediate and working class

To make their data manageable, and give greater meaning to the fig-ures, the Oxford team grouped their first two social categories together and called this 'the service class' (a term borrowed from the Austrian Marxist Karl Renner). They termed social categories 3, 4 and 5 'the intermediate class' and 6 and 7 were called 'the working class'. In general, and unlike Glass, the Nuffield team found that there had been net upward mobility – more people moved up than moved down. This meant that, with few people entering the working class from above, it remained a homogeneous or uniformly consti-tuted class. But with fewer people leaving the service class, and more entering it from below, it became more mixed or heterogeneous, what Goldthorpe termed 'a class of low classlessness' (Bourne, 1979), meaning that its class consciousness and solidarity are low.

As with any statistics in sociology, these tables need to be interpreted carefully.

The changing occupational structure

What has happened in the twentieth century is that the amount of manual work has declined, while service and intermediate occupations have correspondingly increased (*see Table* 3.4). Where manual work made up three-quarters of all occupations in 1911, it was only three-fifths in 1971. At the same time, where roughly only one in 14 jobs was in the service class in 1911, by 1971 one in five jobs were classed in this category. Compounded by the fact that the working class has the highest number of children per family, this means that upward mobility is inevitable, regardless of the degree of openness of the class structure. This makes social mobility studies complex, as they are only immediately comparable over time if the class structure and fertility rates remain constant. This is reflected in *Table* 3.5, which synthesises data from both Glass and the Oxford Mobility Study.

TABLE 3.4   Male occupations, 1911–71 (%)

OCCUPATION	1911	1951	1971
Managerial and Professional	6.9	12.6	21.5
Intermediate	11.9	13.3	14.5
Manual	73.6	68.4	58.8

Source: Goldthorpe, Social Mobility and Class Structure in Modern Britain, 1980.

The level of mobility has been constant, at just below 50 per cent of all men, though there has been a steady increase in upward mobility, and a steady decrease in downward mobility.

Problems of mobility studies

Mobility studies may fascinate statisticians and give number-crunching opportunities to the positivists but how much do they tell us of the realities of the British – or indeed any – system of stratification as well as people's own experience of class and social mobility? The Oxford Mobility Study has been the target of a number of criticisms, both ideological and methodological.

TABLE 3.5   Social mobility rates of men (%)

BIRTH DATE	PRE-1890	1890–9	1900–9	1908–17	1918–27	1928–37
Upwardly mobile	16.5	23.3	23.2	19.9	24.5	30.5
Downwardly mobile	33.0	25.9	24.6	25.3	23.2	20.4
Total mobile	49.5	49.2	47.8	45.2	47.7	50.9

Source: Heath, Social Mobility, 1981.

Rosemary Crompton (1980) has argued that occupations may not be comparable over time because the status of those occupations change, as the debate between writers such as Harry Braverman (1974) and David Lockwood (1958) demonstrates. Being born to a clerical worker at the turn of the century gave you a different status to being born to a clerical worker in the 1960s. The same could be said of printers, with the growth of electronic technology and desktop publishing. Against this, Goldthorpe argues that it is common for work and market conditions to change, but this does not imply changes in class position. In his classification, he did not look at occupational labels, but at a full description of what each occupation entailed.

A second criticism is that Goldthorpe's class 1 – those at the top – is too broad to tell us anything about the chances of reaching the very top, the highest echelons of the ruling class. A narrower band is required. As long as there is homogeneity in the ruling class, where real and effective power resides, as long as the exclusive public schools and old boy networks are in effective operation, then mobility rates at other levels in the class system are less meaningful. Goldthorpe's class 1 contains roughly 12 per cent of all men in work. Other studies of those at the very top – those in élite positions such as company chairmen, chief executives and managing directors – have shown that élite self-recruitment is very high, and entry into this group highly restricted and exclusive.

Women and social mobility

A third, and most damaging, criticism, is that the mobility studies exclude women. As such, they should be retitled 'The social mobility of men'. The suggestion is that women are not permanently in the labour market, therefore any valid measurement is impossible. If this view is accepted, then the role of women in the stratification system goes unresearched.

It is certainly difficult to include all women in a stratification model based on occupation because many women either do not work, work part-time or leave the labour market temporarily to have children. Moreover, many women find themselves pushed into one area of work, particularly secretarial and clerical work, making differentiation difficult. Yet women do play a key role in stratification systems. How can their experience be measured?

There have been a number of attempts. Glass collected information on women in his survey but never used it. Chapman (1984) and Abbott and Sapsford (1987) produced empirically based studies that examine this area. Abbott and Sapsford (using the Social Grading Scale, a similar scale to the Registrar-General's) found that the daughters of professional and managerial workers were much more likely to be down-wardly mobile than their sons, and that the daughters of manual work-ers were less likely to be upwardly mobile than their sons. There is a strong tendency for those at either extreme to gravitate to the centre of the stratification system. In Chapman's survey, only 12 per cent of the daughters of men in the top class managed to remain in that class. They are less likely to be counter-mobile, that is to move up the scale again after an initial decline in their status in commencing employment.

QUESTIONS

1 **What are the differences in the findings of Glass and the Nuffield studies on social mobility?**

2 **What are the main problems with measuring the social mobility of women?**

The overclass

Central to Marxist theory is the concept that there is a ruling class in society, whose power is based on ownership of the means of produc-tion – the bourgeoisie. This has been analysed from a number of angles, raising the following problems:

- Is the term 'ruling class' too simplistic?
- In Marxist terms, do those who own the means of production also rule society?
- Are the few in power better described as an élite? (See chapter 8.)
- Does the group in power still own the means of production, or has it passed into the hands of others?
- Is there a difference between ownership and control?

Wealth If we look at ownership as being related to wealth, then it is clear that this remains in the hands of the few. Despite the abolition of the Royal Commission on the Distribution of Wealth and Income in the early 1980s, it is still possible, through the Inland Revenue, to pic-ture the distribution of wealth in the last quarter of the twentieth century (*see Table* 3.6).

TABLE 3.6   Marketable wealth, United Kingdom, 1976–93

PERCENTAGE OF TOTAL WEALTH					OWNED BY PERCENTAGE OF POPULATION
1976	1981	1986	1989	1993	
21	18	18	18	17	most wealthy 1%
38	36	36	38	36	most wealthy 5%
50	50	50	53	48	most wealthy 10%
71	73	73	75	72	most wealthy 25%
92	92	90	94	92	most wealthy 50%

Source: Social Trends 26, 1996

In 1993, a quarter of the population owned 72 per cent of all marketable wealth, and half the population owned 92 per cent. Alternatively, 75 per cent of the population owned 28 per cent of the wealth and 50 per cent owned only 8 per cent. The sustained owner ship of the majority of wealth by a minority of the population is not enough, though, to show the existence of a capitalist class or ruling class. Further examination is needed of how this wealth is owned, and how it is used.

Managerialism   The idea that the owners of the means of production are individuals or families belongs to the nineteenth century. From the 1870s the growth of the joint-stock company or corporation, characterised by many shareholders, saw what some writers have argued was the transfer of effective power from the owners to the directors of enterprises. This is what Berle and Means (1932) described as 'the managerial revolution'. Where share ownership is so widespread that shareholders are unable to act as a unified group, management control prevails, allowing those in senior management positions to run the enterprise as they wish, free from interference by shareholders. Berle and Means's figures showed that 44 per cent of the top 200 non-financial organisations in the USA were subject to management control in 1932. According to Larner, by 1963 the number had increased to 83.5% (Larner, 1966). Power therefore lay with the controllers, not the owners of capital.

John Scott (1979) argues that while a case can be made for a managerialist stage in the development of US and Japanese capitalism, it is more difficult to apply to other advanced capitalist economies and more recent periods of history. He writes that it is more appropriate to see control as being exercised by a 'constellation of interests' where 'no single majority shareholder has sufficient shares to exercise minority control on their own and any temporary coalition is likely to be countered by another. There is no community of interest among the large shareholders over and above their common interests as shareholders.' Although individual share ownership has increased – from 7 per cent of individuals in 1979 to 25 per cent in 1991 – the proportion of shares they own has fallen.

The group that has become dominant is the financial sector, composed of institutions or impersonal structures such as banks, insurance companies and pension funds. These have become increasingly influential throughout the advanced capitalist economies.

Citing evidence from the USA, Britain, Australia, Canada, France and Japan, Scott is able to conclude that 'the managerial revolution is a myth: salaried managers have not usurped the powers of capitalist

81

shareholders. The joint stock company has not led to the demise of the capitalist class ... but it has produced an important transformation in the structure of property ownership' (Scott, 1986). This view is echoed by Maurice Zeitlin (1989). In America, he says, it is still the case that propertied families hold economic control.

Both Scott and Zeitlin agree that a capitalist class remains in control of modern capitalism, though their hold is now through financial institutions. For Scott, there are four groups visible within this class: the entrepreneurial capitalists, actively involved in their personal property; rentier capitalists with personal investments in many different companies; executive capitalists with an official post in a joint-stock company; and finance capitalists holding many directorships in several companies.

That this capitalist class exists does not mean that they are necessarily the ruling class. For those, like Scott, who are close to Marxism, this immediately draws them into the debate between Ralph Miliband and Nicos Poulantzas (see chapter 8). Scott's own analysis (1991) uses Gramsci's concept of a power bloc, emphasising the use made by the capitalist class of the machinery of the State.

QUESTIONS

1 **How has the distribution of wealth and income changed between 1976 and 1989?**

2 **Can it be argued that there is a unified ruling class, whose power is based on ownership of the means of production?**

Embourgeoisement

From his vantage point in the middle of the nineteenth century, Marx argued that it was in the laws of capitalist development that the class structure of capitalism would eventually polarise into two distinct classes – an increasingly small and increasingly wealthy bourgeoisie, and an increasingly large and increasingly impoverished proletariat, joined by those members of the petty bourgeoisie who had been pushed down into the proletariat by the process of the centralisation of capital.

Proletarian consciousness

Eventually, as the proletariat became poorer and poorer – increasingly immiserated – they would make two key realisations. Firstly, the nature of their exploitation would become clear as they understood that they had a common identity and common cause. A class in itself would become a class for itself as it achieved class consciousness. Elements of this process were emerging in Marx's own lifetime, for example with the formation of the International Working Men's Association, with Marx as its first General Secretary. Secondly, as the system fell into stagnation and decay, the proletariat would realise that the bourgeoisie had become a decadent class, morally unfit to rule and unable to develop the forces of production any further. The only choice left was for the proletariat to take control of the means of production for themselves. This socialist revolution would be the first stage towards a communist, classless society.

A century and two world wars later, many sociologists were arguing that elements of a classless society had indeed emerged, though not in the way that Marx had foreseen. Industrialisation had run its course and polarisation had not taken place. On the contrary, the middle class had grown in number, and the working class had become relatively more, and not less, affluent. Consuming goods had become as much part of their lives as producing them. The traditional working class depicted by writers such as Dennis, Henriques and Slaughter (1956) was fragmenting. Important sections of the working class had become better off, gaining a stake in capitalism. Class conflict was disappearing as workers had come to share the same goals as their employers. They had undergone a process of embourgeoisement, whereby they were taking on the norms and values of the middle class. Working-class culture was disappearing. There was no longer any real difference between the lifestyle and attitudes of the middle class and the affluent working class.

This was the argument put forward in the 1950s and early 1960s by a series of writers (Abrams et al., 1960; Butler and Rose, 1960; Mogey, 1956; Young and Wilmott, 1957 and Zweig, 1952) echoing similar arguments in the USA. Some psephologists, for example, used this argument to explain the victory of the Conservative Party in the elections of 1951, 1955 and 1959. Other sociologists, though, were far from happy with the idea of abandoning one of the key concepts in sociology. In the early 1960s a research team was set up to investigate the truth of the embourgeoisement theorists' claims.

The Affluent Worker   In what has become one of the best-known and important studies of the British working class, Goldthorpe, Lockwood, Bechhofer and Platt (1969) chose to study selected working-class groups in Luton, where they thought the conditions for embourgeoisement would be most clearly present. At three industrial sites (Vauxhall Motors, Skefco Ball Bearings, and Laporte Chemicals) and in their homes, they conducted a detailed examination of the norms, values, attitudes, economic circumstances and lifestyles of 229 blue-collar and 54 white-collar workers.

Their findings are presented under three headings: economic, political and relational. Under the first they found that although manual workers might, on occasion, earn the same amount as the non-manual workers and possess similar consumer durables, their wages were not earned in the same way. The manual workers had to work longer hours, in shifts, frequently taking on overtime. They had less job security, less opportunities for promotion, and fewer of the fringe benefits enjoyed by the non-manual workers such as sick pay and pension rights. Moreover, they were distinguished by their instrumental attitude to work. Work was not a means to finding satisfaction or fulfilment; it was simply a means to an end, and that end was found in their pay packet.

The term 'relational' referred to who the workers spent their free time with. Here they found scant evidence that the manual workers associated with white-collar workers, from inside or outside the workplace. Most of the time was spent with family or friends drawn from the same class. Unlike the non-manual workers, their time was spent in informal, unstructured activities.

At a political level, the team found little evidence to suggest that these workers were not aligned to either trade unions or the Labour Party. Of their sample, 80 per cent had voted Labour in 1959, and 87 per cent were members of trade unions, though in both cases they found that these decisions were made, again, largely on the basis of instrumentalism. It was the workers' belief that Labour and the trade unions could preserve their status as affluent workers.

Privatisation

What was a new trend, though, was the increasing number from both classes who were becoming more home-centred or privatised, with the men spending more time at home with the children and doing DIY. This was not a result of one class adopting the norms of another, but of a process of convergence between the two.

What *The Affluent Worker* showed was that there was no evidence for the original hypothesis. The working class had not undergone a process of embourgeoisement. New trends, though, were discernible. Male workers spent more time at home and they saw work as a way of earning the money necessary to buy consumer goods. Trade unions and the Labour Party were supported to help them become more affluent. The workers they had studied were therefore 'privatised instrumental collectivists'.

Criticisms of *The Affluent Worker*

As well as creating a great deal of interest, and becoming the model for further research, *The Affluent Worker* has also provoked a great deal of criticism. Some of this is aimed at the research methods used.

Although they felt unable to say that their study was generalisable for all affluent workers, they claimed at the time that the Luton group were 'prototypical', containing the seeds of future trends in the working class. As T. H. Marshall argued at the time (1970), this is an ambitious claim, as the aim of their study had been to test the embourgeoisement thesis, not detect future trends in the working class. A different research design would have been necessary to do this. Doubts have also been raised about the composition of the research group, in that many of the workers who had moved to Luton in the 1950s had come from the depressed areas of the north-east and Scotland: 'Far from being the vanguard of the working class, a significant section of the work force has to be understood as labour peripherally recruited and therefore untypical. Prototypicality, given this finding, would be an even more unsubstantiated claim' (Grieco, 1987).

In the 1990s, Fiona Devine (1992) undertook a second study of the Vauxhall car plant at Luton, by now shrunk in size from the 22,000 workers of the 1960s to 6,000 under the impact of a global recession. Her aim was to reinvestigate the concept of privatised instrumental collectivism. Having interviewed 62 men and women at the Vauxhall plant, she argues that the portrait painted by The Affluent Worker team was too simplistic. Her respondents had moved to Luton to escape redundancy and job insecurity and to find cheaper housing. Many had done this while at the same time maintaining strong kinship and friendship links. Their lives were not exclusively family- or home-centred, yet neither were they wholly public or communal. 'Bettering' themselves and their families was a dominant aspiration of all the interviewees. Their individualism was tempered by an awareness of how others in their class also had to work for a living and of the unequal distribution of wealth and income. They still looked to trade unions and the Labour Party to improve not only their own lives but the lives of others like them, although they were critical of, and disappointed by, the shortcomings of both unions and the party.

Devine argues in her research that the connections between individualism, privatism and instrumentalism are not as strong as The Affluent Worker proposed, and that working-class lifestyles and values have not changed as much as they had suggested. Workers accept that they have to earn a living under capitalism, although they do not necessarily accept the social order determined by capitalism, nor are they necessarily committed to this system. Their class consciousness is evident from a sense of solidarity with others in a similar financial position to themselves.

The issue of the class position of the skilled working class remains a live issue today. Although the term 'embourgeoisement' is now rarely used, it is frequently argued that the working class has fragmented into at least two different layers, definable in terms of hopes, aspirations and patterns of consumption: the 'new' and 'traditional' working class. These arguments are considered below and in chapter 8.

QUESTIONS

1 **Can you see any evidence that embourgeoisement is occurring today?**

2 **Where would a research team go in Britain in the 1990s to test the embourgeoisement thesis?**

3 **What is Weberian about the approach of *The Affluent Worker* authors to the question of embourgeoisement?**

Proletarianisation

As we have seen, part of Marx's projection about the development of the class system under capitalism concerned the argument that sections of the middle class would become depressed into the proletariat. In the process, they would adopt working-class norms and values. In other words, they would undergo a process of proletarianisation. As with the concept of embourgeoisement, this idea continues to be keenly debated. In many ways, the proletarianisation debate is the mirror image of the embourgeoisement debate, with sociologists taking similar theoretical positions and employing similar analytical tools. It is mainly a debate between Marxists and Weberians. Specifically it is a debate about the class position of clerical workers.

Lockwood

In *The Black-Coated Worker*, David Lockwood (1958) presents us with evidence that suggests that clerical workers have undergone a process of proletarianisation since the nineteenth century. Holding the position of a clerk implied the high wages and status accorded to those possessing the skills of numeracy and literacy. This situation has changed as the proportion of clerks in the workforce has increased – from 0.8 per cent in 1851 to 13 per cent by the 1950s. Wages have also dropped to a point where they are roughly equivalent to those of the better-paid manual workers. What was once a high-wage, high-status occupation for men has become comparatively low-paid, low-status work dominated by women.

The task Lockwood set himself was to determine whether these changes were enough to indicate that a process of proletarianisation had taken place. He argued that clerks' position could be best understood by reference to three criteria: work situation, market situation and status situation. The first refers to how much they earned, how secure they were in their jobs and what their chances of promotion were. The second refers to the labour process and social relations at work of the clerical workers. The third defines the amount of prestige these workers had in the wider society.

Although Lockwood found that it was now the case that some clerical workers earned less than some of the manual workers on the same site, he found that their conditions of service were preferable in that they were less likely to be made redundant, worked shorter hours, had greater access to fringe benefits and had greater opportunities of promotion.

The labour process of clerical work did not resemble manual work. It did not take place on factory floors, their work still involved the acquisition of skills and specialisations. Their work had not been routinised, nor was it as easy to replace a clerical worker as it was a manual worker.

Status ambiguity   Their status situation, though, had changed. This was because there was both a greater supply of clerical workers and a greater demand for clerical work, and because clerical workers were predominantly female. Although this amounts to a decline in status for these workers, this is not enough to say that they are now proletarian. Nor are they middle class – this is what Lockwood calls a situation of 'status ambiguity'.

Braverman   Writing sixteen years later, and from an explicitly Marxist perspective, Harry Braverman (1974) will have none of Lockwood's Weberianism. Clerical workers, he clearly states, are now proletarian. As with manual work, non-manual work has suffered at the hands of Taylorism (see chapter 6). It has been standardised and routinised in the era of monopoly capitalism. He dates the earliest attempts to apply Taylorist principles to office work from the publication of W. H. Leffingwell's *Scientific Office Management* in 1917.

The proletarianisation of clerical work has advanced relentlessly. By 1960, the Systems and Procedures Association of America had produced a manual entitled *A Guide to Office Time Standards: A Compilation of Standard Data Used By Large American Companies*. In true positivist tradition, everything that could be measured, was:

	Minutes
Open and close	
File drawer, open and close, no selection	.04
Folder, open and close flaps	.04
Desk drawer	.014
Open center drawer	.026
Close side	.015
Close center	.027
Chair activity	
Get up from chair	.033
Sit down in chair	.033
Turn in swivel chair	.009
Move in chair to adjoining desk or file (4ft max.)	.050

Source: Braverman, Labor and Monopoly Capitalism, 1974

87

According to Braverman, the widespread application of these timings shows clear evidence that there is no longer any difference between the labour process of manual and non-manual workers.

The continued attempt by some sociologists to maintain this distinction is itself ideological as far as Braverman is concerned: 'This terminology is … considered serviceable by those who are alarmed by the results of a more realistic terminology – those, for instance, whose "sociology" pursues apologetic purposes. For them, such terms as "white collar employees" conveniently lump into a single category the well-paid, authoritative and desirable positions at the top of the hierarchy and the mass of proletarianised inferiors in a way that makes possible a rosier picture: higher "average pay" scales etc.'

Attempts to operationalise the concept of class stratification frequently founder on the issue of how routine non-manual workers should be classified. John Goldthorpe (1980) has conceded that in his study of social mobility (see above) some of those he classed as routine non-manual – the personal service workers (Class 3) – would be better reclassified as working class, although he continues to see secretaries as part of the middle class.

Wright Erik Wright's (1985) first attempt to construct a Marxist class model centred on the concept of exploitation through relationship to the means of production, foundered on the problem of where to place routine, non-manual workers. Sometimes he placed them in a category of semi-autonomous workers, who have some control over their work, at other times he placed them in the same category as workers taking it as understood that they had been proletarianised. This was the key difference between his model and that constructed by Goldthorpe. Later he decided to place this group in either the working class or the new middle class according to the qualifications they possessed, their job title, and how much control – or autonomy – they had over what they did at work. In doing so he found himself moving closer to a Weberian model of class.

As with so many debates in sociology, part of the disagreement here stems from different uses of the same terms. Proletarianisation can be used to describe different social changes. It can refer to the changing nature of work, for example through deskilling, where technological changes mean that the same job now requires less skill to carry it out. It can refer to changing political consciousness, for example white-collar workers becoming active trade unionists. It can also refer to the experience of downward mobility. In one of the most recent studies of social class, Gordon Marshall *et al.* (1988)

argue that, however it is defined, there is no contemporary evidence for proletarianisation.

Proletarianisation refuted In a study drawn from a national random sample of 1,315 male and female workers in 1984, they found that it was mainly manual workers who claimed that their work had been deskilled. Over 90 per cent of routine non-manual workers did not believe that their jobs had been deskilled. Nor did they report that they experienced less autonomy over the labour process than manual workers. The research team did not find any evidence of significant downward mobility for either male or female routine non-manual workers, at any stage in their working lives. They were as likely to identify themselves as middle class as working class, and more likely to vote Conservative than Labour. Marshall *et al.*'s unequivocal answer to this question is that proletarianisation is not taking place.

As we can see, the most heavily researched area in the sociology of class concerns the question of where to draw the line between the working and middle classes. How this is done depends, as ever, on the perspective used to conceptualise class.

QUESTIONS

1 **How can non-manual workers be described as proletarian?**

2 **What is the best way of describing the class position of clerical workers?**

The underclass

In the same way that the concept of embourgeoisement dominated the sociology of social class in the 1950s and 1960s, in the 1980s and 1990s the argument that a new underclass is emerging – or re-emerging – in the class structure of advanced industrial societies has become a central focus of debate.

As with many concepts in sociology, all the main contributors have a clear idea of what it is they are describing but there is little agreement on the exact nature of what it is that is perceived, or why it exists. The underclass debate is no different. There is disagreement over why an underclass exists – is it a structural or a behavioural phenomenon – and who belongs to it? There is also doubt expressed about whether the concept of an underclass is a useful one or not. Many of the arguments are similar to those surrounding poverty (see chapter 9). In this section we look at the argument that a black underclass can be distinguished.

The idea of a newly emergent underclass has a long history. Marx described the lumpenproletariat and Hitler waged war against the

Untermenschen, and in modern usage the idea of an underclass has been used by writers such as Anthony Giddens (1973), Jordan (1973) and Rex and Tomlinson (1979), but it is in later works that the term itself has been refined and tested.

The term 'underclass' generally means a substratum of society somewhere below the working class, economically and socially distinct from the rest of society. Characteristically, they live in inner-city areas, are dependent on State benefits, are likely to be caught up in crime, are perhaps drug addicts, were conceived when their mothers were in their teenage years, or become teenage parents themselves, have children who frequently miss school, or missed school themselves.

A black underclass?   To many writers, in Britain and America, there seems to be a disproportionate number of people from ethnic minorities in this class. This is the group studied by Rex and Tomlinson (1979) and in the USA by W. J. Wilson (1987). Thus, for Wilson, 'today's ghetto neighbourhoods are populated almost exclusively by the most disadvantaged segments of the black urban community', some of whom are 'engaged in street crime and other forms of aberrant behaviour as well as families that experience long-term spells of poverty and/or welfare dependency. These are the populations to which I refer when I speak of the "underclass".' It is partly for historical reasons that black people have accumulated in inner cities, especially in the northern USA, many of whom have been left high and dry as jobs have moved out, along with some of the more affluent black and white working class. What remains are poor blacks.

This type of structural explanation for the emergence of a black underclass is echoed by neo-Weberian views that emphasise the status inequality that results from racial discrimination leading to, for example, black workers being confined to the secondary labour market which is characterised by low pay, poor promotion prospects and little job security.

Conflict theory   A number of sociologists doubt the usefulness and appropriateness of the concept of an underclass. Marxists see no ethnically differentiated substratum of the working class but the common disabilities of class being experienced by people who happen to be black. R. Miles (1982), looking at migrant labour, argues that 'migrants occupy a structurally distinct position in the economic, political and ideological relations of British capitalism, but within the boundary of the working class. They therefore constitute a fraction of the working class.'

Rather than engage in a sterile debate about whether ethnic minorities are part of the underclass or a fraction of the working class, it is perhaps more helpful to see the similarities between the Marxist and Weberian positions. Both agree that racial discrimination has a socio-economic basis and this racism is widespread and affects all blacks. They further agree that the only jobs available to some blacks are those that whites are unwilling to undertake, particularly manual labour (making them a replacement population) and that they have an experience of life and a consciousness different to the white working class.

Yet there are also important difficulties attached to any attempt to equate ethnicity with membership of an underclass. The underclass is far from exclusively black. Both Townsend (1979) and Field (1989) describe an underclass without specific reference to ethnicity. Field's underclass is simply composed of elderly pensioners, lone parents and the long-term unemployed (see chapter 9).

It is also important to disaggregate the groups so often described as the 'ethnic minorities'. The experience of West Indians, Asians, Indians, Pakistanis, Bangladeshis and African Asians of life in Britain is not uniform. African Asians and Indians in particular have a class profile similar to that of whites. Largely for this reason a shared colour-consciousness has not emerged.

The underclass concept refuted

In the same way that the idea of a black underclass is problematic, so is any concept of a homogeneous group that can be described as an 'underclass'. In the same way that not all of those so categorised are necessarily criminals, or teenage parents, or black, so too are they not necessarily a static group. If it does exist, it is a class that people – except perhaps the long-term unemployed – move into and out of. Nor, according to Bradshaw and Holmes (1989) are even the long-term unemployed part of a separate group. 'In no sense', they argue, are they 'a detached and isolated group cut off from the rest of society. They are just the same people as the rest of our population, with the same culture and aspirations but with simply too little money to be able to share in the activities and possessions of everyday life with the rest of the population.'

It therefore seems to be the case that, while social divisions and inequality in society have become more pronounced in recent decades, few sociologists are willing to unreservedly describe the emergence of a new underclass, black or otherwise. The term has been criticised for being a stereotype of a heterogeneous group, inadequately describing the experience of all black people, all lone parents, all women, or even all of the long-term unemployed. At worst, it has been seen as a dangerous concept, used by some as a euphemism for race while playing down the existence of discrimination. It has been used as an umbrella term to attempt to link social problems such as the rise in lone parents, ethnic discrimination, relative poverty and increasing criminality that, as Jencks and Peterson (1991) argue, are in reality only tenuously linked. The case for the emergence of a distinct and separate underclass remains problematic.

QUESTIONS

1 **Does an underclass exist?**

2 **Given the evidence presented, who may belong to it?**

The obsession with production

In viewing class as an aspect of stratification, the Registrar-General, Hall and Jones, Marxists, and to some extent Weberians, all accept the importance of viewing social divisions principally as based on the way people live their lives as providers of goods and services. The focus is on what people do in their working lives. This view has caused increasing problems for sociologists in recent decades.

By focusing on production, occupation and employment, only a particular sector comes into view. We learn little about those who are not part of the formal economy, for whatever reason, whether they are in education, retired, unemployed, housewives, sick and disabled, or institutionalised.

Excluding these groups has caused many problems. New directions have had to be taken to discover the importance of unpaid domestic labour, the 'informal' economy or what it is like to be unemployed or never intending to work again. Very little has been written concerning the sociology of disability. These areas slipped out of focus because of the centrality of paid work in sociological analysis. Now sociologists are discovering and uncovering whole new areas to study.

Not only does measuring stratification by formal work role hide as much as it reveals, but it no longer tells us very much about how people behave. This argument is at the heart of current thinking in the sociology of politics – for example in the partisan alignment debate which examines the relationships between class and voting behaviour. It is also important in the focus on consumption in the sociology of the community.

Self-provisioning and consumerism

The view that formal work roles may not be as significant as previously supposed has been taken up by Marxists such as Manuel Castells (see chapter 13) as well as non-Marxists such as Ray Pahl

(1984). Pahl's argument is that a fundamental change has taken place in the nature of work. Full-time work has come to play less of a part in people's lives as the domestic sphere has taken over. With people mending their own cars, building extensions, doing their own decorating, growing their own food ('domestic self-provisioning'), the home, not the workplace, is now the centre of most people's lives. Yet he claims the people who engage in self-provisioning are not the unemployed, with time on their hands, but those in work – those with money who choose to make time. As many of the working, domestic self-provisioners are also home-owners (or mortgage-owners), there now exists a marked and visible social division between the 'middle mass' and those without their own homes and the opportunity to work, formally or informally.

Public and private divisions

For Pahl, this division is now more important than that between manual and non-manual workers. Two distinct sectors exist: the public world of council housing, State pensions, public transport and the National Health Service, and the private world of home ownership, private pensions, the motor car and, increasingly, private health insurance (*see Table* 3.7).

Your life chances are increasingly being determined by whether your consumption pattern is private or public, what Patrick Dunleavy (1979) has termed 'consumption sector location'. This could, for example, be the key to understanding why the Conservative Party won four consecutive elections between 1979 and 1992. It also means that sociologists now need to move away from the study of the workplace, and move into other people's homes, the privatised world of millions of individuals.

This is not a new debate in sociology. Changes in lifestyles and consumption were at the heart of the post-war assertions – when there was also a sustained period of Conservative government – that sections of the working class were undergoing a process of embourgeoisement. As we know, the 'Affluent worker' studies found this hypothesis to be unproven, and class and occupation remained key sociological terms.

TABLE 3.7 **Household tenure in Great Britain (%)**

FORM OF TENURE	1914	1945	1951	1961	1971	1981	1987
Owner-occupation	10	26	29	43	53	54	64
Local authority rental	0	12	18	27	31	34	26
Private rental	90	62	53	31	16	12	10

Source: A. H. Halsey (ed.), British Social Trends Since 1900, *Macmillan, 1988*

The debate can therefore go in two directions – one, to greatly emphasise the importance of consumption (in its widest definition). The other is to recognise that before there can be consumption there must first be production. If this is the case, the concept of 'relationship to the means of production' must be redefined in such a way as to not only include those in paid employment, but all members of the population, working or not. This is a problem that neo-Weberians and feminists will be more willing to solve than neo-Marxists.

QUESTIONS

1 **Is occupation the most important indicator of people's class?**

2 **What are the problems of this indicator?**

Sex and gender

The simplest and most widely accepted explanation (outside academic circles) of divisions and inequalities between men and women is the biological one. This emphasises the biologically given fact of 'sex'. Men are stronger, superior in intelligence and physically adapted for an outgoing role. Women are soft, caring, and built mainly for childbearing. Different male and female behaviour can be attributed to differences in sex. This type of explanation is known as biological determinism, although some notable sociologists (for example Talcott Parsons, 1959) have also leaned in this direction. Thus men play 'instrumental' and women 'expressive' roles within the family.

The great majority of other social scientists have, for a long time, been highly sceptical of this argument. As Oakley (1972) and others have argued, the roles of men and women change from society to society and from time to time within the same societies. There is nothing inevitable about male or female behaviour. How they act in society is a consequence of that society's conception of gender roles – the culturally accepted definitions of masculinity and femininity. Differences between men and women are as much socially produced as they are biological. Sociologists are interested in gender, not sex.

Gender role socialisation

From this point of view, how men and women behave is a result of a process of gender role socialisation. Individuals internalise social roles. The traditional ideologies about men being 'masculine' and women being feminine are not difficult to reconstruct. You are probably doing it now, in your mind. We live with it in the media and have been brought up with it. The traditional associations with male and female gender roles are so strongly internalised that it shocks us when they are transgressed – when a female plumber, surgeon, engineer, or a male nanny, au pair or beautician is mentioned. In Western industrial societies, males performing social tasks traditionally asso-

Women are increasingly taking on non-traditional roles: a woman welder.

ciated with females are so few that they are seen as the leaders of a change in social values and are termed 'new men'. They are seen as oddities by the media and regarded with suspicion by some feminists. This highlights the social acceptance of the traditional, normative behaviour according to gender roles and people's dismay when a man takes on a role considered appropriate for the 'inferior' sex.

Gender role socialisation is carried on by parents who choose blue for boys (strong, cold colour) and pink for girls (weak, warm, delicate). It is reflected in cards, presents and hospital name tags. From birth the physical handling of boys and girls is different. Boys are encouraged to look around and stimulated to be active; girls are hugged, protected and encouraged to be passive and 'take care'. Boys develop physical strength and girls cultivate fragility and weakness. Women are encouraged into domestic roles. Notions of romance, marriage and motherhood all tend to pressure girls into these roles which can then exclude other possibilities in their lives which are available to men. They may give up at school and see marriage as an important goal, or they may find it difficult to enter professions on the same terms as men. Social (and employers') expectations are that they will break off their career to have children and look after them. Resisting this role is seen as a form of deviance. Men (who also become parents) are not seen in this way.

Class and gender

The models of class presented so far have seen class in terms of occupation and have been geared to the measurement of the experiences of men. In recent decades it has become clear that this bequest of the 'founding fathers' creates a sociology in which it seems that women are bolted on as an afterthought. The sociology of gender that has emerged in recent decades is in fact an attempt to make up for the omission of women from sociology.

Classical Marxism, for example, argues that all forms of stratification are subordinate to that of class. Marx's economics are constructed on the assumption that surplus value is generated by paid labour at the point of production. He has little to say about unpaid labour. It was left to Marx's friend and collaborator, Engels (1884), to explain how women's exploitation was caused by capitalism, and specifically the link between the State, private property and the family.

'Malestream' sociology

This is generally true of most 'malestream' sociology to date, and since the 1970s a series of books and articles have exposed sociology's intrinsic sexism. Women have only been assumed to exist as appendages of men. Furthermore, the models of class we have looked at so far assume that they are married, live in families, and if they work they earn less than their husbands. The Oxford Mobility Study, for example, was conducted on the assumption that families, not individuals, are the fundamental units of society. As individuals, women are therefore thought not to have an independent experience of class, but are classified according to the occupations of their partners.

Limitations

The limitations of studies based on this assumption are obvious, as Acker (1973) has pointed out. Not all women are married or live with men. Some households may contain couples where the woman is the higher or only earner. Not all women work in paid labour. Most single-parent families are headed by women. Finally, it is not necessarily the case with working couples that they have the same type of occupation and therefore the same class position in their hours of work, regardless of their domestic situation. Seeing class in this way obscures any understanding of the position of women in society.

In defending what has come to be seen as the 'traditional' view, John Goldthorpe (1983, 1986) has countered these claims by stating that, statistically, it is reasonable to say that most people do live in families, and that the head of that household is usually a man. Women are intermittent, limited and conditional members of the labour market. It is not patronising or sexist to devise a model of class that acknowledges that women are socially subordinate to men, because this is a known and measured reality. Indeed it is the starting point for feminist analysis. In situations where there are dual-career households they can be analysed according to who has the salient or most prominent occupation, measured by wages and the amount of qualifications needed to get that job.

It is nevertheless maintained by many theorists that the relationship between women, class and gender is more complex than this traditional view claims. Many writers have argued that there is sufficient empirical evidence to show that men occupy their class position *because* women occupy an inferior one: class structures are gendered. Marshall *et al.* (1988) state that their research shows that men have higher absolute rates of mobility than women, receive higher rewards, and are more highly paid for their qualifications. Only 2 per cent of highly qualified men are in routine non-manual jobs compared with 32 per cent of equally qualified women. Crompton and Jones (1984) found that only 12 per cent of female clerical workers had reached supervisory positions compared with 36 per cent of their male counterparts, and only 1 per cent of women got to management, compared to 34 per cent of men. The effect of women's employment is to privilege men.

Within sociology there is a lack of agreement about what is the basic unit of analysis in society. Where some maintain that it is the family others argue that married women in full-time employment should also be included. This would reveal what Britten and Heath (1983) call the 'cross-class family'. Marshall *et al.* see men and women as individuals in families, while Stanworth (1984) and Giddens (1973) argue that women and men have to be accounted separately in any account of stratification. Delphy (1981) takes the argument further than this when she claims that married women constitute a class separate to men because, whether in paid labour or not, they all engage in the same unpaid labour at home, and many are solely dependent on men for access to money. This is what she calls the 'domestic mode of production'.

The idea of women as a homogeneous class has itself been seen as problematic. Among feminists, there has been little agreement about what it is that pushes women into their shared oppression, with radical feminists emphasising men and marriage, and Marxist feminists highlighting the issue of women and class. Anne Phillips (1987) has suggested that the most effective way of understanding the complex position of women is to recognise the equal importance of gender and class as parallel oppressions.

Black women and gender

While the debate about the relationship between gender and stratification continues, new dimensions to the argument continue to surface. Black women have found little to describe their experiences in the sociology of gender to date (Joseph, 1981) and highlight the stereotypical way in which they have been portrayed by white feminist writers and others. Black women have more experience of the labour market than white. The stereotypical image of the passive, home-bound Asian woman is unfounded by statistics that reveal that, in fact, there is a higher percentage of Asian women in employment than white women (Barrett and McIntosh, 1985). West Indian and Asian women continue to work in sectors of the labour market which largely employ women (genderised employment), particularly in semi-skilled manual labour.

Similarly, many writers are beginning to realise that the concept of gender focuses almost exclusively on the experience of women. A new sociology that reconceptualises the role of men is also emerging from within the concept of masculinity.

QUESTIONS

1 How does the term 'sex' differ from the term 'gender'?

2 Why has gender been ignored by sociologists until recently?

3 What are the problems with the treatment of gender in traditional models of class?

Race and ethnicity

Although they are often thought to mean the same thing, the terms 'race' and 'ethnicity' are not interchangeable. Race refers to the attempt by biologists and others to classify humans according to physical characteristics into different racial groups. The largest categories are usually called 'Mongoloid' (of Asian and American descent), Negroid (sub-Saharan African) and Caucasian (European, North African and Middle Eastern).

Apart from the problems involved in fitting humanity into one of three groups, sociologists and others have been extremely wary of this type of classification. Some of them have asked: 'Why bother?' In whose interests is it to see people in this way? Racial classification is a hangover from the era when it was believed – mainly by Europeans – that some races were naturally superior to others, with Caucasians as the most superior of all.

This argument is no longer seen by anyone, apart from by a few right-wing think-tanks, as having any evidence. It falls into the trap of biological reductionism, attributing human behaviour solely to physical factors. This is the nature side of the nature–nurture argument which, as we saw in chapter 2, sociologists explicitly reject.

Ethnicity

As with the debate around sex and gender (which has many parallels to the race–ethnicity argument), sociologists agree that there are nevertheless culturally defined differences between different ethnic groups in society. This is known as ethnicity, and is variously defined. Yinger (1981) defines ethnic groups as 'a segment of a larger society whose members are thought, by themselves, and/or by others, to share a common origin and to share important segments of a common culture, and who, in addition, participate in shared activities in which the common origin and culture are significant ingredients'. According to Jeffcoate (1984), an ethnic group is a 'comparatively small and powerless group whose culture differs in significant respects from that of the majority and which is possessed of a sense of shared ancestry and identity and committed to self-preservation through endogamy [closed kinship networks through marriage] and the initiation of its young'. It is important to notice that, despite the difference in emphasis in these definitions, neither makes any reference to race and racial characteristics. Thus, it could be argued, the Irish in mainland Britain constitute an ethnic minority.

Officially, though, the population of Great Britain is usually described as in *Table* 3.8.

TABLE 3.8 Ethnic groups in Great Britain, 1991

	%	'000s
White	94.27	51,981
West Indian	0.83	455
African	0.30	163
Indian	1.52	836
Pakistani	1.00	550
Bangladeshi	0.27	149
Chinese	0.26	142
Arab	0.13	73
Mixed	0.60	331
Other	0.29	160
Not stated	0.55	303
All ethnic minorities	5.18	2,859

Source: Labour Force Survey, 1990 and 1991

Ethnic minorities can be absorbed into the majority culture to different extents. A fully absorbed ethnic group exhibits no discernible separate ethnic identity. The French Huguenots are a frequently cited example of this phenomenon. Integration describes a group which, while maintaining its own ethnic identity, participates fully in social life, such as British Jews. Pluralism describes situations where minorities exist as subcultures within the majority culture, with different norms and values, frequently speaking a different language and participating mainly in the life of this subculture. The theoretically impossible situation of separation would describe a minority at odds with the dominant culture. Some have suggested that this describes Rastafarianism in Britain.

Ethnicity and stratification

As with women, there is no agreement about how ethnic minorities should be perceived as a stratified group. From a Marxist point of view, although racial discrimination and prejudice are recognised to exist, class remains the dominant form of oppression. This argument is common to the analyses of Castles and Kosack (1973), Hall (1978a) and Miles (1982). What matters is class, not ethnic identity. It is capitalism that turns social groups into ethnic minorities by moving them around the world as migrant labour. Racial distinctions made by the working class serve only to divide them.

From a Weberian point of view, ethnic minorities constitute separate status groups. For Rex and Tomlinson (1979), among others, ethnic minorities in Britain constitute separate strata of the class system, beneath the working class, distinguishable as an underclass.

In the same way that black women have argued that they have a different experience of sexism to that of white women, so too have they laid claim to a different experience of racism to that of black men. Although they are generally located further down the class system than white women, the type of work they do and the pay they earn is more comparable with this group than with black men (Cook and Watt, 1987). This adds yet another dimension to the sociology of stratification, and further emphasises the interplay between class, gender and ethnicity.

QUESTIONS

1 **In what ways does the debate around race and ethnicity resemble that concerning sex and gender?**

2 **How does the term 'race' differ from 'ethnicity'?**

3 **Are the Irish in Britain an ethnic minority?**

Age

In the same way that we are happy to use terms such as 'working class', 'middle class', 'masculine' and 'feminine' without ever defining precisely what we mean, so we also use terms describing age without putting an exact figure against them. When does infancy end and childhood begin? When do you cease to be an adolescent and become an adult? When do the middle-aged become old? Are all 'old' people the same or are there groups among them, such as the 'young elderly' and the 'elderly elderly'? If you are 70, are you 'old' or simply 'as old as you feel'?

Age and the law

These questions can lead to a number of enquiries about past and present perceptions of age, yet what is important here is to recognise that age is a significant way of defining status within society, and one way that society is stratified. The most obvious forms of stratification or inequality exist at either ends of the age scale. If you are 'young', a number of legal rights are denied to you throughout your youth, and are gradually gained with increasing age, ending with the right to stand for Parliament at 21 years. (You can vote from the age of 18 years.) At the age of 65 (for most men and now women) you are obliged to retire from your employment, and make do with whatever savings and pensions you have for the rest of your life. At 70 you will have to reapply for your driving licence. Although it is not always the case, power in industrial societies tends to be concentrated among those who are middle-aged – approximately 40 to 60, though when middle-age begins and ends is as hotly contested as any other age-band.

The main ages that sociologists have been interested in studying are childhood, youth and old age. All three, it is argued, are phases of life that have come to take on distinct identities in industrial societies in the twentieth century. If the parameters of these phases vary from time to time and place to place, then they cannot be absolute or fixed stages of life, but products of the society that they inhabit; these concepts of age are socially constructed.

Childhood

As a result of historical research, Philippe Ariès (1962) concluded that the idea that children should be treated separately from adults, and that childhood is a separate and distinct phase of life, dates back only a few centuries. Before 1600, he claims, 'the idea of childhood did not exist … as soon as the child could live without the constant solicitude of his mother, his nanny or his cradle rocker he belonged to adult society'. The separation of childhood from adulthood is a product of later centuries, particularly, in Britain, the Victorian era of child legislation, reforms in child labour, and the imposition of compulsory education.

CHILDREN: RIGHTS AND RESPONSIBILITIES

Growing up is marked by a continuous succession of years in which new rights and responsibilities are gained.

- **At five** children can drink alcohol in private although they must also receive full-time education.

- **At ten** they can be convicted of a criminal offence if it can be shown that they know the difference between right and wrong.

- **At twelve** they can buy a pet without a parent being present.

- **At fourteen** they must pay full fare on public transport, and can be held fully responsible for a crime. If convicted, boys can be sent to a detention centre, and convicted of rape.

- **At sixteen** they can leave school, whereupon they become eligible to pay prescription charges and for some dental treatment. They can also buy fireworks, premium bonds and enter a brothel legally.

(See also: M. Rae, P. Hewitt and B. Hugill, First Rights: A Guide to Legal Rights for Young People, National Council for Civil Liberties (now Liberty), 1983)

Perspectives on childhood

Although the historical accuracy of this view has been disputed – by, for example, Linda Pollock (1983) – the emergence of childhood as a distinct phase has been variously explained by sociologists. Thus for functionalists, the growing complexity of industrial societies and the increasing division of labour leads to the need for an extended period of primary and secondary socialisation. For Marxists, it is clear that the emergence of childhood results from the transition from feudalism to capitalism and the growth of wage labour. As with female labour, the costs of reproducing labour become the responsibility – and burden – of the wage earner. Labour power is reproduced without cost as the worker pays for children's upbringing, not the employer. In the same vein, feminists such as Shulamith Firestone (1970) see this same process intensifying the patriarchal position of the male breadwinner over his wife and children, as economic and political power is appropriated to him.

The role played by children in the family is, according to J. Hood-Williams (1990) better described as 'age patriarchy'. Contrary to the functionalist view he argues, with clear echoes of David Cooper (1972; see chapter 4), that the study of childhood should presume 'the existence of antagonistic relations within families' and should focus attention on 'the differential distributions of power, work, violence and rewards. All this is at some distance from analyses which study children through concerns around play, pedagogy, development or even mass media and markets.'

All these views reflect the observation that, in the same way that concepts of childhood have differed from time to time and from place to place, so also there is nothing fixed about the status of children: their role is socially constructed and is not a consequence of the 'nature' of children. A clear example of this is the difference between the roles of children in the developed and less developed worlds, with child labour prevalent in the latter. Childhood is a central fact of age stratification in particular and stratification in general.

In the light of this perception, childhood has become of increasing interest to sociologists. It throws doubt on any studies (such as those of Jean Piaget (1954)) that view childhood behaviour as biologically determined, with generalisable and universal phases of development. For interactionists, there is also clearly a need to examine not only the passive aspects of children's lives – undergoing socialisation – but also how they are active in creating their own child-centred view of the world, and their own distinct culture. (Discovering this world has obvious problems for the participant observer!)

Childhood in transition

Iona and Peter Opie (1967) claimed to have identified a 'self-contained community in which children's basic lore and language seem scarcely to alter from generation to generation'. This view of childhood as separate and unchanging is now open to doubt. In industrial societies, Neil Postman (1985) argues that children are becoming increasingly empowered, speaking more for themselves, conscious of their own rights, becoming sports and media stars, and, increasingly, watching the same programmes and enjoying the same music as their parents. Children are no longer seen as 'economically worthless but emotionally priceless'. With children becoming increasingly expensive to raise, and work becoming more and more home-centred, V. Zelizer (1985) argues that, in a newly democratised domestic setting, the phenomenon of 'housechildren' could emerge along with that of 'househusbands'.

QUESTIONS

1 **What are the problems in deciding when childhood ends and youth or adolescence begins?**

2 **What is meant by the term social construction?**

3 **How is childhood and youth a social construction?**

Youth

Youth is present only when its presence is a problem, or is regarded as a problem

Dick Hebdige, Subculture, 1979

As Geoffrey Pearson (1983) shows, adolescents have continually been seen as a social problem since at least the mid nineteenth century. Groups such as the 'Peaky Blinders' emerged in the 1880s, and anti-Nazi youth cultures even existed in wartime Germany (the Edelweiss Pirates). As a distinct social group, however, youth only became an important sociological concern in the 1950s.

The main focus has been on the concept of 'subculture' – a group with its own norms, values, leisure pursuits, and sometimes even a uniform, coexisting within mainstream culture. The supposed disrespect for authority and conventional morality and the sometimes illegal and organised activities of these groups have also led to intense media attention and the labelling as modern-day 'folk devils' of groupings such as teds, mods, rockers, skinheads and punks in Britain, and hell's angels in America (see chapter 15).

Explanations for youth behaviour and lifestyles encompass many areas: from peer group formation to pluralism, from increasing social mobility to changing class structure, from the extension of the school-leaving age to the emergence of a distinct youth labour market, and from new patterns of consumerism to the very fact of age itself.

This latter approach is the one taken by S. N. Eisenstadt (1956) who, looking at youth from a functionalist point of view, argues that a distinct phase of life is necessary in society to allow the transition from the particularistic values of the home to the universalistic values of the rest of society. The phenomenon of youth and youth cultures is society's solution to this problem of transition. If conflict exists, it is essentially emotional, and results from young people's sense of marginalisation and powerlessness while developing the values and relationships that allow them to stand on their own two feet. The main point is that youth cultures are functional to society and in fact help maintain social order.

The obvious point that not all young people experience the transition to adulthood in the same way and that some people are more marginalised and powerless than others was made by American subcultural theorists from Albert Cohen onwards (see chapter 14). As youth and youth cultures were further investigated, dimensions of class, ethnicity and gender, as well as of age, were also developed.

In the mid 1970s the Birmingham-based Centre for Contemporary Cultural Studies examined the links between youth, class, pop culture and social life – for example, Hall and Jefferson (1976). Focusing mainly on working-class youth, they argued that youth cultures were attempts to solve problems, not necessarily of age, but which affected the working class as a whole. Simply put, the old values of hard work and pride in the job were being challenged by the new consumer affluence. As old traditional communities disappeared, young people tried to re-establish working-class values in their own way. The search for a uniform style and the links with certain types of music were all interwoven in a complex way. These are not 'real' solutions to the social problems but 'magical' ways to deal with them. Strange clothes – teddy boy's Edwardian dress, skinhead's braces and boots, mod's suits and parkas and stripey trousers and Doc Martens of the grunge generation of the early 1990s – and conflict with parents are seen as ways of coming to terms with the problems of forming an identity against a rapidly changing class and cultural backdrop.

A central question asked by these writers concerns the extent to which youth cultures can be seen as a form of resistance to the dominant culture, gaining 'cultural space' to call their own. The concept of hegemony, most closely associated with the Italian Marxist Antonio Gramsci, is central here (see chapter 2). Youth subcultures, by the fact of their very existence and the symbolic messages they transmit, threaten the dominant ideology, punching holes in the hegemony. The most distinctive youth cultures take over and claim symbols for themselves, whether it is a Lambretta scooter (an old man's vehicle before the mods got hold of it), skinheads in workmen's boots or punks with safety pins through their noses.

Other writers have not seen youth cultures in the same romantic way. What appears as resistance can equally well be seen as an elaborate way of acquiescing to the dominant ideology. Resistance through ritualistic leisure pursuits does not really solve the problems of poor education and unemployment. The ability of youth cultures to resist dominant values is severely limited, and their artefacts are soon taken over by commercial interests and turned into mass market consumer items. Any political ideology can effectively use youth groups to further their ends, as with the extreme right and the harnessing of skinheads across Europe. Furthermore, by focusing on the most identifiable youth cultures, the ordinariness of growing up for most young people remains unexamined.

Skinheads: an expression of age, class, gender and ethnicity.

McRobbie and Garber (1976) ask whether girls do not appear in subcultural studies because of the sexism of malestream sociology or because there are no female youth subcultures. Their answer is the latter. The culture of femininity which places a high value on passivity, and allows girls less free time, marginalises them into the position of onlookers, reading romantic magazines and thinking about boys. Girls escape into fantasy rather than rebel. If they do resist, it is by acting in a male way or by getting pregnant. Later research by Sue Lees (1986) confirms most of this argument, showing how the behaviour and attitudes of adolescent girls continue to be seen in terms of male opinion. For example, their behaviour is controlled by the use of pejorative labels like 'slag'.

Black youth is a largely under-researched area of the sociology of youth, yet, whether it is as 'rude boys' in the 1960s (whose style was partly copied by mods and the earliest skinheads) or as Rastas in the 1970s and 1980s, they have made crucial contributions to the definition of youth subcultures. Rastafarianism, with its view of white civilisation as 'Babylon', is closer to a counter-culture than it is to a subculture.

Little has been said about youth culture in recent years, partly because of scarce funding but also, as many sociologists have argued, because there is perhaps little more to say. 'The spectacular sub-cultures of the 1950s and 1960s are now impossible' (Willis, 1990). Wider groups than working-class young people have appropriated subcultural styles, particularly for marketing purposes, while the declining numbers of young people, youth unemployment and homelessness, and increasing numbers of adolescents in full-time education have removed the social basis for distinctive youth cultures. Could it be, as Mark Abrams argued as early as 1959, that a 'teenager' is now little more than a marketing category?

QUESTIONS

1 **What youth cultures exist today?**

2 **How distinctive are the norms and values surrounding their behaviour?**

3 **What social conditions have been identified behind the emergence of post-war youth cultures?**

Old age

The 'rising tide' The number of elderly people has been steadily increasing in Western societies throughout the twentieth century, with the proportion of people of retirement age becoming politically significant. At the turn of the century a little over 6 per cent of the population of Great Britain was over 65 years old. By 1931 this had risen to nearly 10 per cent, going up to 15 per cent by 1951 and almost 25 per cent by 1991. It is projected to rise to around 27 per cent by 2021. The age at which people actually retire is also falling, as the idea of 'natural wastage' – encouraging people to take early retirement – gains popularity. This proportionate growth is sometimes referred to as the 'greying' or 'rising tide' of the population (*see* Figure 3.1).

The main reason for the increase in the number of the elderly is not necessarily that people are living longer, but that less people die in their early life. A much higher proportion of young people reach old age. It is not the case that people are now expected to live longer once they reach old age. The consequence, however, is that there are proportionately less people paying taxes to pay for those not engaged in waged labour, and a larger section of the population that is relatively powerless.

Figure 3.1 Population of pensionable age in the UK

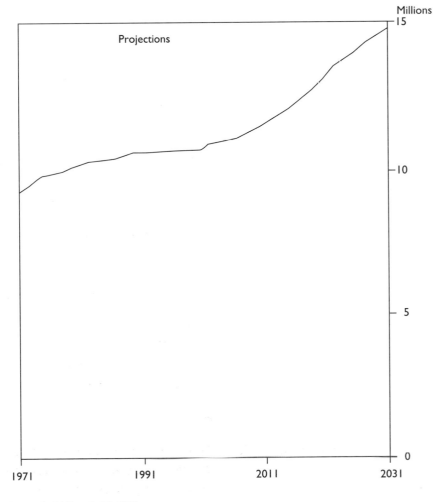

Source: Social Trends 21, 1991

A number of theories have been advanced to try and explain why it is that the elderly come to be devalued and poorly treated in advanced industrial societies. Robert Butler (1975) argues that:

> *Our attitudes towards the old are contradictory. We pay lip service to the idealised images of beloved and tranquil grandparents, wise elders, white-haired patriarchs and matriarchs. But the opposite image disparages the elderly, seeing age as decay, decrepitude, a disgusting and undignified dependency. Childhood is romanticised, youth is idolised, middle age does the work, wields the power and pays the bills, and old age, its days empty of purpose, gets little or nothing for what it has already done. The old are in the way.*

From a functionalist perspective, the elderly need to be progressively disengaged from socially important roles in order for others to take over, and for society to function without disruption. Happiness comes from the recognition that more competent people are taking their places. Age-based ascribed status has been replaced by the greater importance of achieved status. Retirement is essential to make way for others.

Ageism

Others have argued that this view of ageing is insufficient, and that the elderly, like other groups suffering social discrimination, are the victims of the ideology of ageism, which is as powerful and harmful as sexism and racism. There is no necessary reason to suppose that, as people age, they become any more miserable, inflexible, unproductive or isolated than anyone else. These forms of behaviour result from cultural and social expectations, labelling and self-fulfilling prophecies. By obliging people to retire, we create a distinct subculture, based on age. This subculture either accepts their new role passively, or resists it, as the 'Grey Panthers' of the USA have.

The elderly and class

With the growth in the numbers of the elderly, and the increasing phenomenon of early retirement (which may simply be another term for unemployment), the class position of the elderly is a growing question in sociology. This is part of the general move away from viewing stratification purely in terms of paid employment. Two views have been put forward. Proletarianisation theory sees the elderly as a homogeneous group, pushed towards poverty by the fact of age, and constituting an underclass. Labour-market continuity theory sees social inequalities persisting into old age as a result of previous market position. Thus, the age at which people retire is determined by class, as is the amount of income they will receive after retirement. Those in higher classes will receive higher occupational pensions and payments from unearned income such as shares. Income differentials are narrower than among those still in work, but are sufficiently wide for the experience of old age to continue to be structured by class.

As the elderly become a more significant social group then, as with gender and ethnicity, sociology too will have to change its focus away from conventional class-based views of stratification to take on the growing realisation that age is an important and significant form of stratification. This is beginning — but only beginning — to be reflected in the available literature.

QUESTIONS

1 **How can the class position of the elderly retired be measured?**

2 **In what ways are the elderly a significant group in society?**

Disability

The traditional understanding of stratification is that it should mainly be concerned with class. In recent decades the concept of other forms of stratification — gender, ethnicity and age — have been bolted on. An even more recent understanding is that disability, however defined, also constitutes an important — and relatively under-researched — aspect of stratification.

Disability is not simply an aspect of social class, and should not be viewed as being concerned solely with the location of the disabled within the labour market since many disabled people never enter the labour market, or withdraw from it permanently, or develop their disability on retirement. In these situations, it is not possible to be seen as both unemployed and disabled, or to relate disability to an occupational definition of social class.

Disability can originate in three ways: it can exist at birth or be developed in early childhood, it can result from a later illness or injury or from the process of ageing. Official (OPCS) statistics show that 15 per cent of adults suffer some form of disability (Martin *et al.*, 1988). Disability is more prevalent in the North, Scotland and Wales, among the elderly and among greater numbers of women than men as a consequence of women living longer.

Disability and class
Social class is an important factor in the distribution of disability, and the data echo much of what *The Black Report* found concerning the general public profile (see chapter 10). Manual workers are more likely to have a disability than non-manual workers, and skilled workers are less likely to be disabled than semi-skilled and unskilled workers. Generally, disabled workers earn lower incomes, are more likely to be in debt and live in poorer housing than their colleagues at work. It has also been argued by, among others, C.C. Harris *et al.* (1987), that many workers, when retiring from work through ill health, assume a 'disabled' identity as a consequence of their mar-

ginalisation. The strong association between class and disability has led Richard Jenkins (1991) to assert that 'being working class can be disabling'. (See also Walker and Townsend, 1981.)

Moreover, being disabled is an expensive business. It may affect other members of the family or household in their role as 'carers' (particularly women), interfere with the earning pattern of others, and may keep the disabled person permanently outside the labour market. 'In this sense', Jenkins (1991) argues, 'disability may be said to be a factor contributing to the production of stratification in its own right.' It is this observation that prevents him from stating that the disabled could be seen as an underclass or a status group, but disability is clearly to be considered as an important dimension of an already highly stratified society.

QUESTIONS

1 **Would a functionalist or Marxist approach to disability be possible? What aspects would interest feminists? What problems might they encounter?**

2 **Do you agree that disability is an aspect of social stratification?**

FURTHER READING

M. Brake, *The Sociology of Youth and Youth Subcultures*, Routledge and Kegan Paul, 1980

C. Buswell, *Women in Contemporary Society*, Nelson, 1993

G. Fennel, *The Sociology of Old Age*, Open University Press, 1989

J. Goldthorpe *et al.*, *The Affluent Worker in the Class Structure*, Cambridge University Press, 1969

S. Hall and T. Jefferson (eds.), *Resistance through Rituals*, Hutchinson, 1976

G. Marshall *et al.*, *Social Class in Modern Britain*, Routledge, 1993

D. Mason, *Race and Ethnicity in Modern Britain*, Oxford University Press, 1995

J. Pilcher, *Age and Generation in Modern Britain*, Oxford University Press, 1995

J. Westergaard, *Who Gets What? The Hardening of Class Inequality in the Late Twentieth Century*, Polity Press, 1994

4 The family

INTRODUCTION

The discussion on the family begins by examining the view of the functionalist perspective and then goes on to look at the ideas of Marxism and feminism. You will then move on to a discussion about the disadvantages of the nuclear family. The next section looks at the effect of industrialisation on the family. The discussion then moves on to look at power and labour within the family and the chapter finishes with a discussion of the family in the 1990s.

Sociology and the family

Trying to explain society entails arriving at conclusions about the reasons for social behaviour. Themes like nature or nurture, free will and determinism and the relationship between the individual and the culture of society are central issues. Is intelligence, however we define it, passed on genetically, or is it a product of nurture, of socialisation? How is culture, with its restrictive norms and values, forced into children, so that they may become 'social beings'? The first contact which a child has with culture is through whoever is providing nurture – caregivers. In most societies, this role is taken by the biological or adoptive parents of the child, in a family situation.

Functionalists claim that the family exists in all societies, that it is the 'natural' way to live and reproduce. The family is important in society, and society is important in the family. Societies ritualise and reinforce family life through celebrating the various stages in the individual's experience of the family – births, deaths and weddings, Christmas, holidays, parties and visits. The family dominates the media in sitcoms, soaps, ads and serials.

Sociologists have devoted a lot of time and effort to studying, analysing and arguing about the family. It is the place where society is shaped and passed on to be reproduced generation after generation. The answers to questions about nature and nurture, culture and the individual, free will and determinism are never found, but arguments arise, as usual, about theories. A lot of the ground work on the family, and particularly the family in Britain before and since industrialisation, was carried out by sociologists who were 'pro-family', and they raised anxieties about its possible decline. Throughout the 1960s and 1970s radical perspectives within Marxism, feminism and interactionism also pointed to the apparent break-up of the traditional family form, but they did so gleefully, seeing the family as the breeding ground for the justification of inequalities in society – between men and women, capitalists and workers, and parents and children in families.

What is the family then? According to your point of view, it's a place of love and security which produces and trains future members of society and sustains adults in their daily lives; it's an emotional, repressive 'rat's nest' which twists and distorts the personality; it's a patriarchal structure which ensures the domination of women by men or it's an offshoot of the mode of production and provides 'factory fodder' for the ruling classes.

Functionalism and the family

Functions of the family

The theory which looks for a function in every aspect of social life has spent a lot of time listing and explaining the many functions of the family. Society has certain basic needs which must be provided if the structure is to continue to be stable. It needs a steady supply of new members, to continue its existence. These new members have to be initiated into the rights and wrongs, taboos and laws, norms and values – the culture – of their society. Whilst undergoing this long period of initiation, the would-be social beings need food, clothing and shelter. The family provides all these things, and therefore it is seen as the 'natural' way to organise human life. The functionalists examine the ways in which family forms and structures meet the needs of society, and they go on to look at the relationship of the family 'organ' to the other organs in the organism of society. They find that the family way is the best possible way of meeting the basic needs of society, and that the relationship between the family and society is on the whole smooth and harmonious. The family 'feeds' the education system which provides workers who look after families. Relations between family members are also mainly positive, and the family form is said to provide well-balanced, socialised human beings who are in full agreement with the aims and goals of their society, and fully equipped to take their place within it. Functionalism has always been a 'pro-family' theory then, and the debate between the functionalists and the so-called 'anti-family' theories – Marxism, feminism and interactionism – is still going on.

Parsons' two basic functions of the family

Talcott Parsons' ideas about the role of the family in the socialisation process have been influential in the analysis of the family. His work, which mainly appeared in the 1950s, reflects the importance of the family in the functionalist view of society, the leading view at that time. He concentrates on what he calls the two 'basic, irreducible functions' of the family:

1 to reproduce and socialise children;
2 to maintain and stabilise adult personalities.

Parsons himself reflects the popular psychological thinking of the time in using a watered-down version of Freud's ideas to explain how the biological needs and desires of the individual must be formed and controlled to fit in with the moral requirements of society. Sex was central in Freud's theory of individual development, and functionalists acknowledge its importance — where would society be without it? However, the sex drive is powerful and needs to be controlled, social approval is given only to expressions of sexuality between the 'right' people (male and female) in the 'right' place (bedroom) and at the 'right' time. Society makes rules first and foremost about sexuality, and parents have to instil these rules into the personalities of the children they reproduce.

Socialisation

The values of society have to be internalised, and Parsons uses his 'do it yourself' psychoanalysis to explain the process of 'internalisation'. Socialisation is a process — a sequence of stages which have to be passed through. Primary socialisation takes place within the family, and is therefore of great importance. Parsons uses a ladder metaphor to explain the progress of the individual through the stages of socialisation. When you climb a ladder, you always keep one foot on the rung below as you progress to the next rung. Each stage of socialisation is linked, and the connections lead you all the way up to society. Parsons sees society as a set of systems and subsystems. The family exists as a subsystem of society. Relationships within the family such as mother/child, father/child, mother/father are also subsystems. All these subsystems lock together, and make it possible for the culture of society to enter into the family through the adult roles, and, from the adults acting out their roles, into the children. Parsons' sociological works are littered with boxes which are split up into four smaller boxes, with smaller boxes being further divided. His family box considers the roles of men, women and children in society and in the family.

Gender role development

The family can be divided in terms of roles, the leading/following roles which always emerge in small groups, and the instrumental/

Figure 4.1 Parsons' model of family roles

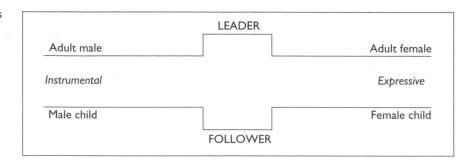

expressive roles (*see Figure* 4.1). The instrumental role is active, it is concerned with ideas and goal attainment which are external activities taking place in the outside world. The expressive role is one of custodian and caregiver, and it is concerned with internally directed activities. The adult male is instrumental and leads his male offspring in this arena, for example teaching him to hunt, taking him to football matches or teaching him to drive. The adult female is expressive and leads her daughter in this field, teaching her to give care, cook and clean, gather berries or go to the supermarket. The family system, then, functions for society, and gender roles are reproduced within the family.

Internalisation

Internal voices of moral authority are a product of culture. Freud claimed that psychological and sexual development were one and the same. Parsons himself spends time analysing the psycho-sexual development of the individual. He sees socialisation as a two-sided process, on one side the individual, and on the other side the culture of society. Culture must get into the individual in some way, but it is not something which just sits on top of what is already there. It must actually become the personality of the individual, it must inform and shape that person. Moral judgements, senses of right and wrong, must become the framework on which the individual is constructed. The individual grows up to look at the world and to deal with other members of society on the basis of these moral roles. If he or she goes against this morality then it feels wrong, they feel uncomfortable, aware of a sense of wrong-doing. They feel guilty. In order to experience this guilt, the morals of society must be so deeply ingrained that the person does not know they are there. They are simply part of that person. How does this internalisation of the voice of society take place?

Development of adult personalities

The Freudian model, which Parsons borrows from selectively, sees this process of socialisation as a set of stages in which conflict must be resolved; for example, the conflict between the base and instinctive desires of the individual (the urge to rape and/or kill others) and the social and moral requirements of society. For Freud the conflicts are never resolved, just more or less successfully repressed.

Parsons, however, makes little mention of any conflict in this process and has been criticised for giving us a picture of passive, conformist and 'over-socialised' individuals. The parental voice is successfully internalised when the child comes to recognise the authority and leadership of the 'instrumental' father figure. Any actions which the individual is then tempted to perform will be considered in terms of consequence – what would the father say if I did such and such? The voice of reprimand and discipline, which used to be external when the child was small, has been internalised and the child becomes the regulator of its own behaviour. Therefore, well-balanced adult personalities emerge from the 'child factory' and take up their places in society. However, the problem does not always run as smoothly as this.

Parsons acknowledges that there may be difficulties. Deviant parenting could lead to conflict. If the socialising agents do not balance out their role they could overdo the nurturing, expressive role, ultimately leading to incest. The taboo against incest functions to prevent this though, and on the whole there is little conflict. Strain may be experienced whilst undergoing socialisation, but the male child has more problems than the female as he has first to struggle free of the mother/child subsystem, then to get out of the whole family system itself (escaping into another family). He then becomes the instrumental leader in his own family, having internalised the moral structure of society. The analysis of adult sex roles in Parsons' theories of the family has received a lot of criticism.

Maintenance of adult personalities

Family roles are enshrined outside the individual, within society. These duties and obligations have been internalised, and anyone who goes against them will feel the vengeance of moral conscience, through guilt. Adult roles, then, entail working through one's daily duties and responding to the pressures of the world. This activity is a strain, and possible conflict is avoided because the family performs the second of Parsons' basic functions – the maintenance and stabilisation of adult personalities. The family home is a haven where the pressures of the outside can be escaped. The parents can indulge in childish behaviour through the children, for example, by playing with their toys. They can recharge their batteries and relax in a harmonious environment, free from the strains and stresses of everyday life. This appears to be a function which services males, for the female rarely escapes her place of work to 'recharge'. There is also a naive ignorance of family strain and conflict. Parsons is also criticised because he seems to have based most of his ideas upon middle-class American families, taking no account of culture, class or other factors. Many of his ideas are based upon the research of a fellow functionalist, George Murdock.

The family defined

George Murdock is famous in sociology because he gave a definition of the family which has been memorised by sociology students for exam purposes ever since. According to Murdock, the family is 'a social group characterised by common residence, economic co-operation and reproduction. It includes adults of both sexes, at least two of whom maintain a socially approved sexual relationship, and one or more children, own or adopted, of the sexually co-habiting adults.' Murdock is also famous for the piece of research upon which he bases this definition, as he claims to have found this family in one form or another, in every society he looked at – over 250 in all. This study – *Social Structure* – gives functionalists a good basis for their claim that the family is a 'universal' form, in other words it exists all over this planet. The societies that Murdock studied range from the simplest to the most complex. Some cultural groups still live in nomadic hunter–gatherer bands, and these give Murdock his historical ideas about sex roles: men hunt, women gather.

The hunter–gatherer bands move from place to place, building temporary shelters (a man's job requiring physical strength) and clearing trees and planting crops (women's work requiring small fingers). The men then go out to hunt (an aggressive, fast, brutal business) whilst the women stay at home making curtains out of bamboo leaves and looking after the children. They need to be at home with the young babies, and therefore they provide the caring, 'expressive', emotional role. These roles have survived into the larger, more complex industrial societies which Murdock looks at, noting that men are involved in economic production, politics and fighting wars, and women are still putting up curtains. The nuclear unit is still the dominant way of organising family life – why?

Sex and reproduction

According to Murdock, the nuclear unit is the best way of getting what you need. Sex needs are provided for. Note the definition of the family – 'at least two of whom maintain a socially approved sexual relationship'. The socially approved bit depends upon the norms and values of the society in question. The family provides an outlet for sexual needs. Reproduction is another necessity for which the family provides. The human infant relies upon its parents for a longer period than any other animal – there are no cultures (as yet) where you have to go off and build your own house as soon as you have learned to walk. The child needs a safe place to grow, and the family is there.

Economic and educational functions

Economic co-operation means working together to produce the materials of life – food, shelter, etc. If you have a 'common residence' someone has to pay the rent. So families work together. The last family function outlined by Murdock is what he calls 'education', i.e. socialisation of children. As these functions – sexual, reproductive, economic and educational – are performed so well in the nuclear family form described by Murdock, it would seem to be the best possible form. It 'fits' the needs of society and of individuals. He identifies this structure in all societies, sometimes surrounded by an outer ring of extended family, and sometimes isolated – the nucleus itself. According to this view, male and female roles are dictated by biology, and again their apparent 'universality' proves that they are 'natural'. Although Parsons and others have based their views of the family and sex roles on Murdock's study, ever since the voices of Marxism and feminism began to be heard in sociological circles, they have been severely criticised.

Criticisms of Murdock

The main criticism of Murdock is that of bias. Murdock is a Western male, and as such has been socialised into a culture which only admits the existence of the 'one man, one woman, two children, good sex and lots of happiness family model'. He sees what he has been taught to see, and this is because he applies his male, Western eyes to the groups he is 'studying'. Critics point out that his definition is too narrow and limiting, and many 'family' structures cannot be included. The gender role argument is challenged, as critics offer up examples of women who build, hunt and fight, and men who shop, gossip and bicker over vegetables. Margaret Mead's work is usually cited (although this has also been challenged, for example by Freeman). Even some of the groups studied by Murdock show a lack of traditional gender roles. This debate has developed into a sociological analysis of the family from perspectives which are in opposition to most of the functionalist ideas. This sociology, far from seeing the family as a positive and valuable institution, sees it as confining, restrictive and harmful to the individual and society.

QUESTIONS

1 **What are the 'functions of the family'?**

2 **What are 'expressive' and 'instrumental' roles?**

3 **How does the family develop and maintain balanced adult personalities?**

4 **What is Murdock's view of the family and what criticisms have been made of it?**

Marxism, feminism and the family

The main statement of the Marxist position on the family comes not from Marx but from his lifelong friend Friedrich Engels (1884). Engels' study of the family was written to contribute to a contemporary debate on the social position of women in the late nineteenth century, and to enlarge on Marx's theory of historical materialism (see chapter 1).

Women and children as private property

On publication, it immediately caused controversy across Europe and the debate about whether Engels was working along the right lines or not has yet to die down. Engels traced the history of the family as a social unit back to when he believed it emerged, at approximately the point where hunters and gatherers became farmers, when concepts of private property became distinct. Without saying why it applied exclusively to men, Engels argued that at this point in history men needed ways of knowing what was theirs; they made women and children part of their private property through the institution of the family, and secured for their own children the right of inheritance of their property.

Abolition of the family

It follows for Engels that if private property and the family emerged at the same time, then there will be no place in a society without private property for the traditional family structure which, Engels argued, exploits women in the capitalist era. 'Within the family', Engels wrote, the man 'is the bourgeois, and the wife represents the proletariat.' In other words, the set-up of the family, with the man having all the economic and legal power, is effectively a trap for women. But Engels believed that this is not necessarily a fixed position for women, and that 'the first condition for the liberation of the wife is to bring the whole female sex back into public industry … this in turn demands that the characteristic of the monogamous family as the economic unit of society be abolished.' For women to be truly free, they must have a way of securing their own livelihood, and the implication of this is that the family as we know it must disappear.

In the hundred years since it was written, Engels' text has been continuously influential, particularly in what was known as the 'communist bloc', where his ideas became part of State policy. In the Soviet Union in the 1920s, for example, serious attempts were made by the infant Soviet government to abolish the family as a bourgeois institution, and bring domestic work into social production. For the Russian revolutionary Alexandra Kollontai (1872–1952) this would come about by making all labour paid labour, replacing domestic work with communal kitchens, canteens and laundries. As Kollontai (1977) claimed, 'The individual household is dying. It is giving way in our society to collective housekeeping. Instead of the working woman cleaning her flat, the communist society can arrange for men and women whose job it is to go round in the morning cleaning rooms.' At the same time, married women were given the right not to live with their husbands if they chose not to, or not to move

> **Friedrich Engels (1820–95)**
> *A journalist, social historian and businessman, he is best known as the friend and financial supporter of Marx. He wrote on the condition of the working class and the family, as well as editing the third volume of* Capital *after the death of Marx in 1883.*

with them if they changed jobs. Marriage was secularised and children born to single women were given the same rights as those of married women. These reforms were reversed under the Stalinist dictatorship of the 1930s.

For feminists, Engels has been equally influential, and many feminists have found it worthwhile to consider his ideas, for example Rosalind Delmar (1976), and recognise that, in the first place, he 'asserted women's oppression as a problem of history, rather than of biology' (Delmar).

The origins of patriarchy

But there are also serious flaws which feminists see in Engels' work. As with many other male writers, his view that women's situation will improve by becoming waged workers is seen as simplistic. He naively suggests that all the familiar aspects of a patriarchal society, such as the unequal distribution of power and wages within the world of work (see chapters 3 and 6) and men's attitude to women, would automatically improve if the nuclear family was replaced by a different form of economic organisation. It could be argued that patriarchy originates from men's sexuality instead. Then the problem facing women would not be the family itself but men.

Meeting the needs of capitalism

From a Marxist-feminist point of view, the exploitation of women in the family serves the interests of a capitalist economy. After all, they point out, women reproduce and service the next labour force (their children) for free, they also service the existing labour force (their husbands) without any extra cost to the bourgeoisie, and when they themselves go out into the world of paid work, they do it for less than men! It follows that it would require a different economic system to liberate women. As well as examining how the family under capitalism benefits the capitalist class, Michele Barrett and Mary McIntosh (1982) also point out that the way in which the family excludes non-family members at the same time as maintaining the conviction that life within the family is the most correct and appropriate way to live leads to other forms being seen as abnormal or even deviant. The consequence of this ideological belief, they argue, is that many people are misguided in their belief that the family is the only appropriate structure in which to live.

Non-Marxist feminists do not believe that women would necessarily be free in a different economic system. It is not capitalism as such, and the way that the family is structured under capitalism that oppresses women, but men and patriarchy.

Alternatives to the housewife-mother role

From this perspective, it is a mistake to see the problem for women originating in capitalism, and to wait for a post-revolutionary solution. The problem of women's built-in subordination in the family has to be tackled now. This realisation leads to a number of feminist positions on the family, all attempting to challenge women's housewife-mother role fundamentally. There have been many suggestions about how to abolish the housewife-mother role and thus the family as it currently stands, and the belief is that this would lead to the end of gender-role socialisation in the family. One idea is to move towards gay-parenting where parents would be either homosexual or lesbian. Other ideas include: conceiving and gestating babies outside the womb; collective child-rearing on the lines of communes and kibbutzim; and professional parenting, where after being born children are handed over to 'professional parents'. Some would say that middle-class parents, by using nannies and boarding schools, have been using this idea for a very long time.

Male domination in the family

The central place that the family has occupied in feminist thought means that it is an area they continuously return to, as the title of the book *What is to be Done about the Family?* (1983) makes obvious. In her introduction to this collection of essays, Lynne Segal makes it clear what contemporary feminists have to say about the anti-family movement of the 1960s: 'Missing from the 1960s critique of the family and sexual repression was any real awarensss or analysis of the male domination integral to existing family arrangements, and of a heterosexuality in which women have been seen as sex objects for men.' In considering the capitalism/patriarchy debate, she comments that 'The isolation of housework and the alienation of paid work become conflicts felt not only between different family members, but experienced every day within the life of each working woman. The needs of capitalism itself then interfere with the family ideal, partially undermining male authority and separating family members from each other both physically and emotionally, just as its demands for a mobile workforce have broken up wider family and community networks of support and friendship.' She continues: 'We know that until men's attitudes to domestic work change – and trade unions make the links between work and home, demanding working conditions adjusted to domestic needs to enable men and women each to participate fully in both spheres – then male privilege at home and work remains unchallenged.' Like Barrett and McIntosh, she argues that 'family ideology needs to change, so that "the family" no longer suggests the married heterosexual couple with children, dependent on a male wage, but instead a variety of possible family forms'.

She concludes by arguing that a social structure 'where men and society generally assume responsibility with women for child-care, domestic life and the care of all dependent people, could move towards solving many of our "family" problems'.

Men have made a variety of responses to the challenge of feminism.

QUESTIONS

1   What does it mean to say that women's oppression is a problem of history and not of biology? Why should feminists find this of interest?

2   What do Marxist-feminists mean when they argue that the family meets the needs of capitalism?

3   What is meant by patriarchy? When did it originate?

4   Why does Segal believe it is necessary to break down the barrier between the domestic sphere and the world of employment?

The death of the family

In its examination of society, sociology is willing to borrow from other disciplines. Psychology and anthropology (in-depth cultural studies) have both offered explanations of family life which concentrate on its internal workings rather than upon its relationship with the social structure. It is stretching a point to label them 'interactionists' but this is how their views are often presented. Unlike Marxism, which analyses conflict within the family from a structural point of view, these theories explain conflict and tension in the family as a result of psychological tensions between individuals. Rows and fights arise because of warring selves and the stifling emotional atmosphere of 'home bitter home'.

Edmund Leach

The anthropological contribution comes from Edmund Leach, a professor of social anthropology at Cambridge University who argues that 'Far from being the basis of the good society, the family, with its narrow and tawdry secrets, is the source of all our discontents' (Reith Lecture, 1967). Leach was lecturing on the nature of violence in society, and his point was that the family had become a strong, inward-looking unit, which narrowed and restricted individual expression and built up barriers against the world 'outside'. Family life is on the one hand very intimate. Parents and children are forced to spend more time together in modern society because hours of work are shorter, holidays longer and labour-saving devices cut down time spent on housework. Now everyone can sit arguing around the TV, or more likely sit in front of TVs in separate rooms. The parents' class and other prejudices are passed on, and this causes more barriers against society. Leach's comments created a lot of fuss amongst academics, leaders of public opinion and the media. It helped to generate the anti-family thinking which attacked the happy functionalist picture.

The Leach–Fletcher debate

The functionalist Ronald Fletcher (1988) has produced an argument which criticises the critics. He is sufficiently angered by Leach's phrase, 'it is the source of all our discontents', to give it as the title of his chapter on Leach. He criticises the lack of empirical evidence and says that Leach was being 'provocative' and 'sensational'. Most of Fletcher's criticism is based on the continued existence of the family as proof that it is a good thing. It is a haven, and all the emotional tension exists in the outside world. If it was not a wonderful institution, people would not keep choosing it. Women particularly yearn for it, and this had proved the feminists wrong as well. Fletcher goes back to the same old functionalist assumptions and ignores the stronghold that the ideology of the monogamous conjugal bond of the family has in society. Leach was pointing out that the family had possibly become too intimate, to the point of suffocation, and that perhaps alternative ways of living could be attempted. In the hippy spirit of the late sixties he advocated some form of commune based perhaps on the kibbutz. However, these alternatives have not been altogether successful perhaps because of the power of prior socialisation. People could not bring themselves to share everything equally because greed and selfishness are passed on as part of the norms and values of society.

R.D. Laing

R.D. Laing (1927– 89)
Psychiatrist and psychoanalyst who became one of the best-known critics of psychiatry in the 1960s. A major theme of his work has been to look at the effect of others on the actions of individuals; this led him to look at the way labels, like mental illness, could be applied to people.

Another voice of the sixties was Ronald Laing, a psychiatrist specialising in treating schizophrenia. Laing became a notorious media figure, compounding his reputation as junkie and drunkard and, again, accusations of sensationalism cloud the points he was making. In *Sanity, Madness and the Family* (1970) he and a colleague Esterson explain their ideas about the role of the family in causing psychological disturbance and schizophrenia. This is a condition stereotyped by many as 'split-personality' but there is a wide-ranging variety of behaviours which are called 'schizoid'. Nowadays, most psychologists accept the view that it is a biological and genetic disorder, although Laing's ideas on the role of the family in causing it still have some support. He claimed that the reasons for the bizarre behaviour which usually surfaces in the late teens were cultural, and the family and society were to blame. 'The experience and behaviour that gets labelled "schizophrenic", is a special strategy that a person invents in order to live in an unliveable situation.'

The murdered self

According to Laing's theory, the individual self, present at birth, has to be suppressed and controlled. The child learns to repress its real self and present one that its parents approve of. This then becomes the person, and the real self is 'murdered'. Parents, having killed off the real child, then proceed to subject the model child to an emotional network based on guilt and fear. Parents are not to blame for this, as they are functioning in a sort of zombie trance, their real selves having been murdered years ago. The child may accept the hypocrisy and madness that passes for society, and the functionalists would probably call this a successful internalisation of norms and values. Some, however, cannot keep their real self down, and it begins to emerge and disturb the false harmony. The individual then cannot cope, and schizoid behaviour becomes a release. The more extreme the parental response, the worse things get. In these cases there is often a history of incest, abuse or extreme conflict, and it is these 'environmental stressors' which provoke the so-called breakdown. Laing maintained that it was more of a 'rebirth' of the true self than a breakdown, and critics claimed that he encouraged patients to celebrate their madness and indulge in it as a release.

The family causes 'madness'

The label given to Laing's ideas, 'anti-psychiatry', came about because he was convinced that the usual treatments for schizophrenia – giving schizophrenics electric convulsions, filling them up with drugs, putting them into a strait-jacket – could not help when the problem was in the family relationships. His methods of treatment entailed talking about what was happening. If the walls shrink away when you touch them and the chairs scream when you sit down on them, it may be something to do with the fact that your father has been raping you since you were thirteen. In this case, Laing's patient was encouraged to leave home and learn judo, and not meet her father again until she could defend herself. By placing the blame for schizophrenia and many other illnesses and unhappinesses upon the family, Laing created a social and sociological controversy.

Cooper

David Cooper (1972) takes Laing's theories a step further and uses a more Marxist perspective. The reason for all the tension and guilt is to be found in the contradictions of capitalism. His own studies as a psychiatrist had shown him that the family is an ideological conditioning device. It 'reinforces the effective power of the ruling class in any exploitative society by providing a highly controllable paradigmatic form for every social institution. So we find the family form replicated through the social structures of the factory, the union branch, the school (primary and secondary), the business corporation, the church, political parties and government apparatus, the armed forces and general and mental hospitals.' The abolition of the family will be part of any destruction of capitalist social relations.

The radical nature of these ideas, the underlying Marxist view and the sensation they caused in the 1960s and 1970s have led to much discussion and even a film based on the case studies. They have also attracted much criticism within sociology, particularly from the functionalists. Ronald Fletcher's main criticism as before is: How can you make generalised statements about all families when you have only studied a few, highly abnormal ones?

Criticisms of Cooper and Laing

Fletcher agreed with Cooper and Laing that 1 per cent of the population is likely to be diagnosed as schizophrenic. But Fletcher saw this as a small proportion, and said that the 99 per cent who are not diagnosed must come from 'normal' families. Why have there been no studies of normal families? Although Laing claims that he did this, Fletcher cannot find it anywhere! This is a good criticism, particularly from a positivist viewpoint, but there is nothing new about it.

Lack of scientific objectivity

Fletcher then criticises the ideological basis which underlies the ideas and leads Cooper and Laing to call for the 'abolition' of the family. The 'mish-mash' of philosophy, psychiatry, religion and revolution, particularly as used by Cooper, makes him the extremest of the extreme in Fletcher's eyes, as this sentence reveals: 'It is hard to believe that anyone could have taken *The Death of the Family* seriously.' He goes on to criticise the jacket blurb and selects passages to ridicule. There is no science or objectivity in any of Laing, Cooper and Esterson's work, and the jargon of revolutionary ideology does not cover up this weakness. Fletcher rounds off his criticism by sniggering at the dedications in *Sanity, Madness and the Family*, *The Divided Self* and *The Death of the Family*: 'To our parents, children, brothers and sisters'.

Concentrating on such trivialities is amusing and highlights the back-biting that lurks underneath the so-called academic objectivity of the family of sociologists, but Fletcher again fails to give any new criticisms or even to explore old ones. The most telling point is when he discusses Laing's claim that 'normality' is actually insanity, and vice versa. It would seem that Laing advocates madness, yet he has a job whose aim is to cure it. Fletcher misses the point. Curing madness for Laing meant dealing with the ills and inequalities of society. For functionalists, this is a non-starter, because society is a lovely place, and families make it that way!

As the publication of Fletcher's book shows, the 'anti-family' views have now fallen out of fashion, and family psychiatry has moved on from the days of Laing and Cooper. It is still the case that most people experience family life, that the family (single or dual parent) is still seen as the most desirable way to bring up children, and very few, if any, signs are emerging that alternative forms to the family (such as collective child-rearing) are gaining popularity. The family may have changed its form and function but it is as much with us today as it ever has been.

QUESTIONS

1 **What are the main points of Leach's view of the family?**

2 **How do the radical psychiatrists argue that the family can produce psychological disturbance?**

3 **What is the case for abolishing the family?**

Industrialisation and the changing structure of the family

For at least the first half of the twentieth century, it was universally assumed that there was a clear pattern in the relationship between industrialisation and the changing structure of the family. This assumed that in a pre-industrial society, the extended family (with three generations) was typical, and under the pressure of the move to the factories and the city, the family shrank to become nuclear (or two generations). Such a belief is explicitly stated in Burgess and Locke's standard text of 1945, *The Family*. Sociologists built theories to explain how the two-generation family came to be typical. Two examples of this are William Goode (1963) and Talcott Parsons (1959).

The industrialisation debate – Parsons

The essence of Parsons' argument is as follows. In the family, an individual's status is ascribed – the role they play in the family is not of their own choosing, it is given to them. If you are a son or a daughter, there is nothing you can do about it. You will always be a son or daughter. In a pre-industrial society, where social mobility was highly restricted, social status was similarly ascribed. If you were born into a serf family, then the probability was that you would die a serf. In all areas of life, your status was ascribed, or given to you.

Role conflict

Industrialisation brought about huge and important changes among which, according to Parsons, the increasing social and geographical mobility of the population was central. Social status was no longer ascribed but achieved. Individuals, not through birthright but their own abilities, could move up and down the social structure. (Whether there is any hard evidence for this is considered in chapter 3.) Conflicts began to appear in the extended family structure, where upwardly mobile children began to challenge the authority of their parents, especially if they had more influential jobs – what Parsons calls role conflict. The conflict between private and ascribed (particularistic values) and publicly achieved status (universalistic values) inevitably produces the nuclear family, whose two-generational structure prevents role conflict. Furthermore, the 'isolated nuclear family' (a phrase greatly associated with Parsons' work) continues to specialise as a social agency as it undergoes a process of 'structural differentiation', whereby the traditional roles within the family become taken up by outside agencies such as the workplace, schools, hospitals, social workers, police and so on.

Anderson

The accounts by Parsons and others of the way that the extended family of a pre-industrial society became the nuclear family of a developed industrial society provide a very clear, neat and logical way of demonstrating how functionalist sociology works. This type of account dominated the way that sociologists looked at the family in the middle of the twentieth century. As Michael Anderson (1980) writes: 'We now know, of course, that the fundamental proposition [which sees the] family form and process as a functional consequence of the demands of industrial society … is hopelessly over-simple … Indeed, it is a special irony that at least some forms of early industrialisation in Britain actually increase people's dependence on kin (and even their ability to live with them and near them) to a level unknown for hundreds of years (at least) before.' His argument is reinforced by Chris Harris (in Anderson, 1980). 'Industrialisation has no more transformed the family than colonialism disrupted the segmentary kinship system of some peoples. One does not have to be a Marxist, merely historically informed and conceptually competent, to recognise the whole debate about industrialisation decomposing the extended family to be the empirical and philosophical nonsense that it is.' It is empirical nonsense because there is no hard evidence to support this view of the transforming effect of industrialisation on family structure.

Laslett

In a seminal work a group of family historians, organised by Peter Laslett, presented evidence from across the industrial world which argued that: 'The wish to believe in the large and extended household as the ordinary institution of an earlier England and an earlier Europe, or as a standard feature of an earlier non-industrial world, is … a matter of ideology' (Laslett, 1972). From 1970, he says, 'demographers generally had come to recognise that the nuclear family predominates numerically almost everywhere, even in underdeveloped parts of the world'.

Household sizes

For England, in particular, the evidence of the dominance of pre-industrial nuclear families seems conclusive, whether it is J.C. Russell (1948) finding an average household of 3.5 people in 1517 England, Hallam's (1961) figure of 4.68 per household in the late thirteenth century in South Lincolnshire or Laslett's own figure of 4.75 in the period 1600–1900 from which he concludes: 'In England … the large joint or extended family seems never to have existed as a common form of the domestic group at any point in time covered by numerical records.' This is not to say that the extended family did not exist, or was insignificant, but that the nuclear family in everyday life is dominant through history and geography.

The British working-class family in the 1950s

Again, to the surprise of many sociologists, it was still possible to find close-knit kinship ties among working-class communities as late as the mid 1950s. Willmott and Young (1960) discovered what they described as 'a village in the middle of London. Established residents claimed to "know everyone". They could do so because most people were connected by kinship ties to a network of other families, and through them to a host of friends and acquaintances. Ties of blood and marriage were local ties.' In their study of East London (1957) they 'were surprised to discover that the wider family, far from having disappeared, was still very much alive in the middle of

London.' The extended family survived in this community as a hang-over from the industrial revolution. In research into other areas of East London, in the newer estates of Greenleigh and more middle-class Woodford, Willmott and Young found that the pattern of kinship had become looser (*see Table 4.1*).

TABLE 4.1 Proximity of parents – Woodford and Bethnal Green (%)

PARENTS' RESIDENCE	WOODFORD	BETHNAL GREEN
Same dwelling	9	12
Within five minutes' walk	7	29
Elsewhere in the same borough	15	13
Outside the same borough	69	46
Total %	100	100

Number studied: Woodford, 394; Bethnal Green, 369

Willmott and Young (1960) argue that localised 'extended families' – family groups spreading over two or more nearby houses – are the distinctive feature of kinship in the East End. In Woodford they are rare.

The symmetrical family

By the time of their third, and most wide-ranging, study of the family and kinship networks in the London area, Willmott and Young (1973) perceived, like many other family sociologists, a pattern to the changing structure of the family before, during and after industrialisation. Synthesising all the available knowledge, they identify four characteristic phases in the development of the family:

Stage 1: the pre-industrial nuclear family (pre-1750)
Marrying late, with their own parents dying early, few families had surviving grandparents. Typically, families constituted their own economic unit of production.

Stage 2: the industrial extended family (1750–1900)
With families living in the city, more children survived, grandparents lived longer and the focus of production became the factory. The central family tie was between mother and daughter with, Willmott and Young claim, the father becoming pushed out of the home and into the pub. Remnants of this lived on in mid-1950s Bethnal Green.

Stage 3: the modern nuclear family (from 1900)
This is the world of the family beyond Bethnal Green, of two generations per household, father not in the pub but at home (a process sociologists call privatisation) wallpapering or watching the TV and helping enough around the house for Willmott and Young to perceive a movement away from segregated and towards conjugal roles:

men are 'more fully home-centred because they are less work-centred. They can more easily leave their work behind them when they leave the premises in which it is done ... Wives have been getting more involved in work, especially when in the kinds of job which have such a hold over men.'

The principle of stratified diffusion

Stage 4: the managing director family
This does not exist yet as a widespread social phenomenon, but is a projection made by the authors, based on trends they identify among the upper middle class. It is their belief – according to what they grandiosely name 'the principle of stratified diffusion' – that the lifestyle of the middle class today will be adopted by the working class tomorrow, as it becomes more affluent. Having become more home-centred in stage 3, the working-class worker will begin to become more work-centred, with work physically intruding into home life. With technology changing the nature of work, and under the impact of feminism, more and more women will be drawn out of the home and into the world of work. 'By the next century,' they write, 'society will have moved from (a) one demanding job for the wife and one for the husband, through (b) two demanding jobs for the wife and one for the husband to (c) two demanding jobs for the wife and two for the husband. The symmetry will be complete. Instead of two jobs there will be four.' It is this final assumption that the family division of labour will become symmetrical that feminists, and others, took exception to, though Willmott and Young are careful to say that, in adopting Gorer's (1971) term, they do not mean that there will be egalitarianism, or total equality, within marriage, merely symmetry.

QUESTIONS

1 **How does Parsons believe that social change has influenced family structure?**

2 **Do Anderson and Laslett reach the same conclusions about family structure?**

3 **How similar is Willmott and Young's stage 3 family to the understanding you have of your own and others' family life?**

4 **Does 'the normal family' exist?**

Power and labour in the family

Patriarchy

A patriarchal society is one where men hold the power – economic, social and political. Women are second-class citizens, discriminated against, dependent upon and dominated by men. These relationships are reflected in the family, and also reinforced and strengthened by what goes on in families. Marxist-feminism places this within the context of a capitalist society. Overthrow this and patriarchal power will disappear along with ruling-class power. There will be an equal division of labour in the home. Radical feminism does not agree, and sees patriarchy as separate from class. A radical restructuring of gender roles is necessary. The family structure would be the first to go. Liberal feminists believe that change is possible within capitalist society, and that helping women as individuals and as groups to become aware of their oppression will eventually lead to equality. Power and labour in the home form the basis of this analysis, and it picks up the debate about the changing family structure.

Shared conjugal roles

Some sociologists, Willmott and Young in particular, have proposed that the family in modern society is becoming symmetrical, with both parents working inside and outside the home. Housework and childcare in these circumstances will be equally shared. The 'symmetrical family' and also the 'privatised' family of Goldthorpe and Lockwood, *The Affluent Worker* (see chapter 3), is a far cry from the 'here's your housekeeping, why isn't my dinner on the table?' family of the 1950s in Bethnal Green. The home, with its comforts and attractions, and its endless opportunities for creative outlets (wallpapering, gardening) is the place to be! Needless to say, this analysis does not meet with feminist approval, and they question Willmott and Young's evidence for the existence of shared conjugal roles. Ann Oakley, a much quoted feminist, has produced one of the most influential studies of housework (1974a), which traces the role of women in families from pre-industrial times through to industrial societies. Far from leading to equal relationships, marriage and family duties turn women into unpaid slaves, whose productive output is unrewarded by wages and therefore not worthy of being referred to as 'work'.

A gender-neutral society?

The pre-industrial woman took a more active role in society, running parts of the agricultural production unit as well as working in the home. As industrialisation altered this pattern, men 'went out' to work and in latter-day industrialised society women had become almost totally isolated within the home. Society expects women to care for home and children, it is their responsibility. Willmott and Young are being much too optimistic about the growth of joint conjugal roles. They have responded to these criticisms from Oakley and others by saying that roles are more equal but women are still responsible for the home. Oakley is 'anti-family' and insists that a new society, gender-neutral, is needed before new family structures can evolve. She does not go into detail on this new world, which is a weakness in her analysis.

Elizabeth Bott (1957) coined the term 'joint conjugal roles' to describe situations where couples both work outside the home and

HOW MUCH IS THIS JOB WORTH?

Position vacant: Housewife

Applications are invited for the position of manager of a lively team of four demanding individuals of differing needs and personalities. The successful applicant will be required to perform and co-ordinate the following functions: companion, counsellor, financial manager, buying officer, teacher, nurse, chef, nutritionist, decorator, cleaner, driver, child-care supervisor, social secretary and recreation officer.

Qualifications: *Applicants must have unlimited drive and the strongest sense of responsibility if they are to succeed in this job. They must be independent, and self-motivated, and be able to work in isolation and without supervision. They must be skilled in the management of people of all ages. They must be able to work under stress, for long periods of time if necessary. They must have flexibility to perform a number of conflicting tasks at the one time without tiring. They must have the adaptability to handle all new developments in the life of*
the team, including emergencies and serious crises. They must be able to communicate on a range of issues with people of all ages, including public servants, school teachers, doctors, dentists, tradespeople, business people, teenagers and children. They must be healthy, creative, active and outgoing to encourage the physical and social development of the team members. They must have imagination, sensitivity, warmth, love and understanding, since they are responsible for the mental and emotional well-being of the team.*

Hours of work: *All waking hours and a 24-hour shift when necessary.*

Pay: *No salary or wage. Allowances by arrangement, from time to time, with the income-earning member of the team. The successful applicant may be required to hold a second job, in addition to the one advertised here.*

Benefits: *No guaranteed holidays. No guaranteed sick leave, maternity leave or long service leave. No guaranteed life or accident insurance. No worker's compensation. No superannuation.*

share tasks inside it. 'Segregated' roles describes the situation when the man goes out to work and the woman stays at home to work. These are tied in with class, according to Bott. A working-class background gives a tight-knit kin and friendship group. Wife and husband know each other's family and friends, the network is not widely dispersed, all the friends know each other. The couple are forced by the norms of this tight network to conform to traditional ideas about marriage and duties. So the woman does the housework – if she did not, their female relatives and friends would criticise her. If her husband did the ironing, he would be laughed at in the pub. The loosely knit kin and friendship group of a middle-class couple means that there is less influence from any one group. The husband and wife concentrate on each other more, and may have separate friendships and activities. They are then freer to change roles and share work at home, as there is no rigid value system or peer-group pressure. Joint conjugal roles are more likely here.

Many studies have criticised these ideas, pointing out that in middle-class, so-called 'dual career' families, it is still the woman who takes time off when the children are ill. The debate about power and labour in the home goes on. Some believe that women will attain equality in this area and have equal economic power in the home, taking decisions together with men. There are some indicators that this is already happening and that the rigid roles of the families found in Bethnal Green in the south, and in mining and fishing industries in the north, are a thing of the past. However, the 'new man' image which pervades the 1990s may be an over-optimistic assessment of the progress of the women's liberation movement.

The 'new man' – myth or reality?

The sexism of sociology has been challenged, and the male-biased ideas of the likes of Willmott and Young have been much criticised. Women are still largely isolated in the home or in low-paid, often part-time work. Careers mean 'sacrificing' parenthood and family, but only for women. Conjugal role studies abound, and they still show that men's tasks around the home are generally restricted to gardening, maintenance and repairs, doing the dishes after one meal and taking out the rubbish. Everything else is done by women, and they are not paid. As many feminists have pointed out, society could not afford to pay at comparable rates for manual labour.

If the family, the cradle of society, is based upon such blatant exploitation, then it is no wonder that there is conflict, tension and strain within it. Sociologists are still arguing about the various solutions to these conflicts, and their arguments are based on their theoretical differences. The way you look at society influences the explanations you give for its various behaviours. The family is no exception, and the widely varying accounts of what families are all about reflects the theoretical differences involved.

Feminist criticism of the family is based on their understandings of the nature of patriarchal power. These power relationships are rooted in the traditional roles which society insists that men and women take up. Being given power in his own 'castle', the male uses it to dominate and suppress his family, especially the women. In this way, gender roles are reproduced, and women in homes throughout the land are restricted and repressed in all forms of social expression. There may have been a slight change in labour and power relationships within families in Britain since the Second World War, but the fundamental basis for male power is still intact. In 1991, English and Welsh law changed to make it illegal for a husband to rape his wife, 73 years after women got the vote. Why did it take so long? Women were fully enfranchised citizens, with political power and rights, except at home.

Following the publication of *The Symmetrical Family* in 1973, a number of empirical studies have found Willmott and Young's assumptions about joint conjugal roles lacking. Rapoport and Rapoport (1976), for example, found that in middle-class families where both partners worked, women's careers were still seen as subordinate to their partners', while domestic matters were chiefly seen as her responsibility.

Elston (1980) found that even in households where both partners were full-time doctors, women nevertheless did the great majority of the shopping and cooking, while men undertook most of the household repairs. Interestingly, in 71 per cent of these medical households it was the women who took time off work when their children were ill.

Such findings led to a questioning of the assumption that conjugal roles were changing among the middle class, let alone the working class. Far from being a present reality, joint conjugal roles and the 'principle of stratified diffusion' were unlikely to be realised in the near future. One reason for Willmott and Young's optimism could be that their own ideas of joint roles did not mean equal roles. They described as 'symmetrical' families where 72 per cent of men studied helped their wife with something other than the washing up more than once a week. This 'something' could include taking their sons out on a Saturday afternoon.

These conclusions are known not only to sociologists. In 1993 the market research group Mintel conducted interviews with 1,500 men and women about how domestic labour was shared out. Their conclusions were that 85 per cent of women living with a man said that they did all the laundry, ironing and cooked the main meal. As many as 20 per cent of the women stated that their partner shared only one domestic task, and less than one in ten thought that their partner shared the cooking equally. Only one man in 100 shared domestic tasks equally.

When the wider question of power in the family is examined, a similar picture emerges. Dobash and Dobash (1980) reveal asymmetry in marriage by focusing on domestic violence. Using Scotland for their case study, they found that a quarter of all cases of violence brought to court concerned men assaulting their wives, although the fines they received were frequently lower than the average parking fine.

QUESTIONS

1 How does Ann Oakley believe the Industrial Revolution changed the position of women?

2 What does Elizabeth Bott believe is the relationship between social class and conjugal roles?

3 Is the 'new man' a myth?

4 Is the job advert for the housewife accurate?

The family in the 1990s

The typical family?

Advertisers love to portray the consumers of their products and services as happy couples with children, gleefully enjoying a new type of breakfast cereal or delighting in the joys of a washing powder that washes whiter than white. Sociologists of the family – particularly Marxists and functionalists – have also been accused of falling into the same trap of building a sociology of the family on the assumption that the typical household or dwelling contains a married couple with children, where the man goes out to work, his wife stays at home to bring up the children and they stay together for life. Statistical evidence gathered over the last 30 years paints an altogether different picture.

Lone-parent families

As *Table* 4.2 shows, the long-term trend is towards a decline in the number of households containing married families with children (32 per cent in 1993 compared with 48 per cent in 1961), while the number of people living on their own, or in lone-parent families, is increasing (27 per cent in 1993 compared with 11 per cent in 1961; and 10 per cent in 1993 compared with 6 per cent in 1961, respectively).

When calculated as a percentage of all families with children (rather than by household), lone-parent families rise to 18 per cent in 1991 (compared to 8 per cent in 1971) of whom more than 94 per cent were headed by lone mothers, and less than 6 per cent were headed by lone fathers. The main reason for this increase is the number of women becoming lone mothers either through divorce or without ever marrying. The number of all lone fathers, by comparison, has stayed constant.

The above statistics have been variously interpreted by politicians and sociologists alike. For politicians of the New Right (see also

TABLE 4.2 Households by type, Great Britain (%), 1961–93

	1961	1971	1981	1991	1993
One-person households	11	18	22	27	27
Two or more unrelated adults	5	4	5	3	3
One-family households					
Married couple with no children	26	27	26	28	28
One to two dependent children	30	26	25	20	20
Three or more dependent children	8	9	6	5	5
Non-dependent children only	10	8	8	8	7
Lone parent with dependent or non-dependent children	6	7	9	10	10
Two or more families	3	1	1	1	1

Source: Social Trends 25, 1995

chapter 8), the breakdown of the nuclear family and the rise of lone-parent families has momentous consequences for the rest of society, particularly as it is claimed that children of lone-mother families, deprived of fatherly help and guidance, are more likely to be brought up in poverty, fail at school, turn to crime and become social problems. With three-quarters of all lone mothers dependent on the State for their income, it has become a political priority for all parents to attempt to restore 'family values' and end a situation where fathers play a minimal and temporary role.

Marriage

Not only does it appear that the nuclear family is breaking down but, it has been claimed, so too is the institution of marriage. *Table 4.3* shows that, while there has not been a significant drop in the total number of marriages, the type of marriage has changed markedly with the declining number of first-time marriages being supplemented by the number of remarriages.

TABLE 4.3 **Marriages by type, 1961–90**

UNITED KINGDOM	1961	1971	1981	1990
		THOUSANDS		
First marriage for both partners	340	369	263	241
First marriage for one partner only	36	54	74	75
Second marriage for both partners	21	36	61	60
Total marriages	397	459	398	376

Source: Office of Population Censuses and Surveys; General Register Office (Scotland)

Divorce

Divorce statistics present a similar picture. Much of the dramatic increase in the number of petitions for divorce filed (overwhelmingly by women) can be accounted for by the enforcement of the 1969 Divorce Law Reform Act in 1971 (1977 in Scotland). This made 'irretrievable breakdown' the sole criterion for divorce, and this could be shown if couples had lived apart for five years or more: the empty shell marriages had eventually cracked. For Ronald Fletcher, 'Without any doubt whatever, the Divorce Law Reform Act of 1969 marked a juncture of the greatest significance in the changing and developing nature of the family and marriage in Britain.' The 1984 Matrimonial and Family Proceedings Act further liberalised divorce by allowing couples to file for divorce after their first wedding anniversary. In 1990, almost 10 per cent of all marriages ending in divorce had lasted less than three years, and almost 70 per cent of marriages ended in divorce in less than fifteen years. *Table 4.4* clearly indicates the rising trend in divorce.

Does this mean that the family and marriage are disappearing institutions? There are a number of responses to this question. The above

Divorce

■ *Four in 10 marriages are likely to end in divorce*

■ *Divorce is bad for your health – divorced men aged 25 to 50 are twice as likely as married men to die prematurely*

■ *Admission rates to mental hospitals are between four and six times greater among the divorced than the married*

■ *Divorced people smoke more, drink more, and have higher rates of unsafe sex*

■ *Divorced people are four times more likely to commit suicide*

■ *Divorce costs £6.5 million a week – in 1992 £3.4 billion was spent in welfare payments, legal costs and health care*

■ *Companies lose £200 million a year through absenteeism and impaired work because of marriage breakdown*

■ *By 1993 176,000 children under 16 had families broken by divorce*

■ *Women are keener than men on divorce – 70 per cent of petitions are filed by wives*

■ *51 per cent of divorced men live to regret it, saying they would have preferred to stay married, compared with 29 per cent of women*

Source: One Plus One

TABLE 4.4   Divorce, 1961–90

ENGLAND AND WALES	1961	1971	1981	1990
Petitions filed (thousands)	32	111	170	192
Persons divorcing per thousand married people	2.1	6.0	11.9	12.9

Source: Social Trends 23, 1993

evidence can be interpreted as saying that they are. Thus, for Jon Bernades (1990), the variation and diversity of family types leads him to state that 'there is no such thing as "the family" and in reality no such things as "normal families"'. Similarly, Gubrium and Holstein (1990) argue that the continued emphasis on 'the family' is ideological: 'the family is as much idea as thing'. The way forward for the sociology of the family is not by examining the relationship between society and what is thought of as 'the family' (the macro view) but to discover the subjective meaning given to the family by its members.

For social historians, these statistics are nothing new in British life. Peter Laslett (1982) points out that the present situation, where there are more people living outside the nuclear family (solitaries) than in it, is nothing new: 'When Britain was still a pre-industrial society ... something like 30 to 35 per cent of all groups were constituted in the same way, and among the solitaries and the few in institutions, a high proportion were the old and the very old, just as is the case in the 1980s.' Moreover, in the mid nineteenth century, at the height of the Victorian era, the illegitimacy rate reached a three-hundred-year peak, and was at a similar level to that of today.

Other writers have put forward other arguments against any notion that the family and marriage are threatened institutions. Firstly, although the number of divorces is high, it is nevertheless the case that most people who do divorce remarry. The divorce rate does not indicate that people have lost faith in marriage but, in their search for a satisfying relationship, are keen to get out of a bad one. Secondly, although the structure of the family has changed in recent decades, it is not the case that alternatives to the family, such as communes or kibbutz-style arrangements, are taking their place.

QUESTIONS

1 **Is marriage as an institution breaking down?**

2 **What are the problems of being a lone parent?**

3 **Does 'the typical family' still exist?**

FURTHER READING

P. Abbott and C. Wallace, **The Family and the New Right**, Pluto Press, 1992

R. Fletcher, **The Abolitionists: Family and Marriage under Attack**, Routledge, 1988

D.H.J. Morgan, **Family, Politics and Social Theory**, Routledge, 1988

A. Oakley, **Housewife**, Allen Lane, 1974

J. Pahl, **Marital Violence and Public Policy**, Routledge, 1985

S. Warde and N. Abercrombie, **Family, Household and the Life-Course**, Framework Press, 1994

P. Willmott and M. Young, **The Symmetrical Family**, Routledge and Kegan Paul, 1973

5 Education

It's a sort of a challenge, coming to school thinking 'How can I outwit the teachers today?' The teachers are the establishment, they've done things to you, you don't like what they've done, how can you get back?

'Joey', P. Willis, Learning to Labour, 1977

INTRODUCTION

The chapter begins with a discussion of how the major sociological perspectives view education systems. You will then go on to look at the role of the State in promoting the education system in Britain. The new vocationalism and recent educational reforms are then examined. The following section examines data on differential educational achievement and then goes on to look at various sociological explanations. The chapter concludes by looking at the reasons for differential educational opportunities for boys, girls and ethnic minorities.

What is education?

If primary socialisation begins at home, then the school is the first taste of secondary socialisation the human encounters. It is here that the transition from the particular values of the family to the general values of society is made.

Education selects and categorises the human animal, ensuring that it is well equipped to take its place within society as a useful, functioning member of the productive process. It can be seen as stamping out originality, creativity and imagination and substituting passive, unquestioning conformity to social rules and obedience to authority. Its purpose may be to instil discipline and respect or to give everyone an equal chance to broaden their intellectual and emotional life. Some people would say it provides a small minority with an intensive, high-quality process of intellectual stimulation until they are 21 years old, and gives the majority a lower quality, basic education until they are 16. Others believe it operates to reproduce the capitalist class system, gender roles and patriarchal relationships. At school pupils learn to read, write, calculate, fight, smoke, and develop social and sexual relationships.

Differential educational achievement

All of this (and more) can be found in education, and as usual the definition you choose depends on your theory. Where you look and what you find, and therefore how you explain it, all depend upon whether you use a functionalist, Marxist, feminist or interactionist perspective. The arguments about education all revolve around the question of differential achievement. Why do some groups of people – members of the working class, some ethnic minorities and women – tend to 'fail' at school in comparison with whites, males and the middle class? Why do girls and boys do better in different subjects? It is already obvious that there are some complications here, and there are no 'right' answers, just good or bad arguments. The secondary socialisation process ensures that the general roles of social life are experienced, and there is great stress laid upon the role of the school in training for 'citizenship', i.e. learning your duties and responsibilities as a member of your society. There is a great deal of functionalism in educational policy.

Why do we go to school?

Functionalist explanations

The functions of education

According to functionalists the aims of education are to maintain social stability, keep society running smoothly, and resolve conflict. The magic word of functionalism is consensus – the shared agreement about the goals and values of the social structure. The individual has to submit to this higher order, which exists outside themselves, which was there before their birth and will continue to exist after their death. The whole is greater than the sum of its parts. The social system is more important than the parts which make it up. Individuals have no importance except as members of society. They must sacrifice a certain level of individuality, and learn to fit in and co-operate with the greater whole. The family provides the first stage in the socialisation process, but in the home the child is a 'special' and particular individual. School provides the next stage, where the child learns that far from being important it is just another person, with new duties and responsibilities.

Meritocracy and consensus

The most important value in post-industrial societies is meritocracy – success or failure in the education system and position in the system of stratification depends on individual merit and achievement. The whole of society is meritocratic and, as Parsons points out, the school is a 'microcosm' of society, a small-scale replica, in the same way that the family is. The school 'bridges' the gap between family and work. Meritocracy is the idea that a system, with its duties, responsibilities and rewards, is based on equality of opportunity. It is fair. If you work hard, you will achieve to the best of your abilities, and will be rewarded on that basis. Ability is to do with talent, and the functionalists are essentially in agreement with Eysenck on the subject of intelligence. 'Talent' is innate, and varies from individual to individual. All individuals are given an equal chance to realise their full potential. Those who are most talented and work hardest get the highest rewards. They become head girls and boys, they get the cups and the certificates, the gold stars and lollipops. Those with less talent get less reward, and they accept this inequality as right and proper, knowing that they have all had a fair and equal chance.

This is how functionalism explains 'differential achievement'. White, black, middle or working class, male or female, it makes no difference. If you have the skills and are prepared to work, then you will succeed. Of course, the harder you work, the more you expect to get for it, and so high-status degrees, leading to high salaries, the so-called 'glittering prizes', are your right. The rest are left to share out the duller prizes, but do so cheerfully, knowing that it is all they are worth and deserve. This view is outlined by the functionalists Davis and Moore in their explanations of social inequality (see chapter 3).

Education as a subsystem

In the 1950s through to the 1970s, mainstream sociology was based on these ideas about education. Talcott Parsons considered education as another subsystem within the social system. In a complex essay published in 1959 he gives his 'structural functionalist' analysis of the school (1959b). He tries to outline the way the structure of a class is related to society. He uses a single class, which is a subsystem within the school, as a model. If schools have functions, this is where they are put into practice. These functions are as an agency of socialisation and to sort people out into their various adult roles – jobs. The school is the 'focal socialising agency' and is based on meritocratic principles. Parsons acknowledges the influence of class, which he calls 'socio-economic status', on achievement.

Parsons the empiricist

He used a sample of 3,348 Boston schoolboys (a good positivist base?). He shows that 80 per cent of boys whose fathers are in 'major white-collar' jobs intend to go to college. Of boys whose fathers are semi- or unskilled only 12 per cent have that intention. So, if you are of high status and high ability, the chances are you will get to college; if you are of low status and low ability it is much less likely. He also points out that boys with low ability and high status also go to college – one with 'low academic standards'. He does not say what happens to boys with low status and high ability. High ability here seems to mean a mixture of two things: intellectual skills in the formal curriculum and an acceptance of the 'moral component' of education. The latter, as defined by Parsons, is 'respect for the teacher, consideration and co-operativeness … good work habits'. Achievement is 'living up to the expectations imposed by the teacher as an agent of the adult society'.

Selection

The teacher sorts out those best able to achieve in this sense and differentiates between the children accordingly. This sorting into levels leads to the 'allocation of adult roles'. If you are good at your work, well behaved, and accept that teacher knows best, you will go on to get a good career and salary. The teacher is an extension of the parent, but there are important differences which are necessary if the school is to perform its function. She (and in Parsons' example primary schoolteachers are usually women) is an adult in a superior role to the child. However, the role is occupational, teaching is her job, and her 'family' of children is large. She teaches them 'universalistic' or general and society-wide values, and she must respond to their performance of tasks, not their emotional needs.

Teacher and pupil roles

The teacher must be hard: 'She is not entitled to suppress the distinction between high and low achievers just because not being able to be included in the high group would be too hard on little Johnny.' The child must accept the role of the teacher, and respond to that. This is a major step in the socialisation process, and leads the child to accept the value system and therefore their own status in it. Parsons emphasises the importance of family and school sharing the same value system if the child is to succeed. There is a relationship between ability, social status and the process of education. Internalising values and giving a high performance leads to favourable chances in the selection of adult roles.

Criticisms of Parsons

However, critics point out that the 'fairness' of the school system is by no means proven by Parsons, and that he uncritically accepts the status quo. Often, those children who do not succeed come from low-status backgrounds, and Parsons does not address this properly. The education system works to ensure that some groups monopolise success and others are left to fail, and this follows through into the job and career structure. Those who succeed come to school already equipped to do so; they receive good responses from teachers and go on to prepare their own children in the same way. The value system which is such an important part of the school, according to Parsons, comes from one small group in society and benefits them at the expense of others, who are defined as 'low ability' and 'low achievers'.

QUESTIONS

1 **In what ways can education be regarded as secondary socialisation?**

2 **What are the key functions of education from the functionalist perspective?**

3 **How do functionalists regard education as a subsystem?**

141

Marxist explanations

Bourgeois ideology and the reproduction of capitalism

For Marxists, the economic base, and the relationship between capitalists and workers which is carried on there, shapes the rest of society, the superstructure. Control of power in the base is maintained at the level of ideas in the superstructure. This set of ideas, according to Marxism, comes from the ruling class. It is an ideology. It presents children with a view of society, and their place within it: you should be punctual, polite, respectful of authority; you should work hard to receive rewards; you should be disciplined and do your duty. These are all part of an education system which works to reproduce the capitalist system. Schools must provide the new society with leaders, managers and a great mass of workers for unskilled, semi-skilled and skilled manual labour. This last and largest group must 'fail' in the education system. Those who accept the ideology passed on in school become the 'successes' of the system, and go on to higher education. Capitalist relations of production are reproduced and correct ideas and attitudes instilled into individuals. Education is not just about passing on knowledge – in fact a great deal of that commodity is actually withheld from most students.

There was no mass education for the working classes in the early stages of capitalist Britain. There was a fear that an educated workforce might get 'ideas'. At that time any attempts by workers to improve themselves intellectually often led to their imprisonment. As capitalism advanced and needed more literate and numerate workers, educational reform began, leading to the lengthy time spent in school in contemporary capitalism. The ruling class uses the system to reproduce inequalities. The skills and knowledge necessary for individual success in a capitalist society – supposedly fair and meritocratic in the way it gives rewards – have to be passed on in some way to the children of the ruling classes. The pattern of working-class failure and middle-class success is not accidental, but necessary. Marxist analysis tries to point out the processes which help it to come about.

Private education

The existence of a private education system ensures that the highest-status skills and knowledge, which lead to the top positions – ruling-class ones – are passed on to an exclusive group. The major public schools and universities fill the top economic and political positions. (Elite groups are examined elsewhere – see chapters 3 and 8.) Private education signals the existence of ruling-class educational privilege in its most obvious form. The ways in which inequalities are reproduced in State schools has generated more research. However, one influential Marxist voice on education used no research, putting forward theory instead.

Althusser

Louis Althusser (1971) puts forward a view of ideology which tries to explain how secret and unconscious it is: 'Ideology is a process which takes place behind our backs.' We cannot see it, but before we can think about it we are a part of it. Ideology calls out to us and invites us to see ourselves in certain ways. By going along with it, we become victims. We believe we are that person. Education in modern societies perfects this process. Children are given a set of ideas which they use to understand the world. They are not allowed to examine and discuss these ideas, just accept and believe them. The child is trapped in a position created for them by another group of people – the ruling class. The individual is then controlled and easily controllable, and goes on to conform to the position given to them in the capitalist world of work.

Repressive and ideological State apparatuses

Althusser points out that there are two ways to rule, by force or by consent. The State can use force at any time, and the forces it uses are called repressive State apparatuses (RSAs) by Althusser. The police, used in strikes and riots, and the armed forces are examples of RSAs. Rule by coercion is not easy, it is expensive, and sooner or later must fail. To gain the consent of the masses by constructing their ideas for them is a much better option. RSAs are replaced by ideological State apparatuses (ISAs) and their role is to pass on capitalist norms and values. It is much better to have workers going more or less willingly to work than having to march behind them with machine guns. People go and stand in smelly, hot, noisy factories for eight hours at a time, performing boring tasks because they want to, or know that they have to. Why don't they all take over the process, kill the bosses, divide up the profits and run the factory between themselves? Not because they think someone will come and shoot them but because they do not see it that way! They see a fair and necessary system. They turn up, do the job, get paid, go home and spend their wages, then come back and they see this as their role in life. Education has become the most influential ISA, replacing the church according to Althusser. Knowledge is passed on in school, but it is 'wrapped up' in ruling-class ideology. Economic history, for example, is presented from a ruling-class viewpoint, where the benefits of capitalism outweigh the disadvantages. Historic working-class resistance is presented from the employer's view. Patriotism and duty are all mixed up with 'facts'. The process which Durkheim applauds as necessary and good is painted in a different light by Althusser. Knowledge is distorted by ideology.

Criticisms of Althusser

His vision of education is of a conveyor belt. The mass of pupils are pushed off the belt at the age of 16 with rule-following, worker attitudes. The next group, ejected at 18 or so, become the managers with leadership values and an order-giving attitude. The smallest group stay on the belt indefinitely becoming 'ideologues', the 'top' minds of the ruling class. Education passes on ideology in a subtle, complex way. Children are programmed to 'fail' or 'succeed' and this is necessary to reproduce the relations of capitalism.

As stated, the main criticism of Althusser is the lack of supporting and empirical research. The essay was a small part of his work, which suggests material for research and thought. Althusser was a philosopher, not a sociologist, but his ideas have influenced modern Marxist sociology.

Bowles and Gintis: correspondence theory

Two American Marxists who could be said to apply Althusser's ideas on education are Bowles and Gintis. Their 1976 study explores the relationships within a school and those in the workplace. The whole structure is mirrored, with heads, senior staff and teachers in school; directors, managers and middle managers in the workplace in authority over workers or students. Students learn about hierarchies. Workers do not control their labour. They have no choice over what they produce, no say in its exchange or who has the profits. Students study what the school tells them to, they do not 'own' the end product of their labour. Knowledge is presented as 'compartmentalised'. Students do as they are told, they learn to value time (punctuality), hard work and the reward system: a certificate for a good project, a 'bonus' for working hard, i.e. 'extrinsic rewards'.

Bowles and Gintis found, after studying American secondary schools, that the most original, imaginative individuals were not encouraged, as there was not much room for non-conformity in capitalism. The rule-following, conforming type was most acceptable, and these individuals come mainly from the middle classes. Working-class under-achievement was the pattern they uncovered, even in the functional 'classless' USA. These students were ejected first and became workers, manually skilled and conforming to the role that had been allotted. The next group, mostly middle class, became the new middle classes, and the smallest, most élite group went on to higher education. The system of rewards and punishments, orders and obedience, the lack of pupil control over their own education – the hidden curriculum – are all said to correspond to the demands of work. They point out the process whereby knowledge and skills are made exclusive to a few, yet attitudes and opinions are transmitted to all.

Criticisms of Bowles and Gintis

Whilst influential, Bowles and Gintis' book has been subjected to a number of criticisms from Marxists and non-Marxists alike. Both have claimed that it is inadequate to argue that the educational system is shaped solely by the demands of a capitalist economic system.

To state this is to posit a determinism reminiscent of the crudest functionalism. For some Marxists, such as Giroux (1984), echoing Poulantzas (see chapter 8), the educational system is 'relatively autonomous' from the rest of society, and is to a large extent able to determine its own direction.

They have been criticised for seeing working-class pupils as passive and for making the assumption that everything that is taught in school is necessarily learnt. Other studies, even from within the Marxist perspective (Willis, 1977), have shown working-class pupils to be anything but passive.

Gender and ethnicity

It has also been claimed that their analysis suffers by ignoring the issues of gender and ethnicity. AnnMarie Wolpe (1988) sees a contradiction in the way that they claim that 'the family's impact on the reproduction of the sexual division of labour is distinctly greater than that of the educational system'. They appear to be arguing that girls are socialised mainly at home and boys at school. 'Girls' ideas', she says, 'have, according to their analysis, been formed in the family. Schooling cannot be as important for women because of the greater power of the family structure and its teaching on sex roles ... In one fell swoop they eradicate any importance of education in girls' lives.'

There is also a problem with the claim that school prepares people for a life of work. In the USA, Gloria Joseph (1988) states: 'There exists a significantly large body of Blacks and Latinos who are not in the economic work force at all.' What Bowles and Gintis have to say misses this ethnic dimension. Similarly, it could be said that significant numbers of British school-leavers will experience long periods of unemployment before they eventually find work. How has school prepared them for this? This is the question the theorists of the 'new vocationalism' (see page 149) seek to answer.

Bowles and Gintis reply

Bowles and Gintis (1988), aware of these arguments, have made an effort to reply. Against the key point that cultures of resistance exist in schools they argue that 'Such cultural dynamics, far from contradicting the correspondence principle, in fact reinforce it. We would welcome, although there does not appear to exist, a strong argument to the effect that the structure of education is the product of contested class, gender, racial and other relationships.' In other words, it remains the case that education is a key agent of the dominant ideology.

QUESTIONS

1 **What is an 'ideological State apparatus'?**

2 **What do Bowles and Gintis mean by the 'correspondence principle'?**

3 **What would Marxists have to say about the national curriculum?**

The State and education in Britain

Any understanding of the sociology of education demands an examination of how the education system came into existence, the forces that determined its shape, and the assumptions made by various educational reformers in framing their legislation.

For the affluent, a form of education has been in existence for many hundreds of years, including public schools for the nobility, and grammar schools for the merchant classes. For the overwhelming majority of the population there was no systematic attempt at education. This was occasionally justified on the grounds that education for the masses would threaten to disturb the social order – they might start asking too many questions. Prior to 1870, schooling was largely provided by the various denominations of the church, seeking to improve the moral character of the young.

State intervention

Three years after a significant breakthrough was made towards working-class enfranchisement (see chapter 8), the Liberal government under Gladstone, against the prevailing philosophy of 'laissez-faire', began an important intervention in the lives of individuals when Forster put the Elementary Education Act through Parliament. From 1870 the State ensured an elementary education – religion, reading, writing and arithmetic – for all children from five to ten years old. In the next few decades, attendance became compulsory, State schools became free, and by 1918 the school-leaving age had been raised to 14.

There is no single reason why the State became so hugely involved in the lives of its citizens at this time, effectively laying the basis for the modern Welfare State. The main factor, however, lay in the need for a literate and numerate population at a time when Britain's main industrial competitors were catching up and threatening to overtake Britain's industrial performance. Further major educational legislation was to follow world wars in which the poor general level of education in Britain was exposed.

Despite being TUC policy since 1890, and also despite intense agitation between the two world wars, secondary education as a right for all children up to the age of 15 was not achieved until, in the closing stages of the Second World War, R.A. Butler passed the Education Act of 1944. This was the first brick laid in the modern Welfare State, taking on the first of Beveridge's 'five evils' – ignorance.

The tripartite system

Up to 1944, only working-class children who 'showed promise' were likely to win a scholarship into a grammar school. After the

1944 Act, all children would attend a type of secondary school, for which they were selected on the basis of an intelligence test: the Eleven Plus examination. Pupils could go in one of three directions after they had taken the test, depending on the kind of aptitude, skills and abilities they had displayed. Children revealed to be logically minded and articulate by the test would receive the academic education offered by grammar schools. Practical and technically minded children would go to technical schools and those who had not shown promise attended secondary modern schools.

Equal value   These three types of secondary school – which made up the 'tripartite system' – were intended to have 'parity of esteem'. In other words, no single part of the tripartite system would be seen to be a more important or valuable form of education than any other. However, private sector education remained virtually untouched by the biggest restructuring of British education to date. This remains the case today.

Another intention of the Act was to create a genuine educational meritocracy in which naturally intelligent children would be allowed to develop to the maximum of their educational potential, following selection at the age of 11. By the time of the 1963 Robbins report, which stated that: 'a course of Higher Education should be available for all those who are qualified by ability and attainment to pursue one and who wish to do so', it was clear that equality of opportunity and parity of esteem in education had not been achieved. More money was being spent on grammar schools than on the two others, and more children of non-manual workers, with the same IQ (intelligence quotient) as the children of manual workers, were going on to higher education. No one believed the three schools were of equal value. The later findings of the Nuffield Study (Halsey *et al.*, 1980) echoed the observation that the 1944 Act had done little to increase upward social mobility for the working class.

Instead, it was argued that the tripartite system had a strong tendency to reproduce the wider system of stratification, where the children of middle-class professionals attended grammar schools, children of the skilled working class went to technical schools and children of the semi- and unskilled manual working class attended secondary modern schools. As increasing amounts of evidence were gathered to reinforce this argument, the notion of under-achievement was formulated.

There had been a provision in the 1944 Act for local authorities to set up an alternative form of secondary education to the tripartite system, and some LEAs (for example in London, Leicester and Anglesey) set up a form of schooling that dispensed with selection at the age of 11. Instead of sending pupils on to one of three schools, they all attended a single school – a comprehensive.

Comprehensive schooling

The idea of comprehensive schooling had, since 1946, been attractive to the Labour Party, and following its election in 1964 it set about redressing the shortcomings of the tripartite system by introducing comprehensive education on a national basis. By 1988 (with the school-leaving age raised to 16 in 1971–2), State education in the UK had become effectively comprehensive, though the tripartite system still lives on in isolated pockets (*see Table* 5.1).

TABLE 5.1   School pupils in State secondary education in England 1971–91 (%)

	1971	1981	1991
Middle schools	1.9	7.0	3.2
Secondary modern	38.0	6.0	1.6
Grammar	18.4	3.4	1.8
Technical	1.3	0.3	0.1
Comprehensive	34.4	82.5	92.5
Others	6.0	0.9	0.8

Source: Department for Education (adapted from Social Trends 23, *1993)*

Comprehensivisation of secondary education was achieved in the face of enormous opposition from many quarters, particularly defenders of grammar schools and those who believed that education must still be able to cater for the 'bright' kids and that the creation of a meritocracy means educational mediocrity. It has been, and continues to be, a political football kicked about between the various political parties. Despite the battle to create equality of opportunity in education, it remained the case that in 1991 7 per cent of all pupils, and 20 per cent of boys and 15 per cent of girls over 16, attended independent or fee-paying public schools.

With the passing of the Conservative Government's Educational Reform Act in 1988, a major series of changes in the nature of State education were set in train. The Act aimed to enforce the teaching and learning of a national core curriculum; introduced standard assessment testing at the ages of seven, eleven, fourteen and sixteen; it gave schools the right to 'opt out' of local authority control and be centrally funded; and it gave greater powers to school governors. Also it abolished the Inner London Education Authority. The realisation of these objectives has proved more difficult than the passing of the Act for all concerned.

QUESTIONS
1 Why did the State take on responsibility for free and compulsory education?

2 What is meant by the tripartite system?

3 Why were three types of school – grammar, technical and secondary modern – set up after 1944?

The new vocationalism: the future of education?

In a famous speech in 1976, the then Prime Minister, James Callaghan, argued that 'it is vital to Britain's economic recovery and standard of living that the performance of manufacturing industry is improved and that the whole range of government policies, including education, contribute as much as possible to improving industrial performance and thereby the national wealth'. In saying this, Callaghan began the 'Great Debate' about the future of educational provision, which focused specifically on how it serves the demands of industry.

The need for change

In the following year a Government Green Paper, *Education in Schools*, targeted three areas where it believed that schools failed industry: a decline in standards with basic skills no longer being adequately taught while 'fringe' subjects were overemphasised; a neglect of the fundamentals of discipline such as good manners and the motivation to work hard; and finally the failure of the education system to provide enough scientists, engineers and technologists.

These themes (without the stress on manufacturing industry) were taken up by the incoming Conservative government in 1979. Part of the solution was seen to lie in giving a greater role in education to Department of Employment agencies such as the Manpower Services Commission (changed to the Training Agency), the Technical and Vocational Educational Initiative and the Technical and Vocational Educational Extension. By the mid 1980s the Youth Opportunities Programme had become the two-year Youth Training Scheme and a Certificate in Pre-Vocational Education was available in schools and colleges. Later initiatives include the industry-led National Vocational Qualification (NVQ) and the General National Vocational Qualification (GNVQ).

The sceptic's view

The motivation behind this new emphasis on vocational qualifications, on skills and competence, has been viewed sceptically by some sociologists, as is clear in the title of Bates *et al.*'s book *Schooling for the Dole?* (1984). In this searching examination of the new vocationalism, the authors argue that the emphasis on personal and life skills in vocational training may be a euphemism for accepting the social control of the workplace in unquestioning fashion.

Finn, one of the authors, argues that it is not the case that school-leavers are ignorant of the world of work. Most young people, particularly the educational 'failures', have experience of part-time work while at school, as well as unpaid domestic labour and the work disciplines of the school. Another of the authors, Moore, argues that industrial training is in any case the chosen responsibility of industry. In a rapidly changing industrial environment, it is difficult for anyone, let alone educationalists, to know what future training needs are: 'the dismal history of manpower forecasting suggests that no-one really knows what industry needs, and the relative isolation of teachers from the world of work as well as the worlds of their pupils suggests that they are in no position to know what their needs are'.

Moreover, it is a false assumption that schools can provide occupationally relevant characteristics in their pupils – all they can do is provide literate and numerate labour. Job allocation happens on the job, through promotion, training and retraining, giving the lie to both functionalist and Marxist arguments concerning the role of schools in placing pupils in the world of work.

QUESTIONS

1 **What is meant by the new vocationalism?**

2 **What do the initials NVQ and GNVQ mean?**

Differential educational achievement

Differences in educational achievement are usually measured by examination results, sixth form (or post-compulsory education) entry, by those gaining places in higher education, and choice of subject. The three forms of stratification that are evident from these data are social class, gender and ethnicity. It is important to note here that the tables discussed below are numerical, positivistic indicators, and the usual anti-positivist arguments about the constructed nature of 'social facts' should be borne in mind.

Class The picture of academic achievement by social class is consistent. The largest survey is that undertaken by Halsey, Heath and Ridge (1980). Using the database generated by the Oxford Mobility Study (see chapter 3), as well as the three-way split of service, intermediate and working classes, they found that boys from the service class (the top strata) had 40 times more chance of attending a public school, and three times more chance of attending a grammar school than a boy from the working class (in a period when the tri-partite system was largely still in place). The 1944 Act had, in the 1950s and 1960s, made very little difference to a working-class boy's chances of rising through the academic ranks: he had four times less chance than a service-class boy of still being in school at the age of 16; eight times less chance of being in school at 17; ten times less chance of being in school at 18 and 11 times less chance of being at university.

Higher education
While it was true in 1980 to say that, in absolute terms, more working-class boys were at university (2 per cent), the number of intermediate and service-class boys had also increased, but at faster rates (6 per cent and 19 per cent). In relative terms, then, the number of working-class boys at university, compared to other classes, had shrunk, not expanded. The 1944 Act and post-war university expansion had led to, if anything, a proportionately smaller working-class entry. The observation that the Welfare State has in reality benefited the middle class most is discussed further by Julian Le Grand (see chapter 9).

A similar picture emerges from statistics collected in the early 1990s (*see Table 5.2*). Many commentators have argued that one of the strongest correlations known to sociologists is that between social class and educational achievement and under-achievement.

TABLE 5.2 Highest qualification held by socio-economic group, 1992–93 (%)

	Professional	Employers and managers	Intermediate non-manual	Junior non-manual	Skilled manual and own account non-professional	Semi-skilled manual and personal service	Unskilled manual	All persons
Degree	61	19	21	3	2	1	-	12
Higher education	16	19	29	6	9	4	2	13
GCE A-level	7	16	12	13	14	7	3	12
GCSE, grades A–C	7	21	20	35	23	21	12	22
GCSE, grades D–G	1	7	5	16	15	12	10	10
Foreign	4	3	3	3	2	4	3	3
No qualifications	3	15	10	24	36	51	70	28

Source: Social Trends 25, 1995

Gender
The pattern of boys' and girls' educational achievement is more complex. In the years 1975 and 1976, 18 per cent of all male school-leavers in the United Kingdom had at least one A-level or Higher, compared with 16 per cent of females. By 1990–91 girls had taken a clear lead: 29 per cent compared with 25 per cent (*see Figure 5.1*). In the same years, more boys than girls were leaving school without any GCSE qualifications.

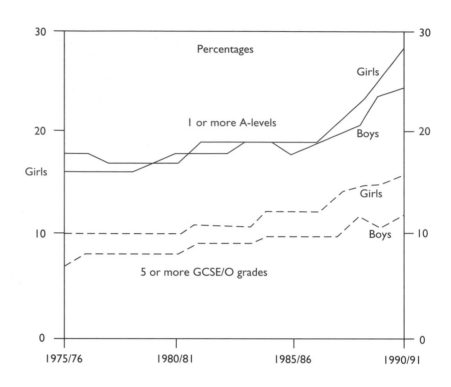

Figure 5.1 Highest qualification attained by school leavers: by sex, 1975/76–1990/91

Source: Social Trends *24, 1994*

While females do better than males at A-level, there are fewer women in higher education, taking a degree, than there are men (*see Table* 5.3). It is more common for women with A-levels to leave full-time education and not go on to university than it is for men.

TABLE 5.3   Male and female students in higher education (thousands)

| | MEN | | WOMEN | |
	1980/1	1991/2	1980/1	1991/2
Full-time undergraduates	277	385	196	361
Part-time undergraduates	178	201	73	163

Source: Social Trends *24, 1994*

There is also a clearly genderised pattern of subject choice at university, where the majority of students studying education, medicine, dentistry and health, languages and literature, and music, drama and art are female, as *Figure* 5.2 shows.

Ethnicity   With regard to ethnicity, patterns of educational achievement are similar to those for employment and unemployment. As *Table* 5.4 shows, whites and Indians have similar profiles, and Pakistanis and Bangladeshis do particularly less well. Amongst Pakistani and Bangladeshi women 68 per cent have no educational qualifications whatsoever.

Figure 5.2 Female students as a percentage of all students: by selected full-time degree courses, 1981/82 and 1990/91

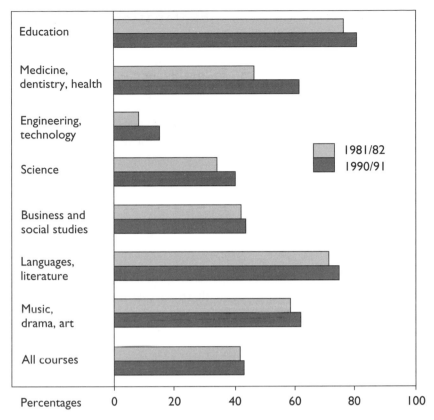

Source: Social Trends 23, 1993

TABLE 5.4   **Highest qualification level of the population by ethnic origin and sex, 1988–90 (%)**

	WHITE	WEST INDIAN/ GUYANESE	INDIAN	PAKISTANI/ BANGLADESHI	OTHER
Highest qualification held					
Males					
Higher	15	–	19	8	22
Other	57	58	51	40	56
None	29	36	30	52	24
Females					
Higher	13	16	13	–	20
Other	51	52	46	28	52
None	36	32	41	68	28
All persons					
Higher	14	11	16	6	24
Other	54	55	49	34	54
None	32	34	36	60	25

Source: Social Trends 22, 1992

QUESTIONS   1 How does male and female educational achievement compare?

2 How did Halsey et al. obtain their data? What period does it cover?

Explanations for differential educational achievement

Intelligence

Genetics Very many people would attribute their failure to gain qualification at school to the 'bungalow factor': they haven't got anything upstairs. Other people have – they were born intelligent, and this is the reason why some do well at school, and others do not. Schools simply separate those who are able from those who are not. There is nothing you can do about it.

Those who think this way agree with a school of psychology that argues that intelligence is innate, a quality that you inherit from your genetically 'intelligent' forebears. Three educational psychologists – Cyril Burt, Hans Eysenck and the American, Arthur Jensen – have all devoted their professional careers to proving this belief. Of these three, Cyril Burt has had the greatest influence on educational policy in Great Britain.

Burt The world's first educational psychologist, Burt grew up at the turn of the century at a time when the 'science' of eugenics was fashionable. According to eugenics, there is a natural hierarchy among humans, based on genetic superiority. Burt (1943) himself argues that 'the higher IQs (intelligence quotients) found among children of the fee-paying (i.e. public school) classes represent inborn differences partly inherited from parents who themselves owe their superior incomes to their superior mental efficiency'. In other words, people are wealthy as a result of their 'natural intelligence', not 'intelligent' as a result of their wealth. A similar argument has been advanced to explain the relatively poor health of the lowest income groups (see chapter 10).

Burt's theories, which were based on years of extensive empirical research – in one case involving 40,000 families in a London borough – became the intellectual justification for the formation of the post-war tripartite system, and the process of selection through the Eleven Plus. The Spens Report of 1938 – the basis for the 1944 Act – stated that 'intellectual development during childhood appears to progress as if it were governed by a single central factor usually known as "general intelligence" which may be broadly described as innate all-round intellectual ability. It appears to enter into everything which the child attempts to think or say or do, and seems on the whole to be the most important factor in determining his work in the classroom.'

Burt's disciples

For decades, Burt's ideas dominated thinking in this area. All that schools needed to do was measure an individual's intelligence and educate them appropriately in one of the three types of schools where, as Eysenck – Burt's student at University College, London – states, 'What children take out of schools is proportional to what they bring into the schools in terms of IQ.' What Eysenck means here is that, if you are not very intelligent anyway, no matter what kind of school you go to or what kind of teaching techniques were used, you will never get anything out of it.

Even more controversially, another Burt disciple, Arthur Jensen (1967) has argued that there is a racial dimension to genetically determined intelligence: blacks are less intelligent than whites.

Criticisms of Burt

Unfortunately for Burt, Jensen and Eysenck, it came to be generally believed that Burt's research – which largely determined British post-war educational policy – was essentially fraudulent. In the mid 1970s (Burt died in 1971) very big question marks were placed against the status of his research. No one, for example, has ever been able to locate at least five of the research assistants that he claimed to have employed. Nor have they been able to identify the London borough from which the 40,000 families that form the basis of his 1961 study came. His statistical work, particularly in his research on identical but separated (and therefore differently socialised) twins, has been widely criticised for improbability and impossibility.

One of the most hard-hitting attacks on Burt and those who have claimed evidence for the existence of biologically determined or innate intelligence in humans comes from within natural science. In *The Mismeasure of Man*, Stephen Jay Gould (1981) argues that the idea of intelligence has been reified – that is, what is really an abstraction has become something that is thought to have a demonstrable physical existence, like height or weight. The belief emerges that intelligence is located in the brain and can be measured. From this it follows that people can be ranked according to their measured intelligence.

The fallacy, for Gould, lies in believing that intelligence exists in the first place. This is apparent in the remark made by the inventor of intelligence tests, Alfred Binet, that intelligence can be defined as 'what my tests measure'. Intelligence only exists as a concept because craniologists and psychologists claim it does. Gould reinforces this point by claiming that what has been called objective intelligence testing merely reflects the social prejudices of those who make use of the reified idea of intelligence. In the year the Butler Education Act was passed, Gunnar Myrdal (1944) argued that it was generally true of biological arguments about human nature (sociobiology) that 'They have been associated … with conservative and reactionary ideologies. Under their long hegemony, there has been a tendency to assume biological causation without question, and to accept social explanations only under the duress of a siege of irresistible evidence.' The popularity of such arguments reflects the political fashion of the times.

The rehabilitation of Cyril Burt

Having been widely discredited in the 1980s, attempts have been made in recent years to restore Burt's name, and therefore the concept of innate and inherited intelligence. This is mainly due to the publication of two books, the first by Robert Joynson (1989) and the second by Ronald Fletcher (1991). Both these books claim that the attack on Burt was unfair and unjustified. Fletcher in particular seizes on the media's readiness, at the height of comprehensivisation, to accept too readily that Burt was a fraud, and that his evidence was insufficient and lacking vigour.

The publication of these works, coupled with a growing dissatisfaction among teachers concerning mixed-ability teaching, and the persistence of differential rates of achievement among pupils, has led to a growing conviction within organisations such as the British Psychological Society that Burt's work was not based on falsifications and deceptions: the belief is now increasingly widespread that he might have had a point.

Why educationalists were so willing to believe Burt at the time, and so unwilling to drop his ideas once they were queried raises a number of questions about ideology and the sociology of knowledge. What is important for sociology is whether ideas of innate intelligence can continue to have any relevance. The answer must be that they do not. There is no quality that we can isolate and call 'intelligence'. Neither an 'intelligence' gene nor a part of the brain that deals with intelligence have ever been discovered. What we know, we have learnt as the result of socialisation. Our knowledge is culturally constructed – the sociological arguments are surely overwhelming. Cyril Burt and the 'innate intelligence school' are as relevant to the sociology of education as Cesare Lombroso is to the sociology of crime and deviance (see chapter 14).

Explanations of differential achievement, under-achievement or under-attainment have taken two directions in the sociology of education: those based in the home and what goes on there, and those based in the school and what happens there, between teachers and pupils, pupils and pupils, and teachers and teachers.

QUESTIONS

1 What is 'innate intelligence'? How can it be measured? Is it a political or ideological issue?

2 Describe the ideas put forward by Cyril Burt.

3 What is meant by 'reification'?

The home

J.W.B. Douglas

J.W.B. Douglas (1964) carried out a survey of over 5,000 children born in 1946. This longitudinal research followed the children throughout their primary school education until they sat the Eleven Plus and were sent on to different secondary schools in the tripartite system. Overall, he found working-class children do less well in ability tests, and he offers explanations based on the home background, parental attitudes, the parents' hours of work and interest in their children's schooling. In one famous passage he points out that fewer working-class parents visit schools on parents' evenings, and it is usually the mother who shows up, whereas middle-class parents turn up together and assertively demand their sons' and daughters' educational rights in elaborated code (see pp. 158–59), seeing the head as well as the teacher. Parental encouragement is seen as a factor in performance, and Douglas seems to suggest that this can be measured by a positivist type of proof. Social action theorists would also look at the possible reasons behind these differences: factors in, or affecting, the home, e.g. jobs, hours of work, the need for one parent to look after the children, etc. This study, and another influential but smaller-scale study carried out by Jackson and Marsden in the 1940s and 1950s, formed the backdrop for arguments which suggest that it is home background, and particularly parental participation in education, which explains working-class under-attainment.

Criticisms of home-based explanations of under-achievement

The implication is that if the State provided spacious homes with quiet places for children to study, a well-stocked library, collages and charts on the wall, classical music, educational outings, educational computer programs, and parents who can spend a lot of time supplementing education, and motivating their children, then everyone would go to university and earn enough to provide those things for their children. Critics of these home-based explanations point out that what is happening here is a culture clash. Speech codes and parents' educational achievements, attitudes towards jobs, careers, ambition, life and death differ according to class. The culture of the working class is at odds with that of schools and society. Their interests and valued skills are ignored or given low status, and there are no explanations given as to the value of university education and all those things taken for granted by the middle classes. Working-class children may rebel, become indifferent, give up and consistently fail to see what the point is – what use is algebra if you believe you are going to work in a supermarket?

There is also the point that behind the statistics there are a number of possible but unexplored interpretations of parental involvement in their children's education such as lack of money for babysitters, shift-working or previous humiliation by teachers in their own schooling, none of which necessarily means that parents are not concerned about or involved in their children's education.

QUESTIONS

1 **What are the problems of measuring parental involvement?**

2 **How important is a child's home life to their success in school?**

Language codes

Basil Bernstein (1961) is one of the most quoted names in the argument that working-class children and middle-class teachers often communicate ineffectively because of different 'language codes'. He is a British sociologist, often associated with functionalism, although he does not necessarily claim the title for himself. Language codes are a small part of his detailed and complex output, and this argument should be considered in context. The argument revolves around the two types of language in use and the way the education system expects you to express yourself using only one.

> **Basil Bernstein (1924–)**
> A British sociologist of education, known especially for his work on the relationship between language, social class and achievement.

Restricted and elaborated codes

Restricted code, he argues, is abbreviated, less grammatical, punctuated by ums, ers, you knows and body language. Total, explicit detail is unnecessary, as everyone knows what you are talking about. Bernstein's suggestion is that this code is used by middle- and working-class people, particularly children and adolescents. Most youth cultures and each teenage generation have their own slang words, often a code to shut out the older generation. Middle-class children also have access to an elaborated speech code, which is used more by their parents. This is more detailed, 'elaborated' upon, giving references to all things which are needed for a full understanding. The user of elaborated code does not take it for granted that you know what they are talking about, and so they explain in depth. The middle-class parent uses elaborated code when talking to the children, and explains and reasons with them. They are expected to respond in the same way. Working-class parents use restricted code themselves, and their children therefore have no experience of elaborated code, except from their teachers at school.

Abstract ideas

Bernstein's research with children involved showing them cartoon pictures which told a story and asking them to write down what was happening. Children who were used to elaborated code could write the story in full detail, so that the pictures were not needed in order to understand what was happening. Working-class children only wrote the bare bones of the story, and the pictures were vital to get an understanding. He also used interviews to discuss various ideas, so-called 'abstract' concepts, for example religion or truth. Children with restricted code were supposedly unable to express ideas like this in the same way as those using elaborated code.

This ability to deal with abstractions is important in intellectual training, and middle-class children go on to universities to do degree courses which deal with theory — like sociology. The argument, when Bernstein's work was popular in the 1960s and 1970s, seemed to suggest that if you used restricted code, you were unable to cope with so-called 'high status' education. The schools use elaborated codes, because heads and teachers are middle class. Education is geared towards a middle-class definition of what intelligence is. Anyone who comes to school without the accepted speech code will only have limited success.

Labov What made some sociologists angry was the assumption that the working class could not cope with abstract concepts because of a 'language barrier'. William Labov (1969), one of Bernstein's strongest critics, pointed out that interviewing working-class children in a formal situation, using a middle-class interviewer, was likely to embarrass and restrict them. His own interviews, performed in a more relaxed setting, produced different results. He found that when they felt confident and secure, the children could express their views on abstractions without any problem, often being forceful and articulate. In one interview, for example, he asked an American black boy why he thought God would be white. 'Why?', he replied, 'I'll tell you why! Cause the average whitey out here got everything, you dig. And the nigger ain't got shit, y'know? Y'understan? So-um-for in order for that to happen, you know it ain't no black God that's doing that bullshit.'

This suggests that there is a problem of confidence at the heart of speech and expression, and that the response of teachers to the different ways in which pupils express themselves could be an issue. If middle-class teachers only listen to the ideas articulated by children who are the best users of middle-class speech patterns then the ideas, views and potential of working-class children are undervalued. More recent sociology has addressed the role of the school in constructing 'failure' for some groups of children by ignoring or devaluing their culture, but it was Bernstein's arguments which were among the first to try to explain working-class failure in terms of something being 'wrong' at home.

QUESTIONS
1 How does elaborated code differ from restricted code?

2 How does Labov criticise Bernstein?

3 How important is language in interviewing?

4 Which language code is this textbook written in?

Cultural deprivation

In the 1960s the concept of 'cultural deprivation' was put forward to describe and explain what was happening to prevent certain children from doing well in school. According to this their inability to rise above the basics at school was due to the cultural norms, values and attitudes they brought to the school, evident from their language, life experience, personality, and even their ability to think.

Compensatory education

To compensate for this deficiency, a number of schemes were put forward in both Britain and America, with the aim of making up for this perceived cultural deprivation. In the USA in the mid 1960s the Johnson administration spent billions of dollars on 'Operation Headstart', targeting resources on the 'underprivileged'. In Britain, following the Plowden Report of 1967, four educational priority areas were identified in Liverpool, Birmingham, South-East London and Yorkshire. These were given extra funding, resources and staff in an attempt to enrich the cultural development of the children.

In neither project was any significant improvement discovered. The schemes continued to be defended on the grounds that they had been targeted at children of the wrong age, or for too little time, or – in Britain – with insufficient funding.

Criticisms of the cultural deprivation theory

Others have argued that, as with theories of cultural deprivation in the sociology of crime, health and poverty, those at the bottom of the pile should not be blamed for what appears to be their own inadequacy. Nell Keddie (1973), amongst others, has argued that the concept implies that the culture that the targeted children are part of is in some way deficient. No human can be 'deprived' of culture as it is part of socialisation. What the arguments suggest is that anyone who is deprived of middle-class cultural values is in some way lacking.

According to these critics, the education system, run by the middle class, discriminates against any cultural views which differ from its own. What schools should recognise is 'cultural difference', not deprivation. Working-class culture should be recognised and valued. Those not exposed to middle-class culture in schools would not then under-achieve.

QUESTIONS

1 What would be included on the timetable of a school which valued and rewarded working-class cultural skills?

2 How does cultural deprivation differ from material deprivation? Could one be the cause of the other?

3 Why did schemes of compensatory education fail?

The school and the classroom

As the tripartite system began to merge into comprehensive education, sociologists moved into the classroom, using observation techniques to further their understanding of why some pupils do better at school than others. In these studies, the focus came to be less on the external factors that contribute to differential educational achievement and more on how the organisation of the school, and the teachers within it, contribute to the way the students behave.

Hargreaves and streaming

Three important studies form a complementary sequence of enquiries into secondary modern, grammar and comprehensive schooling. In the first of these, David Hargreaves (1967) used a variety of information-gathering techniques, including teaching, to reach the unsurprising conclusion that students in higher streams have a greater commitment to the values of the school. His main point is that it is the division of the school into streams — student groupings according to levels of academic ability — which creates pupil subcultures. These, he says, are of two main types. Those at the top of the streaming system (which went from A to E in the school he examined) form an academic culture which values hard work, compliance with authority and being well turned-out. At the other end are what he oddly called the 'delinquescents', a subculture which values breaking rules, fighting, smoking, winding up the teachers and bending dress codes.

Hargreaves argues that the school compounds the divisions between the different groups in the way that staff allocation and the structure of the timetable place the two subcultures in separate streams. Like Becker's 'outsiders' (see chapter 14) those in the bottom stream become deviant as a common response to the problem of being labelled 'inferior' and 'not worth the effort'.

Lacey

In a similar vein, and also working as a teacher, Colin Lacey (1970) found the same negative effect of streaming prevalent in grammar schools where lower-stream boys were pushed into lives focused outside the school, for example in coffee bars, but not completely into the kind of 'delinquescent' culture described by Hargreaves. In another work Lacey (1975) presents evidence to suggest that when streaming was abandoned in favour of mixed-ability groupings, those academically at the bottom improved their performance in exams, although the most 'able' registered no change.

Ball These findings were echoed by Stephen Ball's later study (1981) where again he found that grouping students by ability helped form pupil subcultures and that changes away from banding within the school meant that disciplinary and behavioural problems lessened. But it did not necessarily lead to egalitarianism within the school, as teachers continued to make distinctions between 'bright' and 'dull' students, with the 'bright' ones being favoured and encouraged onto better things. Other students were 'cooled out', gently persuaded to drop whatever academic aspirations they may have had on the grounds that they were 'not up to it'. They left school believing that in some way they simply were not intelligent enough, yet this system of stratification within the comprehensive school, Ball says, is actually teacher-defined. Comprehensivisation has not led to equality of opportunity for all up to the leaving age of sixteen.

Rutter and school ethos Michael Rutter (1979) tried to show, through a six-year longitudinal study and the collection of a mass of statistical information, how objectively similar inner-London secondary schools could be organised to produce different levels of ability and success: 'Schools do indeed have an effect on children's development and it does matter which school a child attends.'

What matters, Rutter argues, is the quality of the interaction between teacher and pupils, the atmosphere of co-operation, the sense that classes are well planned and prepared. A 'good' school is not necessarily well equipped, but is measured by its overall 'ethos' or value system as determined by indicators such as attendance, academic achievement and behaviour of pupils inside and outside the school. These qualities usually go together, and can be summed up as reflections of the professional organisation and ability of the teaching staff, whether traditional or progressive.

Rutter's work has been heavily criticised, however, mainly for dwelling on what happens in the school, at the expense of variables such as gender, ethnicity, class, what kind of primary school children had attended, or the influence of parents, and what happens to the children when they leave school, once their fifteen thousand hours are up.

Keddie and the teacher's response The part played by teachers in defining the students' ideas of their own ability is now well documented. Nell Keddie (1971) demonstrated that different types of knowledge are made available to students in different streams, and that questions from different streams are differently treated. Children in the bottom stream are taken less seriously than those in the top streams. As she relates, she asked a teacher whether any pupil had asked in class (as they had in some other classes) 'Why should we do Social Science?' The teacher replied: 'No, but if I were asked by C stream I would try to sidestep it because it would be the same question as "Why do anything? Why work?"' Keddie then asked: 'What if you were asked by an A group?' and the response was: 'Then I'd probably try to answer.'

Yet it is not the case, Keddie argues, that those in the top stream and most favoured by the teachers are necessarily the brightest. They are seen to be succeeding because they match up to the teacher's idea of how an ideal student appears and behaves. 'Good' students do not seek to challenge the fundamentals of what the teacher is presenting, they do not exhibit scepticism about the power structure of the school, the classroom and the knowledge served up within the school. 'Good' students have values and attitudes which match the teacher's values and attitudes.

Although the above studies are based on investigations of how schools can define notions of 'good' or 'bad', 'success' and 'failure', and are couched in the language of interactionism, using concepts of labelling, self-fulfilling prophecies and 'teacher's definitions of the situation', it is a mistake to see them as studies rooted purely in phenomenology. All of them acknowledge the influence of social structure and environmental factors. It is better to see these as studies where sociologists have used whatever methods they feel appropriate to their investigation without being bound by the constraints of one or other perspective. This is a common theme in an area as wide and widely studied as the sociology of education.

QUESTIONS

1 **What are the main differences between home- and school-based explanations of under-achievement?**

2 **What impact has interactionism had on the sociology of education?**

3 **What are the main criticisms of concepts of labelling and the self-fulfilling prophecy?**

Knowledge and status

Middle-class knowledge

M.F.D. Young (1971) and others assert that the causes of under-achievement are to be found in the interactions between individuals and school. Who controls knowledge? Who defines what is important to learn? Why are some subjects 'high' status, some 'low' status?

They argue that the middle classes have a monopoly on knowledge. They succeed in education and are in a position to state what is and what is not important. Literacy and numeracy skills, reading, writing and arithmetic, abstract subjects, classical studies, Latin, Greek, sciences, maths are all considered types of knowledge worthy of the schools. Bricklaying, carpentry and physical development are undervalued, secondary, low-status subjects. This split mirrors the working-class—middle-class culture divide. The things which working-class culture values most are immediate, practical skills, which can be used to help everyday existence. Being 'good with your hands', able to do things helps you now, whereas months and years of study of abstract maths seems irrelevant.

The children who accept the teacher's idea of what knowledge is will do well. To argue with the teacher about the value and worth of the lesson does not help you. It is not seen as original or challenging thinking, just trouble-making – deviance. The 'brightest' pupils accept the teacher's total control of knowledge, and they live up to this definition in the classroom. The 'failures' rebel and argue along the lines of 'what use is this?' and are seen as unintelligent. They are left to create what meanings they can from their situation, dossing around and bunking off until they can leave school and get a job or go on the dole. Working-class failure is built into the system, and the interactions between teachers and pupils help to make sure that the failures take place. The definition and control of knowledge is done by the middle classes for the middle classes, and they go on to secure their hold on education, knowledge, intelligence and success.

QUESTIONS

1 **What is seen as 'high status' knowledge in school?**

2 **Is it true to say that the middle and working classes value different types of knowledge?**

3 **Should manual skills have a higher educational status?**

Counter culture

Paul Willis (1977) used a Marxist perspective to inform his research, which was carried out over a two-year period in a manufacturing district near Birmingham ('Hammertown'). He spent time, however, observing, interviewing and participating with a main study group of twelve working-class 'non-conformist' pupils in a tough secondary modern school. Willis was trying to show that there is a strong relationship between factory shop-floor culture and school culture. Responsibility for their actions is allocated to the individuals, or their group, and they are seen as taking an active part in their own failure. The class basis of this is always present in the ways the boys make sense of school. They use ideas which come from their parents, ideas about work. The 'shop-floor counter culture' is the way workers inject some humour and have a laugh at work, while still getting the work done. This humour is sexist, cruel and aggressively 'anti-intellectual'. The boys' fathers revel in the macho aspect of manual labour. They earn good money, work hard, have a laugh at the bosses, whom they see as weaklings, who could not lift a sledgehammer if they tried. They accept their status and are suspicious of authority.

This culture is used and re-created by their sons, who see school as a necessity, a bore unless you spice life up a bit by winding up the staff, fighting, thieving, and avoiding schoolwork. Their rebellion is subtle, obeying the rules but doing so only when necessary, smiling, nudging, playing the innocent. They take the model which teachers offer – 'you listen to me, learn and you will get on' – and turn it upside-down. They are giving their lives some colour and interest by weighing up the teachers, destroying school property, scorning the kids who do accept the teacher's model by calling them 'earoles' or 'lobes'. They call themselves 'the lads'. The lads are aware of their non-conformity. They form a small, extreme group, which creates a cultural space for itself and, from the teachers' point of view, ruins the educational process.

Willis's study is long and overcomplex in its language, but as a piece of ethnographic research it is excellent reading. The creativity of the disruption is a proof of the imagination and humour these boys possess, an originality and wit which is only allowed expression in their working futures when they play practical jokes on their workmates to break up the boredom of another working day. This passage describes a class which a junior teacher is attempting to 'teach', a mistake which a senior member of staff would not make:

> In such classes, advertising jingles are sung in unison to break the period up like a television programme. Regular 'news flashes' contain wicked mixtures of all that is known to give the teacher apoplexy. In one case the teacher has told 'the lads' never again to mention the school moped which they had been pestering him to let them ride, and never again to mention Picasso, whom he had once unwisely been drawn into describing at length. A raucous advertising jingle is interrupted for an 'important announcement': Picasso has just been seen riding through the school gate on a stolen school moped.

Cultural style 'Havin' a laff' is the sole reason for being at school. They are rebels, and look down on the 'earoles', although knowing full well what will happen. They accept that the 'earoles' will 'succeed' and go on to get better jobs, but they see that as damnation. They want to embrace their future as manual labourers, because that is where they will be able to continue to express their cultural style – swearing, fighting, sexism, physical labour and easy money. The culture they are embracing – fatalistic, harsh, humorous, manly – is the only way to live. They oppose school values, and this opposition fits in with their class culture. Willis emphasises that their parents may not encourage this, but in the end the culture of their class is available to them. They take this culture, which is the shop-floor response to boredom and alienation, and rework it into their school situation.

The comparative studies Willis carried out, for instance with middle-class anti-school groups in a grammar school, shows that they have similar attitudes to 'the lads' in their anti-school activities, but when the middle-class non-conformist gets home he faces a cultural attitude to career and society which mirrors that of the school. This child cannot use the shop-floor counter culture and rework it at school, so the anti-school activities and attitudes are less extreme, unsupported by the class culture.

Cultural space and cultural reproduction

Willis shows how individual and group creation of a cultural space at school, a way to get through the day, having 'a laff' and not working, is related to the class structure of society and the nature of work under capitalism. The lads create their own failure, and do so willingly, rejecting all the middle-class educational values. They are active in ensuring their own 'failure', but they see it as success. The schools and teachers are forced into aiding and abetting this, since there are no methods acceptable in education to try to alter it. These boys are said by staff to deserve their fate. They rebel at school and thus ensure that capitalism continues, as the class structure is reproduced. Working-class kids get working-class jobs because their whole cultural style insists that they must. They do not trust pen-pushers, but respect honest manual labour. They have actually conformed, willingly participated in reproducing the system, and their conformity is a product of their rebellion.

The Marxist-interactionist aspect of this study makes it an interesting example of the new approach to sociology in the 1970s. One of the main criticisms of Willis is the sexist ignoring of girls' voices in the study – how do *they* see 'the lads', *their* work, and *their* future? The girls are relegated to the role of 'the missus' by the lads, and their mothers say even less. The fact that Willis studied only boys has led some to remark that the subtitle to his work should really read 'How working-class boys get working-class jobs'.

Another problem is that he neglects ethnicity in a school with a substantial number of Asian and Afro-Caribbean students. He has also been criticised for the extent of his 'participation' with the lads, some critics suggesting that he encouraged their behaviour. For example, in one interview he talked to two pupils who told him how they broke into the school. Is this ethical? The most telling criticism is that you cannot generalise from a small, unrepresentative sample. However, this study does provide insights into the two sides of the argument about working-class under-achievement. Class culture, the home and parents' attitudes are important, but the individual social action which reproduces these attitudes, and the interaction between cultures and individuals in school is complex, subtle and loaded with meaning. Willis states that it is most difficult to understand why working-class kids let themselves fail and they leave the middle-class jobs for middle-class kids. His analysis of class, culture and the school goes some way towards answering that, but within a Marxist framework. Education is firmly rooted in the ideological superstructure, and the social processes take care of themselves. Capitalism sits back and lets it happen.

QUESTIONS

1 **How does the analysis given by Willis differ from that of Bowles and Gintis?**

2 **Are the 'lads' unintelligent?**

3 **What is the relationship between ideology and the reproduction of capitalist social relations of production?**

Gender

Girls' experience of school has always been different to that of boys. This is as old as, if not older than, the growth of State intervention in education in the late nineteenth century. In this period, the central motive behind educating girls was that they should become either knowledgeable companions for men if they were middle class (an approach pioneered by Cheltenham Ladies College), or domestically able if they were not. Working-class girls were uniformly taught needlework, cooking and domestic science, in an age where the highest profession any woman could aim for was that of governess. The first women's higher education college, Queen's College, was instituted with the sole aim of training governesses. Women were not allowed to take degrees at the University of London until 1878, at Oxford until 1920, and on equal terms with men at Cambridge until 1948 – although they were allowed to attend some lectures after 1872!

Sexism in education has persisted into the twentieth century and is reflected in numerous government reports. The 1926 Board of Education report – *Education of Adolescents* – advocated an expansion of

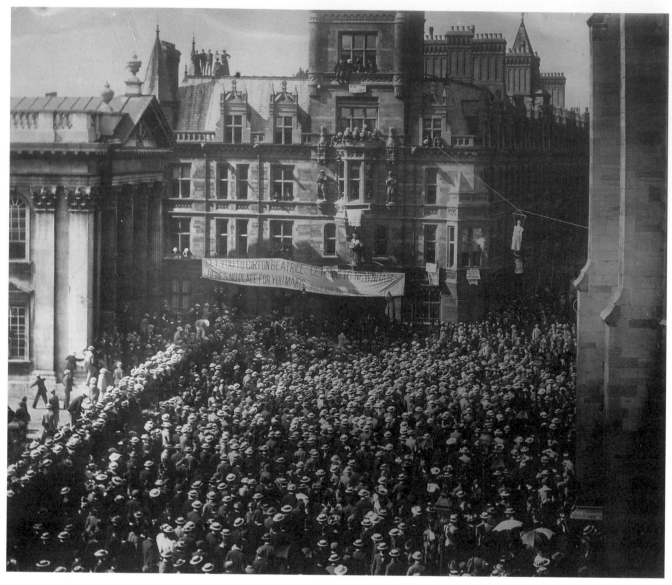

Sexism in education: male students at
Cambridge University demonstrate against
the admission of women in 1897.

the housecraft syllabus for girls on the grounds that 'Greater efficiency in the housewife would go far to raise her status in the estimation of the community', by which they mean the male community. In the year before the 1944 Act, the Norwood Report accepted
the view that the destiny for a boy might be to get a job and be academically successful, while for girls it was to marry and raise children, neither of which require academic success. In the same year as
the Robbins Report, the Newsom Report, *Half our Futures* (1963)
argued that 'In addition to their needs as individuals, girls should be
educated in terms of their main function – which is to make for
themselves, their children and their husbands a secure and suitable
home and to be mothers.'

The problem of equality

In a different climate, the Sex Discrimination Act of 1975 made it illegal for girls and boys to be treated differently at school, and demanded equal school curricula, with both boys and girls moving out of their traditional subject areas. The Act, however, did not say how this was to happen, and there has been a considerable debate about whether co-educational (mixed) or single-sex schools are more beneficial to girls. The evidence to date – Harding (1980) and Kelly (1981) – suggests, for the reasons given below, that girls achieve better academically when boys are out of the way.

Sexual divisions in education

As *Figure* 5.3 shows, there is a pattern to girls' under-achievement in schools. They are not more likely to drop out of education after sixteen, but they are concentrated in particular areas. They are heavily biased towards arts subjects and away from science in higher education (universities) and over-represented in further education, being less likely to take enough A-levels at eighteen to qualify for higher education. There are important consequences of this pattern, the most important being that women become excluded from the world of high technology and pushed towards clerical and service jobs which pay less. It also means that girls do not fulfil their educational potential.

Figure 5.3 Percentage of school leavers with grades A–C at GCSE: by subject and sex, 1990/91

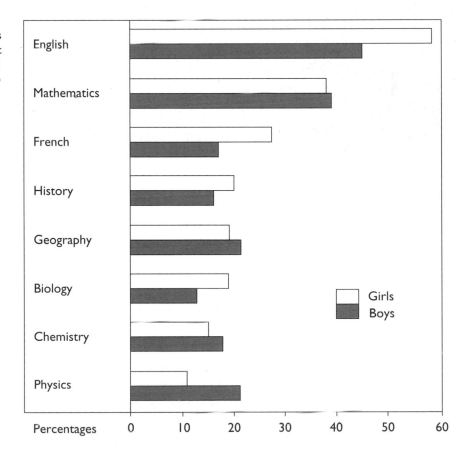

Source: Social Trends 24, 1994

Stereotypes   In trying to explain why this is so, the concept of a stereotype – a fixed image based on traditional ideas of what someone is or should be like – has been greatly used. The stereotype of girls and boys persists throughout life – not least in education. Girls are domestically inclined, and are centred on the 'internal' world of the home, where they serve men. At school, they opt for subjects that do not challenge their feminine self-concept, making biology their only foray into the scientific domain. Boys, being more outgoing and aggressive, are interested in the 'external' world of discovery and adventure, science and engineering, subjects that confirm their masculinity.

It is only when educationalists have tried to break down these stereotypes that they have found how deep-rooted they are, among pupils, teachers and the wider society. All three work together to make schooling a gender-based experience, and sociologists have looked at all three areas in their efforts to understand why girls fare differently to boys at school and after.

Confidence   For Carol Dweck (1972), girls in mixed schools have a different profile in the classroom to boys. Boys are more the subject of the teacher's focus than girls, they are disciplined more, while girls are only likely to be picked up for academic mistakes, not their conduct. Girls believe that if they do well, it is because they have worked hard or have been lucky, not because they have more ability; boys attribute their success to their ability but if they fail they blame it on bad luck or lack of effort. Doing well becomes a question of confidence, which teachers fail to bolster in girls. Lacking confidence, girls resist new challenges, learn 'helplessness' and correspondingly lower their aspirations and academic goals. This pattern, Dweck argues, is present for girls even when they become university undergraduates. Males, on the other hand, suffer none of these problems of self-assurance and even entertain wildly exaggerated ideas about what careers lie ahead for them.

This argument can be extended to examine the different types of knowledge and techniques involved in studying arts and science subjects. Subjects such as French, German and Spanish, as well as being once considered 'appropriate' for Victorian middle-class girls as conversational arts, develop by building on an existing knowledge base. Science subjects, such as physics and chemistry, progress through constantly taking on new ideas and concepts, at the same time continuously exposing students to the risk of failure. Biology, however, which does not carry the same masculine identification as other natural sciences, is perceived differently.

The visibility of girls and women

Tessa Blackstone and Helen Weinrich-Haste (1980) suggest that differential educational achievement can be overcome if three areas are tackled. First, positive role models are needed. This involves textbooks where role images are not gender-based, or where girls are seen doing unstereotypical things. This also applies to teachers: women should teach technology and men domestic science and more women should occupy senior positions in schools. Secondly, teachers themselves should raise their expectations of what girls are capable of, as they are a key contributor to reinforcing gender roles. In a series of interviews with seven classes of boy and girl pupils, Michelle Stanworth (1983) collated information that revealed that the students themselves claimed that boys stand out more vividly in classroom interaction, are four times more likely to join in a discussion or make comments in class, twice as likely to demand help or attention from the teacher and to be asked questions, and five times more likely to be the ones to whom teachers pay attention. The third area is pupil motivation. Girls need to be encouraged to develop a sense of independence, self-reliance and belief in their own ability. They suggest that single-sex schools may help girls in their most 'vulnerable' (to losing confidence) years, and science courses should be compulsory up to the age of sixteen. The national curriculum is a move in this direction.

Sharpe

Sue Sharpe's interviews with Ealing schoolgirls reinforce these ideas (Sharpe, 1976). Although a majority of her respondents expected to stop work for only a few years when their children were small, they nevertheless saw marriage as a career in itself and success in male-dominated areas as abnormal and unattractive. What they have to overcome is the force of their socialisation: 'by the time a girl reaches adolescence,' she says, 'her mind has usually been subjected to an endless stream of ideas and images incorporating sexist values'.

Christine Griffin (1986) found that deviant girls are deviant in a different way to boys. In attempting to replicate Paul Willis's study, *Learning to Labour*, she found that while 'most young men "hung around" in those "gangs of lads" which have provided the foundation for so many studies of youth cultures and subcultures, young women either had one extremely close "best" girlfriend, or spent time with a small group of two, three or four female friends. At the most basic level, there was no clear similarity between the social structures of female and male friendship groups.'

The structure of gender inequality

This is not to say that the position of women in the labour market will necessarily change simply because their schooling has become more genuinely egalitarian. As Carol Buswell (1991) warns:

'Education may occasionally help individuals to change their class but it cannot change their sex, and thus the structural position of women becomes an important aspect of understanding the educational experiences, achievements and choices of girls.' It is the awareness of inequalities outside of school that will continue to contribute to girls' performance while still in school, no matter how 'gender-free' that experience may be.

It must also be said that, in discussing the relative performance of girls and boys in school and considering the problem of gender-stereotyping, the very notion of 'girls' as a single undifferentiated, homogeneous group is itself a stereotype, as with notions of age, ethnicity or class. Girls can individually and collectively be bright or dull; noisy or quiet; riotously uncontrollable and wild or passive, dutiful and co-operative.

QUESTIONS

1 **Why have girls been treated differently in the education system?**

2 **What policies have been developed in order to overcome the problem of differential achievement by gender?**

Ethnicity

Ethnic minorities in Britain have provided and continue to provide new statistical patterns for sociologists to explain. It is highly misleading – if not racist – to see all non-whites as an undifferentiated mass, lumping them all together as a single ethnic minority. The pattern of educational results shows different levels of achievement between different groups. Broadly speaking, Indians have the same level of attainment as whites, while West Indians and Bangladeshis, by contrast, consistently under-achieve. A number of arguments, backed by research, have been put forward to explain this pattern.

The patterns which emerged in the 1960s showed that some children of Asian origin were under-achieving, mainly due to language barriers, but that once this is overcome they achieve on a level with white middle-class children. If the categories are further divided there are differences within the Asian group according to caste and class.

Afro-Caribbean British children have also been shown to under-achieve, although again this problem is complicated by, for example, gender differences. Why does this group under-achieve? Some of the explanations which have been offered are similar to those used to explain social class under-achievement. 'Disorganised' families, the lack of encouragement, poor housing and attitudes to white authority have all been blamed.

Ethnocentricity   Experiments in compensatory education have attempted to remedy this under-achievement, but have had little success. However, explanations which look into the classroom provide more insight. The British government's policy toward education in the 1950s, 1960s and most of the 1970s was to ignore cultural differences and educate all children into a white, British culture. This was reflected in the reading schemes which showed an all-white home and society. Blacks were invisible or in low-status roles such as bus conductors or maids. Enid Blyton's Noddy was mugged by golliwogs; the black witch and the black wood held evil; the white prince and princess were beautiful and good. At a higher level, history gave a glowing account of the wonder and kindness of the British, extending their Empire all over the world and civilising 'savages'. There is a great deal of argument about the effects of these factors, and some argue that a childhood of Noddy and the golliwogs does not make you a racist or a sexist. However, the unconscious internalisation of negative images may leave a stereotype lurking in your head, which makes you racist without you knowing it.

Class   As with other aspects of educational attainment, class is seen as an important dimension of ethnicity, and it has been suggested that Indians and African Asians (most of whom were thrown out of Uganda and Kenya in the 1970s) occupy a higher class position than either West Indians or Bangladeshis. This is a consequence of the differing historical factors behind their immigration into Britain. It then follows that class plays a role in their educational lives in the same ways discussed elsewhere in this chapter. Similarly, it has been asserted that, for historical and cultural reasons, it has been easier for Indians to fit into British culture. Some commentators have also pointed to the disproportionately high number of single-parent Afro-Caribbean families, with insufficient time and money to support their children during their school years.

Gender   Numerous studies have also shown that Afro-Caribbean girls do better than boys while at school. In trying to understand why this happens, Mary Fuller (1980) found that, while black girls are unwilling to show it, they recognise the importance for their futures of getting good qualifications. At the same time they are determined to achieve them without compromising their positive self-image as black and female or showing their teachers, or the boys, that they are too keen. Outwardly, they appear to be uninterested and indifferent to what is happening in the classroom.

It is less clear why Afro-Caribbean boys become unmotivated and develop forms of resistance to school. Racism in the curriculum, from teachers, and in the wider society have all been suggested as contributory factors, but they have not as yet been confirmed by research. These three factors, of course, remain essential to any understanding of the relationship between ethnicity and educational under-achievement.

The white middle-class teacher

Unconscious, or covert, racial differentiation can be a part of teaching practice. The teacher is most likely to be white and socialised by a British culture which some anti-racist thinkers claim is riddled with racism. Their outlook and background is white and middle-class, steeped in the glories of the British Empire when it was the 'white man's burden' to educate, Christianise and 'civilise' the blacks. Four hundred years of these attitudes cannot be changed overnight. Teachers may use stereotypes of West Indians as deviant or unintelligent or subnormal. Labelled in this way, meeting racism in reading books, textbooks and from other children, black youths are forced to react and often 'fail'. Stereotypes of being good at sport and music actively work against them: being given time off lessons to practise basketball or to play in the steel band leave gaps in a pupil's education.

Multicultural and anti-racist education

The pattern of under-achievement was so marked that it was recognised by Afro-Caribbean parents in the early 1960s, and voluntary Saturday schools, staffed by black parents and teachers, to supplement the basic education have been operational for many years. During the 1970s and 1980s, a policy response to this discrimination was developed – 'multicultural education'. The idea is to provide an education in cultures which exist alongside and within white, middle-class culture. Non-European history, languages and religion were injected into the curriculum in many inner-city, mixed-race schools. However, schools in parts of the country where there were few ethnic minorities (middle-class areas) did not take this up, and the children who needed it most, those whose only meeting with other cultures was in racist texts, never experienced multiculturalism.

The latest direction in education criticises this approach as worthless. Anti-racist educationalists say that multiculturalism merely dabbles in cultural differences, and dressing everyone up in saris or listening to calypsos and reggae does not address the real issues of racism, prejudice and discrimination. Leading children to believe that there is racial equality and respect for all cultures in society does not do children any favours. British society is racist, and education should address the issues of discrimination, prejudice and racial hatred.

QUESTIONS

1 **What is the pattern of educational achievement by ethnic group?**

2 **What explanations have been offered for differential educational achievement of some ethnic minority groups?**

FURTHER READING

R. Burgess, *Sociology, Education and Schools*, Batsford, 1986

R. Deem, *Women and Schooling*, Routledge and Kegan Paul, 1988

J.W.B. Douglas, *The Home and the School*, MacGibbon and Lee, 1964

D. Gill, B. Mayor and M. Blair (eds.), *Racism and Education*, Sage/Open University Press, 1992

A.H. Halsey *et al.*, *Origins and Destinations*, Clarendon Press, 1980

A. Pollard *et al.*, *Education, Training and the New Vocationalism: Experience and Policy*, Open University Press, 1988

M. Rutter *et al.*, *15,000 Hours*, Open Books, 1979

P. Willis, *Learning to Labour*, Saxon House, 1977

P. Wood, *Sociology and the School*, Routledge and Kegan Paul, 1983

6 Work and leisure

There is no greater modern illusion, even fraud, than the use of the single term work to cover what for some is … dreary and painful and for others is socially reputable and economically rewarding.

J. K. Galbraith, The Culture of Contentment, 1992

INTRODUCTION

The chapter begins by looking at definitions of work and leisure. It then goes on to a discussion of the way the founding fathers of sociology viewed work and leisure. The next section goes on to examine sociological theories of worker motivation in the work process, discussing the work of F.W. Taylor, Mayo, Blauner, Goldthorpe and Lockwood, Mallet, Gaillie, and Braverman. The next section goes on to look at the extent and causes of industrial conflict. You will then go on to examine the relationship between gender, ethnicity and work. The future of unemployment is then discussed. Finally, the relationship between work and leisure is explored in detail.

Work, non-work and leisure

Problems of definition   Everyone knows what work is, yet it is a difficult concept to define. There is a similar problem with leisure. It is easy to understand work as paid labour, something you travel to and from – 'going to work' – and leisure as activities undertaken outside of work. The distinction seems clear, but grey areas abound. Is a car worker or plumber at work if they spend a weekend mending their own car or installing their own central heating? Do full-time volunteers or burglars work? Do house-wives work? If you are unemployed and go to a library for something to do, is it leisure-time you are using? Do professional, multi-million-aire golfers play golf as a leisure pursuit, or – even if they give the prize money away – are they still nevertheless working? Are we at leisure when not working, or is there another area of non-work?

Work   In attempting definitions of these terms, many writers suggest that the distinction between work, non-work and leisure will be blurred, as old certainties, such as lifetime employment with one employer, using one set of skills, disappear. Work is frequently thought of as meaning the same as labour and employment, although only the concept of employment implies a social relationship between employer and employee. For this reason, it is more accurate to describe people as unemployed rather than out of work. Both 'work' and 'labour' carry wider connotations, and are thought of as activities necessary for survival.

Leisure The term 'leisure' presents similar difficulties. One of the main writers in this area, Stanley Parker (1983), identifies three broad groups of definitions: the 'residual' type of definition that sees leisure as existing when people are not working, a wider definition that sees leisure as a positive activity, and what he calls the traditional or classical view which emphasises contemplation, enjoyment of self in search of knowledge, debate, politics and cultural enlightenment. Leisure is not necessarily free time. If work is 'time that is not your own' because it is time bought by an employer, client or customer, then time that is your own, non-work time, becomes leisure when it is used positively or creatively. This is still an unsatisfactory definition. What needs to be examined is the quality of the use of work time and leisure time, and the way the two concepts are related.

A work–leisure continuum To heighten these distinctions, Parker describes a continuum where work – 'sold time' – stands at one end, and leisure – 'choosing time' – at the other. In-between are three categories: work-related time or work obligations (such as getting ready for or travelling to work), existence time spent doing things like eating and washing, and the category of non-work obligations or semi-leisure such as gardening or taking the dog for a walk. Even then, these activities are not carried out in isolation or separately: while engaging in primary activities (like eating) we can also listen to the radio as a secondary activity. There are also many people for whom these distinctions are hardly perceivable. Do mothers at home (or, less frequently, fathers), the retired or unemployed, experience work, work obligations, physiological needs, non-work obligations and leisure separately?

Work and leisure have different meanings to those who participate in them, depending on the kind of activities they undertake. Work may be an opportunity to be creative, to use a skill, to have responsibility and mix with people. These, we could say, are its positive functions. Yet work may also bore you to death, restrict your development through alienation and deskilling and be seen as a total waste of time – a waste of a life.

The founding fathers and industrialisation

Durkheim To understand the importance sociologists give to the role of work in society we need first to look at how the founding fathers viewed the changing nature of their own societies. From a functionalist point of view, industrialisation is part of social evolution. The most stable society copes with change yet still holds together. Durkheim characterises these changes as the movement from mechanical solidarity, where there is very little difference between people and the roles they play, to organic solidarity where roles become more specialised and differentiated (see also chapters 1, 7 and 13).

As societies grow larger and more complex, the way in which order is kept – the means of social control – must change to handle the complexities of a highly differentiated division of labour. Industrial society is a web of interdependent relationships, where individuals can only exist through co-operation with others. That this concept of order is tied up with the structure of society reflects the main concerns of functionalism – the generation and maintenance of stability and consensus. Both Durkheim and Herbert Spencer were fascinated by the process of an increasing division of labour, the splitting and fragmentation of work tasks into many smaller ones, and the creation of new tasks and roles in the interests of greater productivity.

Durkheim (1893) was aware, however, that this increasing specialisation brought problems, where some individuals became 'no longer anything but an inert piece of machinery, only an external force set going which always moves in the same direction and in the same way'. The resulting anomie or normlessness was a product of a rapidly changing society. The pace of early industrialisation was rapid, the vast changes brought about by new technology and a new system of social relationships were difficult to keep up with and left individuals feeling lost and helpless in the maze of new social conditions. There were no rules to recognise or follow; order had not yet been created from the chaos. When order did emerge, the social inequalities which had seemed so sharp and brutal, so unfair and cruel, would disappear. Moral regulation would be restored on the lines being established by professional associations. Social inequality would nevertheless remain as 'social inequalities exactly express natural inequalities'.

> **Herbert Spencer (1820–1903)**
> Victorian sociologist and an important figure in evolutionism and social Darwinism. His functionalism influenced structural-functional sociology via Durkheim and Malinowski.

Marx

For Marx, work, production and creativity should be at the centre of life. A fulfilled, satisfying existence involves producing artefacts, food and materials which would be owned and shared by all. The worker would be a fully active part of the productive process, exercising creative powers and feeling ennobled by the work they do.

In his lifetime, though, industrial societies were capitalist societies based on class conflict, exploitation and bourgeois control. One group is oppressed and forced into a life of meaningless activity which has as its end result nothing more than high profits and a luxurious life not for themselves but for the capitalist class. Labour produces marvels, palaces, beauty, technology and skill, but only for the ruling class. The worker shares in none of these but is left with only the world of animal functions to give meaning to existence, concentrating on personal adornment, eating, drinking and sex. Marx welcomed the technological innovations associated with the capitalist mode of production when it overthrew the feudal mode of production, but these technological innovations were misused as a tool of oppression and misery, when they could have been used for the greater benefit of all. The capitalist mode of production produces selfishness and alienation.

Alienation   By alienation Marx meant more than the consequences of the division of labour. He was referring to the way capitalist social relations alienates workers from their creative nature, their 'species-being', whereby the full fruits of their labour are expropriated – effectively stolen – from them, leaving them as wage slaves, less than human, with the capitalist machine crushing the life out of them, allowing no control over what they make or the speed and technique with which they make it. Selfishness and alienation are a product of the capitalist mode of production, not innate human qualities: 'The mode of production of material life determines the general character of the social, political and spiritual processes of life. It is not the consciousness of men that determines their being, but on the contrary, their social being determines their consciousness' (Marx, 1859). The only resolution to this situation was for the workers to take control of the means of production for themselves.

Although Marx and Durkheim considered the same social structures, they reached very different conclusions about how these large and mysterious systems worked. This reflects the power of theoretical concepts in determining the nature of social exploration. The two theorists began from a different set of assumptions about the basis of society, social order and social change.

Criticisms   If developments in capitalist social relations may not have proved Marx correct, many Marxists, amongst others, would argue that Durkheim's idealistic and optimistic version of industrial society based on a consensus over morals and natural inequality has not materialised either. The functionalist view of social change is of a slow, steady progress towards a system based on co-operation and shared values, the collective conscience which binds all together. This assertion has been extensively discussed in the debate about embourgeoisement (see chapter 3).

QUESTIONS

1 **What does Marx mean by the term 'alienation'?**

2 **What is meant by the 'division of labour'?**

Worker motivation and the experience of work

Sociologists of work have been interested in how technology, work organisation, class conflict and the profit motive have contributed to workers' experience of work and notions of job satisfaction or alienation. Their stance on these issues, and the theoretical assumptions behind them, have created a substantial and rich body of writing, which has also made an important and distinct contribution to the study of methodology in sociology.

Taylor

Scientific management

In the first decades of the twentieth century two models of work motivation caused considerable debate within sociology. The publication in 1911 of F.W. Taylor's *Principles of Scientific Management* led to new methods of work organisation which were eventually to spread across the world. As a management consultant in the USA, Taylor was interested in the question of maximising worker output and efficiency, and overcoming the phenomenon of 'goldbricking' or 'soldiering', where workers conspire to slow down the rate of production in order to keep their rates of pay high.

His answer to this was to remove control from the workers and transfer it instead to a management layer. This could be achieved by, firstly, greater division of labour whereby each work task would be reduced to its simplest form. This would remove any notion of skill from the tasks the workers would be required to do and allow individual work tasks to be carried out more quickly. Secondly, managers would control the pace of production and control the production process. Thirdly, time and motion studies would allow cost accounting and individual targets to be set. In advocating the adoption of these principles, Taylor took a monetary view of worker motivation, believing that they will trade interest and satisfaction in their work for the higher economic rewards that would result from greater productivity, not only from higher wages but also possibly from profit sharing.

Taylor's ideas were taken up and developed most widely by the car manufacturer Henry Ford, who between 1908 and 1914 introduced mechanised mass production and the assembly line, with each worker being asked to undertake a specific simple and repetitive work task for the then (1914) high wage of $5 per day. This was

> **F.W. Taylor (1856–1915)**
> *'Taylorism' is often used as another term for scientific management. Taylor was a consultant at the Bethlehem steel works in the USA where he conducted his experiments into improving productivity of workers. He believed that management should organise the production process to make it efficient and that workers should be given the incentive of wages paid in relation to the level of their productive output.*

brought in, however, partly to combat absenteeism. The spread of this work organisation around the world, creating a new level of management responsibility, is known as 'global Fordism', characterised by mass production of a few types of commodity. It has also meant that the car industry has been the subject of considerable interest to sociologists throughout the twentieth century, particularly theorists of the 'labour process approach'.

Mayo

The 'Hawthorne effect'

> **Elton Mayo (1880–1949)**
> *Australian-American social anthropologist who greatly influenced managerial practices world-wide. Mayo tried to counter the ethics of the school of scientific management. He argued that workers needed more than economic incentives to make them work hard. It is the task of management to apply sociological principles to the study of work to understand how to overcome the alienation of workers from the co-operative work processes.*

The second school of work-motivation studies also emerged out of attempts to increase productivity. This was the Hawthorne studies carried out by an American sociologist, Professor George Elton Mayo, between 1927 and 1932. He wanted to find out why there was so much grumbling and dissatisfaction among the 30,000 employees at the Hawthorne Works of the Western Electric Company in Chicago. His original idea was to attempt to increase productivity by playing with the light switches. He took one group and increased the intensity of illumination, measuring the expected increase in their productivity levels. However, the group who had been left in the dark had been working harder as well. They then reduced the illumination for the group who had a taste of the bright lights, and found that this made them work even harder. So the lighting was not the important factor, but something was encouraging these employees to get their noses to the grindstone.

Further research involved a five-year programme with a selected group of female workers, whose output was recorded, and who were involved in all the details of the observation. They were put through a complex series of shift and work changes: one break, two breaks, a break plus free meal, early finishing times, all of which produced changes in output, which mostly increased. For example, when they left at 4.30 p.m. instead of 5 p.m. output went up, but when this was changed to 4 p.m. output stayed the same. The largest increase was recorded when the women were put back on normal working conditions: no breaks, Saturday work and no free meals or early leaving. When the women had been working under these conditions before the research they had produced 24,000 relays (an electronic part) per week. When they were returned to exactly the same conditions after all the research, this had gone up to 30,000 a week, the highest ever recorded.

It seems difficult to believe that during the five years that this went on for, the researchers were not aware that the main factor affecting output was *their presence*, and this has become the standard criticism of observation as a research method – the 'reactivity' of the subjects, i.e.

181

their response to being observed. Could the involvement of the workers in both pieces of research have heightened their sense of importance, their interest in work and their job satisfaction? It could be claimed that it was this new sense of actually being involved with something meaningful that decreased the workers' sense of alienation. It certainly shows how problematic this kind of research can be.

The importance of the Hawthorne studies for sociologists and theorists of industrial relations is that they showed a different dimension to worker motivation, particularly that productivity is as much affected by the amount of interest shown in the work done as any other factor, and that informal interactions between workers are important to production norms. The findings of what became the human relations school point to significant other factors than financial motivation, such as psychological needs, in understanding worker motivation.

QUESTIONS

1 **What is meant by Taylorism? What would be the advantages and disadvantages of employing it?**

2 **What are the most important factors in increasing workers' productivity? How important is money?**

3 **What is meant by the 'Hawthorne effect'?**

Blauner

Blauner's (1964) study is famous for attempting an operational or working model of the alienation concept. However, he annoys Marxists by rejecting the Marxist viewpoint, as Blauner claims that alienation is not a product of class position in capitalism. For him, it is the nature of the work and the type of technology which are important. He provides a watered-down version of the concept of alienation, reducing it to a variety of work satisfaction as measured by workers' attitudes.

Alienation exists, he says, 'when workers are unable to control their immediate work processes, to develop a sense of purpose and function which connects their jobs to the overall organisation of production, to belong to integrated industrial communities, and when they fail to become involved in the activity of work as a mode of personal self-expression'.

He first split the concept into four separate, measurable segments, taken from M. Seeman (1959):

1 *Powerlessness*: Do workers feel that they have any control over their work? Do they feel that they have some power in the work situa-

tion, that they contribute to decisions? Or are they powerless, unable to contribute anything other than labour?

2 *Meaninglessness*: Does work mean anything to those involved in it? Do they approach the factory gates in eager anticipation of tasks which give them a sense of purpose? Or is work meaningless, boring, repetitive, with no point at all other than earning money?

3 *Isolation*: Do workers feel an accepted part of society? Does the job have high or low social status? Do they have the respect of others? Another aspect of this is whether workers are socially integrated at work or isolated individuals, restricted in communication with their fellow workers by the disciplines of the shop floor and working process. A high degree of isolation would encourage alienation.

4 *Self-estrangement*: Are the workers involved in their work, or do they cut themselves off, dream of other things, divorcing themselves from their actions, becoming like robots, automatic and unthinking, concentrating on the next tea-break, smoke-break and so on?

Measuring alienation

If all of the above are present to a high degree, then Blauner would claim that alienation exists. As mentioned above, the cause of alienation lies not in capitalist class relations but in the level of technology. Attitudes to work and job satisfaction depend upon how highly skilled the job is. Does it take skill or is it a matter of pulling levers and pushing buttons? To test out these ideas, Blauner looked at work methods in different types of industry and tried to measure and compare levels of alienation. Each industry is an example of a different technological method (*see Figure 6.1*).

Printing

The printing industry was used as an example of 'craft industry' – this was in the days of typesetting by hand, which is now being rapidly replaced by electronic publishing. Skill, judgement and initiative were an integral part of the job. The division of labour was low, as the job was not split up into smaller tasks using specialised skills. Each worker was highly skilled and worked on their own initiative. There was a high demand for this work, leading to job security, a strong union and high wages. Their sense of powerlessness was low because they had a high degree of control over the work process and conditions. The meaninglessness levels were also low, as the workers had knowledge of the whole process and each product was unique and individual. Their sense of isolation was similarly low, printing being a well-respected skilled trade. The social community provided in the mainly small, decentralised workshops meant high integration within the workplace too, unlike the case of the Ford workers quoted above. All this obviously means that their self-estrangement is low, as the traditional, highly skilled work brings with it a sense of identification and intrinsic satisfaction. The questionnaires Blauner used show that this particular craft had the highest level of job satisfaction. Automation has brought a deskilling of printing, and levels of satisfaction may have changed.

Mass production

The second area of industry examined by Blauner was 'mass production'. This means the mechanisation of crafts such as weaving and textiles, with a high division of labour where tasks are reduced to simplicity, e.g. machine-minding. Such industries are characterised by labour intensiveness, poor job security, and the use of a lot of employees at the lowest-paid end of the labour market such as ethnic minorities and women. The tasks are routine, paced by machines and strictly supervised. The powerlessness is high, with control out of the workers' hands entirely – the machine has the power; you have to stand in the same place all day and cater to its every whim. The textile worker and others who experience similar working conditions should feel the meaninglessness and isolation at its highest pitch, but, he found, they do not. Their lives are given meaning by their community, a traditional tight-knit social group. The boring jobs and low pay are overridden by loyalty to the company and social network. Self-estrangement is high though, as there is little involvement with the actual work. For the large numbers of women in the industry there may have been social pressures and 'role-strain', with conflicting ideas created by sexist ideologies concerning childcare and housework. For these women, the social integration within the factory must have provided relief from the boredom and arduousness of being a housewife, but it did not mean they loved the actual work involved. In this case, influences outside, from the traditional community, counteract the alienating consequences of technology and the boring, meaningless activity which occupies most waking hours.

Assembly work

The 'assembly line' has the highest levels of alienation, with no community life as a substitute. There is no control, as the line determines the speed of work entirely. The worker does not have to move, and the supervision is absolute. The work is routine, standardised and social isolation is high. Workers are not integrated at work, nor do they have a high standing in the eyes of society – no tradition or skill, just high wages and a media-led reputation for laziness. Powerlessness, meaninglessness and isolation are at an all-time high then, and the self-estrangement scaled similar heights. Workers were hostile to the work, and only put themselves through it for the pay –

a purely instrumental attitude. The shifting communities of workers, moving to where the work was, with high lay-off rates and low job security meant that there was social alienation and no traditional occupational community. This is Goldthorpe's privatised worker and Willmott and Young's symmetrical family, drawing the curtains and shutting out the dull reality of their lives, taking comfort from all the things advertised on the TV which they can afford, replacing their estrangement from themselves with a commitment to consumerism.

Figure 6.1 Technology and alienation

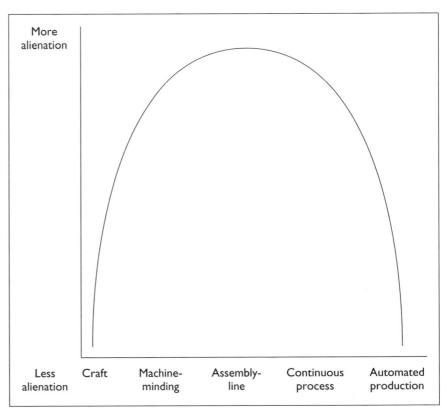

Source: adapted from R. Blauner, Alienation and Freedom (1964).

Continuous process technology

However, the U-curve in job alienation, low in pre-mechanisation and at its highest with assembly-line technology, turns back down when the results of the automation–continuous process technology are examined. Blauner's examples of this are the oil and chemical industries. The trend towards alienation is reversed, and control, integration and involvement are restored to the worker. The division of labour is low as each worker is a highly skilled, responsible team member. Powerlessness and meaninglessness are low, as operators have control, monitoring dials, gauges, using initiative and working with others. They have a knowledge of the whole process, and can re-train in other jobs within the plant. The social integration is high within the workplace populated by highly satisfied workers with good promotion chances. This compensates for the lack of traditional status, and self-estrangement is also low, as the work is found satisfying.

Consensus In examining these areas, Blauner has identified important variables relating to job satisfaction: the division of labour, the social organisation of the industry and the economic structure within which they operate. However, the overriding factor for Blauner is the type of technology employed. His conclusions were that automation in industry will bring alienation at work to an end. There will be consensus, consultation and co-operation between management and worker, instead of conflict and control. Loyalty to the firm will mean that the worker in automated industry will be middle class in out-

Automated production: the end of alienation at work?

look and status. Blauner's optimistic conclusion has been criticised in a number of ways. Research carried out by other sociologists does not support Blauner, particularly that of Goldthorpe and Lockwood, who found that attitudes and behaviour relating to work were little influenced by technology.

Blauner is aware of the shortcomings of his methodology, which is mainly based not on his own work but on a study by Elmo Roper in 1947, carried out over twenty years before the publication of Blauner's book. This was a questionnaire given to 118 printing workers, 419 textile workers, 180 automobile workers and 78 chemical workers, chosen as a quota sample. Blauner's own research was based on interviews with 21 randomly chosen chemical plant workers, as well as a limited amount of observation in the same industry. He is well aware of the problems of generalising these data in order to reach any meaningful conclusions about alienation at work, commenting that the industries he investigated cover only three million of the US workforce, and that it would be impossible to characterise industries such as iron and steel as based on craft, machine-tending, assembly-line or continuous process technology.

Goldthorpe and Lockwood

Goldthorpe and Lockwood (see also chapter 3) used a social action approach to investigate 'affluent' workers. They found the same pattern of job satisfaction as Blauner, with skilled maintenance workers enjoying their jobs more than machinists and assemblers. Their findings show that workers had very similar attitudes to work, despite the technology used. They all had 'instrumental' attitudes to work: work is only performed for pay – extrinsic as opposed to intrinsic motivation. As all workers had this attitude, Goldthorpe and Lockwood claim that this orientation to work was brought to work, not created there. Loyalty to the firm can be found anywhere, as long as pay is high. A decrease in wages leads to a downturn in loyalty. Goldthorpe and Lockwood claimed that the process workers, whom Blauner claimed would be highly satisfied, were the most likely to be critical and hostile. Goldthorpe and Lockwood conclude that this is due to the fact that their pay was lower than that of assembly-line workers. Work companionship was also much less likely amongst the process workers.

Critics of Goldthorpe and Lockwood have pointed out that their sample was not representative: it consisted of married men between the ages of 21 and 46, 86 per cent of whom had dependent children, in a town of migrant workers, whose high geographical mobility was caused by moving specifically for the high wages. A high percentage of these affluent workers were downwardly mobile in social terms, possibly from skilled manual workers. In Goldthorpe and Lockwood's study then, there was no support for Blauner's argument that automation will lead to a decrease in alienation.

Mallet

Integration and conflict

Serge Mallet (1963), a French Marxist, does agree with Blauner on this point, believing that greater integration of workers will be a result of increased automation. However, as a Marxist he sees this increased integration amongst workers as helping them develop a political consciousness and realising their common position of conflict with management and owners. Automation will encourage the proletariat to become a 'class-in-itself'. The workers in automated industry will become the leaders of class struggle. However, the main criticism of Mallet's ideas is that he does not give details of any research to support them.

Gallie

Blauner revisited

Duncan Gallie (1978) has studied the effects of automation in four automated oil refineries, two in France and two in Britain. One of his reasons for carrying out this work was his questioning of the methodology of both Blauner and Mallet. Studying the same industry in two different countries enabled him to assess the effects of technology independent of national or regional factors. Different cultural attitudes should not interfere with the findings.

This research found little support for either Blauner or Mallet. Gallie concludes that automation on its own has no effects. There were many differences in attitude between French and British workers, and these could be traced back to historical and cultural differences. A theory which claims that technology on its own can affect job satisfaction ignores the cultural context in which the industry exists. This cultural context is much more influential than the method of production. The most common attitude to work was indifference and this existed in both countries. Workers received similarly high wages, but the British were satisfied with this whilst the French were not. Gallie found a higher level of co-operation and consensus between British workers and management, with antagonism and conflict marking that relationship in the French refineries. Gallie concludes that these differences in job satisfaction are due to the French working class being more committed to socialist values than the British. French management was more autocratic and paternalistic than the British, which led to conflict with the workforce. The role of trade unions was also different, with the French unions taking a left-wing, ideological role, while the British unions were concerned with pay and conditions rather than overthrowing capitalist society.

From these studies, it becomes apparent that attempting to measure job satisfaction and alienation is full of methodological problems. To concentrate on a single factor, such as technology, and ignore the social and cultural context, and other non-technological factors like age, gender, pay and job security may lead to a distorted picture of workers' attitudes to work.

However, there are some factors within the workplace which affect these attitudes:

- where work is controlled by machines
- where the task is fragmented
- where the task is repetitive
- where the work is unskilled and needs little training
- where the workers are isolated

There also seems to be a trend towards higher levels of satisfaction in manual jobs as they become automated, while those in the professions may become more dissatisfied as their jobs become automated and bureaucratised.

QUESTIONS

1 **What factors are thought to result in alienation at work?**

2 **What methodological problems are involved in the study of job satisfaction and alienation?**

3 **How is technology related to the experience of work?**

Braverman

The American Marxist, Harry Braverman (1974), describes what he believes are the consequences of an ever-increasing division of labour under developed capitalism. Capitalism is geared towards the pursuit of profit, not towards the attainment of consensus or social solidarity, as functionalism proposes. A consequence of this need to maximise profits is the general and progressive deskilling of jobs. As we have already seen, capitalists have been aware of the advantages of an ever-increasing division of labour for centuries, particularly because fragmentation can lead to huge increases in productivity— output per person. The logical result is total automation of everything – factories, petrol stations, railway lines, food and drink dispensers and hotels. This necessarily involves a devaluing and downgrading of human skills, often ending in redundancy. Humans are a by-product, so much so that job-loss is referred to as 'natural wastage'.

According to Braverman, the resulting increase of routine mechanical work, simple and monotonous, will cut down the barriers within the working class. Crafts which in the past enjoyed status and respectability, through skill and high wages, have gradually disappeared with mechanisation and automation, as in the printing industry. The high hopes held out for the morale-boosting team work in the process industries are unfounded. The working class melts into one big, semi-skilled, homogeneous group, with similar pay and boredom levels. Braverman challenges the view that skill levels have increased. The end result of this deskilling would see an end to distinctions between manual and non-manual work, between the traditional and new working class, because some skills would disappear and technology would mean a levelling of skills. This not only increases profits, but it also increases control. Capital cannot rely on its workers, due to the conflict of interests, so control is vital.

Control of labour

Theories of management, as in Taylor's 'scientific management', recognise the need for managers to monopolise 'brain work'. They conceive of and plan the ideas, while workers, under strict control, execute them. The more separate these two areas, the more efficient. New machine technology will incorporate this control, as the machine decides on time and motion. Control of labour is therefore more easily achieved given this technology, but it is always a vital part of capitalism, and as such, control of labour is independent of technology.

Criticisms of Braverman

Braverman's thesis has been criticised on a number of points. The first is that he gives us a picture of an inert, passive workforce, which does not fight back against management control. He neglects trade-unionist class consciousness and worker resistance to management. He also assumes that all managers will adopt scientific management techniques. This is not always the case, and some management strategies are designed to give workers some autonomy in their work situation. In making these sweeping assumptions, Braverman depicts a homogeneous, lifeless working class, rendered helpless through deskilling. There is no reference to differences within the working class, except a somewhat romantic view of the skilled artisan of the past. There is no historical analysis of the social conditions of craftworkers and therefore no comparison between their lives and those of deskilled workers in late capitalism. Braverman has uncritically adopted the myth of the 'golden age' of craftworkers, living in cosy, productive family units. He is also accused of using an individualistic, task-centred idea of skill and the labour process, thinking in terms of the individual manager's 'conceptions' and individual worker's 'executions'. Labour is reorganised, as a result not of class struggle, the key Marxist assumption, but of managerial design. An important point here is that although Taylorism takes capitalist control to its logical conclusion, management has always had control in its hands. The control brought about by deskilling and Taylorist methods is simply a new and stricter form of capitalist control. Other factors which play a part in the production process are the size and availability of labour markets – workers have more power when they are in scarce supply. Trade-unionism and politics are also important, but again, ignored by Braverman. Furthermore, he has also been criticised for over-estimating the extent to which Taylorism has been taken up, and not appreciating that many new jobs require as much or more skill than the jobs which have disappeared.

Methods of control

Taylor's views on how to increase efficiency in production centre around the process and the product, not the producer. High output for low cost was the goal. Workers were to be given no part in the planning, leaving them free to put all their efforts into the execution of management's plans and were to be selected for their strength, skill, disposition, and those best suited to the task got the job. One problem was social integration in the workplace. A way of stopping it was to cut any movement on the shop floor to a minimum. Henry Ford once boasted of the numbers of disabled people who could be employed on the assembly line. He was not a champion of disabled people but was pointing out that some jobs on the line only needed one arm. The immobility of workers cuts down on the amount of time spent drifting around the factory avoiding work. The compensation for all this – the motivation – is extrinsic: money. It is this brand of management which Braverman sees as uniting the working classes in dissatisfaction.

Beynon

Working for Ford

Beynon's (1973) research argues that informal social groups can create a sense of identity and purpose even in situations where there is a detailed division of labour. In the Ford factory where Beynon's study was carried out, workers were well aware of management's attitudes, and much bitter, shop-floor humour deals with the role of being 'another machine'. In one factory, the standing joke was a tale of a worker who had dropped dead on the line, and the first thing the foreman did was to 'clock him out', ensuring that he would not be paid for any minutes after he had died. Beynon points out that the fact that 'the line never stops' becomes something to be challenged, beaten in various ways. They have to keep up with it, or better still, get ahead of it and have a laugh or half a fag. The line determines pace, and the worker who cannot keep up with it is sacked. Beynon's research shows the attitude of workers to the 'timings':

> *They decide on their measured day how fast we will work. They seem to forget that we're not machines, you know. The standards they work to are excessive anyway. They expect you to work the 480 minutes of the eight hours you're on the clock. They've agreed to a built-in allowance of six minutes for going to the toilet, blowing your nose and that. It takes you six minutes to get your trousers down.*

The speed-up process Beynon found that the main enemy of the workers was the 'speed-up' process. This means a systematic increase in the pace of work demanded by the line. Speed up the line, and the workers adjust their pace, working faster, sometimes without being aware of it. 'Making time' – getting a few sections ahead then taking a break – becomes more difficult, and the worker is suspicious. When he started work, the line speed was 30 cars per hour, he left with it moving at 35 cars per hour. So, the workers devise strategies to deal with this, again showing the importance of informal group norms in the workplace. The most effective response is walking out.

> *The lads said 'sod you', we're not doing it. It worked as good as anything else you know. We just said no, and if they pushed it, we just went home.*

Forms of resistance Walk-outs did not always happen, there were other methods available: sabotage of machinery, pulling the safety wire and stopping the line, deliberately doing a bad job so the work was sent back. Beynon sees this as workers defending the last remaining part of their autonomy to control. These methods are used in other jobs. Ditton's (1977) research into bread delivery drivers shows that they resort to 'fiddling' the books, adding extra on to people's bills. Informal norms control the fiddling, ensuring that it does not go too far (for example, it was not fair to 'do' old people). Crusting up stale loaves so they feel fresh through the wrapper and selling them as fresh improves the delivery driver's income and avoids boredom – it's a laugh!

Braverman accuses social science studies of bias towards management, seeing workers as a 'problem' if they use these methods of resistance. Deskilling, speeding up the line and strict supervision all threaten workers' dignity, pride, independence and privacy. These are valuable things, and protecting them is a rational act.

The human relations response

Volvo The human relations model tries to take account of these ideas (see also chapter 7). Poor industrial relations are said to be the result of poor communication between management, poor group cohesion and overall weak management. In the human relations model, there is less attention paid to conflicts of interest, and more stress upon harmony and equilibrium. An example of this model in practice is the Volvo car assembly plant at Kalmar, Sweden. In the mid 1970s Volvo attempted to change the nature of assembly-line production from the workers' viewpoint. Jobs would be meaningful and interesting. Technology would not be allowed to set the pace or influence discipline. Volvo turned to the new methods because they had to — workers were definitely not attracted to the car plants, with high absenteeism and people quitting their jobs.

Attitudes to work have changed because people are more informed, more likely to ask questions, and need to understand the reasons behind what they are doing. More rights have been given to unions, there is more control over factors such as lighting, heating, ventilation, and the right to call a halt if there is potential danger. Rules regarding sickness leave and pay are more relaxed. Work has to be made as rewarding as possible with team work, job rotation, talking on the job, in short the 'small workshop atmosphere'. The belt, with all of its connotations of pace-setting and technological control, has been replaced by computer-controlled trolleys, which carry parts around the plant. The workers have been given rest rooms, fridges and saunas, toilets, showers, fitted carpets in the coffee rooms. The human relations model seems to be flourishing there, but the fact that absenteeism is still high (around 12 per cent) shows that workers are not all that keen to get involved in this way. Critics say that it is the nature of Swedish society which forced these changes. From a Marxist viewpoint, the workers are still there to make profits for the employer and are exploited because the full value of their labour is not paid for. The 'softer' management methods are just a new facet of ruling class ideology.

QUESTIONS

1 Why does Braverman suggest that capitalists want to deskill the work process?

2 What would be the effect on the working class of making them a semi-skilled, homogenous group?

3 Can you think of any ways that workers might gain control of the work process?

4 Is it possible for management to structure the work process so that workers are not exploited?

The future of work

Braverman's ideas have certainly been influential and his work remains controversial. More recent writers have analysed work and the labour process in a similar way, for example Harley Shaiken (1986) and David Noble (1984) who both argue that Taylorism (or Fordism as it is sometimes called) lives on.

Fordism

Other writers are less sure, believing that the 'Fordist' age is being superseded by 'post-Fordism'. Fordism means mass production techniques using machines and labour trained to undertake only one task where the workforce works with relative job security in a hierarchically structured organisation, collectively negotiating their wages and producing goods for a mass market. The epitome of this was the assembly-line method of car production pioneered by Henry Ford, symbolised by his statement on consumer choice: 'You can have any colour you like, as long as it's black.'

Post-Fordism

Post-Fordism, sometimes called 'flexible accumulation' or neo-Fordism, is the pattern for the future, based on projecting currently observable trends. Here, there is less job security for those outside the 'core' of the employment market as many companies will sub-contract others to undertake specific tasks for specific markets (batch production and niche marketing), using micro-electronically controlled multi-purpose machines. Cheap mass-produced products will be less popular, as higher quality products appeal to more discerning consumers. Workers will increasingly work in groups or on their own, possessing more skills than before, and being paid on their individual performance. The four areas of change are therefore the labour process, workers' contracts, the goods produced and the technology involved in producing them. The key concept is flexibility, and these trends are the most observable in the most advanced capitalist economies.

Factories are not only becoming smaller, but the number of people working in them is also shrinking, with only 300 factories employing more than 1,000 people. British manufacturing produced approximately the same amount of goods in the late 1980s as it did in the early 1970s – with about two million less workers. In the 1980s, for the first time in British industrial history, the number of workers employed in non-manual work overtook those doing manual work, rising from 37.5 per cent in 1961 to 52 per cent in 1984.

Whether Fordism is no longer a dominant influence in the world of work depends on views of how far it was considered to have spread in the first place and how successfully it has been superseded by other practices. Alain Lipietz (1993) sees the New Right policies of British and North American political and industrial leaders in the 1980s as intensifying rather than replacing Fordism, failing to successfully transplant Far-Eastern ideas of work organisation such as 'just in time', 'continuous improvement' and 'total quality man-

---

FORDISM AND POST-FORDISM

Fordism	Post-Fordism
Economy, competition and production process	
Protected national markets	Global competition
Mass production of standardised products	Flexible production systems/small batch/niche markets
Bureaucratic hierarchical organisations	Flatter and flexible organisational structures
Compete by full capacity utilisation and cost-cutting	Compete by innovation, diversification, sub-contracting
Labour	
Fragmented and standardised work tasks	Flexible specialisation/multi-skilled workers
Low trust/low discretion, majority employed in manufacturing sector/blue-collar jobs	High trust/high discretion, majority employed in service sector/white-collar jobs
Little on-the-job training, little formal training required for most jobs	Regular on-the-job training, greater demand for knowledgeable workers
Small managerial and professional élite	Growing managerial and professional service class
Fairly predictable labour-market histories	Unpredictable labour-market histories due to technological change and increased economic uncertainty
Politics and ideology	
Trade-union solidarity	Decline in trade-union solidarity
Class-based political affiliation	Declining significance of class-based politics
Importance of locality/class/gender-based lifestyles	Fragmentation and pluralism, global village
Mass consumption of consumer durables	Individualised consumer choice

---

agement'. The resistance to this new culture, he argues, has contributed to the West's economic decline.

One key indicator of the demise of Taylorist thinking would be the disappearance of the idea of work-task design based on a separation of thinking from doing. It is argued, however, that the emergence of practices such as 'multi-skilling' do not overcome this duality as they mean only that the number of tasks a worker can be expected to undertake has increased, not that the work tasks themselves have become enlarged.

Many writers now argue that the traditional focus on manual work is now out of date, and that the focus for sociologists of work should move to the service sector, where diverse forms such as job-splitting, job-sharing, self-employment, part-time working, temping, agency work, flexi-working, contract working, home-working and telecommuting need to be examined.

New technology Doubt exists as to whether new office-based technology, such as computers, demands 'enskilling' and 'reskilling' (Straussman, 1985) of workers or 'deskilling' (Shaiken, 1986). Other writers such as Kling (1991) argue that demands on skill are dependent on the type

195

of technology used. New technology can also be used, he argues, to enhance the image of an organisation as efficient, competent and rational, whether it is or not, as these are difficult to measure. In clerical work, Baran (1988) argues that multi-activity jobs in insurance where 'work has been electronically reintegrated' are 'not necessarily translating into greater autonomy or task variety on the job: on the contrary, numerous workers may be much more closely supervised'. In these new fields, it is still possible to detect the dead hand of Taylor at work.

QUESTIONS

1 **In what ways may work change in the future?**

2 **What evidence is there to suggest that we live in a post-Fordist era?**

3 **How would you characterise the labour process of a fast food outlet?**

The extent of industrial conflict

Strike statistics

Official strike statistics provide some basic data on industrial conflict. As with all statistics, interpreting what they mean involves an understanding of how they are collected. The figures are collected by the Department of Employment, and include only strikes which lasted more than one day and involved more than ten workers. Calculations of how many workers are involved in the strike may be misleading because of the difficulties of knowing who actively supports the strike and who has been laid off as a consequence of the strike. The statistics similarly do not reveal how many workers in other industries have been made idle as a result of a strike elsewhere. Nor is it possible to know how many days were lost per striker, because some workers may make up the time afterwards, or may return to work during the strike. One strike may cause massive distortion to the statistics, for example the 27,135,000 days lost in 1984 which were largely due to the year-long conflict between the National Union of Mineworkers and the National Coal Board (British Coal) (*see Figure 6.2*).

Strikes as a social problem

Moreoever, focusing on strikes reveals only one aspect of industrial conflict: some industries may be strike-free but have high rates of absenteeism or labour turnover. A strike involves conscious, collective action, it is 'a temporary stoppage of work by a group of employees in order to express a grievance or enforce a demand' (Griffin, 1939). Losses of production because people either do not turn up to work or walk out on the job because they hate the way they are dehumanised by work are less-discussed forms of grievance, but no less a problem for management. It may be the case that more days are lost through workers having bad backs than being on strike.

Figure 6.2 Labour disputes: working days lost, 1971–93

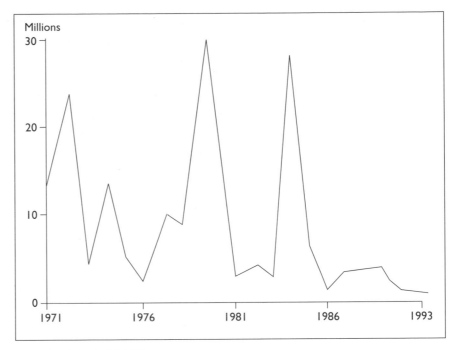

Source: Social Trends 25, 1995

Similarly, some writers, such as Hyman (1972), see strikes as only one side of a structural problem. Focusing on strikes avoids looking at how employers use their power. For 'as well as the lock-out, conflict with the employee can take the form of plant closure, sackings, victimization, blacklisting, speed-up, safety hazards, arbitrary discipline, and so on. The routine practices of employers do not count as "industrial conflict"; they are part of the normal, repressive reality of work.' The main area of industrial conflict studied by sociologists is nevertheless the strike.

Two questions need to be asked: Why do strikes happen at all? Why are some industries more prone to strikes than others? In many ways, some sociologists see these as the same question, arguing that strikes are a product of the wider social structure and the conflict between labour and capital in general, and the organisation of the labour process in particular. A number of causes of strikes have been suggested, and the parts played by 'agitators', communications, community integration, technology and the system of industrial relations have all been examined.

Agitation   Management and the media frequently refer to shop stewards as 'agitators' but this has been given little credence by social scientists, largely because shop stewards are elected officials, and represent the opinion of the members who elected them, and also because they cannot agitate successfully without there being widespread grievances in the first place. It is also observed that trade union officials, including shop stewards, are just as often involved in preventing strikes as they are in fomenting them.

Communication   Poor communication between management and workforce has received more critical attention, particularly from those writers working within the human relations tradition. Scott and Homans (1947), looking at wartime Detroit, then centre of the American car industry, and W. H. Whyte (1951) see strikes as caused by the fact that workers and management simply do not talk to each other enough: 'In the long run a number of strikes seemed to stem from faulty communication' (Scott and Homans, 1947). The key problem of this approach is that it does not adequately explain why some industries appear to be more strike-prone than others. It could also be the case that more information, for example concerning planned redundancies, management salaries or profit margins, could lead to more strikes, not less.

Integration   The industries that have been most strike-prone in the industrial West in the twentieth century have been those that are at the heart of industrial development, particularly mining, shipbuilding, dock-work, iron and steel and motor-vehicle manufacture (*see Table* 6.1). Kerr (1964) argues that strikes in these industries reflect the employees' high degree of integration as workers with 'their own codes, myths, heroes, and social standards', with a relatively low level of integration into the wider community. Concomitantly, workers who are less likely to strike will be more closely integrated into the wider community.

TABLE 6.1   Some strike-prone British industries: annual averages

| | STRIKES PER 100,000 EMPLOYEES | | | | STRIKER-DAYS PER 100 EMPLOYEES | | | |
	1966–70	1971–5	1976–9	1980–2	1966–70	1971–5	1976–9	1980–2
Docks	140	154	126	93	286	401	126	214
Coal-mining	67	67	100	124	109	1,056	38	94
Motor vehicles	51	44	41	36	206	359	1,812	166
Shipbuilding	50	41	23	19	110	320	96	119
Iron and steel	31	38	33	13	65	114	119	1,030
All industries and services	12	11	10	6	24	59	57	32

Source: Hyman, Strikes, 4th edn, 1991

Technology   Technology is also believed to play a major role in determining the character of industrial relations. This point is argued by three writers: Woodward (1958), Kuhn (1961) and Sayles (1958). For Kuhn the key point is the extent to which the organisation of technology allows what he calls 'fractional bargaining', that is, *ad hoc* bargaining outside institutional structures such as trade unions. New technology, he says, gives rise to 'regular changes in work methods, standards or materials; the opportunity for considerable interaction between workers; the grouping of the labour force into a number of roughly equal departments; and the sequential processing of materials into a single end product.'

Criticisms   The problem with such explanations, as many of the authors are aware, is that they veer towards monocausality and technological determinism, and do not take into account wider influences on behaviour. To broaden the picture, Dunlop (1958) describes an 'industrial relations system' of workers and their organisations, managers and their organisations and governmental agencies all concerned with the work-place and work community. Further variables on behaviour are technology, market and budgetary constraints, and wider power relations. Collectively, he says, these factors create 'an ideology or a commonly shared body of ideas and beliefs regarding the interaction and roles of the actors which helps to bind the system'. It is the culture of such a system that encourages or discourages the development of strikes.

Such explanations clearly have their roots in structuralist explanations informed by a positivist philosophy. For Eldridge (1968), any analysis of industrial conflict must examine 'the interaction of cultural, economic and organisational factors'. Within this interaction, it is necessary to perceive how the situation is seen and defined by the actors, as well as understanding the goals and motives they bring to the situation.

This point is neatly made in an influential British study by Goldthorpe et al. (1968): 'The attempt to provide explanations from the point of view of the "system" entails the neglect of the point of view of the actors involved … The orientation which workers have to employment and the manner, thus, in which they define their work situation can be regarded as mediating between features of the work situation objectively considered and the nature of the workers' response.' This study reveals, for example, different attitudes to absenteeism in mining and the steel industry. Amongst miners it was seen as acceptable to take a day off; however, this was frowned upon by steel workers.

Similarly, there may be differing definitions of how to use the strike – as a weapon of the first or last resort, for example, partly depending on how seriously management will take threats of strike action. For Hyman (1972), 'the meanings attributed to a strike will vary so much between situations where stoppages are routine and those where they are unprecedented that it is unhelpful to define it as the same action in both cases. Where the significance of their action is so differently regarded by the strikers themselves, the precipitating causes are likely to be similarly distinctive.' Once again, the interplay between social structure and social action is central to the understanding of social phenomena.

Other forms of action

Although strikes are the most documented form of industrial conflict, they are not the most representative. Most workers strike rarely, if at all. According to Clegg (1979), 'there can be little doubt that the overtime ban is now the most common form of industrial action'. The phenomenon of the strike may be in decline. As we have seen, the most strike-prone industries, involving heavy manual labour, are themselves shrinking in Great Britain, and many of their former workers are now unemployed. Also trade-union membership has been in decline over the same period. Moreover, a series of laws in the 1980s weakened the position of trade-unionists and the ability to strike. It may well be that, in the twenty-first century, the focus of industrial action will move away from manual labour and the strike, and more towards non-manual labour and other forms of industrial action. For Hyman, there is nevertheless always 'the inevitability of industrial conflict in a society in which the main purpose of industry is profit, and in which the relationship between employers and workers is dominated by the drive to extract surplus value from the labour of men and women'.

QUESTIONS

1 **What forms of industrial action can be taken?**

2 **How do structuralist and interactionist views of industrial conflict differ?**

3 **Why are some industries more prone to strikes than others?**

Women and work

Women have always occupied a disadvantaged position in the labour market, having been increasingly excluded from it throughout the nineteenth century, to a point where, as Ann Oakley (1974a) shows, it was seen as natural that a woman's place was in the home. The law backed the rights of employers not to employ women or to pay them less money than men for the same work. Indeed, the 1842 Mines Act, which bans women from underground work in mines, is still in force. In both world wars, women were sucked into the labour force and immediately thrown out again when men returned to reclaim 'their' jobs when the wars ended. This situation persisted until two pieces of legislation were passed in the 1970s. These are the 1970

Equal Pay Act (enforcing the same pay for the same job regardless of sex) and the 1975 Sex Discrimination Act, which banned discrimination in employment on the grounds of sex alone.

The effects of these Acts are unclear. The picture of who works within the world of paid labour is changing. Although men have always outnumbered women in the workforce in peacetime in the twentieth century, their share in paid labour is declining. In the recession-hit years of the 1980s and 1990s, the number of men in work declined from 13,810,000 in 1984 to 13,655,000 in 1993, while the number of women in employment increased from 9,765,000 in 1984 to 11,210,000 in 1993 (see Table 6.2). The picture is more complex than this if these figures are disaggregated into full-time and part-time work.

TABLE 6.2 Full- and part-time employment by sex 1984–93 in the UK (thousands)

| | MALES | | FEMALES | |
	FULL-TIME	PART-TIME	FULL-TIME	PART-TIME
1984	13,240	570	5,422	4,343
1993	12,769	886	6,165	5,045

Source: Social Trends 24, 1994

Pay Although women are a growing proportion of the paid labour force (their position as unpaid domestic labourers remains unrecognised in official statistics), it is still far from the case that they are paid equally to men or are evenly distributed in the labour force. Women's earnings as a proportion of men's earnings in all sectors has hovered around the 70 per cent mark since the passing of the Equal Pay Act (see Table 6.3).

TABLE 6.3 Average gross weekly earnings for full-time employees, July 1994 (£s)

	MALES	FEMALES	ALL
Non-manual occupations	434	284	366
Manual occupations	285	185	266
All	367	267	331

Source: Employment Gazette, Nov. 1994

Vertical segregation These statistics can be explained by an examination of the location of women in the workforce. It remains the case that the top positions in most workplaces are dominated by men. In 1992, women still constituted less than 1 per cent of chief executives and members of boards of directors, less than 2 per cent of chief executives in local authorities, less than 3 per cent of permanent secretaries in the Civil

Service and 4 per cent of all judges. In trade unions, less than 3 per cent of general secretaries were female. The virtual absence of women in these top positions is frequently described as 'vertical segregation', or the 'glass ceiling' that women encounter as they progress in their careers but beyond which very few go.

Horizontal segregation

Secondly, women are also segregated within the labour market by the work that they do. While men dominate professional and managerial posts in general, as well as jobs in science, engineering, technology, security services, construction, transport, mining and transport, women form the vast majority of workers in lower grades in education, health, clerical and office work, catering, cleaning and other personal services. This is known as the horizontal segregation of work.

One consequence of this is that women not only earn less than men on average but that they dominate the worst-paid jobs. Using the Council of Europe's decency threshold, in 1991 79 per cent of all women working part-time in the United Kingdom were classed as low paid. Of the total of all workers, part-time and full-time, classed as low paid, 65 per cent were women.

To explain the location of women in the labour force, Barron and Norris (1976) argue that the labour market is made up of two sectors: a core or primary sector of highly paid secure employment with promotion possibilities, and a peripheral or secondary sector of low-paid, insecure employment with low promotion prospects often involving unskilled work. Women occupy the secondary sector of this dual labour market. This analysis draws attention to the belief that women are only seen as temporarily in employment, on loan from their main roles as wives and mothers, developing less of an industrial consciousness, and are less likely to join trade unions and to demand as much pay as men. This largely stereotypical view has been challenged by a number of writers (for example Dex, 1985) for its simplistic division of the labour market into only two sectors, and its assumption that women 'accept' lower wages. The role of male trade unions in alienating and excluding women is not examined and it is unable to explain why women in the same jobs as men do not get promoted when the men do, and why some women in the primary sector continue to be relatively less well paid.

A reserve army of labour?

From a more Marxist point of view, women are an industrial 'reserve army' of labour, sucked into and expelled from the world of work with the ebb and flow of capitalist and economic fortunes. According to this theory, women will be the last to be taken on in times of expansion, and the first to be thrown out with recession.

Evidence for this theory, however, is slim. As we have seen, in the 1980s the number of women in work increased, while the number of men fell. As women earn on average less than men, the cost to the capitalist of employing them is also less. To explain why women are located in specific sectors (horizontal segregation) some writers (Walby, 1986) have highlighted the role of trade unions in preventing women from entering traditionally male areas of employment.

Unpaid labour   Behind the world of paid labour lies an unquantified level of unpaid labour undertaken by women. This is as carers, for children, relatives and partners, where it is argued they are the slaves of wage slaves. In Ann Oakley's (1974a) study of housewives, women did at least 48 hours, at most 105 hours and on average 77 hours of domestic labour, whether in full-time employment or not. It is the low status accorded, culturally, to this work that may be the key to women's poor standing in the formal labour market where, for some writers, the work women do can be seen as an extension of their domestic role, providing for and cleaning up after men.

As Rosemary Crompton (1991) has argued, there is a paradox in government policies resulting from documents such as the 'Griffiths Report' (*Caring for People: Community Care in the Next Decade and Beyond*, 1989) which has resulted in the closing of many State institutions delivering care for the mentally and physically ill. This is that the idea of the community caring for those being kept out of institutions in reality implies that women will take on this unpaid work. Yet this is occurring at a time when women are increasingly sucked into paid labour, and there is a shortfall of young people entering the labour market.

QUESTIONS   1   **Could Blauner's categories of meaninglessness, powerlessness, self-estrangement and isolation be applied to domestic labour? What likely results would this enquiry bring?**

2   **What do the terms 'vertical' and 'horizontal' segregation mean?**

3   **How effective has legislation been in improving the position of women at work?**

Ethnicity and work

Using data from the *Employment Gazette* compiled in the late 1980s, it is possible to build up a picture of the location of members of the ethnic minorities (principally West Indians, Guyanese, Indians, Pakistanis and Bangladeshis) in the British labour market. This group composes 7.9 per cent of all those under 16, 4.7 per cent of all those of working age, and 0.9 per cent of the population who have reached the State retirement age. The focus is therefore on the 1,600,000 who are of working age.

When we examine participation in employment further in terms of the positions people occupy (*see Table* 6.4), a pattern similar to that of women in employment emerges, with vertical and horizontal segregation. However, it is wrong to generalise too much and view 'ethnic minorities' as homogeneous and undifferentiated.

TABLE 6.4   (a) Job levels by ethnic group, 1988–90, males (%)

	WHITE	AFRO-CARIB	AFRICAN ASIAN	INDIAN	PAKISTANI	CHINESE
Professional/Manager/Employer	27	12	27	25	12	30
Other non-manual	20	19	30	18	16	19
Skilled manual	33	39	26	29	34	10
Semi-skilled manual	15	23	13	24	31	36
Unskilled manual	4	6	3	4	6	4

(b) Job levels by ethnic group, 1988–90, females (%)

	WHITE	AFRO-CARIB	AFRICAN ASIAN	INDIAN	PAKISTANI	CHINESE
Professional/Manager/Employer	11	8	7	10	4	16
Other non-manual	56	54	58	47	42	53
Skilled manual	5	4	9	5	7	2
Semi-skilled manual	22	25	25	34	45	20
Unskilled manual	7	9	1	4	2	9

Source: Labour Force Surveys 1988–90, in Reena Bhavnani, Black Women in the Labour Market: A Research Review, *Equal Opportunities Commission, 1994*

Horizontally, men from ethnic minorities are over-represented in the distribution, hotels, catering and repairs sector, as well as in the health services. Women from ethnic minorities are also over-represented in the health services and some parts of manufacturing, but they are more evenly represented alongside white women than men from ethnic minorities.

As with women, similar theories exist to explain the nature of this segregation. Rex and Tomlinson (1979) advance the idea of a dual labour market in which Asians and West Indians are confined to the secondary sector, and systematically disadvantaged by comparison with whites in similar (but not identical) class and status positions.

Looking at immigrant workers in France, Germany, Switzerland and Britain, Castles and Kosack (1973) advance the Marxist-oriented concept of a reserve army of labour. Immigrant labour is used, like female

TABLE 6.5   Employment participation rates (%), Spring 1995

	WHITE	BLACK	INDIAN	PAKISTANI/ BANGLADESHI	OTHER	ALL ETHNIC GROUPS
Males						
Working full time	72	49	65	41	51	71
Working part time	5	8	7	8	8	5
Unemployed	8	21	10	18	12	9
Inactive	15	22	18	33	29	15
All (=100%) (thousands)	16,993	273	306	216	224	18,017
Females						
Working full time	38	37	36	12	30	38
Working part time	29	15	19	6	16	28
Unemployed	5	14	7	7	8	5
Inactive	28	34	38	75	46	29
All (=100%) (thousands)	15,420	296	279	191	238	16,428

Source: Social Trends 26, 1996

labour, to provide a pool of surplus labour on which capitalism can draw in order to keep wage levels low and profits high. As such they form the bottom strata of the working class. It is in the interests of the capitalist class to encourage these divisions within the proletariat. *Table* 6.5 shows the labour market position of ethnic groups in the mid 1990s.

The experience of ethnic minorities in the labour market, as with women, is probably far too complex to be comprehensively understood and can lead to meaningless generalisations. Behind the term 'ethnic minority' lie the diverse experiences of West Indian men and Bangledeshi women, Indian managers and Pakistani labourers, some in professional organisations, others in non-unionised sweatshops. A lot more research is needed in the area of race and ethnicity.

QUESTIONS

1 **Compare and contrast the position of ethnic minorities in the labour market with that of women.**

2 **How can the location of ethnic minorities in the labour market be explained?**

Unemployment

Unemployment and the sociological imagination

When, in a city of 100,000, only one man is unemployed, that is his personal trouble, and for its relief we properly look to the character of the man, his skills, and his immediate opportunities. But when in a nation of 50 million employees, 15 million men are unemployed, that is an issue, and we may not hope to find its solution within the range of opportunities open to any one individual. The very structure of opportunities has collapsed. Both the correct statement of the problem and the range of possible solutions require us to consider the economic and political institutions of the society, and not merely the personal situation of a scatter of individuals.

C. Wright Mills, 1959

Measurement

Unemployment statistics are among the most controversial statistics issued by governments. Until 1913, for example, the figures were collected not by the State but by the trade unions operating unemployment benefit schemes. The Department of Employment, from whom unemployment statistics now originate, considers that only statistics collected since 1923 are truly accurate, particularly in showing fluctuations in unemployment. There are six different estimates of the level for 1921, for example. In the inter-war period, the changing status of some workers as insured confuses the picture because unemployment insurance schemes were the main way of gauging unemployment levels.

Since the National Assistance and National Insurance Acts of the late 1940s, the unemployment figure is believed to be more reliable and consistent. This figure included anyone drawing unemployment benefit and those, such as school leavers, newly arrived immigrants and married women, who were registered at the Department of Employment as seeking work but not entitled to draw benefit.

Statistical massaging? Following the election of the Conservative government in 1979, and the rapid rise in unemployment in the early 1980s, the official measurement of unemployment was changed nineteen times up to 1987. For example, those on youth training schemes who would otherwise be unemployed, those seeking part-time work only, and those seeking work but not registered unemployed were all excluded. At the same time, the number of people in the labour force was increased by adding the self-employed. The number of people unemployed as a percentage of the labour force therefore automatically decreased. As unemployment is a highly political issue, the way in which the number of unemployed is calculated has become the subject of debate not only between sociologists, but politicians as well. Arguments persist as to what the 'real' rate of unemployment is, with those on the Right suggesting that some of those registered as unemployed are not genuinely seeking work (as they may, for example, be already working in the hidden economy), and those on the Left arguing that many more people are in fact unemployed than the official statistics show (*see* Figure 6.3).

Figure 6.3 Claimant unemployment and job centre vacancies

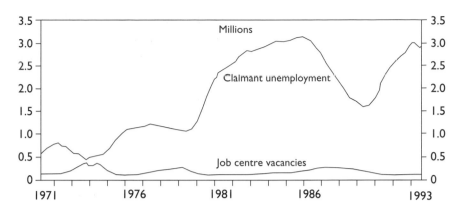

Source: Social Trends 24, 1994

Who is unemployed?

It is possible to build up a sociological profile of the unemployed according to age, gender, ethnicity and region.

Region An analysis of unemployment by region shows that, traditionally, the hardest-hit areas tend to be those furthest from the metropolitan centre. Hence, the areas worst hit by unemployment in the twentieth century have been Northern Ireland, Scotland (particularly Strathclyde), South Wales, the North-East and North-West regions of England, as well as the West Midlands (*see Table 6.6*). Within these areas, it has been in the industries most closely associated with the Industrial Revolution – coal, steel, shipbuilding, textiles and mechanical engineering – that the highest rates have been recorded.

TABLE 6.6 Unemployment rates by region

UK	PERCENTAGE OF ALL ECONOMICALLY ACTIVE	
	1989	1994
Northern Ireland	15.4	11.5
North	10.7	11.7
Scotland	9.8	9.9
North West	8.8	10.2
Yorkshire and Humberside	8.0	9.8
Wales	7.9	9.4
West Midlands	6.9	9.9
East Midlands	6.0	8.3
South West	4.8	7.5
East Anglia	3.8	7.4
South East	3.1	9.6

Source: Social Trends 25, 1995

Changing geography of unemployment In the 1990s, however, the geography of unemployment has altered radically, with falls in Northern Ireland and substantial increases in the traditionally high employment areas of the South East, the South

West and East Anglia (*see Table 6.6*). This is because of the 'white-collar' character of the early 1990s recession, with substantial job losses being suffered in financial services, as well as in construction, mining, and the manufacture of cars and computers. It is therefore becoming simplistic and inaccurate to say that unemployment is a particular problem for the North rather than the South, inner-city rather than suburban areas, and industrial rather than urban areas. Post-war unemployment is no longer confined to areas where heavy industry was the main source of jobs.

Age By age, the highest percentage of those unemployed are men over 50 and both sexes under 30 (*see Table 6.7*). In absolute terms it is men and women in their twenties who have been hardest hit. The likelihood of experiencing long-term unemployment (more than twelve months of continuous unemployment) increases with age, though older people may also see themselves as 'prematurely retired', which is how unemployed men over the age of 60 are officially classified.

TABLE 6.7   Unemployment by sex, age and duration, Spring 1993

UK	1993 (%)	UNEMPLOYED FOR OVER 12 MONTHS (%)	TOTAL (THOUSANDS)
Males			
16–19	22.0	25.8	192
20–29	16.4	44.2	666
30–39	10.3	51.3	404
40–49	8.8	52.5	317
50–64	11.9	53.5	377
65 and over	4.6	–	–
			Total men 1,967
Females			
16–19	16.0	18.4	126
20–29	10.2	28.5	321
30–39	7.0	17.2	207
40–49	4.7	32.6	142
50–59	5.6	38.1	106
60 and over	3.9	–	–
			Total women 924
			Total 2,891

Source: Social Trends *24, 1994*

Ethnicity Ethnic minorities, particularly those of Pakistani, Bangladeshi or 'black' origin, experience higher rates of unemployment than whites (*see Figure 6.4*).

How unemployment has been experienced is of great interest to sociologists. The main findings are that it is experienced differently according to social group, the amount of time employed prior to

Figure 6.4 Unemployment rates: by ethnic group, Spring 1993

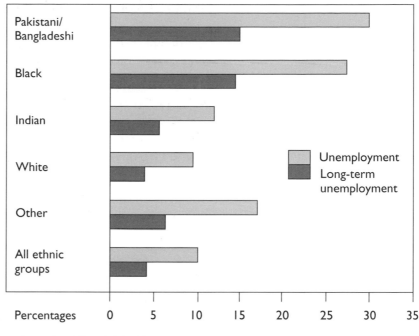

Source: Social Trends 24, 1994

unemployment and the amount of social support, though whether you are young or old, male or female, black or white, working class or middle class is also seen as important.

Social class Social class is seen as important by sociologists because unemployment may affect different areas of life for different social classes. Ashton (1986) argues that 'if you are a doctor for whom work is a central life-interest and you lose your job, the experience is likely to be different from that of an assembly-line worker for whom work is boring, monotonous and physically demanding'. The main impact is felt in three areas: work identity, financial situation and identity within the family. For the doctor, he says, the main problem will be that his social identity through work will be threatened. This will not be the same for the assembly-line worker, where the main problems are that on losing their job they will have only short-term financial security, while their family identity (as breadwinner) will be threatened by unemployment, in a way that their work identity will not. These three areas are least problematic for females seeking part-time work, mainly housewives returning to the job market.

Youth unemployment For youths, the problem is mainly that the possibility of having a work identity is threatened, while access to adult status is delayed and dependence on the family is enhanced. Social class is also a factor here, with work and success seen as of central significance to the attainment of young people's self-identity. This will be undermined by long-term unemployment. Lower working-class youths, who do not expect much from work, have in any case developed ways of 'doing nothing' and what frustrates them is lack of money. For them, unemployment is 'just part of the everyday experience of the labour market' (Ashton, 1986) mitigated by membership of peer groups.

The growth of government youth training schemes since the late 1970s has attracted the critical attention of many sociologists. The number of schemes points to the depth and extent of youth unemployment, which in turn has been seen as a reflection of the fact that the number of unskilled jobs has declined, that part-time service sector jobs are taken by married women, and that traditional 'school-leaver' jobs in clerical work are being replaced because of new office technology.

Paul Thompson (1983) argues that, first, these training schemes are evidence that schools, contrary to Bowles and Gintis (1976), do not train youths directly for work, and secondly, that such schemes are mainly designed to produce a pool of semi-skilled workers prepared to receive low wages in a newly restructured youth labour market.

Gender

The picture for young women is different (as Griffin argues, 1985). Young females rely more on work as a means of breaking out of the parental home and domestic isolation. If they cannot do this, they are likely to be obliged to take on additional domestic responsibilities. For women who have left home but cohabit with a partner, being without work means any financial independence they may have is threatened. Several sociologists, however, have argued that, as women's main source of identity is as mother and housewife, and work will be fitted in with domestic responsibilities, their identity is unthreatened by unemployment. For women working full time, this does not apply to the same extent.

Ethnicity

For people from ethnic minorities, the problem of unemployment is compounded by racism in employment practices, despite the fact that this is illegal. According to Roberts (1984), unemployment among Afro-Caribbean school-leavers was 10 per cent above that for whites even where they had left school with superior qualifications. They have more difficulty in finding work, and will be out of work for longer if they lose their jobs. Once they are convinced that this is happening because they are black they may then retreat into ethnic subcultures such as Rastafarianism, refusing to work for whites and do their 'trash' jobs.

Unemployment and health

Given that different groups experience unemployment differently, there is general agreement that unemployment usually has deleterious effects on mental and physical health: 'it is not in serious dispute that research shows that unemployment can impair psychological health in many people' (Haworth and Evans, 1987).

Sinfield (1981) suggests that the psychological pattern following redundancy is firstly to feel shocked or surprised, then optimistic, then pessimistic and finally fatalistic as the adjustment to the idea that unemployment will not be short-lived is made. The initial feeling that an unexpected holiday has been gained, giving opportunities to undertake jobs around the house and to use time as they please becomes a meaningless, unremitting series of unremarkable, uneventful days with nothing to look forward to, as this quotation from Binns and Mars (1984) shows: 'I'll tell you about daily life. I sit in this chair peeking out of a wee slit in the window looking at the world. Not that it changes much from day to day, though somebody did take away the railings this morning. That was interesting.'

QUESTIONS

1 **Why are social characteristics such as age, gender, ethnicity and class important when studying unemployment?**

2 **How has the geography of unemployment changed in this decade? What reasons might there be for this?**

> **W. Beveridge (1879–1963)**
> British social reformer, politician and architect of the Welfare State. Early in his life Beveridge campaigned for old age pensions, free school meals and government action to help the unemployed. As a civil servant he produced the Beveridge Report, which became the blueprint for the modern welfare state in Britain.

Causes

The only sovereign remedy yet discovered by democracies for unemployment is total war.

W. Beveridge, 1944

Unemployment, a term first coined in the 1880s, has been a persistent but periodic problem in modern British socio-economic life. Its most severe periods have been in the inter-war period, and at the start of the 1980s and 1990s, though some writers believe that the experiences of pre- and post-Second World War unemployment are not comparable. This is because of the relative lack of post-war protest against unemployment, compared with the continuous campaigns of inter-war organisations such as the National Unemployed Workers Movement (see Croucher, 1987), changes in attitudes to work, leisure, and the existence of universal benefits. Nevertheless, the causes of unemployment remain hotly debated within the world of politics, sociology and economics.

Common-sense ideas about unemployment might point to idleness, people getting too much on the dole, too many people living in Great Britain, or new technology taking away people's jobs. Very few of these ideas are academically accepted. The unemployment of the last twenty years cannot easily be explained by sudden mass outbreaks of laziness or increases in unemployment benefit.

Keynes's General Theory

For many writers, the long period of more-or-less full employment following the end of the Second World War can be explained by the adoption, at governmental level, of the economic ideas of John

211

> **J.M. Keynes (1883–1946)**
> *A Cambridge economist who produced a major work called* The General Theory of Employment, Interest and Money *(1936). He believed that governments could have a major role to play in introducing economic policies to reduce or eliminate unemployment.*

Maynard Keynes (1883–1946). Put briefly (though explained fully by Keynes, 1936), Keynes believed that the State could intervene in the workings of the market economy, stimulate demand, and keep unemployment low. The belief that Keynes had solved the problem of unemployment is clearly put by Michael Stewart (1972): 'the basic fact is that, with the acceptance of the General Theory, the days of uncontrollable mass unemployment in advanced industrial countries are over. Other economic problems may threaten; this one, at least, has passed into history.'

The New Right

Such certainties dissolved in the 1970s with the breeching of full employment levels, and the appearance of simultaneous rising inflation and economic stagnation: 'stagflation'. It was the persistence of stagflation, and Keynesianism's apparent inability to deal with it, that led to the revival of monetarist theory in economics, and the New Right in politics. From this point of view, unemployment occurs because of impediments to the smooth workings of the labour market. As Patrick Minford (1982) argues: 'the proximate cause of unemployment is excessive high wage costs, produced either by high wages or by low productivity'. There are, he says, two major distortions in the UK labour market which prevent real wages and productivity from adjusting naturally to shifts in technology, demand and industrial structure, and from relocating those freed from one sector into other sectors. These are the operation of the unemployment benefit system and the power of trade unions to raise wages relative to non-union wages.

A similar kind of argument was put forward by Marx, and has been taken up by writers in the tradition he established. The difference is that he sees unemployment, or the creation of reserve armies of labour, as a central and persistent feature of capitalist development. The main point here is that, in the struggle to keep profits high, the bourgeoisie in periods of stagnation need to force wages down, and therefore create unemployment until profits return to acceptable levels. The only way to end unemployment is to end a system based on the need for profit. (Why profits need to be kept high is explored in chapter 3.)

New technology

One of the most popular beliefs concerning unemployment is the role played by new automation taking the place of human labour. There are two arguments here. On one side, the labour-replacing nature of automation is uncritically accepted. However, others point out that automation and robotisation will increase productivity (and therefore economic growth) and free labour to undertake other productive tasks. For Marx, if machinery ultimately comes to take the place of labour, then the creation of surplus value cannot occur.

Those who see new technology as unimportant point out that the introduction of technology is a constant feature of the process of industrialisation, and cannot therefore account for rises and falls in unemployment. This is disputed by Jones (1986) who argues that information technology is having consequences not witnessed since the earlier days of the Industrial Revolution. This is because, unlike other new technologies, microelectronics allows output in industry to be increased while inputs such as capital and energy, and particularly labour, can continually be reduced. The service sector, he says, will suffer job losses most dramatically, leading to a social choice between the possibility of leisure for all, involving the restructuring of work commitments, or unemployment for a growing number.

If automation does lead to unemployment, then it leads to severe consequences for the economy at a macro or national level. In the first place, it means the State takes on a heavier burden in paying unemployment benefits, and secondly, those still working are taxed more heavily (directly or indirectly) to meet this cost.

Equilibrium

The return to mass unemployment since the mid 1970s has provided the opportunity to test the accuracy of two theories of unemployment: the equilibrium theory and the saturation of labour markets theory. In the first, which is closely allied to classical or New Right thinking on unemployment, areas of high unemployment will produce low wages, while areas of full employment witness wage rises. Equilibrium will result as workers move from low to high wage regions (the thinking behind the former Conservative MP Norman Tebbit's famous 'Get on your bike' speech) and employers relocate from high wage to low wage regions. There is little evidence that this did in fact happen in the 1980s.

Saturation

In the second theory, new jobs will be created not in areas of high unemployment, but in areas of low unemployment and economic buoyancy. This is because the workers in these areas already possess the skills that new industries need and other services are also available, whereas workers in high unemployment areas have only the skills of outmoded industries, and need to be retrained, an expensive option for many growth industries. The saturation theory best explains the pattern of unemployment in the 1980s, although it should also be noted that some of the new businesses of the late 1980s and early 1990s also encountered severe problems.

Types of unemployment

The full employment that Beveridge wrote of was defined by him as less than 3 per cent of the workforce unemployed. Britain has therefore experienced mass unemployment continuously since 1975.

Different types of unemployment are identifiable. *Frictional unemployment* refers to the unemployment of workers temporarily between jobs, or in the process of being matched to a job. This type of unemployment can exist in times of full employment.

Structural unemployment exists when the occupational and industrial structure of the economy changes. Unemployed workers need to be retrained or relocated into new jobs, if there are any.

Seasonal unemployment affects workers whose jobs only exist during certain periods of the year. It is expected that, for example, unemployment rates will rise in agriculture, construction and tourism in the winter months, and seasonal adjustments are made to unemployment statistics to reveal the underlying rate.

QUESTIONS

1 **What are the causes of unemployment?**

2 **Is a return to full employment possible?**

Leisure

Perspectives on leisure

The emergence of two distinct concepts of 'work' and 'leisure' as industrialisation advances has been differently viewed by the main perspectives in sociology.

Functionalism
The functionalist view sees work and leisure as interlocking parts of the social system. As Dumazedier (1974) argues, leisure is necessary to help people adjust to their social situation and for the maintenance of social order. Leisure helps people to rest between work periods, and those who engage in leisure pursuits during work-time are seen as deviant. The three main aspects of leisure are relaxation, entertainment and personal development.

Weber
In the Weberian view what were originally loosely organised and uncoordinated activities have become increasingly rationalised, systematised and rule-bound. The same forces that have changed the nature of work (see above) have also changed leisure pursuits. The underlying forces that come to control leisure pursuits are the same as for work. A good example of this is the way football and rugby football have developed since the middle ages into highly rule-bound activities (Dunning and Sheard, 1969).

Marxism
For Marxists work in a socialist society will not lead to alienation but will be fulfilling in itself. The need for leisure will be transformed.

Under capitalism, the key issue is the battle for the workers to wrest free time from the employing class and to develop their own distinctive culture, sometimes called 'popular culture'. The most significant use of the time gained from the reductions in the working week as a consequence of the Ten Hours Act in the nineteenth century onwards, was for political and trade-union meetings. There is also the emphasis, as in the study of youth cultures, on the concept of gaining 'cultural space' from the dominant ideology (see, for example, Clarke, Critcher and Johnson, 1979 or Clarke and Critcher, 1985).

Feminism Whether women experience anything that can be called 'leisure' in the same way that men do is of particular interest to feminists. Rosemary Deem (1986) argues that women's opportunities for leisure are different from those of men in the private world of the home, as well as in the outside, public world. As interest in the sociology of women's leisure has grown, a number of studies have argued that women's opportunities for leisure are limited by men, partly because of their control over women's sexuality. This can prevent or constrain journeys out at night, or they may be prevented from going to pubs and discos by their partners. Writers, such as Deem (1990), argue that as women, generally, do not riot, kick each other in the vicinity of football grounds and create public disorder, public provision for their leisure needs is relatively neglected, as placating their needs is seen as less urgent or necessary.

In general women in full-time employment have less leisure time than men (*see Figure 6.5*). Moreover, as Deem (1988) points out: 'men's leisure is often out of the home and may revolve around sport ... and informal group activities like going for a drink. Women tend to spend more leisure time at home (sometimes through necessity rather than

Figure 6.5 Free time in a typical week: by sex and employment status, Great Britain, 1992–93

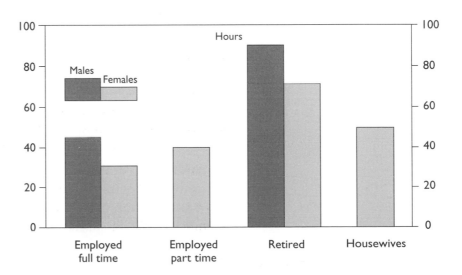

Source: Social Trends 24, 1994

215

choice), whether alone or with friends … Once out of their teens, the-yare seldom involved in sport.' Within the home, the only place that is seen as a woman's exclusive place is the kitchen. Among women, those with least leisure time are mothers of children under five. Generally, according to Deem, leisure for women is a reward extended grudgingly for good behaviour and well-executed housework.

QUESTIONS

1 **Define work and leisure. What other time uses can be identified?**

2 **How do functionalist and Weberian views of leisure differ?**

The changing pattern of leisure activities

The impact of industrialisation

Early industrialisation is associated with a loss of free time, and the introduction of new time disciplines and orientations by employers. This is an aspect of the 'Protestant work ethic' described by Weber (see chapter 11). Marrus (1974) estimates that, in the Middle Ages, one third of the year was devoted to leisure. According to Wilensky (1963) the typical working day of 12 hours, with a two-hour rest in 1700, became a working day of between 14 and 18 hours a century later. During the course of the nineteenth century, the reduction of the working day became the focus of intense industrial and political agitation, and led to the Ten Hours Act of 1847 though, as with much industrial legislation, this was only achieved for certain work-ers in certain industries. As *Table* 6.8 shows, time spent at work has shrunk ever since.

TABLE 6.8   Changes in the working week 1870–1965

DATE	WORKING HOURS	WORKING DAYS
1870	70	7
1900	60	6
1950	44	5
1965	40	5

Source: Wilensky in Smigel, Work and Leisure, *1963*

Since the mid 1960s, basic work hours have not fallen dramatically, while the amount of overtime worked is increasing, as *Figure* 6.6 shows.

The indications are that when overtime is included in working time, the amount of actual hours worked on average is no shorter than the 44–48-hour working week characteristic of the period before the Second World War. This is contrary to Gorz's (1984) estimation that a working life will eventually involve only 20,000 hours of labour per person.

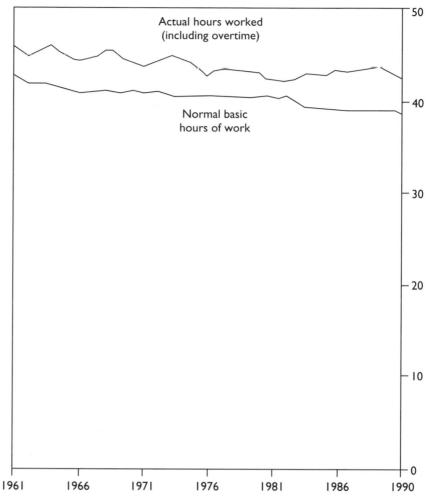

Figure 6.6 Weekly hours of work in the UK (full-time manual employees)

Actual hours worked (including overtime)

Normal basic hours of work

Source: Social Trends 22, 1992

By comparison with the nineteenth century, workers in the twentieth century have more leisure time. Once employment, travel and essential activities are subtracted, the picture shown in *Table 6.9* emerges.

One of the main ways in which leisure time has been gained is through paid holidays. These are steadily increasing in length (*see Figure 6.7*).

TABLE 6.9   Free time by sex and employment status (1990–91)

| | FULL-TIME EMPLOYEES | | PART-TIME EMPLOYEES | HOUSE- | RETIRED |
	MALES	FEMALES	FEMALES	WIVES	
Weekday free time (hours)	4.5	3.3	5.4	8.4	11.6
Weekend day free time (hours)	12.1	10.3	9.5	9.3	13.6

Source: Social Trends 22, 1992

Figure 6.7 Percentage entitled to annual paid holidays of duration

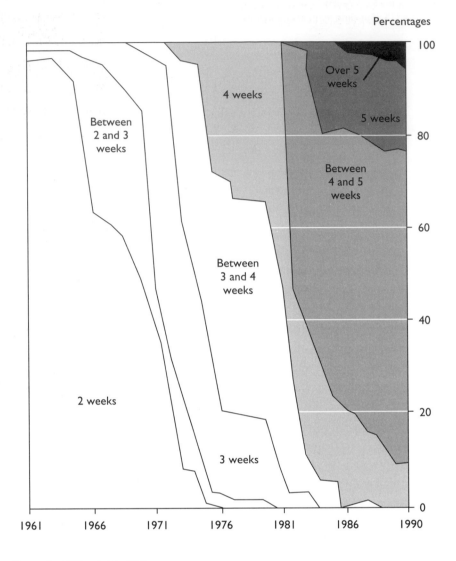

Source: Social Trends *21, 1991*

Whether you have a holiday away from home at all, and how long this holiday is for, is related to social class (*see* Figure 6.8).

Many left-wing writers are critical of the way leisure-time is used, arguing that the free time that does exist is nevertheless absorbed and reclaimed by the dominant culture of capitalism. Leisure and money are inseparable. To participate in some sports it may be socially necessary to wear the appropriate kit bearing the right brand names. Advertising may have a powerful influence on the choices people make when spending their money in their free time. Jeremy Seabrook (1984) argues that, far from being an escape from work, many leisure activities are nostalgic attempts to return to the industrial past. Model railways can be seen as nostalgia for the days of steam and sailing is a sublimation of centuries of

Figure 6.8 Number of holidays per year:
by social class in Great Britain

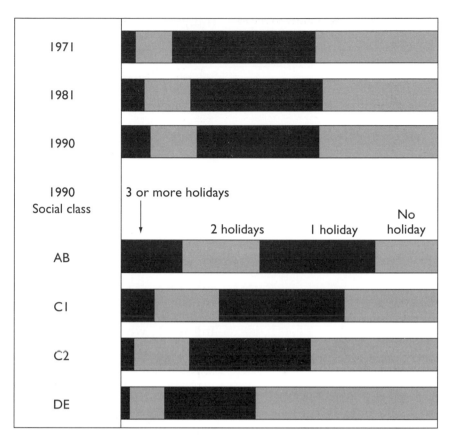

Source: British National Travel Survey, British Tourist Authority

naval history. The interest in crafts, pottery, embroidery, sewing, weaving, and the creation of working museums suggest a powerful impulse to escape the modern world to a time when there was a personal input into work. The needs which leisure activities are called upon to answer are perhaps far more profound than the words themselves suggest.

Deem (1988) sums up these issues: 'it is easier to see fundamental changes taking place over long periods of time, so that there is clearly a vast difference between a factory worker's experience of leisure in the mid nineteenth century and the same worker's experience of leisure in the late twentieth century. But the differences may be less great than we suppose; certainly fewer hours of employment are involved and for many in full-time employment there is more paid holiday entitlement. But activities such as drinking are just as prevalent now as then even though new leisure activities like TV, videos and home computer games have appeared.'

The relationship between work and leisure

The idea that what people do in their spare time is directly or indirectly related to what they do in their work hours is disputed. Bacon (1975) finds no strong evidence: 'To a considerable extent, the

219

things that people choose to do in their free time are unrelated to the nature of their employment.' Roberts (1974) argues that 'at the levels of individuals' life-styles, leisure interests are often only weakly related to characteristics of people's jobs, though types of work do have some bearing upon leisure interests'.

Patterns of work and leisure

Stanley Parker (1983) argues that three patterns are perceivable. Some people extend their working life into their leisure hours – their leisure time is clearly identified with their working life; others have leisure patterns that are deliberately opposed to their work, where the content of the two worlds contrasts; the third group display a neutrality about the type of leisure they choose – the content of work and leisure is separate, but not deliberately so.

The relationship between work and leisure, Parker believes, is determined by the nature of the work. Highly autonomous or self-directing work, where people's abilities are used intensively, produces an extension into leisure. This is true, he says, of the social workers he studied, and also of successful businessmen, doctors, teachers and self-employed workers. Neutrality includes minor professionals other than social workers, and the oppositional pattern is characteristic of unskilled manual workers, assembly-line and oil-rig workers and tunnellers. Another significant variable is the type of education the workers have had.

Unemployment and leisure

The return of mass unemployment from the mid 1970s onwards has, for many writers, falsified the claim that a leisured future lay beyond the work ethic of a post-industrial society. When unemployed, people watch more television, do more housework and reading, but go out less. They do not necessarily increase or decrease the amount of sporting, religious, community, creative and outdoor activities. If anything, studies (for example Kelvin *et al.* 1984; Miles, 1984) have shown that people reduce their leisure activities when they become unemployed. This is true even where local authorities have provided low-cost or free leisure facilities.

The implication is that the work ethic is still strong, and that unemployed people have difficulty in seeing leisure as an end in itself, or as a viable alternative to employment. However, the problem seems to be mainly financial, though there is also difficulty in learning how to structure free time. This is also a problem for retired people.

Neither leisure, nor unemployment, it seems, can meet the five characteristics of employment outlined by Jahoda, Lazarsfeld and Zeisel

(1933): time-structuring, shared experiences outside the family/household, goals and purposes additional to their own personal ones, personal status and identity, and enforced activity.

QUESTIONS

1 How has leisure-time changed in the past 300 years?

2 How are class and gender related to leisure-time?

FURTHER READING

R. Deem, *Work, Unemployment and Leisure*, Routledge, 1988

K. Grint, *The Sociology of Work: An Introduction*, Polity Press, 1991

R. Hyman, *Strikes*, Macmillan, 1991

J. McIlroy, *Trade Unions in Britain Today*, Manchester University Press, 1988

R. Roberts, *Youth and Employment in Modern Britain*, Oxford University Press, 1995

S. Wood (ed.), *The Transformation of Work: Skill, Flexibility and the Labour Process*, Routledge, 1992

7 Organisations

Without something to belong to, we have no stable self, and yet total commitment and attachment to any social unit implies a kind of selflessness.

Erving Goffman, Asylums, 1961

INTRODUCTION

The chapter begins by looking at how the classical sociological thinkers, Marx, Durkheim and Weber, viewed organisations. You will then go on to examine bureaucracies in more depth, focusing on the work of Merton, Blau, Selznick and Gouldner. The chapter then focuses on formal and informal organisations and the work of Erving Goffman. The next section discusses the differences between mechanistic and organic forms of organisational structure, moving on to examine the structuralist model of Etzioni. Contemporary issues are examined in the debate over post-modernism and the 'Japanisation' of British industrial organisation. The chapter closes by looking at trade unions and professional associations.

The sociology of organisations

Organisations and social change

This branch of sociology is concerned with the analysis of organisations: how people, acting together according to a set of rules, with a given set of duties and responsibilities, can attain certain objectives. The use of the word 'organisation' suggests that these sets of relationships are similar to organs within an organism, connected and interdependent. The development of industrial society saw the growth of organisations in the modern sense. Pre-industrial classical societies were organised and were capable of amazing feats of organised activity – the pyramids, Stonehenge, Roman roads and cities, Greek democracy. The difference is that industrial societies are *based* upon organisations, they are central to their existence. Therefore, these organisations must be more tightly controlled than those of the past, which were often based upon friendship, corruption, family loyalty, and were much less efficient than the bureaucracies of today, which have come to be thought of as cold and impersonal. This is because they are run according to principles enshrined within the institution, not determined by individuals. Marx, Durkheim and Weber were concerned with the role of the organisation within the changing structure of society. As usual, the different theoretical assumptions give rise to differing explanations of this role.

QUESTION 1 **What organisations are you a part of, for example school, work, unions, social and leisure clubs?**

Marxism

Classical Marxism

According to Marx, organisations under capitalism arose out of the need to extract surplus value from the working class and keep that surplus for the capitalists. All forms of organisation, except those expressly formed to overthrow capitalism, exist to further the needs of the ruling class. Public organisations, as opposed to private ones, exist to help maintain control through ideology and political domination. State institutions are a good example, education being the most important 'ideological state apparatus' (Althusser, 1971). The domination of one class by another is reproduced in the nature of organisations. Like everything else under capitalism, organisations have been used for the ends of one group only. The increased efficiency of production, which should be a liberating factor in working people's lives, is used as a weapon against them. Marxists say this is due to the implicit exploitation in the social relations of capitalist production. Workers don't get a fair slice of the profits, yet they do the work. Capitalist organisations exist to increase control and domination of the worker.

QUESTIONS 1 **How could organisations be used in a way that Marxists would see as non-exploitative?**

2 **According to Marxism, what are the main goals of a capitalist organisation?**

Functionalism

Social solidarity

Durkheim was also interested in the way organisations developed along with industrialisation. A key concept of functionalism is 'social solidarity'. How does society continue to hold together, particularly given the wide variety of possible behaviours open to individuals in large-scale industrial societies? Organisations play an important role in integrating individuals into society.

Individuals need to feel that they belong to something which is greater than themselves. If this sense of belonging is not fulfilled, then there would be a potential for 'social pathology', a breakdown in the smooth running of the social structure with individuals involved in deviant and possibly disruptive behaviour because they have no sense of social responsibility towards others. Without some form of common, organisational bond to provide aims and goals of a collective nature, society would begin to break up.

In Durkheim's analysis, the organisation acts as a vital go-between which unites the individual with the wider society. Without organisations, isolated individuals would not feel that they played an active role in society. As members of organisations, they are given an opportunity to take part in social decision making. Acting as part of a larger team, with given duties and responsibilities, the individual feels an active and useful member of the organisation, and therefore of society. Organisations give people a sense of 'position' in society, of knowing where they fit into the overall structure. This position carries with it a sense of 'social value', and this helps the individual to integrate, take up their post and revel in the social value attached to it. The complexities of a wide division of labour give organisations a vital function in society, with this underlying or 'latent' function of maintaining solidarity through the integration of individuals into society.

QUESTIONS

1 **How do functionalists explain the relationship between individuals and organisations?**

2 **If individuals are committed to the values of an organisation, why is there a need for rules and hierarchies?**

Weber and bureaucracies

Weber occupies an important position within the sociology of organisations. From his vantage point at the turn of the nineteenth century he was able to observe industrial societies as they passed into the twentieth century. Each society is unique, according to Weber, and must be viewed as the product of unique historical and cultural developments. However, common to all industrial societies was the development of bureaucratic organisations. Unlike Marx, who sees this as yet another aspect of capitalist control, and Durkheim, who sees organisations as necessary for promoting solidarity, Weber sees bureaucracies as the most efficient institutions for getting the job done. This was in contrast to the non-bureaucratic forms of organisation which existed before industrialisation. The 'nature' of organisations had altered with the new, efficiency-demanding, rationalised society.

Traditional society

Traditional, pre-industrial social organisations were often little more than clan or kinship groups. Status within them was based upon nepotism: getting favours for your nephews, sons, cousins or friends of the family. There were no clearly expressed rules and hardly even a proper hierarchy. The goals of these organisations were not tightly defined and pursued, and they did not need to be. The traditional society, with its limited division of labour and slower pace of production, did not have the requirements for specified goals and highly developed processes of control through a hierarchical power system, all of which were necessary for industrial society. This need for a network of individuals, each paid a salary for a clearly defined set of tasks, required a fundamental change in the way organisations worked.

Weber's analysis of bureaucracy is a good example of his concept of the 'ideal type' (see chapter 3). The ideal type is a model, an abstraction of what an organisation should be, and as it is a model, you cannot expect to come across its exact match in reality. It is used as a guide for the researcher to compare with reality and see how closely the real thing, in this case an actual organisation in society, matches up to the model – the ideal type. Weber outlines the characteristics of the bureaucratic organisation, and offers this model to use as a way to measure the workings of organisations.

QUESTIONS

1 **How do modern organisations differ from traditional ones?**

2 **What is meant by a hierarchical power system?**

The characteristics of bureaucracies

Bureaucratisation

For Weber, the word 'bureau' encompasses both the official posts and the material apparatus – files, equipment and technology, rules and hierarchy – which make the process of bureaucracy work. Management is based upon written documents, and managers utilise this power in carrying out their duties. Bureaucracy means 'rule by office', and it is this which characterises industrial society. Weber looks back to the Middle Ages for the origins of the process of bureaucratisation, beginning with a gradual separation of home and office. The household became a private place, cut off from the business world. In pre-industrial society, there had been no such disconnection, and the family was the centre of both consumption and production. Business correspondence began to be separated from private correspondence, and personal fortunes were distinguished from business assets. Once this process had begun, it became necessary to introduce the hierarchy of control and rules which characterise the modern industrial organisation.

Rational-legal authority

Weber (1922) discusses the way in which the activities necessary to maintain the bureaucracy are fixed and described as 'official

225

duties'. The people who carry out these duties are given authority and there are rules which govern the use of this authority. The system will ensure that duties are carried out and that those who perform them are suitably qualified. These duties, authority and responsibilities are the daily business of the organisation. The system is more important than mere individuals, who have to fit into the office hierarchy. Weber sees this as a structure of supervision, with positions graded according to authority. He calls this 'subordination and superordination'. Management within this structure is 'reduced' to a strict obedience to the rules. All cases dealt with by the bureaucratic organisation are judged according to the rules, not on individual merit. This ensures that all cases are dealt with fairly and no one receives special benefit or favour. Anyone who has tried to get extra payments from the DSS, for instance, will understand this. This is a technically superior, efficient form of organisation, which makes the smooth running of industrial society possible, in both the public sphere – for example, State organisations – and the private sphere – business. This rational pursuit of clearly defined aims and goals, using the processes of legally organised rules and hierarchies of authority, is called 'rational-legal' bureaucracy. It was also, however, a potentially dangerous source of a new, blind, bureaucratic power.

Weber thought and wrote himself into at least two serious psychological depressions as a result of this analysis. On the one hand he believed the superior efficiency of bureaucratic organisations was obvious, and the hierarchical, impersonal nature of these institutions should ensure fairness and equality of treatment. The 'faceless bureaucracy' which people criticise should work to their advantage. On the other hand, the possibility of bureaucratic power getting out of control alarmed Weber. He could foresee a situation where bureaucracies only existed to maintain and perpetuate their own power. This would stifle social change, and only the existence of dynamic, imaginative leaders in society could combat suffocating bureaucratic control. The nightmare of the human individual – the 'social actor' of social action theory – locked in and unable to exercise free will, helplessly incarcerated in the 'iron cage of bureaucracy', must have followed Weber to his grave.

Informal aspects

Weber's work is definitely important in providing an understanding of the workings of bureaucracies. By comparing them with pre-industrial organisations, he shows what is new about the bureaucracy, in particular its formalised, rational system of organisation, and the way this fits industrial society. He is also aware of the negative potentials, in the form of massive bureaucracies wielding too much power. However, Weber's description of the characteristics of bureaucracies does not address their informal aspects. He shows the need for fairness in recruiting individuals, and how the system should make sure that only those with the necessary qualifications should be entrusted with authority. The human agency is missing from this analysis, and people obviously affect the organisations they are a part of. Interactionist approaches explore this aspect of organisations.

Power in a hierarchy such as a bureaucracy becomes concentrated at the top. If everyone is subordinate to those above them, then the real power is at the highest level. Organisations tend to become 'oligarchies', where only a few exercise real power. The Weberian view sees power as a product of the bureaucratic hierarchy, but ignores the possibility that this power is in the hands of a small group.

Some of these questions are answered by the development of a new sociology of organisations in the 1950s, mainly in the USA. These studies were concerned with particular organisations and how they worked at a micro level. This shifted the analysis away from the role of organisations within the wider processes of social change – the main concern of the classical theorists.

QUESTIONS

1 **How does Weber explain the need for bureaucratic hierarchies?**

2 **What is the negative side of bureaucratic power?**

3 **Which aspects of bureaucratic institutions does Weber's analysis miss?**

The dysfunctions of bureaucracies

In the immediate post-war period, new studies of organisations emerged. In the main, these studies were critical of Weber's ideal type of bureaucracy. The work of sociologists like Merton, Blau, Selznick and Gouldner borrows from and develops the Weberian view of organisations as efficient institutions. This microanalysis revealed weaknesses within organisations, flaws which are a direct result of bureaucracy. There was a gap between the model of bureaucracy, the ideal type, and the reality. Bureaucracies spawned 'bureaucratic personalities', 'bureaucratic inertia' and, last but not least, 'red tape'. Merton (1949a) and Blau (1955) highlight the costs of bureaucratic organisation. The efficiencies of the system lead to the necessary breaking of the rules, in order to get the job done. This analysis of the informal aspect of organisations – the 'social action' within bureaucracies – is the main strength of the 1950s debate. It is perhaps fair to say that Weber himself was more concerned with large, public, State bureaucracies than with the workplace, although he knew about and was a supporter of Taylorism (see chapter 6). Using Weber's model as a yardstick, the realities of different types of organisation emerge on closer analysis, as Merton and Blau show.

Merton Merton saw that the very elements which lead to efficiency in general produce inefficiency in specific instances. He draws attention to the following possible bureaucratic dysfunctions:

- *Impersonality:* Clients of various State organisations may expect staff to be sympathetic and interested in them as people. Bureaucratic procedures emphasise the importance of objective, impersonal treatment.

- *'Red tape':* The rule systems so beloved of bureaucracies can become the be-all and end-all of the organisation. The maze of regulations may cause staff to lose sight of the original goals for which the rules were made. These rules could make the organisation less effective.

- *Inflexibility:* Training staff to follow rules rigidly can produce inflexibility. A situation may arise where the organisation's goals could be achieved by bending the rules or ignoring them for a while but the bureaucrat has not been trained to be adaptable or innovative. They will stick to the very letter of the law, and efficiency will be reduced.

Blau Blau's work is concerned with case studies which highlight the existence of informal structures within the larger organisations. These can and do help efficiency, and go some way towards putting right the various inefficiencies caused by the rules of bureaucracy. Blau's original research followed the working life of employees of a federal agency in Washington DC. They worked on individual cases which involved complicated tax laws. They were officially forbidden from discussing cases with each other, but were reluctant to consult their bosses. So they broke the rules, discussed details and asked each other for advice on a regular basis. The outcome of this rule-breaking was more efficiency on the job. The agents learned from each other and pooled their experiences. This gives them an insight which would not have been available had they played it by the book. So informal structures can promote efficiency.

QUESTIONS

1 **Outline some of the dysfunctions of bureaucracy.**

2 **What is an 'informal structure' in an organisation?**

Formal and informal organisations

From a theoretical point of view, it can be assumed that if an organisation functions because it has goals then in functionalist theory, all else will become targeted on this goal. The reality, however, may be more complex. By engaging in participant observation, working as an assistant to an athletic director in an American asylum, Erving Goffman (1961) produced an altogether different insight into the means by which organisations meet their goals. As he wrote: 'Often we find that if the principal ideal aims of an organisation are to be achieved, then it will be necessary at times to by-pass momentarily other ideals of the organisation, while maintaining the impression that these other ideals are still in force.'

Total institutions   Asylums are an extreme form of organisation, what he calls 'total institutions'. These include prisons, boarding schools, mental hospitals, monasteries and military barracks; in short, any institutions which have 'an encompassing tendency', and which are closed off from the outside world, often physically, by walls, wire and fences. Interwoven with the official aims of the organisations are a whole set of 'underground' goals and practices which operate invisibly but are often a vital part of the functioning of these institutions – the 'underlife of public institutions'. In order to understand this underlife, Goffman concentrates on the world of the inmates. Indeed, critics would say he over-identifies with them.

Mortification of the self   The patients in the mental hospital which Goffman studied had often been forcibly committed, or tricked into admission by an alliance between their family, friends and the agents of social control in the shape of the police, social workers, doctors and psychiatrists. Goffman calls this the 'betrayal funnel'. They were de-personalised, humiliated and deprived of the most basic rights. Their total lack of autonomy was continually pressed home to them by, for example, being forced to beg attendants for a light or permission to go to the toilet. This contributes to what Goffman calls the 'mortification of the self'. Patients make a 'primary adjustment' to this formal organisational demand. They can then be easily controlled. However, humans develop complex social responses to such formal demands, and a process of 'secondary adjustment' helps to create a new self, squeezed into the spaces which are not filled by the rules and regulations. Goffman (1961) writes: 'Our sense of being a person can come from being drawn into a wider social unit; our sense of selfhood … can arise through the little ways in which we resist the pull. Our status is backed by the solid buildings of the world, while our sense of personal identity often resides in the cracks.'

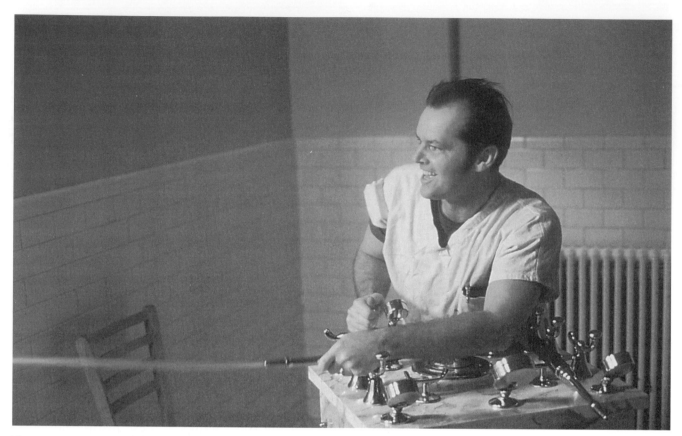

Not everyone is successfully socialised into the norms and values of total institutions: Jack Nicholson as McMurphy in *One Flew over the Cuckoo's Nest*.

Secondary adjustment

Secondary adjustments involve creating some sort of living space for yourself without clashing with the rules. Urinating on a radiator, which quickly dissolves the liquid and adds to the pungent ward atmosphere, has the advantage of relieving oneself without having to ask, and wait for, permission. Using rooms and materials for your own comfort when you should be doing something else, and 'getting in' with attendants and staff are ways of creating a space in which to exert some control over self and situation.

The most popular 'mode of adjustment' identified by Goffman was 'playing it cool'. This entailed a way of getting along with staff, using free spaces and time for personal satisfactions, generally 'getting along' and 'making do', carving out a self without antagonising the formal structure. 'Building up a life' means 'stashes', communication systems, free places, territories, new 'currencies', for example tobacco and sweets. Patients use 'bargains, wit, force and cunning' to provide these arrangements, which are taken for granted – primary adjustment – in ordinary social situations. Every institution, no matter how 'total', has its 'damp corners' – the kitchen, sick bay, workshops – in which 'secondary adjustments breed and start to infest the establishment'. It is these damp corners and cracks in the organisation which Weber's ideal type fails to consider.

The interactionist sociology of the 1950s provides these extra insights into human actions and their consequences for organisational aims. Conflict and personal definitions of the situation exist in formal organisations, and so the functionalist assumption that there is consensus about goals and aims is challenged. The managerial definitions are not always accepted, and as David Silverman (1970) points out, the interactionist approach provides a useful theoretical perspective in the study of organisations. As Goffman (1961) says:

> Whenever we look at a social establishment ... we find that participants decline in some way to accept the official view of what they should be putting into and getting out of the organisation. Where enthusiasm is expected, there will be apathy; where loyalty, there will be disaffection; where attendance, absenteeism; where deeds are to be done, varieties of inactivity ... Wherever worlds are laid on, underlives develop.

QUESTIONS

1 What does Goffman mean by secondary adjustments?

2 How has Goffman's work provided a new insight into the sociology of organisations?

3 What criticisms could be made of this work?

Mechanistic and organic organisations

Once the social action theorists had analysed the internal workings of organisations, and highlighted the importance of informal groups, theories of management attempted to use new models to explain how control operates in organisations. Burns and Stalker (1961) provide an important analysis. In their view, an industrial organisation exists to carry out a specific task. A sugar-processing plant is there to turn molasses and other ingredients into bags of sugar. The organisation depends firstly upon people, who have to be employed. These people are given their particular part of the overall task, and the nature of this task depends upon the division of labour and available technology. The members of the industry co-operate, and this is achieved through organisation. Members have certain rights allotted to them to control others and themselves. They have duties and responsibilities to transmit and receive information. The management system of the organisation decides how these rights, duties and responsibilities are organised and achieved. Management systems vary according to the particular task of the institution.

Aims of the organisation

Decisions and actions are organised and controlled by management, and all members of an organisation are recruited to act as resources to help achieve the task of the organisation. The people allow themselves to be controlled and organised in order to ensure that the bags of sugar keep rolling off the end of the conveyor belt. Their activities are directed, the management system is operating, and this is the 'working organisation' of the industry.

Burns and Stalker point out that humans are not always willing to be used as resources in a process. Contracts offer wages in return for the mental and physical resources of individuals, and this should help keep the task chugging along, but people have other, private purposes and in most organisations they will try to pursue these, rather than the official purposes of the organisation. This is what we have been calling the 'informal structure' and what Goffman calls 'secondary adjustments'.

Management systems therefore have a more complicated task than just directing and organising the pursuit of official aims. They also have to devise ways of making sure that informal structures do not hamper the efficiency of the organisation's main task. Burns and Stalker's main concern is with the way the working organisation is 'directed' by the managing director, whose main function is to manage and direct the pursuit of the official task, in this case to make sure sugar is produced. This 'head of managers' monitors the task, people and materials, notes change, reorders the system when it needs it, and controls the 'sub-managers'. The managing director also ensures that individual commitment is made to the organisation, not in any self-interest, but acting as a figurehead to bolster the loyalty of the workers.

The work of Burns and Stalker proposes two 'extremities of form' which management can take – ideal types arising from their research. They criticise the 'sociological ideology' of most interpretations of organisations, emphasising their concern with the real world. The two types are 'mechanistic' and 'organic'. These terms are reminiscent of Durkheim's theory of solidarity (see chapters 1 and 12).

Mechanistic and organic types

The characteristics of 'mechanistic' forms are:

- the overall task is broken down into specialised tasks – the division of labour
- the specialised tasks are 'abstract' in that they are pursued separately from the end concern. (People try to improve the machine which glues the sugar bag, forgetting the end product – a bag of gluey sugar.)

- superiors reconcile these tasks by joining them together
- each role has defined rights, obligations and technical methods
- these rights, obligations and methods are transferred into responsibilities in a functional position
- a hierarchic control, authority and communication structure – the 'pecking order', 'chain of command', 'procedures'
- this hierarchy is confirmed by the controllers at the top, who reconcile all the tasks and ensure the end product
- communication between superior and subordinate – 'up and down' the pecking order
- operations and working behaviour are governed by superiors
- staff are loyal and obedient
- knowledge of tasks within are more important than general, external knowledge – you could be a brilliant sociologist but you know nothing about packing sugar

The 'organic' model is less rigid, more flexible, adaptable to change, problems and new conditions. These are the organic characteristics:

- specialist knowledge and experience contribute to the overall task of the concern
- individual tasks must be seen 'realistically', as part of the overall concern, not as separate
- interaction will lead to redefinition of individual tasks
- 'responsibilities' are the province of everyone, and should not be passed up the line – 'the buck stops here' syndrome must go
- commitment is more than a technical term – it should be spread to the whole concern
- control, authority and communication should be a network of interactions, and people work in their roles because of community and co-operative interests rather than being forced to by impersonal contracts
- everyone may have knowledge which can be used in the control network – the all-knowing boss would not exist
- communication and information should travel in all directions not just up and down
- emphasis is on information and advice rather than instructions and decisions
- loyalty and obedience are replaced by commitment to the task
- externally recognised knowledge and experience are valid, not just internal know-how

Human relations   It is clear that, for Burns and Stalker, the organic system (with its multidirectional communications, its recognition of the ideas and knowledge of individuals, its emphasis on less formal controls and its ethos of listening and advising rather than rigid order structures) is the preferred and more efficient system. The two forms neatly outline the differences between 'scientific management' (mechanistic) models and 'human relations' (organic) models. In the latter, individual commitment is strongly emphasised, as if all this informality will buy the heart and mind of the worker more effectively than a mere contract to the cold face of mechanistic organisation. There is recognition of seniority and expertise, but it is not used for control. The workers' co-operation is ensured by commitment to the goals and values of the organisation. The workers are important and feel important, so they are less likely to develop self-interest. Most organisations are to be found somewhere between these two poles.

QUESTIONS

1   **What are the most important differences between mechanistic and organic forms of organisation?**

2   **What are the similarities?**

3   **Which form do you think is most common in Britain now? Can you suggest examples?**

Scientific management, human relations and structuralist models

Amitai Etzioni (1964) summarises the three main theories of organisations. He distinguishes between 'scientific management', 'human relations' and 'structuralist' analyses.

Goals   Scientific management theories are referred to as 'goal-models'. These include work based upon the ideas of Taylor (see chapter 6) and they concentrate upon the analysis of how efficiently an organisation achieves the goals it is set up to realise: 'organisations are social units (or human groupings) deliberately constructed and reconstructed to seek specific goals' (Parsons, 1960). Etzioni asks whether goals should be seen as all-important, the 'masters' of an organisation, or whether they can be seen as secondary, the 'servants'. Organisations have other problems to solve, which arise out of the work situation – problems of morale and problems which arise because of human needs, which cannot be assessed by timing people shovelling coal or going to the toilet, which is what the early Taylorist time and motion studies ended up doing. He poses the question 'Do organisations ever fully achieve their goals?' and in answering it shows that if a particular organisation ever does achieve its goals, it will either fold up and go away, or it will construct new goals in order to maintain its existence. If the various organisations which fund cancer research were successful, and a cure was found, what need would there be for the organisations?

Means

> **R. Michels (1876–1936)**
> German social and political theorist. His most famous work Political Parties (1911) explained the loss of any revolutionary potential by the socialist movements of Europe at that time by pointing to the tendency for the organisations to give rise to oligarchical hierarchies which promoted the leaders rather than the ideals. This became known as 'the iron law of oligarchy'.

In this way, Michels' 'iron law of oligarchy' (rule by a few) is used to show that the self-interest of those involved in organisations always comes to the fore. Means become goals, goals become means. A socialist organisation which begins life intending to promote a socialist revolution soon becomes more concerned with pursuing its own existence, and the original goal becomes the means which allows the small group of individuals to achieve their own personal aims, keep a steady job, secure public position and perhaps wealth. How many British trade union and Labour Party leaders become peers of the realm, members of the established élite which they were supposed to be defending their workers from or working to dismantle and replace? A study based merely upon the analysis of efficiency in reaching goals misses all this. In fact, few organisations ever achieve their goals.

Systems models

The second wave of ideas, spearheaded by the work of Elton Mayo in the 1920s, is termed the 'human relations' model, or 'systems model'. These use a method which looks at the system in operation, how it pursues goals and also how it deals with all the other issues and problems which arise in a social situation where human interactions are involved. Systems models compare one organisation with others, not to see how efficient it is at achieving goals, but to compare levels of oligarchy – some organisations manage to be less oligarchical, and these are the ones that rely on human relations, increased communication, workers taking part in decisions, and less of a hierarchy – Burns and Stalker's organic model, for example. The advantage of this method of analysis is that the 'unintended consequences' of goal achievements are highlighted. Etzioni's example is the bank which is totally efficient in its goal of making money. Goal-model research would highlight this and claim that the organisation was using maximum efficiency. The systems model could uncover the alienation and dissatisfaction of staff, low morale and the possibility of widespread fraud and embezzlement, to 'compensate' for the harsh regime they are working under. Human relations models seek to explain the needs of humans as individuals, and how these become an important factor in the workings of any organisation. These needs can also become more important than the organisation's original goals, and the 'iron' bit of Michels' law of oligarchy suggests that all organisations tend to get sidetracked into a set of operations which are devised to prolong the life of the institution, fatten the salaries and boost the public status of those at the top.

Structuralism   The problem with systems models is one which plagues most interactionist research: research based on this model is too time consuming and therefore expensive. Structuralist approaches combine the classical, formal systems approach and the human relations model, based on informal systems. Whereas scientific management ignored conflict, the structuralists recognise it, see it as inevitable and sometimes desirable in helping the organisation function. Weber, with his ideal type of bureaucracy, is the first structuralist, as his social action theory looks at both goal-related and human-needs aspects of organisations. The school of thought is broad enough to include Marxists, and the whole thrust of structuralist models is to avoid the narrowness of early Taylorism or the simplicity of Mayo's work on human relations. A combination of both types of approach is needed for a full understanding of how organisations work.

The structuralist approach considers the growing trend towards new managerial techniques which emphasise the need for decentralisation in the workplace and flexibility in decision making, thus allowing more autonomy for the workers. The hierarchies which develop in the old-style bureaucratic structures are more to do with the plans and strategies of management than a direct result of organisational goals. Marxist writers are quick to point out that all forms of control exist to help exploit the worker, and substituting wage increases with token schemes of power sharing is only another way of exploiting the proletariat.

The 'intrapreneurial' model proposed by Atterhead (1985) in *Table* 7.1 is a good example of how the new, flexible organisation is meant to work. How widespread is such decentralisation? Although many organisations are responding to social scientists' pleas for more flexibility – and this appears to be happening when you look at the way decisions are made and tasks are allotted in the workplace – an

TABLE 7.1   Centralisation and decentralisation

BIG CORPORATION CULTURE		INTRAPRENEURIAL CULTURE
Control	⟷	Trust
Meddling	⟷	Protection
Boss	⟷	Mentor
Instructions	⟷	Visions
Planning	⟷	Flexibility
Orders	⟷	Viewpoints
Alienation	⟷	Participation
Fragmentation	⟷	Wholeness
Rules	⟷	Customers

Source: Sven G. Atterhead in Clutterbuck, 1985

analysis of new information technology shows that long-term planning is more firmly centralised in the management sphere. For example, General Motors has a company called Electronic Data Systems to co-ordinate the activities of its many organisations throughout the world. Management is really controlling a huge, global factory. In the component plants, flexibility and decentralisation are apparent, but the oligarchical few are still controlling the keyboard. Japanese organisations, renowned for their efficiency, are characterised by hierarchical rule, with status in the hierarchy being recognised by size of desk and depth of bow.

As Thompson and McHugh (1990) point out, companies still increase their overall size, through mergers and monopolies, despite their increased decentralisation. Behind the scenes, there is still a powerful unit which directs and controls. We are back to Michels' iron law. The Japanese encourage worker integration, and even if British workers in Japanese-owned firms start singing company songs every morning, vowing to increase productivity and pledging allegiance to their work group, there will be a forceful, bureaucratic organisation looming in the background. As Stewart Clegg (1979) points out, the new bureaucracy is based upon democracy and collectivism, but it is still a bureaucracy at heart. As we shall see, in his analysis of the 'post-modern' organisation, Clegg argues that Japan has managed to supersede the old Weberian model of bureaucracy.

QUESTIONS

1 **How do structuralist views of organisations differ from those of scientific management and the human relations model?**

2 **Other than increasing output, productivity and efficiency, what organisational goals are considered in this chapter?**

3 **What is Michels' iron law of oligarchy?**

Modernism and post-modernism

Stewart Clegg argues that contemporary Japanese industries have developed a new style of organisation since the Second World War. He distinguishes between 'modernist' – those based upon the Weberian model which was also called 'Fordist' because Ford was the first industry to use the authoritarian, bureaucratic form – and 'post-modernist' or post-Fordist organisations which are based on the flexible 'organic' model used by Burns and Stalker and supported by the human relations approach.

Japan The Japanese version of this emerged as a response to the economic crisis of the 1970s, which continues to dog the world economy. The modernist structure was struggling to survive, for all the usual reasons, mainly that the need for surveillance in hierarchies became too expensive and efficiency was falling. Clegg suggests that the modernist organisation will be an outdated system in the future, relegated to underdeveloped countries. The centralisation behind all this decentralisation continues to exist, but the way Japan has responded is perhaps unique, due to post-war social conditions.

The post-modern organisation

The stress in the post-modern organisation is upon all the factors mentioned in discussion of previous models – flexibility, less authoritarianism, collective decision-making and less supervision. Workers are committed to the company, not their occupation, and they are seen as contributing towards 'core-competencies' (Prahalad and Hamal, 1990). All expertise is used to help further the organisation's interests through a system of cross-unit relationships; 'contracts' and workers are 'multi-skilled'. As Clegg shows, this applies to about a third of the Japanese workforce – those who are on the inside, part of the company for life, with all the benefits and lifestyle options which this brings. These lucky few enjoy the advantages of post-modernism, becoming committed through the attraction of this security and a process of organisational indoctrination.

Core and periphery

Singing the company song was mentioned above, but 'spiritual training' goes deeper. Workers are subjected to a Moonie-like programming into social co-operation, responsibility, reality-acceptance and perseverance in tasks. Encouraging commitment by a process as blatant as this would, to a Marxist, be a straightforward construction of 'false-consciousness', without even the subtlety of ideology. Spiritual training is a process which takes place in front of your eyes. These 'core-workers' tend to be mostly male, with women very heavily marginalised. Indeed, two-thirds of the workforce, those employed externally to the companies, are in seasonal jobs and do not enjoy the benefits of the post-modernist organisation. This could be the organisational type of the future. The picture of a society characterised by a secure, well-paid minority and a hard-pressed, marginalised majority echoes the existence of a 'dual-labour market' (see chapter 5). Lifestyle options are restricted to the few, who enjoy private pensions, health schemes, education, all aided by the company, whilst the rest struggle on. Perhaps the future will see an 'immiserated' proletariat. The post-modernist organisation has substituted authoritarian control with commitment and a high degree of connection between worker, task, leaders and goals. As control has improved, so has efficiency. The dated, modernist bureaucratic structure is being thrown out and old methods of worker–management relations are becoming redundant and fossilised.

QUESTIONS
1 What are the characteristics of the post-modern organisation?

2 Why have post-modern organisations emerged in Japan?

Trade unions and professional associations

The interests of most of those in the world of employment are organisationally divided into three sectors: trade unions, representing manual and white-collar workers, professional associations representing more senior and higher status employees and employers' organisations representing employers, such as the Confederation of British Industry and the Institute of Directors. At the same time, many employers and employees are unrepresented by any organisation. All three types of organisation have long histories, paralleling the growth of industrial societies. It is since the Second World War, and the growth of corporatism, that they have been of particular interest to sociologists.

Corporatism

Corporatism is a term used to describe the phenomenon of the State co-operating with employers' organisations and trade unions to formulate an industrial policy, principally aimed at smoothing the process of bargaining over wages and conditions of service without undue industrial strife. In Britain, this 'voluntary corporatism' was exemplified at a national level by the creation of the National Economic Development Council in 1962, made up of members of trade unions, employers' organisations and representatives of the Conservative government, and taken further with the creation of a National Enterprise Board under Labour in 1975. At a local level it involved a move to industrial democracy through the increasing involvement of trade union shop stewards in processes of negotiation and consultation.

Richard Hyman (1989) offers a number of reasons for the emergence of corporatism in Britain: first, the State desired to intervene in wage settlements in order to control inflation; secondly the State itself had become increasingly involved as a major employer as more and more industries and services became nationalised; and thirdly the co-operation of the other two sides of this tripartite agreement could be useful in solving wider social and economic problems.

Trade-union power

Over time, however, the perception grew that trade unions had become too powerful, out of control and were overstepping the line between industrial relations policy and wider political concerns. This had become apparent as early as 1968, when the government-commissioned Donovan Report remarked that 'Britain has two systems of industrial relations. The one is the formal system embodied in the official institutions. The other is the informal system created by the actual behaviour of trade unions and employers' associations.' In other words, the national system was failing to work. Hyman himself claims that this was because the status of national union leaders was deliberately overstated in order to gain the co-operation of their membership.

Fear of trade-union militancy grew throughout the 1970s, with miners' strikes bringing down the Heath government in 1974, culminating in the Labour government's inability to prevent the 1978/9 'winter of discontent' when many unions, in both the private and the public sector, refused to obey government-imposed limits to wage rises. Ostracised by the hostile Conservative governments from 1979, they left the NEDC in 1982 and the era of corporatism had effectively come to an end, to be replaced by the discipline of more anonymous 'market forces' and a series of measures designed to deregulate the labour market by the Conservative government.

Trade unions

Trade unions became effective when they were made legal in the nineteenth century, following the repeal of the Combinations Acts in the 1820s, allowing workers to collectively represent themselves and protect their interests in the workplace through their union and eventually at a national level through the Trades Union Congress, dating from 1868. Having first embraced skilled workers, union membership filtered down to semi-skilled and unskilled workers by the end of the nineteenth century. Membership continued to grow throughout the twentieth century up to the early 1980s. At its maximum in 1980 more than 50 per cent of the registered workforce were members of unions (*see Figure 7.1*).

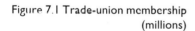

Figure 7.1 Trade-union membership (millions)

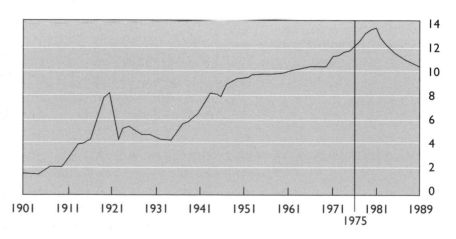

Source: Social Trends 22, 1992

European trade unions The main purpose of trade unions is to collectively protect the interests of their members, particularly with regard to their pay, conditions of service and employment rights. British trade unions can be distinguished from many others in the industrial world in a number of ways. First, because they organise not by plant or employer, as for example in Germany ('industrial unionism'), but by trade. In a place of work there may therefore be a number of different unions which may co-operate through joint shop stewards' committees. A second difference is their relatively high density of membership, i.e. the percentage of unionised members of the workforce compared with the overall workforce.

As we know from the work of Duncan Gallie (see chapter 6), trade unions in France and Britain, for example, interpret their role differently, with French trade unions being more willing to see themselves as ideological leaders, trying to raise the political consciousness of their members, and entering into wage negotiations at a national level, removing most workers from the decision-making process. This means, Gallie argues, that French and British workers have different attitudes to their work and their employers.

In the twentieth century, as unions have become part of the apparatus of industrial relations, they have also become increasingly organised and bureaucratised, employing full-time officials and a hierarchical power structure, mirroring the structure of the firms their members work for. For many writers, the existence of legitimate, organised unionism has reduced the potential for conflict, easing their transition into becoming conduits of the dominant value system.

Functionalism This observation informs much of the functionalist view of unionism. For writers such as Parsons and Davis and Moore (see chapter 3) the value consensus in society implies that a consensus similarly exists between employers and employees, where benefits are made from working co-operatively, with each having their own particular role. Strikes are explained as minor problems of communication and adjustment or as necessary breaks from the monotony of work. In stable democracies, union officials provide a line of communication to the workforce for the management, preventing unofficial (or 'wildcat') strikes, not sanctioned by the union. They are not seen as agents of class conflict.

Pluralist theorists are more willing to recognise differences of interest between employers, seeking to keep costs down, and employees, seeking to use their union to maximise wages. These differences are not so great, however, that they prevent co-operation and coexistence. Conflict, where it exists, can be minimalised through institutionalised annual pay rounds, agencies such as ACAS and industrial tribunals. The emphasis here is on trade unions as incorporated rather than marginalised organisations, participators in the process of creating an industrial and social democracy. This vision, put forward by writers such as Ralf Dahrendorf (1959) in Britain, and Lipset (1964) in America, seems less plausible now, given the developments of the last two decades, as well as the high level of strikes throughout the 1970s.

Feminist writers have been sharply critical of the role played by unions throughout industrialisation, seeing them as patriarchal organisations formed partly to keep women out of paid labour. Writers such as Rubery (1980) and Walby (1986) claim that they contribute to the genderisation of labour by preventing the claims of women as skilled workers being recognised, while seeking to maintain the definition of some men's work as skilled, for example in clerical, textile and engineering work. Even in unions with a largely female membership, it remains the case that the majority of full-time officials are male.

Marxism   Marxism views trade unions with ambivalence. At one level, they are evidence of the existence of a separate working-class consciousness, formed to resist exploitation at the hands of the bourgeoisie. At another level there is the belief that trade unions can only ever develop an 'economistic' level of consciousness, concerned more with improving the lot of workers under capitalism than struggling for a new social formation or tackling the issue of control over the labour process. Only a revolutionary party can unite the trade-union movement towards this end. More than a hundred years after the death of Marx, unions show very little sign of wanting to negotiate more than the terms of their obedience to employers. For some writers they have failed even in this limited ambition, being unable to prevent mass unemployment, the collapse of the manufacturing sector in the early 1980s or a substantial decline in union membership.

In the last quarter of the twentieth century, unions have undergone a series of changes to their legal and political powers. The Employment Acts passed by the Conservative government in 1980, 1982, 1988 and 1990, as well as the Trade Union Acts of 1984 and 1993 (which Hyman describes as a campaign of 'coercive pacification') restricted and weakened trade-union activity and the return of mass unemployment meant that membership began to fall steadily to the present day, both in absolute terms and as a percentage of the civilian workforce in employment. Between 1978 and 1987, for example, membership fell from 13.1 million to 10.2 million, while registered unemployment rose from 5.7 per cent to 10.7 per cent, reaching 13.5 per cent in 1985. By 1992, only 36 per cent of the labour force belonged to a trade union. This picture, however, is complicated by a number of factors, particularly the changing composition of the workforce, shifting away from men working full time in manual jobs. At the same time, the number of strikes, measured in days lost per worker, has also fallen to an all-time low. In 1993, Wage Councils, setting a minimum wage in some industries, were abolished.

The debate on trade unions

For some writers (for example Purcell, 1982 and Bassett, 1987) the power and influence of trade unions has been fatally damaged, particularly because of the changing composition of the workforce and the changing nature of employment terms and conditions. Thus the 'traditional' blue-collar male trade unionist, working full-time as part of a close-knit industrial community, is disappearing, being superseded by more part-time, white-collar and female workers, none of whom are usually associated with the class consciousness necessary for solidaristic action. The introduction of compulsory competitive tendering in the public sector has also allowed some public-sector employees to favour non-unionised companies. At the same time, there has been a growth in individually, rather than collectively negotiated contracts, performance-related pay and the implementation of the practice of human resource management and total quality management, emphasising the importance of individual commitment to enterprises. All of these have worked against the existing trade-union philosophy of collective action.

Other writers (such as Kelly, 1988 and Grint, 1991), however, argue that the diminution of trade-union power has been overstated, and that it is more realistic to see a pattern of stability and continuity. Union organisation and collective bargaining remain intact, and many national agreements continue to exist. The number of union convenors and shop stewards has not markedly fallen, and in areas such as public-sector employment union membership has actually increased. The cause of the decline in overall membership can be found not in the changes listed above but in the fact of the downturn in the business cycle. Union membership and strength will therefore be restored with an upturn in the business cycle. It remains the case that wages have continued to exceed the rate of inflation, and significant victories have been won in areas such as the railways and motor vehicle industries. New industrial relations practices, such as the introduction of no-strike agreements, have received a lot of publicity but have not become widespread. They are confined to new companies, particularly those from the Far East, that have set up in Britain. Similarly, new legislation has not been widely used by employers. Compulsory ballots on union and political affiliation have shown overwhelming support for Labour Party membership. Finally, doubts have been expressed about the allegedly low level of class consciousness and the existence of a golden age of class solidarity. Trade unions have survived hostile conditions before, particularly in the inter-war years, and they will successfully survive them again.

Trade unions in the future

Trade unions are undoubtedly under pressure to change. Those most willing to change are characterised as modernists or realists and those wishing to resist change are seen as traditionalists or dinosaurs. Some have earned the wrath of other trade unionists by being willing to enter into single-union and no-strike agreements and other unions have had to merge or consider merging, leading to the phenomenon of 'conglomerate unionism'. Many hope for improved fortunes with economic upturn and the election of a Labour government, though they will not necessarily benefit from either.

Professional associations

Higher and lower professions

Professionals differ from manual and routine non-manual workers in that they specialise in the development and dissemination of technical knowledge. Following the Registrar-General's classification (see also chapter 3) they can be split into two levels – the higher professions, including lawyers, architects and doctors, and the lower professions (sometimes also described as semi-professionals) made up of occupations such as teachers, nurses and social workers. What distinguishes these two levels is the extent of training and qualifications needed to take up these posts.

It is the task of professional associations in particular to define and preserve the standards and ethics necessary to each profession. Thus it is the relative success of organisations such as the British Medical Association, founded in 1832, in defining the standards and ethics required of medical practitioners that has allowed this group to be accepted as being of professional status.

Professional associations are normally thought to represent the interests of the higher professions, the Law Society in the case of the legal profession and the British Medical Association in the case of doctors. The status of groups representing the lower professions is less clear. In some ways they clearly have the character of the higher professions in terms of status and tradition, in others they more closely resemble trade unions, being increasingly more inclined to engage in the kind of collective actions typical of traditional unions.

This is particularly true of teaching unions and, increasingly, nursing.

In the 1980s almost all professional groups came under fire from a Conservative government which perceived their existence as a restriction on the free market for labour. Traditionally autonomous groups such as lawyers and doctors found themselves targeted for professional restrictive practices, as with the control of house conveyancing by solicitors, or barristers' claims to sole representation (or 'right of audience') of clients before the upper courts. Significantly, however, lawyers, through their professional associations, have been one of the few groups to resist such attacks successfully and their monopoly remains, in practice if not in law.

Functionalism

The discussion in chapter 10 on sociological perspectives of the medical profession is also relevant to this discussion of professional associations. Thus, from a functionalist point of view, the professions, through their associations, are a microcosm of a cohesive moral community, the ethics of which will, according to Barber (1963) and Halmos (1970), following Durkheim, spread out into the whole of society, particularly industry, setting a model of consumer relations (see also Parsons, 1951). They also integrate professionals into an occupational group, providing ethical standards and a code of practice. Because they serve the community, as well as their clients, professionals are consequently highly rewarded for playing their roles and given high status.

Other writers (for example Johnson, 1972) have argued that professions have gained their status not through altruism but self-interest, by preventing competition to keep their market value high and by encouraging the public to believe their services are necessary rather than optional. In the words of the Parrys (1976), this amounts to a 'strategy for controlling an occupation in which colleagues set up a system of self-government' in which the professional associations play a central role. This forms the core of the neo-Weberian view, emphasising occupational closure, through the control of training, supply and entry, and the claim that their behaviour is exemplary and necessarily self-regulating, preventing others from performing the same tasks, as doctors achieved with the Medical Registration Act of 1858, following the formation of the BMA in 1832. Teachers professionalised later and therefore failed to gain such a strong hold on their profession, failing, for example, to control entry to it.

Marxism

Marxists believe that this emphasis on autonomy is overstated, seeing the professions instead as agents of capital, with the higher professions in particular occupying an intermediary position between the bourgeoisie and the proletariat. They are increasingly losing their independence and are becoming directly employed by the bourgeoisie in large companies. Following Braverman, this perspective sees the end of this process as an accelerating division of labour and the proletarianisation of the lower professions in particular (see also chapter 3).

From a neo-Marxist perspective, Ehrenreich and Ehrenreich (1979) break with the orthodox two-class Marxist analysis in claiming that a professional-managerial class, not owning the means of production but 'whose major function may broadly be described as the reproduction of capitalist culture and capitalist class relations', exists between the bourgeoisie and the proletariat. This class exists like any other, empirically distinct through its own reproduction, but paid out of the surplus produced by the proletariat, although the professional-managerial class are also wage labourers. Professional associations serve to maintain the independence of this class from the ruling class, although ultimately their interest is in maintaining the capitalist system.

The perhaps obvious criticism from within Marxism of this theory is that it does not take into account the proletarianising tendencies that exist within the professions that other Marxists such as Braverman claim, even though as fellow Americans they are all aware that the professions in the USA are better organised than they are in Europe, though in both continents it is the case that professionals are increasingly becoming directly employed by large organisations as in-house workers. Other neo-Marxists such as Erik Olin Wright (1985) deny the existence of a separate class of professionals but see them instead as occupying a contradictory class location, possessing some of the characteristics of the other two classes.

These organisations may therefore be seen as serving a primarily integrative role; as largely autonomous organisations self-interestedly defining their own role; or as agents of capital subject to the control and direction of the bourgeoisie. Since the Second World War, they have come under the increasing scrutiny of the State, initially with the aim of co-ordinating industrial policy. More recently they have struggled to sustain their identity and position in an increasingly deregulated and insecure labour market.

QUESTIONS

1 **How do Weberians view the professions?**

2 **How has the position of trade unions changed since the Second World War?**

3 **How important are political factors in determining the role of these organisations?**

The end of organisations?

In the past, society did not depend upon organisations, but the Industrial Revolution and the development of capitalism created the 'organisational human', a being socialised to move between different forms of organisation – for example family, school, work and sports club. The core of the middle-class value system, with its emphasis upon neatness, punctuality and conformity, is geared towards producing the organisational human, prepared to live within and depend upon organisations. Organisations have changed dramatically from the original, strictly hierarchical bureaucratic organisations towards the flexible, democratic organisation – the human resources, or human relations model. There seems to be some relationship between the degree of regulation in a society between State and industry, and the degree of organisation, and particularly the amount and depth of interactions, between State and organisations. With decentralisation of society comes decentralisation of organisations. Some organisations, which attempt to span a variety of smaller organisations, specifically unions and professional and employers' associations, lose their aims and therefore their power and influence as a result.

This still leaves a major issue in the sociology of organisations. They exist to put large numbers of humans in situations to pursue certain goals – whether it be to produce goods, educate people, cure their ills, rehabilitate or punish offenders or organise political interests. All these things need effective systems of control, making sure that people pursue organisational interests, not their own. Perhaps the so-called flexible, democratic, post-modernist ideal is just a more effective way of control – giving people the illusion that they are directing their own lives, when they are really being directed and used to their full potential as 'human resources'.

FURTHER READING

D. Beetham, **Bureaucracy**, Open University Press, 1987

S. Clegg, **Modern Organisations: Organisation Studies in the Postmodern World**, Sage, 1990

R. Dingwall and P. Lewis (eds), **The Sociology of the Professions: Lawyers, Doctors and Others**, Macmillan, 1983

E. Goffman, **Asylums**, Anchor Books, 1961

G. Morgan, **Organisations in Society**, Macmillan, 1990

D. Pugh et al., **Writers on Organisations: An Introduction**, Penguin, 1989

P. Thompson and D. McHugh, **Work Organisations: A Critical Introduction**, Macmillan, 1995

8 Politics and power

The State is a group of humans who have successfully monopolised the legitimate use of violence in a given territory.

Max Weber

INTRODUCTION

This chapter begins by focusing on notions of power, authority and ideology. Functionalist, Marxist, élitist and pluralist theories of power are then examined in some detail. You will then go on to look at the role of the State in Britain, which is followed by a discussion of political parties and their respective political ideologies. The chapter closes with an examination of changing sociological explanations for voting behaviour, with a discussion of class (partisan alignment), dealignment, issue voting and rational choice models.

Power and authority

Ideology and false consciousness: cartoonist Steve Bell's view of the 1992 election result.

Power relationships exist everywhere in society, whether between domestic partners, parents and children, teachers and students, police

and citizens, priest and congregation, editor and readers or newspaper magnate and editor. According to the roles we play, we are all relatively more or less powerful. Many sociologists have argued that people seek power over others to compensate for the lack of power they possess in other situations, for example at work between employer and employed – or more frequently, between workers and their immediate bosses. So what do we mean by this term power?

Weber   The clearest explanation comes from Max Weber. According to Weber, power exists where one individual or group is able to get their way over another group – to oblige them to act or behave in a certain way – whether the others resist or not. As he puts it, power is 'the probability that one actor within a social relationship will be in a position to carry out his own will'. The power that some possess over others may be recognised by the passive group as legitimate – legally acceptable – in which case it will be seen as 'authority'. Power not recognised as legitimate is coercion or force.

Three dimensions of power   Steven Lukes (1974) has argued that three views of power have been articulated. The difference between them is the number of dimensions to power that is perceived.

The *one-dimensional view* focuses on the behaviour of decision makers, the decisions they make, the central issues that are decided on, and the forms of conflict that are openly observable. This view of power is most appropriate to élitist and pluralist views.

The *two-dimensional view* looks at power in terms of decisions that are made, as well as decisions that are not made – it looks at what are potential as well as actual issues. As Bachrach and Baratz (1963) argue, the two-dimensional view questions who it is who sets the agenda concerning the decisions to be decided on, and what other issues they are able to block from becoming areas for public discussion.

The *three-dimensional view* is similar to the two-dimensional view in questioning who sets the agenda for decision making, but goes further by arguing that some fundamental issues never emerge because, under the hold of propaganda or ideological control, no other possible alternative is imagined or considered.

Other views of power have sought to move the term away from the idea that it is something to be possessed or not – you either have power or not. Power can also be seen as a potential and something that can be generated. Societies, and organisations within them, can become more or less powerful according to the degree to which the potential power is organised. For Michael Mann (1986), power can be mobilised in ideological, political, military and economic forms. None of these forms of organisation automatically possesses power. It only becomes – or ceases to be – effective when its organisational form allows it. Thus, if the modern State has power, it is due to the immense amount of organisational ability that it now possesses.

The term authority is not synonymous with the term power. Authority is the exercise of legitimate power. The two do not always co-exist. People may have the authority to carry out an action, but be unable to carry it through because they lack the power (such as a teacher trying to keep a class quiet). On the other hand, people may be able to succeed in their actions without the legitimacy to do so, as with one country invading the territory of another. In this case, they would have power without authority. They would then seek to make this power legitimate.

Weber distinguished between three different types of authority in society: traditional, charismatic and rational-legal. In the first, order is maintained on the basis of established custom and procedure – 'we've always done it this way'. The authority once possessed by the aristocracy is a good example of this. In the second, individuals or groups maintain authority because of the particular qualities they possess, particularly leadership, that make people want to follow them. Jesus Christ is a good example here. The third refers to authority that is maintained because of the importance given to formal rules which are followed regardless of the individuals enforcing them. Respect is given to the position someone holds, not to the person holding the position. Bureaucratic authority is what Weber had at the front of his mind here, where norms have a semi-legal status (see also chapter 7).

QUESTIONS

1 **How do the one-, two- and three-dimensional views of power differ?**

2 **How does power differ from authority?**

3 **What is Weber's view of power and authority?**

Theories of power

Functionalism

There is very little writing of any substance that has appeared – especially in the last twenty years – that articulates the concept of power from a functionalist point of view. The paucity of such material points to the conclusion that this is one of the weakest and least elaborated areas of functionalist theory.

Parsons   As ever, it is with Talcott Parsons that we will find the most comprehensive attempt to theorise power from a structuralist perspective (for example in *Politics and Social Structure*, 1969). His argument proceeds in a manner that closely resembles his ideas on stratification. Power, like social inequality, originates from the collective needs of the whole society. The amount of power in society can be measured by the degree to which collective goals are being realised. There is a difference between what a society wants – for example an increasing standard of living – and its ability to attain that goal. Power, for Parsons, exists as 'a facility for the performance of functions in and on behalf of the society as a system'. A society is at its most powerful and efficient when these goals are being effectively realised – what Parsons calls a 'variable-sum' notion of power. In the same way that stratification is necessary, so too is it vital for some to have more power than others. These powerful individuals or groups will exercise power on behalf of the wider society.

In a Western democracy, some are powerful because that power has been entrusted or 'deposited' with them, in much the same way that money is placed in a bank by creditors. And in the same way, that trust can be withdrawn through elections when the electorate feels it needs to withdraw it. The possibility of sectional interests of the State holding on to power for its own sake is therefore unconsidered.

Criticisms of the functionalist view   The shortcomings of functionalist – or Parsonian – theory here are glaring, and it is no surprise that little work has been done recently on its application. Parsons is effectively limited to describing Western democracies, and there is a strong sense that he is really only thinking of democracy in the USA. He makes what many see as a naive assumption about the efficient working of a democratic system and citizens' ability to express their will through it – this is perhaps a result of the consensual nature of American politics, where the differences between Republicans and Democrats are not as great as they have traditionally been between Conservatives and Labour in Britain.

QUESTIONS   1 **Define what Parsons meant by a variable-sum concept of power.**

2 **What are the shortcomings of the functionalist viewpoint of power?**

Marxism

The State in Marx's lifetime   From Marx's point of view, an understanding of the nature of the State is simple. It is, he said, 'but a committee for managing the whole affairs of the bourgeoisie'. By this he meant that the State existed to referee Victorian capitalism and act on behalf of the bour-

251

geoisie to maintain their class control over the proletariat. And at first sight, this point of view seems persuasive. In his lifetime, 1818–83, the great debates within the State took place between a fading aristocracy and a rising bourgeoisie. Only those who owned or possessed a certain amount of property could vote, and some with enough property could vote twice. The claims of the working class for political participation through organisations such as the Chartist movement were ignored or suppressed. The State represented the interests of one class in society, which enabled it to control and direct key parts of the superstructure such as the police and the army. The State was the political expression of ruling-class power. In a Communist society, Engels predicted, the State would become obsolete and 'wither away'.

After Marx died, and as the proletariat gained the right to participate at a political level through voting, a debate developed between Marxists: would the working class, through its own political organisations, be able to take control of the State and use it for its own ends, or did the State itself need to be transformed out of all recognition in order to truly represent the working class? This debate raged in the early decades of this century, mainly between German Social Democrats and Russian Bolsheviks, with anarchists on the fringe making their own unique contribution.

Bolshevism With the establishment of Soviet government by 1922, following the Russian Revolution of 1917, the Bolsheviks put their own ideas into practice, at first by spreading the idea of government by local councils of workers, soldiers and peasants. Yet, while arguing that the State in the capitalist West represented the 'monopoly of violence', the Soviet State in the 1930s under Stalin was to unleash State violence on a scale that paralleled Hitler's, giving rise to the term 'totalitarian' to describe the similarities between the two State-centred systems of Nazism and Communism.

For Western Marxists, the State outside totalitarian countries continued to be seen as a system of social control run either by or for the owners of the means of production. Important differences emerged as to how the ruling class maintained their control, particularly in Marxist debates of the late 1960s and early 1970s between Ralph Miliband and Nikos Poulantzas, who represented what have come to be seen as the 'instrumentalist' and 'structuralist' wings of Marxist theories of the State.

Miliband Ralph Miliband's (1969) view is a basic restatement of Marxism in order to counter more conventional ideas of the State prevailing at the time, such as pluralism. For Miliband, a clearly visible capitalist ruling class exists, in both the élite positions of industry and the élite positions of the State. The State is simply an instrument of the capitalist ruling class, the individual members of whom are closely linked to the leading positions in the State through ties of family, religion, education and culture. In finance, in industry and the State, there is a single homogeneous class.

There is an abundance of evidence to support this view. For example, the Conservative Prime Minister, Alec Douglas-Home's Cabinet of 1963 contained 21 members who had attended public schools – one of the key agencies of ruling-class reproduction. Mrs Thatcher's first Cabinet of 1979 contained seven ministers who had, at some time or other, attended Eton. In 1983, the heads of both the Civil and Foreign Service, the Chief of Defence Staff, the editor of *The Times*, the chairman of the BBC, the governor of the Bank of England and four of its directors had all attended Eton. In the 1992 general election one-third of the Conservative MPs who were elected described themselves as company directors. Of all Conservative MPs, 47 per cent had been educated at a public school. Exactly the same proportion had attended Oxford and Cambridge universities, as had 22 per cent of Labour MPs. In the same year, *The Whitehall Companion* showed that the eight largest government departments are run by permanent secretaries who went to fee-paying private schools, of whom only one did not attend Oxbridge. Of all the graduates in the highest grades of the Civil Service, more than half had attended these same two universities (see also chapter 3).

Poulantzas   Yet for the Marxist Nikos Poulantzas this focus on the profile of individuals is mistaken. He argues against Miliband (1969). It does not matter who it is who runs the State, whether they are from Eton or a south London comprehensive, whether their father was a merchant banker, an unemployed gnome maker or even if they are a grocer's daughter from Lincolnshire. The point is that the structure of society is capitalist. There is therefore a structural guarantee that the State will serve the needs of the leading capitalists, even if those running the State are not actually of the capitalist class themselves. It cannot be any other way, because the structure of a capitalist society demands this of the State. The State may, according to Poulantzas, be 'relatively autonomous' or self-directing, where an institutional separation can exist between the political power existing in the State and economic power in society's base. At this level, the professionals who run the State will be able to overcome what divisions may exist within the capitalist class and make any necessary concessions to the working class.

Structural super-determinism   In putting forward this view of the State, Poulantzas has provoked a great deal of criticism. One strand of it comes from Miliband, who asserts that Poulantzas is guilty of 'structural super-determinism', by which he means Poulantzas simplistically accepts the literalness and automatic nature of the economic base necessarily determining the superstructure, or that because a society is capitalist it necessarily follows – simply by assertion – that the State serves the interests of the capitalist class. A second objection is the almost structural-functionalist nature of Poulantzas' argument. He appears to argue that, simply by existing, the State must be functional to the needs of capital.

Gramsci and hegemony

Somewhere between Miliband's instrumentalism and Poulantzas' (and Althusser's) structuralism lies the analysis of Antonio Gramsci (1891–1937). He was an Italian Communist who, having spent many years fighting for communism, spent many more years in jail under Mussolini in Italy. Much of his best-known work – for example the *Prison Notebooks* – became popular in Europe in the 1970s and 1980s. One of his most important ideas is the concept of hegemony, by which groups in society gain intellectual leadership (see also chapter 2). Whoever holds hegemony in society holds the dominance of ideas. By making a division between political society or the formal institutions of the State (particularly the police and the army) and civil society (which may be the family, the church, trade unions, the media, education system and so on), Gramsci is able to highlight the difference between capitalist control through the State and, more importantly, their ideological control and domination of civil society. It is the wrong approach, Gramsci argues, for the working class to target its struggle solely on the State. What they must first do is establish their own ideological supremacy in civil society through the permeation of a revolutionary class consciousness. At all levels, he says, they must win the battle for ideas to gain hegemony. The division between ideological State apparatuses and repressive State apparatuses also re-emerges in the work of Louis Althusser.

Neo-Marxism and the State

In *The Context of British Politics* David Coates attempts to construct a neo-Marxist model of the British State (Coates, 1984). Employing Gramscian concepts and seeing the State as more fluid than Miliband and Poulantzas, Coates argues that the main pressures on the State derive from the demands of international and domestic capital, in the form of banks, finance houses and large businesses. Industrial capitalism, by comparison, is much weaker. The power and influence of the ruling class is divided rather than monolithic, made up as it is of many constituent parts. At the same time, its ideological control over the working class is far from total. The proletariat, as individuals, possesses 'dual consciousness'. At times they are under the sway of hegemonic control, at others, in the grind of their daily lives, they realise the serious deficiencies of capitalism and grope towards class consciousness.

To maintain control, the State is occasionally prepared to make real concessions in its power, for example to trade unions or in the form of public ownership. This is true for the long period of economic expansion in the decades following the Second World War. Economic contraction creates crisis in which ideological dominance, in the harsher form of Thatcherism, is far harder for the ruling class to maintain.

QUESTIONS

1 How do modern Marxist views of the State all differ from that of Marx in the nineteenth century?

2 How does Poulantzas' view of the State differ from Miliband's? What does he mean by relative autonomy?

Elitism

Classical and modern elite theories

Phe theories which are gathered together under the heading of Pélitist' are wide and varied. It is necessary to distinguish between 'classical' élitist theories (so called because they came first and are the oldest, classical models) and modern élite theories. One of the most important things to do is to distinguish between Marxism as an élite theory (in which the ruling class can be seen as an élite group) and the rest. The most famous names in classical élitism, Vilfredo Pareto (1978; first published in 1902), Gaetano Mosca (1896) and Robert Michels (1911), were spurred to write in reaction to Marx's theories.

Pareto's work is considered to be the classic refutation of Marxist economics and sociology. It is said that of all anti-Marxist writing, this book caused Lenin the most concern.

Lions and foxes

Pareto was a positivist and followed Durkheim's lead in criticising Marxism for having no scientific validity. However, he did have time for some of Marx's thinking: 'There is in Marx a sociological part, which is superior to other parts and is often in accord with reality. Marx has one very clear idea – that of class conflict.' However, Marx's *Capital* was criticised as vague and obscure. Pareto was willing to admit that class conflict was real, but it was caused by more than just the economic base. He believed that some individuals were innately superior. According to Pareto these superior individuals wanted power, whereas the mass of mankind was politically inactive. For him political movements could only ever be the work of active minorities; the élites. Most people in society are passive instruments in the power struggle. The élite fall into two categories – 'lions' and 'foxes'. Lions are strong, brave and rule forcefully and with little fear of the outcome. Their leadership is direct and open, with little political cunning or trickery. Foxes on the other hand are cunning manip-

---

Vilfredo Pareto (1848–1923)
Italian economist and sociologist. He is well known as an élite theorist believing in the inevitability of élite circulation to regenerate élites in power. The advent of new social élites to power maintains the social equilibrium.

ulators, manoeuvring politically behind the scenes. They rule through manipulation and deceit, and overcome their political enemies by stealth rather than direct, forceful action.

These élites sometimes hold power and are sometimes in opposition throughout history. Changes in political fortunes are a consequence of the inevitable tendency for the ruling group to become decadent, soft and ineffective leaders. When this happens, that power structure gives way to the next, foxes step down and lions take over or vice versa. This 'theory of circulating élites' is said by Pareto to be reflected in the past two thousand years of human society. Critics of Pareto usually criticise the simplicity of his basic ideas. Although the characteristics of 'lions' and 'foxes' can be found in certain leaders, the theory relies on the psychological make-up of individuals, and is therefore considered to be weak when applied to social structure, where many other factors intervene.

Mosca

> **Gaetano Mosca (1858–1941)**
> *An Italian political theorist and one of the founding fathers of élite theory. He is best known for his work* The Ruling Class *(1896) in which he argued that a political class, monopolising power and the advantages it provides, is a universal feature of all societies.*

Gaetano Mosca had a similar aristocratic approach when it came to talking about 'natural' superiority in some social groups. Mosca believed that the masses were unfit to rule, and at best they could be allowed no more than to participate as voters in a representative democracy. Mosca believed in the right of the upper classes to rule by birth. Only those from old established families could possibly have the intellectual and leadership abilities necessary to carry the burden of power. He gradually came around to accepting that representative democracies could work, but he believed that this was true only when the élites formed the leadership of political parties, and therefore ensured that power only changed hands between one élite group and another. Any attempts to allow the masses a share of power would be disastrous. Democracy was only acceptable in that it keeps the majority politically inactive for most of the time. As long as real decisions are taken by those with the correct family backgrounds, then democracy poses no threat to the stability of the élite leadership.

Michels and oligarchy

Robert Michels was a friend of Mosca, and his work can be considered as belonging to the classical élite explanations of power. He saw bureaucracy as an enemy of individual liberty, and claimed that democratic organisations are based upon the bureaucracy which is needed to organise them. This necessity for a rigid hierarchy comes about because of the sheer size and complexity of democracies, and also because the masses need leadership from above. According to Michels, the leadership in any organisation tends to separate from the masses because of their knowledge and ability to work the dense bureaucratic system. Matters of process, points of order, minutes, agendas, sub-committees, reports, complex voting systems, arcane language and ritualised events all help to mystify the role of the leadership. Keeping power becomes the goal of bureaucracies, and the wants and needs of the masses are secondary. Capitalist and communist societies are ruled by these élites, the 'oligarchies' whose main interest is to maintain their own power. The masses are content to leave it to the experts.

Michels, Mosca and Pareto see no benevolence in democracies such as those that have developed in the West or in any possible communist state. Elite groups rule, and the main difference when compared with Marx's ideas is that none of these thinkers sees any chance of the masses ever taking power from the hands of the élite. For Pareto and Mosca the masses lack the psychological and intellectual skills which seem to be a natural property of the upper classes. For Michels that section of the masses which led any revolution would seize power for itself and become another élite, oligarchical group based on bureaucratic organisation and which would work hard to maintain its own privileged position and prevent the masses from taking part in the power structure.

Testing for democracy Critics of Soviet communism point out that this was the case there following the 1917 Revolution despite its claims to represent the highest form of democracy. Others argue that democracy still works, even though élite groups dominate the process. For them the real test is to look at how well or badly the needs and interests of the masses are being served. Even if the majority of politicians, leading industrialists, bankers and the leadership of the armed forces come from the same backgrounds – private schools and the 'best' universities – if the systems they control can be shown to serve the needs of the people, then democracy still works. Examinations of power-sharing in modern societies do not always reflect this. C. Wright Mills (1956), an American sociologist, developed a theory which has come to be known as 'modern' élite theory. The main difference between this and the 'classical' élite theory of Pareto, Mosca and Michels is that Mills takes a critical view of élite groups in the USA.

C. Wright Mills: the military–industrial State Mills distinguishes three groups: the military, economic and political élites. He claims that they effectively form a closed group, barring people from other parts of society from any real political participation. Membership of the three groups is often interchangeable, for example powerful military figures, who may have business interests, may go from military to political service. It is considered normal for politicians to have business interests, and business is active in politics, not least through financing political parties and individuals. This interlocking, self-serving group of élites has a monopoly of power, and therefore runs society not by bending to the collective will of the people, but by maintaining and increasing its own power. Representative democracy just serves to disguise the existence of the élite leadership.

Although at times his ideas seem to take on a Marxist tone, Mills is analysing American society from an élitist perspective, and there is no suggestion that power exists solely within the economic base or that communist societies would be any better. Mills does seem to argue that there should be a way to share power so that the needs and interests of the majority, rather than a select minority, should be served. However, the pluralist view of power in Western democracies claims that this is exactly what happens – the minority élite only exist so that they can use their political expertise to answer the demands of the mass. The pluralists argue that the proof of the political pudding is in the decision-making process. If you analyse the decisions which are made and work out in whose interests they are made, you will find that all groups in society are receiving equal benefit from the role of the élite groups. If not, the people would throw out one élite and vote in another.

QUESTIONS

1 **How do the views of the classical élite theorists differ from those of C. Wright Mills?**

2 **What evidence is there to suggest that power is in the hands of a few?**

Pluralism

A plurality of views

'Pluralist' is a label which describes the view of power adopted by social theorists who envisage a plurality of many different groups competing for some say in the political process. The State, far from being the capitalist-controlled and directed committee described by Marxism, is a neutral body, open to influences from all groups in society, not serving the interests of an élite minority.

Political parties are seen as an important part of this process, as are pressure groups. The various combinations which arise in democracies to fulfil the needs of groups of people are in competition, and the State bends to the will of those best able to get their voices heard.

State neutrality

Requests for State action are put forward by pressure groups and political parties and the State must process these demands and take decisions which represent the majority interest. If the State consistently took decisions in favour of any one group at the expense of the others, then at elections there would be a shift of power, another government would be elected, and their policies would be formulated to best serve the demands of the majority groups in society. The whole thing depends upon the neutrality of the State in processing the demands made upon it. The plurality of interests ensures that the élite groups do not manipulate the power they hold to serve their own interests.

The State maintains a balance in society, making sure that all is fair. Pluralist evidence is usually to be found in the analysis of decision-making processes in democratic societies. Robert Dahl (1961), Polsby (1963) and others claim that an examination of key decisions taken should show an overall balance of interests being met by those holding political power, at both national and local government levels.

A frequent criticism of this argument is that it does not go deeply enough into political processes or the real nature of power. To get at the real issues, it is necessary to examine the processes by which issues emerge in the political arena in the first place. This argument insists that élite groups control this process by making sure that demands which could pose a real threat to the élite power base never surface as public issues – this is the power of non-decision making. For Marxists, a clear example would be the issue of private ownership of the means of production or the massively unequal distribution of wealth in the hands of a few. These are issues that no interest group or political party raises at general elections or any other time, because to do so would fundamentally challenge the power of the bourgeoisie and encourage the formation of working-class consciousness. According to Marxists, the issue the pluralists miss is that effective power does not reside in the State but in the private ownership of the means of production.

Elite pluralism   To take account of the unequal distribution of power, and to overcome some of the weaknesses of classical pluralism, more recent pluralist theorists acknowledge that in a great many cases decisions are made by organised groups without direct – and sometimes even indirect – reference to the mass of the population. Furthermore, some groups are more powerful than others, according to whether they are seen as insiders in the political system whose voices are frequently heard, such as the CBI, or outsiders, such as the Campaign for Nuclear Disarmament. It can also be the case that some pressure groups have no effective access to the ear of government, though this may mean they have to find new ways of exerting pressure. A good example of this would be the way that environmental groups have moved from being seen as 'cranks' to serious and influential organisations.

This view, put forward by writers such as Richardson and Jordan (1979) and Budge (1983), has been described as 'élite pluralism' or 'neo-pluralism'. It propounds the view that difficult and unpopular issues can be forced onto the political agenda through the democratic process, against the will of some élite groups, while accepting that there is not a 'level playing field' of power. In such a situation governments cannot rule by force, and cannot manipulate affairs simply to suit themselves.

QUESTIONS

1 **How many of the 'dimensions of power' are expressed in the pluralist view?**

2 **How many interest groups would want to be involved in trying to enable or prevent the sale of tobacco?**

3 **What is meant by non-decision making?**

What is the State?

Powers of the State

Just about everywhere we turn in modern life we encounter the State. The State in some form is present when we post letters, use money to buy stamps, watch BBC television, travel abroad bearing passports, go to school, or attend further or higher education. The State obliges birth, marriage and death to be registered. It takes a cut from every pound you earn. The roads you walk and drive on belong to the State. The State can declare you insane and institutionalise you. It can kick your door down at five in the morning and arrest you under the Prevention of Terrorism Act. It can conscript you and send you to war. The State can remove all your belongings if you do not pay the council tax. Clearly, the State is a powerful and diverse organisation. It is easiest to think of it in three parts: legislature, executive and judiciary.

At the heart of the State is its ability to draw up and pass laws. These are then enforced by the executive – the agents who carry out or execute the will of the legislature. In a democracy, the legislature is the representative or delegated body partly or wholly elected by the people in periodic elections. In the United Kingdom this is the House of Commons and the House of Lords. The House of Commons is the more important and powerful of the two. The House of Lords is not elected by the people.

The executive carries out the orders of the legislature. In Britain, once an Act of Parliament is passed it is the job of civil servants to make sure that these new laws are enforced. The executive is divided into ministries, headed by ministers who meet together in twice-weekly cabinet meetings. Between them, these people head executive power in the modern British State.

The third arm of the State is the judiciary. This is primarily responsible for interpreting laws once they have been passed, and enforcing them in the courts. The judiciary includes untrained magistrates and highly trained and experienced High Court judges in the Old Bailey in London.

The growth of the State

> ### The story of the vote
>
> *Although the UK boasts the 'Mother of Parliaments', full adult suffrage is a relatively recent achievement. These are the key dates in its development:*
>
> 1832   *The electorate rose from 478,000 to 813,000 in a population of 24m (or one in every seven adult males).*
>
> 1867   *The electorate rose from 1,430,000 to 2,500,000, in a population of 30m (or one in three adult males).*
>
> 1884   *The electorate rose from 3,000,000 to 4,900,000 (or two in three adult males).*
>
> 1918   *All adult males over 21 and, after a long and intense struggle, women over thirty were able to vote.*
>
> *It is important to note that, before 1918, entitlement to vote was based on a property qualification, not a simple matter of right or citizenship.*
>
> 1928   *All women over 21 were enfranchised.*
>
> 1970   *All adults over 18 allowed to vote.*

In the past 150 years, the State has grown in size to play a role in people's lives in a way unthinkable in early Victorian Britain. In the era of *laissez-faire* or free-market economics of the nineteenth century, the guiding belief was that the State should play as little part as possible in the lives of its citizens (the vast majority of whom were unable to vote). This principle was slowly eroded as the century progressed, as the working class gained the right to vote and as local government spread (municipalism). At the same time that the Liberal Party came under serious threat from the rise of the Labour Party, it found itself using the power of State, in the First World War, to conscript workers into the army and send them off to fight and possibly to die. This was the very opposite of the principle of minimising government intervention in the lives of citizens.

After the Second World War, when the State again conscripted its citizens, it maintained the central role it had come to play in the war (through, for example, rationing) with the creation of the Welfare State by the Labour government of 1945–51 (see chapter 9). The broad commitment of all the major political parties to the maintenance of the Welfare State meant that there was a long period of what has been described as consensus politics. The divide between Labour and Conservative politics had become very narrow, best expressed in the term 'Butskellism', where the budgets of one Chancellor of the Exchequer – Butler, for the Conservatives – were very similar to those of the Labour Chancellor – Gaitskell. Both Labour and Conservative parties in this period were strongly influenced by the economic ideas of John Maynard Keynes who advocated government intervention in market economies to keep unemployment rates low.

The end of consensus

This long period of consensus came to an end in the turbulent last years of the 1974–79 Labour government and any notion of political consensus disappeared entirely in the years of the Thatcher Conservative government (1979–90). According to Thatcherist ideology the State should again play a minimal role in people's lives, yet where it did intervene it should be forceful and strong. In the 1980s, the theme was 'rolling back the frontiers of the State', in the field of taxation and by privatising industries and services such as gas, water and electricity. It is a fiercely debated point whether, as Prime

Minister, Mrs Thatcher succeeded in contracting State power in favour of individual freedom, or merely centralised the State more than it already had been.

QUESTIONS

1 **What is consensus politics?**

2 **How has the role of the State changed in the twentieth century?**

Who controls the State?

The official view of who controls the State in the United Kingdom is that it is ultimately controlled by its citizens. Any citizen has the freedom to form a political party, or to vote for a political party which may then in turn take control of the machinery of State. In reality, in the United Kingdom only one of two political parties is likely to take power, the Labour or Conservative Party, although smaller parties such as the Liberal Democrats or an Ulster Unionist party may come to hold the balance of power if no party has an overall majority in an election.

First past the post

Voting in general elections, held at the most every five years, is done on the basis of the 'first past the post' system. The United Kingdom is divided up into 659 roughly equal electoral areas called constituencies, containing approximately 85,000 electors each. Electors elect one Member of Parliament (MP) for each constituency on the basis of a simple majority. The political party that gains 330 MPs or more in this way is guaranteed an overall majority in the House of Commons, and the ability to turn their policies into law.

It does not at all follow, however, that the party forming a government does so by virtue of a simple majority of votes. Mrs Thatcher's Conservative governments of the 1980s, for example, won power with between 42 per cent and 43 per cent of votes cast. This does not include those registered to vote who did not do so (which takes the figure down to around a third of the electorate) or even those eligible to register to vote who did not even do so, for whatever reason. In 1979, for example, the Conservative Party won 339 seats, 70 seats more than the Labour Party, with the votes of less than a third of all adults over the age of eighteen (*see Table 8.1*).

Similarly, it does not follow that the party gaining power even wins more votes than other single parties. The winning party only needs to win majorities in half plus one of all constituencies. How it performs in the remaining constituencies then becomes unimportant. This can lead to anomalous situations as shown in *Table 8.2*.

TABLE 8.1   Mrs Thatcher's government 1979

		TORY VOTES AS PERCENTAGE OF:	
Votes cast for Tories	13 697 690		
Total votes cast in election	31 220 010	Total votes cast	43.9
Electorate	41 093 264	Electorate	33.3
Total adults over 18	42 100 000	Total adults over 18	32.5
Total population	55 822 000	Total population	24.5

Source: compiled from Butler and Butler (1994)

TABLE 8.2   Voting in general elections – 1951 and 1974

	LABOUR	CONSERVATIVE	LIBERAL
(a) 1951 (Total seats = 625)			
Votes	13 949 105	13 718 069	730 552
Seats	296	320	6
(b) 1974 (Feb) (Total seats = 635)			
Votes	11 661 488	11 928 677	6 056 713
Seats	301	296	14

Source: compiled from Butler and Butler (1994)

As we can see, this system of electing a government contains many strange quirks and anomalies. For example, the Liberal Party gained more than six million votes in February 1974 and yet won only 14 seats, while the party that came to form the government received less than twice as many votes as the Liberals and yet gained twenty times as many seats.

Critics of this system, particularly Liberal Democrats, argue that the only fair form of electoral system would be proportional representation, where the number of seats gained reflects the overall number of votes cast. Parties that do form governments under the existing system, however, are unlikely to want to change the system that brings them to power, and it is improbable that they will do so unless forced to in a power-sharing agreement with the Liberal Democrats. The Labour Party does at least seem willing to consider this possibility, though it is unlikely ever to be taken up or even considered by the Conservative Party.

Turnout   Defenders of the system, however, can point to the fact that, although the party that gains power rarely does so with a majority of the electorate's votes, it is nevertheless the case that the vast majority both of those who have registered to vote, and of those entitled to vote, do so in a general election. In 1979, for example, when the electorate totalled more than 41 million people, over 31 million (or

76 per cent) turned out to vote. At the same time, the adult population over eighteen numbered 42,100,000, meaning that 74 per cent, or almost three-quarters of those over eighteen, voted in the 1979 general election. These figures are representative: since 1935 the highest turnout has been 82.5 per cent (1951), with the lowest only 71.2 per cent (1935). In this way, it can be said, the electorate legitimates the electoral system itself every time it turns out and votes in a general election.

Once a party is elected into government, even with an overall majority, they do not have a free hand to govern as they wish. Opposition parties and dissenters within the government's own ranks can try to influence the course of legislation as it passes through the Houses of Parliament (the Commons and the Lords), through debates in the Chambers, in committees and in votes on amendments to the three readings of Bills.

Pressure groups

Outside of the Houses of Parliament, pressure groups exist to influence the course of legislation at all its stages, as well as to encourage political parties to adopt new policies. Two types of politically oriented pressure groups can be discerned – interest or sectional pressure groups who protect the interest of their members, of whom trade unions and professional associations such as the British Medical Association (see also chapter 7) are among the largest. Promotional pressure groups exist to draw attention to specific issues and causes, whether it is the environment (in the case of Greenpeace and Friends of the Earth) or poverty, as with the Child Poverty Action Group and Save the Children. A wide range of methods is used to draw their campaigns and interests to the attention of Members of Parliament and the general public, from demonstrations and boycotts to media campaigns and lobbying MPs in the House of Commons. Some groups are able to claim success in meeting short-term objectives (such as the Anti-Poll Tax Campaign of the late 1980s) while others have longer-term objectives and need to maintain continuous pressure, as with campaigns to make roads safer.

If pressure groups and the wider public are unable to influence the course of legislation, then three courses of action remain possible: to disobey the law, for example by withholding payments or mass trespasses; to challenge it in the courts, in the United Kingdom or in Europe; or by voting out the government in a general election and replacing it with a government which will adopt that particular cause.

Pluralism

It is the existence of all these courses of action, persuasion and protest that persuades many people, particularly those at the heart of the system, of the truth of the pluralist case that the electorate gets the government it deserves. In various ways it is continually able to let its elected representatives know of the depth of feeling concerning the way they are being governed, and that the epicentre of power is therefore always shifting to reflect the public's mood.

This is, of course, only one view of what the State is and how it is controlled, focusing on how decisions are made and seeing the State as a referee between different groups, with no interests of its own. As we have seen above, from a functionalist point of view, the State can also be seen as an instrument responding to the majority will, enabling society as a whole to focus its energy. The Marxist approach, on the other hand, begins from the assertion that the State is a committee for managing the affairs of the bourgeoisie, an instrument of class rule that will itself wither away when class divisions disappear. Elite theorists see the State as a vehicle for élite opinion and interests.

The autonomous State

An entirely different point of view (though hinted at by some Marxists) is to see the State as a self-interested organisation, an independent force with its own rules of action. This is echoed in Skocpol's (1979) claim that the State is a 'structure with a logic and interests of its own not necessarily equivalent to, or fused with the interests of the dominant class in society, or the full set of member groups in the polity'.

In the same vein, other writers have observed that the ideological persuasion of the political parties when in government makes very little difference to the way Britain is governed. As Rose (1984) argues, necessity, rather than ideological consensus, has usually held sway: many policies would have come into being regardless of who was in power, with only slight shifts of emphasis in practice. All parties have sought to increase economic growth and sustain the basic provisions of the Welfare State – education, health and social security. Even the Thatcherite campaign of privatisation was part of a global phenomenon in industrial societies and is unlikely to be immediately reversed by any incoming Labour government. In matters of foreign policy, there have been barely perceptible differences in the conduct of each party's foreign ministers.

This phenomenon has been explained in three ways. First, convergence theorists (see chapter 12) have argued that industrial societies have a developmental logic of their own, posing the same choices at particular stages of development; second, there is the claim that government ministers are unable to outwit and outmanoeuvre the vested interests of their civil servants who have political priorities of their own, as well as a large say in how ministers are advised and what information they receive; third, the innate conservatism of the British electorate prevents any government or party from straying too far away from the political centre.

The Thatcher governments

Many commentators are willing to accept that the years of 'consensus politics' from 1945 to the mid 1970s can be characterised in this way. The extent to which the Thatcher governments (from 1979 to 1990) changed the role of the State in British political life has been more keenly debated. Part of the reason for this is the contradictory nature of the Thatcher government's record, and the difference between its rhetoric and what really happened. It was certainly Mrs Thatcher's stated intention to break with the past when she remarked that 'For me, consensus seems to be the process of abandoning all beliefs, principles, values and policies' (Kavanagh, 1985).

In attempting to release the population from the grips of the State, more people nevertheless became dependent on it as recipients of welfare benefits, particularly unemployment benefit. The rate of crime rose and prisons became fuller. Private housing and farming continued to be subsidised. Controls were exercised over the ability of local government to run its own services and some (particularly in education) were taken into central control, although many others were put out to tender. New and unelected quangos (quasi-autonomous non-governmental organisations) were created in many areas including the privatised public utilities. The power and influence of trade unions and public sector professionals were markedly reduced while the business and finance community were given a greater say in government decisions, although the manufacturing sector was substantially reduced in size.

None of this suggests that power became more pluralised, unless the élite pluralist model is followed, although the interests of what is frequently described as the 'establishment' (the Church of England, BBC, the universities, and higher civil service) were also challenged. On the other hand, the importance given to the ethics of capitalism in this period would support the Marxists' model.

The sovereign State?

Many sociologists have argued that the focus on the State, or the nation State as a sovereign body, exaggerates its importance in an increasingly interdependent and globalised world where transnational political organisations such as the European Union and the United Nations are becoming increasingly important, although they are still relatively ignored by sociologists. At the same time, issues of ethnicity, national identity and small-scale nationalism remain as strong as ever, as developments in the new nations of the former

Soviet bloc and the former Yugoslavia show. Sociologists need to examine international and local developments as much as national developments in their search for the epicentres of political power in society.

1 **What evidence is there for a pluralist view of power?**

2 **In what ways is the United Kingdom a democracy?**

3 **How can pressure groups exert influence on the course of legislation?**

Political parties and ideology

Marxism and ideology

As with many other terms in sociology, the word ideology carries different meanings according to the context in which it is being used. In its broadest usage it refers to any belief system holding a particular group together (see also chapter 2). In other senses, particularly those given by Marxist sociologists, it refers to a belief system that, while claiming to represent the truth, is in reality a set of distorted ideas. To Marxists, the concept of bourgeois ideology not only denotes the value system of the capitalist class, derived from their position as owners of the means of production, but also the view that this belief system constitutes a false consciousness, a false view of reality. Furthermore, only a classless society and the application of scientific Marxism can show the world as it is and break away from this world of illusion. The term ideology therefore carries great importance within Marxism and consequently has been much debated within Marxist thought, particularly by writers such as Louis Althusser and Antonio Gramsci.

Outside of the Marxist perspective, the term ideology is used to refer to the ideas, values and beliefs of discrete power groups in society. In Bill Jones's (1991) formulation, it can be described as 'a comprehensive and systematic perspective whereby human society can be understood together with a framework of principles to guide future action'. According to Jones, an ideology has four components: a perspective or set of assumptions about human nature and the world; a critique of why that perspective is better than any other; a set of objectives concerning political goals and a set of prescriptions of how these objectives should be realised in practice. Political objectives are described in ideological terms, for example as fascism, communism, socialism, liberalism and conservatism. In the 1960s, the American sociologist Daniel Bell had this sense in mind when he declared The End of Ideology (1961), indicating that real differences between political parties no longer existed, having been replaced by a consensus on political values. It is in this sense that it is explored in this section.

It is through political parties that political ideologies eventually become policies and legislation. The concept of party was of particular interest to Weber (1922–3) who defined it as any group seeking to pursue 'communal action no matter what its content may be'. Sociologically, Weber says, they represent interests 'determined through "class situation" or "status situation", and they may recruit their following from one or the other respectively. But they need be neither purely "class" nor purely status parties. In most cases they are partly class parties and partly status parties, but sometimes they are neither.'

Forming the ideology is a complex process drawing on a range of ideas of thinkers, from Marx on the left to F.A. Hayek on the right. More immediately, policy 'think tanks', such as the Adam Smith Institute or the Policy Studies Institute, also exist to contribute ideas, arguments and research to this process. Within political parties, particular figures may play the role of ideological leaders, seeking to develop their party's policy in a particular direction. This would be the case with the former Conservative MP Sir Keith Joseph or one of the founder members of the short-lived Social Democratic Party, Roy Jenkins. Through books, pamphlets, speeches, newspapers and even videos, their ideas will be disseminated to elected representatives, party officials and activists, the politically interested and eventually, at election time, the electorate. The battle to try to make these ideas seem 'common sense', the only political possibility, is described as a hegemonic struggle. The way the New Right, under Margaret Thatcher, won the ideological battle in the late 1970s, ending the era of consensus politics, can be described as a 'hegemonic shift'. It amounted to, in Stuart Hall's (1978) phrase, 'the great moving Right show', and highlighted the way that traditional left-wing and centrist policies and solutions were falling out of favour in all areas of political life. The New Right attempted to redefine the way people thought about themselves in relation to the State.

Numerous attempts have been made to understand the relationship between political parties and the ideologies they expound. It often appears in the form of a continuum with 'left-wing' ideas, such as equality, the redistribution of wealth and common ownership, at one end, and 'right-wing' ideas, encompassing individual freedom and free enterprise, at the other. Applying this to the political spectrum in the United Kingdom it can be shown as in Figure 8.1.

This type of model does not always work – it is difficult, for example, to include Ulster Unionist parties such as the Democratic Unionist Party or nationalist parties such as Plaid Cymru on such a scale because of the importance given by them to nationalist causes. Nor does it easily describe the Green Party who, unlike the parties named above, reject the idea of economic growth as a fundamental objective. No model exists to solve this problem.

Some writers have suggested that a more realistic or representative way of seeing all this is as vertical and horizontal axes as in Figure 8.2.

Figure 8.1

Left wing	Centre	Right wing

| SWP | Labour | Lib Dems | Tories | BNP |

Figure 8.2

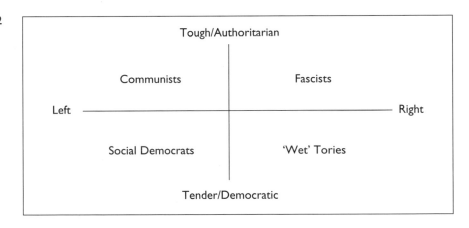

The Conservative Party

The modern Conservative Party emerged from the Tory party of the eighteenth and nineteenth centuries, seeking to protect the power of the landed gentry against the claims of the rising bourgeois class and its doctrine of anti protectionism and *laissez-faire* economics. In the late nineteenth century it redefined itself under Benjamin Disraeli to appeal to a new generation of working-class voters, in the process becoming a 'popular' party and surviving the threat of the rise of the Labour Party and the decline of the Liberals. Following the end of the Second World War it committed itself to the broad aims of the Beveridge Report (see chapter 9) until sections of the party became convinced that the organisation of the Welfare State was hastening Britain's decline.

The election of Margaret Thatcher as leader of the party in 1975 and as Prime Minister in 1979 began a radical change of direction, ushering in the politics of the New Right. 'Thatcherism' had five major objectives: to promote free trade and minimise State intervention in the economy; to squeeze out inflation through tight control of the money supply; to promote individual choice by breaking the power of State monopolies; to curb the power of trade unions and reduce the role played by corporate bodies in government decision-making; and to enforce strict obedience to the rule of law and those in authority. The strong emphasis on free market economics aligned the party more closely to the values of nineteenth-century liberalism: it was these values that Thatcher had in mind when she championed the 'Victorian values' of thrift and hard work.

Some writers (such as Stuart Hall, 1978) have doubted whether Thatcherism amounted to a coherent ideological position as such, withdrawing the role of the State in some areas, particularly the industrial sphere, while increasing it in others such as law and order. For this reason it has been described as 'authoritarian populism', carried on after her fall in 1990 in a more diluted form by John Major.

The Labour Party

The Labour Party is effectively as old as the twentieth century, defining itself as a democratic socialist party, seeing the State as instrumental in achieving its aims of increased social justice and equality. For much of its life it has committed itself to Clause 4 of its 1918 constitution, seeking to bring about 'common ownership of the means of production, distribution and exchange'. After 1945, when it won a landslide victory in the general election, it took large sections of the economic infrastructure such as the mines and railway network into public ownership by nationalising them. At the same time, it consolidated the Welfare State, for example through the creation of the National Health Service and a universal scheme of National Insurance. In 1995, under the leadership of Tony Blair, the Labour Party agreed to alter Clause 4 as part of a programme of modernisation (see p. 271).

The immediate post-war Labour government was perhaps the most radical and reforming of the twentieth century (though many would argue that it nevertheless failed to create anything resembling a democratic socialist society). In the long periods since then that it has been out of power – in the 1950s, 1980s and 1990s – it has sought to redefine itself as the party of the affluent (particularly those living in 'middle England') as well as the disadvantaged.

In 1994, following fifteen years out of power, the election of Tony Blair as leader of the party provided Labour with the opportunity to provide a new statement of its values and drop its central commitment to nationalisation. It did this in 1995 by changing its party constitution and describing itself as a party seeking to create 'a society in which power, wealth and opportunity are in the hands of the many, not the few', achieved through a 'dynamic economy, serving the public interest, in which the enterprise of the market and the rigour of competition are joined with the forces of partnership and co-operation to produce the wealth the nation needs and the opportunity for all to work and prosper, with a thriving private sector and high quality public services, where those undertakings essential to the common good are owned either by the public or are accountable to them'.

Critics of this move say this makes it harder than ever to distinguish much of the Labour Party's ideology and stance from other parties. It has also been frequently observed that, in changing Clause 4, the long battle begun by the breakaway 'Gang of Four' in 1981, founding the Social Democratic Party, has now been won as the Labour Party under Blair is now, in effect, the party that Williams, Rodgers, Jenkins and Owen sought to fashion all along.

The Liberal Democrats

The present Liberal Democrat Party exists as the result of a merger between the Social Democratic Party (which itself split away from the Labour Party in the early 1980s) and the Liberal Party of the nineteenth century. The Liberal Party itself emerged from the Whig Party, playing an important part in laying the foundations of the Welfare State (see chapter 9) before being eclipsed by the Labour Party in the second quarter of the twentieth century. It has been out of power ever since, although it briefly shared power with the Labour Party in the 'Lib–Lab Pact' of the late 1970s. As the third party in British politics, it does not expect to form a government in its own right (although it is a major player in local government), with its only hope being a hung parliament, where no single party has overall control through a simple majority. In these circumstances it would join any coalition government that may be formed on the condition that it introduced a form of proportional representation (see p. 263).

In terms of values, the Liberal Democrats stand for a mixed economy, supporting the aim of improved funding for public services such as health and education, but sharing some of the Conservative Party's hostility to trade unionism and the organised labour movement. The Liberal Democratic Party struggles to maintain a policy of political 'equidistance' from the main parties, at the same time as co-operating with sections of the Labour Party at local government level.

Voting behaviour

Partisan alignment

In the early post-war years, the sociological view of voting behaviour was based on social class. There were two main classes: the working class, who consistently saw themselves as such, identified themselves with the Labour Party, and would always vote for it; and the middle class who saw themselves as middle class and identified themselves with the Conservative Party, consistently voting for that party. This pattern of class loyalty was deemed regular and predictable enough for writers such as David Butler and Donald Stokes (1974) to describe it as one of 'partisan alignment' (*see* Table 8.3).

This was also clear from an analysis of the way the two leading parties dominated the overall share of the votes cast (*see* Table 8.4).

TABLE 8.3 Voting patterns, 1945–59 (%)

CLASS	AB	C1	C2	DE
Conservative	85	70	35	30
Labour	10	25	60	65

Source: Tapper and Bowles, 1981

TABLE 8.4 Labour and Conservative share of votes cast, 1945–59 (%)

	CONSERVATIVE	LABOUR	CONSERVATIVE AND LABOUR
1945	39.6	48.0	87.6
1950	43.4	46.1	89.5
1951	48.0	48.8	96.8
1955	49.7	46.4	96.1
1959	49.4	43.8	93.2

Source: The Guardian Guide to the House of Commons 1992, Fourth Estate Ltd, 1992

Allegiance to one of the two main parties on the basis of class came about through a process of political socialisation. These values were learnt from others in much the same way as any other key aspect of socialisation. They came from people met with in everyday life, particularly at home and in schools. People voted according to their class image of the society they lived in.

Deviant voters

As the case for partisan alignment seemed clear, attention turned to the problems of why a minority of people voted against their class – 'deviant voters' – while others changed their allegiance from one election to another – 'floating voters'. Why, for example, did 10 per cent of AB class voters vote Labour and 30 per cent of DE class vote Conservative on average in the period 1945–59?

The phenomenon of the working-class Tory was explained by the tendency to deference that exists in part of the working class. By 'deference', writers such as McKenzie and Silver (1968) meant the willingness on the part of workers to believe that an individual would make a good politician simply because they already possessed a high, and often ascribed, status. This pattern, however, was dying out as working-class voters became increasingly interested in the specific policies each party was offering. In identifying this new phenomenon of 'secular' voting, McKenzie and Silver anticipated the direction of later theories of voting behaviour, or psephology.

Middle-class Labour voting, Frank Parkin (1971) argued, could be understood in a similar way. Public sector professionals, such as teachers and social workers, did not perceive their work in an instrumental way, but identified with the wider altruism of the Labour Party and its commitment to the public sector.

Butler and Stokes (1974) themselves believed that deviant voting could be understood within the concept of partisan alignment. As the skilled working class became more affluent and underwent a process of embourgeoisement, they argued (see chapter 3), they would be more likely to vote Tory as an expression of their new values because the lines of class division had shifted. As we know from *The Affluent Worker* studies of the 1960s (Goldthorpe *et al.*), however, as well as from the work of Eric Nordlinger (1967), the opposite was closer to the truth. Psephological trends and patterns were still best explained by the nature of an individual's political socialisation within their class.

Partisan dealignment

The early 1970s were watershed years for both political parties, especially the Labour Party, and for political sociologists. From the elections of 1974, many commentators argued that it was now more accurate to talk of partisan dealignment than of partisan alignment. As with the intervening elections from 1974, the 1987 election appeared to show clear evidence of partisan dealignment when the statistics were analysed by class and by looking at the combined Conservative and Labour vote (*see Tables 8.5 and 8.6*).

It was difficult to argue the case for partisan alignment when the Conservatives were gaining a clear majority of the skilled workers' vote, with 40 per cent compared to Labour's 32 per cent. Equally, it was difficult to discern a two-party system, based on the dominance of two parties, when the Labour Party gained only 30.8 per cent of the vote while the Alliance gained 22.6 per cent (see Table 8.6).

TABLE 8.5 Voting patterns (%) by class, 1987

	AB	CI	C2	DE
Conservative	60	51	40	33
Labour	10	20	32	41
Lib/SDP Alliance	28	27	26	24

Source: MORI

TABLE 8.6 The Conservative and Labour vote (%), 1974–87

	CONSERVATIVE	LABOUR	CONSERVATIVE AND LABOUR
Feb 1974	37.8	37.1	74.9
1979	43.9	37.0	80.9
1987	42.3	30.8	73.1

Source: The Guardian Guide to the House of Commons 1992, *Fourth Estate Ltd, 1992*

Class decomposition

Political sociologists such as Sarlvik and Crewe (1983) argue that this dealignment can best be explained by divisions that are present in both the working and middle classes and the motives behind voting choices. In voting terms, there are now two perceivable working classes: the traditional and the new. Where workers live, whether they are home-owners or not, whether they belong to trade unions and whether they work in the public or private sector as well as their occupations all have to be taken into account. Belonging to a trade union and not owning a house increases a propensity to vote Labour. It is also important to realise that voters make 'rational' decisions about how they vote, based on experience, knowledge and policy preference rather than on the grounds of simple class identification and loyalty. If a political party is not offering what voters want, no matter which class they appear to represent, they will not vote for them.

A similar pattern was discernible among the middle classes where there was also division between private sector workers, two-thirds of whom voted Conservative, and public sector workers, less than half of whom voted Conservative. This figure had declined since 1983. The process of class dealignment seemed to be gathering pace.

Rational-choice voting

In a longitudinal study of a group of voters from 1959 to October 1974, Himmelweit, Humphreys and Jaeger (1981) dispense with concepts of political socialisation and develop the concept of rational choice by voters. Voters, they say, behave in the same way as any other consumers faced with important financial choices. 'Brand loyalty' (which would correspond with partisan alignment) does not necessarily exist. The voter–consumer will make their choice according to the policies which are on offer at the time, and if they are unhappy with their choice they may well change it at the next opportunity. Some critics have claimed that it is difficult to draw valid conclusions from this study as it is based on an ultimate sample of only 178 men living in the greater London area, the majority of whom were non-manual workers. Nor are we able to discover the basis on which these voters made their choices in the first place.

A new model of class

Other writers are less convinced that class can be so quickly discounted. Heath, Jowell and Curtice (1985) argue that a more sophisticated model of class than those previously employed needs to be considered. Their own model, used to examine the 1983 election, sees five classes, which are defined in terms of labour-market position, and incorporate both men and women:

- the *salariat* are managers and professionals who wield power in the workplace and over their own working lives – vote Conservative (54 per cent) or Alliance;

- *routine non-manual workers* on low wages with little control over the labour process – vote Conservative (51 per cent) or sometimes Alliance (31 per cent);

- the *petty-bourgeoisie* and self-employed who neither employ workers nor are employed by others – strong Conservative vote (71 per cent);

- *foremen and technicians* who supervise others – vote Conservative, but not in the majority (48 per cent);

- *all forms of manual workers* who are most likely to vote Labour (49 per cent in 1983).

As their results from viewing class in this way proved inconclusive, they then devised an 'odds ratio' which compared the way that class strata voted in elections with the way they ought to vote in terms of class alignment. This revealed, far from conclusively, that the working class and salariat vote was not significantly less partisan in 1983 than at other elections in the previous 20 years.

Other factors also needed to be taken into account, not least of which was the fact that, while the manual working class has shrunk as a proportion of the labour force, the number of people in non-manual jobs has increased. Even if this decline had been fully reflected in the Labour Party's share of the vote in 1983, however, they could have done much better than they actually did. Yet it seems clear that people do not vote on the basis of issues, as the Labour Party were thought by voters to have the best policies on the most important issues. The Labour Party failed because of its overall image in the eyes of the voters and it did not manage to match this to the individual policies it campaigned for.

The 1992 election

The 1992 election results give little firm support to any of the above theories. According to Ivor Crewe (1992) there was a slight increase in class-aligned voting, although as this was from 44 per cent in 1987 to only 47 per cent of all voters voting according to their class in 1992, this is hardly enough to argue for the rebirth of partisan alignment. Moreover, he notes that Heath, Jowell and Curtice's 'odds ratio' fell to a historically low level.

The picture is more complex than this, according to Crewe. Largely because of the recession, 'the new and traditional working class continued to vote differently but the gap was much narrower. The swing to Labour was larger among working-class owner-occupiers than council tenants, among private-sector than public-sector workers (who actually swung to the Conservatives), among those without a union card than those with one, and among manual workers in the South than those in the North or Scotland' (*see Table 8.7*). The real reason, Crewe says, that Labour lost in 1992 was because of lack of belief in the Labour Party leader as a potential Prime Minister.

Gender and voting behaviour

Although the main debate in voting behaviour centres around the concept of class, age and gender are also important factors. Women have always formed a significant constituency for the Conservatives.

It has generally been thought that men are more aligned to the Labour Party than women because they are more likely to be engaged in the organised labour movement, to belong to a trade union, and have a sense of solidarity as industrial workers. Women, at home, are more likely to be concerned with family values and issues and will vote for the party that campaigns hardest on these issues, usually the Conservative Party. Some writers have argued that it was because women were seen as a bloc against the rise of the Labour Party that they were enfranchised in 1918.

TABLE 8.7   (a) How the new working class voted, 1987 and 1992

	LIVES IN SOUTH 1987 1992		OWNER- OCCUPIER 1987 1992		NON-UNION 1987 1992		WORKS IN PRIVATE SECTOR 1987 1992	
Conservative	46	40	44	40	40	37	38	32
Labour	28	38	32	41	38	46	39	50
Lib/SDP	26	23	24	19	22	17	23	18

(b) How the traditional working class voted, 1987 and 1992

	LIVES IN SCOTLAND/ NORTH 1987 1992		COUNCIL TENANT 1987 1992		UNION MEMBER 1987 1992		WORKS IN PUBLIC SECTOR 1987 1992	
Conservative	29	26	25	22	30	29	32	36
Labour	57	59	57	64	48	55	49	48
Lib/SDP	15	15	18	13	22	16	19	16

Source: compiled from Ivor Crewe, 'Why wasn't Thatcher returned with a landslide?', Social Studies Review, September 1987; and Ivor Crewe, 'Why did Labour lose (yet again)?', Politics Review, September 1992

In the 1980s, however, the 'gender gap' in voting was temporarily reversed, with more men than women voting Conservative. One reason for this appears to be that younger women, attracted by Labour's image as a 'caring' party on issues such as health and education, were more likely to vote Labour than older women, while younger men were attracted by Mrs Thatcher's 'macho' image and voted for her. The gender gap was restored in 1992, with John Major as the Conservative leader (*see Table* 8.8).

Age and voting behaviour

Analysis of voting behaviour by age alone shows that support for the Conservative Party increases as people grow older, while it decreases for the Labour Party. Two forces are thought to be at work here: on the one hand, each new political generation of first-time voters forms a loyalty to a political party that stays with them for many

TABLE 8.8   Sex and party choice in general elections 1964–92

		CONSERVATIVE	LABOUR	LIB/SDP (ALLIANCE)
1964	Men	40	48	11
	Women	46	42	12
1970	Men	44	49	8
	Women	51	41	8
1983	Men	46	30	24
	Women	43	28	28
1992	Men	38	36	19
	Women	44	34	16

Sources: Nuffield Studies, 1964–70; Guardian, 13.6.83; Daily Telegraph, 14.4.92

years. In the late 1940s this would have been the Labour Party, in the 1980s, the Conservative Party. However, as people get older they become wealthier and more prosperous. They therefore become less dependent on the Welfare State, and are less concerned about those who are. In this way, they become more likely to vote Conservative, thus class and age combine as factors in voting behaviour.

Opinion polls

Finally, it is important to realise that most of the statistics presented above are only accurate in the sense that they are computed from the replies given to opinion pollsters at the time of each election. In other words, they are figures gathered by polling organisations such as MORI, Harris and Gallup, not official statistics or even primary data gathered by sociologists. It is frequently the case that different commentators will cite different figures in their account of an election, because of the number of polling organisations. These data are generated by taking a stratified sample of the electorate across a random selection of constituencies and asking them a series of questions about how they would vote in a general election. This is what sociologists would call a closed-ended structured interview.

In the 1992 general election, opinion polls became an issue in themselves. Prior to election day, very few of the 57 polls conducted showed a Conservative lead, and if they did it was by a margin of 1 per cent or less. Even when polling had been completed, exit polls (where voters are asked how they voted as they leave polling booths) predicted a Conservative victory of only between 4 and 5 per cent. In the end, the Conservatives won by a clear margin of 7.6 per cent (42.8 per cent to Labour's 35.2 per cent).

This underestimation of the strength of support for the Conservatives raises questions about interviewers' ability ever to get the truth out of their respondents. It may be, for example, that the interviewee does not yet know what they think. After the election, many polling organisations argued that a significant number of people had either made up or changed their minds in the days and hours before voting. It may also have been the case that a disproportionately high number of people who answered 'Don't know' then went on to vote Conservative and could not be accounted for by statistical margins of error. Another argument is that, because of what is seen as the selfishness associated with voting Conservative – putting yourself and your family first – enough people hide this fact from the pollsters as to seriously underestimate the real Conservative vote. It was also suggested that a substantial number of respondents who said they would vote Labour did not do so as they had not paid their poll tax and were therefore not eligible. It could also be that respondents do not take opinion polls as seriously as they take entering a ballot box, and use the interview as a way of venting short-term grievances, before reluctantly voting Conservative anyway.

Whatever the reasons, unless the questions and the way they are asked change and opinion polls become more accurate, it will be a long time before they are taken with any seriousness and credibility again. This clearly has implications for quantitative sociological research in general and structured interviews in particular. It is for these reasons that some political parties (the Labour Party, for example) are turning to qualitative methods to learn more about the electorate's view of them.

QUESTIONS

1 What is meant by partisan alignment and dealignment? Which best explains trends in voting behaviour?

2 How does the voting behaviour of women differ from men?

3 How reliable are opinion polls?

FURTHER READING

T. Bottomore, *Political Sociology*, 2nd end, Pluto Press, 1993

D. Butler and D. Kavanagh, **The British General Election of 1992**, Macmillan, 1992

E. Goot and M. Reid, *Women and Voting Studies*, Sage, 1975

P. Hirst, **The Pluralist Theory of the State**, Routledge, 1993

R. Levitas (ed.), **The Ideology of the New Right**, Polity Press, 1986

S. Lukes (ed.), **Power**, Blackwell, 1986

C. Mackinnon, **Towards a Feminist Theory of the State**, Harvard University Press, 1989

G. Marsh (ed.), **Pressure Politics: Interest Groups in Britain**, Junction, 1983

J. Scott, **Who Rules Britain?**, Polity Press, 1991

9 Wealth, welfare and poverty

I've worked myself up from nothing to a state of extreme poverty.

Groucho Marx

INTRODUCTION

This chapter begins with a discussion of poverty and the development of the Welfare State in Britain. You will then look at some of the sociological research into poverty focusing on the work of Booth, Rowntree, Townsend, Pen and Field. The next section discusses the problems with the measurement of poverty. This is followed by an examination of the explanations for poverty, looking at functionalist, culture of poverty, structural determinants and situational constraints explanations. Gender and ethnicity and their relationship to poverty are also examined. The chapter finishes with an analysis of the success and future of the Welfare State.

Poverty and the Welfare State

Laissez-faire
The guiding principle of politics in the nineteenth century in Britain was that of *laissez-faire* (let it happen). The dominant ideology held that industrial capitalism would best develop with minimum State interference and that inequalities in wealth would be evened out as economic development progressed and then everyone's standard of living would improve. Economic opportunities were there for all to take, and those who missed out failed to take them because of their own fecklessness and idleness. If you were poor, then it was probably your own fault, and your problem.

Poor Laws
The options open to anyone who fell on hard times were few. The Elizabethan Poor Laws of 1597 and 1601 became highly punitive following the amendment of 1834. The central principles were that no 'relief' (from poverty) would be given to the able-bodied except through the workhouse, and that this relief should bring a worse standard of life than that of the worst-off labourer – the principle of 'less eligibility'. This system was to survive until well into the twentieth century. The alternative was to turn to the charitable institutions of private philanthropists.

As the nineteenth century progressed, the principle of minimal State interference began to be gradually eroded through, for example,

Charles Booth (1840–1916)

A shipowner who became famous for his work on poverty. Booth started his research on poverty in London to disprove claims made in the Pall Mall Gazette that a quarter of Londoners lived in poverty. Booth found that the figure was far worse.

public health legislation and the Factory Acts. By 1891 the State was providing free and compulsory education for all children up to the age of ten partly as a consequence of the realisation that British industry was beginning to lose ground to its main competitors. By the turn of the century, considerable evidence was available to show that there had been little or no 'trickle down' of wealth to the poor and Marx's concept of capitalist development 'immiserating' or 'pauperising' those at the bottom was gaining credence.

Studies on poverty

Two key studies emerged from English philanthropists to confound those who continued to believe that poverty was a small-scale and individual problem: Charles Booth's *Life and Labour of the People of London*, published in seventeen volumes between 1889 and 1903, and Seebohm Rowntree's *Poverty: A Study of Town Life* (1901) which investigated poverty in York where Rowntree's family were one of the main employers in the chocolate industry. These two works represent the first real systematic studies of the nature and extent of poverty.

Rowntree

Seebohm Rowntree (1871–1954)

An industrialist with a major interest in unemployment and social welfare which led him to undertake a number of population surveys to measure the extent of poverty in York.

Both studies used similar measurements for their definition of poverty, based on the needs of a family of two adults with three children. Rowntree, in his study of poverty in York, took advice from medical scientists as to what exactly were the minimum requirements in terms of food and clothing in order for an individual to simply subsist. He then gave these a financial value. To be above his poverty line a family of five needed an income of 21s. 8d. a week (about 108p). He found that if this amount was used correctly, without any spending on 'luxuries' or waste, 7,230 people or 9.91 per cent of the population of York were in 'primary' poverty.

Rowntree described the lives of those living in primary poverty. They must, he said, 'never spend a penny on a railway fare or omnibus. They must never purchase a half-penny newspaper or spend a penny to buy a ticket for a popular concert. They must write no letters. They must never contribute to church or chapel or give help to a neighbour. They cannot save, nor can they join a sick club or a trade union. The children must have no pocket money. The father must smoke no tobacco and must drink no beer. The mother must never buy any pretty clothes. Should a child fall ill it must be attended by the parish doctor; should it die it must be buried by the parish. The wage earner must never be absent from work for a single day.'

When those who were extravagant, or spent their money 'unwisely' (secondary poverty), were added, he calculated that 28 per cent of the population of York were in poverty. If this was worrying to a factory owner, then the main cause of their poverty was even more so: 51.96 per cent were in poverty due to low pay.

Charles Booth's study indicated that 30.7 per cent of the population of London were in poverty. The evidence from both sources showed that, at the heart of the vast British Empire, at the height of its power, when it was sucking in wealth from all over the world and after more than a century of industrial advance, more than a quarter of its population did not have enough to live on from one week to the next. The Boer War fought against Afrikaner farmers in South Africa (1899–1902) provided further evidence when 60 per cent of recruits were found to be physically unfit for service.

Poor Law reforms

In the best British tradition, the Conservative Party, on its last day in government in 1905, formed a Royal Commission to investigate the Poor Law and consider its reform. This took until 1909, when the Commission, which included Charles Booth, issued its 47-volume report. This actually consisted of two reports, a majority report and a dissenting minority report, produced by the left-wing members of the Commission.

Liberal government reforms

Although the recommendations of both reports were largely ignored, the Liberal government, inspired by Lloyd George, did make some important inroads into the principle of non-intervention by the State. In 1908, old age pensions were introduced at 5s. (25p) per week for those over 70, and in 1911 compulsory health and unemployment insurance was introduced for workers in selected industries. Even then, however, the health insurance covered only the worker, not their family. Three years later Britain was at war, with 282,000 people still living in workhouses. By 1916, when Lloyd George became Prime Minister, the principle of non-intervention was completely abandoned when the Liberal government conscripted all men between 18 and 40 into military service. Of every nine conscripts examined, four were totally unfit for service and another two were fit only for supporting service.

In the inter-war period, despite two periods of Labour government, there was no return to the reforming zeal of the years immediately prior to the First World War. In 1921, 2,038,000 insured workers were unemployed. In 1922, two million people received Poor Relief. Unemployment never fell below one million throughout this decade, and began to rise steeply as the decade ended. By 1932, 23 per cent of all workers were out of work, with as many as 60 per cent of shipbuilders unemployed. Throughout this inter-war period, those not eligible for unemployment benefit had only the ministrations of the Poor Law between them and starvation.

It would be a mistake, however, to see the inter-war years as being entirely characterised by depression. For those still in work, real

The Welfare State 1944–48 and the battle against 'the five evils'

Ignorance: to be defeated by free secondary education for all, following the 1944 Education Act. Set up the 'tripartite' system.

Squalor: to be defeated by the New Towns Act 1946, creating a ring of new towns (e.g. Stevenage and Harlow) around London. Also the Town and Country Planning Act (1947).

Idleness: to be defeated by a commitment to maintaining 'full employment', through following the economic policies of J. M. Keynes – 'Keynesianism'. In 1944 a White Paper on employment was followed by Beveridge's book Full Employment in a Free Society.

Disease: to be defeated by the setting up of the National Health Service, following the 1946 National Health Act. From 5 July 1948, all health care and treatment was free to all at the point of delivery.

Want: to be defeated by a universal National Insurance Scheme (following the 1946 Act) and a National Assistance Act (1948) whose opening words were: 'the existing Poor Law [of 1601 and 1834] shall cease to have effect'. Also, family allowances were initiated from 1943.

The end of poverty?

wages rose by 50 per cent between 1918 and 1938, and increasingly affluent lifestyles developed. This is reflected in Rowntree's second poverty survey in York in 1936, where he found, using similar standards as before, that only 18 per cent of the population were now in poverty, although low pay still accounted for 42 per cent of these cases. Three years later Britain was at war again.

Wars produce fundamental social and economic changes. The State takes an ever-increasing role in directing the economy. Women are brought into the workforce as unemployment falls, and children may be evacuated into non-urban areas. Politicians and citizens unite around a common cause. The welfare of the people once again becomes a central political issue.

In the Second World War there was a widespread determination not to return to the socio-economic conditions prevalent after the First World War. To this end, the coalition government commissioned a report into how the welfare of the people could be improved, in the advent of peace. Written by a civil servant, William Beveridge, the 1942 *Report on Social Insurance and Allied Services* is the most important document in twentieth-century British social policy. In it, Beveridge identified five 'giants' or 'evils' to be eradicated: disease, ignorance, squalor, want, and idleness.

The Beveridge Report, as it became known, was immediately popular, and the belief that the Labour Party was the party most intent on implementing its recommendations was largely responsible for its winning of 393 seats compared with the Conservatives' 212 seats in the election of summer 1945. Before this, in 1944, Butler passed the Education Act that provided free secondary education for all (see chapter 5). Following the landslide Labour victory, there was an intense flurry of legislation that comprehensively established the Welfare State, with the aim of caring for its citizens 'from the cradle to the grave'. This legislation was put through against a background of post-war economic adversity that found the Labour government being forced to consider introducing prescription charges in 1949, and then charges for false teeth and spectacles. The free provision of such items was undoubtedly necessary and popular, with 187,000,000 prescriptions written, 8,500,000 dental patients treated and 5,250,000 pairs of glasses prescribed in the first year 1948–49, yet the rapid introduction of charges for some of these caused the chief architect of the NHS, Aneurin Bevan, to resign.

Nevertheless, it was widely believed that the newly founded Welfare State was improving the standards of living for all. In his third, and final, survey of poverty in York, in 1950, Rowntree found that only 1.5 per cent of people lived in poverty. The battle, he was able to conclude, was over – at least in his lifetime.

QUESTIONS

1 **What were the main factors that led to the creation of the Welfare State?**

2 **What does the term Welfare State mean?**

3 **What influence has ideology had on the development of the Welfare State?**

4 **What is the difference between primary and secondary poverty?**

The sociology of poverty

In the 1950s, anxieties concerning poverty in the UK were largely dispelled, as politicians were able to claim that the British people had 'never had it so good', and the idea of the embourgeoisement of the working class gained ground (see chapter 3). In many ways, it was believed that the social problems of the first half of the century had been overcome, and that a new consensus existed.

The rediscovery of poverty

This new mood did not satisfy some sociologists, who argued that poverty still existed, though a new perception of its nature was needed to identify it. It was argued by, for example, Wootton (1959), Abel-Smith and Townsend (1965), Coates and Silburn (1970) and Kincaid (1973) that the problem of poverty had far from disappeared. In the work of these sociologists, poverty in Britain was 'rediscovered'.

Abel-Smith and Townsend argued that the State's poverty line – the National Assistance level (later Supplementary Benefit, and now Income Support) – was set too low to reflect a normative standard of poverty. If the poverty line was set 40 per cent higher than the National Assistance level (i.e. 140 per cent of National Assistance, a figure chosen by the two researchers to reflect their concept of what was needed to be out of poverty) then a different picture emerged. According to information supplied to them by the Ministry of Labour, the official number in poverty in 1953 of 1.1 per cent increased to 7.8 per cent when recalculated by the authors, and the official figure of 3.8 per cent in 1960 should be revised upwards to 14.2 per cent. From these new statistics, poverty ceased to be mainly a problem for the elderly (who represented 68.1 per cent of those in poverty according to Rowntree in 1950) and principally a problem of low pay (40 per cent of those in poverty in 1960, according to Abel-Smith and Townsend, were low-paid). Low

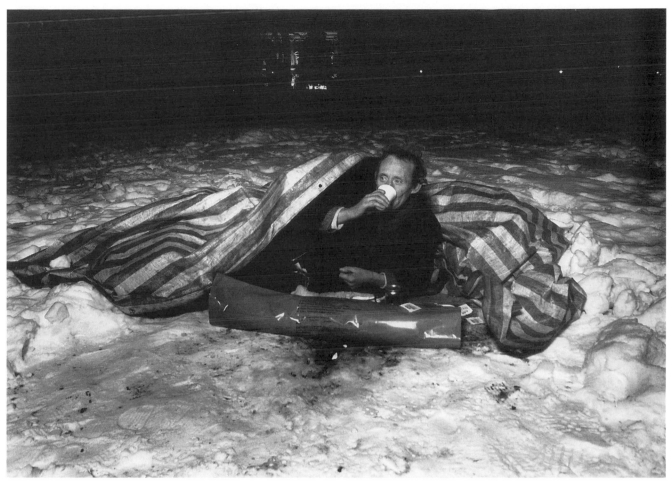

Absolute poverty in Britain in the 1990s:
a homeless man attempts to sleep in
the snow.

pay was also the chief cause of poverty in Rowntree's surveys of
1899 – 52 per cent – and 1936 – 42 per cent. Statistically, there was
no reason why low pay should have disappeared as a problem, as
the earnings of the lowest-paid 10 per cent of income earners had
remained constant at just above two-thirds of the average wage
through the century, reflecting an unchanging wage structure,
despite the Welfare State.

Poverty in the United Kingdom

In a later, and more widespread, study undertaken between 1968
and 1969, Townsend (1979) enlarged on the principles established
in his earlier works, this time basing his research on three forms of
measurement. The first was the State or Supplementary Benefit standard, showing 6.1 per cent of households, and 9.1 per cent of
income units (or individuals), in poverty. According to the relative
income standard (those with incomes of less than 50 per cent of the
average for households of their type), 9.2 per cent of households
and 19.6 per cent of income units were living on the margins of

poverty. By the deprivation index (see pp. 287) 22.9 per cent of households and 25.9 per cent of income units were in poverty. This meant that 12.5 per cent of the population were in poverty. In particular, Townsend pointed out that 'Elderly people who had been unskilled manual workers and children in the families of young unskilled manual workers, especially those with substantial experience of unemployment, sickness or disablement and in one-parent families, were most likely to be poor.'

The new underclass The publication of Townsend's book revived controversies around the concept of poverty not witnessed since Rowntree. New evidence has continued to be amassed. Frank Field (1989) details how he believes a new 'underclass' has emerged in Britain since the optimistic decades of the 1950s and 1960s. As evidence, he cites the number of those receiving National Assistance/Supplementary Benefit/Income Support as increasing from an initial 963,000 in 1948 to 2.8 million in 1979, and 4.9 million by 1988. In 1949, 1.5 million were dependent on Supplementary Benefit alone. This figure increased to 4.4 million in 1979 and 8.2 million in 1988.

Field observes that the type of group most vulnerable to poverty has changed in the course of the twentieth century. Booth and Rowntree found that a vast majority of those in poverty were on low wages, or were wage-earners with large families of five or more children. Between the wars, poverty was increasingly associated with unemployment, as well as low wages. In the immediate post-war period the concern was with old age. From the 1980s, the focus has returned to low incomes. The underclass now, Field says, consists of the long-term unemployed, particularly school leavers who have never had a job, and those older workers who have been without work for very long periods; single-parent families, whose number doubled between 1979 and 1988, particularly those dependent on welfare for long periods of time, and elderly pensioners who are entirely dependent on old age pensions and Income Support. These people belong to 'an underclass that sits uncomfortably below that group which is referred to as living on a low income' (see chapter 3).

QUESTIONS 1 **What does the term poverty mean to you? How would you define it?**

2 **According to Field, who are the new underclass?**

3 **How was poverty rediscovered?**

The measurement of poverty

There is now no agreed measure of the extent of poverty in the United Kingdom. Most people would agree that it exists, but how much there is and why it exists depend on how it is defined and measured. The amount of poverty perceived depends on where the line is drawn.

Absolute poverty

Rowntree, in 1899, drew his line according to what has become known as an 'absolute' standard. After consulting nutritionists, he then estimated the average nutritional needs of adults and children, translating these needs into quantities of different foods and then into their cash equivalent. He then added minimum sums for clothing, fuel and household sundries according to the size of family. Families were in poverty, he said, if their 'total earnings are insufficient to obtain the minimum necessaries for the maintenance of merely physical efficiency'. Even this absolute standard changed in 1936 (eventually becoming the basis of Beveridge's figures for the amount of National Assistance) when additional necessities were added, and as John Veit-Wilson (1986) observed even Rowntree's conception of poverty was relative, not absolute. The State's measure of poverty – the Income Support level – is an absolute measure in that it attempts to meet basic physical, and not cultural, needs.

Relative poverty

Most conceptions of poverty are relative. Townsend (1979) is in no doubt about how he conceives poverty: 'Individuals, families and groups in the population can be said to be in poverty when they lack the resources to obtain the types of diet, participate in the activities and have the living conditions and amenities which are customary or are at least widely encouraged or approved, in the societies in which they belong.' Here, the emphasis moves away from what humans need to exist to what the society they live in expects in terms of living standards. The poverty line is always moving. So how can it be fixed at any one time?

Deprivation index

Townsend's own answer was to compile a 'deprivation index' comprised ultimately of twelve items the lack of which, he argued, pointed to poverty. This included things such as not having a week's holiday away from home in the last twelve months, children not having a party at their last birthday and households not having a fridge. Built into this index is the realisation that poverty is both material and social. In a later work (1987) he makes a distinction between deprivation and poverty, where the former implies unmet need and the inability to participate in activities, and the latter describes the lack of material resources that causes this deprivation.

The main problem with this type of index is that it is subjective: it is based on what Townsend and his research team believed constituted poverty. Yet the index includes items such as 'does not have fresh meat … as many as four days a week' (number 4), 'has not had a cooked breakfast most days of the week' (number 9) and 'household does not usually have a Sunday joint (3 in 4 times)' (number 11). In Townsend's carnivorous world, poverty clearly exists when the bacon is not being brought home.

Subjective definitions

Neither Rowntree nor Townsend seem concerned with what people themselves believe is poverty – what subjective ideas of poverty are. To correct this, in 1983, Mack and Lansley (1985) asked 1,174 people what were necessities in contemporary Britain. Where more than 50 per cent of the respondents agreed on the necessity of items, then the authors decided that it meant that those without them lived in poverty. This gave them 22 items on their list, ranging from heating living areas of the home if it's cold (agreed by 97 per cent) to 'two hot meals a day for adults' (64 per cent) and 'presents for friends or family once a year' (63 per cent). This index revealed that 7.5 million people, or 13.8 per cent of the population of Britain lived in poverty, as defined by its population.

A similar piece of research by the British Social Attitudes Survey found that only a quarter of people believed that those 'who had enough to buy the things they really needed, but not enough to buy the things most people take for granted' were living in poverty, while 55 per cent defined having enough to eat and live but not to buy other needed items as poverty, and 95 per cent accepted that not having 'enough to eat and being able to live without getting into debt' meant poverty. One wonders what the other 5 per cent thought?

QUESTIONS

1 **How can absolute and relative poverty be distinguished?**

2 **What was Townsend's purpose in developing a deprivation index? What problems are associated with using this index?**

3 **How might the concept of subjective poverty be criticised? What are its merits?**

4 **Do definitions of absolute, relative and subjective poverty remain constant over time?**

5 **Why are women and ethnic groups vulnerable to poverty?**

Why does poverty exist?

No one really argues that poverty does not persist in Great Britain. The debates around poverty concern its nature, extent and causes. A number of theories in sociology have been developed to explain its persistence.

The functions of poverty

From the functionalist point of view, if poverty is a prevalent feature of society, then it must in some way be functional, although it is clearly dysfunctional to those in poverty. Poverty must serve a social function. This argument has been elaborated by Howard Gans (1973). He delineates fifteen ways in which poverty can be functional, for example:

- Poverty helps to ensure that dirty, dangerous, menial and undignified work gets done.
- The poor help to uphold the legitimacy of dominant norms by providing examples of deviance (e.g. the lazy, spendthrift, dishonest, promiscuous).
- The poor help to provide emotional satisfaction, evoking compassion, pity and charity, so that the affluent may feel righteous.
- Poverty helps to guarantee the status of the non-poor.
- The poor add to the social viability of non-economic groups (e.g. fund-raising, running settlements, other philanthropic activities).

'A functional analysis', he says, 'must conclude that poverty persists not only because it satisfies a number of functions but also because many of the functional alternatives to poverty would be quite dysfunctional for the more affluent members of society.' 'Phenomena like poverty', he concludes, 'can be eliminated only when they either become sufficiently dysfunctional for the affluent or when the poor can obtain enough power to change the system of social stratification.' The poor, he suggests, will always be with us.

The culture of poverty

Other analyses focus on the norms and values of those in poverty, rather than the society that requires poverty. This group of theories argues that a distinct subculture of poverty is identifiable. For Oscar Lewis (1961), 'poverty in modern nations is not only a state of economic deprivation, of disorganisation, or of the absence of something. It is also something positive in the sense that it has a structure, a rationale, and defence mechanisms without which the poor could hardly carry on. In short, it is a way of life, remarkably stable and persistent, passed down from generation to generation along family

POVERTY DESCRIBED

Oscar Lewis, The Children of Sanchez (1961), gives the following descriptions of the lifestyles of the poor. They are characterised by 'a miscellany of unskilled occupations, child labour, the absence of savings, a chronic shortage of cash, the absence of food reserves in the home, the pattern of frequent buying of small quantities of food many times a day as the need arises, the pawning of personal goods, borrowing from local money lenders at usurious rates of interest, spontaneous informal credit devices organised by neighbours, and the use of second-hand clothing and furniture'.

The poor live in 'crowded quarters, [with] a lack of privacy, gregariousness, a high incidence of alcoholism, frequent resort to violence in the settlement of quarrels, frequent use of physical violence in the training of children, wife-beating, early initiation into sex, free unions or consensual marriages, a relatively high incidence of the abandonment of mother and children ... little ability to defer gratification and plan for the future ... a belief in male superiority [and] a corresponding martyr complex among women'.

The structural determinants of poverty

lines.' These subcultural features can be found in any major city, whether in London, Glasgow, Paris, New York or Mexico City. In another study (1958), he argues that 'by the time slum children are aged six or seven they have usually absorbed the basic values and attitudes of their subculture and are not psychologically geared to take full advantage of changing conditions or increased opportunities which may occur in their lifetime.'

Despite the clearly value-laden concepts underlying this theory, it has been discussed at governmental level, both in the United States in the 1960s – at the time of the battle against 'cultural deprivation' and 'Operation Headstart' – and in Britain, in particular by Sir Keith Joseph, the former Cabinet minister and intellectual mentor to Margaret Thatcher.

It is also a theory that has come under sustained fire. Lewis, in particular, is seen as looking only at *some* people in poverty, and abstracting their characteristics. Lewis himself was aware of this: 'my rough guess would be that only about 20 per cent of the population below the poverty line in the US have characteristics that would justify classifying their way of life as that of a culture of poverty'. Many other people are poor, but do not necessarily behave in the way Lewis describes, as Rossi and Blum (1968) conclude: 'our review of the literature concerning poverty does not support the idea of a culture of poverty in which the poor are distinctively different from other layers of society'. A research programme set up by Sir Keith Joseph failed to identify a cycle of deprivation. Rutter and Madge (1976) found that 'At least half of the children born into a disadvantaged home do not repeat the pattern of disadvantage in the next generation. Over half of all forms of disadvantage arise anew each generation.'

Other criticisms are that, firstly, the theory concentrates on those in poverty, without examining the possibility that the cause of their poverty may originate from the society in which they live. In other words, poverty may be structurally determined. By concentrating on the individuals – or more particularly the families – involved, the theory of a subculture of poverty, Townsend (1979) says, encourages 'the recurrent prejudice that poverty is the fault of individuals and family or community groups rather than of society itself'.

As we know, to become part of a subculture you must be socialised into its norms and values. This theory suggests that poverty is something you learn from your parents, as an attitude and a way of life. From this perspective the solution to your poverty is that you must be socialised out of it, hence the wide range of schemes launched to this end, for example the Department of Social Security's 'Restart' programme. Is this the sociology of poverty or the poverty of sociology?

Situational constraints

The idea of 'situational constraints' takes issue with the culture of poverty argument and claims instead that the behaviour of the poor is simply a consequence of the constraints of the situation in which they find themselves, with little money and few opportunities to get hold of any more. If their situation was to change then – contrary to Lewis's claim – so too would their behaviour. There is no fixed culture of poverty, and the poor are only detached from everyone else because of their financial position.

This is the central argument of Elliot Liebow's *Tally's Corner* (1967), where the behaviour of a group of black men on low incomes was explained by him as a response to their awareness of their likely future. He makes it clear that they share the aspirations and values of mainstream society, from a stable family life to well-paid, full-time employment. However, an overstated and temporary culture of manliness among the men developed to compensate for their poverty, their sense of failure and their inability to support a family. This cultural response is not seen as an important or permanent aspect of their lives.

Marxism – the problem of wealth

Other views of poverty point to the structure of society as its cause, not those in poverty themselves. For Marxists, poverty is a consequence of the ownership of capital by a few people, at the expense of the rest of society. When most of a society's wealth is in the possession of a handful of people, then we are all in a sense relatively poor. Inequality is essential to capitalism, and a consequence of its exploitative dynamic. The problem of poverty is not the poor themselves but the rich, as R.H. Tawney (though not himself a Marxist) observed in his well-known statement: 'what thoughtful rich people call the problem of poverty, thoughtful poor people call with equal justice the problem of riches'. If you are poor, it is because someone rich has got the wealth that is, by rights, yours. Their wealth, not your poverty, is the problem.

Weber and market position

The Weberian view stresses the weak market position of the poor – their poverty is the consequence of a lack of bargaining power. This is a common feature of those who are most vulnerable, particularly the unemployed, low-paid, single parents and the elderly. Recognising this, and adopting a position close to neo-Weberianism, Peter Townsend makes a number of recommendations in order to eliminate poverty, including payment of incomes to dependants, a legally enforceable right to work, and restricting the grip of professional organisations.

Gender and poverty   Feminists have stressed the feminisation of poverty, pointing out that those who suffer most from poverty are women. Women have always been particularly vulnerable to poverty. In 1908, three out of five Poor Law recipients were women, in 1983, three in five Supplementary Benefit recipients were women and in 1992 62 per cent of those in receipt of Income Support were female. As Millar and Glendinning (1989) argue: 'the conditions under which women obtain access to resources, the levels of those resources, women's control over resources and their degree of responsibility for the welfare of others in deploying material resources – all these are factors which make women more vulnerable to poverty, and which shape women's experience of the impact of poverty'. There is a hidden poverty within the family that means that women experience poverty more intensely than men in that, for example, they are more likely to feed others before themselves when little food is available. It also falls largely to women to manage poverty, and they consequently have a disproportionate amount of their time caught up in this activity.

Ethnicity and poverty   It is also argued that poverty disproportionately affects ethnic minorities in Britain. Despite the paucity of statistics specific to ethnic groups, Leech and Amin (1988) argue that 'there has been an increased racialisation of poverty: blackness and poverty are more correlated now than they were some years ago ... the condition of the black poor is deteriorating'.

Immigration policy   A number of reasons have been put forward for this. Immigration policy has made it difficult for some groups to approach welfare services. The 1971 Immigration Act specified that wives and children could only enter the United Kingdom if those who were going to finance them were able to do so without using public funds. This was defined in 1985 as meaning Income Support, Housing Benefit and Family Credit. This emphasis discourages eligible groups from taking up benefits although it does not prevent the portrayal of some ethnic groups as 'scroungers'. This is compounded by the weak market position of many ethnic minorities who are either unemployed or in low-paid work and the fact that, proportionately, there are more young people in ethnic minorities than there are in the population as a whole. While there are proportionately less pensioners than among white groups, the younger age profile of ethnic minorities means that they are more vulnerable to changes in Child Benefit, Family Credit and Income Support. Afro-Caribbean – though not Asian – families are more likely than white families to be headed by lone parents.

QUESTIONS
1 What are the functions of poverty?

2 How can wealth be regarded as a problem?

3 In what ways can the 'culture of poverty' thesis be criticised?

4 To what extent does the extract from Oscar Lewis's *The Children of Sanchez* describe the plight of the poor in Britain today?

Has the Welfare State succeeded?

Any analysis of whether the Welfare State has been a success depends on how the role of the Welfare State, through its gradual evolution from the nineteenth century, is interpreted.

Elimination of the 'five evils'

One way is to ask whether Beveridge's five giants or evils – squalor, ignorance, disease, want and idleness – have been eliminated, as he intended. Clearly, want and idleness persist in a society where 2.5 million people were unemployed in 1991, nearly 3 million were unemployed in 1993 and there were never less than 1.5 million unemployed throughout the 1980s (see chapter 6), and where a growing proportion of people below retirement age are dependent on Income Support.

Unequal use and distribution

Another is to ask whether the aim of making the services of the Welfare State available to all has brought about a corresponding equality or even equality of opportunity, in society. Again, the answer is that it has not. A great deal of evidence has been amassed pointing to this conclusion. In the NHS, as early as 1971, Julian Tudor-Hart felt able to identify an 'Inverse-Care Law', whereby health care resources are distributed in inverse proportion to need. In other words, those who most need health care are least likely to get it, and vice versa. There is still a distinct system of stratification within the education system, with those outside the State system – the public schools – being disproportionately represented in higher education. A.H. Halsey, A. Heath and J.M. Ridge (1980) argue that there is no evidence of increased upward mobility from the working class as a result of compulsory secondary education. Julian Le Grand (1982) observes that it is the middle classes who make most use of State education, as it is their sons and daughters who are most likely to go on to higher education. Yet it is the working class, who make relatively less use of universities, who will pay their taxes and finance their degrees. Similarly, income tax relief on mortgages also favours the middle class more as they are more involved with the purchase of domestic property. In general, he says, 'the richest group receives nearly twice as much public subsidy per household as the poorest group' as a result of housing policy. For Le Grand, it clearly is not true that the Welfare State has brought about equality, in fact the opposite may be true because of the unequal use of the Welfare State's resources.

Distribution of wealth

The evidence from changes in the distribution of wealth and income can also be construed in the same way. By wealth is meant the individually owned assets of the population over the age of 18. This mainly describes the value of dwellings, assurance policies, pensions, stocks and shares. These are usually calculated by the Inland Revenue from the estates of people on their death. The collective wealth of the British people was thought to total £2,270 billion in 1991. Throughout this century a few people have held a disproportionate share of this wealth.

The small downward distribution of wealth in this period (*shown in Table 9.1*)can be mainly accounted for by the wealthiest distributing their wealth to friends and relatives before they died, to avoid paying estates duties and the increase in the value of houses. It is nevertheless the case that the overall wealth of the bottom 90 per cent increased from 8 per cent before the First World War to 21 per cent after the Second World War.

The main change to the post-war distribution of wealth was the introduction by the Labour government in 1974 of a capital transfer tax, designed explicitly to prevent this redistribution from the wealthiest to their relatives before death. This in turn was amended by the introduction of inheritance taxes by the Conservative government in 1981 and 1986, which once again made it easier to transfer assets prior to death, as *Table* 9.2 shows.

TABLE 9.1   Long-term trends in the distribution of private property (%)

	1911–13	1936–38	1954
Richest 1% owned	69	56	43
Richest 10% owned	92	88	79

Source: Westergaard and Resler, 1976

TABLE 9.2   Distribution of wealth (%)

	1976	1986	1991
Most wealthy 1%	21	18	18
Most wealthy 10%	50	50	50
Most wealthy 50%	92	90	92

Source: Social Trends 24, 1994

Although these statistics are calculated in a slightly different way to the earlier series (excluding estimates for hidden wealth), they still show that half the population owned only 8 per cent of the wealth and that 50 per cent of the wealth was owned by only 10 per cent of the population in 1991.

Distribution of income

While there has been relatively little legislation surrounding wealth in the United Kingdom, taxes on income – what people earn in terms of wages and salaries – are the continuous focus of political interest.

As we can see in *Table* 9.3, the highest earners suffered a loss in their share of overall income, both before and after tax, though the chief benefactors were the middle-income earners, not the bottom 10 per cent of earners. Thus there was no redistribution of income from the highest to the lowest earners in the post-war period.

TABLE 9.3   Distribution of income in the UK before and after tax

PERCENTAGE SHARE OF TOTAL INCOME						
	Before tax			After tax		
	Top 10%	Next 60%	Bottom 30%	Top 10%	Next 60%	Bottom 10%
1949	33.2	54.1	12.7	27.1	58.3	14.6
1959	29.4	60.9	9.7	25.2	63.5	11.2
1967	28.0	61.6	10.4	24.3	63.7	12.0
1978/9	26.1	63.5	10.4	23.4	64.5	12.1

Source: A. B. Atkinson, 1983

The 1980s

It is in the period since the election of the Conservatives in 1979 that trends in the distribution of income and fiscal policy have come under the greatest scrutiny, despite that government's decision in the early 1980s to abolish the Royal Commission on the Distribution of Wealth and Income. The general thrust of Conservative fiscal policy has been to lower income tax, particularly for the highest earners, and instead raise revenue where necessary though indirect forms of taxation such as Value Added Tax (VAT). There has therefore been a shift away from progressive to regressive taxation. Thus top rates of income tax of 83 per cent in 1979 were reduced to 40 per cent for the highest earners in 1988, while VAT has been increased from 7.5 per cent to 17.5 per cent and the range of goods and services on which VAT is charged has been widened. The government's own figures show that in the 1980s £31.4 billion was lost to the Treasury as a consequence of these changes in income tax. Those who gained were the top 1 per cent of taxpayers who saved an average of £33,300 per year or 27 per cent of all the tax cuts made, while the top 10 per cent of taxpayers saved £6,000 or 48 per cent of all tax cuts. The bottom 50 per cent of tax-payers gained an average of £400 per year or 15 per cent of all tax cuts on income. All of these gains have to be offset against other forms of tax increase and also changes in the benefit system have to be taken into account. This broader picture is revealed in the calculations of the Institute of Fiscal Studies (an independent 'think tank') concerning net gains and losses in this period. These clearly show that, on average, the group that benefited most in the 1980s was already the most wealthy, as *Table 9.4* shows.

A similar study by the same organisation in 1994 showed that, as a result of the tax changes made in the budgets between 1985 and 1993, including the changes to be brought in in 1994 and 1995, the bottom 40 per cent of income groups would be worse off, losing between £1.10 and £3.00 per week, while the top 10 per cent of households gained an average of £31.30 per week.

This same trend can be shown in a different way. The Department of Social Security's own statistics show that in the 1980s the amount of disposable income available – what is left over after taxes, national insurance and pension contributions have been paid – rose for the richest fifth but fell for the poorest fifth (*see Table 9.5*).

Numerous studies all show increasing income inequalities in the United Kingdom from the 1980s on. In 1994, a study by the Department of Economics at Swansea University showed that the poorest 5 per cent of the population saw their real income (adjusted to take account of inflation) fall between 1979 and 1991 before taking account of housing costs, while the richest 5 per cent saw their income increase 58 per cent. When rent and mortgage payments are taken into account, the bottom sixth of the population are revealed as being worse off than they were in 1979.

TABLE 9.4   Distributional effects of tax and benefit changes 1979–92 by income decile

DECILE	AVERAGE GAIN/LOSS (£ PER WEEK)	% GAINING	% LOSING
First (poorest)	−1	48	40
Second	2	66	24
Third	2	65	27
Fourth	4	69	24
Fifth	9	81	13
Sixth	13	84	10
Seventh	15	85	10
Eighth	21	89	7
Ninth	25	90	7
Tenth (richest)	87	92	6
All	18	77	17

Source: E. Davis et al., Alternative Proposals on Tax and Social Security, Commentary No. 29, Institute of Fiscal Studies, 1992

TABLE 9.5 **Distribution of individual disposable household income (%)**

	BOTTOM 5TH	NEXT 5TH	MIDDLE 5TH	NEXT 5TH	TOP 5TH
1979	10	14	18	23	35
1990–91	7	12	17	23	41

Source: Social Trends 24, 1994

Marxism and welfare capitalism

There are a number of responses to these observations. Marxists argue that, in the light of the way the Welfare State evolved, there is no reason why greater equality should emerge. None of the central legislation of the twentieth century has fundamentally attacked the position and privilege of the wealthy. The Keynesian economics that underlay the developments after the Second World War were based not on a fundamental redistribution of wealth but on the principle that a fully employed working class could pay for these services out of its own tax and national insurance contributions. As O'Connor (1973) points out, the State under capitalism has to assist private capital to remain profitable while at the same time helping to make the existing economic and political order of society appear acceptable. The Welfare State provides the appearance of an egalitarian society, with a better-educated and healthier workforce, while in reality the structure of a deeply unequal society persists. The Welfare State is a palliative, a sticking plaster over a gaping wound.

The New Right

From the point of view of the New Right, the aims and objectives of the Welfare State are fundamentally flawed, as Rhodes Boyson observed.

In Britain the State now decides how half or more of a man's income shall be spent, how his family should be educated, how their health care should be organized, how they shall save for misfortunes and retirement, what library and in many cases what cultural provision they should receive, and where and at what cost they should be housed.

The present Welfare State, with its costly universal benefits and heavy taxation, is rapidly producing an economic and spiritual malaise among our people. Planned, introduced and encouraged by good men who believed that State intervention would bring both economic and spiritual returns, the end-product is completely different.

The National Health Service was introduced by men of compassion who wished to improve the health of the poor and to remove the worry of medical bills. The end-result has been a decline in medical standards below the level of other advanced countries because people are not prepared to pay as much through taxation on other people's health as they would pay directly on their own and their families'. Long queues in surgeries, an endless waiting-list for hospital beds, and the emigration of many newly trained doctors are among the unexpected results. Small wonder that more and more people are looking to some form of private insurance to give them wider choice in medicine and surgery.

Unemployment schemes and other social security benefits have been universalized and increased to their present level because people remembered the millions of unemployed and the poverty and deprivation of the 1930s. But all they do is to provide encouragement for the lower paid with large families to become unemployed or to go sick. Similarly, millions of workers are encouraged to break the monotony of factory routine by strikes when meagre strike pay can be augmented by supplementary benefits to their families and tax rebates for themselves. The reliable and industrious worker looks with irritation and animosity at his idle fellows whom he helps to maintain and the general sense of responsibility and personal pride declines. National economic strength and personal moral fibre are both reduced.

State education, introduced 100 years ago by men and women concerned first to provide the benefits of universal literacy and later to develop leisure and cultural pursuits, is more and more coming under control of the trendy 'expert', who seeks to make his name at the children's expense while he gathers his money from the state. There is little choice of school either by type, discipline or area and the neighbourhood comprehensive school with a complete egalitarian ethic could have disastrous effects upon educational standards.

Housing subsidies and rent controls, also introduced by good if short-sighted middle men, have produced the appalling slums and homelessness of the present day. Many working-class families are virtually prisoners of their council houses since they would lose the subsidy – and perhaps a roof – if they moved elsewhere. The large tower blocks with their tragic effect upon young and old inmates would never have multiplied in a free market where the producer has to take careful account of the preferences of the sovereign consumer.

The result of all this extra State interference financed by taking over 50 per cent of the gross national product in taxation has been not the production of an economically viable society but what might be called rampant stagflation, that is to say stagnation in production and raging inflation which further destroys belief in the future. The moral fibre of our people has been weakened. *A State which does for its citizens what they can do for themselves is an evil State; and a State which removes all choice and responsibility from its people and makes them like broiler hens will create the irresponsible society.* In such an irresponsible society no one cares, no one saves, no one bothers – why should they when the State spends all its energies taking money from the energetic, successful and thrifty to give to the idle, the failures and the feckless?

Rhodes Boyson, 'Down with the Poor', 1976

The philosophy of this group is based on the socio-economics of nineteenth-century *laissez-faire* and the corresponding 'Victorian values'. These emphasise self-help, the virtues of the family as the basic social unit, and the non-intervention of the State in everyday life. The existence of State handouts to the unemployed encourages dependency, is a disincentive to work, and an unfair burden on the tax-payer. Attempts to create greater social equality are ultimately a block on economic growth, for example in the case of progressive taxation, 'you do not make the poor richer by making the rich poorer'. The monopoly of State provision also prevents freedom of choice.

These were the arguments that underlay the decade of Thatcher government in the 1980s. There is no small irony in the fact that in a period dedicated to 'rolling back the frontiers of the State' public expenditure on social security increased in real terms by 40 per cent between 1979 and 1987. Although this is partly due to the increasing numbers of single-parent families and the elderly, the bulk of the increase has been caused by the rise in unemployment. In real terms, more is now spent on the Welfare State than ever before.

The social democratic view

A third view, broadly known as the 'collectivist' or 'social democratic' view, argues that the Welfare State has been beneficial and at least partially successful. Despite its shortcomings, Wilding (1986) argues that, as well as being popular, 'the achievement of the last forty years has been considerable ... Welfare State policies are an efficient way of meeting social needs, such policies are the most effective way of supplementing, complementing and correcting the shortcomings of the economic market; Welfare State policies are the only satisfactory way of meeting needs which other traditional sources of welfare can no longer supply; the Welfare State is an important mechanism for securing political stability; it provides a basis on which to build a genuine welfare society and, finally, the Welfare State is based on values which are the necessary basis for fair and civilised life.'

QUESTIONS

1 Has the Welfare State succeeded?

2 Has the gap between the rich and the poor been closed since the end of the Second World War?

3 Which group in society benefited most by the tax changes of the 1980s?

4 How is the Welfare State criticised by:
   (a) Marxists
   (b) the New Right?

5 Follow the news and try to establish the differences between the policies of the Conservative and Labour parties on the development of the Welfare State.

The future of the Welfare State

The question of the future of the Welfare State is ultimately a political one, but many commentators are agreed that whichever political party is in power it has to face a range of social and economic realities. These include the demography of a society where the population is not projected to decrease until at least the year 2025. The dependency ratio, comparing those of economically active age against those over 65 and under 16, is also projected to keep shrinking. In 1991, 64 per cent of the population were between 16 and 64 years old; however, by 2025 it is projected that this will have decreased to only 61 per cent. This immediately implies that there will be less earners available to pay income tax. Such calculations must also take into account the number of people actually working. In 1993, only 66 per cent of men aged between 55 and 59 were classed as being in employment. The 'greying' of the population has serious implications for the future of the Welfare State, but discrimination against the 'active elderly' also carries significant implications.

The family Changes in the structure of the family are also important, in particular the rising number of single-parent families, the dissolution of the family through separation and divorce, the increase in the average age of marriage, the trend towards increased cohabitation, and women's increased participation in the workforce. The apparently irreversible move away from the traditional nuclear family challenges the social policy of any political party that believes that caring begins in the home.

Political parties need also to take into account what is politically possible in any vision they may have of the Welfare State in the future. Successive elections in the 1980s and 1990s appear to have revealed an electorally significant proportion of the electorate unwilling to pay for the welfare of themselves and others through high levels of direct taxation. Parties rarely win elections on the grounds that they will increase taxation, and, increasingly, membership of the European Union will restrict a governing party's ability to raise taxes or annul taxes at will as the EU moves towards fiscal uniformity.

The affordable Welfare State It is for these reasons that many writers (for example George and Miller, 1994) believe that all political parties are restricted to projections concerning the 'affordable Welfare State', broadly agreeing to run a mainly privately owned economy in pursuit of higher rates of economic growth, low inflation and low rates of taxation. All are agreed that there will be no return to the 'welfarism' of the early post-Beveridge years. In all but a few areas of political life, the argument that public spending in itself is a drain on the economy has won out.

Few political parties, however, are willing openly to support calls for the demolition of the Welfare State on the lines attempted in recent years in New Zealand. Some pressure groups such as the Adam Smith Institute (1994) have called for exactly this, arguing that the State should phase itself out of responsibility for paying for unemployment and invalidity benefits, retirement pensions and health care. In this way, they argue, families would cease to be imprisoned by the State and would be free to escape the squalor of their lives, breaking the dependency culture. As we have seen, whether such a dependency culture exists and possesses these properties, is a matter of keen sociological debate.

In the 1990s, the leadership of the Conservative Party has been careful to distance itself from such calls, claiming instead that any changes they make at most amount to a move away from the Welfare State to a 'welfare society', which is still committed to providing basic levels of old age pension, child and unemployment benefit.

Calls to encourage increasing participation by individuals, families and companies in taking direct responsibility for their own welfare have nevertheless been interpreted by opposition parties as the beginnings of the creation of a two-tier or residual Welfare State, where universal benefits are replaced by selective and means-tested benefits. At the same time, market forces have been introduced into former 'command sectors' of the economy, with schools, hospitals and doctors managing their own budgets and trust funds. The end result, its critics say, is that it is no longer possible to talk about a truly National Health Service, a truly free and universal education system, and a coherent and comprehensive system of welfare provision for those who need it.

Commission on Social Justice   The Report of the 1994 Commission on Social Justice (the Borrie Commission, which was set up by the Labour Party and was in many ways intended as a Beveridge Report for the 1990s) makes three possible projections and looks at the form the Welfare State could take. They call these projections a 'deregulators' Britain', a 'levellers' Britain' or an 'investors' Britain'. The first option sees the State pulling out of intervention in social and economic life, in the way advocated by the Adam Smith Institute, leaving the free-market economy to hold sway. The second posits the redistribution of wealth without any clear idea of how the wealth will be created. The third combines 'the ethics of community with the dynamics of a market economy'.

301

The Labour Party supports the third position. Its leader, Tony Blair, argues that this means that 'while retaining the values of the Welfare State, we must be more ambitious' and provide 'a helping hand to success and achievement throughout life, enabling people to gain the security and independence of a good job at a fair wage and not a life on benefit' (*Guardian*, 14.7.94).

Thus, the future of any Welfare State depends, as ever, on political views about the role of the State, the amount of money available to finance it, the underlying social and demographic factors, and the political will to carry reforms through.

QUESTIONS

1 **What demographic and social factors will influence the future of the Welfare State.**

2 **In what ways can the Welfare State be 'afforded' in the future?**

FURTHER READING

L. Bryson, *Welfare and the State: Who Benefits?*, Macmillan, 1992

J. Clarke *et al.*, *Ideologies of Welfare*, Hutchinson, 1987

D. Dale, *Feminists and State Welfare*, Routledge and Kegan Paul, 1986

H. Dean and P. Taylor-Gooby, **Dependency Culture**, Harvester/Wheatsheaf, 1992

R. Klein and M. O'Higgins (eds.), **The Future of Welfare**, Blackwell, 1985

D. Marsland and R. Segalman, **Cradle to Grave: Comparative Perspectives on the Welfare State**, Macmillan, 1989

M. Rutter and N. Madge, **Cycles of Deprivation**, Heinemann, 1976

P. Townsend, **Poverty in the United Kingdom**, Penguin, 1979

W.J. Wilson, **The Truly Disadvantaged**, University of Chicago Press, 1987

10 Health

INTRODUCTION

The chapter begins by outlining the history that led to the development of the NHS. It then goes on to examine the relationships between health and social class, geographical locations, gender and ethnicity, and the various explanations that have been put forward for these relationships. The social factors involved in health and illness are discussed. The chapter concludes with a discussion on the role and power of the medical profession.

Towards a National Health Service

Poor Law Infirmaries

Following the 1834 Poor Law Amendment, workhouses were ordered to set up sick wards – the 'Poor Law Infirmaries' – which, from 1848, were centrally administered by the General Board of Health. These infirmaries became the main public providers of health care, alongside charitable and voluntarily run hospitals and hospices. Although some workers had insurance schemes that would pay for treatment from doctors and hospitals, for most people the infirmary was where they went when they fell ill, and it was a popular belief that few would be cured in such places.

Growth of national insurance

As a consequence of the general alarm about the poor health of the population at the turn of the century, an increasing number of workers gained health insurance under the 1911 National Insurance Act. This move failed to prevent an epidemic of 'flu in the years immediately following the First World War, in which more British people died than in armed combat during the war!

'Free at the point of delivery'

In 1929, following the creation of a Ministry of Health in 1919, the administration of Poor Law Infirmaries was taken up by local authorities. Hospitals were now municipal. As is common during wartime, this devolution of power was reclaimed by central government in 1939, with the formation of an Emergency Medical Service covering day-to-day control of both voluntary and municipal hospitals. Casualty services became free at the point of delivery.

The cost of health This principle was made general with the formation of the NHS in 1948, although it soon broke down when the full cost of such a policy was realised. This rose remorselessly, from £437 million in 1949 to £27,000 million in 1990. Even this amount, many groups believe, is still not enough, and there is intense political debate over the funding of the NHS. Private health insurance is increasing, with 7.5 million people covered by 1994. The Labour Party has argued that the NHS is being gradually privatised, with the creation of NHS trusts, and the increasing number of services that are no longer entirely free at the time of use.

QUESTION **Is there an infinite demand for health care?**

The social construction of health

Measuring health In order to assess the health of an individual, group or society, forms of measurement have first to be found. This immediately causes problems. There are two main indicators: mortality and morbidity, where mortality refers to death and morbidity to sickness. Of these two, mortality is the easiest to measure, although the causes of death, both in the long and short term, may be more difficult to ascertain. In the short term – the direct cause of death – the debate around suicide can be cited (see chapter 14). In the long term, the question 'why did someone die when they did, and of that particular cause?' is one that produces a variety of answers.

At first sight, the biological explanation that an individual can die of 'natural causes', that there is a biological time clock that simply expires at a certain point, is persuasive. Alternatively, someone may be 'unlucky' and develop the symptoms of a terminal illness – it could just as easily have happened to someone else. Sociologists dispute both ideas: that health and illness are simply biological processes or merely matters of chance.

Social causes Against these explanations, the sociological view points to the fact that life expectancy varies from time to time, and from place to place. It is higher in an urbanised society than a rural one, and increases as that industrial society develops. Even in an industrial society there are clear differences in life expectancy between social classes, within the occupations constituting each social class, between men and women, between ethnic groups, and between regions. For most sociologists, the existence of these statistical regularities points to social, economic and environmental causes of mortality, rather than causes based on biology or chance.

The role of medicine and the medical profession

A number of reasons have been put forward to explain why life expectancy has increased, including improved diet, declining fertility, sanitation, the decline of infective diseases, and improved medical care. Of these, the role of medicine and medical care is disputed. The evidence available suggests that conditions such as tuberculosis were beginning to disappear long before effective vaccines and medical treatment emerged. McKeown (1976) claims that hospitals in the nineteenth century were as likely to kill, for example through the spread of disease, as they were to cure. In the first third of the twentieth century, infant mortality fell most sharply during the First World War (1914–18), when 60 per cent of doctors had joined the armed forces, suggesting that the real cause of decline was temporarily improved living standards (rations, full employment) for the very poorest during wartime.

Health care in the United Kingdom is geared towards curing people when they are ill, not preventing them becoming ill in the first place. As some have cynically suggested, the NHS could be renamed a 'National Illness Service'. Doctors have a vested interest in people being ill, as have drug companies. Yet if illness and disease are socially and environmentally caused and produced, why do we turn to the medical solution in times of illness? This is explored further in the next section.

QUESTION   **Are health and illness medical or social issues? Can they be both?**

Inequalities in health

Health and social class

The Black Report

In 1977, the Labour government set up a Royal Commission, under the chairmanship of Sir Douglas Black, the Department of Health and Social Security chief scientist, to investigate how successful the NHS had been in meeting its aims in the immediate post-war period, implicit in which was the idea of meeting everyone's healthcare needs equally, regardless of age, class, ethnicity, region or gender. The main aim of the commission was to discover whether inequalities in health had lessened since 1948.

The answer was that they had not. The commission found, using mortality rates and the Registrar-General's table, that whatever way mortality was tabulated, people in social class I (see chapter 3) were less likely to die than those in social class V, and the classes in between had rates in accordance with their position between I and V. Whether using the mortality figures for stillbirths, for infants (up to the age of 12 months), for children up to the age of 14 years, or for adults of working age (15–64), the occupational mortality statistics for 1970–72 show that your chances of living, or living longer, are greater the higher your social class. There is a particularly pronounced increase in the jump from the semi-skilled workers of social class IV to the unskilled workers of social class V. The picture is still roughly the same if the statistics are disaggregated into causes of death, with the clearest correlations between social class and illness being shown in diseases of the respiratory system, in both males and females, and accidents, poisoning and violence, among men in adulthood, and the least clear correlations being shown in tumours and congenital anomalies in childhood and malignant tumours in adult women. As the report, which was eventually published in 1982 as *Inequalities in Health*, *the Black Report* edited by Townsend and Davidson, argues: 'if the mortality rates for Social Class I had applied to Classes IV and V during 1970–72, 74,000 lives of people aged under 75 would not have been lost.' The report discusses four possible ways of explaining why these apparent inequalities in health exist:

I The artefact explanation

From this point of view, the form of measurement used in *The Black Report* is suspect. Although the mortality ratios are standardised to take into account the proportion of people nationally in each social class, they are nevertheless unrepresentative and inaccurate. Social class V, for example, is unrepresentative in terms of age. Workers in this class are generally older than those in other classes, as younger and better trained recruits to the labour force will enter the increasing number of skilled occupations. Older people are more likely to feature in mortality statistics, therefore social class V has the highest mortality ratio. The statistics used by *The Black Report* are therefore artefactual, or made up – invented.

2 Theories of natural and social selection

Put simply, this group of theories argues that people are not ill because they are in social class V, but in social class V because they are ill. Illsley (1955) found, by looking principally at maternity, that upwardly mobile women were likely to be the most healthy. Building on this, Stern (1983) argues that upward and downward mobility are the effects, not causes, of good or bad health. If you are wealthy but in poor health, you are vulnerable to downward mobility. If you are poor but in good health, upward mobility is more likely than for those in the same and adjacent classes in worse health. Social mobility becomes a genetic, not a social phenomenon. The only accurate way of measuring the relationship between health and class is to use an individual's class of origin, not their class of destination. As the statistics are recorded, it is no surprise that social class

V, into which the unhealthy have sunk, records the highest mortality rates.

3 Theories of material deprivation and structural explanations

Neither of the first two theories discussed are based on sociological factors. The theorists of material deprivation locate the causes of premature mortality and ill-health in the material or physical circumstances of people's lives. In particular, they point to whether people are employed or not, what income they receive, what their conditions of work and security of tenure are, how happy they are in their work, and their possession of wealth and property. This position is closest to that of Marxism in explaining inequalities in health.

There is certainly a strong correlation between mortality statistics and measures of relative material deprivation. What is more difficult to establish is causation – does one circumstance (in this case their class position) cause another event (in this case a mortality rate) to occur? Is it enough to say that because one thing happens at the same time as another that one, therefore, causes the other? It is because of this problem that some people have pointed to the need for the following explanation.

4 Theories of cultural deprivation and behavioural explanations

One of the reasons that it is difficult to argue that ill-health and premature death are caused by material deprivation is that the main causes of death are no longer directly related to want. The diseases most typical of poverty and malnutrition are infective diseases. These are the illnesses Beveridge had in mind when he located 'disease' as one of the five evils. These infective diseases have largely been stamped out. The main killers today are degenerative diseases associated with smoking, a rich diet and inactivity: diseases of the respiratory and circulatory system, as well as cancer. This points away from the problem of not having enough to looking at how people use what they do have.

The sociology of smoking

As in theories of educational under-achievement and poverty, it is the culture of groups – their norms and values – that is highlighted here. Health care is the responsibility of individuals. Only they can properly make choices about how to look after their own bodies. Everyone, for example, is now aware that there is a strong correlation between smoking and lung cancer, and government health warnings state unequivocally that 'smoking causes cancer'. Yet there is also a strong correlation between cigarette consumption and social class. Smoking is a cultural habit most prevalent among manual workers, particularly the unskilled. If premature death in this social class is to be reduced then this cultural practice has to change, or be 'recoded'. Young people have to find other ways of marking the transitions from childhood to adolescence to adulthood. Women need to find symbols other than cigarette smoking as a means of asserting personal independence.

It is more difficult, however, to assert that manual workers smoke more because of cultural rather than material deprivation. Why did they start smoking? Why do they continue? Stress at work would be a material factor. 'Being sociable', expressing group solidarity, a sense of fatalism, or an inability to defer gratification are cultural factors.

Reactions to *The Black Report*

The publication of *The Black Report* during the first Thatcher government caused immediate controversy. Attempts were made to suppress and limit its publication. New and further research, however, was commissioned and undertaken to determine whether health inequalities were statistical mirages, the result of the struggle of the fittest to survive, or the consequences of material or cultural deprivation.

The Health Divide

In 1987, the Health Education Council (now the Health Education Authority) published *The Health Divide: Inequalities in Health in the 1980s*, a review prepared by Margaret Whitehead. Using data collected up to the mid 1980s, and thus updating the base years of 1970–72 used in *The Black Report*, she finds 'convincing evidence of a widening of health inequalities between social groups in recent decades, especially in adults. In general, death rates have declined more rapidly in the higher than in the lower occupational classes, contributing to the widening gap. Indeed, in some respects the health of the lower occupational classes has actually deteriorated against a background of general improvement in the population. There was also a widening gap between manual and non-manual groups in their rates of chronic sickness from 1974 to 1984, and during the late 1970s the gap widened for acute sickness too. The exception to the widening trend was in relation to deaths in babies under one year.'

Having collated this evidence, she then reviews new research on the four explanations offered in *The Black Report*:

I The artefact explanation
She rejects the arguments of those such as Illsley (1986) and Jones and Cameron (1984) that the Registrar-General's classification artificially inflates the size and importance of mortality and morbidity differentials, and renders comparisons meaningless. While agreeing that this classification could be bettered, 'the recent evidence continues to point to the very real differences in health between social groups which cannot convincingly be explained away as artefact. On the con-

trary [new evidence suggests] the Registrar-General's classification may under-estimate the size of the social class gradient in health.'

2 Theories of natural and social selection

New data have emerged principally from Illsley's finding that taller women tend to move up the social classes at marriage, whilst shorter women tended to move down at marriage, and Wadsworth's evidence (1986) that seriously ill boys were more likely than others to experience a fall in occupational class by the time they were 26. Yet, she remarks, in both studies the size of the selection effect suggests that it accounts for only a small proportion of the overall differentiation between the social classes.

3 and 4 Materialist/structuralist and cultural/behavioural theories

Whitehead notes a trend towards arguing that the distinction between the two explanations is becoming increasingly artificial, as one explanation frequently cannot be separated from the other, and that they are strongly interrelated.

As *Table* 10.1 shows, everyone is smoking less, but the rate of reduction is still determined by class. Similar gradients exist for alcohol consumption, food and nutrition (such as consumption of white and brown bread, fresh fruit and vegetables, and fats) and exercise in leisure, particularly swimming and walking.

New evidence, however, points away from cultural and behavioural explanations for these patterns. Calnan and Johnson (1985), for example, compared the health beliefs of women from social class I and social class V and found no difference in beliefs about concepts of health and the perception of vulnerability to disease: 'The importance of the "culture of poverty" model as an explanation of poor service use and health-damaging behaviour may have been over-estimated in the past, and new appraisals of health behaviour are needed.'

TABLE 10.1   Prevalence of cigarette smoking by sex and socio-economic group (%)

| | | SOCIO-ECONOMIC GROUP | | | | | | ALL OVER 16 YEARS |
		A	B	C1	C2	D	E	
Men	1972	33	44	45	57	57	64	52
	1984	17	29	30	40	45	49	36
	1990	16	24	25	36	39	48	31
Women	1972	33	38	38	47	42	42	42
	1984	15	29	28	37	37	36	32
	1990	16	23	27	32	36	36	29

Source: Social Trends, 23, 1993

There is now a wealth of information that socio-economic or material factors, specifically housing conditions and income, strongly influence cultural behaviour. Graham (1984) argues that low use of preventive health services by poor families may be the result of an economic decision: 'for poor families in particular, a rational decision may be one which rejects professional care. The mother may choose instead to invest her limited resources of time, money and energy in other areas of family health – in food for the family for example, or in keeping her children warm.' Some actions, such as smoking, may be the only way that mothers can stay sane and act responsibly towards their family, as it helps relieve tension, without having to leave the room. Socio-economic factors, Whitehead concludes, play an important part in determining class-based forms of behaviour concerning health.

Health and region

In the same way that mortality and morbidity rates vary from country to country, and by class, age, ethnic group and gender, there are also distinct regional differences (*see Table* 10.2). *The Black Report* found that mortality rates were lowest in the South and South East of Britain, and highest in the North and North West. These differences have persisted into the 1980s. The pattern remains the same if examined by class and gender. Social class I men and women have lower standardised mortality ratios in the South than in the North.

The obvious explanation for these regional differences is material deprivation which, as Whitehead suggests, 'may be the key to the North/South gradient', yet there is a similar pattern between regional differences and smoking (*see Table* 10.3).

TABLE 10.2 **Mortality of men and women in different regions of Britain 1979–80 plus 1982–83 (direct age-standardised death-rate per 1,000)**

REGION	MEN 20–64	SINGLE WOMEN 20–59	MARRIED WOMEN 20–59
Britain	5.57	1.43	2.23
England & Wales	5.43	1.41	2.17
Scotland	6.92	1.62	2.89
South West	4.82	1.32	1.93
South East	4.88	1.29	1.97
Wales	5.86	1.43	2.34
North West	6.37	1.69	2.52
North	6.43	1.53	2.50
Strathclyde	7.14	1.66	3.06
Central Clydeside	7.86	1.78	3.23

Source: Townsend, Phillimore and Beattie, Inequalities in Health in the Northern Region: An Interim Report, 1986

TABLE 10.3 Prevalence of cigarette smoking by region – persons aged 16 or over Great Britain, 1984

REGION	% SMOKING CIGARETTES
Scotland	39
Wales	37
England: North	36
North West	35
South East	31
South West	30

Source: General Household Survey, 1984

It was also, notoriously, people in the North to whom the then Under-Secretary of State for Health, Edwina Currie, was referring when she claimed that their failure to look after themselves produced their poor health profiles.

Health and gender

Women have lower mortality rates than men, as shown in *Table* 10.4 from *The Black Report.*

TABLE 10.4 Death rates by sex and social class

	MALES	FEMALES	RATIO MALE TO FEMALE
I	3.98	2.15	1.85
II	5.54	2.85	1.94
IIIN	5.80	2.76	1.96
IIIM	6.08	3.41	1.78
IV	7.96	4.27	1.87
V	9.88	5.31	1.86

Adapted from Occupational Mortality 1970–72, *death rates per 1,000 population, published by HMSO and compiled by the Registrar-General*

In 1984, the life expectancy of men was 71 years and 77 years for women. On the other hand, women seem to suffer more sickness in their lifetime than men, as *Table* 10.5 suggests.

TABLE 10.5 General practitioner (NHS) consultations in Great Britain, 1984 by social class and gender

SOCIO-ECONOMIC GROUP	AVERAGE CONSULTATIONS PER PERSON	
	Males	Females
Professional	2.9	4.1
Employers/managers	3.5	4.4
Intermediate/junior non-manual	3.7	4.6
Skilled manual	3.7	4.9
Semi-skilled manual/personal service	4.0	5.4
Unskilled manual	4.3	5.5

Source: Adapted from Hilary Graham, Women, Health and the Family, *1984*

Interpreting the statistics   Interpreting these statistics highlights many of the methodological problems involved in the sociology of health. The artefact explanation would argue that women may visit their doctors more often than men because they often do so on behalf of others, especially children, and that if they live longer than men there are therefore more elderly women than elderly men visiting the doctor. A further problem is that the official statistics used for mortality in *Table* 10.4 measure married women according to their husband's occupation, further distorting the figures. (This problem is discussed further in chapter 3.) Leeson and Gray (1978) point out that if maternity and disorders of the breast and reproductive tract are excluded, then more men than women are hospitalised.

Female longevity   Other reasons for women's longevity have been put forward although any generalisations are inevitably prone to stereotypical portrayals. In their first twelve months, boys have a higher infant mortality rate suggesting that, genetically, it is boys who are the weaker sex. Through their socialisation as men they try to ignore minor illnesses and do not care for themselves properly. Men are more aggressive, take more risks, form the majority of car drivers and motor-cyclists, and generally lead more hazardous lives than women. They manage stress differently as they are not socialised into showing their emotions in the same way as women. At work, more men work full time than women, and they tend to work longer and more unsociable hours, working in areas of higher risk and hazard, and taking on greater responsibility than women. They are more prone to industrial accidents and diseases, and at home they will want to be the ones who climb up ladders and crawl over the roof. Finally, until the 1990s they retired at a later age than women.

For theorists of social selection, the fact that women live longer than men (and records show this to be true as far back as 1838) is evidence of their superior genes, suggesting that women have a greater aptitude to survive than men. However, other evidence suggests that women have not always, on average, outlived men and their life expectancy can be lower as it is, for example, in Nepal and Bangladesh. Similarly, the gap in life expectancy has changed over time, particularly in the mid twentieth century.

The materialist explanation argues that gender differentials in mortality rates are based on occupation. This would explain why female rates were at their relative lowest at the point of their greatest exclusion from the labour market. Overall, the fact of work and occupation causes premature death.

From a cultural/behavioural point of view, there is clear evidence that male and female behaviour is different: men smoke more and drink more than women. Although there is still very little empirical research on this question in Britain, Waldron (1976) argues that in the USA men die at twice the rate of women from seven of the major causes of death: coronary heart disease, lung cancer, emphysema, motor-vehicle and other accidents, cirrhosis of the liver and suicide. Given that these account for 75 per cent of the sex differential in mortality, Waldron concludes that gender differences in behaviour are more important than genetic factors.

QUESTIONS

1 Do the findings of the Black Report differ from those of *The Health Divide?*

2 Using the four possible explanations cited in the Black Report, decide which you find the most useful in explaining inequalities of health by:
(a) social class
(b) gender
(c) region

3 Which of the Black Report's four explanations are sociological? How does material deprivation differ from cultural deprivation?

4 Are official statistics on mortality and morbidity reliable?

Health and ethnicity

The relationship between health profiles and ethnicity is problematic. In the first place, it is far from clear what the concept of ethnicity means and how it should be used in understanding the experience of health by different ethnic groups. Death certificates, for example, record country of origin but do not show ethnic group membership for the increasing proportion of second-generation black British. The same is true for white Britons born outside the United Kingdom. Furthermore, how should people of mixed parentage be categorised?

Mortality

From the studies that have been undertaken to date, for example Whitehead (1987) and Mares et al. (1987), the evidence is that members of ethnic minorities die from mainly the same causes as the rest of the community, that is from cancer and circulatory problems. However, people of Afro-Caribbean and Indian, Pakistani and Bangladeshi descent are more likely to die from cancer of the liver, diabetes and tuberculosis. Asians suffer from a higher than average incidence of heart disease and osteomalacia (softening of the bones) and there is a greater possibility of infant mortality for mothers who were themselves born in the Indian subcontinent. Afro-Caribbeans are more likely to die from strokes and hypertension (high blood pressure), to be diagnosed as mentally ill and to receive electro-convulsive therapy (ECT). All ethnic minorities are more likely to die from accidents, poisoning and violence.

Explanations As with social class, attempts to explain the patterns of health differences experienced by different ethnic groups have focused on genetic, cultural and material factors. In the earliest explanations it was thought that there was likely to be a higher incidence of mortality from subtropical diseases. There is, however, very little evidence for this. While it is true to say that one in every 300–400 people of Afro-Caribbean descent develops sickle-cell anaemia, and people from the Mediterranean, Middle East and Asia inherit thalassaemia (a blood disorder), they are not exclusive to these groups and have been found among members of the white population. There is therefore thought to be little – or no – link between 'race' (defined biologically) and mortality.

Greater emphasis is given to other factors. The cultural argument has tried to explain high perinatal mortality among Asian mothers by their low attendance at antenatal classes and high rates of coronary heart disease for Asians in general by the use of ghee in cooking. Similarly, diabetes has been blamed on a high carbohydrate diet. Against this it has been argued that equivalent groups in the Indian subcontinent suffer lower rates of heart disease (Coronary Prevention Group, 1986).

The 'material' argument sees physical factors as overriding these other arguments. From this point of view what matters most are the consequences of racism and the low class position occupied by most members of ethnic minorities in the United Kingdom (see also chapters 3 and 6). Their poor health profiles can be best explained by bad housing, unemployment, low pay and the greater likelihood of working in hazardous or unhealthy jobs such as textiles and footwear. High rates of long-term unemployment, low job security, too much shift work and working nights lead to stress which in turn leads to high blood pressure. As Mares *et al.* found, deaths from hypertension are four times as common in men living in the UK who were born in the Caribbean than they are among their white counterparts and six times as common in women.

Among others, McNaught (1987) has argued that racism is a factor in both type of housing and employment that people from ethnic minorities get, as well as in their relationship with organisations such as the National Health Service, which has been slow to adapt to the demands of a multicultural society. Racism in the NHS can be seen in the employment of large numbers of black people in ancillary work (such as catering or cleaning) and in the less prestigious aspects of nursing or medical work. It can also be seen in the organisation of the NHS which needs to be adapted to accommodate the different cultural and religious beliefs of different ethnic groups. Language, hygiene (for example, the importance of washing in running water to Moslems) and death rites are all important factors which should be taken into account if the NHS is to be truly accessible to all British citizens regardless of ethnic origin.

QUESTIONS

1 **How important are material and cultural factors in explaining the health profiles of ethnic minorities?**

2 **How important is social class to an understanding of the health profiles of ethnic minorities in the United Kingdom?**

3 **How important is it that the NHS adapts itself to a multicultural society? How much of a bearing might this have on the health of ethnic minorities?**

Doctors and patients

The sick role

Sociologists have contributed a number of theories to explain the power of the medical profession in Western societies. For Talcott Parsons (1951), doctors are necessary because, by identifying people as sick, they enable people to adopt a 'sick role' whereby they can escape their social obligations for a short period of time. Doctors regulate and control behaviour to the extent that they decide when people should and should not go to work. This is 'motivated deviance', in which doctors co-operate. The patient is socially allowed to be ill and exempt from some social duties as long as they take reasonable steps to get better and use the available medical services. The function of doctors is to facilitate the sick role for patients.

In this argument Parsons is assuming that illness is a temporary phenomenon. This falls down when chronic or long-term illness is considered as it both allows a more explicit and threatening form of deviance to challenge the social system, and also questions the competence of the medical profession, as they are unable to find a cure for the illness. As someone who studied psychology before moving on to sociology, Parsons regarded most illness as psychosomatic – only in the patient's imagination – and simply another opportunity for role-playing.

Marxism and the medical profession

For Marxists, the existence of a curative rather than preventative model of health care is a consequence of capitalism. As Navarro (1976) argues, the dominance of the medical profession in health care helps obscure the social and economic causes of illness, the resolution of which demands political, not medical, action and initiatives. While health care may be free at the point of delivery (though this is increasingly less true), there are also vast profits to be made, firstly by companies selling drugs and high-tech equipment to hospitals, and secondly through the ability of industry to ignore and bypass health and safety legislation where prosecutions are rare and fines negligible and which permits activities such as cigarette smoking. Health care is still primarily about profit and the relative powerlessness of consumers.

Weber
The power of the medical profession itself is the focus of the Weberian view. This is best illustrated by Friedson (1975) who emphasises the way in which the medical profession monopolises the practice of health care, through legal–rational means (see also chapter 7). As such, it is a highly secretive, autonomous organisation, successfully preventing outside intervention in its practice even on behalf of the ruling class. (The medical profession was also the group that the then Minister for Health had most trouble with in setting up the NHS in 1948 until he 'stuffed their mouths with gold'.) The medical profession, according to Friedson, has successfully brought about the untested belief that it knows best, as industrial societies have come to place a high status on 'scientific' knowledge, partly due to the successes of the medical profession in eliminating some diseases. Primarily, the profession exists to serve its own interests, not those of the ruling class, and certainly not the interests of the consumers of medical care.

Iatrogenesis
Ivan Illich (1975) provides a radical critique of the way health care has evolved, focusing on the concept of iatrogenesis or doctor-originated illness. This happens in three ways. Clinical iatrogenesis results from the actual practice of medical health care, for example through the use of humans as 'guinea pigs', because of the side-effects of drugs (treatments where the cure is worse than the illness), and through addiction to prescribed drugs. Social iatrogenesis can be characterised by the way that, for example, birth and death have become medicalised. Here he is thinking of the way that the birth process has come under the control of doctors, not mothers, and is geared to doctors' demands. In reaction to this clinical control campaigning organisations were formed, such as the National Childbirth Trust, which aims to help mothers regain some control over childbirth. It also led to attempts to minimise the medical side of childbirth which causes anxiety to mothers. The French obstetrician Leboyer encouraged women to give birth in a warm bath in low lighting which greatly reduced the stress. Thirdly, Illich claims that cultural iatrogenesis has resulted in individuals abdicating responsibility for their own health to a self-regarding

medical profession and alienating technology. As with education, a return to smaller scale and more democratic structures is required.

Doctors' power over women   Similar points have been made by feminists. Ann Oakley (1981) finds little evidence to suggest that technological intervention in childbirth is beneficial for mother or child. Generally, doctors have a great deal of control over women's fertility, through controlling access to some types of contraception and to abortion. The contraceptive pill in particular, a form of birth control targeted at women, not men, has come under strong criticism for its side effects, such as depression, excessive weight gain, headaches, nausea and even loss of sex drive.

QUESTIONS

1 What is the 'sick role'? How is it functional for the individual and society? How might it be dysfunctional?

2 What is meant by the term iatrogenesis? Think of other examples of what Illich means by this term.

3 What have some sociologists said are the effects of the power of the medical profession?

4 In what sense could medicine be said to be a part of the capitalist mode of production?

FURTHER READING

J. Gabe *et al.*, *The Sociology of the Health Service*, Routledge, 1991

H. Graham, *Women, Health and the Family*, Wheatsheaf Books, 1984

I. Illich, *Medical Nemesis*, Marion Boyars, 1975

J. Mitchell, *What is to be Done about Illness and Health?*, Penguin, 1984

M. Senior, *Health and Illness*, Macmillan, 1996

D. Silverman, *Medical Sociology*, Sage, 1988

S. Taylor and D. Field, *The Sociology of Health and Health Care: An Introduction*, Blackwell, 1993

P. Townsend and N. Davidson (eds.), *Inequalities in Health: The Black Report*, Penguin, 1988

11 Religion

Man makes religion, religion does not make man

Karl Marx 1844

INTRODUCTION

The chapter introduces the subject through examining the work of the major sociological perspectives on religion. The next section goes on to examine the debate over secularisation. Finally, some religious sects are investigated.

What is religion?

Sociology and religion

Sociologists have long been fascinated by religion, not in order to argue theological points but rather to explain the symbols, rituals and practices of religion in relation to the structure of society. What the theories give us, then, are explanations regarding the social significance of religion. The sociological researcher is concerned with how religion is used to help keep society together, how it helps to maintain the status quo, or whether it can help bring about changes in society. The metaphysical and theological discussions are secondary. Most sociologists start from the position that any religious belief system can be explained in purely secular, non-spiritual terms. Christianity, Islam, Hinduism, Buddhism, Sikhism, Hare Krishna or any set of religious beliefs can be looked at as social phenomena without making any judgement on their spiritual aspects. Sociological theorists are interested in what religions have in common and the social consequences of these factors.

Functionalism

Answer these questions for yourself before you read this section:

- What functions does religion perform to help maintain social stability?
- Does religion impede or encourage social change?
- Is the role of religion in society changing?

For functionalists, religion is an organ in the organism, a subsystem within the system, an interlocking and necessary institution which plays a role in the creation and maintenance of the value consensus. It acts as a conservative force within society, a brake upon social change. The internalisation of a traditional religious belief system and the formal hierarchies which represent it ensures that any social change that occurs is slow, part of social evolution, rather than rapid, with disturbing structural changes which threaten cohesion and stability.

Durkheim

For Emile Durkheim, in *The Elementary Forms of Religious Life* (1912), the importance of religion lay in its division between the sacred and the profane. Through religion, sacred objects were created in society in such a way that society itself became sacred. In his research into the customs and beliefs of aboriginal groups he argues that religion has a role to play in maintaining 'mechanical solidarity', where law is automatic and final. The law of the gods is absolute. How 'organic solidarity' is maintained in larger societies, where rules and values are more flexible, is more complex. The construction of the 'collective conscience' or value system, which underpins law and order, is more problematic.

If you take Christianity as an example, sacred things include the Bible, altar, church, holy water and the cross. The last is a form of execution yet it has acquired religious significance because Christ was put to death on it. As Durkheim says, any object can be invested with a symbolic meaning. It is the belief system which gives it that importance. But what do sacred objects symbolise?

The value system

According to Durkheim, religion is a disguised way for people to worship society itself. The sacred objects come to stand for the value system, the all-powerful, integrating force which has an existence above and beyond the existence of human individuals. The value system is a social fact, existing before you were born, continuing to exist after your death, more powerful than you, a vital element which keeps society together and is therefore worthy of worship. Durkheim's view of religion has been criticised as being idealistic — society has been placed upon the altar and deified. Are religious believers really just worshipping society?

Rites of passage

Rather than concentrating on the global social significance of religion, other functionalists have examined religious rituals and ceremonies to see their significance for individuals. Acts of collective worship are supposed to reinforce social values, so just by being there you are taking part, consenting to the consensus. Why do drunken groups always turn up at church for midnight mass on Christmas Eve? Christenings, weddings and funerals always fill churches with people who are 'just there for the family' but they are nevertheless taking part in a ritual ceremony which serves to integrate them into a community of moral values and beliefs. Funerals help to heal the rift in society and fill the gap left by the deceased. Individuals can mourn and grieve in public, communally, and this reassures them that although their loved one has gone, the community remains. Sooner or later somebody always says 'life goes on' and society goes on with as little disruption as possible. The christening welcomes the new individual to society, the ritual promises they will live life according to the church's (social) values. The worship of society is evident in the fuss made of young babies on these occasions – they are the future of society.

Criticisms

However, like any other organ, the church may lose its power and therefore its functions in society. Does the church really still provide the basis for normative behaviour, the values and morals? Talcott Parsons claims that these are enshrined in the Ten Commandments, but how many people can recall them even if they have had a Christian religious socialisation? The fact that most modern industrial societies are multicultural – there are many forms of religion in Britain and the USA, for example – means that the moral codes may be in conflict. Or have secular values taken over? Is it not a modern value to actually covet your neighbour's possessions and wish you could afford them? Success in financial terms could be said to be the main value of modern industrial societies.

QUESTIONS

1 **Can societies exist without some form of religion?**

2 **What does Durkheim mean by saying that when we worship God, we worship society?**

3 **How may religion be a conservative force in society?**

Marxism

Marxist views of religion place it in the ideological and legal superstructure of society. Religion assists ruling-class ideology by helping to keep the workers in a state of false consciousness, preventing them from realising that they are being exploited. Religion stops the development of the proletariat as a 'class-for-itself'. Revolutionary class consciousness is kept at bay by the laws and promises of religion. Although Christianity was a religion which grew out of oppression, which sustained and comforted people whose lives were miserable and hopeless, it also promised eternal salvation to compensate for earthly misery. If you live a 'good' life, without complaining about your conditions and put up with poverty and exploitation, you stand a better chance of getting to heaven. Rich men will have similar difficulties getting through the pearly gates as camels would have in squeezing through the eye of a needle.

The church and the bourgeoisie

In arguing that 'religion is the sigh of the oppressed creature, the sentiment of a heartless world and the soul of soulless conditions. It is the opium of the people' Marx (1844) tries to show how religion muffles and deadens the harsh experiences of working-class life, and makes it slightly more bearable. This has the long-term effect of preventing social change, putting a stop to revolutionary activity. The role of the church as capitalist landowner and employer (particularly in the nineteenth century) is further evidence that religion is one more ideological tool used by the ruling classes to control and oppress the workers. The popularity of Methodism with the new manufacturing middle class of the 1900s and the attempts to coerce workers into attending services are further evidence. The middle classes were perturbed by the apparent irreligiosity of the workers. Their promiscuity, gambling and drunkenness were seen as a threat to 'respectability', a key ideological concept at the time. Bible study, so-called 'rational' recreations – educational talks, visits, hobbies – were meant to educate the worker into a decent, sober existence. The pub and the music hall were godless, heathen pursuits.

However, there is evidence to suggest that when it came to opiates and 'spiritual gin' (Lenin), the British working classes preferred the real thing. Horace Mann's 1851 religious census showed that very few working-class people attended church with any great regularity. Perhaps the internal segregation in some churches (middle-class people had their own section) contributed to this. Both Marxist and functionalist theories are forced to see the church as a conservative force, preventing social change from occurring too rapidly. The functionalists note the positive aspects of this, that it maintains stability and keeps society together, and the Marxists point out the negative aspects – religion is seen as a ruling class ideological prop which offers pie-in-the-sky salvation in return for suffering on earth while the bourgeoisie continue to profit.

QUESTIONS

1 **What does Marx mean by 'the opium of the masses'?**

2 **Why is religion important to the ruling classes?**

Weber

Weber's social action theory allows him to take a more flexible view of the role of religion, particularly in explaining how social change may occur. His argument is that each society has to be looked at as a unique entity, with a history and a social structure which has developed due to a special set of circumstances. In some circumstances, religion may promote and encourage social change rather than oppose it.

As outlined in chapter 1, Weber's perspective on social structure allows him to analyse the rise of capitalism and the influence of the Protestant work ethic upon capitalist ideas and vice versa. The effects of religion on society can be flexible, sometimes acting as a conservative force, holding back change, at other times reinforcing the values which promote and encourage new forms of production in society. Weber's more flexible, interpretive and structural analysis allows him to reflect upon the power of religious thought in everyday life at certain stages of history.

The Protestant Ethic

In *The Protestant Ethic and the Spirit of Capitalism*, Weber argues that the regime imposed by Calvinistic puritanism ensured hard work, thrift, sobriety and the accumulation of wealth. Societies such as Germany, Britain, and later the USA, were developed through this underlying religious ideology. Capitalism flourished with religious justification, although no causal relationship was put forward by Weber. In other words, he did not claim that Calvinism caused capitalism or the other way around. The similarities between the two systems of belief were so great that they were attracted and flourished together in an 'elective affinity' – a partnership of values and guides to existence. Weber shows that the socio-economic structure of society often coincides with the deeply felt beliefs and meanings which individuals hold about their experiences. The powerful explanations of existence in any society at any time may come together to form a world-embracing ideology that helps transform social structure and sets the scene for new sociological analysis. Weber's ideas contain the seeds of the secularisation debate, as can be seen in his comments upon the change from religious to scientific explanations of reality. This leads to the rationalisation of thought and the so-called 'disenchantment' of the world.

Disenchantment

Disenchantment is a failure of belief in the power of magic in general to explain the world. Religion plays its part, but the eventual rational, scientifically based society is no longer dependent upon bizarre rituals. The laboratory experiment, the ballot box vote, the political conference will replace religious rituals like mass and holy communion. The other founding fathers did not disagree with Weber about the declining importance of religion in advanced industrial societies, but they were certainly divided as to how and why it occurred.

QUESTIONS
1 What is, for Weber, the relationship between religion and the rise of capitalism?

2 How do Weber's views differ from those of two other founding fathers?

The debate about what secularisation means

Measuring secularisation

Secularisation is generally thought to be the process of the decline of religious influence upon social life. The problem is: how do we measure that influence? Should we use statistics: positivistic indicators like church attendance, marriages, christenings and funerals (*see Table 11.1*)? Or should we rely on more qualitative indicators: belief- and meaning-based data on how religion pervades your inner soul and existence – non-positivistic, interactionist research. As usual there are some big sociological ideas to look at, with the arguments and problems which run through sociology churning under the surface.

TABLE 11.1   (a) Church membership of larger denominations, 1910–85, Great Britain

	ANGLICAN	PRESBYTERIAN/ CONGREGATIONAL	BAPTIST	METHODIST
1910	3,685,386	2,108,973	418,194	841,294
1950	3,249,342	2,053,059	337,203	744,815
1985	1,825,911	1,388,598	154,290	436,049

(b) Churches per 100,000 population 1910–85

	C OF E	BAPTIST	CONGREGATIONAL
1910	64	11	18
1940	52	9	13
1985	38	6	4

Source: Halsey, A.H. (ed.), British Social Trends since 1900, *Macmillan, 1988*

Wilson

Bryan Wilson (1966) defines secularisation as: 'The decline of the influence of religious institutions, thinking and practices upon social life.' He uses hard social data, statistics on all aspects of religious life, to prove his thesis that secularisation is indeed taking place, as earlier writers had predicted. His critics, who analyse religion from an interactionist perspective, point to the fallacy of the 'social facts' of his data, in the same way as Durkheim's critics point to the problems in trusting suicide rates (see chapter 14). The foremost critic is David Martin, who claims that the alleged decline of religion cannot be measured in statistical terms. The figures do not tell us whether people go to church for religious reasons, social reasons or because they have to be seen to be 'respectable', as Martin

323

(1978) says was the case in nineteenth-century England. Studies into the decline or growth of religious belief in people's minds can only be properly carried out using interactionist methods. However, to look back at Wilson's definition – the decline of 'the influence' of religion on 'social life' – perhaps his methods do prove what he is claiming. Attendance at church, the status and number of the clergy, the use of church ritual to signal important points in the life cycle (birth, marriage and death) do show, in however crude a way, that the influence of religious institutions, thinking and practices upon social life is indeed declining. The statistical evidence has all the answers to a positivist's prayers.

Wilson's evidence

Wilson (1977b) himself argues that:

- in 1950, 67 per cent of the children born alive in Great Britain were baptised in the Church of England; in 1973, this was the case for only 47 per cent.

- in 1952, about 28 per cent of those aged 15 years in England were confirmed in the Anglican Church; the proportion was below 20 per cent by the mid 1970s.

- some 6.5 per cent of the population took Easter communion in the Church of England in 1953; 20 years later, fewer than 4 per cent did so.

- Methodists had three quarters of a million members in 1952; their membership fell by a third by 1977.

- in the same period, the number of Baptists fell from 300,000 to 185,000.

- Congregationalism and Presbyterianism present a similar picture.

- in the early 1950s, no more than 10 per cent of those polled did not believe in God; by the mid 1970s this had risen to 36 per cent. Less than 40 per cent of people believed in life after death.

Shiner

In a review of the literature on secularisation, Larry Shiner (1971) analyses six different usages and points out their weaknesses:

1 Decline of religion

Symbols, doctrines and institutions lose influence. Research in this area shows that even the members of different faiths may doubt some of the doctrines of their religions: did Christ *really* come back from the dead; did Mohammed *really* speak to an angel; do Catholics *all* avoid using contraceptives? The usual problem with this definition of secularisation is that it assumes a 'golden age of religion' when everyone believed, when the religious authorities were all-powerful and pews were filled. In fact, no such age actually existed. Even the Middle Ages were full of disbelievers.

2 Conformity with this world

A crucial stage in any religious movement is when it turns away from the supernatural and becomes more concerned with this world. Will Herberg (1955) describes the differences between 'conventional' religions in a society, and the 'operative' religions which provide the meaning and value system. Those who belong to the 'conventional' religions (Judaism, Islam, Christianity) actually reflect the values of the 'operative' religion of American society – secular, non-religious values. This has the social effect of bringing the diverse cultural groups in American society together under a value system which may be at odds with the views of each 'conventional' religion.

Again, the difficulties of measuring these shifts of belief away from the scriptures and into everyday life prove impossible to untangle. What could be happening is that people choose to emphasise the aspects of their belief system which are in accord with their lifestyles and the expectations made of them, while ignoring other aspects. Does this mean that they 'believe' any less than their ancestors, who also tailored their beliefs to fit in with 'the world'? Shiner argues that 'increasing secularisation' implies a move away from religious belief, when what in fact is happening is simply a shift in the emphasis of religious belief.

3 Disengagement

According to this definition of secularisation, society is no longer defined and controlled by religion, and so religious belief is 'disengaged' from the social sphere, and becomes a private, inward matter, with no need of corporate institutions. It is confined to the private sphere of life and is no longer an issue of public importance.

There are examples of this in the growth of the State as provider and regulator of public functions, for example education and welfare, which used to be controlled by the church. Another aspect of this definition is the intellectual disengagement of philosophy and thought from supernatural to physical, rational, scientific influences. The problems of deciding whether disengagement actually means that belief is less strong than in the past are obvious. How does the fact that the State has taken over certain social functions, and religion has withdrawn from them, prove that supernatural beliefs have declined? The churches may be as strong as ever but now concentrate more upon specifically spiritual concerns. Parsons

(1965) uses a similar idea which he calls differentiation, by which he means that the functions of the church become refined, 'purer', and it is free to concentrate on the sphere of doctrine and creed. Robert Bellah (1964) agrees that this differentiation is a signal of change and that it signifies evolution rather than secularisation. Any rejection of the supernatural and of doctrine are just new ways of using religion, not evidence of a move away from it.

4 Transposition of religious beliefs and institutions

Under this definition of secularisation, aspects of religious belief are 'taken' from religion and given a social, secular nature. Examples are psychoanalysis as a secular form of confession, the spirit of capitalism as a secular 'Protestant work ethic', and the Marxist revolution as a secular Judaeo-Christian Messianic revolution. The 'transposition of beliefs' definition suggests that society steals the most attractive ideas in a religion and strips away their supernatural coverings. This view of secularisation is open to the criticism that it is not clear which came first, the religious or the secular version. Are they really the same thing? And if they are, then does it really matter what form the belief or practice takes if it is performing the same function for society and individuals?

5 Desacrilisation

In this definition of secularisation, everything in the world is described and explained in rational-causal terms. Weber called it 'disenchantment' – the move away from magical explanations toward scientific ones. A prehistoric person kept away from lightning because they knew it was an expression of the anger of the gods, and a modern person keeps away because they know it is a big electric charge. Whatever we think it is, it can still kill you if it hits you. The main problem with this definition is that it is based upon the assumption that religious systems necessarily try to explain these physical events. The Hebraic God has given the world over to men to control and understand; the religion has in effect 'desacrilised' itself in its own beliefs. When the religion itself admits that rational-scientific explanations are valid, how does this prove secularisation?

6 The move from 'sacred' to a 'secular' society

This last definition is much more general. Secularisation here refers to the acceptance of political, legal and social decisions which are based on rational grounds, and the acceptance of change. The concept of social change through stages is considered here, but the problem again is measuring just what was a 'sacred' society and deciding what is a 'secular' society.

These six definitions of secularisation have some overlaps and some obvious differences. They have all been used in empirical research, and all have been shown to be occurring. This shows why it is important to understand the definition being used when a sociologist claims that they have evidence for secularisation. Shiner argues that to think of 'religious' versus 'secularised' is to limit the argument to a 'polarised' concept. One problem is that the split between the functions of the church and the functions of the State occurs in Western societies, but not necessarily in other societies. Another is that to polarise secular activity and religious activity, and to claim that when there is a lot of secular activity, religious activity is in decline is also false. In many periods of history, both secular and religious activities were wide-ranging. The final problem in the religious–secular polarity is that it supposes that religion is an 'entity' which can be measured in some way. Bryan Wilson and others define religion in terms of institutional practices and then proceed to measure their decline.

The myth of secularisation

As David Martin (1978) argues, it is impossible to develop criteria to distinguish between the religious and the secular, because the belief systems combined under the name religion are so varied and diverse. Martin suggests that the concept of secularisation has become a 'tool of counter-religious ideologies' which is used to attack religion. Peter Glasner (1977) also has problems with the concept as it has been used, claiming that it has become 'mythicised', no longer related to empirical evidence, and is ideological and confusing. Each social structure needs to be analysed on its own merit, and a specific way of measuring 'religiosity' in that structure needs to be developed before any research can be usefully attempted.

QUESTIONS

1 In what ways can secularisation be measured?

2 How can it be argued that secularisation has not taken place in industrial societies?

3 What does the secularisation debate tell us about the positivist/interactionist divide in sociology?

A secular world?

Secularisation and industrialisation

From one point of view then, it can be argued that industrialisation, and the advances in science and technology that it brings in its wake, contributes to a decline in the importance of religious thought and action in society. This position – the secularisation thesis – can be demonstrated statistically through the falling numbers of people either attending church, being baptised, taking communion, and so on, while at the same time scientific explanations of phenomena replace religious ones. As Gilbert (1980) argues, 'the enhanced mastery over nature, and the increased material comfort and security that have gone hand-in-hand with modernisation, have guaranteed a human preoccupation with the present life and temporal world'. It therefore remains the sociologist's task to explain the fit between industrialisation (or modernisation) and secularisation by employing the concepts described above.

The counter-argument

Those sceptical of this argument, however, question the validity of such indexes of secularisation, claiming at the same time that the religiosity of earlier periods of history cannot be taken for granted. In our own age, moreover, new evidence seems to continually point away from the secularisation thesis. In Britain, for example, the organised church does still play a high-profile role in British life. It would be unthinkable if the next monarch were not crowned by the Archbishop of Canterbury in Westminster Cathedral. The 'Lords Spiritual' play an active life in the House of Lords and play an influential role in promoting or combating legislation on a range of issues from Sunday trading to more secular legislation. Religious programming is a marked feature of Sunday television, and comments made by members of the clergy can still provoke national debate and discussion. Other religious organisations and smaller Christian churches (such as the Seventh-Day Adventists) retain strong and even growing memberships. Figures on private and house-based worship are difficult to obtain but may nevertheless indicate thriving activity, while interest in the occult, tarot and astrology – as well as superstition – remains widespread. In Northern Ireland, the labels 'Catholic' and 'Protestant' have described the groups at the heart of the conflict. While the organised church appears to be in decline, it seems also to be the case that cults and sects are proliferating.

Outside Great Britain, organised religion continues to play a major role in shaping post-war world events. In the USA the Baptist church and particularly the Baptist Minister, Dr Martin Luther King, played a central role in the civil rights movement in the 1960s. This leadership was itself challenged by the Nation of Islam sect and the figure of Malcolm X. In both examples religion was the main organising force behind social change. In the Reagan era of the 1980s the American New Christian Right sought to gain political power while trying to change social policies on issues such as abortion and how accounts of the Creation were taught in school. Evangelists became both popular and wealthy enough to be able to broadcast from their own television stations.

Secularisation has not been synonymous with industrialisation in the Middle East where, Ernest Gellner (1992) remarks, 'Islam is as strong now as it was a century ago. In some ways, it is probably much stronger.' This could not be more clearly demonstrated than by the revolutionary overthrow of the Shah of Iran by the followers of Ayatollah Khomeini at the end of the 1970s. In Latin America Catholics have broken away from papal authority and, calling themselves 'liberation theologists', have backed popular campaigns against autocracy and poverty. In Eastern Europe, both the Catholic and Protestant churches were active in the revolutions of 1989, particularly in East Germany and Poland, where many members of the Solidarity trade union (such as Lech Walesa, who eventually became the President of Poland) were to become members of the new post-communist government with full papal approval.

Wilson How then can the persistence of religion in an increasingly industrial (and some would say post-industrial) world be explained? Bryan Wilson (1982) argues that the new religious movements are profoundly 'anti-cultural'. He sees them as forces making for the destructuring of society and personality rather than playing the traditional role of agencies of socialisation and social control. They are unable to channel religious expression into a form that might have significant repercussions for the social and political structures of modern society. In this view, new religions are further evidence of secularisation in society, attempting to compensate for the more demanding features of a secular society.

Other writers have argued that what unites groups such as those of Eastern Europe and others who have turned to religion is that it has been used as a form of cultural defence in defining their nationality and ethnicity against the threat of more powerful forces. It is a feature of the make-up of national or imperial organisation that groups at the periphery differ ethnically from those at the centre, as with Catholicism and Presbyterianism in Northern Ireland and Scotland. In the case of some Third World countries the rise of religion represents the rejection of Western values as the expected modernisation failed to emerge.

The growth of evangelical Protestantism in what has been seen as a traditionally Catholic South America has been seen by writers such as David Martin (1990) as reflecting the aspirations of particular groups in a time of rapid cultural transition, echoing the adoption of Methodism by the working class in England during the Industrial Revolution.

Islam   Ernest Gellner sees no necessary contradiction between the revival of fundamentalist Islam and modernisation. We know from Weber, he says, that modern economies are 'orderly, sensitive to cost-effectiveness, thrifty rather than addicted to display, much given to the division of labour and the use of the free market. It requires those who operate it to be sensitive to the notion of obligation and their fulfilment of contract, to be work-oriented, disciplined, and not too addicted to economically irrelevant political and religious patronage networks, nor to dissipate too much of their energy in festivals or display … Reformist Islam would seem to be custom-made for the needs of the hour.'

For Steve Bruce (1988), the rise of the New Christian Right in the USA is another example of cultural defence, though it is only weakly linked to any notion of ethnicity. It is linked more to regionalism and the idea of periphery (see chapter 12), and is particularly important in the states of the deep South which had always been peripheral in American economic, social and cultural life. Bruce explains this phenomenon as the reaction of these states to the permissive era of the 1960s and 1970s at the same time as they became relatively more prosperous and important to the US economy. What is of most importance in understanding this movement, however, is the New Christian Right's lack of political success, only ever being able to influence a handful of senators, and only achieving limited change in general social and moral values – they never did become the 'moral majority'.

Once again, whether contemporary societies are seen as secular or not depends on the perspective adopted and the terms used to define that perspective. For both sides of the argument there is plenty of evidence to suggest that their point of view is the correct one. Empty churches and the separation of church from State certainly do suggest the declining importance of religion, though as many have been quick to observe, this applies only in the case of Western Europe and not in other parts of the world. It could be argued with equal conviction that religion does not die out in importance in society but simply evolves and changes its form.

QUESTIONS

1 **How can the term 'secularisation' be defined?**

2 **Are Western societies becoming more or less secular?**

3 **Can the revival of Islamic fundamentalism be successfully accounted for?**

Church, denomination and sect

When people stop believing in God, they don't believe in nothing,
they believe in anything.

G. K. Chesterton

It is not only what people believe but the form that belief takes that tells us much about the roles of religion in society. Hence sociologists have constructed typologies of religious forms encompassing all religious organisations, small or large.

Troeltsch   Attempts to classify different forms of religious organisation usually date from Troeltsch's (1931) church–sect distinction: 'the Church is that type of organisation which is overwhelmingly conservative, which to a certain extent accepts the secular order, and dominates the masses'. At its most developed, the church makes use of the State and the ruling class and becomes an integral part of the social order, represented particularly in the upper classes.

Sects, however, are 'comparatively small groups; they aspire after personal inward perfection, and they aim at a direct personal fellowship between the members of each group ... their attitude towards the world, the state and society may be indifferent, tolerant or hostile, since they have no desire to control and incorporate these forms of social life'. They mainly draw their membership from the lower classes, working upwards from below. They are mainly interested in the supernatural and a direct and personal union with God.

Niebuhr   At about the same time as Troeltsch (and also Weber, mining the same seam) was writing, Niebuhr (1929) argued that sects should be best understood as split-offs from the church, unable to accept the church's compromising tendencies. Over time, however, this new sect either disappears or takes on church-like features and the same process happens all over again. The life-span of a sect, necessarily, is short-lived. Niebuhr also identified denominations (for example, Methodism) as intermediate strata between church and sect. They are larger and more established than sects, but do not yet have the same wide appeal as the church.

Yinger   Yinger (1957) further redefined this typology and defined six types: the universal church; the ecclesia (less successful than the church in incorporating sect tendencies); the class church or denomination (less successful than the ecclesia and limited by class, racial or regional boundaries); the established sect; the sect (still unsure of its relationship with the world); and the cult (at the farthest extreme from the universal church). It is the nature and types of sects and cults that have been of most interest to sociologists.

Wilson   In developing these ideas, Bryan Wilson defined sects as ideological movements having as their explicit and declared aim the maintenance and perhaps even the propagation of certain ideological positions. He identified seven types: conversionist (concerned to change the self or gain salvation, as with the early Methodists and the Salvation Army); revolutionist (trying to overthrow the world before Armageddon, as with the Jehovah's Witnesses); introversionist (practising withdrawal from the world, such as the Quakers in the eighteenth century); manipulationist (engaged in a special teaching to enable members to rise above the world); thaumaturgical (which believe that people can experience the supernatural in their lives, as with Spiritualists); reformist (attempting to change the world slowly, for example the Quakers in the twentieth century); and Utopian (attempting to create perfect societies on earth, as the Tolstoyans have attempted).

Wilson accepts that it is the nature of these organisations to undergo change, caused by both internal and external factors. Internal factors can include the recruitment of a second generation or the need to sustain revolutionary zeal. External factors concern how the sect relates to, and is affected by, the outside world. Manipulationist and introversionist sects only emerge at certain stages of social and cultural development, for example as a consequence of the development of metaphysical thought, or when social institutions have developed a certain degree of autonomy from each other. They are unlikely to develop in non-Christian societies, where thaumaturgical and revolutionist sects are more characteristic, particularly in societies responding to missionary Christianity. Jamaican Rastafarianism is a good example of this revolutionist response, which is typical of a pre-literate society. Conversionist sects, however, are linked to the rise of individualism. Reformist sects are derived from other religious organisations and Utopian sects are limited to stages of social development in which traditional cultural values are being challenged.

Glock and Stark   Glock and Stark (1965) argue that the church–sect dichotomy ignores many of the different forms religious movements take. In generalising and extending this theory, they build at the same time on Merton's (1949) view that social change arises because of an imbalance between cultural goals and the cultural means to attain them (see also chapter 14). Groups and individuals lacking these cultural means may be described as deprived. Deprivation, then, is 'any or all of the ways that an individual or group may be, or feel, disadvantaged in comparison either to other individuals or groups or to an internalized set of standards'.

Glock and Stark identify five types of deprivation: economic deprivation due to income inequalities; social deprivation due to lower social status; organismic deprivation due to physical or mental deformities; ethical deprivation as the result of value conflicts (as in the case of Luther and Wesley, early leaders of the Protestant movement); and psychic deprivation which occurs when people 'find themselves without a meaningful system of values by which to interpret and organize their lives'. The experience of this deprivation leads to change, which may or may not take a religious form. If it does, then the religion may only attempt to compensate for rather than attempt to conquer such deprivation (except organismic and psychic deprivation). The form that new religious movements take, and their chances for survival, depend on the type of deprivation that spurred their formation as shown in *Table 11.2*.

TABLE 11.2 **Deprivation and new religious movements**

TYPE OF DEPRIVATION	FORM OF RELIGIOUS GROUP	SUCCESS EXPECTATIONS
Economic	Sect	Extinction or transformation
Social	Church	Retain original form
Organismic	Healing movement	Becomes cult-like or is destroyed by medical discoveries
Ethical	Reform movement	Early extinction due to success, opposition or becoming irrelevant
Psychic	Cult	Total success resulting in extinction through transformation or failure due to extreme opposition

Source: Glock and Stark (1965)

Wallis Roy Wallis (1984) claims that the 1960s and 1970s witnessed a proliferation of new religious movements in the West. They were only new, however, in the sense that they were either reworkings of the dominant indigenous religions based on Judaeo-Christianity such as the Jesus People, or imported from other traditions, as with the International Society for Krishna Consciousness (ISKCON) and the Divine Light Mission. The Unification Church of the Reverend Sun Myung Moon managed to combine both indigenous and exported religions.

These new movements can be categorised into three types: world-rejecting, profoundly rejecting the world around them as corrupt and beyond redemption, as with the Children of God; world-accommodating, neither accepting nor rejecting the surrounding society, such as Neo-Pentecostalists; and world-affirming, accepting most of the goals and values of the wider society. This latter group is typified by psychologically based groups such as Scientologists.

Behind the emergence of these new religions, Wallis believes, is what Weber described as the process of rationalisation in industrial societies whereby 'life has become organised in terms of instrumental considerations: the concern for technical efficiency; maximisation of calculability and predictability; and subordination of nature to human purposes'. The disenchantment that results from living in such a routine and predictable world leads many, particularly the young, to search for meaning to an otherwise pointless existence.

Barker and the Moonies

Wallis's general points are backed by Eileen Barker's (1984) study of people who had joined the Moonies. Using in-depth interviews, Barker sought to understand the rationale behind becoming a member of such a group – why would anyone join a church which had, as one of its articles of faith, the belief that its leader, Moon, was ordered to set up his church after experiencing a vision in which Jesus told him he was the Lord of Creation? Moon's mission was therefore nothing less than to be the Second Coming, complete with his own rewritten version of the Bible.

According to Barker, members of the sect are not brainwashed in any conventional sense, although at their first workshop meetings potential new recruits are encouraged to think evocatively about their memories, hopes, fears and even guilt, and the opportunity of joining a loving and caring community is offered to them.

A certain type of person is attracted to the Unification Church: 'those who have responded have tended to be overwhelmingly between the ages of 18 and 28, predominantly male, disproportionately middle class and usually unmarried', while Home Church or Associate members tend to be older, female, of a slightly lower class (although still disproportionately middle class) and, frequently, married.

Push factors for recruitment

Becoming a Moonie offers an outlet for youth's idealism, its need to experiment and its rebelliousness. They will be expected to give up material aspirations (at a time when they have very few material things to give up). But becoming a Moonie is more than this: it attracts people whose idealism outweighs their materialism because 'it is a religion that offers to change this world, for everyone, so that it is a better world – indeed the best of all possible worlds .... It will be a world in which a loving, caring God has a loving caring relationship with each individual, and in which each individual will also find him or herself as an integral part of a God-centred family'

(Barker, 1984). Each individual is given tasks to perform and goals to achieve, such as recruiting new members or fund-raising, in such a way that everyone has a clearly described role and a goal.

Moonies are recruited against a backcloth of general disillusionment and discontent. Many of them see the world as 'a divisive, turbulent, chaotic society, characterised by racial intolerance, injustice, cut-throat competition and lack of direction ... everything is relative to the utilitarian interests and desires of a pleasure-seeking, money-grubbing, power-hungry population'. This form of rejection of the material world is only the latest in a series of rejections by middle-class youth dating back to at least the 1960s – indeed, these cults are a result of the failure of the hippy movement of the 1960s to deliver real social and personal change, or to give meaning to a young person's existence. This is what the Unification Church provides. It offers freedom from directionless choices and an opportunity to belong, to do something of value and to be of value. There are therefore, for Barker, more reasons to believe that people join the Moonies as a result of a rational, calculated choice than because of brainwashing.

The importance of sects

As we can see, sects have been of particular interest to those writers concerned with the sociology of religion. As Beckford (1986) argues, although the actual number of people involved or likely to be involved in sects amounts to a small proportion of the population in Europe and the USA, they are nevertheless important not only to the sociology of religion but to sociology itself. Sects give us insight into future social trends. They represent an 'extreme situation' which, precisely because it is extreme, throws into sharp relief many of the assumptions hidden behind legal, cultural and social structures. They could be described as 'social and cultural laboratories where experiments in ideas, feelings and social relations are carried out. They are a normal aspect of social life and a critical guide to societal problems and prospects.' It could, however, be argued that in focusing on sects and new religious movements, we have learnt a lot about a little, at the expense of ignoring an in-depth understanding of the meaning of religion to the vast majority of the rest of the population.

QUESTIONS

1 If sects proliferate, does it indicate that a society is becoming more or less secular?

2 What is the most helpful way to typologise religious organisations?

3 Why do Moonies have a particular appeal to young, middle-class people?

FURTHER READING

E. Barker, *New Religious Movements*, E. Mellen Press, 1989

S. Bruce, **Religion in Modern Britain**, Oxford University Press, 1995

D. Martin, **Tongues of Fire: The Explosion of Protestantism in Latin America**, Blackwell, 1990

R. Robertson (ed.), **Sociology of Religion**, Penguin, 1978

W. Swatos, *A Future for Religion? New Paradigms for Social Analysis*, Sage, 1993

R. Wallis, **The Elementary Forms of the New Religious Life**, Routledge and Kegan Paul, 1984

B. Wilson, **Religion in Sociological Perspective**, Oxford University Press, 1982

12 World sociology

The country that is more developed industrially only shows, to the less developed, the image of its own future.

Karl Marx

INTRODUCTION

The chapter starts by investigating the ideas of Durkheim, Marx and Weber. After examining convergence theory the next section goes on to discuss modernisation theory and the work of Rostow, alongside dependency theory, focusing on Frank. The chapter goes on to look at alternative development strategies, aid and development. The chapter closes by speculating on issues in development sociology in the 1990s, featuring specifically the work of Immanuel Wallerstein.

The founding fathers and social change

Although the ideas of Durkheim, Weber and Marx are often taught as different and opposing theories there are many important similarities in their interests and work which also need to be appreciated. All three lived and worked in societies that were undergoing rapid transition from rural to urban, from agricultural to industrial societies, and it is the nature and implications of this transition that principally interested them. They were all concerned to discover why societies changed.

Durkheim

This process of change was the subject of Durkheim's first published work, his doctoral thesis in 1893. In it he contrasts two types of societies: the traditional and the modern. The traditional society roughly corresponds to a pre-industrial or agricultural society, though what chiefly characterises it for Durkheim is its value system. This, Durkheim says, is composed of norms and values which are rigidly adhered to and which do not vary from village to village or settlement to settlement. He terms this 'mechanical solidarity' (see chapters 7 and 13). Modern societies are characterised by a high density of population and the struggle for scarce resources. In order to overcome these two potential problems, societies learn to increase and share their resources through what Durkheim sees as an ever-increasing division of labour. This necessitates the breakdown of the traditional self-sustaining community and the adoption by more

The breakdown of mechanical solidarity

and more individuals of increasingly specialised roles, in order to produce more. In this way, members of society become more interdependent and as a result specialised institutions form that arc devoted to the meeting of particular needs, for example in the fields of politics, religion, education and the economy. This more complex and integrated society he terms 'organic' which, because of its diversity and complexity, demands that individuals follow less rigid social norms and values. As the division of labour increases, society becomes less cohesive and social integration more difficult to maintain.

Criticisms of Durkheim It must be pointed out here that Durkheim is describing social change not explaining why it happens. This absence of explanation creates an inherent problem for more recent attempts to apply his ideas of why societies develop and change. Similarly, his ideas are based on a very small amount of historical evidence.

Weber Max Weber's interest in social change is more focused and historically based than Durkheim's, and is principally concerned with the emergence and development of Western capitalist economies (see chapter 11). One of the aspects of this development, springing from early Protestantism, is the emphasis on rationalisation in the business world which results in the never-ending search for efficiency in all areas to beat off competitors and satisfy consumers' demands. When this drive for efficiency is combined with the early Protestants' distaste for extravagance and their conviction that 'the devil makes work for idle hands', then capitalism develops and flourishes, tradition is edged aside and individualism triumphs.

The common ground occupied by Durkheim and Weber encouraged some sociologists in the post-war period to synthesise aspects of the two theorists' ideas into a new theory concerning why and how pre-industrial societies would become industrial. The resulting theories of 'modernisation' are dealt with below. (See Modernisation and underdevelopment, pp. 341–46.)

Marx Marx's theory of social change tries to explain change in all societies. His answer is simple. It is ringingly declared in the first lines of his *Communist Manifesto*:

> *The history of all hitherto existing society is the history of class struggles. Freeman and slave, patrician and plebeian, lord and serf, guild-master and journeyman, in a word, oppressor and oppressed, stood in constant opposition to one another, carried on an uninterrupted, now hidden, now open fight, a fight that each time ended, either in a revolutionary reconstitution of society at large, or the common ruin of contending classes.*

In this short extract, Marx (Engels is credited with co-authorship, but never wrote a word!) is expressing his belief that human history can be understood as a series of progressions from one epoch or period of history to another. Although a period of 'primitive communism' is sometimes identified, Marx highlights three main phases: classical society such as ancient Greece and Rome (where the fundamental class conflict is between freemen and slaves); feudal society (where the fundamental class conflict is between lords and serfs); and in the period of his own life, capitalist society (where the fundamental class conflict is between bourgeois and proletarian).

The materialist conception of history

The motor that drives history from one epoch to the next, through a series of revolutions, is, according to Marx, class struggle. As the oppressed struggle against the oppressors of each epoch, new classes and class formations emerge. In his own age, Marx claims, 'modern bourgeois society ... has sprouted from the ruins of feudal society' but 'has not done away with class antagonisms'. Yet it has simplified the process of class struggle where one great class – the proletariat – stand poised to overthrow the bourgeoisie, and in the process end pre-history and inaugurate classless society or communism. Marx spent most of his mature life studying how this transition to a communist society could come about.

Like Durkheim and Weber, Marx is greatly interested in the transition from pre-industrial to industrial society, or what he calls feudalism to capitalism. It is this theory of history, known as historical materialism, and the detailed analysis of the dynamics of capitalist development to which Marx devoted himself, that inform one of the main theoretical attempts to understand the sociology of development since the Second World War: dependency theory (see pp. 344–46).

QUESTIONS

1 How do the views of Durkheim, Marx and Weber differ on what causes social change in society?

2 What is meant by 'the materialist conception of history' in Marxism?

3 What aspects of development did Durkheim fail to take account of?

Convergence theory

In the late 1950s and 1960s in the USA, it became increasingly argued that all industrial societies, whether capitalist (as in the West) or nominally communist (as in the Soviet bloc) will eventually exhibit features that are essentially similar, particularly in terms of the structure and dynamics of their stratification systems. This is because, regardless of the dominant political ideology, industrialisation itself has its own logic of development. This argument is most particularly associated with Kerr *et al.* (1960). Behind this argument lay the observation that the Soviet Union – despite the claims of Nikita Khrushchev, General Secretary of the Communist Party of the Soviet Union – would never become fully egalitarian. As the prevailing functionalist perspective argued at the time, systems of stratification are permanent, inevitable and necessary.

Industrial society

To this, Kerr adds the dimension that in industrial societies, stratification systems reflect the technological demands of the specific level of industrial development, where a range of skills is required of the labour force. It is further argued that in order to co-ordinate and manage development, all advanced industrial societies require advanced management techniques, central economic planning and large governmental bureaucracies. The logic of industrialisation is that the shape and structure of all advanced societies will eventually converge. From a sociological viewpoint, societies' technological demands make them essentially similar, regardless of how they might package and market themselves ideologically.

Criticisms of convergence theory

A number of important objections have been raised against these attempts to compare capitalist and socialist or communist societies in this technologically deterministic way. John Goldthorpe (1966) argues that the class structure of industrial societies is determined not by technological demands but by whether market forces (in the West) or political forces (in the East) are at work. This produces different economic and status priorities, as Parkin (1971) shows. In the Soviet Union of the 1960s, manual workers tended to be better paid than lower white-collar workers, who also received fewer fringe benefits than their counterparts in the West. Rates of social mobility were higher in the USSR, a society that had rapidly transformed itself from agricultural to industrial within two generations. Income differentials were smaller and the most powerful in the Soviet Union were not owners of capital, but members of political bureaucracies. In these important ways the industrial East and West are not directly comparable.

Perhaps one of the main things we can learn from these works is that, once again, the old certainties of the post-war era have become increasingly untenable. In the 1980s, under the twin banners of Reagonomics and Thatcherism (see chapter 8) profound attempts were made in the West to shift society away from bureaucracy, nationalisation, State direction and intervention and the security of the Welfare State and to allow economies to be regulated only by market forces. At the same time, the Soviet bloc has disappeared, East and West Germany have reunited and the Communist Party of the Soviet Union has been dissolved, as the economy stagnated. The New Right claim that the necessity of market forces was the driving force behind developments in the East and the West. Does this, and not technology, truly reveal the real motor of industrial change and advance?

QUESTIONS

1 What is meant by 'technological determinism'?

2 What is convergence theory?

3 Do the events of the 1980s and 1990s suggest that the societies of East and West are converging in their social structures?

Modernisation and underdevelopment

Imperialism and colonialism

As Durkheim and Weber approached their final years, European countries – mainly Britain and France – owned or had control of huge areas of the globe. For a time the British Empire dominated a quarter of the earth's land surface. Britons laid claim to territory in every part of the world. It was, as was proudly claimed at the time, 'the Empire on which the sun never set'. The struggle for imperial control was in the background of both major world wars of this century. The dissolution of both the French and British empires in the period after the end of the Second World War was not achieved without widespread bloodshed. In India the people struggled for independence against the colonial authority, Britain. The final political settlement led to the division of the subcontinent between India and West and East Pakistan. In Algeria there was a bitter independence struggle against the French. Although these empires no longer formally exist (the British Empire is now called the Commonwealth), it has been argued that the racist and colonial attitudes that underlay the empires – that the white man was superior – live on and continue to have damaging effects in the present, in both the North and the South.

It is now the case that almost all parts of former colonial empires are formally politically independent of their imperial masters, although remnants of imperialism continue to live on. Africa, in particular, has seen an enormous wave of newly independent states in the 1960s and 1970s, though few, if any, achieved independence without a struggle by the indigenous population. A complex example of this is Zimbabwe, formerly Rhodesia, where the black population fought a lengthy civil war (costing about 28,000 lives) against the armies of the white settler population, who themselves had rebelled against their British masters in 1965. White Rhodesia finally became black Zimbabwe – at least politically – in 1980. Almost overnight, war leaders who had been branded 'terrorists', were welcomed across the world as international statespeople.

Bretton Woods

As the Second World War came to an end, leaders and key economists of the allied forces (mainly American and British) met in Bretton Woods in the USA and agreed to form two institutions to aid and oversee the recovery of the global economy. These were the International Monetary Fund and the International Bank for Reconstruction and Development (more commonly known as the World Bank), both of which, in the Cold War that immediately followed the end of the Second World War, were to become twin agents in the spread of capitalism throughout the non-communist world.

New explanations of how and why the non-industrial areas of the world would become industrial were also proffered, often explicitly to attract what was becoming known as 'the Third World' (as opposed to the First World in the West and the Second World of the Soviet bloc) to the Western path of development.

Modernisation theory

To explain how change would come about, a new generation of mainly American sociologists returned to the ideas of the founding fathers and sought to apply their ideas to the post-war world. Hence Talcott Parsons (1951) argued that traditional societies become modern by overcoming ascription (see chapters 3 and 4) and becoming achievement-oriented and rational, with jobs allocated and rewarded on the basis of achieved skills and hard work. This notion of achievement-orientation is a central concept to a school of theory that, in the 1950s, became known as 'modernisation theory'. Achievement-orientation is only possible if innovation and entrepreneurship are also possible. More importantly, they must become accepted and rewarded cultural norms.

Rostow's five stages

The best-known modern statement of how traditional societies become modern was expressed by W. W. Rostow (1960). In it, he elaborates on five stages:

1 The traditional society
This is characterised by limited and low productivity, pre-Newtonian science and technology, agriculture, tightly knit kinship systems and 'long-run fatalism': 'the assumption that the range of

possibilities open to one's grandchildren would be just about what it had been for one's grandparents'.

2 The preconditions for take-off

It is realised that not only is economic progress possible but judged to be good, and 'new types of enterprising men come forward' to drag the traditional society out of its historical rut. Slowly, investment, infrastructure and commerce as well as the nation state grow bigger.

3 Take-off

The traditional society is finally broken with and economic growth accelerates rapidly, as new technologies appear in quick succession. Industries make high profits which they immediately reinvest, and the new class of entrepreneurs expands. Agriculture is commercialised.

4 The drive to maturity

This is recognised by steady rates of economic growth, and technological change as the norm with a workforce moving from heavy industry and mineral extraction to more skilled areas of manufacture such as engineering. 'This is the stage in which an economy demonstrates that it has the technological and entrepreneurial skills to produce not everything, but anything that it chooses to produce.'

5 The age of high mass-consumption

Industry turns from making capital goods (things for making other things) to consumer goods (things for final use). People become producers and consumers, with a growing amount of disposable income. Everyone wants, and expects, one day, to have, a house, central heating, a fridge, a full chest-freezer, a microwave, satellite TV, a compact disc-player – whatever consumer goods are available.

Alongside Parsons (see chapter 13) and Rostow, writers such as Eisenstadt (1966), McClelland (1961), Lerner (1964), Hagen (1962) and Lewis (1954) – though with different emphases – provided the core of modernisation theory.

Criticisms of modernisation theory

A number of increasingly trenchant criticisms have been made of these writers' ideas. The traditional–modern dichotomy, it has been objected, is too vague. As with Durkheim, little is said about why societies modernise. Some societies, such as Saudi Arabia, have modernised without abandoning much of their traditional culture. Ascription is still an important factor in Japanese society, one of the world's most modernised in Rostovian terms, and the existence of meritocratic, achievement-based societies is still far from proven in the most industrial societies (see chapters 3 and 5). Kinship systems do not necessarily weaken with industrial advance, if indeed they were ever so extended (see chapter 4) in pre-industrial societies, and it has been argued that these family and kinship ties do not necessarily hold back development within peasant cultures.

Yet the most important omission from modernisation theory is an understanding that the traditional societies in question do not start from scratch but have undergone decades and often centuries of domination by other countries whose only interest in those countries was often to extract as much wealth from them as possible. This criticism is enlarged upon and developed in what is effectively the opposite of modernisation theory: dependency theory.

QUESTIONS

1 How does Talcott Parsons suggest traditional societies become modern societies?

2 What are Rostow's stages of economic growth?

3 What are the major criticisms of these analyses?

Dependency theory

The development of underdevelopment

Not only does dependency theory draw attention to the experiences of many Third World countries of colonisation and rule by foreign powers, but it argues – starting with Kwame Nkrumah, former President of Ghana (1965) – that although former colonies may have achieved a semblance of political independence, they remained (and could not fail to remain) economically dependent on the advanced capitalist countries, and increasingly on multinational companies.

Frank

At the same time in South America (a region formally free of Spanish and Portuguese colonialism for over a century), the evidence seemed to be growing that exposure to advanced capitalism did not aid development but the very opposite: it caused underdevelopment. Working within a broadly Marxist tradition, writers such as Frank (1967) argued vehemently that the effect of imperialism was to distort the economies of Latin America, which had become geared to the export of raw materials. Many of these economies were dependent on only one agricultural product: they were monocultures. The imperial powers had also encouraged the formation of a 'comprador' bourgeoisie whose ownership of the means of production was only at the behest of foreign buyers at what he calls 'the metropolitan centre' so these countries will never be able to develop economically. They will get poorer, not richer, the last link in an international chain of dependency. The only real choice for the people of these countries is to break with imperialism through socialist revolution.

Wallerstein's world systems theory

As statistical evidence piled up to support Frank's claim, so too did the number of writers broadly subscribing to the idea of dependency, not only in Latin America but other areas of the world too, for example Africa, analysed by Rodney (1972). The belief that doing business with the West harmed, not helped, economic development, was present in the revolutionary and anti-imperialist movements in China (1949), Cuba (1959), throughout the war in Vietnam in the 1960s, Chile (1970–73), Nicaragua and Grenada (1979). A more recent and all-embracing example of dependency theory is Immanuel Wallerstein's world system theory. This has similarities with Frank. Wallerstein's 'core and periphery' can be compared with Frank's 'metropolis and satellite', although he argues that parts of the world system are capitalist even where they are fuelled by slave and not waged labour (the hallmark of capitalism for orthodox Marxists). In fact, he sees these as essential to the operation of the world system in the same way as some feminists see unwaged domestic labour as essential to capitalism. In Wallerstein's view, the Soviet bloc of countries is not separate from Western capitalism. This bloc represents (or rather represented) a different form of capitalism, not socialism.

Criticisms of dependency theory

As with modernisation theory, there are a number of important criticisms of dependency theory. The idea of dependency is too vague – many countries and economic systems are dependent on others without becoming less developed, as with Canada's dependence on the USA, or the USA's dependence on Middle Eastern oil (though in this case, it has been argued that the USA will go to war to maintain this supply, as in the case of the Second Gulf War of 1991). Secondly, dependence is difficult to measure. If it means that a net surplus of invested finance is extracted then it may be termed exploitation, but it does not account for the infrastructure – roads, railways, telephone and sewage systems for example – that may be laid down and left in the process. Thirdly, there is increasing evidence to suggest that 'homegrown' or indigenous development is emerging in some Third World countries. These are now termed the newly industrialising countries (NICs) and include Brazil, Mexico, Argentina, India, Iran, Israel, South Africa, South Korea and Taiwan. Frank (1981) terms these 'intermediate semi-peripheral and sub-imperialist economies' indicating that he sees them as being intermediate between the rich metropolitan centres and the poor peripheral areas.

Newly industrialising countries

It is the status of these NICs that has led to an enormous debate, especially within the neo-Marxist school. One of the most important challenges to Frank and the dependency school is to be found in Warren (1980). At its broadest, Warren's argument is that the dependency school misinterprets both Marxism and Leninism, specifically on the subject of historical materialism. For Marx, capitalism is a transitional stage between feudalism and socialism. The role of the bourgeoisie is to develop the forces of production to their limits within capitalism, when the industrial working class takes over the means of production in a socialist revolution. This stage cannot be bypassed (though Marx does make unhelpful references to 'the Asiatic mode of production'), and in any case, is already happening. Against 'the underdevelopment fiction' which 'maintains that the peoples of the Third World have been getting steadily worse off ever since the industrial revolution in the West', Warren argues that 'the period since the Second World War has seen titanic strides forward in the establishment, consolidation and growth of capitalism in the Third World, with corresponding advances in material welfare and the expansion of productive forces'. Moreover, it is un-Marxist to see this period in any other way – no one has ever claimed that capitalist development was either uniform or without fundamental problems of dislocation and distribution.

Warren While not arguing specifically against Warren, Frank nevertheless maintains that, in none of the economies of the NICs 'is there any prospect that the masses of the population will in the foreseeable future share the benefits of … growth … to any substantial extent. On the contrary, in several of these countries the relative and absolute population that is excluded from any benefits of economic growth is rising as increasing numbers of people are either super-exploited or bypassed by the productive process.'

The debate does not end there. John Taylor (1979), for example, argues against Warren's view of indigenous capitalist development in the Third World by pointing out that much of their industrialisation is based on import-substitution of consumer goods – making things yourself that would previously have been imported – though they still import the machinery (capital goods) that makes the consumer goods. Third World development is still hugely dependent on multi-national companies, which themselves increasingly do not produce finished goods in any one country, but produce component parts all over the world. For example, the printed circuit board may be made in the Philippines, capacitors in Taiwan, casing in Germany and the final assembly of the computers may happen in Wales. Can it be argued that this development is genuinely indigenous?

QUESTIONS

1 What does dependency theory owe to Marxism?

2 What is Warren's criticism of dependency theory?

3 What is meant by indigenous development?

Alternative development strategies

So far we have looked at the concept of industrial development uncritically. Modernisation and dependency theories do not necessarily ask whether industrialisation is desirable or not; they debate whether and when it will happen or, indeed, if it has already begun in the Third World. Outside of this debate, a third area of discussion and analysis extends around the question of whether industrialisation is either desirable or inevitable. Grouped together, these are known as alternative development strategies.

Since the earliest days of the Industrial Revolution, the desirability of the changes wrought by industrialisation has been continuously questioned, and a number of alternatives have been tried. An early example is the British socialist Robert Owen in the early nineteenth century and his vision of a 'co-operative commonwealth' of industrial villages, first attempted in New Lanark, Scotland. Similar philosophies and movements spread across Europe and are generically known as 'populism'.

Ujaamaa

They have been a force too in the pre-industrial countries of the Third World. Following the 1967 Arusha Declaration post-independence Tanzania, in East Africa, geared its socio-economic policies to a self-reliant rural development in which all the trappings of large-scale industry, including a wealthy and exploitive capitalist class, were actively prohibited from emerging. This policy of 'rural socialism' is known in Tanzania as '*ujaamaa*'. There are networks of villages where land is largely communally worked and owned. The shortcomings of this programme, such as lack of infrastructure, tools and machinery, and local rather than State-led initiatives and knowledge have been highlighted by, among others, Gavin Kitching (1982). These criticisms would be rejected by the former President of Tanzania, Julius Nyerere, as too narrow. For him, 'Development brings freedom, provided it is development of the people. But people cannot be developed; they can only develop themselves. For while it is possible for an outsider to build a person's house, an outsider cannot give the person pride and the self-confidence in themselves as human beings. Those things people have to create in themselves by their own actions.

They develop themselves by what they do; they develop themselves by making their own decisions, by increasing their own knowledge and ability and by their own full participation – as equals – in the life of the community they live in' (Nyerere, 1973).

The distinct path taken by President Julius Nyerere's Tanzania differs in an important respect from the roughly comparable case of China. There, following the revolution of 1949, the Communist Party has used the State more decisively to develop an agricultural society backed by a strong industrial sector, without heading exclusively for full-scale industrial advance at the expense of the peasantry and the agricultural sector. In the 1990s, however, they are now widely assumed to be attempting to develop a capitalist economy – led by the Party – as quickly as possible.

The Green movement

A further objection to industrial development in the Third World points, not so much at the hardships and rigours of development, but at the problem of resources. Ecologists point out that industrial development in the Third World demands resources of energy and raw materials that simply are not there and would increase the problem of global pollution. For ecologists, unrestrained and unplanned industrial development means unrestrained and unplanned pollution of air, sea and earth. Western development, up to now, has been based on an environmental exploitation which cannot be sustained.

Small is beautiful

One arm of the anti-industrial school of thought proposes that technological development is possible without the creation of the large-scale industrial sites characteristic of industrial development. What is needed is 'appropriate' or intermediate technology, serving the local demands of the community, where reliance on materials outside the locality is reduced to a minimum. In everything, the guiding principle, as expressed by Schumacher (1973), is 'small is beautiful', particularly in Third World technology where cheap and labour-intensive strategies are advocated.

Alternative development strategies generally advocate small-scale, locally based low-tech lifestyles, attempting to avoid the potential horrors of industrialisation and argue that this is the most appropriate path for poor societies to take. When advocated by theorists from advanced industrial societies, where a high standard of living is taken for granted, it is difficult for Third World governments to see anti-industrial strategies and appropriate technology programmes as anything other than ways of keeping the Third World backward and poor, a permanent jumble-sale economy without growth and development. Why should they be prevented from industrialising because the West has polluted the world? This is a problem for the West, not the developing nations. The way out of poverty and backwardness, Kitching argues, against the alternative strategies, is industrialisation and economic growth.

QUESTIONS

1 **Why would a less developed country want industrialisation?**

2 **What are the arguments against industrialisation?**

3 **What does Schumacher mean by small is beautiful?**

Aid and development

By about 1960, when the Bretton Woods institutions – the IMF and the World Bank – had largely completed their initial task of rebuilding the economies of Europe, initiated by the 1947 Marshall Plan, they turned their attention more fully to the rest of the world. Their task, as they saw it, was to aid the development of the rapidly decolonising Third World to achieve what had now been identified by W. W. Rostow as the 'take-off' point for industrialisation. In order to achieve this, a number of institutions were created, for example the International Development Association of the World Bank, giving cheaper loans on preferential terms to the poorest of what were becoming termed 'Third World' or 'less-developed countries'.

Forms of aid This was undertaken in a number of ways, involving direct foreign investment, loans from private banks, developmental assistance from First and Second to Third World governments, or voluntary aid such as Oxfam or Bob Geldof's Band Aid. Governmental aid can take a number of forms: it can come from one or more countries to another (bilateral and multilateral aid); it can be in the form of a grant or a loan; aid can be given with or without the expectation or requirement that the receiving country uses the money to buy goods from the donor country ('tied' aid) or to finance particular programmes and projects only.

The very word aid carries with it the notion of doing good, as expressed by the report of the 1969 Pearson Commission of the World Bank on the value of aid. Since then, however, this accepted wisdom has been fundamentally challenged on all sides.

In the early 1970s the conditions of trade and commerce which had developed after the Second World War deteriorated. The decision of the US government, under President Nixon in 1971, to end the free convertability of dollars into gold, followed by the quadrupling of the price of crude oil by the oil producing and exporting countries

(OPEC) in 1973–4 fundamentally changed the world economic climate. The most important consequence for the financial world was that, with Western banks now awash with the surplus capital invested by the richer OPEC countries (petrodollars), large-scale and widespread loans were made by Western banks to Third World countries. But in order to reduce domestic inflation, the same banks found themselves having to increase interest rates, which in turn meant Third World borrowers had to pay back more – hence 'when the West sneezes, the Third World catches pneumonia'.

The debt crisis

The consequent attempts, particularly by the IMF, to reschedule debt repayments from the borrowers had led to increasingly austere conditions in Third World countries, and the phenomenon of 'IMF riots' by the poor against price rises. Soon, the world realised it had a debt crisis of enormous proportions on its hands.

There are a number of ways of seeing this relationship between the North and South (as the 1980 Brandt Report, a United Nations commission headed by the former German Chancellor, Willy Brandt, describes it). The first is that it is in the mutual interests of both the North and the South to overcome the debt crisis, if only because a debt-free South will be able to buy goods from and regenerate the economies of the North.

The second view of the relationship between North and South asks the question: Is this interest really mutual? This view owes much to the dependency school of thinking, and comes mainly from two writers: Teresa Hayter and Cheryl Payer. The titles of Hayter's books leave little doubt about her view of aid: *Aid as Imperialism* (1971), *The Creation of World Poverty* (1981), and, with Catherine Watson, *Aid: Rhetoric and Reality* (1985). Similar conclusions can be drawn about Cheryl Payer's views: *The Debt Trap* (1974) and *The World Bank: A Critical Analysis* (1982).

Aid as a political weapon

These works point to the twin Bretton Woods institutions of the IMF and the World Bank as creators, not of development, but of dependency and poverty. For these writers, aid is a political weapon, targeted on and used to control strategically important economies. The aid goes, not to those who need it most – the poor – but to the already wealthy, who then become indebted to the agencies of the First World. Anti-inflationary packages lead to reduced government spending, devalued local currencies, more foreign investment and a failure to break from the need to export traditional primary products. 'Much of this aid,' Watson and Hayter argue, 'fails to alleviate poverty even in the immediate context in which it is provided; and its overall purpose is the preservation of a system which damages the interests of the poor in the Third World. To the extent that it is effective in this underlying purpose, aid from the major Western powers therefore probably does more harm than good to the mass of the population of the Third World.'

The view from the New Right

The third view, most closely associated with the New Right (see chapter 8), comes from writers such as Peter Bauer (1976 and 1981) and Deepak Lal (1983). This is a similar argument to that concerning the Welfare State in advanced countries – people can only help themselves, and attempts to help are often misguided. The West should not offer preferential treatment to people who should be pulling themselves up by their own bootstraps (assuming, of course, that they have any boots!). Aid is not necessary for industrialisation. The West did without it, as have the East Asian 'Gang of Four' – South Korea, Taiwan, Hong Kong and Singapore – and so must the Third World. What is necessary is a change in values towards entrepreneurship and achievement-orientation. Aid only aids torpor and sloth, as well as being a highly inefficient use of capital. Moreover, the existence of aid only confirms the status of a country as being part of the Third World. As Bauer (1981) puts it: 'The Third World is the creation of foreign aid: without foreign aid there is no Third World.' Only unfettered free markets produce economic growth and development.

Philosophies of aid

Within the aid world itself there are massive differences of philosophy and opinion on how to assist or work with any large group of people struggling to leave desperate poverty behind. Most of these differences arise from the organisation's view of modernisation and dependency. But in the translation from theory to practice the roots have become obscured. World Bank projects for example are generally based on the premise that a massive injection of capital and/or technology will raise people's productivity and thus automatically their standard of living (although it is gradually being accepted that neither of the two assumptions holds true). Such projects are mostly designed without any reference to the population's wants and needs. Consequently the vast majority are failures and the Third World is littered with their debris, ranging from tractors to entire fish-canning factories which were set up without considering the access to markets.

Non-governmental organisations such as OXFAM and Christian Aid tend to be more prudent about the kind of projects which they recommend or support and more concerned that the population is involved in planning and implementation. They also recognise that some, at least, of the problems stem from international economic and political structures and focus some of their resources on education about development and campaigning work in this country.

Freire

A small but increasing number of aid projects are based on a philosophy which developed from the work of Paulo Freire (1972 and 1976). He states categorically that any help which is founded on assumptions of superiority and inferiority is both wrong and bound to fail. All that a 'change agent' – an external facilitator or catalyst – can do is encourage people to analyse their problems and come up with their own solutions. Freire himself found that appropriately designed literacy programmes were an extraordinarily effective tool for such 'conscientisation'. The translation of such theory into practice ranges from encouraging political activism (so Freire himself had to leave two right-wing countries – Brazil and then Chile), to encouraging communities to participate in planning their own projects, to simply ensuring that the community understands enough about a project to provide a labour input willingly.

The whole issue of participation absorbs large amount of energy. As more and more projects fail to demonstrate their total sustainability once their initiators have left, even massive bureaucracies like the UN or World Bank are being forced to re-examine their whole structure and ethos. There is increasing recognition of the value of 'local knowledge' – technical knowledge is occasionally no longer seen as the exclusive possession of the Western world. 'Participation' and 'empowerment' have thus come to replace 'efficiency' and 'progress' as the buzzwords of the 1980s and 1990s.

The issue of participation became particularly acute where women were concerned. Most aid projects had no understanding of the position of local women and very often caused it to deteriorate, while at the same time foundering themselves because the women were not involved.

Criticisms of New Right theories

Against Bauer, and New Right thinking, it can be argued that it is not only free-market economies that have developed industrially. The Soviet Union, Japan, Singapore, Taiwan and South Korea were State-led in their development, though the outcomes were very different. Secondly, it has been argued that the West did the initial development through its exploitation of its colonies, for example through the slave trade, though this is dismissed by Bauer as a 'windfall', compared to the opportunities available to the Third World for technological and capital investment from the First World. Thirdly, there is an ideological problem with the use of the word 'free' as in free market to denote the 'free world' of the Cold War age. Many of the NICs were anything but free societies. Chile in the 1970s and 1980s had a free market economy but the government was authoritarian to the point of using terrorism against its own citizens when they resisted the regime.

Most criticisms of aid programmes, then, have their ideological roots in either modernisation or dependency theory. For the New Right, entrepreneurs in the Third World will lift their countries out of their pre-industrial condition. Aid will only distort the necessary free-market conditions. The radical critics of the IMF and World Bank, however, see these institutions not as interveners in a natural process or doers of good but as key agents of First World imperialism, contributing to the continued dependence of the Third World on their imperialist masters.

QUESTIONS

1 **Is aid good or bad for industrial development?**

2 **Do Left and Right agree on aid? How similar are their arguments?**

3 **Why have some attempts to aid less developed countries failed?**

4 **How do the attentions of rich countries affect the development of poor ones?**

5 **How have the policies of the IMF and the World Bank been criticised?**

6 **How has aid been criticised by the New Right?**

Development sociology in the 1990s

The main theories of development and underdevelopment were conceived in an atmosphere of optimism and belief in progress and advance in the three decades following the Second World War. There were two strong possibilities: 'traditional' societies would either modernise and emulate the path of development taken by Western countries, or they would see the West as degenerate and parasitic which would lead to them breaking their links and finding their own course of development, broadly influenced by the example set by the Soviet Union.

As the century draws to a close, many writers have begun to argue that fundamental changes have taken place in the way the world is structured both politically and economically that render both models of modernisation and dependency effectively redundant. These developments have important implications not only for the sociology of development but for sociology as a whole.

A changing world The world political map has changed fundamentally with the collapse of the Soviet bloc and the rapid move from central planning to a free market economy. Not only has an alternative model of development disappeared but with it a belief in economic planning. Only a handful of countries, such as China, Cuba and North Korea, are even nominally communist (although China's current economic growth is part of a pattern of State-led capitalist development in Asia). At the same time, with the Cold War apparently at an end, it means very little to describe the world as divided into First, Second and Third Worlds when the world is becoming increasingly linked, economically, politically and culturally. As private companies become larger and larger, the nation State is no longer the main focus of international analysis.

Changing theory

At a theoretical level, belief in grand-scale, all-embracing theories that seek to explain long-term historical trends and changes – described by post-modernists as 'metanarratives', such as functionalism or Marxism (see chapter 16) – have themselves come to be regarded with increasing suspicion, as has the belief in the possibility of the spread of enlightenment and rationalism, when evidence to the contrary abounds.

Similarly, the assumption that a complex and diverse world, whose population has different cultures, histories and identities, can be adequately comprehended by grandiose theories such as modernisation and dependency theory has been profoundly questioned. This assumption has been seen as ethnocentric (based only on the values of your own culture), élitist and simplistic: the view of white intellectuals in the West. As Edwards (1989) argues, existing development theory has very little relevance for those engaged in field work.

At the same time, the situation for what can be described as less developed countries, the South, or even the Third World remains pressing (*see Figure 12.1*). The 1991 Human Development Report of the United Nations Development Programme reported that in this part of the world:

- 180 million children suffer chronic and severe malnutrition;
- 1.5 billion people lack basic health care or safe water;
- over 2 million people are without safe sanitation;
- 1 billion adults are illiterate and 300 million do not attend school;
- more than 1 billion people live below the United Nations' poverty line;
- income per head declined in the 1980s in Latin America and sub-Saharan Africa;
- one urban dweller in five lives in that nation's largest city.

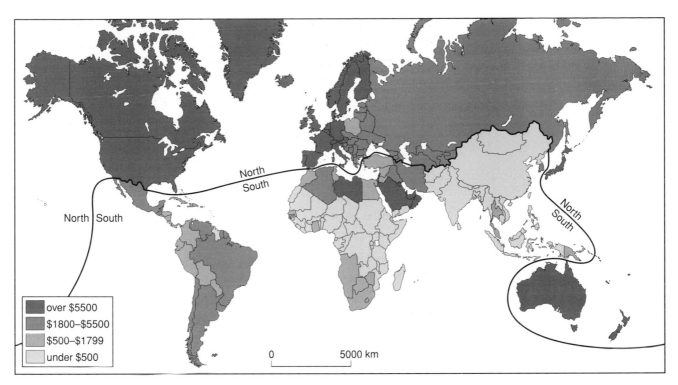

Figure 12.1 North and South (GNP per capita, 1990)

Various ways out of this impasse have been put forward. Most people agree that existing development sociology has to change by incorporating and placing greater emphasis on new areas of enquiry, and restoring the place of others, such as social anthropology, comparative historical sociology in the tradition of the founding fathers, and even geography. It is also strongly argued that sociologists and others need to reconceptualise their view of the world as being globally linked and that this fact needs to be the starting point of any analysis.

Transnational corporations

The basic assumption of theorists looking at the world as a global or world system is that there is now a single dominant economic system in the world whose principal actors are no longer interested in or need to serve national interests. These are huge capitalist organisations operating transnationally, seeing the world as without borders, manufacturing and selling products that have become household names across the world. The largest transnational corporations (TNCs) like Ford, Shell and Pepsico each have annual sales way in excess of the gross national product of most less developed countries. In the 1992–3 financial year, the American investment bank Goldman Sachs made a pre-tax profit of 2.6 billion dollars mainly shared between the firm's 'general partners'. In 1991, Tanzania, with a population of 25 million people, had a gross domestic product of 2.2 billion dollars (or less than $100 per person).

Although Immanuel Wallerstein's world systems theory, outlined above (p. 345), argues that there is an international division of labour between core, semi-peripheral and peripheral countries, and describes a world economy, he has been criticised for his continued emphasis on countries rather than TNCs as the key actors on the world stage, and for the overriding importance he gives to economic factors in determining political and cultural affairs.

Globalisation

More recently, Sklair (1991) advocated a theory of globalisation based on the view that the owners and managers of TNCs now constitute a transnational capitalist class (TCC) (which includes State bureaucrats and pro-capitalist politicians) engaged in 'transnational practices', by which he means global political, economic and cultural–ideological activities.

Crucial to the development of these TNCs is the emergence of a global culture, promoted throughout the world by transnational media organisations, using satellite technology, spreading the culture–ideology of consumerism across the globe. In the march of global capitalist advance, all aspects of local culture are either subsumed, marginalised or destroyed: 'TNC's, transnational capitalist classes and the culture–ideology of consumerism operate systematically to transform the world in terms of the global capitalist project.'

As Sklair freely admits, there are many problems standing in the way of global theorising, which is still at an embryonic stage. These include political and economic blocs such as the EU and the North American Free Trade Area, the rise of Islamic fundamentalism throughout the Islamic world (as well as other religious fundamentalism), and the fragmentation of Eastern Europe and the former Yugoslavia into resurgently nationalistic states. Yet it still remains the case that transnational corporations are superseding national and international organisations in importance, and development theory has to take this fully into account.

QUESTIONS

1 **How useful are the concepts of modernisation and dependency in understanding the world today?**

2 **What is meant by the term 'globalisation'? What evidence is there that it is occurring?**

3 **How useful is the term 'Third World' in the 1990s? What alternative term might you use?**

FURTHER READING

D. Banerjee (ed.), *Marxian Theory and the Third World*, Sage, 1985

T. Barnett, *Sociology and Development*, Routledge, 1991

J. Ferrante, *Sociology, A Global Perspective*, Wadsworth, 1992

T. Hayter and C. Watson, *Aid: Rhetoric and Reality*, Pluto Press, 1985

J. Momsen, *Women and Development in the Third World*, Routledge, 1992

W.W. Rostow, *The Stages of Economic Growth*, Cambridge University Press, 1960

L. Sklair, *Sociology of the Global System*, Prentice-Hall, 1995

M. Waters, *Globalisation*, Routledge, 1995

A. Webster, *Introduction to the Sociology of Development*, Macmillan, 1990

13 Community and locality

INTRODUCTION

The chapter introduces the topic through the work of Ferdinand Tönnies and Georg Simmel. There then follows a discussion of the problems of defining the term community. The next section examines the terms rural, urban and suburban, looking at the work of the Chicago School, Pahl, Gans and Bennett Berger. The chapter continues with a discussion of the sociology of the city, concentrating on the Marxist perspective of Castells. Following this section you will examine the notion of the inner city and the 'zone of transition' alongside the theory of housing classes. The chapter closes by taking a look at sociological explanations for riots in the inner cities and the movement of the middle classes from cities into rural areas.

The community: the history of an idea

Marx, Durkheim and Weber are considered to be the most important social theorists and their ideas continue to be discussed and analysed. Other writers, for example Comte and Spencer, have subsequently fallen out of fashion. One of the thinkers whose ideas gained currency for a considerable period is Ferdinand Tönnies (1855–1936) who developed some key concepts in sociology which continue to be used.

Tönnies and *Gemeinschaft* Tönnies (1887) wanted to understand the forces at work behind the growth of industrial societies. Where Marx saw class struggle, Durkheim the division of labour and Weber the Protestant ethic and rationality, Tönnies encapsulated his view of industrial change in two ideal types: *Gemeinschaft* and *Gesellschaft*. As with many words translated from other languages (particularly German sociological ones) the precise meaning he gives to these terms is difficult to capture in English. *Gemeinschaft* is most frequently translated as 'community' and is contrasted with *Gesellschaft*, which is translated as 'association' or 'society'. Tönnies' concept of community is a romantic

Ferdinand Tönnies (1855–1936)
German sociologist who coined the terms Gemeinschaft *(community) and* Gesellschaft *(association). These concepts were used by Tönnies in his explanation of the transition from feudalism to capitalism and are used in similar ways to the functionalist particularistic and universalistic values.*

concept, embracing the idea of a homogeneous group of people, who are united organically by ties of kinship, and have shared norms and values, which are usually of a religious nature. The kind of community or *Gemeinschaft* he had in mind was similar to that of the traditional, pre-industrial community, where everyone knew, and was possibly related to, everyone else and nothing much changed – there was little social and geographical mobility and status was ascribed (see chapter 3). The family and the church ensured that a moral consensus was maintained.

Gesellschaft

The opposite of *Gemeinschaft* is *Gesellschaft*: association or society. By this he means societies where face-to-face relations have become impersonal, superficial and short-lived. Everything is large scale, and the main tie between people is not sentimental but contractual. Ideas of kinship, friendship and neighbourhood have broken down.

Underlying these two concepts are philosophical assumptions about human nature. *Gemeinschaft* and *Gesellschaft* express the concepts of natural and rational will, where the former concerns instinctual needs, habits and inclinations and the latter describes an artificial form of behaviour, where rationality is cold, calculating and unnatural. These two concepts, which are also identifiable in Weber's writings, are clearly heavily value-laden, favouring community over association or society. These terms, as Tönnies intended, have most frequently been used to describe the difference between pre-industrial and industrial societies, although they have also been used to describe the difference between urban and rural societies.

Simmel and the Formal School

Georg Simmel (1858–1918) was also a contemporary of Durkheim, Tönnies and Weber with whom he founded the German Sociological Society in 1910. His own theories mark the beginning of the 'Formal School' (largely associated with Simmel himself), and he was influential in the thinking of the Americans Talcott Parsons and Robert Merton. He himself developed Tönnies' ideas in an essay in which he argued that cities required inhabitants with a certain type of personality if they were to survive its demands (Simmel, 1903). They must be cold, calculating and self-interested. In the pace of city life there is no time to see others in any way except as objects. This new way of life can be a liberation for some after the closed and suffocating ways of small-town life, allowing creativity, but at the same time the city may leave others who cannot survive as down and out, homeless or suicidal.

Georg Simmel (1858–1918)
German sociologist who is a principal figure in the development of 'formal' sociology. He believes that society is neither organism or real totality, but is the product of the sum total of interactions between the members who make up its constituent parts.

Weber: The City

It was largely Simmel's ideas that Max Weber was building on when he wrote *The City* (published posthumously, 1958). He acknowledged Simmel's argument that the city broke down personal relationships, but tried to broaden this view, incorporating it as a subpart of his own theory, examining social actions, social relations, social institutions and the concept of 'the urban community'. Social institutions encapsulate the sum total of social relations, which in turn encapsulate the sum total of social actions, the ultimate units of analysis for the sociologist.

The urban community itself was a trading and commercial entity which at its most full blown has traditionally been composed of a fortification, a market, a court of its own and an at least partially autonomous legal system and therefore 'an administration by authorities in the election of whom the citizens participated'. What Weber is really seeking to understand is how and why cities have arisen throughout history.

The writings of Tönnies, Simmel and Weber form the modern foundations for twentieth-century investigations into the effects of the community on rural, urban and suburban ways of life.

Pattern variables   Tönnies' use of two contrasting concepts in order to understand social life is a familiar feature of sociological theory. Marx contrasts capital and labour, Weber traditional and rational-legal authority. Other contrasting concepts, identified by Nisbet (1966), are status and class, the sacred and the secular, alienation and progress, and tradition and modernism. The *Gemeinschaft–Gesellschaft* division is also discernible in Talcott Parsons' conception of the pattern variables underlying social action. These are:

- Affectivity versus affective neutrality (immediate contrasted with deferred gratification)
- Universalism versus particularism (norms and values held widely in society contrasted with norms and values of a particular group such as the family)
- Quality versus performance or ascription versus achievement (people are seen by others according to who someone is or by contrast they are seen according to what they have achieved)
- Diffuseness versus specificity (broad-based contrasted with narrow social relationships; the former concern many aspects of social exchange whereas the latter concern few aspects of social exchange).

The first set of variables describe community, whereas the second set describe society. Parsons' (1959c) own specific definition of community is 'that aspect of the structure of social systems which is referable to the territorial location of persons (i.e. human individuals as organisms) and their activities ... When I say "referable to" I do not mean determined exclusively or predominantly by, but rather observable and analysable with reference to location as a focus of attention (and of course a partial determinant) ...The population ... is just as much a focus of the Study of Community as is the territorial location.'

Problems of definition

One of the problems that has beleaguered the sociology of community is the lack of an agreed definition of what the term means. The depth of this problem was highlighted by Hillery (1955) who identified no less than 94 definitions, although he was able to condense these down into 16 broad headings, which can then be sub-grouped into three components: area, common ties and social interaction. Ultimately, all that can be reliably said according to Hillery is that 'all of the definitions deal with people. Beyond this common basis, there is no agreement.'

This definitional problem had been unresolved when Newby (1979) asserted that, for the analysis of English villages, 'The word ... is so value-loaded that no judgement on whether contemporary trends in rural society have or have not brought about a "loss of community" ... is realistically possible.' The community is simply what community studies analyse.

More recently attempts have been made to revive the concept of community, focusing on the idea of a community as a locality and a symbolic boundary. These have emerged partly out of dissatisfaction with the use of concepts such as class in the context of the decline of the nation-state, and the impact of global factors, where class may be experienced differently from one place to the next. Thus, the concept of class is not uniform but can be applied differently according to how densely populated an area is by working-class people, or whether workers are employed in public- or private-sector industries in locally or multinationally owned companies. Belonging to a class is interpreted differently in different situations. This may lead to differing perceptions of class for each group and the emergence, for example, of 'neighbourhood effects' in voting behaviour (see also chapter 8). Gender and ethnic dimensions further complicate this picture and are also evident in local political activity.

Locality and locales

In rejecting the term 'community' because of its over-emphasis on insularity, continuity and stability, Philip Cooke (1989) argues that the term 'locality' better expresses the rights of citizens in the area where they work, consume and live. A locality is 'the base for a large measure of individual and social mobilisation to activate, extend or defend rights, not simply in the political sphere but more generally in the areas of cultural, economic and social life'. This definition overcomes the vagueness of Giddens' (1984) definition of 'locales' – 'a room in a house, a street corner, the shop-floor of a factory, towns and cities, the territorially demarcated areas occupied by nation-states'. This, for Cooke, is merely a synonym for space.

Cohen (1985) has attempted to define the community as a 'symbolic boundary'. This recognises that the word community is widely used by many people, but – contrary to functionalist assumptions – they have different interests and the term is rarely used to mean the same thing. Appeals are made, however, to the symbolic importance of defending the interests of that community, whether it is a mining area, a middle-class district or a nation.

QUESTIONS

1 How does *Gemeinschaft* differ from *Gesellschaft?*

2 How do Tönnies, Simmel and Weber differ in their views of urban life?

3 Why is 'the community' so difficult to define?

4 What do television soap operas depict – *Gemeinschaft* or *Gesellschaft?*

Rural, urban and suburban

'Folk Society'

As with many other aspects of sociology, the European ideas of Tönnies and Simmel were developed most extensively in America, where repeated attempts were made to investigate the importance of where people lived in determining their social attitudes and behaviour. One example is Robert Redfield's 'Folk Society' (1947). Building on his earlier study of the rural areas of the Yucatán peninsula in Mexico (1941), he characterised 'folk' or rural society as lying at one end of a rural–urban continuum. Rural society is, he says, 'small, isolated, non-literate and homogeneous, with a strong sense of group solidarity. The ways of living are conventionalised into the coherent system we call "a culture". Behaviour is traditional, spontaneous, uncritical and personal: there is no legislation or habit of experiment and reflection for intellectual ends. Kinship, its relations and institutions, are the type categories of experience and the familial group is the unit of action. The sacred prevails over the secular; the economy is one of status rather than the market.'

'Urbanism as a way of life'

The other end of the continuum has been most famously described by the Chicago School's Louis Wirth (1938). He believes three features of urban life are particularly important: size, density and the heterogeneity of the population. These factors mean that urban and rural dwellers live qualitatively different lives. Size causes people to be continuously on the move in their daily lives, with work demands meaning that they never stay long enough in one place to establish anything other than impersonal relationships. A high level of density makes people irritable and increases tension between them, and heterogeneity expresses the fact that many social groups, with a great number of cultural backgrounds and histories, sit uneasily side by side. The result is a way of life in which urbanites lose the intensity of primary relationships, experience weaker social controls, and treat other people as simply means to ends. The rural–urban divide is clear: 'the city and the country may be regarded as two poles in reference to which one or other of human settlements tend to arrange themselves'. It also follows that suburban areas, when developed, should also exhibit distinctive characteristics beyond the urban end of the continuum.

Criticisms   Having asserted the existence of distinct rural and urban ways of life, the ideas of writers such as Redfield and Wirth have been extensively challenged, tested and ultimately found to be unhelpful. When Manuel Avila (1969) visited two of the four Mexican villages studied by Redfield he found not stagnation but an interest in market economics, economic growth and a strong interest in self-improvement. Change is not confined to urban areas, nor are peasants unable to adapt to urban life, as Oscar Lewis (1961) shows (see chapter 9).

Pahl   A major assault on the concept of the rural–urban continuum comes from a number of works by the British sociologist Ray Pahl. Following his own empirical studies of commuter villages in Hertfordshire (1965a), and studies by writers such as Young and Willmott (1957), he squarely addressed the rural–urban continuum concept. He concludes that: 'Any attempt to tie particular patterns of social relationships to specific geographical milieu is a singularly fruitless exercise. Some people are of the city but not in it, whereas others are in the city but not of it; the *Gemeinschaft* exists within the *Gesellschaft* and the *Gesellschaft* within the *Gemeinschaft*' (Pahl, 1968). This last point has strong echoes of Willmott and Young's study of 45 couples in Bethnal Green with 902 relatives living in the borough or the one next to it (see chapter 4). From this they argue that there is 'a strong sense of community; that is, a feeling of solidarity between people who occupy the common territory, which springs from the fact that people and their families have lived there a long time'. This is exactly what writers such as Wirth believed did not exist.

Like Pahl, the American sociologist Howard Gans, examining urban and suburban areas, found little evidence of any necessarily distinct urban lifestyle. Whyte (1956) had already shown that an egalitarian community ethic existed in the suburban area of Park Forest he studied, where the central activity was child-rearing, and the key values were flexibility and the capacity to adjust. Believing that this study (on which Gans had also worked), and others, such as that conducted by Seeley, Sim and Loosely (1963), were contributing to the idea that people changed when they moved into the suburbs, Gans spent several years enlarging on his statement that 'ways of life do not coincide with settlement patterns'. For one suburban study he even bought his own house in Long Island, New York State, to study community life as a participant observer (Gans, 1967).

The *Levittowners* Although he is in no doubt that there is a community in the suburb he studies – 'Levittown' – it is best defined as 'an administrative-political unit plus an aggregate of community-wide associations'. Most Levittowners would be better described as 'sub-locals for they are home-orientated rather than community-orientated'. This leads to his central point that people's lives are principally influenced not by their geographical location but by their social class and their stage in the family life cycle.

What Gans believes Wirth has described, 'and not too accurately', is the way of life in the inner city, or 'zone of transition' as it is sometimes known. This is in any case, Gans says, composed of a number of relatively homogeneous groups: the 'cosmopolites', the unmarried and childless, the 'ethnic villagers', the 'deprived', 'trapped' and downwardly mobile, people whose lives are dominated by the fact of 'residential instability', who, for varying reasons, do not stay in any one place for long. What Wirth does not describe is the outer city and the suburbs.

Although the type of residence changes, moving from the inner to the outer city and the suburbs does not necessarily mean that people's behaviour changes. If suburbs are more homogeneous than inner cities, it is 'as a result of factors having little or nothing to do with the house type, density or location of the area relative to the city limits ... The sociologist cannot, therefore, speak of an urban or suburban way of life' (Gans, 1962).

Although Gans is specifically taking issue with Wirth, he is also taking on those writers who have created what many critics have described as 'the myth of suburbia'. Behind this myth lies a stereotyped view of suburban life, whether in America or the United Kingdom. Synthesising these two traditions, Thorns (1973) identifies five common elements: child-rearing, family-centredness, active social lives, a homogeneous and middle-class population and political conservatism, although it was believed that American suburbs had a higher population turnover than British ones.

Working-class suburbs Bennett Berger (1960) attempted to explode this stereotype because 'one suburb is apt to differ from another not only in the price range of its homes, the income characteristics of its residents, their occupational make-up, and the home-to-work travelling patterns of its breadwinners, but also in its educational levels, the character of the region, the size of the suburb, the socio-geographical origin of its residents, and countless more indices'. The main reason for the existence of the myth and the stereotype is that the focus of research on suburbs has been limited to middle-class ones. In his own study of Militipas, he set out to show how suburbs could be working class, middle class, or both, and it is these class characters which are their dominant feature and the key variable.

QUESTIONS

1 What is the importance of 'size, density and heterogeneity' to Wirth's understanding of urbanism?

2 How important is place or location in determining forms of human behaviour?

3 Is a 'working-class suburb' a contradiction in terms?

4 What is suburbia?

5 What criticisms of the rural–urban dichotomy can be made?

The city

Castells By the mid 1970s, the sociology of community – and urban sociology in particular – seemed to have lost direction. A series of books and articles by the Spanish Marxist Manuel Castells attempted, and almost succeeded, in throwing away the map altogether.

In his main text Castells (1977) argued that there was no good reason for studying urban areas as distinct and separate entities. People lived similar or different lifestyles regardless of whether they lived in urban or rural areas. Urbanism does not produce distinct forms of behaviour. What matters is the structure of the society producing the forces acting on urban areas. Urbanisation does not have a logic of its own, but is merely an expression of the level of capitalist development. Riots, slum housing, traffic congestion and other features of urban life are the consequences of private ownership of the means of production and the accumulation of capital by the few. It is not cities which should be studied, but capitalism.

Collective consumption Cities do matter, but they have to be viewed in the right perspective. For Castells, they are 'spatial units of collective consumption': simply places where the mass of people are housed, schooled, kept healthy and moved to and from the workplace in a way that places a minimum cost on the owners of capital and allows them to transfer the costs of producing and reproducing the labour force to the 'relatively autonomous' State (see chapter 8). The city, run by the State, is the cheapest way of servicing labour for the demands of capital. That is why cities exist.

It will not always stay this way, however. The massive costs to the State of running urban facilities such as transport systems, schools and hospitals will eventually lead to cutbacks in spending, and the consequent radicalisation of city dwellers as collective consumers. New broad-based 'urban social movements' will be thrown together and these will engage in increasingly bitter and bloody battles with the State, as happened in the events of May 1968 in Paris. The State will no longer be able to suppress the revolutionary ardour of the working class with the trappings of the Welfare State, and will be revealed to all as the instrument of class control by the bourgeoisie. The city is the arena of class conflict. The correct focus for urban sociologists is the latter, not the former.

For a short period, Castells' argument influenced many groups inside and outside the world of academic sociology, seeming to explain why so many cities seemed to be collapsing into chaos and disorder across the Western world. At that time New York went bankrupt and Paris and London experienced sustained rioting. It was also quickly realised, not least by Castells himself, that his argument contained serious flaws.

Criticisms of Castells

Like the French Marxist, Louis Althusser, and the Greek Marxist, Nicos Poulantzas, who influenced him, Castells often wrote in obscure and dense language, giving few concrete examples of what he had in mind. He does not explain why, or where, urban dwellers will develop a collective awareness and take to the streets in protest. He simply assumes they will, as the result of structural determinants. In the same way, whatever the State does, whether it makes concessions or represses, it does so because the bourgeoisie wills it.

Production and consumption

Many Marxists were unhappy with Castells for shifting the focus of struggle from the point of production of goods – the factory – to the point of consumption – large urban areas. Cities also reduce the costs of production by grouping factories and offices together and facilitating the circulation of goods, money and labour. They are units of collective production, as well as consumption. Moreover, cities are also features of 'socialist' societies, themselves exhibiting many urban problems and inequalities.

Other sociologists have responded to Castells by arguing that there are as many factors likely to prevent the development of an urban social movement as there are to encourage it. As Rex and Tomlinson (1979) have argued, there are not just one or two but many housing classes. Equally, not everyone has children in school, and those who do not see themselves as consumers of welfare services may instead see themselves as private individuals and consumers preferring to hold out for tax cuts. This has been an important factor in British politics since the 1980s, and echoes the former Prime Minister Margaret Thatcher's famous comment that 'There is no such thing as society. There are individual men and women and there are families.'

Castells' later work

In the face of this criticism, Castells himself changed direction and took issue with many of the key ideas of his previous work (Castells, 1983). He addressed the problems of concrete examples, structural over-determinism, the emphasis on class rather than gender or ethnicity, and the belief that the Communist Party and trade unions were necessarily agents of human liberation. Finally, he saw the concept of collective consumption as too narrow, excluding the wider questions of cultural domination and State power. Nevertheless, Castells opened up many rich areas of debate for urban sociologists to consider, particularly the question of whether where we live influences how we live.

In Britain in the 1980s a number of developments loosely based around environmental issues led some sociologists to argue that 'new social movements' were emerging, qualitatively different to social movements of the past (which were concerned with money, the workplace and bureaucratically organised forms of resistance), and yet were still not equivalent to the forms of action described by Castells.

New social movements

These new movements are concerned with personal freedom and the rights of the individual in relation to issues such as gender and the environment. Their form of organisation is usually non-hierarchical and decentralised, and decisions are made directly and without the mediation of representatives. Where older movements (such as the labour movement) might have used negotiation, compromise and elections in pursuit of instrumental aims, new movements use direct and symbolic action in pursuit of radical social change. A good example of this would be the women's peace camp at the Greenham Common NATO base throughout the 1980s, though there are elements of the new movement in campaigns against trunk roads, superstores, the Anti-Poll Tax Campaign, environmental pollution and in the emergence of new age travellers.

The debate about why these new movements have emerged and why they have taken particular forms is part of a wider discussion about whether Western societies have left the industrial and urban age behind and have entered a post-industrial and post-urban age where, as Beck (1992) and others argue, the problem of subsistence – mere survival – has been largely solved.

QUESTIONS

1 **What does Castells mean by 'spatial units of collective consumption'?**

2 **What is Marxist about Castells' approach?**

3 **What are the criticisms of the analysis of the city produced by Castells?**

4 **What is a new social movement?**

The inner city: a zone of transition

Urban zones

The identification of a zone of transition – a place where there is a high turnover of residents – in the centre of cities dates back to the concentric zone theory developed by Ernest Burgess of the Chicago School (see Park and Burgess, 1925, and Figure 13.1). The zone of transition is typically a run-down area where there are few plans for long-term investments and development, many multi-occupation houses, a high crime rate and little sense of community (however defined).

The zone of transition is a social jungle in which everyone is fighting for survival, until they are able to move out like ripples in a pond, into the more stable and relatively affluent outer rings.

Figure 13.1 *Burgess' concentric urban zones*

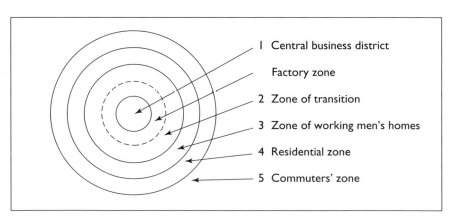

1 Central business district

Factory zone

2 Zone of transition

3 Zone of working men's homes

4 Residential zone

5 Commuters' zone

The theory has been criticised for its ideological assumption that urban development is a natural and neutral process, a response to impersonal market forces free from the influence of the business community, politicians and planners. It has also been criticised because of its inability to explain the frequency of riots in these areas. Despite these criticisms, many sociologists have sought to develop the concept of the zone of transition for their own distinctive research. Among the best known in Britain is the work of John Rex and his associates.

Rex and Moore Rex and Moore (1967) attempted to explain why, in particular, ethnic minorities come to be concentrated in inner-city areas. In their study of the Sparkbrook area of Birmingham, Rex and Moore used the Weberian concepts of market situation, status and lifestyle (see chapter 3) to develop their theory of housing classes in order to explain what they saw as racial segregation. They decided that the best indicator of class is housing and they were ultimately able to identify seven 'housing classes', competing in a 'class struggle' for scarce and valued resources. These were:

1 The outright owners of large houses in desirable areas
2 Mortgage payers who 'own' whole houses in desirable areas
3 Local authority tenants in houses built by the local authority
4 Local authority tenants in slum houses awaiting demolition
5 Tenants of private house owners
6 House owners who must take lodgers to meet repayments
7 Lodgers in rooms

Classes 6 and 7 describe inhabitants of the zone of transition.

According to Rex and Moore, it is your position within one of these classes, not your occupation, that defines social behaviour: 'membership of a housing class is of first importance in determining a man's associations, his interests, his lifestyle and his position in the urban social structure'.

In a later paper Rex (1968) argued that in the zone of transition he found that there were four classes:

1 The lodging house proprietors
2 The lodging-house tenants
3 The slum dwellers
4 The 'respectable' tenants of private houses.

Racism It is because of institutional racism, from those whom Pahl (1975) called 'Urban Managers' and 'Urban Gatekeepers', and also social racism, as well as the poor market position of newly arrived immigrants, that people from ethnic minorities become trapped in what should be a zone of transition. The potential consequences of this entrapment are clear to Pahl: 'Any attempt to segregate the inhabitants of this area permanently is bound to involve conflict. The long-term destiny of a city which frustrates the desire to improve their status by segregationist policies is some sort of urban riot.'

Events subsequent to the publication of their book have vindicated this prediction, with riots in the inner cities (London, Birmingham – the Handsworth and Lozells area studied by Rex and Tomlinson (1979) – Liverpool and Bristol) becoming a feature of Britain in the 1980s, as well as of other major world cities such as Miami, Los Angeles, Lyons and even Seoul in South Korea.

Rex and Tomlinson: the inner city defined

Rex and Tomlinson (1979) describe the inner city as follows:

> It is essentially the archaeological residue of an Edwardian or late-Victorian industrial working-class culture and society. It usually includes a declining number of factories; a park of some grandeur, but somehow now under-used and gone tatty; a football ground which still brings noisy and turbulent crowds onto the street, but which is essentially divorced from ordinary domestic living; demolition sites, whose future has been pencilled in by planners, but which is uncertain and unknown to the local populace; some odd pockets of boarded-up houses not yet demolished; old working-class shops, some with garish fronts as they are taken over by the supermarket chains; and, finally, the huddled, though often tree-lined terraces which actually constitute lodging-house zones, general improvement areas and housing action areas.

The theory of housing classes has not survived as well, however. It has been pointed out that, for example, the idea of 'urban leapfrogging' out of the inner zones is erroneous to many of the people who both want to, and enjoy, living in the inner city and have no desire to live in the suburbs. Many ethnic minorities have managed to move into middle-class suburban areas. Rex and Moore themselves agree that the number of housing classes could be continually modified and increased, as no two people are in exactly the same position in the housing market, where the main struggle is between the middle classes and the working classes. Finally, they effectively put the cart in front of the horse by viewing class distinctions as determined by housing, for, in order to buy a house, people need money, and to get money most people need an occupation. Rex himself, because of these criticisms, was eventually to see the theory of 'the underclass' (see chapter 3) as more helpful in explaining the position of ethnic minorities in Britain.

QUESTIONS

1 **What is meant by 'housing classes'? How useful is this concept?**

2 **How real is the claim that inner cities are qualitatively different from other urban areas?**

3 **Why are inner-city areas usually the most run-down areas of a city?**

Urban disorders

The Scarman Report

Although rioting has been a persistent feature of inner-city life across the industrial world, very few writers locate the inner city itself as the cause. After the Brixton 'riots' or 'disorders' of 1981, Lord Scarman, in his report to the government, identified five factors:

1 high unemployment, particularly among the young, especially blacks;
2 widespread deprivation, most markedly in the poor quality of housing, educational and social service provision, recreational facilities and high levels of crime;
3 widespread racial disadvantage and discrimination, with members of ethnic communities suffering racism and abuse from authorities, the white community and each other;
4 political exclusion and powerlessness – people in these areas have little or no access to the structures of power that may be able to alter decisions affecting their lives;
5 mistrust of, and hostility to, the police. Conflict between the police and some of the inner-city inhabitants is frequently the spark that ignites the riots. As Scarman remarked, the Brixton 'riots were essentially an outburst of anger and resentment by young black people against the police'.

This liberal view of the riots is not the only one. The New Right sees rioting principally as a breakdown of law and order: simply 'crimes', or even the product of politically inspired and organised conspiracies. A radical view sees collective violence of this nature as the opposite of irrational and purposeless behaviour. Rather, it is seen as the only effective means of protest open to politically marginalised groups.

Endless pressure

Stuart Hall (1987) remarks that what is missing from most accounts of urban unrest involving the black population is any real sense of what constitutes the lived reality of those who experience social deprivation. Ken Pryce's (1979) participant observation study of the black community of St Paul's in Bristol is one example of sociology's attempt to overcome this problem.

One point Pryce stresses is that the idea of an 'ethnic community' existing in any meaningful sense, simply because black people live in the same area, is simplistic: 'The only unity is an external one, in the form of common services utilised by all. Beneath the romantic's illusion of a tight-knit, friendly, organic, warm harmonious community, the divisions are deep. There is much suspicion between

Riots: a breakdown of law and order or
effective protest by the dispossessed?

groups.' 'Endless pressure' comes from being without work, living in
substandard housing, being harassed by the police, racism, short-
lived marriages, and because of the few opportunities for change.

Paul Gilroy (1987) attempts to see disorders from a subjective and
radical view in emphasising the oppressive role of the police in
many of the riots of the 1980s, drawing attention away from factors
such as unemployment and the notion of irrational or mindless
behaviour on the part of the rioters. The mass media and some sociologists fail to observe the sense of liberation that temporary control
over a community can induce. Gilroy's wider argument concerning
the way he believes black people have been 'criminalised' in Britain,
however, has been seriously criticised (see chapter 14).

QUESTIONS
1 How do the explanations for the Brixton riots put forward by Lord
   Scarman differ from those of the New Right?

2 What problems are associated with the concept of an ethnic
   community in inner-city areas?

Rural suburbanisation

One of the distinguishing features of industrialisation in Britain is that it happened earlier than in any other country. Great Britain is perhaps the society furthest removed from its peasant past. According to the United Nations Demographic Yearbook, in 1985 only 8 per cent of the British population lived in rural areas, while only 2.5 per cent of the population are economically active in rural areas (*see Tables 13.1 and 13.2*).

TABLE 13.1   UK urban dwellers (% of total population)

1950	1985
84	92

TABLE 13.2   UK rural population (millions)

1950	1985
8.1	4.5

Although the rural population is in decline, it is important to recognise that two movements are at work: people are leaving rural areas and moving into urban areas – 'rural depopulation' – while at the same time, people are leaving urban areas and moving to rural areas, though not necessarily to work there – the 'suburbanisation of rural communities'.

'Urbs in rure'   For Ray Pahl (1965b and 1968), just as there are urban villages in cities, so too are there metropolitan or commuter villages in the countryside.

Focusing on Hertfordshire, Pahl discerned six social groups living in villages that were effectively dispersed cities:

1 large property owners
2 the salariat (business or professional people)
3 retired urban workers (with capital)
4 urban workers (with limited capital in cheap housing)
5 rural working-class commuters
6 traditional ruralites

The largest of these groups is the salariat, the business and professional strata who are of the city but not resident in it, living suburban lifestyles in a 'village of the mind', experiencing *Gemeinschaft* and *Gesellschaft* simultaneously.

Newby   Whether the type of community these out-migrating groups hope to find actually exists, or indeed ever existed, is discussed by Newby

(1979). The rural working class, historically, has lived together because they had to, experiencing 'the mutuality of the oppressed'. Whether the concept of community, 'the ideology of communion', meant or means anything to this group is difficult to discern. As Newby remarks: 'it is virtually impossible to generalise about whether there has been a perceptible "decline of community" in the English village'.

The new urban, middle-class, car-owning newcomers to rural areas bring with them the potential for conflict and conflict of interest, particularly in the fields of housing and the environment, where houses become scarce resources and prices rise, and the countryside is seen, not as a working environment, but something picturesque, ancient and unchanging.

The new immigrants themselves are not a homogeneous group but are themselves variously commuters, weekend cottagers, holiday-home dwellers, and retired couples, many of whom are attracted by the prospect of living in a 'real community'. Conflicts may arise with the indigenous population over different concepts of community – the newcomers' concept may be 'associational', involving membership of educational, artistic or theatrical societies and perhaps the building of a 'community centre' whereas the longstanding residents' concept may be of a natural and spontaneous community of people built up over time from the experience of living and working together. As Newby remarks: 'To a farm worker, a community centre represents the antithesis of what he understands by "community".'

QUESTIONS

1 **Does the term rural still mean anything in an advanced industrial society?**

2 **Why would people in urban areas choose to move into a rural area?**

FURTHER READING

C. Bell and H. Newby, **Community Studies**, George Allen and Unwin, 1971

J. Benyon and J. Solomos, **The Roots of Urban Unrest**, Pergamon, 1987

P. Cooke (ed.), **Localities**, Unwin Hyman, 1989

J. Kingdom, **No Such Thing as Society? Individualism and Community**, Open University Press, 1992

H. Matthews, **British Inner Cities**, Oxford University Press, 1991

H. Newby, **Green and Pleasant Land? Social Change in Rural England**, Wildwood House, 1985

A. Scott, **Ideology and the New Social Movements**, Unwin Hyman, 1990

14 Crime and deviance

INTRODUCTION

This chapter starts by looking at the early explanations for crime: physiological, psychological, functionalist and subcultural. You will then go on to look at the Marxist explanation, examining the work of Quinney, Chambliss and Pearce. The chapter continues with a discussion of the interactionist perspective, focusing on labelling and the concept of the 'self-fulfilling prophecy'. Control theory, women and crime, and ethnicity and crime are then discussed. The chapter moves on with a review of sociological approaches to understanding white-collar crime and goes on to look at the critique of official crime statistics. The next section focuses on contemporary explanations for the causes of crime, examining Left idealism, new administrative criminology, New Right realism and Left realism. The debate over suicide is then discussed, with the chapter closing with a look at the sociology of murder.

Before sociology: Cesare Lombroso

Lombroso's study

Cesare Lombroso (1835–1909) was an Italian doctor working for the Italian army. He believed that criminals share common physical characteristics, and to prove this he set about measuring and quantifying certain physical features. He used a number of devices in this task, including a dynamometer (to measure physical strength), a craniograph (to measure the skull) and a pelvimeter (to measure pelvic strength).

In all, he studied over 400 prisoners, whom he compared with an equivalent number of Italian soldiers. Lombroso (1876) then concluded that: criminals have disproportionately long arms; hard expressions; shifty glances; large ears; twisted, upturned or, in the case of thieves, flattened noses and frequently upturned mouths; extra fingers/toes; and upturned nipples. Murderers, he discovered, have bushy eyebrows and beak-like noses.

The fact that they shared these features, he said, was evidence that people who commit serious crimes do so because they are genetically abnormal. They provide evidence of atavism – a throwback to a previous, less civilised age. Their criminal nature has decanted them from society into prison. Crime, he says, 'mingles with all kinds of degeneration: rickets, deafness, monstrosity, hairiness and cretinism, of which crime is only a variation'. The soldiers, by comparison, exhibited none of the characteristics of the criminals.

There are a number of problems with Lombroso's study. He only studied the characteristics of people who had already been caught and sentenced. They may have been arrested because of the way they looked and therefore aroused suspicion. This idea lives on in the folk myth that people with 'their eyes too close together' or eyebrows that meet in the middle cannot be trusted. He does not take into consideration those criminals who were never caught. The prisoners may have had abnormalities because of poverty and malnutrition. These are therefore class and not criminal characteristics. They may well have been rejected by the army for these characteristics, which is why they did not resemble the soldiers.

Women

While Lombroso was keen to differentiate between types of men, his view of women was more general and sweeping, claiming (Lombroso and Ferrero, 1895) that: 'Women have many traits in common with children; ... their moral sense is deficient; ... they are revengeful, jealous ... in ordinary cases these defects are neutralised by piety, maternity, want of passion and sexual coldness, and an underdeveloped intelligence.'

Lombroso's work is a good example of the belief that only some people are predisposed towards deviancy, and their behaviour can be explained through the discovery of characteristics and traits that determine this predisposition towards deviance. Although his work is no longer accepted as valid, the idea of 'deviant natures' has continued into twentieth-century criminology.

The psychological perspective

'Mad' and 'bad' individuals

The psychological perspective also locates deviance and its causes within the individual. 'Bad' or 'mad' blood, or evil spirits possessing the reluctant innocent, are ideas which, though they have disappeared from medical practice, still retain their form and shape within more modern and advanced theories. They occupy a place in some areas of mainstream thought, growing from the seeds of everyday, commonsense assumptions. Was the 'Yorkshire Ripper' really mad as his defence and the press would have us believe? Why was this a good defence?

Treatment   Some of these notions about the causes of deviance have led to harsh physical practices supposedly to cure the physical problem. 'Trepanning' (drilling or cutting) involves opening the skull to let out evil spirits. It used to be a great favourite, with most of the bad people in question dying from the operational trauma. This was superseded by attempts to locate the areas of the brain which advances in psychology had decided upon as the site of the impulse to misbehave, where centres of aggression could be isolated by the surgeon's knife. This was trepanning under a clinical guise, and ranged from lobotomies which entailed carving out various parts of the frontal lobe to the more refined leucotomies which pinpointed smaller areas of a malfunctioning, deviant brain. The end result is Jack Nicholson in *One Flew Over the Cuckoo's Nest* – a walking zombie.

Neurology   Other groups of psychologists – neurologists, who are interested in the biology of the brain and the nervous system – are interested in the excitatory and inhibitory substances which are transmitted through the central nervous system, propelled by electrical impulses. The levels of these drug-like chemicals, called neurotransmitters, are said to determine aspects of behaviour. 'Dopamine', large levels of which are found in the brains of deceased schizophrenics, is of particular interest. (For alternative explanations of this complex condition see chapter 4.) Dopamine excess causes 'inappropriate behaviour' – a cultural construct if ever there was one! – where garbled speech and auditory and visual hallucinations are the result. The question is, which came first, the condition or the high level of the neurotransmitter? Psychologists will now point to genetic explanations for this particular form of deviance, but this does not explain entirely why only certain people develop schizophrenia, usually in late adolescence, and why in some cases it is easily controlled and in others it is a continuous and debilitating condition.

At this point, explanations begin to veer towards the cultural, admitting that environmental 'stressors' can be located in the family, peer groups or social class. The best social science renders the nature–nurture debate an artificial one, acknowledging that biological, psychological and cultural factors all play a part. This compartmentalisation is a common situation within social science, as representatives of each discipline tend to stress the importance of their own explanations. Their theoretical spotlight shines only on certain selected 'facts'.

Eysenck and personality   A further psychological perspective is provided by Hans Eysenck (1975; see also chapter 5). Eysenck's Personality Questionnaire

(EPQ) is perhaps the most detailed and exhaustive analysis of what makes a 'personality'. Designed from a positivist point of view – that the essence of personality can be measured and quantified – Eysenck's questionnaire is cunningly contrived to ask the same question over and over again in a slightly different way, something like a desperate teacher in front of a class intent on improving their powers of non-verbal communication. The EPQ will present a picture of an individual around the concepts of introvert and extrovert personality. The balanced personality comes somewhere between these two extremes, with anyone scoring high on either end of the scale being classed as a deviant, if not psychopathic, personality.

The common thread that runs through these psychological explanations of deviance is that they all concentrate on internal causes of what is deemed to be deviant behaviour. From 'mad' or 'bad' explanations, evil spirits, and excess brain chemicals to the apparently innate criminal behaviour described by Eysenck, the influences and constraints of the wider social and cultural environment are ignored or given a back seat.

Sociological explanations

The essential difference between this type of explanation and sociological ones is that sociologists are interested in the relationship between the individual and culture, and how both help to create each other. Some explanations point to the structural, economic backdrop of the social system, others concentrate on the meanings and understandings which are constructed through interaction between individuals, between individuals and groups, and between individuals and those in power. Explanations which look for the causes of deviance solely within the individual lack this broader aspect, and suffer as a result. The concept of deviance is a social construct. If it were not then all societies would have exactly the same laws, with no cultural variation. The way the concept is constructed as a result of interactions has to be an important factor.

QUESTIONS

1 **How do sociological explanations of deviance differ from the non-sociological?**

2 **How does Eysenck measure personality?**

3 **Can deviant characteristics be inherited?**

Functionalist theories

Mechanical solidarity

For functionalists it is consensus which is the basis of social stability. It is within this framework that deviance, and the deviant act, must be explained. In exploring the differences between small-scale, pre-literate societies and large industrial social systems, Emile Durkheim noticed that an important aspect of social solidarity was different concepts of law and order. Mechanical solidarity, he observed, existed in smaller groups, where the limits of acceptable behaviour in all social areas are obvious to all. Anyone who breaks the law by sleeping with a parent, commits a murder, steals, is traitorous or breaks any religious taboos will accept or expect punishment – the social sanction which applies to that particular crime or deviant act. Retribution is 'mechanical'.

Organic solidarity

In the more complex organ of industrialised society, there is more choice in all areas of social life, so individuals are free to choose adult roles, religious beliefs, sexual practices and so on. What can possibly keep this society on the straight and narrow? Durkheim's answer is 'organic solidarity', upheld by a 'moral conscience' which ensures that all members of society are instilled with a sense of the importance of the larger social structure, so that their existence within society depends upon the well-being and maintenance of that structure. Collective values, moral codes, ethics, 'a sense of right and wrong' not only influence individual actions but are a central part of the social being. Internalisation, as Parsons says, consists of living and breathing the value system, seeing the world through norm-coloured spectacles. Any transgression has to be explained in terms of the inability of the individual to 'connect' adequately with the collective conscience, that is, poor socialisation.

Suicide and integration

Durkheim's famous study *Suicide* (1897, see pp.412–16) highlights integration as an aspect of socialisation where various social attributes lead individuals to volunteer for death. If you are young, male, not Catholic, or unmarried you are a high suicide risk. Your degree of integration affects your desire to remain a smaller part of the whole. With family responsibilities, and a caring church, you are much more likely to wish to remain and support your dependants than to end it all. Deviance, then, is the product of the inability to mesh with the greater value system, for whatever reason.

Internalisation and conflict

As usual, the functionalist spotlight has picked out explanations stemming from the need to maintain stability, so transgression of the value system reflects an inability to negotiate it appropriately. Breaking the law goes against the consensus wishes of the majority. Those who engage in these activities are grappling with their own guilt, as they are going against their very personalities, the social being constructed through the socialisation process. Critics (for example Dennis Wrong; see also chapter 2) have pointed out that this conception of individuals overdoes the ease of internalisation, where little or no resistance appears evident. There is a parallel here.

The basic assumptions of functionalist theory determinedly play down conflict within the social system; conflict within individuals is likewise ignored.

Changing the law

The internalisation of social norms and values is by no means easy, and it is questionable whether it is ever complete, but is rather a continuous process of internal battles which are mirrored in external battles in society. Would laws regarding homosexuality have been changed in Britain if socialisation had been a perfect, one-way process?

Deviance and social change

This aspect of deviant behaviour – the first signs of a new pattern of behaviour – is encompassed within Parsons' ideas concerning social evolution. Change is the product of deviance, from within which new behaviour patterns emerge. Again, the conflict within existing values is not satisfactorily explained, and we are left with the questions: Why do some people deviate and not others? Why do those who indulge in different behaviour tend to come from similar areas of society? Functionalist explanations which are more recent than Durkheim's study attempt to provide answers to these questions, but before we examine them, it would be useful to look at one more theoretical aspect of this argument.

The functions of deviance

Social facts exist in relation to society as a whole. The functions of each aspect of society need to be examined in order to place them within the whole. What are the functions of deviance? How does it contribute to the maintenance of society? Surely behaviour which goes against the grain of social acceptability is destructive, dysfunctional and a disease in the organism? In one sense it is seen in this way by functionalism, and a rapid spread of deviant activity – drug use, non-heterosexual sex, or violence which is not officially sanctioned – are seen as potentially leading to a breakdown of society. However, in another sense, as we have seen, deviant behaviour can lead to social change, as with the scientist who labours against professional opinion and subsequently makes a breakthrough which benefits all humanity. In this sense deviance can be seen as functional.

It can also be seen as functional in so far as it helps to define what is acceptable behaviour. As long as we have violent behaviour, we need laws and sanctions which condemn and prevent it. The variety of sanctions which can be applied here is enormous, and depends on the context. It may be being kept in at playtime for bullying or it may mean ten years in prison for committing grievous bodily harm. Even the level of harm is taken into account, harm that is actual or grievous being defined by law. Now, imagine a society where physical violence was unheard of. How would unacceptable behaviour be signalled? How would we know what we can and cannot do? An eyebrow raised in anger could get you a suspended sentence, a dirty look two years. Swearing might become a capital offence. The point here is that deviance can be functional in that it lets us know where to draw the line. We must then toe the line or be defined as deviant.

Merton and cultural explanations

From a statistical point of view, deviant and criminal behaviour is more apparent in the working classes. The functionalist Robert Merton has evolved an explanation which attempts to deal with this. For Merton (1949) deviance is born out of reaction to the values and norms of society. The major value is success, defined financially. The norm to achieve this goal is hard work. Merton used males for his analysis, reflecting the main area of concern. Merton does not enter into a debate about sexism, mainly because he and his society at the time – 1940s USA – were sexist. Young working-class males were well aware of the goals of their society, they just lacked the ability to score. Frustrated by lack of qualifications, they are left to devise an alternative means of scoring the goals – the foul. Merton goes on to construct a table which he believes explains why certain people deviate – the football pools of misbehaviour. How many crosses you get against your name determines the causes and nature of your particular brand of deviance. This is known as Mertonian 'strain' theory (*see* Table 14.1).

TABLE 14.1 **A typology of modes of individual adaptation**

MODES OF ADAPTATION	CULTURAL GOALS	INSTITUTIONALISED MEANS
Conformity	+	+
Innovation	+	–
Ritualism	–	+
Retreatism	–	–
Rebellion	±	±

+ = *acceptance; – = rejection; ± = rejection of prevailing values and substitution of new values*
Source: Merton, 1949

The gap between goals and means

Inability to achieve the goals of society, due to a problem in engaging in the norms which are beyond an individual's control, which cannot be grasped and used, leaves the individual in a condition of anomie, a lack of norms, 'normlessness'. People can suddenly be thrown into this situation for various reasons: the loss of a loved one, marriage breakdown, abrupt financial disaster or success being the most obvious. Disaster leaves you with goals but without the means to achieve them, windfall success leaves you with a lifestyle you can move beyond but without a map to show you how to advance. Hence pools or lottery winners who either say 'It won't stop me going to work' or who decide to 'Spend! Spend! Spend!'

Deviance and the working class

Merton's table attempts to deal with different types of deviance, with type being awarded according to class position. The lower classes are most likely to 'innovate'. Lacking the accepted norms of success, they operate using a new set, which they have adapted in order to realise the goals. In short, they steal, lie and cheat their way to financial success, as they know they would never reach the top through the legitimate route, which for them is manual labour.

The lower middle class

The lower middle class is the most likely to produce the 'ritualist' deviant. This is the person who has long since given up their pretentions to success, and, unable to drop their socialisation, always plays by the rules. They therefore 'go through the motions', no longer expecting success, conforming to failure, and becoming petty, rule-minded sticklers.

By far the most active deviants, and in Merton's words 'the true aliens', are the retreatists, who reject and retreat from the values, refuse to pursue wealth, and live unconventionally. He goes on to characterise these people more distinctly as 'pariahs, outcasts, vagabonds, tramps, chronic drunkards and drug addicts'. Rejection of the norms and values of society and a commitment to replace these with a new order form the response of the 'rebels'.

Criticisms of Merton

The first criticism is in Merton's wide use of the word 'deviant'. Would the ritualist, with a narrow and conforming lifestyle, be classed as deviant by the rest of society? Some of these forms of deviance carry severe social sanctions, others none at all. This arises from the functionalist concern with consensus and the fixation with the goals of success being financial. It comes back to the same old criticism. Functionalists are obsessed with the mainstream values of society, and use these as the yardstick against which all behaviour is assessed, so conflict must be deviance!

The intrinsic sexism in what Merton says is evident in his failure to see that the one social group which most clearly suffers an imbalance between cultural goals and the cultural means to attain them is that of women. Statistically, though, this is the least criminal group in society.

Another problem area for Merton's theory is that too many people are pushed into too few categories. Merton's famous list of retreatists quoted above shouts this out to the discerning social observer. The 'types' he mentions under the drop-out category are subcultures in their own right, from acid-heads to alcoholics.

Albert Cohen and subcultural theories of deviance

Various American sociologists have come up with theories which attempt to refine the broader type of explanation. Albert Cohen (1955) focused on the inabilities of working-class boys (girls are again ignored) to catch up with the 'American Dream', in the same vein as Merton. Cohen's new angle is that individuals do not respond to this frustrating position on an individual basis – they find mates in a similar predicament and, together, reject the dominant system of values, goals and norms.

This, claims Cohen, explains what Merton does not, that is, groups of youths acting out their deviance in uniform patterns, and types of deviance which bring no monetary gain and therefore cannot be classed as 'innovative'. Cohen goes on to elaborate on this subcultural theory, calling inability to achieve success 'status frustration', which leads to the creation of norms and values in direct opposition to those of mainstream society. He locates the cause of failure within the home and environment, a classic case of 'deprivation theory' (see chapters 5, 9 and 10). This insists that the cultural values of the working class are in some way deficient. This 'deficiency' leads the boys to fail academically, and so they seek status elsewhere – and where else than among their mates!

In subcultural territory, anything goes, anything which in any way threatens those in secure, successful positions – teachers, police, politicians, sociologists and so on – is accepted. The 'toughest kid in the school' may get into trouble with teachers, but it is a hard-won title and his mates will think he is 'well hard'. Cohen's explanation is about taking success where you find it.

There are other, closely related yet slightly differing subcultural explanations. They tend to view deviance from a structural stance, attempting to show how patterns of behaviour are related to the wider social group. The constraints of society create the context in which subcultural values are constructed and acted out.

Cloward and Ohlin

Cloward and Ohlin (1961) use class subcultures, particularly criminal ones, to explain various types of deviance. They claim to have uncovered yet another aspect of deviance not dealt with by Merton: the existence of groups who engage in stealing to counterbalance their failure to succeed 'legitimately' – criminal subcultures – and those who gain their status by fighting – conflict subcultures. Another group is formed by working-class 'wimps' who cannot succeed. These people fail exams, and cannot steal or fight, so they become junkies, drunks and weirdos – these are retreatist subcultures.

Miller   Walter Miller (1962) has yet another angle, pointing out that working-class subculture is on the whole geared towards 'toughness, smartness and excitement'. This three-pronged concern with life in the fast lane entails being a good fighter and a fast-talking hustler who seeks thrills and pleasure. Miller goes on to point out the predominance of peer-group pressure among the working class. Nowhere else will you find such conformity, not to mainstream culture but to their own value systems. Status and security are to be found in the peer group, and any behaviour which helps you attain this status is therefore desirable.

Sociological work   An analysis of the sociological work being done reveals a composite picture. Merton starts the ball rolling with an analysis of the relationship of individuals to the value system. The subcultural thinkers pick the ball up and stagger with it. The point is that Cohen, Miller and others build upon and develop Merton's ideas, in varying directions. Taken as a whole, they do provide a comprehensive explanation for deviant behaviour, each attempting to address issues which others have ignored. Cohen takes Merton a step further by explaining group reactions rather than individual ones. Cloward and Ohlin look at the different reactions of these groups. Miller goes further with his view of working-class values and the importance of peer-group conformity.

Criticisms   Imagine you are born into the lower working class. You live in the inner city. Your culture is 'deficient' in that it leads you to 'fail' educationally. This means that you will not get a high-earning career, but you are still exposed to the goals of success in financial terms. So you become a thief or a fighter according to your peer-group values. If you cannot thieve or fight you fall into a drop-out subculture. 'Status' is won by adhering to oppositional values, but to be street smart, thrilling and exciting is an overriding necessity. Is this the end of the story?

Old youth cultures   People's understanding of deviance depends on their class, gender, peer group and neighbourhood. Once you become socialised into alternative goals, you live by their code. If you look back at British society since the 1950s (see chapter 3) you will find various expressions of 'deviant' reactions to social norms. If the subcultural theories were correct, then we should see seventy-year-old teddy boys swaggering and staggering around town centres, swapping stories with sixty-year-old rockers in cracked leathers with tarnished studs, glowering at fifty-year-old mods. They in turn then rev up their ancient Lambrettas and swerve past thirty-year-old skinheads, who still take pleasure in beating up ageing hippies who keep getting their Afghan coats trodden on by the platform heels of forty-year-old glam rockers with Aladdin Sane haircuts who sneer at punk rockers pushing prams and choosing curtains.

Of course, there are isolated examples of all these – the perennial Elvis fans and hippies who have not realised that the sixties are over – but the majority have progressed into mortgaged greyness, criticising the tunelessness and meaninglessness of rap and other contemporary music in much the same way that their parents criticised the Rolling Stones.

Sykes and Matza   Sykes and Matza (1962) point out that the entire subcultural argument is too sweeping and too deterministic. Individuals conform or otherwise in various ways. Not everybody tattoos swastikas on their forehead and ACAB on their fingers, and a lot of those who did have saved up their wages to have the marks of subculture removed. Sykes and Matza point out that subcultures are the proverbial 'phase he's going through', and this will be followed by other, possibly more conforming phases, shifts, transitions into the boring stability of adult life.

Miller's three-pronged value system, according to Sykes and Matza, consists of 'subterranean values', which attract all youths, middle- and working-class alike. The difference is that middle-class youth can afford (or rather their parents can afford) to indulge these needs for toughness, smartness and excitement legitimately. For example, whereas Daddy might buy you a Porsche so you can indulge your speed fantasies, less affluent youths will steal somebody else's.

Techniques of neutralisation   The most telling point that Sykes and Matza make is that of 'neutralisation' techniques. When apprehended, how many kids stick to their subcultural values rather than shutting their mouths, nodding meekly and paying the price, accompanying this with various excuses and apologies? Sykes and Matza provide a shrewd criticism of the tendency for sociologists, and particularly those in the structural school, to be too deterministic in the search for a comprehensive explanation. Real life is not so easily confined, and inconsistencies keep spilling over the edge of neat, self-contained explanations.

QUESTIONS
1 How can it be argued that deviance is functional for society?

2 What does Merton mean by 'cultural goals' and 'cultural means'? What is the importance of the relationship between the two?

3 Are Merton and the subcultural theorists in agreement?

4 If you are young and live in the inner city, are you doomed to deviate?

Marxism and crime

A non-romantic notion

As with other areas of what we now call sociology, Marx did not write anything that he or Engels might have described as 'a theory of crime and deviance'. What we know of their ideas in this area were formulated while developing what they believed was a scientific analysis of capitalist development and the emerging revolutionary role of the working class. Crime bore no romantic connotations to them, and in some writings they were scathing of criminals, referring to them as 'lumpenproletarians'. These are the peripheral and unproductive working class who find ways of avoiding selling their labour to the bourgeoisie, but still earn a living through burglary, theft, black-marketeering and robbery. They are parasitic on the working class, draining their revolutionary power.

It was not until the 1970s that, with the apparent deficiencies of functionalist and interactionist accounts of crime and deviance exposed, new theories emerged from within the Marxist tradition. A good example of this is Richard Quinney (1975).

Quinney and economic determinism

His approach is that of an economic determinist. It is the need to produce that brings people together in society, and it is out of the economy that laws, religious beliefs, family forms, and types of ownership emerge. His position (which has firm roots in Marxism) is that it is the economic arrangements that prevail — the mode of production in Marx's term — and from which everything else in society springs. The pattern and nature of crime must therefore originate from the mode of production. Since the breakdown of the feudal era in Britain, we have lived under the capitalist mode of production in which the means of production are owned by a few (the bourgeoisie) to whom everyone else (the proletariat) eventually has to sell their labour power. (This is explained in much greater detail in chapter 3.) The source of crime lies in the unequal distribution of wealth and power, and for this reason it is essentially a material problem, about the struggle for things.

A class State

For Marxists (see chapter 8), the State in a capitalist society is not neutral. It does not play the same role as a referee in a football match, but is biased in favour of one side: those who already own all the wealth. The law as we know it, heavily biased towards property rights, emerged with the rise of capitalism and is a central means of enforcing the interests of the dominant capitalist class — those who are already 'winning'. There are any number of examples that Marxist historians have found to illustrate this point, for example the removal of common land and creation of poaching laws in the eighteenth century.

Crimes of control

Although the State under capitalism makes the laws of the land, it is not all-powerful, being subordinate to the capitalist class, and obliges even those who stand to benefit most from its workings, the employers, to abuse it in an attempt to maintain the existing system. What results are crimes of control. These can take many forms, such as police brutality on the streets and in police cells, crimes at governmental level like the Watergate scandal of the 1970s which resulted in Richard Nixon being forced to resign as President of the USA, or crimes of economic domination committed by big business, ranging from deliberate pollution to price-fixing in order to protect or increase profits. What ultimately links these crimes is the fact that capitalism makes a god of money and profit, and the crimes of the rich and powerful emanate from the greed on which the capitalist system feeds and depends.

Working-class crime

Within the working class, it is a different picture. The lumpenproletariat either consciously or unconsciously directs their crimes against the capitalist system, for which they incur the wrath and vigilance of the police, or, as a result of the way that life under capitalism has dehumanised and alienated – 'brutalised' – them, they commit crimes against their own class. Only people without any conception of class consciousness and solidarity would break into another house on the same council estate and raid someone else's gas meter. The 'honest' working class will direct their struggle against exploitation in the workplace through industrial sabotage, deliberately damaging machinery in order to slow down the pace of production. Nearly all crime among the working class is actually a means of survival, an attempt to exist in a society where survival is not assured by collective means. Crime is inevitable under capitalist conditions.

It is Marx's argument that as the capitalist system grows, the cycle of booms and slumps in production will get longer and longer. In slump periods there will be more and more unemployed, the reserve army of labour. Quinney adds that crime will increase, and there will be greater demands for more and more police. When the costs of policing become so great that they are no longer economic, then the State will drop its mask of neutrality and the bourgeoisie will resort to direct political rule through dictatorship. In these new conditions, all crime will become political as the workers realise the true nature of the way they are governed. They will unite against the common enemy – the bourgeoisie – and overthrow them. The result will be a socialist society, run by workers for workers. In this society, as there is no inequality, no system based on greed, no want, no alienation, no repression, the problem of crime will disappear along with the need for police and prisons.

Criticisms of Quinney

It is perhaps too easy to see the flaws in Quinney's argument. Does all law protect and advantage only the powerful? Would this explain laws on abortion or homosexuality, traffic laws and child abuse? Can there be an explicitly Marxist account of why Dennis Nielsen or the Wests killed people and hid their bodies under the floorboards? It also seems contradictory to see the working class as one day passive victims of the capitalist system and the next as potentially revolutionary and destroyers of the same system. Quinney is unwilling to acknowledge that the working class has struggled to achieve rights under capitalism that were hard-fought: the right to strike, to form unions, to vote, and so on. Finally, the experience of the 1980s and 1990s in Great Britain does not suggest that mass unemployment makes the working class more revolutionary or critical of capitalism. If anything, the proletariat has moved politically to the right, and is no more unified than before.

Crimes of the rich and powerful

A similar study to Quinney's, based on fieldwork undertaken in the 1960s, was carried out by William Chambliss (1978). His central argument is that everyone either is, or is potentially, criminal or deviant. The only question is: why do only some get caught? Being captured is not necessarily a question of misfortune or bad luck, it may well be because you are not paying enough backhanders to the local police force, or contributing enough to their charitable funds. The most successful criminals are the ones who can encourage the police to turn a blind eye to their activities. The police, the business community and organised crime work together. Each stand to gain from each other while publicly condemning crime, in order to mask their own corruption. The real criminal class in America is in reality the rich and powerful.

These arguments are reinforced by Frank Pearce (1976). Why is it, he asks, that we give priority to working-class crime when, on financial grounds, the cost of their crime to the community is negligible when compared to the estimated cost of corporate and white-collar crime? Why stop and harass someone in an old Cortina when the real criminals are in the boardroom? It is because of the way the law is enforced that the working class seem to be the main offenders, yet this is simply a reflection of the way resources are concentrated, and that white-collar and corporate crimes provoke less interest because they appear to be 'victimless'. Yet for Pearce, they should be the real focus of law enforcement. It cannot be a reflection of the reality of the nature of crime in society that the powerful manage to escape the sanction of the law. They can be involved in insider dealing or price fixing or, through decisions made on the grounds of profit, fail to maintain safety standards in workplaces knowing that inspections are infrequent and fines are minimal. The crimes of the powerful, compared to the relatively powerless, go unpunished because it is not the purpose of the law, as it is enforced, to punish them.

Criticisms of Chambliss and Pease

Marxists such as Quinney, Chambliss and Pearce opened up new areas of considerations for sociologists, though others have been wary of following in their path. Marx and Engels themselves left the problem of crime well alone, and subsequent Marxist and radical criminologists have been criticised for a deterministic view of crime. In other words, they have fallen into the trap of saying that certain conditions will always cause certain consequences. Exploited proletarians will turn to crime because they are alienated by capitalism. The police and the courts will side with the rich because that is the way the system is rigged. The State always favours the interests of the ruling class. Formulae such as these are evidence of what has been called 'vulgar' Marxism: simplifying complex social problems by selective reference to evidence that moves towards a picture of an evil, scheming bourgeoisie and a passive, innocent, and intrinsically good working class.

More recent work has tried to move beyond this situation, seeing working-class crime, for example, as more than primitive rebellion, and the State as more than a giant conspiracy in favour of bourgeois interests. The 'New Criminology' attempts to escape vulgar Marxism and portrays criminals as conscious, not passive, actors, and working-class crime as problematic.

QUESTIONS

1 **What is meant by 'economic determinism' in relation to crime and deviance?**

2 **What is the role of the State in dealing with crime?**

3 **What are 'crimes of control'?**

4 **What reasons do Marxists give for the working class committing crimes?**

Interactionism

Interactionists have been responsible for a change in all areas of sociological explanation, and deviance has claimed their attention in particular. They approach the topic from a completely different angle to structural theorists. Most importantly, they do not take the deviant act itself for granted. The interactions between the deviant and society are the focal point. How does society respond to the deviant and vice versa? In their view, deviants are made, not born.

Becker and *Outsiders*   *An* American sociologist, Howard Becker (1963), is perhaps the best-known of the interactionists. Becker was involved in a 'subculture' – that of a night-club musician. These people live their lives in a way that most people find incomprehensible, sleeping by day and working by night. Their value system develops through their lifestyle, and as such has its own set of meanings and values. This is just one group within a larger one, and this alternative society exists everywhere. The interactionists point out that these lifestyles are a central part of society, and norms are constructed and reconstructed all the time. Everything should be analysed in the sense that it arises out of interactions between individuals, groups and society.

Becker's first point is that there is no such thing as a deviant act. But surely murder and robbery are deviant? The interactionists would say 'only if it is not sanctioned.' Even killing is acceptable if it is sanctioned. 'Terrorists' murder people, but they get 'killed' by the army. If a doctor gives you a shot of morphine, then you are a patient, but if it is administered by someone not medically qualified then you are a junkie. Until 1991, if a man forced intercourse on his wife, it was sex. If they were not married, it was rape. The law changed and it became rape in both situations. If a man wears a dress in public (or in private) he is a transvestite. If the Archbishop of Canterbury wears one it is a holy vestment. If you appeared in court wearing a long curly horsehair wig, you could possibly be fined for contempt by someone who is wearing exactly the same thing. Now make up your own examples!

Deviance is relative   Becker shows that it is not the act itself which is deviant but it is the response of society that defines it as deviant. It is not only the response of society in general, but the responses of individuals or groups who have power in society. The proof is to be found in a simple analysis of cultures and historical periods. What is deviant in one culture is acceptable (and sometimes even required) in another. The changing attitude towards homosexuality in Britain in the 1960s led to a change in the law. Is homosexuality, which is no longer a crime between (socially defined) adults in private, still considered deviant in Britain in the 1990s? Relating back to our studies of the family (see chapter 4), in Western societies monogamous marriage is the only legal form but this is not true in all cultures and religions. It is clear from these examples that deviance is in the eye of the beholder, and the collective meanings which arise out of certain situations lead them to be defined as deviant or otherwise. Which people in society have the power to set up those definitions?

The power to define   Becker is perhaps the best-known proponent of 'labelling theory'. The crucial point here is that only those in society who have power can make a label stick. If you steal your sister's pocket money, or if she wears your jacket without permission, you may call each other thief. Will society recognise the label? Will it affect your future career? Will your friends drop you? Unlikely. If you are labelled deviant by those in authority, if you are arrested, charged and convicted of theft, then the police and courts have the power to ensure that this label will stick.

Labelling theory and the self-fulfilling prophecy

Labelling theory works on the basis of the self-fulfilling prophecy. If enough people put the label on an individual, eventually they begin to recognise themselves in terms of the label. If people call you a hooligan, you may as well become one. The labelled individual will soon realise that he or she is being watched – 'Look out for that one, he's a right thief.' All behaviour displayed by that individual is interpreted in terms of the label, and any minor transgression is leapt upon with glee. Others may be indulging in similar or worse behaviour, but this goes unnoticed and/or unpunished, because they have not got the label which signals the 'type' of person they are. The prophecy initially made in the light of an isolated incident is fulfilled, proven correct and, the interactionists insist, it is fulfilled because it is made in the first place. To escape fulfilment, to shake off the label, is extremely difficult. In order to do so the labelled individual would need to behave like a saint.

According to the microsociological approach, concentrating on small-scale interactions between people in society, the individual is more likely to adopt an 'if you can't beat them join them' response. In other words, they start living up to the label, have some fun, and enjoy being a deviant. The media, powerful label makers indeed, used to revile the activities of football fans as 'animal behaviour'. The chant was soon to arise from the terraces to celebrate this newfound bestial status: 'We hate the humans.' The position of the 'animal hooligan', then, is far from one of 'mindless behaviour', but is actually a highly organised, structured existence. The hierarchy on the terraces is well ordered, and fans must progress through a structural pattern, a 'career' of football violence.

The deviant 'career'

Again, Howard Becker has been foremost in defining this idea of 'career', relating to the self-concept of the individuals involved. He considers the problem of becoming a marijuana smoker, an activity that was apparently an important part of the night-club musician's life. The initiate has to learn to smoke the stuff, then learn to perceive the effects, and then go on to enjoy the effects. Then the apprenticeship is completed by learning to hide your habit from the 'straight' world. Being caught, perhaps arrested and so on, could serve to confirm your status, both in your own eyes and in those of society. All other statuses, labels which you own, can be overshadowed by this.

This idea of careers is very important to interactionism, and the progress of an individual through various stages of deviance is well documented. It does not only apply to deviance. Alcohol is a socially accepted form of drug-taking yet acquiring a taste for alcohol is not a one-drink process.

The rewards of following a deviant career clearly do not come from society, but from the feelings of belonging to a group, united in opposition to others, and this helps to form a self-concept which can be lived with. There is an overlap here with ideas on subcultures, where peer-group values can become as, or more, important than mainstream ones. The interactionist approach, however, stresses that it is society's response to deviant acts, and the response of the individual to that social response which leads to a career of deviance. What matters is how individuals come to take on the labels and definitions applied to their behaviour by those they interact with.

The negotiation of deviance

What Becker does is to point out the fragility of such definitions, and reinforce one of the main assumptions of interactionism – that social reality only exists in so far as it is constructed in interactions between individuals. There are no 'true' deviant acts, laid down in tablets of stone, irrefutable and permanent. Rather, there is a process whereby some things come to be defined as deviant, according to the actors involved, the historical period, and the culture. These definitions are open to negotiation; they can and will be changed according to circumstance. They are not fixed immutably in the social structure. This begs a question: 'What about people who indulge in deviant activities, but are not discovered?'

Primary and secondary deviance

Lemert (1967) addresses this issue by distinguishing between 'primary' and 'secondary' deviance. Primary deviance is when the act is not officially labelled as such, whereas secondary deviance is all out in the open. Did you ever steal from your mum's purse or your dad's wallet? Were you caught? If you were, it is unlikely that they called in the police. Many children go through a phase of shoplifting (a euphemism for stealing) but are not labelled as thieves – unless they are caught and publicly punished. Often the local media have the power here. If it is not reported then it is unlikely to produce a deviant label. Older people have been caught in the same act, and despite their pleas of lack of memory, or too much valium, are prosecuted, as all the shop signs warn. However pitiable their plight, or true their pleas, the stigma attached still makes people wonder.

Secondary deviation is the more serious then, in the myopic eyes of society.

Aaron Cicourel

Deviance is to be found in social reactions to an act, not in the act itself. Cicourel (1976), from an ethnomethodological perspective, investigates this in relation to the police and their definitions of certain people as delinquents. He found that the police operated using a stereotype of the deviant as a young working-class male who exhibited certain forms of behaviour. If enough traits were exhibited by the youths, then they and their actions were said to be deviant and legal action was taken. These traits concern class when appearance, type of language used, attitude, father's occupation and living in the inner city were taken as indicators. If a youth was arrested then he was more likely to be charged if he had a criminal record. The whole process was built around complex interactions and meanings systems operated by the police, the courts, the probation service and so on. Middle-class youths were much less likely to be classed as deviant, and this applied even when the acts committed were identical.

This has been pointed out by many sociologists in Britain and elsewhere. In Britain, the activities of students in Rag Week, or rugby players after a match, were more likely to be attributed to high spirits, whereas working-class youths indulging in the same acts were labelled as deviants or even criminals. This shows that there are many factors which affect interactions, and that this complexity cannot be ignored when considering what society describes and reclassifies as criminal or deviant.

The relative simplicity of structuralist ideas, in particular functionalist views, has to be mentioned here. In all areas of sociology, the straightforward explanations are initially attractive but, on closer analysis, prove to be much less comprehensive. However, the interactionist perspective is not without its own faults and criticisms.

Criticisms of the interactionists

The first criticism and the one most often aimed at labelling theory and the self-fulfilling prophecy, is: what causes the individual to deviate in the first instance? In other words, how and why do they attract the attention of the labellers? Interactionism is very weak here, and explanations have to be taken from social structure, environment and subculture. Interactionists initially disregarded such causes, preferring to concentrate on the resulting interactions between individuals and those in authority. The theoretical assumptions upon which microsociological approaches rest are most apparent here, and this leads us to the second criticism: interactionist explanations are 'context bound'.

Structuralist critics point out that no interaction takes place in a social vacuum, and that such factors as social class, the economic substructure and the wider social system are the most important factors in determining the outcome of small-scale interactions. This type of criticism is associated with other weaknesses in microanalysis. Is it really little more than descriptive social comment, at best a form of social psychology? What is the point of studying small and marginal groups such as night-club musicians, or hippies and homosexuals?

At the end of a long, expensive research project, the microsociologist is left with a mere description, albeit rich in quality, reporting meanings and experiences of individuals, from which they cannot generalise or establish universally applicable rules. Here we have the standard positivist criticism of phenomenological schools of thought: what is the point?

Response to criticisms There are two answers to this type of criticism. The first is that interactionists play down the relevance or importance of quantitative, scientific data. They are principally interested in internal meanings and these cannot be explained by tables of figures, graphs and equations. Second, in a response more typical of contemporary sociology, both interactionists and structuralists in fact recognise the importance of each other's analyses and explanations. As we have seen, Cicourel and others recognise the importance of social class, subculture and culture in their explanations. In this way statistical information, 'social facts' gathered from the larger-scale methods of research, can be used alongside the smaller-scale data, providing a richer and more detailed explanation of the wider picture. These are the seeds sown by the Weberian approach which stresses understanding, *verstehen* (see chapter 1), bearing fruit.

Free will There is further major criticism, related to the interactionists' understanding of social action and social agency. It ignores the autonomy of the individual, their ability to control their own life, and the struggle of free will over determinism. Interactionists see the individual as passive not active. Alvin Gouldner complains that Becker's deviants seem to be totally passive accepters of any label which society slaps on them. Gouldner's famous phrase is 'man on his back'. He means that we do not just accept labels or live out the prophecies which others make. We can and do fight back, we reject the stigma and forge our own path. In short, our free will is stronger than this school of thought would have us believe.

This criticism finds support among those who accuse interactionists of being soft, liberal and looking for excuses for the deviant. If you break formal or informal laws, and get caught, you can always blame it on society, parents, police, environment, home life or education. How many people have never said at some time in their lives 'I didn't ask to be born, did I?'

Gouldner's criticisms undoubtedly carry some weight, and have provoked a debate which still continues. Becker points out that interactions are much more complex than the simplistic views stated in the various criticisms. He agrees that not all those who come to be labelled as deviant continue to develop deviant careers. However, he stresses that there are social pressures which make it difficult for those labelled as deviant to avoid their lifestyle, and in cases where they feel their lifestyle is better than that required by society, they willingly adopt deviant attitudes.

It is clear from the above that there are still many arguments and debatable points. As with all advances in sociology, interactionism is full of holes. However, most sociologists would agree that it has uncovered another aspect of deviant and criminal behaviour and the response of society to that behaviour. Sociologists take on board these new ideas, and they have to be considered as additions to existing ideas rather than replacements.

QUESTIONS

1 **What does it mean to say that deviance is historically and culturally relative?**

2 **What is meant by a 'self-fulfilling prophecy'? How might such a prophecy be fulfilled, and how might it be refuted?**

3 **How is deviance negotiated?**

4 **What are the most important criticisms of interactionist theories of deviance?**

Control theory

Hirschi   Alongside subcultural, labelling and many other theories, a theory of deviance exists under the heading of control theory, first put forward by Travis Hirschi (1969). In this work, based on questionnaires given to a random stratified sample of 5,545 children in schools around San Francisco, California, Hirschi critically examines the central sociological concept of socialisation. There is nothing deterministic or automatic about this process of learning how to conform to the dominant norms and values in society. Left to themselves, humans would do anything they pleased. Hirschi, and others such as Stephen Box (1971), are interested in understanding how and why individuals opt into social control, knowing all the time that there are alternatives.

Hirschi identifies four factors: attachment, involvement, commitment and beliefs. By attachment he means the extent to which individuals are sensitive to the thoughts, feelings and expectations of others. The more attached to others you are, the less freedom you have to deviate. Involvement concerns the amount of time individuals have to get up to no good; commitment refers to how much of an investment people have made in things such as education, a career or being socially respected. Delinquent behaviour would jeopardise this investment. Finally, by belief he is referring to the intensity with which people believe they should obey the law, or some laws in particular. So the less socially attached, involved, committed and believing you are, the greater is your freedom to deviate.

The question is not why do most people obey the law but why doesn't everyone break it? An understanding of why people make a social bond with the society in which they live needs to be carefully examined. As Box writes: 'Occurrence of special circumstances is not necessary to bring about the freedom to deviate; freedom is there all the time as a human possibility. It is lost when humans surrender themselves to others' reputations and moralities. It is regained, perhaps only momentarily, when they cease to care about others or perhaps their own social selves, or find segments of conventional morality distasteful.'

Box himself cites five factors that make people likely to deviate: the ease with which they will be able to conceal their deviance; the amount of skill needed to carry out the deviant act; having the necessary resources; the approval of peers; and a belief that status will be gained from carrying out the act. With juvenile delinquency in mind, he adds the question, 'Why would someone who is willing and able want to?'

Criticisms of control theory

The answer is strongly connected to an individual's beliefs that an initial deviant act is the most rewarding line of activity they can pursue, and that they remain unpersuaded by the rest of society's arguments that the risks are not worth taking.

Box himself is aware of the shortcomings of control theory, stating that it relies too much on what he calls 'situational subjective explanations' where there is too much emphasis on the individual and not enough on the role of the social structure. An attachment to school, for example, is important, but the class character of that school will itself play a part in determining the level of attachment. It is for this reason that the methodological approach taken by writers such as Paul Willis (see chapter 5) is to be commended.

Furthermore, while it may succeed in providing the framework in which primary deviance may be explained, it says little or nothing about secondary deviance, when individuals have become habitual criminals and eventually recidivists. Finally, it has nothing to say about the crimes of the powerful, having mostly juvenile delinquents in mind.

QUESTIONS

1 **What factors does Hirschi identify as important in preventing deviance?**

2 **What is meant by the phrase 'situational subjective explanations'?**

3 **What criticisms can be made of control theory?**

Women and crime

Little is known, and even less has been researched, concerning the relationship between women and crime. The main reason for this is because, statistically, women have always been a tiny minority of those engaging in crime.

Before the rise of feminist theory in the 1970s, accounts of women's criminality had gone little further than Lombroso and Ferrero's (1895) failure to find a clear correlation between criminal women and their biological characteristics. Furthermore, they argued, although women were less advanced along the evolutionary scale (and therefore more likely to be criminal), the process of natural selection had bred out those women who tended to crime as these 'masculine' women were less likely to find male sexual partners to reproduce with.

Adler Adler (1975) attempted to discern a correlation between an increase in female criminality and the movement for women's liberation, with greater opportunities arising for crime with more women out of the home and in the workplace. Female criminality, she argued, could therefore be seen as an index of the degree of liberation achieved by women.

This initially persuasive theory is the latest in a long line of arguments that have emerged when rises in female crime rates have been detected but, as with so much of the study of criminology, the argument is found wanting because the statistical evidence is thought to be inaccurate. Adler's statistical series, based on figures from the USA between 1960 and 1972, showed rates of increase for juvenile and adult female crime higher than those for male crime. Her data were dogged by the fact that her base for women was very low. A rise in serious crime of 500 per cent can in reality be the difference between one murder by women in one year and five in the next.

A more important question, for writers such as Frances Heidensohn (1985), is: 'Why are there so few female criminals?' There are, at first sight, two possible answers to this question: the statistics are misleading, or women really do not engage in crime at the same rate as men.

Official statistics

Officially, convictions for serious or indictable offences are split approximately 80:20 between men and women, and there are approximately 33 times more men in prison at any one time in Great Britain than women. Even figures for shoplifting, traditionally thought of as a 'female' crime, show that more men are consistently captured and convicted than women.

Social control

Bizarrely, Pollack (1950) explained this pattern by stating that, because women had to hide the fact of menstruation, they are good at hiding things in general, for example their criminality. More modern research, based on self-report studies – such as those of Mawby (1980) – indicate that the proportion of male to female crime corresponds with the reality of people's experience. Nor does it seem to be true that women are dealt with more leniently by the police and courts (the 'chivalry thesis'). If anything they are treated as doubly deviant because they have broken both the stated laws of the land and the unstated laws of feminine behaviour. Moreover, if charged with serious crimes, they are much more likely than men to be seen as suffering from psychological problems than seen to be simply guilty (see Carlen, 1985 and Allen, 1987). Heidensohn argues that women's low involvement in crime reflects the constraining nature of the way they are socialised, when compared to men. Control over their behaviour is exercised through the family, the school, among peers, by the media and by more formal agents of social control. While this may contribute to an explanation of the relatively low rate of female crime, this control theory, which contradicts Lemert's (1967) argument that 'social control leads to deviance', does not explain why some women engage in crime. Carlen suggests that this will most easily occur when girls are brought up in care in adolescence, away from the tight gender roles learnt in families where there is a male breadwinner and a female carer.

Women are as capable as men of committing any crime, whether murder, as in the cases of Myra Hindley and Rosemary West, or child sexual abuse. The 'borstal girls' studied by Anne Campbell (1981) fought in pubs, in streets, and at home, used weapons and broke bones, yet there is general agreement that this violence remains on a far smaller scale than that carried out by men. Most women's experience of crime is as victims.

Given the paucity of evidence concerning women's criminality, the focus on gender and crime has brought out the positive emphasis on crime as male, an expression of their masculinity. This is clear from studies of football violence, such as Dunning *et al.* (1988), where the focus of their study is on three aspects: masculinity, excitement and territory.

QUESTIONS

1 **How can women's low involvement in crime statistics be explained?**

2 **If there were more high-ranking women criminals, would there be more high-ranking women police officers?**

Ethnicity and crime

If the picture of women and crime shows a relative under-representation, an analysis of the criminality of ethnic groups in Britain reveals, at first sight, exactly the opposite. There are, proportionately, far more blacks than whites brought to court and sent to prison. They have a higher crime rate. While this can be explained by the fact that black people are concentrated among the working class and, some argue, the 'underclass' (see chapter 3), who in turn have higher crime rates, many sociologists have argued that a more profound analysis is needed.

Differential processing

The evidence is that black people have a different experience of justice to white people. According to the Home Office, the prison population in 1991 was classified as being made up of 16.5 per cent black males and 32.1 per cent black females, whereas they make up 5 per cent of the population nationally. They receive longer prison sentences and are more likely to have probation recommendations ignored. Afro-Caribbean youths are more readily remanded in custody and given custodial sentences, even when they have fewer previous convictions than white youths (see Smith, 1994).

As ever, the use of the term 'black' has to be carefully examined. Close analysis shows that groups of Asian descent should be distinguished from Afro-Caribbeans. In 1991, for example, men of West Indian, Guyanese and African origin represented 10.3 per cent of the prison population but only 1.8 per cent of the total population, while Indians, Pakistanis and Bangladeshis represented 3.0 per cent of the prison population and 3.4 per cent of the overall population.

For Daniels (1968), these figures cannot be explained by institutional racism, as all minorities suffer equally from such discrimination. The difference lies, he believes, in the patterns and expectations of immigration. Afro-Caribbeans came from islands modelled administratively on Britain, and they spoke English. Believing they were entering the same culture, they were initially outgoing and thus surprised to meet racism and hostility. Asian groups came from cultures already different organisationally and linguistically from Britain and therefore relied on their own resources and communities on arriving in Britain. Afro-Caribbeans therefore placed themselves in situations where they were more likely to encounter racism and discrimination. From 1969 onwards there was also an inflow of well-educated petty bourgeois Asians from East Africa.

As Gilroy (1987) writes, the years between 1972 and 1976 'saw the definition of blacks as a low crime group turned around 180 degrees'. For this writer, their resistance to discrimination and exploitation has politicised them and for this they have in turn been criminalised.

Stuart Hall (1978a) argues that, in this period, young blacks were stereotypically associated with the 'mugging problem', which allowed the police to use stop-and-search methods and saturate black areas with police. The belief emerged in schools, courts, police and government agencies that 'immigrants' had difficulty in meeting British demands for the rule of law. The position of the State seemed to be that black people should be disciplined and punished if they would not be contained. For many writers, however, the real problem was the entrenched racism of those in power, clearly evident in policing and immigration policy.

If Irish nationalists in the United Kingdom are seen as an ethnic minority, then they present a specific example of this approach, where all aspects of the legal process have been intensified to maintain control, from the way the army has been used to internment without trial and the arbitrary use of the Prevention of Terrorism Act. This view is held by Hillyard (1987). This issue remains an underdeveloped area of sociological research.

For 'Left realists' such as John Lea and Jock Young (1984), the relationship between ethnicity and crime has been oversimplified. There are many factors which point to the fact that blacks are not simply the victims of institutional racism, although they accept that this nevertheless exists. The great majority of crimes (over 90 per cent) are brought to the police's attention by the public. It may well be the case that black people do commit more crimes than other groups, but, equally importantly, they are also more likely to be the victims of such crimes.

From this perspective, it is more worthwhile to examine the sense of relative deprivation, the subculture, marginalisation and willingness to challenge law and order experienced by young blacks in Britain, especially Afro-Caribbeans. By marginality Lea and Young mean the way young blacks feel pushed to the edge of society, doing less well in school, getting badly paid jobs, being likely to be unemployed, and with few outlets for political expression; relative deprivation refers to their greater expectations of material success compared to older generations, which are nevertheless thwarted by life in Britain; and subcultures emerge out of the mismatch between aspirations and the constraints of reality.

QUESTIONS
1 **How does Left realism differ from earlier theories of ethnicity and crime?**

2 **Are some ethnic minorities more prone to crime than others? If so, why?**

White-collar crime

Sutherland
For the first half of this century, most studies of crime focused on what is usually called 'ordinary crime', dealing with criminal activity such as theft, robbery, burglary, vandalism, assault and murder, where there is typically a perpetrator and a victim. The publication of Edwin Sutherland's *White Collar Crime* in 1949 added a new direction to criminology by bringing crimes committed either for or within businesses into the picture.

Since the publication of this book, the study of white-collar crime has become more, not less, important, not least because the ratio of white-collar to manual jobs has increased throughout the century, to the point where they now outnumber blue-collar jobs in the industrial world. Defining exactly what is meant by white-collar crime, however, has proved more problematic.

Sutherland himself defined it as 'crimes committed by persons of high social status and respectability in the course of their occupations'. Later writers have sought to introduce a distinction between white-collar crimes carried out by employees against a company (such as fraud or embezzlement) and crimes committed by the companies themselves in pursuit of maintaining or increasing their profit margins. These 'corporate crimes' can cover activities as varied as contravening pollution laws, neglecting health and safety legislation or breaking the Food and Drugs Act.

Corporate crime

The diverse nature of corporate crime means that it is not usually revealed in police statistics, issued by the Home Office or Central Office of Information, but separately in information issued by government bodies such as local government environmental health departments, the Ministry of Agriculture or Customs and Excise. These crimes are therefore not defined and labelled in the same way that ordinary crime is, and continue to escape the attention of many criminologists, attracted to more 'glamorous' forms of crime.

Clarke (1990) argues that ordinary and white-collar crimes differ in that white-collar criminals commit crimes in places where they can normally be expected to be found and the police are unwilling to enter. Furthermore, such crimes are often seen as 'complaintless' and frequently resemble legal behaviour, as in the cases of fraud and confidence tricks, where the presence of the victim appears as voluntary. Organised crime syndicates, such as the Mafia, may choose to resemble legitimate businesses and legitimate businesses may employ corrupt or illegal organisations to secure loan repayments, avoid taxes or to discipline labour. In this way, the distinctions between legal, semi-legal and illegal activity become blurred. How corporate crime in particular can be explained is itself the cause of much debate. Businesses, like conventional bank robbers, are principally concerned to make money but, unlike bank robbers, are already making money in an orthodox and legal way. Why should they then turn to crime?

From a positivist point of view, Clinard and Yeager (1980) argue that variables such as company size, growth rate, diversification, market power and resources mean that some businesses, for example the oil, pharmaceutical and motor vehicle industries, are more likely to offend than others. Passas (1990) attempts to use Mertonian strain theory (see pp. 381–82) to explain corporate crime as an 'innovative' response to the strain of meeting cultural expectations of maintaining profits and surviving in highly competitive markets.

The Marxist view

Marxist-influenced explanations have sought to show white-collar (particularly corporate) crime not as exceptional but as endemic to capitalism. Where legal means are blocked then companies will resort to illegal means. As Pearce (1976) argues, for these companies, 'business is business'. This is at its clearest in the Third World, where unregulated and unscrupulous capitalism thrives. Against this, many writers have argued that the quality of goods and safety records improve as capitalism develops and the goodwill of clients and staff needs to be maintained. A further distinction needs to be made between what is seen as good for capitalism as a whole, such as anti-trust laws, and what only benefits individual capitalist concerns. Poor records on corruption, pollution and safety were also common in communist countries. Abuse may therefore be due to the absence of market pressures.

Crime and the State Attention has also been focused on the way governments appear to have encouraged or allowed corporate crime by being deliberately weak on regulation, by deregulating activities altogether, or (as some have argued with the rapid exploitation of oil from the North Sea) by turning a blind eye to safety issues because of a company's importance to the balance of payments. In such cases, white-collar crime is tolerated because the interests of the State and business coincide.

The issue of political will thus looms large, even at as fundamental a level of consideration as why some activities become criminalised in the first place. However, many, including Nelken (1983), argue for 'coherence without conspiracy' in explaining the low level of white-collar prosecutions, which they say is due to problems of definition, the complexity of the issues and the cost, as well as the need to maintain the goodwill of businesses. Nevertheless, Cook (1989) shows that Social Security fraud is treated differently and more severely to a very similar kind of crime: tax fraud.

QUESTIONS

1 **What are the differences between white-collar crime and working-class crime?**

2 **What is meant by the term corporate crime?**

3 **What is the Marxist explanation for corporate crime?**

Official statistics

The official statistics supplied by the Home Office for crimes notified to the police and crimes that have led to arrest and conviction are the basis for our commonsense awareness of what the social profile of a criminal is. This is the main information that has been available to sociologists for them to build up theories concerned with these patterns. The statistics tell us that criminals are overwhelmingly male, disproportionately black, predominantly working class and generally under thirty years old. They live mainly in cities, and since the Second World War, their activity has been on the increase at an alarming rate.

If, for example, we look at serious or indictable crime, the statistics tell us that, in England and Wales, where there were 525,000 known indictable offences (of which 7,000 concerned violence) in 1951, these figures had shot up to 3,661,000 offences in 1985 (of which 122,000 were crimes of violence). The evidence, at first sight, is clear: England and Wales have suffered huge rises in the serious crime rate, with violence in particular being a major cause for concern.

Interpreting the statistics

These statistics can be explained in a number of ways. They can be seen as evidence of a society in decline, where lawlessness and disrespect for the law is rife. When crime statistics rise there are habitual calls for more police and tougher sentences to deter criminals. Blame is placed on parents, and single parents in particular, for failing to bring up their children with proper respect for authority. Lack of 'discipline' is frequently cited and action is called for to restore the disintegrating fabric of society.

Are there other ways of seeing these figures? The criticism of Durkheim's use of official statistics tells us that we should be at least wary of any official statistics which claim to be 'social facts'.

Limitations of statistics

What we are dealing with here are crimes known to the police. The obvious question to ask is: 'What about the crimes not known to the police?' They are nevertheless crimes, although they never become statistics. They are the 'dark figure' of crime. For a wide range of reasons, people, whether victims or not, simply do not always inform the police when they witness or are victims of a crime. As Figure 14.1 shows, the crime with the highest dark figure is vandalism.

Crime surveys

A more accurate picture of the 'real' crime rate can be gained by undertaking sample surveys of people's experience of crime. Four such surveys have been undertaken by the Home Office, with 1981, 1983, 1987 and 1992 as the base years. The 1988 survey by Mayhew *et al.* (1989) claims that for every 100 offences committed:

- only 41 are reported
- only 26 are recorded
- only 7 are cleared up
- only 4 result in a caution or conviction
- only 3 result in a conviction

This process of 'crime shrinkage' means that 93 per cent of all crime is never cleared up. It also implies that at any time, the 7 per cent clear-up rate could inflate itself towards 100 per cent if the priorities of the police, the courts, the public and 'public opinion' change.

Figure 14.1 Recorded and unrecorded crime in England and Wales: by type, 1987

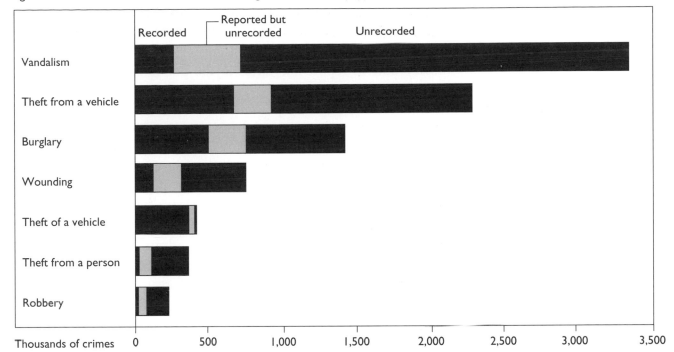

Source: Social Trends 22, 1992

In the specific cases of rape, domestic violence and child abuse there has been a marked change in the way that these crimes are perceived in recent decades. They are more likely to be reported to the police now, because there is a greater confidence than before that the claims of women and children will be taken seriously and offences against them will be recognised as crimes. Domestic violence is less likely to be accepted as something to be endured. This does not, of course, prevent a male-dominated judiciary from occasionally making comments and advising juries in ways that make it clear that their sympathies are not always with the victims. Each time this happens, confidence in the judiciary is dented, for example when judges decide that women are guilty of 'contributory negligence' if they are raped hitch-hiking home from a party in a short skirt. The suggestion is that women in these situations are in some way 'asking for it' and that when they say 'No' they mean 'Yes'.

We are not suggesting that it is the case that women, children and other victims of violence have perfect trust and confidence in the police and judiciary, but where this confidence and sense of injustice does increase, then it can lead to statistical increases without the actual incidence of crime going up. It may even have gone down, but there may be a much higher rate of reporting.

An increase in crime? This is certainly one way that sociologists have explained the apparent increase in the crime rate. Other important contributory factors may be the increase in the number of people who own phones (so they can report to the police with greater ease). Also it is more necessary now to report burglaries to the police in order to make an insurance claim. Another area that has been highlighted is the increased amount of manpower as well as surveillance and information technology now available to the police. The police now routinely use cars, radios, cameras, computers and highly advanced forensic techniques in their battle against crime. There are more police per person. In 1861 the police-to-population ratio was approximately 1:1,000. By 1951 this had risen to 1:694. By the early 1980s this had risen to 1:420. There has also been a considerable increase in the number of civilians (i.e. administrative workers) in the police force. We can therefore say that we are a substantially more policed society than we have ever been before.

It does not necessarily follow, however, that this means that there are more police on the beat, or out looking for criminals. An average force of 2,000 officers might expect to have 100 officers assigned to general patrol at any one time. Studies have shown that as much as 40 per cent of their time can be spent inside police stations, mainly on paperwork. Traffic control also consumes much of their time. It is this side of the police's work that is rarely portrayed by television dramas.

All of this suggests that the world of crime revealed by official statistics needs to be treated with caution. As many sociologists have argued, what appear to be 'social facts' could, on closer examination, be better described as 'social constructions'.

QUESTIONS
1 **Are people committing more crimes today than in previous years?**

2 **How can it be argued that criminal statistics are 'socially constructed'?**

3 **What other sources of knowledge about the extent of crime are there other than official statistics?**

What is the cause of crime?

During the 1980s and up to the present, one thing has become clear to criminologists – the theories developed since the Second World War offer at best only partial explanations of the causes of crime. The main evidence for this is the continued increase in the crime rate in industrialised countries. Although various theories have offered suggestions for reform based on their suggested causes, and in some cases these reforms have found their way into social policy, the crime rate as recorded in official statistics continues to climb regardless (*see* Figure 14.2). This leaves criminology in a crisis, and has prompted a new set of paradigms to attempt to understand why people commit crimes.

Figure 14.2 Notifiable offences recorded by the police

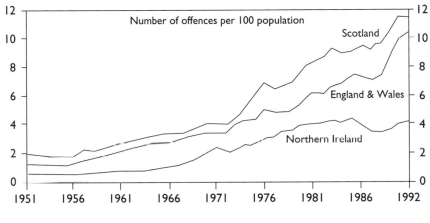

Source: Social Trends 24, 1994

Welfare crime

There has been a psychological response to the failure of the various strands of sociological theory to answer the question 'What causes crime?' The 'social democratic' ideas of the 1950s blamed social conditions and poverty and advocated social reform. This failed and crime rates went up. Marxists offered their analyses, but nobody listened. Crime rates went up. The labelling theorists focused on negotiations between those in control and those who became labelled. Crime rates still went up. All this occurred against the growth of the Welfare State, the elimination of absolute poverty and a return to full employment. This trend is therefore known as 'welfare crime'. A rapid return to Lombrosian views surfaced: the 'neo-classicist' approach which claimed that people 'prone to crime' at birth and those who were inadequately 'conditioned' were the backbone of the criminal classes. The introduction of ideas of the 'hyperactive' child in the 1970s occasioned some people to advocate sterilisation for some parents, to wipe out the criminal strain in human nature. Sociologists and criminologists had to provide explanations, and four paradigms emerged in the 1980s and 1990s as a response. They claim to solve the 'crisis of aetiology', but do they end up as an apology for 40 years of mistaken or partial theorising?

Four new paradigms of criminology

I Left idealism

This paradigm emerged from labelling theory and Marxist analysis, and is represented in the work of Scraton (1985) and Carr-Hill and

407

> **Michel Foucault (1926–84)**
> *French historian specialising in the history of human sciences, penal and medical institutions and sexuality. Foucault is regarded as a structuralist.*

Stern (1979) with some of the main ideas drawn from Foucault (1980). Crime, according to this theory, is caused by inequality and greed. The increasing crime rates are just a reflection of police bias against the working classes and black people. The increase is merely a side effect of more police. This increased police presence causes 'moral panics', police stereotypes reinforce this and the police force cries out for more funding and resources to deal with the crime 'problem' they have helped to create. The amount of crime is exaggerated in order to draw attention away from poverty and exploitation. The role of the police is a political one, relating to control and keeping order, putting down illegal pickets and protecting the State. The public are there to be policed, and the only people who can escape police control are the rich and powerful. The crisis is not one of cause – the cause of crime is the system, which is based on greed. The crisis, according to the Left idealists, is that the police are getting out of control. They advocate policies of decriminalisation and closing down prisons.

2 New administrative criminology

This is not strictly a sociological theory, but one based upon statistical analysis of crime figures carried out by the British Home Office by writers such as Clarke and Mayhew (1980), Clarke and Cornish (1983), and Mayhew and Hough (1983). Points of similarity are to be found with Left idealism in that they both agree that there is no crisis of aetiology. They are both critical of the social democratic theories of the 1950s and 1960s and both paradigms disagree with the response of the New Right, who call for more police and more prisons.

However, when it comes to the cause of crime, they begin to differ. The new administrative criminology (NAC) argues that most crime is opportunist, that is unplanned and carried out on the spur of the moment: an open window, a handbag on the front seat of a car, the empty shop. The best way to deal with this is to improve security measures. Most crime is 'petty', as opposed to 'serious' crime, and the increasing crime rate is caused by people being more willing to report petty crime. The fear of crime is much greater than the reality of crime, and really, statistically speaking, people have little need to worry, if they take the correct security measures.

The most likely victim of crime bears an amazing resemblance to the 'typical criminal' – young, male, single and a heavy drinker. The police play a small role in the detection of crime and arresting criminals, because 90 per cent is reported and solved by the public. The fictional images offered by TV serials, with the police solving crimes by detection, clues and violence mislead us. A realistic police programme would show us images of police dealing with lost property, giving advice, directions and telling people the time but that does not make for exciting viewing. The public play a vital role, and should co-operate with the police in 'Neighbourhood Watch' and other schemes. There is no aetiological crisis as crime is only being reported more. There is no real increase, it just seems as if there is.

The final two paradigms disagree on this, as they both take a 'realist' approach, which accepts that there is a real increase in crime, and also accept that there is no real, overriding explanation as to why this is.

3 New Right realism

James Wilson is the main theorist here, and the title of one of his books *Crime and Human Nature* (1985) gives a heavy clue to the basic assumptions. Crime is caused by a number of factors. Some people are born with a 'proneness to crime', it is a part of their innate physical constitution. There are echoes of Lombroso, Sheldon and Glueck and Hans Eysenck here, and Eysenck's ideas provide another possible causal factor: the importance of social conditioning in the family. The child is socialised inadequately, fails to develop a conscience, and does not know right from wrong. This is compounded by the weak punishments and attractive rewards of crime – crime really can pay. The crime rate has increased, and will continue to rise. This is partly due to the increase in the proportions of young people in the population, who are said to be more impulsive and prone to criminal behaviour. The changes in culture and socialisation in agencies like the family, media, schools and churches mean that people are not being taught respect.

Wilson, being a realist, offers no sure-fire solutions, but points out the difficulties: you cannot change people's physical constitution, and you cannot change the demographic structure. It is both difficult and slow to address the problems of family conditioning, and the culture of American society, and possibly British society, is based upon a grasping, individualistic culture in which everyone is encouraged to grab what they can for themselves. This can lead people to use illegal methods of attaining success.

The New Right advocates a 'trial and error' approach to tackle the crime problem: try various things and see what works. The police are effective if they maintain a high profile, keep order by moving people along and disperse groups. Wilson is adamant that this is the best job that the police do, and the public feel more secure if the police are there to prevent disorder. It is the thought of chaos, 'no-go areas' that frightens the public, so increasing patrols might eventually slow down the crime rate. However, the police are restricted by rules and regulations, and need to be given a free hand. Rather than decriminalise, the New Right approach is to clamp down, give the police powers to control legal deviance, arresting people for being 'suspicious looking', or behaving oddly. Persistent, 'recidivist' criminals should be given massive sentences regardless of their crime, in order to protect the public. The main critic of all these paradigms is Jock Young (1994).

4 Left realist critique

Although there are many points of disagreement between Left and Right realism, there are a number of comparisons. They agree that there is a real problem and people are right to be worried. Both hold that the police–public relationship is vital. Both paradigms agree that little is known, very little can be done and that there is a need for more criminological research. Both paradigms agree that earlier criminological views were partial, and only focused on specific aspects of the problem.

Relative deprivation

New Left realism argues that the main cause of crime is relative deprivation: some people in the social structure feel deprived in relation to the majority of people. The most marginalised groups are the lower working class and certain ethnic minorities. These people feel deprived, and therefore the push towards crime among them is greater. This is much more likely to happen when the political ethos is one of *laissez-faire*, with little or no State control of the economy, so that 'market forces' are allowed to dictate what happens. This was the case in nineteenth-century Britain and under Thatcher in Britain and Reagan in America.

Young stresses that these things only cause crime in certain conditions, in other words, determinism is mistaken. Crime is not inevitable under these conditions, just more likely to occur. The increase in the crime rate is partly explained by the bias amongst those in authority when labelling criminals, but labelling theory does not explain everything. Some behaviour is classed as criminal by all sections of society, so criminal deviance is not merely a product of negotiations. Another factor is the increased sensitivity to crime, which leads to more crime being reported. However, this only gives half of the story, as crime really is increasing, and it is a combination of more crime, less tolerance of crime and more labelling which leads to higher crime rates.

A real approach to crime

The NAC view that the fear of crime is greater than the reality is criticised by Left realism, as there is an undoubted, real risk of crime,

TABLE 14.2 Criminological paradigms, 1980–90

PARADIGM	CAUSE OF CRIME	EXPLANATION OF CRIME RATE	EFFECT OF CRIME	ROLE OF POLICE	ROLE OF PUBLIC	CRISIS OF AETIOLOGY
Left idealism	Inequality, poverty, greed	Reflects police bias, side effect of more police	Police stereotypes, moral panics, more police funding	Political order and control, e.g. strike-breaking	To be policed, unless they are members of powerful groups	Does not exist, no rise in crime just moral panics, only crisis is that police are out of control
New administrative criminology	Opportunist, therefore more security needed	Serious crime is a small part of all crime, petty crime reported more, more opportunities	Typical victim: young/male single/drunk. Fear of crime is greater than reality	90% crime is reported by public. Other demands more time-consuming	Co-operation with police, more Neighbour-hood Watch schemes, more home security	Does not exist, crime is not caused, crime rate is result of increased public reporting
New Right realism	Conditioning, physiology, rewards and punishments of crime	More opportunity, more young impulsive people, no reason not to commit crime	Difficult to change conditioning, part of culture, policing not effective	Police presence encourages informal control to keep 'order'	Good parents, Neighbourhood Watch schemes, help police	Causes are physical constitution, conditioning and the rewards and punishments of crime
New Left realism	Relative deprivation of working-class and black people	Increase in criminal behaviour plus a lower tolerance of deviance	Some areas and some groups are at high risk. Victims those most vulnerable	Should be seen to act justly and fairly	Informal control but not initiated by police, sense of community	Solved – new causation theory of 'relative deprivation'

particularly for vulnerable groups: the elderly, women and children on inner- and outer-city estates. The police play an important role, but if they are seen to be acting unfairly, using brutality, false arrest and so on, then this will lead to more disorder. Social order depends upon a sense of justice and fairness, in the courts, and by the police. This point was amply demonstrated by the events in Los Angeles in 1992, when four white policemen were acquitted of assaulting a black man, after the world had seen them committing it on video. The acquittal led to two nights of riots.

When James Wilson advocates more police and longer sentences, he is encouraging this sort of injustice, which could trigger off more social problems. It is the groups who are marginalised that the police need to co-operate with, and it is just these people who become alienated by blatant injustice. The informal communal controls, which have broken down, are much more effective than 'artificial' systems, like Neighbourhood Watch, which have been imposed by the police.

Reconstructing informal community control means reconstructing the communities, and the Left realist solution is a political one. The crisis of aetiology has been solved, and relative deprivation is the cause of crime. Getting rid of this deprivation means changing society, so getting rid of crime means a new social and political ethos, based upon socialist ideas. The industrial countries with the highest crime rates are those countries with no real socialist parties.

These four new paradigms (*Table* 14.2) are an attempt to cobble together new theories from old. As ever, it is through a battle between these perspectives, in terms of their theoretical coherence, and supporting empirical evidence, that new, more fruitful paradigms will emerge.

QUESTIONS

1 **How does Left idealism differ from Left realism?**

2 **What are the political and ideological assumptions underlying each perspective?**

Suicide

Suicide is a form of deviance. It is so because most people do not do it and because of religious and cultural taboos. The study of suicide also contains in a nutshell the essence of sociological theories and methods.

Suicide is dramatic. It is individualistic and personal. Often it is tragic not only for the person who has committed suicide but for those who are left behind. It might seem that sociology would have nothing to say on this sad subject; surely individual pathology, biology or psychology is more relevant here.

Durkheim's analysis In attempting to get his positivist version of sociology accepted as the way to investigate society, Durkheim (1897) produced a major comparative analysis of the suicide rates among European countries (*see Table* 14.3). The statistical base of the comparison gives the study its positivist, scientific aspect. It has been influential, if only for its large-scale and detailed analysis of what makes people kill themselves. According to Durkheim, personal reasons are irrelevant. Psychological explanations lack scientific validity. A macroanalysis, comparing the only real, social facts about suicide – the national

TABLE 14.3 Rate of suicides per million inhabitants in the different European countries

| | PERIOD | | | NUMERICAL POSITION IN THE | | |
	1866–70	1871–75	1874–78	1ST PERIOD	2ND PERIOD	3RD PERIOD
Italy	30	35	38	1	1	1
Belgium	66	69	78	2	3	4
England	67	66	69	3	2	2
Norway	76	73	71	4	4	3
Austria	78	94	130	5	7	7
Sweden	85	81	91	6	5	5
Bavaria	90	91	100	7	6	6
France	135	150	160	8	9	9
Prussia	142	134	152	9	8	8
Denmark	277	258	255	10	10	10
Saxony	293	267	334	11	11	11

Source: Emile Durkheim, Suicide, 1897

suicide rates between various countries – is needed in order to get at the 'real' reasons for suicide: social reasons. You do not kill yourself; society kills you. This type of explanation works well with positivist and functionalist theory. Functionalists look at external social realities, which are above and beyond individual actions. Positivism relies on measurable, quantifiable details in order to maintain objectivity. In the suicide rates, Durkheim finds both external realities which can be measured and compared between countries, and general laws that can be predicted. The general law on suicide is, he says, that: 'Each society is predisposed to contribute a certain number of voluntary deaths.' In every society, some people 'volunteer' for death. The only thing that varies is the rate from country to country.

Firstly he gathered together secondary data on the number of suicides in various countries. He then examined them in terms of patterns or similarities that may be observed. Next he went on to put forward theories on the social causes of this patterned behaviour. There must be social causes, he argued, because the suicide rates were similar in terms of different countries, different religions and different marital statuses. Individual pathology, psychology or biology did not explain this pattern; sociology did. Suicide was not an act of individual will, it had a social cause. The cause of suicide lay outside the individual. Society causes suicide.

Types of suicide Durkheim argued that social order is possible because society controls or at least severely limits people's behaviour by integration: the process by which we share the values and expectations of others in our society. We are also regulated: society establishes a legitimate set of goals for us and provides some means to achieve these goals. He argued that suicide was the result of too much or too little social regulation. Further, he argued that the form of suicide was determined by an imbalance between these two aspects of social regulation. He cites four different forms of suicide: egoistic, altruistic, anomic and fatalistic. Egoistic suicide occurs when a society is characterised by a lack of integration. Durkheim observed that Catholic societies have a lower rate of suicide than Protestant societies. This is due, he argued, to the individual being integrated into religion and the church which is in turn integrated into the State and civil society. In Catholic societies individuals are encouraged to take their problems to the church and the priest plays a major (some would say intrusive) part in social life. Problems are more likely to be resolved and sins can be forgiven in the confessional. Once forgiven the sinner is reintegrated into the body of the church and by extension, therefore, the wider society. Italy is a strongly Catholic society and has a low suicide rate; Saxony in Germany is strongly Protestant and has a high suicide rate.

Durkheim also observed that married people and especially couples with children were much less likely to commit suicide than single, divorced or widowed people. The family integrates its members and the family is integrated into the wider society. (For a contrary view to this see chapter 4.) Egoistic suicide occurs when an individual lacks or loses group support. They are not part of society; they do not fit in; they are not integrated.

Egoistic suicide

Durkheim considered that egoistic suicide would increase as societies were transformed from traditional (pre-industrial) to modern societies. This is because in traditional societies people are bound together by shared beliefs and values and by ascribed status. This he called mechanical solidarity. In industrial societies the basis of social integration is very different and is based on people needing each other indirectly. The increased division of labour increases differences, creates mutual interdependence and causes organic solidarity which is less strong a force than mechanical solidarity. People are less integrated in modern society, and so egoistic suicide increases.

Altruistic suicide

Altruistic suicide may be regarded as the opposite of egoistic suicide. It occurs when an individual is over-integrated into society. The individual places a greater value on society, the social group or 'the cause' than they do on themselves. They are willing to give up their life for the greater good or glory. Durkheim thought that this form of suicide was greater in traditional societies than in modern societies which place a greater value on the importance of the individual. Some examples of this form of suicide include: soldiers, particularly the élite corps who are trained to place a very high value on the corps, the regiment, the monarch, country or president. It is not just élite soldiers though. In the Battle of the Somme in 1916 60,000 soldiers died in one day, 1.5 million in five months, many of them dying in an appallingly gruesome manner.

In Hindu culture it still occurs that on the death of her husband a woman will throw herself onto his funeral pyre, thus committing 'suttee'. She is nothing without him. The deaths of some 'terrorists' are altruistic, as is the practice of hara-kiri and kamikaze missions. Altruistic suicide is not confined to other cultures nor is it a thing of the past.

Anomic suicide

Anomic suicide is more typical of modern industrial society, argued Durkheim. We can think of anomie as a state in which our old norms and values have become irrelevant in a particular situation or context. This is often due to sudden social change which may result in downward or upward mobility. We can envisage the 'loss', in every sense of the word, for those, once rich, thrown upon hard times. Those who suffer this experience find that their social world and their friends often change. What they experience is being transported into another world full of alien people with alien values and behaviour. What is worse is that there is only one way back home and they cannot afford it.

An example of this form of suicide was provided in the 1929 Wall Street Crash when a number of stockbrokers threw themselves from high office windows. A less dramatic form of anomie occurs to 'skidders' – those who experience downward social mobility. The 1980s and early 1990s has been a period of economic restructuring which has resulted in fortunes being made and lost. It is likely that anomie may be a useful concept to explain much suicide in this period. In any event modern society tends to encourage high expectations of material rewards which are not easy for everyone to achieve. The gap between hopes and reality may result in some people becoming very unhappy with their lot in life.

Perhaps less easy to imagine is a situation in which we suddenly gain a vast amount of money. How would you know who your friends were? Does your lover really love you or just your money? What would you do if you did not work? Do you really want to spend your time with new 'friends'? Such 'problems' may occur for people who win the pools, the National Lottery or inherit a fortune.

Fatalistic suicide

Fatalistic suicide may be regarded as the opposite of anomic suicide. This form of suicide is caused by there being no change. There is no prospect of improvement, no hope. The individual is over-controlled. Perhaps due to misguided optimism Durkheim thought that this form of suicide was of very little importance in contemporary society. He thought that it might be the cause of suicide for slaves or for some long-term prisoners. Fatalism has long been regarded as one characteristic of traditional working-class culture. We might also postulate that 'fatalism' may be a characteristic of the new 'underclass' of the 1980s and 1990s.

The interactionist critique

A very different way of examining suicide has come from that branch of sociology known as interactionism. Two theorists are particularly relevant here: Jack Douglas (1967), a symbolic interactionist, and J. Maxwell Atkinson (1978), viewing suicide from an ethnomethodological stance. These theorists put forward a general critique of positivism, arguing that the social world cannot be studied in the same way as the natural world because human beings have consciousness, their actions are influenced by the meanings or interpretations that individuals put on social forces or external stimuli. What matters is not what goes on outside of the individual (objective reality) but what goes on inside their heads (subjective reality). There are therefore no social facts. Suicide is not an unambiguous social fact to be innocently compiled, tabulated and correlated ready for a scientist to look for explanations or causes (hence the rejection of causality). On the contrary, suicide is a label that is attached to a particular phenomenon after a social process of interpretation, negotiation and decision-making. Suicide is socially defined; it is a social construct.

Interactionists criticise Durkheim for an uncritical acceptance and use of statistics for the above reasons and because these statistics have been compiled by people other than sociologists, often for very different reasons. The quantity and quality of such statistics are open to manipulation and misuse.

Douglas

Suicide does not have a single meaning for everyone within a society or between societies. Thus Douglas argues that we cannot assume that in Catholic societies people do actually commit less suicide than in Protestant societies. In Catholic societies suicide is a mortal sin which results in eternal damnation. Relatives will be severely distressed if it is thought that their loved one committed suicide. The deceased and their family will suffer stigmatisation in the community if such a label is attached. There is therefore a social pressure not to attach this label. A process of negotiation may take place which results in a particular death being interpreted as, say, accidental death.

It may not be the case that single people commit more suicide than married people with families. It is possible that the husband or wife of a deceased person would, being the first on the scene of the death, be predisposed to destroying some of the evidence that a suicide had taken place, for example they may destroy a suicide note, their objective being to avoid social shame or distress to other members of the family. Police and coroners in some senses have to negotiate with those who are left behind. For single people there is no one to cover up their actions, the first person on the scene of the death is more likely to be a stranger with less vested interest in 'bending' the assessment of the cause of death. There is no family to upset and police and coroners are freer to reach their own conclusion.

Atkinson   Atkinson is particularly interested in this process of negotiation and definition. The suicide note is often a major cue which influences this decision positively. Yet, as we have seen, notes can be destroyed by loved ones and murderers may forge suicide notes. Relatively few suicide notes are found at the scene of a death which later becomes diagnosed as suicide.

Evidence shows that the mode of death is given great significance by coroners. Road deaths are usually labelled as accidental. Though a gruesome form of death, this is regarded as a common form of suicide despite it not being labelled as such. Perhaps the thinking here is that because there are a great number of road accidents, it is possible that the death was accidental, and therefore it is acceptable to attach the accidental death label in this circumstance. Hanging, on the other hand, is fairly difficult to do accidentally yourself, therefore it is usually labelled as suicide. This tends to sidestep the fact that it is not particularly difficult to be hanged by someone else, in which case the verdict could be murder.

Death by drug or alcohol overdose presents more difficulties for coroners. The line between getting 'out of it' temporarily and for ever is often a fine one. Coroners tend to use the quantity of drugs taken as a guideline in their decision-making as to whether the death was intentional or not. It seems to be more accepted that the elderly who die from an overdose did so accidentally because they were likely to be confused than a young person who, it is thought, has more awareness and intent as to what they are doing.

Another cue that is often used by coroners is that a person who dies through drowning at sea is more likely to have committed suicide if their clothes were left neatly folded than if they were not. The folding of the clothes implies premeditation and intent or, of course, it could be the usual behaviour of a very tidy person. In the 1970s, the Labour MP John Stonehouse was at first thought to have committed suicide when his clothes were found on the beach neatly folded after he had disappeared. It was later discovered that he had disappeared due to his involvement in fraud.

The 'amplification' of suicide

Atkinson also refers to cultural or social influences which may amplify the real or perceived incidence of suicide. He refers to the widespread view in our society that students are prone to commit suicide due to exam, parental and social pressure. The more students hold this view the more likely they are to contemplate suicide as a solution to their problems. The more coroners share this view the more likely they are to label a student death as suicide. The more suicide verdicts there are on student deaths, the more the media will highlight this. The more the media highlights this, the more students are likely to contemplate it, and so on. Thus society amplifies the incidence of suicide.

Interactionists have argued that suicide is best understood as a form of secondary deviance. They see it as a reaction to stigmatisation, to the application of a label to them. Such labels may include failure, being terminally ill or poor. It is important to know who attaches these labels and how the process works. Coroners are likely to be influenced by the past personal, medical and psychological biography of an individual, particularly if they were prone to being depressed or psychotic.

Interactionists reject the reliance on statistics and instead focus their study on individual cases of suicide and attempt to discover the meaning of the act for the individual suicidee, their family and friends. They then are in a position to discover if there are any patterns to these individual meanings. Such patterned meaning may include revenge, repentance, escape and a cry for help. We may then be able to link these patterns to wide social and cultural influences.

Parasuicides

We can see that in the study of suicide the theoretical perspectives are sharply exposed and opposed. We can say that, even from within the empiricist tradition, strong criticisms have been made of Durkheim's reliance on official statistics of actual suicide rates. Ettlinger and Flordah (1955) found that out of 500 cases of self-injury almost 90 per cent were 'gambles with fate'. These were situations in which there was a very serious risk of death. The individual had made no plans that would ensure their discovery in time. These are not fake suicides, they are not mere attempts to draw attention to oneself; on the other hand they are not suicides because they were not successful. They are known as parasuicides. Most people in this situation are not sure whether they want to live or die. They undertake a 'trial by ordeal' in which the outcome is left up to fate. There are approximately 100,000 admissions to hospitals in England and Wales every year under this category. What is important to note here is that Durkheim and those who have followed in his footsteps did not count these parasuicides. If he had done so he may have come up with very different theories.

It is also necessary to point out that the simple dichotomy of positivism on the one hand and phenomenology (or interpretivism) on the other, is perhaps a false one – or at least not a simple one. Douglas does not escape the positivist trap entirely. He rejects the use of suicide statistics because they are the result of a process of negotiation and are unreliable. He argues that we should focus on meanings. The way to get to these meanings is to carefully study case histories and documentary evidence. Yet these, too, are the result of a process of negotiation. If it is possible to get an accurate description of suicide cases then it is possible to get accurate statistics.

Feminists have also criticised Durkheim for what they see as his sexism. This is evident in his discussion of differential rates of suicide for widows and widowers. A widow is less likely to commit suicide, firstly because 'her sensibility is rudimentary rather than highly developed' and secondly because, being less a part of society, she does not have the same need for social support systems: 'With a few devotional practices and some animals to care for, the old unmarried woman's life is very full. Very simple social forms satisfy all her needs.' Women are less complex and also more the product of nature than society. With women, it is argued, his social analysis breaks down because he fails to see them as fully socially determined as he does men.

A new synthesis

In a recent study of suicide, and in an attempt to escape the problems that have dogged the study of suicide in particular, Steve Taylor (1990) uses a realist scientific approach (see chapter 1) to investigate this phenomenon. In doing so, he believes he is following Durkheim, whose search for the 'structural switches' that influence behaviour has been overemphasised, allowing him to be too readily characterised as a positivist theorist. Unlike Durkheim, however, he stresses not the degree of integration into the social structure but the individual's thoughts and feelings about themselves and the people closest to them.

Taylor categorises suicide in four ways, under two main headings: ectopic and symphysic. Ectopic suicides are inner-directed, demonstrating what a person thinks of themselves. They can be either submissive, when a person is certain they no longer want to live, or thanatative, resulting from someone's decision to gamble with their life (e.g. Russian roulette). Symphysic or other-directed suicides are mainly attempts to let others know how desperate someone is feeling. People commit sacrifice suicides to let others know how much they have been hurt and disappointed. Appeal suicides can often be dramatic attempts to show other people how they feel about others close to them.

In terms of deviance the study of suicide brings to the fore many classic arguments. Does society cause the act? Is it the result of too little or too much constraint, too much or too little integration, too much or too little regulation? These are arguments over the validity of statistics and causal explanations based on them. Suicide can be seen as secondary deviance, the result of a deviancy amplification spiral and a social construct.

QUESTIONS

1 **What are social facts?**

2 **What are social constructs?**

3 **What are the main criticisms of Durkheim's approach to the study of suicide?**

4 **What is the importance of the study of suicide to the theory and methods of sociology?**

Murder

Having looked at the important section on suicide, what issues would you expect to be involved in a sociology of murder? What aspects would the dominant perspectives focus on? Could there, for example, be an interactionist approach? Would the methodological problems raised by the study of suicide re-emerge?

One of the best-known studies of murder has been undertaken by the American M.E. Wolfgang (1958). He looked at the class background of those convicted of homicide, and found that the vast majority, between 90 and 95 per cent, were from the manual working class, although the victims came from a wider class background. Other studies have argued that the motives for homicide differ according to the class of the murderer – middle-class killers are much more likely to have financial motives, and to hire someone to do their killing for them, while working-class murders are far more likely to originate from small arguments about nothing. Katz (1988) found that of 56 upper-class people who had been involved in the killing of their husband or wife, 11 had hired someone to do it for them.

British statistics are revealing. In 1988 there were 592 homicides in England and Wales (Scotland and Northern Ireland have different judicial systems), of which 356 were murders of men and 236 involved female victims. This distinction between male and female is important. 45 per cent of female victims were killed by their partner as opposed to only 7 per cent of male victims being killed by their partner. 13 per cent of female victims were killed by someone unknown to them; 37 per cent of male victims were killed by an unknown attacker.

Of the total of 592 people murdered, 22 per cent were killed by their partners or ex-partners, 51 per cent by someone, such as a relative, who was known to them, and only 27 per cent by a stranger. More than 80 per cent of the homicides of women were of a 'domestic' character. Most murders occur at the weekend. A similar picture emerges from Katz's study, where only 3 per cent of murders were carried out by women killing other women, and in his study only 6 per cent of the victims of female murders were unknown to their killers.

From a positivist point of view, the sociology of murder is substantially about working-class men killing people close to them in their leisure time. Land *et al.* (1990) have taken this a step further and argued, with clear echoes of Durkheim, that the probability of homicide increases the more economically deprived an area is; it increases as population density increases; and it correlates with high divorce rates among males.

Katz has been particularly concerned to understand the normative framework in which murderers exist at the time of the killing. In the case of 'domestic' murders he focuses on ideas of righteousness and sensuousness, or what he calls 'distinctive sensual dynamics'. Usually, killers do not care about the legality of what they are doing, which makes the concept of deterrence problematic. By righteousness he means the killer's belief that what they are doing is morally correct, a defence of respectability (for example marriage vows) or property rights. In some cases the killer's own sense of self-worth has been challenged and humiliated, leading to escalating righteous indignation, often resulting from small arguments that get out of hand.

Marxists see murder in a much broader way, moving away from individuals and anticipating the concept of genocide as a form of war crime. In the mid nineteenth century, Friedrich Engels (1845) wrote: 'Murder has been committed if thousands of workers have been deprived of the necessities of life or if they have been forced into a situation in which it is impossible for them to survive. Murder has been committed if society knows perfectly well that thousands of workers cannot avoid being sacrificed so long as these conditions are allowed to continue. Murder of this sort is just as culpable as the murder committed by an individual. At first sight it does not seem murder at all because responsibility for the death of the victim cannot be pinned on any individual assailant ... But it is murder all the same.'

QUESTIONS

1 **What would an interactionist view of murder focus on?**

2 **How reliable are the statistics of murder?**

3 **How does the sociology of murder compare with its media portrayal?**

FURTHER READING

P. Aggleton, *Deviance*, Routledge, 1991

H. Becker, *Outsiders*, The Free Press, 1973

L. Gelsthorpe and A. Morris, *Feminist Perspectives in Criminology*, Open University Press, 1990

P. Gilroy, **There Ain't No Black in the Union Jack**, Hutchinson, 1987

M. Maguire *et al.* (eds.), **The Oxford Handbook of Criminology**, Oxford University Press, 1994

F. Pearce, *Crimes of the Powerful*, Pluto Press, 1986

P. Rock and D. Downes, **Understanding Deviance: Guide to the Sociology of Crime and Rule-breaking**, Oxford University Press, 1995

J. Young, *Realist Criminology*, Sage, 1988

15 The mass media

INTRODUCTION

The chapter begins by looking at models of the mass media: pluralist, mass manipulative and hegemonic models. The discussion moves on to concentrate on two sociological methods: semiology and ethnomethodology. You will then examine the role of the press, television and bias, news values, agenda-setting and gatekeeping. The chapter then examines television and stereotyping. Attitude formation and the reinforcement of values by the media are then analysed alongside the debate around the suggested link between television and violence. The next section discusses the work of Stan Cohen on the amplification of deviance and the chapter closes with an examination of new technology, the mass media and mass culture.

Sociology and the mass media

The analysis of all the forms of media (visual, audio and printed matter) is a field which has grown rapidly in order to keep up with the rapidly changing means of communication. The fast-changing technologies which bring us media messages lead to a sociology which studies the content and the impact of these various forms of communication, a branch of study which struggles to keep up with its subject matter. It was not until 1991 that the first articles by sociologists and psychologists discussing video games and their effects appeared. The impact of new forms of entertainment and education such as 'virtual reality' have yet to be felt. Sociologists of the media are always a long way behind the area they are investigating.

The sociologists' main concerns are: who controls the content of the mass media and how do the media affect our ideas about society? How much influence do the media have on our political, economic, social and cultural views? Do we accept and believe everything we see, hear and read, or are other social forces more important in shaping our social experiences? Marxists, pluralists, feminists, and the various brands of interpretive sociology all have their competing explanations.

Models of the mass media

Pluralist model

The public gets what the public wants

The pluralist view is the liberal, free-thinking, consensus and pressure-group view, in some ways resembling a functionalist approach in its emphasis on consensus. There are a large number of media outlets, and this plurality of types means that the needs and interests of all groups in society will be catered for. Bias is inevitable, but the public gets what it wants, and you are free to choose your particular brand of bias. If you do not want to see half-naked women and read about lurid sex crimes, buy *The Times* instead of the *Sun* (both owned by Rupert Murdoch's News International). News is gathered from a plurality of sources, again ensuring impartial representations. Anything is newsworthy, depending on the medium used. Anything obscene is not allowed, nor is any seditious material which brings the royal family into disrepute. Anything libellous or against the Official Secrets Act is out but, apart from these, anything goes. There is a wide variety of choice, and the public can discriminate.

The 'uses and gratifications' approach is an important concept in the pluralist model, allowing for:

1 selective exposure – we choose which messages we are exposed to;
2 selective perception – we react to different parts of the message in different ways, according to whether we agree with it or not;
3 selective retention – we remember what we want to remember.

In short, as a viewer, reader or listener you can choose what you want to watch, read or hear, and if you do not like it you can turn it off. If you are exposed to it, you can choose how to receive it, instead of passively taking it in (as proposed by the hypodermic model (see p. 438). After you have been exposed to it, you will only recall the bits you particularly liked or hated. The pluralist model uses this approach to show that, at the very most, the media's influence is restricted to reinforcing the ideas you already hold.

Criticisms of the pluralist model

Critics of the pluralist model argue that if the media are left to market forces, then the range of opinions presented is likely to decrease, as increasing competition means that all media cater to the 'lowest common denominator'. Also, research shows that portrayals of women and ethnic minorities in the media do influence people's

Newspapers
New York Post *and* Boston Herald
(USA)
The Times, The Sunday Times, *the*
Sun, *the* News of the World *(UK)*
Tallozo, Mai Nap, Reform
(Hungary)
The Australian *and 108 other titles
in Australia*
The Fiji Times *(Fiji)*
Post Courier *(Papua New Guinea)*
Sunday Morning Post, Wah Kiu Yat
Po *(Hong Kong)*

Television
*Twentieth Century Fox Broadcasting
and eight other affiliated stations
(USA)*
BSkyB *(UK)*
Antenna 3 *(Spain)*
Seven Network *(Australia)*
Star Television *(Hong Kong)*
Vox *(Germany)*

Books
*HarperCollins Publishers including
Perennial, Zondervan, Fontana,
Grafton, Thorsons and Tolkein, in
USA, UK and Australia*

Magazines
Mirabella, TV Guide *and* FSI
Division *in the USA*
Times *supplements and* Shoppers
Friend *(UK)*
New Idea, TV Week, Australian
Post *and four other titles in Australia*

Criticisms of the
mass-manipulative model

views and ideas, particularly those of children and adolescents. Another argument against pluralism is the concentration of media ownership in a small number of companies. Rupert Murdoch is usually held up as the prime example of this.

The media world is a small one, and those people who work within it come from similar backgrounds, have similar ideas and attitudes. This means that the range of views expressed is limited – a white middle-class outlook.

Pluralists respond to these criticisms by claiming that the media reflect the tastes and opinions of the public. If women and blacks appear in stereotyped, traditional images, then this is what the majority expect and want to see. The debate here degenerates into a 'chicken and egg' situation. The model which is most at odds with that offered by the pluralists is the 'mass-manipulative' model.

The mass-manipulative model

This is a version of the Marxist model, and it sees the bias of the media as a straightforward reflection of capitalist ideological values. There are a few press agencies which monopolise the news. The lives of ordinary people, or any radical viewpoints, are ignored, and a stream of show-business trivia and the lives of the rich and famous are daily fare. In Britain, where the media are partially State-controlled and mainly privately owned, the State and capitalism go hand-in-hand. The so-called press barons are usually rewarded with peerages and knighthoods for a lifetime spent churning out capitalist ideology. Media controllers like Rupert Murdoch and the late Robert Maxwell make no secret of their power and influence over what they publish and show. The capitalists own the media and control distribution. Radical press and independent newspapers are often banned from retail outlets and distribution. When the power of capital works with the government, then the public is served up straight capitalist propaganda.

Pluralists would argue that the concentration of ownership of the media amongst a small group of capitalists does not prove that the content is affected at all. Journalists and others can and do resist attempts from above to control their output. Reports are published and programmes broadcast which are openly critical of some aspects of capitalism, and there is a strong tradition of radical investigative journalism. Newspapers such as the *Guardian* and the *Independent*, which are not owned by the media monopolies, also have a strong tradition and a loyal readership. The main pluralist argument is again that the major factor influencing what the media produce reflects the people's choice. Any attempt to force values upon them would be a bad financial move. Finally, it has been pointed out that both sides of the political spectrum, left and right wing, are critical of the BBC, with the likes of the Glasgow University Media Group highlighting right-wing bias, and Norman Tebbit calling them the 'Bolshevik Broadcasting Corporation'. A third model, which is very similar to the manipulative model, is the hegemonic model.

The hegemonic model

Hegemony is rule through consent from ideological leadership rather than brute force or coercion. It suggests that the mass-manipulative model is too specific and simplistic. The idea of the ruling class spreading their ideology through the media in such a straightforward, mechanical fashion leads us to believe that a group of capitalists sit huddled in darkened rooms plotting just how the news will reflect capitalist ideology that week. Such conspiracy theories do not explain the all-pervasive influence of these ideas. The hegemonic model argues that the media pass over their messages using language and ideas which reflect consensual values.

Gramsci

Antonio Gramsci (1891–1937), an Italian Marxist theorist, whose research was limited due to ten years in Mussolini's prisons, developed and refined the concept of hegemonic political leadership. He makes the important point that any ideological viewpoint is not tied to one class, but is adrift in society, there to be harnessed and used by any group. The dominant group in any society is the one which can pin the greatest number of ideologies to its flagpole. In capitalist Britain, the white middle class has the monopoly on ideological ideas and their use. It is therefore the values of this group which permeate the media. 'Newsworthiness' is defined by this group, as they are the people mainly working within and controlling the media. The values of nationalism, democracy and free-market competition are at the forefront, and most media output is aimed at the lowest common denominator. The middle class is the affluent group, and advertising ensures that a specialist area of the media is reserved for them. For example, the masses get their daily dose of royal family stories from the *Sun* and the *Mirror*. The affluent get theirs from the *Tatler*. 'High' culture or 'low' culture, it's all the same message.

Glasgow University Media Group

The work of the Glasgow University Media Group (see pp. 431–33) is a good example of this approach. If the output of the mass media reflects the values of the ruling class it is because 'most top journalists share a similar social and cultural background with the hierarchies of the state. More importantly, the routine working practices of journalists are informed by the class assumptions of the society in which they live' (GUMG, 1982). In the field of news production, 'the world view of journalists will prestructure what is to be taken to be important or significant ... First it will affect the character and content of specific inferential frames used in the news ... Second it will set general boundaries on where news is looked for, and on who are the significant individuals, the "important" people to be interviewed' (GUMG, 1980).

Three views of the content and effects of the mass media are therefore discernible. Significantly, there are strong parallels here with the sociology of politics, where similar arguments have been put forward. In both areas, some writers have sought to highlight the plurality of ideas and representation in the mass media – for example Gurevitch and Blumler (1977), Tunstall (1983) and Whale (1977) – and the plurality of power groups in a liberal democracy. Ralph Miliband (1969) constructs an instrumentalist view of both the State and the mass media, emphasising the common ruling-class background of both media barons and leading figures in the State. Structuralists (whose position closely corresponds but is not identical to the hegemonic view) such as Graham Murdock (1980) argue that, as with the State, 'proprietors and other capitalists do not need to intervene in newspaper production since the logic of the prevailing market structure ensures that by and large the output endorses rather than opposes their general interests'.

QUESTIONS

1 **Do the mass media represent all groups in society?**

2 **What are the differences between the pluralist and hegemonic models?**

3 **How has the media's portrayal of the royal family changed in the 1990s? What reasons could be given for this change?**

Semiology and ethnomethodology

Ethnomethodology

This section looks at ways of researching the media, concentrating on two methods – semiology and ethnomethodology. The latter theory was developed by Garfinkel (1967; see chapter 1) and proposes that each individual is a sociologist, attempting to make sense of each situation by giving it a structure. From this point of view media research is a waste of time. How can we create a theory or model of the effects of the media if each individual is busily constructing their own version of social reality? Each newspaper article or TV programme will affect each individual in a unique way. Therefore it is not useful to construct models which try to explain the effects of the media upon the group. Research can only be concerned with the way individuals construct their realities, using the media as one of many social influences. Semiology takes a slightly different view.

Semiology

Semiology is the science of the life of signs in society. Anything which has symbolic significance in society can function as a sign, and semiologists study literature, film, art, fashion, billboards and all the areas of the mass media. Each form of media is a 'text' to be read in a certain way containing a hidden, usually ideological meaning. All texts are also 'polysemic' – many messages can be read into each one, as many as human minds are capable of devising. There is a similarity here with the ethnomethodological view, but the semiologists assume that whoever produces the text – author, photographer, biscuit-tin designer – will 'encode' the preferred meanings, the ones they want us to read. This means that they will try to ensure that the meanings which we associate with the text are the ones the text is intended to convey. For example, when a soap powder advertiser uses lots of white-coated scientists to push a product, the association is meant to be with science and its methods as a benevolent force, working to get your clothes as clean as possible. Scientific advance makes you more attractive, cleaner and more odour-free. We could, however, see science and scientists as destructive, cold and calculating, polluting and destroying the earth and its atmosphere.

Encoders and encoding

'Encoders' try to ensure that we go along with their version of the message. We read the connotations of the signs in the intended way. Applying this to the media, we can see that the encoded texts push us into a certain type of understanding of the images. If ideological ideas about the world are presented concerning, for example, family values, honesty, hard work, nationalistic and patriotic messages, pro-capitalist, pro-democracy, racist and sexist ideologies, and presented as encoded messages, then the task of the sociologist of the media is to try to unravel the ways in which the messages are received. Neither type of research can be reduced to statistical, quantitative methods, instead each relies on the qualitative analysis of interpretive sociology.

QUESTIONS

1 **What is semiology?**

2 **What is involved in an ethnomethodological approach to the mass media?**

The press

'Quality' and 'popular' newspapers

The press is usually divided by media analysts into 'quality' and 'popular'. The quality papers are larger, have smaller print, fewer photos, more in-depth analysis of current events and political affairs, especially world news, fewer stories about zany pets and sordid sensationalism, not so much sport and harder crosswords. They are intellectual, analytical and are bought every day by a minority of the newspaper-purchasing public. The popular papers are garish, simplistic with banner headlines, small words in large print, lots of photos and cartoons, 'wacky' stories, an abundance of breasts, pages of sport, competitions, special offers, scandal, gossip and easy crosswords. They cater for the lowest possible taste, are simplistic and easy to read, and most people who buy newspapers plump for them — hence the 'popular' tag. When it comes to the social class of their readership, it should come as no surprise to find that the popular papers are consumed by the lower groups according to the Registrar-General's scheme — the C2, D and E groups, whilst the inhabitants of classes A, B and C1 eagerly devour the offerings of the so-called 'quality' press (*see Tables* 15.1 *and* 15.2). The names of the papers indicate their position — the *Sun* rises every morning, it is bright and cheerful and sheds light on the stories of the day. *The Times* reports events as we live through these times, the *Telegraph* is a dated form of communication, the *Guardian* guards our values and the truth, the *Star* is on another planet, and so on.

Newspapers traditionally support one or other of the main political parties. The method of support may be more or less obvious — from banner headlines insisting that we 'Vote Tory' to stories which present an issue in pro-government or pro-opposition terms.

One of the questions asked by sociologists concerns how much influence these papers have in deciding their readers' voting behaviour (see chapter 8). At this stage you should be in a position to give the arguments which would be presented by the hegemonic, the mass-manipulative and the pluralist viewpoints.

The hegemonic view

This view argues that as all parties represent the same middle-class, pro-capitalist values it does not really matter which paper you read. They all promote the same ideological view of the world. The only choices offered are capitalist choices. The Tories are most closely associated with the white middle-class view, so the press supports them most.

The mass-manipulative view

This view argues that as most of the press is Tory, this ensures capitalist ideology permeates all the papers, whether Labour or Conservative. There is a strong bias towards the Conservative Party.

TABLE 15.1   Reading of national newspapers: by social class and gender, 1993–4

	AB	CI	C2	DE	Males	Females	All adults	Readership (millions)	Readers per copy (numbers)
PERCENTAGE READING EACH PAPER									
Daily newspapers									
The Sun	7	18	29	30	25	19	22	9.9	2.5
Daily Mirror	7	13	22	20	18	14	16	7.1	2.8
Daily Mail	14	13	8	6	10	9	10	4.5	2.5
Daily Express	9	10	8	5	8	7	8	3.5	2.5
The Daily Telegraph	6	6	2	1	7	5	6	2.6	2.6
Daily Star	1	4	7	7	7	3	5	2.2	2.9
Today	3	4	5	3	4	3	4	1.8	3.1
The Guardian	8	3	1	1	3	3	3	1.3	3.4
The Times	8	3	1	1	4	2	3	1.3	2.9
The Independent	6	3	1	1	3	2	2	1.1	3.5
Financial Times	5	2	–	–	2	1	2	7.4	4.2
Any national daily newspaper	61	58	64	59	65	56	60	27.4	–
Sunday newspapers									
News of the World	11	23	36	36	29	26	27	12.4	2.6
Sunday Mirror	9	16	24	21	19	17	18	8.1	3.1
The Mail on Sunday	18	17	11	6	13	13	13	5.9	3.0
The People	6	12	16	15	14	11	12	5.6	2.8
Sunday Express	13	13	9	5	11	10	10	4.6	2.8
The Sunday Times	21	8	3	2	9	7	8	3.7	3.0
Sunday Telegraph	11	4	2	1	5	4	4	1.9	3.1
The Observer	9	4	2	1	4	3	4	1.6	3.2
Independent on Sunday	7	3	1	1	3	2	3	1.2	3.5
Sunday Sport	1	2	3	3	3	1	2	9.0	3.5
Any Sunday newspaper	69	68	72	65	70	66	68	30.9	–

Source: National Readership Surveys (NRS) Ltd

TABLE 15.2   Circulation of national daily newspapers, 1930–95 (thousands)

	1930	1960	1995
Daily Herald/Sun (from 1964)	750	1467	4076
Daily Mirror	630	4545	2492
Daily Star	—	—	754
Daily Mail	1968	2084	1894
Daily Express	1603	4130	1253
Daily Telegraph	222	1155	1052
Guardian	51	190	404
The Times	187	255	673
Independent	—	—	294

Source: compiled from Butler and Butler (1994) and Audit Bureau of Circulation

The pluralist view   For pluralists, there is a fair spread of political ideas and opinions from all sides of the spectrum. You buy the paper that supports the views you agree with, the choice is yours. Against this view, though, surveys show that the majority of *Sun* readers – an indisputably Tory paper (though Murdoch has hinted it may one day support Labour) – actually vote or identify most strongly with the Labour Party.

The two-step flow model suggests that the immediate circle of people around an individual, and particularly opinion leaders within it, steers individuals towards a paper which reflects the viewpoint they hold. Reading the same paper is like being a member of a club which reinforces the views you hold, rather than directly influencing you.

Really bad news: television and bias

In an important series of books (1976, 1980, 1982 and 1985) the Glasgow University Media Group (GUMG) and Greg Philo (1990) systematically investigated whether television lived up to its statutory obligation to present news in an unbiased way.

The technique they used to do this was a form of content analysis. The GUMG video-recorded a series of news programmes and enumerated the number of times an issue was presented, how long relevant actors were given to put their case, how events were described by journalists and in what setting interviews took place.

In their first book they examined the presentation of industrial relations issues, arguing from what they believed was the evidence that some disputes were singled out for particular attention over other, perhaps larger, ones. They found that strikes were displayed as chiefly the responsibility of 'troublemaking' trade unionists rather than 'incompetent' managers, and that other industrial relations issues such as health and safety were comparatively ignored.

In the next book they asserted that the language used to describe industrial disputes was again biased against unions – they make 'demands' and 'claims', while management 'offer' and 'propose'. Management are interviewed in their boardrooms, appearing as calm, rational and reasonable, while strikers have microphones thrust at them on picket lines, frequently with violent backdrops. A consensus, rather than conflict, view of industrial relations is presented, where the management's view is clearly thought to represent the consensus position. This, according to the GUMG, is what television believes is 'balanced'.

The work of the GUMG has made a significant contribution to the wider debate about the ideological role of news journalists, editors and producers. They do not need to be openly biased in the way news is reported – they do not have to tell us what to think – but they can tell us what to think about by making a clear statement about what they believe are the important issues of the day. They do this in two ways, by 'agenda-setting' and 'gate-keeping'.

News values, agenda-setting and gate-keeping

According to their own 'news values' – their own beliefs about what constitutes 'news' – they can set agendas by prioritising some issues over others, most obviously by the order in which they are presented, and the amount of time and resources used to cover them. They can also choose to ignore some issues altogether. Organisations such as the Campaign for Nuclear Disarmament, the Greenham women and gay and lesbian groups have frequently complained that they have had their protests shut out by such 'gate-keeping'.

Sociologists have considered a number of reasons for this selectivity. It has been argued that news values have a logic of their own, independent of what is actually happening 'out there'. Very little of what is called 'news' is in fact new. Much of the news is predictable reporting of the day in politics, particularly in parliament, government statistics, royal engagements, weddings or divorces, or international conferences. Everyone knew these were going to happen. The rest of the reported issues take priority not because they are important (important to who?) but because they are immediate ('news has just come in that…'), dramatic, titillatory or they did or did not involve a national of the home country. As the Provisional IRA learnt, and the British government know, one bomb in London, however small, is worth a thousand in Ulster.

In a more recent work, Greg Philo (1990) attempted not only to analyse the portrayal of the year-long pit dispute of 1984–5 but also to examine the way that viewers had come to think about the strike as a result of this portrayal. He did this by, for example, visiting workplaces and asking workers in their lunch-breaks to write news stories about the strike, stimulated by a series of pictures that could be associated with the events. He found, in a huge number of cases, that the language used, for example phrases such as 'the drift back to work', were identical to those used by television journalists. Most people saw picket lines as violent, although all the actors involved – police, miners and the National Coal Board – believed almost all picket lines to be peaceful.

For Philo, this allows an important conclusion about the power of television: 'The earliest mass communication researchers believed that the media had tremendous power to promote ideas and beliefs. They saw media power as akin to a hypodermic needle injecting society with ideologies and propaganda. Later it became apparent that audiences bring much of their culture and history to their understanding of media messages. However, our current research shows that at least some of the information which is used when these audiences think about the world is itself provided by television and the press. It is also clear that it can be very difficult to criticise a dominant media account if there is little access to alternative sources of information. In these circumstances we should not underestimate the power of the media.'

QUESTIONS

1 **How does the GUMG perceive television bias? Can television news be presented in an unbiased way?**

2 **Is the GUMG biased?**

3 **What is 'content analysis'?**

4 **What did Philo see as the differences between the media portrayal of management and strikers?**

Television and stereotypes

The media abound with stereotypes. Those of working-class people, women and blacks have received the most attention from sociologists. The use of stereotypes has an instant appeal to the media-greedy public. You can avoid thinking about real people if you operate using stereotypes of groups, based on a few exaggerated characteristics. If these stereotypes are reinforced by the media, they become even more rigid and unshakeable.

More people watch television than are exposed to any other form of the media, and so the images and messages presented may be influential. There are numerous examples of sociological research into the whole area of the influence of TV, most of it aimed at the impact upon children and adolescents. Ros Coward (1987) drew the following conclusions from advertising aimed at children:

Children's toys and television

Watching the adverts between children's programmes is like entering a feminist nightmare where boys build up grotesque arsenals and girls endlessly comb the pastel mane of My Little Pony. In September 1987 American children had their first chance to shoot back with 'interactive toys' when 'Captain Power and His Soldiers of Fortune' quite literally hit the screen. In this new form of 'entertainment', the TV programmes are linked to sales of guns and weaponry with which the child is encouraged to participate in the programme ... We are

433

now in an altogether more gendered and imperialistic phase, where violence and owning weapons is seen as a vital part of masculine identity.

Women

Women are presented in the stereotyped feminine roles – dependent victims, sex objects, having their lives dominated by strong, forceful men. Plots which feature female lead characters still have men hanging around to sort out any trouble. Women shown in positions of power are 'out of place', a woman in a man's world, and this provides the story-line. Women politicians, football managers and police superintendents always have a family or love affair story-line. These images certainly reinforce traditionally held views, and the fact that they are changing at all indicates that society is changing, albeit very slowly.

Blacks: funny, threatening or dependent

Black people are also usually portrayed using negative stereotypes. Most young black males on TV are fast-talking hustlers living on the edge of the law, or crack dealers in flashy cars. If black people appear in plays or soaps on British TV, they tend to be the same tired old stereotypes. Asian people are shown in corner shops and Chinese people in restaurants. Black characters are on the periphery of an all-white cast or feature in 'their own' all-black programmes, such as *Desmonds* and *The Cosby Show*. What effect do these media portrayals have? Do they merely reflect the reality, showing what is there, or do they reflect the stereotyped attitudes of a racist society and show what people think is there?

There are very few positive or realistic images of black people on TV. They are usually linked to a social problem, with very little suggestion of any positive social roles they could play. The scheduling of black magazine programmes, and the steady trickle of black characters appearing in such roles as police officers and firefighters, indicate, as with gender roles, a slowly changing picture. The appeal of programmes like *Desmonds* is not confined to blacks, and as programme makers realise this, more positive images will appear. However, there are still a lot of problems in the TV presentation of blacks, and despite the changes, there are still racist overtones in a number of advertisements which, for instance, show barefoot blacks on desert islands drinking soft drinks or rum punches.

Downing (1975) found in a study of news, current affairs and documentary programmes that most of the time devoted to race issues concerned immigration, with the taken-for-granted view that immigration causes problems. If the media focus on crime and problems associated with black people in this way, then white people's anxiety and racist stereotypes could become more firmly entrenched.

QUESTIONS

1 What would be the pluralist answer to the argument that black stereotypes in the media reinforce racism in society?

2 Do the mass media have a responsibility for leading the challenge against racist, sexist and other stereotypes?

The mass media and women

It starts when you sink into his arms and ends with your arms in his sink.

Feminist slogan

Much of the printed and broadcast media targeted at women focuses on them as lovers, mothers and potential housewives, as essentially feminine. An intrinsic part of this femininity is the depiction of women whose lives revolve around the possibility of romance. Why this image of femininity is projected at women, who projects it, and whose interests it serves is the subject of much debate. Do women become involved in romance as part of a great lie that men construct to trap them in domestic roles, or should more men become sensitive to the emotional and expressive issues discussed in romantic fiction and women's magazines? Is the whole notion of romantic love simply a smokescreen through which women cannot recognise their oppression? Do the media shape women's sexuality into one of heterosexuality, passivity and subservience? Do women have any control over the way they are presented in the media?

Teenage magazines

There is much agreement over the nature and intent of magazines aimed at teenage girls, such as *My Guy* and *Jackie*, whose sales can reach as many as half a million copies. These magazines rely on a formula of written stories, photo-stories and problem pages. Certain characteristic features emerge: relationships are heterosexual and monogamous; love and sex go together and are both mystical and magical; the male is dominant while the female is passive and ideally virginal; the male 'takes' the female and she adapts to his needs; and friendships are secondary or unimportant. For Angela McRobbie (in McRobbie and McCabe, 1981) they describe the world of teenage girls in a way that is both limited and limiting. The central message of *Jackie* is that girls' lives should be oriented to capturing and thinking about boys. In doing this, *Jackie* is 'a friendly text book, a manual which works on the assumption that there are no real alternatives to this prescribed goal'.

A similar argument, expressed in a much more virulent tone, is put by the journalist and feminist Polly Toynbee (1978) in her examination of the girls' magazines published by IPC. For *My Guy* and its genre, 'All that matters in the world,' she says, 'is to get an attractive "fella", hold on to him and love him to distraction.' Problem pages encourage the idea that there is something wrong with a girl, if she 'hasn't got a "fella", doesn't want a "fella", feels she's not pretty/developed enough to get a "fella", is passionately interested in playing the violin, hockey, chess, reading books, solving maths problems or mending bikes'. In analysing the function of girls' magazines, Toynbee takes a mass-manipulative view, seeing them as little more than a 'shower of propaganda to those who are most vulnerable'. Against the argument that such publications are not meant to be taken seriously and that even the girls who read them see them as a joke, Toynbee replies 'what's funny? Where's the joke? The joke is that after all these years of battering on for a new deal for women, struggling with Equal Opportunities, Equal Pay, anti-sex discrimination, equal school curricula, striving to release young girls from the stultifying role stereotypes of the past, magazines like these are actually travelling fast in the opposite direction.'

McRobbie, however, is far less willing to concede such a powerful role to these magazines: '*Jackie* cannot be held solely responsible for the narrow and restricted lives many girls are forced to lead. Ultimately, the girl's "career" at home and in the workplace is determined by her social class, her sex and her race.'

Both McRobbie's and Toynbee's articles were written in the 1970s when teenage girls' magazines were at the height of their popularity. In the intervening decades, the image of women in the media has changed. Women's romantic fiction in general is more likely to project their heroines as successful with exciting jobs, though they are nevertheless likely to be read by women doing semi- and unskilled jobs (McRobbie and McCabe, 1981).

The cult of femininity

An altogether different view of women's magazines is given by Marjorie Ferguson (1983). Unlike publications for men, these trace women's biographies — there are magazines for very young girls, teenage girls (*Just 17*), young women, pregnant women, brides-to-be, mothers and housewives (*Good Housekeeping*) not paralleled by magazines for men. These provide a normative direction for the course of women's lives. Ferguson argues that these publications can be best understood through adapting Durkheim's interpretation of the role of religion (see chapter 11). Women's magazines are the organising focus for the cult of femininity. The parallels are that 'the oracles that carry the message sacred to the cult of femininity are women's magazines; the high priestesses who select and shape the cult's interdictions and benedictions are women's magazine editors; the rites, rituals, sacrifices and obligations [offerings] that they exhort are to be performed periodically by the cult's adherents'. What 'every woman knows' is sacred knowledge, where the rituals are beautification, child-rearing, housework and cooking. The totemic object is not men, however, but women. The house equates to the church, with the kitchen as its inner sanctum.

Paraphrasing Durkheim, Ferguson claims that when women read *Woman* magazine, they are worshipping women. Women's magazines socialise women into femininity in a way that men are never socialised into masculinity. The real mystery to be addressed is therefore 'How are men socialised into their male roles?' The issue of masculinity, however, is only just beginning to be addressed by sociologists.

Unlike McRobbie and Toynbee, Ferguson argues that women's magazines play a benign role in improving the collective lives of women: 'For some women, there may be nowhere outside the pages of these journals where they are consistently valued so highly, or accorded such high status. It may be that only within the pages of *Good Housekeeping* or *Women's Realm* do some women find an easy, accessible and regular source of positive self-esteem and social support' as women.

Game shows
In a similar vein, John Fiske (1990) manages to see good in television programmes targeted chiefly at women – soap operas and game shows such as *The Price is Right* which, he argues, have a liberatory dimension for women. Consumer-based quiz shows with mainly women contestants, he says, celebrate women's knowledge, in this case the price of household commodities: 'Two main forms of liberation are expressed in the game show audience's enthusiasm: the first is to give public, noisy acclaim to skills that are ordinarily silenced; the second is simply to be "noisy" in public, to escape from demure respectability, from the confines of good sense that patriarchy has constructed as necessary qualities for "the feminine".' Money is replaced by knowledge, symbolically liberating women from men's economic power. In these ways, Fiske claims, women cannot be seen as the 'cultural dopes' identified by Garfinkel. They are not complicit, and find no pleasure, in their subordination. These game shows can therefore be seen as an example of women using popular culture for their own, more subversive, ends.

The mass media targeted at women can therefore be seen in at least two ways: either, as McRobbie and Toynbee argue, as vehicles for transmitting a limiting and reactionary patriarchal ideology, or, as with Ferguson and Fiske, as an organising force for women, and as one of the few instances in which women are the sole object of their own attention, albeit within a patriarchal culture.

QUESTIONS

1 Is it possible to compare women's magazines with religious cults?

2 Would the content of teenage girls' magazines be any different if they were owned, written and produced entirely by women?

3 How do magazines for women differ from those for men?

Attitude formation and reinforcement

The hypodermic syringe model

The earliest and simplest explanations of the impact of the media upon individuals is known as the 'hypodermic needle model', so called because it proposes that media influence is a direct, one-way process. Messages are injected directly into the individual, and take root there. This is the sort of common-sense explanation that most people might hold. The job of sociology is to get beneath such simplistic explanations, which are all on the surface, and to discover the complex interactions which actually occur. Think for a moment about the hypodermic model. What is wrong with it? Surely it is a reasonable explanation? If you read an editorial in the *Sun*, watch the news, listen to music, watch a video, you receive messages which then influence you. If you read a chapter of this book, you immediately agree with all of the ideas. Or do you?

The hypodermic model is too simple, and the reason why is obvious if you consider the way in which you deal with the media. You weigh up the ideas which are being presented in the light of past experience – what you already know about the subject. These ideas and opinions probably come from a variety of sources – parents, peer groups, teachers, employers, and the media – which are parts of a large and complex social network, bubbles of influence in a sea of socialisation. The models of the media which evolved from the criticisms of the simplicity of the hypodermic model have all tried to explain this complex social network. The first to emerge was the 'two-step flow' model formulated by Katz and Lazarsfeld (1955) (*see* Figure 15.1).

Two-step flow model

The main idea behind Katz and Lazarsfeld's model is that it is a two-way process, between group and individual, the group comprising 'opinion leaders', i.e. people who have social status and influence in certain areas. The media and the group are influenced by the social structure, and in their turn exert some influence upon that structure. The individual interacts with group and media, and is not therefore a passive receiver of messages, as outlined in the hypodermic model.

Cultural model

A similar idea – the cultural model – shows us the individual as existing at the centre of a network of social values, opinions and atti-

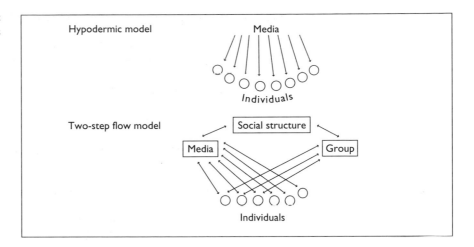

Figure 15.1 The hypodermic and two-step flow models

tudes, the accumulated products of a lifetime of primary and secondary socialisation. We each exist in an ideological maze which informs and shapes our consciousness. Any new messages have to be filtered through this complex pattern of ideas, and we will reject or accept new concepts on the basis of how they compare to our overall, cultural world view. The individual does not sit down in front of the TV screen every night like a blank sheet of paper to be written upon. The messages have to be compared to what has already been written, by a constant barrage of social influences since birth. One thing that the sociologists of the media have discovered is that their impact is not direct and easily traceable, but that a huge amount of social and cultural material has to be sifted through to trace the complicated and subtle influence of the mass media.

QUESTIONS

1 **In your opinion, does advertising succeed on the principles of the hypodermic syringe model?**

2 **What are the two steps of the two-step flow model?**

3 **Does the hypodermic syringe model live on? Are there any groups in society (such as politicians) who believe that the public will do and think what the mass media tell them?**

Violence and television

A woman called Mary Whitehouse, a former primary school teacher turned media analyst, moral guardian and founder of the National Viewers and Listeners Association, is one of the main exponents of the view that seeing violence and sex acts on television has a direct influence upon the actions of individuals, particularly children. The removal of *Child's Play 3* from TV schedules shortly after the killing of James Bulger by two children was a tacit acceptance that watching the film may have played some role in

439

their violent actions. Similarly, the video release of the film *Natural Born Killers*, portraying a couple engaged in random killing, was withheld by Warner Brothers following the shooting of primary school children in Dunblane, Scotland, in 1996. Although the common-sense argument seems plausible that if you watch enough violence on television it makes you more likely to use violence yourself, there is very little research evidence to back it up. Only the most artificially induced, laboratory experiments show any support.

The Bandura experiment   In a famous experiment, three social psychologists – Bandura, Ross and Ross (1961) – used four groups of children to discover the effects of seeing violence, in this case vicious attacks on self-righting or 'bobo' dolls. The first group saw real-life men and women making the attacks, the second watched a film of men and women with mallets, the third watched cartoon characters attacking the dolls with mallets. A fourth group simply sat around as a 'control group'. All groups were then put in rooms on their own with, firstly, toys they were not allowed to touch, and then in a room with mallets and self-righting dolls. Which of the four groups would be more violent to the dolls? The psychologists' conclusion was that 'aggressive behaviour was sharply higher in each of the model conditions in comparison with the control, and further, that most of this difference was due to the direct imitation of the model's aggressive behaviours. Differences between the various viewing conditions – live, film, and television – were negligible.'

The Bandura experiment actually tells us more about learning by imitation in a small-scale situation. The widespread and diverse influences of TV on people living in the real world are much harder to trace. It is very difficult to gauge whether, and how much, people are affected by what they see and hear. Mrs Whitehouse has been criticised for the extremity of her views, for example that Tom and Jerry cartoons lead children to believe that they can walk away unharmed from what could be fatal collisions with frying pans and falling boulders.

Belson   Research into these areas is full of methodological problems. Sociological, as opposed to psychological, research into this area has usually been in the form of field studies, using questionnaires, interviews and in some cases observation. William Belson's (1978) study was based upon in-depth interviews with 1,565 adolescent boys in London, aged between 12 and 17 years. He undertook elaborate sampling procedures, and cross-checked his data by using different interview settings, to try to obtain a conclusion which could be supported. Boys with high TV exposure were compared to those with low exposure, and Belson claims that those who had seen a lot of TV violence had committed 49 per cent more acts of violence than the low-exposure group. However, critics have pointed out that this correlation between high exposure to TV does not really specify violent TV. In fact, it shows that those watching a lot of any kind of programme are more prone to violence.

Dennis Howitt (1982) points out that Belson's results actually show that there are three types of viewer, those with light, moderate or heavy exposures to violence. Of these, it is the watchers of a moderate level of violence who are more prone to it themselves. The low and the high groups are not affected. It appears that Belson's work can be construed in a number of different ways, and is a good example of the difficulties in both methodology and making direct links between TV violence and social behaviour.

The work of Himmelweit (1958) shows different results. She discovered that the effects of TV vary according to the presence of other socialising forces in the child's life. Children not encouraged to read or with no books or comics, and children whose parents spent little time with them, tended to be influenced by their viewing. It is the absence of other forms of stimulation or role models to imitate, which leaves the children to formulate their impressions according to their viewing. In the 1980s and 1990s, children's cartoons are merely long adverts for action character figures. These all portray violence but no bloodshed and people still assume a direct link with the behaviour of children. At the height of the Turtles craze, some primary schools banned Turtle games in the playground, and there were occasional media reports about children going down to the sewers to find their green heroes. All these things indicate a relationship between TV and children's self-image and behaviour, but the research does not, or perhaps cannot, firmly establish this. The network of influences which surround and shape every human being is complex and difficult to unravel. How do adults react to their favourite TV programmes?

QUESTIONS

1 **Does violence on television cause violence in society?**

2 **How important is television as an agency of socialisation?**

The media and the amplification of deviance

Deviancy amplification and amplification spirals

Perhaps one of the most famous sociological analyses of deviance comes from Stan Cohen – *Folk Devils and Moral Panics* (1972). A moral panic occurs when society throws up its arms in horror at behaviour that is perceived likely to cause the breakdown of society. Cohen

441

considers how the media actually make deviancy expand and increase the incidence of 'bad behaviour' which they are actually writing about and condemning. The folk devils of the title were the mods and rockers of the 1960s but the model applies to all the youth cultures and anything which 'disturbs' the public. The underlying idea is that societies going through change, particularly rapid change, are potentially unstable. People need to blame their insecurity upon something or someone, and the mods and rockers played that role. The media, selecting 'newsworthy' events, feed the public's need, and opinion leaders take up the cry. The church, politicians, moral spokespersons, all climb on the bandwagon, and the folk devils are persecuted, while bad parenting and poor schooling are held up to blame. This has the effect of spreading both the deviance and the panic, and things get increasingly worse, in a spiralling effect. Deviancy amplification spirals and a moral tornado is whipped up. The media play an important intermediary role by bringing certain things into the public consciousness, at certain times.

Cohen points out that seaside town disturbances which featured in the onset of the mods and rockers panic had been common since the late 1950s. Why, then, did a few isolated scuffles between rival gangs of youths turn into one of the great British moral panics of the latter part of the twentieth century, spreading new fashions, music and the images of gang warfare into the living rooms and school playgrounds of Britain? Easter 1964 was cold and wet, and groups of youths in Clacton were bored. They rode up and down the streets on their scooters and bikes, wrecked a few beach huts and broke some windows. There were fights and crowds in the streets. The Monday papers, starved of news after the Bank Holiday period, seized upon the events as news, and the following headlines appeared: 'Day of terror by scooter groups' (*Daily Telegraph*), 'Youngsters beat up town – 97 leather jacket arrests' (*Daily Express*), 'Wild ones invade seaside – 97 arrests' (*Daily Mirror*).

Cohen goes on to analyse the amount of exaggeration and distortion of numbers involved, the events taking place and how the language over-stressed the significance of what happened. Old people and respectable families of holidaymakers were often reported as being intimidated by the fighting youths. According to Cohen's research into local press and eyewitness reports, this intimidation rarely took place. 'Deserted beaches' were empty, not because of the fear of violence, but because of the bad weather. In fact, those holidaymakers who did turn out, did so to watch the fighting.

Symbolisation, exaggeration and prediction

In this case, the media are seen as encouraging more occurrences of the kind they are reporting. More police are on hand to cover the next Bank Holiday, there are more mods, rockers and 'innocent bystanders' which lead to more arrests and more media coverage. Even when nothing has happened, headlines screamed the word 'violence' then proceeded to report the lack of it! The mods and rockers were the folk devils of the mid-twentieth century, and there has been a steady stream of replacements in subsequent years. In the 1990s, the 'rave' scene whipped up a minor moral panic, with media impressions of young people out of their heads on hallucinogens becoming the scourge of society. The work of Cohen and others analyses the role of the media in exaggerating and over-reporting events selected as newsworthy at a particular time. Unscrupulous reporting techniques such as 'posing' a screaming mob for photos on the beach could be the real deviance.

Cohen assesses how important the mass media were in organising the youths. At Margate, on the Bank Holiday following the original Clacton 'event', very few of them cited the sense of expectation, created by the media, that something was going to happen as their reason for going, claiming instead that they got the idea of going mainly by word of mouth from their friends. Media publicity during the 'warning phase' was therefore unimportant, reinforcing rather than initiating rumours. During the weekend itself, however, broadcast interviews with mods and rockers did have the effect of encouraging both sides, calling up reinforcements and inviting the youths to act up: 'If one is in a group of twenty, being stared at by hundreds of adults and being pointed at by two or three cameras, the temptation to do something – even if only to shout an obscenity, make a rude gesture or throw a stone – is very great and made greater by the knowledge that one's actions will be recorded for others to see.'

If the media do have a role in amplifying deviance, the central question to be asked is 'How much?' In South Africa in the 1980s, international coverage of township violence under apartheid was eventually banned by the white government on the grounds that it encouraged copycat violence elsewhere. It was also claimed that riots in Britain in the mid-1980s had been at least partly influenced by pictures from South Africa. As Cohen argues, the media may have little influence in creating primary deviance, and they cannot cause it to happen. It is still unclear how far they contribute to the creation of secondary deviance.

The invasion from Mars   In a celebrated radio broadcast in 1938, Orson Welles and the Mercury Theatre Company managed to fool many Americans into thinking that the USA had been invaded by Martians. In a decade that had witnessed the advancement of propaganda techniques in Nazi

443

Germany, the fact that the programme managed to bring many convinced listeners into the street screaming in panic appeared to be further evidence for hypodermic syringe theorists.

For Hadley Cantril (1940) the truth was more complex. First, of the six million people who heard the broadcast, only one million confessed to having been taken in. (Does this mean the other five million were lying?) Furthermore, only 12 per cent of those who were listening at the beginning of the broadcast were fooled. As with today, many people zapped stations to find what they wanted to hear most. Radio was also thought to be a more reliable medium than newspapers, and more likely to tell the truth. The play was performed in the style of a contemporary news programme. Equally important for Cantril was the fact that the play was broadcast on 30 October 1938, the eve of Halloween. It appeared towards the end of a decade in which American self-confidence had collapsed in the depression following the 1929 Wall Street Crash. European politics were focused on the attempts to appease Hitler by, among others, the British Prime Minister Neville Chamberlain. The expectation of war was rife. It was a climate in which there were no longer any certainties and anything – even a Martian invasion – could happen. This is the proper context, Cantril argues, in which the *War of the Worlds* broadcast has to be understood.

QUESTIONS

1 **What 'moral panics' have been presented in the mass media recently?**

2 **Is the spread of a moral panic dependent on the mass media?**

3 **What is meant by the amplification of deviance?**

New technology, the mass media and mass culture

The impact of information technology

In recent decades, the development and spread of new information technologies such as satellite television have engendered many debates about the consequences of their use. One of the first writers to see the possibilities of these changes was the American writer Marshall McLuhan, who argued in the 1960s that communications technology would have two effects: first, it would create a global village where everyone and everything are accessible to the television camera and secondly, it would become the case that 'the medium is the message', that is, how a message is transmitted would become more important than what the message is (McLuhan and Fiore, 1967).

Other theorists have gone further in arguing that the explosion of, and increasing dependence on, information technology have brought about profound changes in the way that societies are organised. Jean Baudrillard, for example, believes that we can now describe a 'post-modern society' (see also chapter 16), characterised partly by an information-based international division of labour that allows increasing freedom of movement. At a cultural level, distinctions between 'high' and 'low' culture have disappeared as new technology makes everything available to everyone, while stylistically, form has become more important than content, and the ubiquity of television means that everything is seen in television codes. McLuhan's global television-led culture is now with us.

The accuracy of such a description, however, has been questioned. At one level, many sociologists are reluctant to accept any argument that technology can lead to social and economic changes, arguing instead that the relationship is exactly the other way round. In other words, they are critical of any tendency to technological determinism. Furthermore, evidence can be cited that queries the notion that the information revolution has been spread evenly throughout the world or even throughout Britain. This has been described as the uneven development of information capitalism. Thus, many areas of Great Britain are not yet equipped with the on-line communications systems necessary to receive new information technologies such as cable and interactive television, and the take-up of these technologies varies according to socio-economic factors. We are still a long way from the full-scale and comprehensive implementation of the information super-highway.

The end of family viewing

What does seem to be the case, however, is that the stereotypical image of the nuclear family sitting together in the front room cheerfully choosing their evening's viewing from a limited range of television stations, is disappearing. This is partly due to the increased number of televisions per household as well as the rapid growth in television stations, a development mirrored by the niche marketing of magazines to a multiplicity of interest groups. The amount of time spent watching television per head has stabilised in recent years at an average 26 hours 44 minutes per week in 1992. Women watch on average four hours per week more television than men, and all statistics show a relationship between social class and viewing, with A and B groups watching less than D and E groups (19 hours and 56 minutes against 31 hours and 54 minutes in 1992). 95% of the population watch TV at least once a week.

This is not to say that greater diversity and choice has necessarily been achieved. It remains the case that satellite television caters for mass-appeal interests such as music, sport, news, children's programmes and American films and light entertainment, ignoring many disadvantaged social groups. New media technologies have not empowered people in the sense that there are an increased number of community-based television networks. In Britain, it is still possible to describe a mass culture based on centrally directed mass media. (See also chapters 2 and 16.)

A global television culture?

Doubts have also been raised, however, about the ability of satellite stations to succeed in creating a global television culture. As we have seen, Rupert Murdoch owns substantial parts of the global media industry. In 1994 he added a controlling share of Star TV to his collection, meaning that he gained access to 2.5 billion people in 50 countries, or 40 per cent of the world's television sets, in a region stretching from Jordan to Japan. Capturing the market in India, however, and hooking the population onto Oprah Winfrey, *Dynasty*, *Baywatch* and *L.A. Law* has not been as easy as first imagined. Cultural differences are complicated by the fact that India possesses 18 official languages, and 1,700 dialects. It remains the case that the most popular programmes are Hindi films transmitted by the State broadcasting station. Murdoch's own response to this realisation was to immediately buy into a local television station. Indian culture, for the present at least, remains resistant to Western broadcasting. The creation of a global mass culture rests as much on social, economic, cultural and political factors as it does on technology.

QUESTIONS

1 Does the global media village exist yet?

2 Why do classes D and E watch more television than classes A, B and C1?

3 Do you agree that a mass culture still exists in Great Britain?

4 Can the Internet be described as a form of mass media?

FURTHER READING

D. Barrat, **Media Sociology**, Tavistock, 1986

J. Downing, **The Media Machine**, Pluto Press, 1980

C. Geraghty, **Women and Soap Operas: The Study of Prime Time Soaps**, Polity Press, 1990

Glasgow University Media Group, **Getting the Message: News Truth and Power**, Routledge, 1993

M. Gurevitch *et al.* (eds.), **Culture, Society and the Media**, Routledge, 1990

D. McQuail, **New Media Politics**, Sage, 1986

D. Morley, **Television, Audiences and Cultural Studies**, Routledge, 1992

J. Winship, **Inside Women's Magazines**, Pandora, 1987

16 Postscript

Playing with the pieces – that is postmodernism.

Jean Baudrillard, Baudrillard Live: Selected Interviews, 1983

It has been increasingly argued in recent decades that fundamental changes have taken place in the way that Western societies are organised, and that these changes are clearly visible in all spheres – economic, cultural, political, social and intellectual. The 'modern' era, with its origins in the seventeenth and eighteenth centuries, has come to an end and has been superseded by a 'post-modern' age. This argument has profound implications for the future of the study of sociology.

Traditional and modern

The modern era can itself be said to have superseded the 'traditional' when the rural and agricultural gave way to an industrial and urban society. This is described by W.W. Rostow (see chapter 12). At the heart of this transition to modernity was the founding of an intellectual tradition that sought to reject old ways of understanding the world based on religious knowledge, and replace it with knowledge based not on faith but on reason. It was out of this movement – usually known as the Enlightenment – that the embryo of sociology was formed, and it is the claims of the Enlightenment project that its new critics – the theorists of post-modernism – are most concerned to contest.

The Enlightenment

Although it was a broad-based movement, the Enlightenment can be described as the collective writings of eighteenth-century French thinkers such as Rousseau (1712–78), Voltaire (1694–1788), Diderot (1713–84) and Montesquieu (1689–1755), who are sometimes collectively known as the *philosophes*, and Scottish writers such as Hume (1711–76) and Adam Smith (1723–90). In a theological age, these writers argued the case for raising the status of science, for a more rational understanding of the world, based on belief in the possibility of the use of reason to increase human understanding of the world in which they lived. At the same time, they sought also to contest the claims of what they believed to be ignorance, prejudice and superstition. Through the use of reason, and their commitment to test all ideas against what their senses told them, they believed that they could come up with a scientific knowledge whereby truths that applied in any situation – universals – could be found to exist.

Underlying this aspiration was the belief that part of this knowledge would lead to improvements in the way society was organised and the way people led their lives. As a secular intelligentsia, they were progressive in their thinking, making claims for the individual as the centre of their analysis, an individual who would be free and allowed to think whatever they dared, without fear of religious or political persecution. In doing so, they opened the door to the possibility of a science of society, to the extent that some have claimed that in the eighteenth century 'sociology' would have been translated as the work that the *philosophes* were doing, before it was further developed by Saint-Simon (1760–1825) and Comte (1798–1857). During the nineteenth and early twentieth centuries these ideas became professionalised and institutionalised by the 'founding fathers' – Marx, Durkheim, Tönnies, Simmel and Weber – and it is their intellectual inheritance, in the form of social science, that has been largely described and discussed in this book.

Post-modernism

The theorists of post-modernism attack the Enlightenment inheritance at its foundations. A project committed to the pursuit of truth, reason, certainty, progress, secularism and control over nature has produced a world which in the twentieth century has witnessed two world wars, continued famine, global pollution, 'ethnic cleansing', the sustained rise of religious fundamentalism and the collapse of the Soviet bloc. It is therefore difficult to conclude that there is an inner logic of history leading to the perfection of the human condition. As Zygmunt Bauman remarks, 'the two-centuries-old philosophical voyage to certainty and universal criteria of perfection and a "good life" seems to be a wasted effort' (Bauman, 1988). This sense of disillusionment is what has been described by one of the most prominent post-modernist writers, Jean-François Lyotard (1984), as 'the post-modern condition'.

This new condition is present in all aspects of life. In philosophy, it is marked by the claims of relativism – there are no universals, and there is no objective or scientific truth. Sociology, which is strongly linked to philosophy, also exhibits the post-modern condition in that in all of sociology's subject areas post-modern thinking is making a significant and subversive contribution. It is no longer possible (if it ever was) to scientifically analyse an increasingly secular and industrial world as if the class structure of an isolated nation-state were the key to understanding behaviour, explaining how people vote, their consumption of 'high' or 'low' culture, or their propensity to criminal acts. Men are no longer the sole breadwinners, living in nuclear families with the same job and a wife for life, with a limited choice of programmes to watch on television. The projections of modernist sociology have been examined and found wanting

Post-industrialism   The growth of service industries and the absolute decline of manufacturing industries, the spread of flexible working, part-time working, temporary contracts, niche production and so on mean that the industrial world has become post-industrial, and Fordist production has become post-Fordist (see chapter 6). In the analysis of stratification the dimensions of age, gender and ethnicity are now seen to be at least as important as the concept of class, which in turn has ceased to be defined simply by the relationship people have to the means of production. Patterns of consumption of goods and services are now thought to be equally as important as an increasing number of people own property and contribute to pension schemes and private health care plans. If there is an overall pattern to be perceived, it is one of diversity and differentiation at all levels.

The boundaries of the nation-state have been breached as capitalism has become a global economic system, marshalled by a stateless, transnational capitalist class. New technologies have also brought about the possibility of a global media village. The main distinction to be drawn in the post-modern era is that between what is global and what is local. New social movements are evident in the way people behave politically, contesting not traditional battles drawn on class lines but uniting to take on planners and supermarket owners in the interest of environmental and neighbourhood protection. The 'green' movement is becoming a force in all areas of life as more and more people attack the equation that 'big' science equals progress. The idea that humans are the most superior life form – anthropocentricity – is being radically attacked. The dominance of traditional religious organisations in the Christian world is being challenged not by full-blooded atheism but by the emergence of sects and an interest in new age religions emphasising individually attained spiritual awareness and fulfilment. New age travellers have challenged modernist notions of community. As family forms diversify into nuclear, single parent and reconstituted families, and as more and more people choose to live alone, the 'post-modern family' has been identified. There are now a great variety of routes by which educational qualifications can be attained, in an education system that has become increasingly localised in its control and administration. Decades of criminological research have resulted in a 'crisis of aetiology' where the causes of criminal behaviour in a welfare society are now thought to be highly complex, if they can be understood at all.

The ubiquity of mass media technologies has broken down the distinction between high and low culture and even the distinction between culture and society. All have become equally indistinguishable from the economy as we become defined as consumers with needs, and cultural artefacts are either used to sell commodities, or have become the commodities themselves. 'Pop' art appears in art galleries, and classic art appears on T-shirts, compact disc covers, and is now commonly used in all areas of advertising. Style and surface have superseded content. Because the world of media signs, symbols and images is central to our discourse, the nature of reality has also been transformed. For Baudrillard, people do not visit Disneyland (or even the recently opened Postman Pat Themepark) to escape America, but because it is America in its 'hyperreal' form. 'Disneyland is presented as imaginary in order to make us believe that the rest is real, when in fact all of Los Angeles and the America surrounding it are no longer real, but of the order of the hyperreal and of simulation. It is no longer a question of a false representation of reality (ideology), but of concealing the fact that the real is no longer real' (Baudrillard, 1988).

Metanarratives

Yet it is at the level of the overarching theories – or metanarratives – in sociology that the most powerful body blows are being aimed This is encapsulated in Lyotard's now famous and frequently quoted declaration that post-modernism can be described as 'incredulity towards metanarratives', where a metanarrative is a grand-scale attempt to show how empirical and rational methods can be used to demonstrate how society as a whole works, revealing its inner logic and dynamic. In sociology, theories such as Marxism, functionalism (particularly Parsons' *Social System*) and feminism, can be described as examples of these 'totalising' theories, seeking to cover an impossibly large subject area, making ridiculously vast generalisations, and in the end only telling stories like any other fiction.

If the progress to truth and absolute knowledge has not been achieved, then what has been created can be better described as stories (narratives) or even 'mythologies' that can never be verified. Positivism, Marxism, and objective science are no more than modern mythologies, comforting people with the pretence that attempts are being made to answer the great questions of existence. The post-modernists (though very few of them accept this title) reject what they see as the pretensions and pomposity of science, particularly social science, claiming that at best it should be seen as 'language games' and 'rhetorical jousting'.

Identity

Even the way we think about ourselves is in transition. Here, the Enlightenment view differs from the sociological, in that, from Descartes on (1596–1650) people were seen primarily as individuals, particularly in the formulation of law, economics and the Protestant religion. An individual's identity was seen as something

Disneyland: fantasy, reality or hyperreality?

that stayed the same throughout their lives. In this sense, their identities were 'centred'. Sociology, particularly through the contributions of writers such as Cooley and Mead (see chapters 1 and 2), sees
people not as isolated, free-standing individuals but as socially constructed in the process of interaction between the 'self' and society,
taking on the roles and identities of the world we live in and are
socialised into.

Post-modernism sees identity as fluid, arguing instead that the
processes of fragmentation and differentiation mean that identities
are continuously changing and even contradictory. We have no fixed,
essential or permanent identity. If we nevertheless believe that we
have maintained the same identity throughout our lives, constructing what Stuart Hall (1990) calls a 'narrative of the self', it is only to

comfort ourselves, in the same way that other narratives and meta-narratives (or mythologies) have been constructed to solve other existential problems.

Traditional identities such as class, family and neighbourhood membership are being eroded away. New identities, however, are not being formed to replace these. For some writers, the mass media and popular culture now provide the sole but nevertheless inadequate frame of reference for the construction of identities. Yet: 'No new forms or institutions, no new ideas or beliefs can now serve to give people a secure and coherent sense of themselves, their place and time, nor are there any longer legitimate and acceptable ways by which they can define themselves to themselves and to others' (Strinati, 1992).

Post-feminism

Writers describing themselves as post-feminists or feminist post-modernists have entered this debate by questioning the feminist assumption that all women can be assumed to live similar lives and share similar experiences. Women's lives are cross-cut by other dimensions such as class, age, ethnicity, 'colour' (whiteness as a racialised category), sexual orientation and able-bodiedness. The way that these identities are perceived (not least by the individual) can change many times in a person's life. As Elizabeth Spelman (1988) argues, metanarratives about 'woman's oppression' therefore become highly problematic, when it is so unclear which woman feminists have in mind.

Resistance post-modernism

In its denial of the claims of the modernist project, two directions have been discerned in post-modern analysis. Lather (1991), for example, contrasts her own 'postmodernism of resistance' against the nihilism and cynicism of a 'postmodernism of reaction', where the latter takes a pessimistic view of the possibility of human emancipation. Such a pessimistic view can be found in the writings of Jean Baudrillard (echoing Nietzsche) who states that 'The mass is dumb like beasts, and its silence is equal to the silence of beasts ... it says neither whether the truth is to the left or to the right, nor whether it prefers revolution to repression. It is without truth and without reason' (Baudrillard, 1983). Elsewhere he argues that post-modernism is 'more a survival among the remnants than anything else' and that 'All that remains to be done is to play with the pieces. Playing with the pieces – that is postmodernism.'

Resistance post-modernism (sometimes called oppositional post-modernism), however, sees possibilities in the diversity and multi-centredness of the post-modern condition. Traditional forms of resistance have broken down but have been replaced by a multiplicity of localised, participatory and non-hierarchical forms, for example within the multi-voiced post-feminist movements.

Criticisms of post-modernism   Many writers have been unwilling to dismiss the Enlightenment project as easily as the post-modernists (such as Lyotard) have done, seeing instead serious flaws in the post-modernist case. A frequently made point is that it contradicts itself in the claim that there are no universal truths – facts that everyone agrees are true. The statement 'all things are relative' sounds very much as though it is itself claiming the status of absolute truth. For sociologists, although no two cultures are the same, comparing cultures can be fruitful even if we conclude that these cultures have different ways of interpreting their worlds.

The Marxist reply   Marxists and neo-Marxists have been particularly active in refuting the post-modernist position, especially because they are one of this group's main targets. Alex Callinicos (1990), as the title of his book shows, is dismissive of post-modernism as a theory, seeing it in Marxist terms, as 'the product of a socially mobile intelligentsia in a climate dominated by the retreat of the Western labour movement and the "overconsumptionist dynamic of capitalism in the Reagan–Thatcher era"'. The implications of this are clear: the class struggle is not over yet and never will be until post-industrialism also means post-capitalism. Furthermore, it is not even the case that Fordism as a form of work organisation has yet run its course.

Modernity is really only a poor synonym for capitalism. Marx made it clear as early as 1848 that this is a highly dynamic system: 'The bourgeoisie cannot exist without constantly revolutionising the instruments of production, and thereby the relations of production, and with them the whole relations of society ... Constant revolutionising of production, uninterrupted disturbance of all social conditions, everlasting uncertainty and agitation distinguish the bourgeois epoch from all earlier ones. All fixed, fast frozen relations ... are swept away, all new-formed ones become antiquated before they can ossify. All that is solid melts into air' (Marx, 1848).

According to Callinicos, Marxist theory continues to be the best living example of 'Radical Enlightenment'. All that has really happened is that some former socialist intellectuals have turned to defeatist posturing as a way of earning a living. Socialist feminists have also made it clear that post-feminism makes little sense until a post-patriarchal society is attained.

Jameson   Less fundamentalist Marxist theorists have been willing to concede some of the post-modernist arguments. Frederic Jameson (1991) agrees that post-modernist analysis is possible at a cultural level, but sees it as 'the cultural logic of late capitalism', where late capitalism has superseded market and monopoly capitalism, even turning culture (as aesthetic production) into something to be bought and sold. While it is true to say that class politics are in abatement, and 'new social movements' are mounting the most successful resistance to global capitalism, it is in the logic of Marxist theory that a transnational proletariat will eventually unite to wage a global class struggle. To date, however, there is scant evidence of this occurring.

Harvey   In a similar vein, David Harvey (1989) agrees that in many respects the way people live their lives has changed rapidly and substantially in recent decades. 'Time-compression', by which he means the way that countries and markets can be reached in hours rather than weeks, or instantly through communication networks, encourages people to think that they live in a fast-moving world. The way work and employment practices are regulated has also changed very quickly. Yet it is also possible to find much continuity present through a period of change, and to find cultural conflicts similar to those described as the post-modern condition in earlier periods of modernity. Unable to choose between modernity and post-modernity as the most useful way of describing the age in which we live, Harvey argues that 'Whatever else we do with the concept, we should not read postmodernism as some autonomous artistic current. Its rootedness in daily life is one of its most patently transparent features.'

Giddens   From a non-Marxist position, Anthony Giddens (1990) also concedes some of the post-modernist argument, particularly their criticism of the view that there is a continuous progression in history, and their view that the 'indubitable foundations' of knowledge that the Enlightenment thinkers sought do not exist: 'no knowledge can rest upon an unquestioned foundation, because even the most firmly held notions can only be recognised as valid "in principle" or "until further notice". Otherwise they would relapse into dogma and become separate from the very sphere of reason which determines what validity is in the first place.' Yet to accept these points does not at all mean that all of post-modernist theory has to be accepted. As with other writers, Giddens argues that the post-modernist position is contradictory, recycling older arguments and mistaking them for something new.

It is contradictory, for example, to argue that, on the one hand, we have moved from modernity to post-modernity, and on the other to say that history has no shape or direction. It is equally paradoxical to write books that say that no knowledge is possible, when the books themselves constitute knowledge. What has been described as post-modernism is better seen as the engagement of critical reason in 'radicalised modernity', in an age where more and more people in the Western world – not simply intellectuals – are becoming more self-aware and inquisitive about the roles that they play. What is happening is that modernity has become more reflexive, looking inwards on itself, which may reflect the overall decline of the West's privileged and hegemonic position in the world, as the process of globalisation gains in intensity. We cannot therefore describe a new post-modern world.

Interactionism   What is perhaps most curious in the debate about sociology raised by the post-modernists is that it is only directed at part of sociology, the scientific or positivistic tradition to which Marxism, functionalism and (to a lesser extent) Weberianism have been the main contributors. Doubts about their scientific status are not new to sociology. Since at least the 1920s interactionist sociologists have raised questions of cultural relativism and have sought to examine the nature of small-scale interactions in the generation of meaning, and the plastic and changing nature of identity. It is at least debatable whether these theorists would recognise much that is new or that they would wish to take issue with in the post-modernist argument.

Sociology therefore approaches the end of the twentieth century engaged in as much debate and controversy as it began it. How the argument between the pro- and anti-metanarrativists will be resolved is as much up to you, the reader, who represents the next generation, to tackle as it is anyone else.

QUESTIONS   1   **In what ways can post-modernism be defined?**

2   **Why do classical Marxists reject post-modernism?**

3   **How could modernity be distinguished from post-modernity?**

4   **Can the economic be distinguished from the cultural?**

FURTHER READING

A. Callinicos, *Against Postmodernism: A Marxist Critique*, Polity Press, 1990

M. Featherstone, *Postmodernism and Consumer Culture*, Sage, 1991

D. Lyon, *Postmodernity*, Open University Press, 1994

G. Ritzer, *The McDonaldisation of Society: An Investigation into the Changing Character of Contemporary Social Life*, Sage, 1992

M. Sarup, *Introduction to Post-structuralism and Post-modernism*, Harvester/Wheatsheaf, 1993

B. Smart, *Post Modernity*, Routledge, 1992

B. Turner (ed.), *Theories of Modernity and Post Modernity*, Sage, 1990

Bibliography

Note: In order to place these texts in their appropriate historical context, dates of first editions have been given where possible.

Abbott, P. and Sapsford R., 1987, *Women and Social Class*, Tavistock

Abbott, P. and Wallace, C., 1990, *An Introduction to Sociology: Feminist Perspectives*, Routledge

Abel-Smith, B. and Townsend, P., 1965, *The Poor and the Poorest*, G. Bell and Sons

Abrams, M., 1959, *The Teenage Consumer*, Routledge and Kegan Paul

Abrams, M. et al., 1960, *Must Labour Lose?*, Penguin

Acker, J., 1973, 'Women and social stratification: a case of intellectual sexism', *American Journal of Sociology*, 78

Adam Smith Institute, 1994, *The End of the Welfare State*

Adler, F., 1975, *Sisters in Crime*, McGraw Hill

Allen, Hilary, 1987, *Justice Unbalanced*, Open University Press

Althusser, L., 1969, *For Marx*, Allen Lane

Althusser, L., 1971, *Essays on Ideology*, New Left Books

Anderson, M., 1971, 'The relevance of family history' in M. Anderson, *Sociology of the Family*, Penguin, 2nd edition, 1980

Anderson, M., 1972, 'Household structure and the industrial revolution' in P. Laslett (ed.), *Household and Family in Time Past*, Cambridge University Press

Ariès, Philippe, 1962, *Centuries of Childhood*, Jonathan Cape

Armstrong, W. A., 1972, 'A note of the household structure of mid-nineteenth-century York in comparative perspective' in Laslett

Ashton, D., 1986, *Unemployment under Capitalism*, Wheatsheaf

Atkinson, A. B., 1983, *The Economics of Equality*, Oxford University Press

Atkinson, J. M., 1978, *Discovering Suicide*, Macmillan

Atterhead, Sven, 1985, 'Intrapreneurship: the way forward?' in Clutterbuck

Avila, Manuel, 1969, *Tradition and Growth*, University of Chicago Press

Bachrach, P. and Baratz, M., 1963, 'Decisions and non-decisions: an analytical framework', *American Political Science Review*, vol. 57

Bacon, A. W., 1975, 'Leisure and the alienated worker', *Journal of Leisure Research*, vol. 7, no. 3

Bagehot, Walter, 1867, *The English Constitution* (Fontana, 1963)

Ball, Stephen, 1981, *Beachside Comprehensive: A Case Study of Secondary Schooling*, Cambridge University Press

Bandura, A. et al., 1961, 'The imitation of film-mediated aggressive models' *Journal of Abnormal Psychology*, 66

Baran, B., 1988, 'Office automation and women's work' in R. Pahl (ed.), *On Work*, Blackwell

Barber, B., 1963, 'Some problems in the sociology of professions', *Daedelus*, vol. 92, no. 4

Barker, E., 1984, *The Making of a Moonie: Choice or Brainwashing?*, Basil Blackwell

Barrett, Michele and McIntosh, Mary, 1982, *The Anti-Social Family*, Verso

Barrett, Michele and McIntosh, Mary, 1985, 'Ethnocentrism and socialist-feminist theory', *Feminist Review*, 20

Barron, R. D. and Norris E. M., 1976, 'Sexual divisions and the dual labour market' in D. Barker and S. Allen (eds.), *Dependence and Exploitation in Work and Marriage*, Longman

Bassett, P., 1987, *Strike Free*, Macmillan

Bates, I. et al., 1984, *Schooling for the Dole?*, Macmillan

Baudrillard, J., 1983, *In the Shadow of the Silent Majorities ... Or the End of the Social and Other Essays*, Semiotext(e)

Baudrillard, J., 1988, in M. Poster (ed.), *Jean Baudrillard: Selected Works*, Polity Press

Bauer, Peter, 1976, *Dissent on Development*, Weidenfeld and Nicolson

Bauer, Peter, 1981, *Equality, the Third World and Economic Delusion*, Weidenfeld and Nicolson

Bauman, Zygmunt, 1988, *Legislators and Interpreters*, Polity Press

Beck, U., 1992, *The Risk Society*, Sage

Becker, H. S., 1963, *Outsiders: Studies in the Sociology of Deviance* (The Free Press, 1973)

Becker, H. S., 1967, 'Whose side are we on?' *Social Problems*, 14

Beckford, J., 1986, *New Religious Movements and Rapid Social Change*, Sage/UNESCO

Bell, D., 1961, *The End of Ideology*, Collier-Macmillan

Bellah, R. N., 1964, 'Religious evolution', *American Sociological Review*, 29

Belson, William, 1978, *TV Violence and the Adolescent Boy*, Saxon House

Bendix, R. and Lipset, S. (eds.), 1966, *Class, Status and Power*, The Free Press

Berger, Bennett, 1960, *Working-Class Suburbs: A Study of Auto Workers in Suburbia*, University of California Press

Berle, A. A. and Means, G. C., 1932, *The Modern Corporation and Private Property*, Macmillan

Bernades, Jon, 1990, 'The family in question', *Social Studies Review*, September

Bernstein, Basil, 1961, 'Social class and linguistic development: a theory of social development' in A. H. Halsey et al., *Education, Economy and Society*, The Free Press

Beveridge, William, 1942, *Social Insurance and Allied Services* (The Beveridge Report), Cmd 6404, HMSO

Beveridge, William, 1944, *Full Employment in a Free Society*, Allen and Unwin

Beynon, Huw, 1973, *Working for Ford*, Allen Lane

Binns, D. and Mars, G., 1984, 'Family, community and unemployment: a study in change', *The Sociological Review*, vol. 32, no. 4

Blackstone, Tessa and Weinrich-Haste, Helen, 1980, 'Why are there so few women scientists and engineers?', *New Society*, 21.2.80

Blau, P. M., 1955, *The Dynamics of Bureaucracy*, University of Chicago Press

Blauner, R., 1964, *Alienation and Freedom*, University of Chicago Press

Blumer, H., 1969, *Symbolic Interactionism*, Prentice Hall

Blumer, H., 1975, 'Exchange on Turner', *Sociological Inquiry*, vol. 45

Booth, C., 1889–1903, *Life and Labour of the People of London*, Macmillan

Bott, Elizabeth, 1957, *Family and Social Network*, Tavistock

Bottomore, T. and Rubel, M., 1976, *Karl Marx: Selected Writings in Sociology and Social Philosophy*, Pelican

Bourne, Richard, 1979, 'The snakes and ladders of the British class system', *New Society*, 8.2.79

Bowles, S. and Gintis, H., 1976, *Schooling in Capitalist America*, Routledge and Kegan Paul

Bowles, S. and Gintis, H., 1988, 'Schooling in Capitalist America: reply to our critics', in M. Cole (ed.), *Bowles and Gintis Revisited*, Falmer Press

Box, Stephen, 1971, *Deviance, Reality and Society*, Holt, Rinehart and Winston

Bradshaw, J. and Holmes, H., 1989, *Living on the Edge*, Tyneside CPAG

Braverman, Harry, 1974, *Labor and Monopoly Capitalism: The Degradation of Work in the Twentieth Century*, Monthly Review Press

Britten, N. and Heath, A., 1983, 'Women, men and social class' in E. Gamarnikow et al., *Gender, Class and Work*, Heinemann

Bruce, Steve, 1988, *Rise and Fall of the New Christian Right: Protestant Politics in America 1978–88*, Clarendon Press

Bruce, Steve, 1990, *A House Divided: Protestantism, Schism and Secularisation*, Routledge

Bruce, Steve (ed.), 1992, *Religion and Modernisation: Sociologists and Historians Debate the Secularisation Thesis*, Clarendon Press

Bruegel, I., 1979, 'Women as a reserve army of labour: a note on recent British experience', *Feminist Review*, 3

Budge, I., 1983, *The New British Political System*, Longman

Burgess, E. and Locke, H., 1945, *The Family*, American Book Company

Burnham, J., 1943, *The Managerial Revolution*, Putnam and Co.

Burns, T. and Stalker, G., 1961, *The Management of Innovation*, Tavistock

Burt, C., 1943, 'Ability and income', *British Journal of Educational Psychology*, 13

Burt, C., 1961, 'Intelligence and social mobility', *British Journal of Statistical Psychology*, vol. 14

Buswell, Carol, 1991, 'The gendering of school and work', *Social Studies Review*, January

Butler, D. and Butler, G., 1994, *British Political Facts 1900–1994*, Macmillan

Butler, D. and Rose, R., 1960, *The British General Election of 1959*, Frank Cass

Butler, D. and Stokes, D., 1974, *Political Change in Modern Britain*, Macmillan

Butler, Robert, 1975, *Why Survive? Being Old in America*, Harper Row

Callinicos, Alex, 1990, *Against Postmodernism: A Marxist Critique*, Polity Press

Calnan, M. and Johnson, B., 1985, 'Health, health risks and inequalities: an exploratory study of women's perceptions', *Sociology of Health and Illness*, 7

Campbell, Anne, 1981, *Girl Delinquents*, Basil Blackwell

Cantril, Hadley, 1940, *The Invasion from Mars: A Study in the Psychology of Panic*, Princeton University Press

Carlen, P. (ed.), 1985, *Criminal Women*, Polity Press

Carr-Hill, R. and Stern, N., 1979, *Crime: The Political and Criminal Statistics*, Academic Press

Castells, Manuel, 1977, *The Urban Question*, Edward Arnold

Castells, Manuel, 1983, *The City and the Grassroots: A Cross-Cultural Theory of Urban Social Movements*, Edward Arnold

Castles, S. and Kosack, G., 1973, *Immigrant Workers and Class Structure in Western Europe*, Oxford University Press

Chambliss, William, 1978, *On the Take: From Petty Crooks to Presidents*, Indiana University Press

Chapman, A. D., 1984, 'Patterns of mobility among men and women in Scotland, 1930–1970', Ph.D. thesis, Plymouth Polytechnic

Cicourel, Aaron, 1976, *The Social Organisation of Juvenile Justice*, Heinemann

Clarke, C. et al., 1979, *Working-Class Culture*, Hutchinson

Clarke, J. and Critcher, C., 1985, *The Devil Makes Work: Leisure in Capitalist Britain*, Macmillan

Clarke, M., 1990, *Business Crime: Its Nature and Control*, Polity Press

Clarke, R. and Mayhew, P. (eds.), 1980, *Designing out Crime*, HMSO

Clarke, R. and Cornish, D. (eds.), 1983, *Crime Control in Britain*, SUNY Press

Clegg, H. A., 1979, *The Changing Structure of Industrial Relations in Great Britain*, Blackwell

Clegg, H. and Adams, R., 1957, *The Employers' Challenge*, Basil Blackwell

Clegg, Stewart, 1979, *The Theory of Power and Organisation*, Routledge

Clinard, M. and Yeager, P., 1980, *Corporate Crime*, The Free Press

Cloward, R. and Ohlin, L., 1961, *Delinquency and Opportunity*, The Free Press

Clutterbuck, D. (ed.), 1985, *New Patterns of Work*, Gower

Coates, D., 1984, *The Context of British Politics*, Hutchinson

Coates, K. and Silburn, R., 1970, *Poverty: The Forgotten Englishmen*, Penguin

Coates, K. and Topham, T., 1986, Trade Unions and Politics, Blackwell

Cohen, A., 1955, Delinquent Boys: The Culture of the Gang, Glencoe Free Press

Cohen, A., 1985, The Symbolic Construction of Community, Tavistock

Cohen, Stanley, 1972, Folk Devils and Moral Panics: The Creation of Mods and Rockers, MacGibbon and Kee

Cole, M. (ed.), 1988, Bowles and Gintis Revisited, The Falmer Press

Coleman, James, 1979, 'Sociological analysis and social policy' in T. Bottomore and R. Nisbet, A History of Sociological Analysis, Heinemann

Commission on the Poor Law and Relief of Distress, 1909, The Poor Law Report of 1909, Macmillan

Cook, J. and Watt, S., 1987, 'Racism, women and poverty' in C. Glendinning and J. Miller (eds.), Women and Poverty in Britain, Wheatsheaf

Cook, S., 1989, Rich Law, Poor Law, Open University Press

Cooke, P. (ed.), 1989, The Changing Face of Urban Britain: Localities, Unwin Hyman

Cooper, David, 1972, The Death of the Family, Penguin

Coronary Prevention Group, 1986, Coronary Heart Disease and Asians in Britain, Coronary Prevention Group/Confederation of Indian Organisations

Coward, Ros, 1987, 'Violent Screen Play', Marxism Today, December

Coyle, Angela, 1984, Redundant Women, The Women's Press

Crewe, I., 1992, 'Why did labour lose?' Politics Review, vol. 2, no. 2

Crompton, R., 1980, 'Class mobility in modern Britain', Sociology, vol. 14

Crompton, R., 1991, 'Women and work in the 1990s', Social Studies Review, May

Crompton, R. and Jones, G. (eds.), 1984, White Collar Proletariat: Deskilling and Gender in Clerical Work, Macmillan

Crosland, C. A. R., 1956, The Future of Socialism, Cape

Croucher, R., 1987, We Refuse to Starve in Silence, Lawrence and Wishart

Dahl, R., 1961, Who Governs? Democracy and Power in an American City, Yale University Press

Dahrendorf, R., 1959, Class and Class Conflict in an Industrial Society, Routledge and Kegan Paul

Daniels, W., 1968, Racial Discrimination in England, Penguin

Darwin, C., 1859, The Origin of Species (J. M. Dent, 1971)

Davis, K. and Moore, W. E., 1945, 'Some principles of stratification', American Sociological Review, vol. 10

Deem, Rosemary, 1986, All Work and No Play: The Sociology of Women and Leisure, Open University Press

Deem, Rosemary, 1988, Work, Unemployment and Leisure, Routledge

Delmar, Rosalind, 1976, 'Looking again at Engels' Origin of the Family, Private Property and the State' in Juliet Mitchell and Ann Oakley, The Rights and Wrongs of Women, Penguin

Delphy, C., 1981, 'Women in stratification studies' in H. Roberts (ed.) Doing Feminist Research, Routledge

Dennis, N., Henriques, F. and Slaughter, C., 1956, Coal is Our Life, Eyre and Spottiswood

Denzin, N., 1970, The Research Act, Aldine

Department of Health and Social Security, 1980, Inequalities in Health, Report of Working Group chaired by Sir Douglas Black. Reprinted as Inequalities in Health: The Black Report, ed. Peter Townsend and Nick Davidson, 1988

Devine, F., 1992, Affluent Workers Revisited, Edinburgh University Press

Dex, S., 1985, The Sexual Division of Work, Wheatsheaf

Ditton, J., 1977, Part-time Crime, Macmillan

Dobash, P. and R., 1980, Violence against Wives: A Case against Patriarchy, Open Books

Douglas, J. W. B., 1964, The Home and the School, MacGibbon and Lee

Douglas, Jack D., 1967, *The Social Meaning of Suicide*, Princeton

Downing, J., 1975, 'The balanced white view' in C. Husband (ed.), *White Media and Black Britain*, Arrow Books

Dumazedier, J., 1974, *The Sociology of Leisure*, Elsevier

Dunleavy, Patrick, 1979, 'The urban bases of political alignment', *British Journal of Political Science*, vol. 9

Dunlop, J., 1958, *Industrial Relations Systems*, Holt

Dunning, E. and Sheard, K., 1969, *Barbarians, Gentlemen and Players*, Oxford University Press

Dunning, E. et al., 1988, *The Roots of Football Violence*, Routledge

Durkheim, E., 1893, *The Division of Labour in Society*, first translated by George Simpson (Macmillan, 1933)

Durkheim, E., 1895, *The Rules of Sociological Method*, first translated by Sarah Solovay and John Mueller (University of Chicago Press, 1938)

Durkheim, E., 1897, *Suicide: A Study in Sociology*, first translated by John Spaulding and George Simpson (The Free Press, 1951)

Durkheim, E., 1902–6, *Moral Education* (The Free Press, 1961)

Durkheim, E., 1912, *The Elementary Forms of Religious Life*, first translated by Joseph Ward Swain (Allen and Unwin, 1915)

Dweck, Carol, 1972, 'Learned helplessness and negative evaluation', *Educator*, vol. 19, no. 2

Dyson, S., 1987, *Mental Handicap: Dilemmas of Parent–Professional Relationships*, Croom-Helm

Edwards, M., 1989, 'The irrelevance of development studies', *Third World Quarterly*, vol. 11, no.1

Ehrenreich, B. and J., 1979, 'The professional-managerial class' in P. Walker (ed.), *Between Labour and Capital*, Harvester Press

Eisenstadt, S., 1956, *From Generation to Generation*, The Free Press

Eisenstadt, S., 1966, *Modernisation: Protest and Change*, Prentice Hall

Eldridge, J., 1968, *Industrial Disputes*, Routledge and Kegan Paul

Elston, M., 1980, 'Medicine: half our future doctors?' in R. Silverstone and A. Ward (eds.), *Careers of Professional Women*, Croom Helm

Engels, Friedrich, 1845, *The Condition of the Working Class in England* (Penguin, 1988)

Engels, Friedrich, 1884, *The Origin of the Family, Private Property and the State* (Penguin, 1986)

Esterson, A., 1972, *The Leaves of Spring*, Penguin

Esterson, A. and Laing, R., 1970, *Sanity, Madness and the Family*, Penguin

Ettlinger, R. and Flordah, G., 1955, 'Attempted suicide', *Act Psychiatrica*

Etzioni, Amitai, 1964, *Modern Organisations*, Prentice Hall

Eysenck, H. J., 1971, *Race, Intelligence and Education*, Temple-Smith

Eysenck, H. J. and Eysenck, S. B. G., 1975, *The Manual of the Eysenck Personality Questionnaire*, Hodder and Stoughton

Ferguson, Marjorie, 1983, *Forever Feminine: Women's Magazines and the Cult of Femininity*, Heinemann

Field, Frank, 1989, *Losing Out: The Emergence of Britain's Underclass*, Blackwell

Firestone, Shulamith, 1970, *The Dialectic of Sex*, Paladin

Fiske, John, 1990, 'Women and quiz shows: consumerism, patriarchy and resisting pleasures' in M. E. Brown (ed.), *Television and Women's Culture*, Sage

Fletcher, R., 1962, *Family and Marriage in Britain*, Penguin

Fletcher, R., 1988, *The Abolitionists: The Family and Marriage under Attack*, Routledge

Fletcher, R., 1991, *Science, Ideology and the Media: The Cyril Burt Scandal*, Transaction

Foucault, M., 1980, *Power and Knowledge: Selected Interviews and Other Writings 1972–77*, Harvester Press

Frank, A. G., 1967, *Capitalism and Underdevelopment in Latin America*, Monthly Review Press

Frank, A. G., 1969, *Latin America: Underdevelopment or Revolution*, Monthly Review Press

Frank, A. G., 1981, *Crisis in the Third World*, Heinemann

Freeman, D., 1983, *Margaret Mead and Samoa: The Making and Unmaking of an Anthropological Myth*, Australian National University Press

Freire, Paolo, 1972, *Pedagogy of the Oppressed*, Penguin

Freire, Paolo, 1976, *Education: The Practice of Freedom*, Writers and Readers Cooperative

Friedson, E., 1975, *Profession of Medicine*, Dodd, Mead and Co.

Fuller, Mary, 1980, 'Black girls in a London comprehensive school' in R. Deem (ed.), *Schooling for Women's Work*, Routledge and Kegan Paul

Galbraith, J. K., 1967, *The New Industrial State*, Hamish Hamilton

Galbraith, J. K., 1992, *The Culture of Contentment*, Sinclair Stevenson

Gallie, Duncan, 1978, *In Search of the New Working Class*, Cambridge University Press

Gans, Howard, 1962, 'Urbanism and suburbanism as ways of life' in A. M. Rose, *Human Behaviour and Social Processes*, Routledge

Gans, Howard, 1967, *The Levittowners*, Allen Lane

Gans, Howard, 1973, 'The positive functions of poverty', *American Journal of Sociology*, vol. 78, no. 2

Garfinkel, H., 1967, *Studies in Ethnomethodology*, Prentice Hall

Gellner, E., 1992, *Postmodernism, Reason and Religion*, Routledge

George, V. and Miller, S., 1994, *Social Policy Towards 2000: Squaring the Welfare Circle*, Routledge

Gerth, H. and Mills, C. Wright, 1954, *Character and Social Structure*, Routledge and Kegan Paul

Giddens, Anthony, 1973, *The Class Structure of the Advanced Societies*, Hutchinson

Giddens, Anthony, 1980, *The Making of Post-Christian Britain*, Longman

Giddens, Anthony, 1984, *The Constitution of Society*, Polity Press

Giddens, Anthony, 1990, *The Consequences of Modernity*, Polity Press

Gilbert, A., 1980, *The Making of Post-Christian Britain*, Longman

Gilroy, P., 1987, *There Ain't no Black in the Union Jack*, Hutchinson

Giner, S., 1976, *Mass Society*, Martin Robertson

Giroux, H., 1984, 'Ideology, agency and the process of schooling' in L. Barton and S. Walker (eds.), *Social Crisis and Educational Research*, Croom Helm

Glasgow University Media Group, 1976, *Bad News*, Routledge and Kegan Paul

GUMG, 1980, *More Bad News*, Routledge and Kegan Paul

GUMG, 1982, *Really Bad News*, Routledge and Kegan Paul

GUMG, 1985, *War and Peace News*, Open University Press

Glasner, Peter, 1977, *The Concept of Secularisation*, Routledge and Kegan Paul

Glass, David (ed.), 1954, *Social Mobility in Britain*, Routledge and Kegan Paul

Glock, C. and Stark, R., 1965, *Religion and Society in Tension*, Rand McNally

Goffman, Erving, 1959, *The Presentation of Self in Everyday Life*, Doubleday Anchor

Goffman, Erving, 1961, *Asylums: Essays on the Social Situation of Mental Patients and Other Inmates*, Anchor Books

Goffman, Erving, 1971, *Relations in Public*, Basic Books

Goldthorpe, John, 1966, 'Social stratification in industrial society' in R. Bendix and S. Lipset (eds.), *Class, Status and Power*, The Free Press

Goldthorpe, John et al., 1968, *The Industrial Worker: Industrial Attitudes and Behaviour*, Cambridge University Press

Goldthorpe, John et al., 1969, *The Affluent Worker in the Class Structure*, Cambridge University Press

Goldthorpe, John, 1980, *Social Mobility and Class Structure in Modern Britain*, Clarendon Press

Goldthorpe, J., 1983, 'Women and class analysis: a defence of the conventional view', *Sociology*, 17

Goldthorpe, J. and Payne, C., 1986, 'On the class mobility of women', *Sociology*, 20

Goode, William, 1963, *World Revolution and Family Patterns*, The Free Press

Gorer, G., 1971, *Sex and Marriage in Britain Today*, Nelson

Gorz, A., 1984, *Pathways to Paradise*, Pluto

Gould, S. J., 1981, *The Mismeasure of Man*, W. W. Norton and Co.

Gouldner, A., 1968, 'The sociologist as partisan: sociology and the welfare state', *The American Sociologist*, 3

Gouldner, A., 1970, *The Coming Crisis of Western Sociology*, Basic Books

Graham, Hilary, 1984, *Women, Health and the Family*, Wheatsheaf

Gramsci, Antonio, 1971, *Selections from the Prison Notebooks*, New Left Books

Grieco, M., 1987, *Keeping it in the Family: Social Networks and Employment Change*, Tavistock Publications

Griffin, C., 1985, *Typical Girls?*, Routledge and Kegan Paul

Griffin, C., 1986, 'It's different for girls', *Social Studies Review*, November

Griffin, J., 1939, *Strikes: A Study in Quantitative Economics*, Columbia University Press

Grint, K., 1991, *The Sociology of Work: An Introduction*, Polity Press

Gubrium, J. and Holstein, J., 1990, *What is Family?*, Mayfield Publishing

Gurevitch, M and Blumler, J., 1977, 'Linkages between the mass media and politics' in J. Curran et al. (eds.), *Mass Communication and Mass Society*, Edward Arnold

Hagen, E., 1962, *On the Theory of Social Change*, Dorsey

Hall, S. and Jefferson, T. (eds.), 1976, *Resistance through Rituals*, Hutchinson

Hall, S., 1978, 'The great moving right show', *Marxism Today*, December, reprinted in S. Hall, *The Hard Road to Renewal*, Verso

Hall, S. 1978a, 'Mugging, the State and the law' in S. Hall et al., *Policing the Crisis*, Macmillan

Hall, S., 1987, 'Urban unrest in Britain' in John Benyon and John Solomos, *The Roots of Urban Unrest*, Pergamon

Hall, S., 1990, 'Cultural identity and diaspora' in J. Rutherford (ed.), *Identity*, Lawrence and Wishart

Hallam, H. E., 1961, 'Population density in medieval Fenland', *Economic History Review*, 14

Halmos, P., 1970, *The Personal Service Society*, Constable

Halsey, A. H. et al., 1980, *Origins and Destinations*, Clarendon Press

Hammersley, M. (ed.), 1993, 'Introduction' in *Social Research: Philosophy, Politics and Practice*, Sage Publications

Harding, J., 1980, 'Sex differences in performance in science examinations' in R. Deem (ed.), *Schooling for Women's Work*, Routledge and Kegan Paul

Harding, S. (ed.), 1987, *Feminism and Methodology*, Open University Press

Hargreaves, D., 1967, *Social Relations in a Secondary School*, Routledge and Kegan Paul

Harris, C. C. et al., 1987, *Redundancy and Recession*, Basil Blackwell

Harvey, David, 1989, *The Condition of Postmodernity*, Blackwell

Haworth, J. and Evans, S., 1987, 'Meaningful activity and unemployment' in D. Fryer and P. Ullah (eds.), *Unemployed People*, Open University Press

Hayter, Teresa, 1971, *Aid as Imperialism*, Penguin

Hayter, Teresa, 1981, *The Creation of World Poverty*, Pluto

Heath, A. et al., 1985, *How Britain Votes*, Pergamon

Heath, A., 1981, *Social Mobility*, Fontana

Hebdige, D., 1979, *Subculture: The Meaning of Style*, Methuen

Heidensohn, Frances, 1985, *Women and Crime*, Macmillan

Herberg, Will, 1955, *Protestant, Catholic, Jew*, Doubleday

Hillery, G. A. Jnr, 1955, 'Definitions of community: areas of agreement', *Rural Sociology*, 20

Hillyard, P., 1987, 'The normalization of special powers: from Northern Ireland to Britain' in P. Scraton (ed.), *Law, Order and the Authoritarian State*, Open University Press

Himmelweit, H., 1958, *Television and the Child*, Oxford University Press

Himmelweit, H. et al., 1981, *How Voters Decide*, Academic Press

Hirschi, Travis, 1969, *The Causes of Delinquency*, University of California Press

Hood-Williams, J., 1990, 'Patriarchy for children: on the stability of power relations in children's lives' in L. Chisholm et al., *Childhood, Youth and Social Change*, Falmer Press

Howitt, Dennis, 1982, *Mass Media and Social Problems*, Pergamon Press

Hudson, B., 1989, 'Discrimination and disparity: the influence of race on sentencing', *New Community*, vol. 16, no.1

Humphreys, L., 1970, *Tearoom Trade: A Study of Homosexual Encounters in Public Places*, Aldine Publishing Company

Hyman, R., 1972, *Strikes*, Fontana (4th edition, 1991)

Hyman, R., 1989, 'What's happening to the unions?', *Social Studies Review*, March

Illich, Ivan, 1975, *Limits to Medicine: Medical Nemesis — The Expropriation of Health*, Marion Boyars

Illsley, R., 1955, 'Social class selection and class differences in relation to stillbirths', *British Medical Journal*, 2

Illsley, R., 1986, 'Occupational class, selection and the production of inequalities in health', *Quarterly Journal of Health Affairs*, 2

Jahoda, M. et al., 1933, *Marienthal: A Study of an Unemployed Community*, Aldine/Atherton

Jameson, Frederic, 1991, *Postmodernism or the Cultural Logic of Late Capitalism*, Verso

Jeffcoate, R., 1984, *Ethnic Minorities and Education*, Harper and Row

Jenkins, R., 1991, 'Disability and social stratification', *British Journal of Sociology*, vol. 42, no. 4

Jencks, C. and Peterson, P. (eds.), 1991, *The Urban Underclass*, Brookings Institution

Jensen, A., 1967, 'How much can we boost IQ and scholastic achievement?', *Harvard Educational Review*, 29

Johnson, T., 1972, *Professions and Power*, Macmillan

Jones, B., 1991, *Politics UK*, Philip Allen

Jones, I. and Cameron, D., 1984, 'Social class: an embarrassment for epidemiology?', *Community Medicine*, 6

Jordan, B., 1973, *Paupers: The Making of the Claiming Class*, Routledge

Joseph, G., 1981, 'The incompatible ménage à trois: Marxism, feminism and racism' in Lydia Sargent (ed.), *Women and Revolution: A Discussion of the Unhappy Marriage of Marxism and Feminism*, Pluto Press

Joseph, G., 1988, 'Black feminist pedagogy and schooling in white capitalist America' in M. Cole (ed.), *Bowles and Gintis Revisited*, Falmer Press

Joynson, R., 1989, *The Burt Affair*, Routledge

Katz, E. and Lazarsfeld, P., 1955, *Personal Influence*, The Free Press

Katz, J., 1988, *Seductions of Crime: Moral and Sensual Attraction in Doing Evil*, Basic Books

Kavanagh, D., 1985, 'Whatever happened to consensus politics?', *Political Studies*, vol. 33

Keddie, Nell, 1971, 'Classroom knowledge' in M. F. D. Young (ed.), *Knowledge and Control*, Collier-Macmillan

Keddie, Nell (ed.), 1973, *Tinker, Tailor ... The Myth of Cultural Deprivation*, Penguin

Kelly, A. (ed.), 1981, *The Missing Half: Girls and Science Education*, Manchester University Press

Kelly, John, 1988, *Trade Unions and Socialist Politics*, Verso

Kelvin, P. et al., 1984, *Unemployment and Leisure*, Sports Council

Kerr, C. et al., 1960, *Industrialism and Industrial Man: The Problems of Labor and Management in Economic Growth*, Harvard University Press

Kerr, C., 1964, *Labor and Management in Industrial Society*, Doubleday

Keynes, J. M., 1936, *The General Theory of Employment, Interest and Money* (Macmillan, 1973)

Kincaid, J., 1973, *Poverty and Equality in England: A Study of Social Security and Taxation*, Penguin

Kitching, Gavin, 1982, *Development and Underdevelopment in Historical Perspective*, Methuen

Kling, R., 1991, 'Computerisation and transformation', *Science, Technology and Human Values*, vol. 16, no. 4

Kollontai, A., 1977, *Selected Writings of Alexandra Kollontai*, Norton and Co.

Kuhn, J., 1961, *Bargaining in Grievance Settlement*, Columbia University Press

Kuhn, T., 1962, *The Structure of Scientific Revolutions*, University of Chicago Press

Labov, W., 1969, 'The logic of non-standard English' in Keddie, 1973

Lacey, C., 1970, *Hightown Grammar*, Manchester University Press

Lacey, C., 1975, 'Destreaming in a "pressurised" academic environment', in S. Eggleston (ed.), *Contemporary Research in the Sociology of Education*, Methuen

Laing, R. D. and Esterson, A., 1970, *Sanity, Madness and the Family*, Penguin

Lal, Deepak, 1983, *The Poverty of Development Economics*, Institute of Economic Affairs

Land, K. et al., 1990, 'Structural covariates of homicide rates', *American Journal of Sociology*, 95

Larner, R., 1966, 'Ownership and control in the 200 largest non-financial corporations – 1929 and 1963', *American Economic Review*, Sept 1966

Laslett, P. (ed.), 1972, *Household and Family in Past Time*, Cambridge University Press

Laslett, P., 1982, 'Foreword' in R. Rapoport et al. (eds.), *Families in Britain*, Routledge and Kegan Paul

Lather, P., 1991, *Getting Smart: Feminist Research and Pedagogy with/in the Postmodern*, Routledge

Lea, J. and Young, J., 1984, *What is to be Done About Law and Order?*, Penguin

Leach, E., 1967, *A Runaway World?*, BBC Publications

Leavis, Q. D., 1932, *Fiction and the Reading Public*, Chatto and Windus

Leech, K. and Amin, K., 1988, *A New Underclass? Race, Poverty and the Inner City*, Child Poverty Action Group

Lees, S., 1986, *Losing Out: Sexuality and Adolescent Girls*, Hutchinson

Leeson, J. and Gray, J., 1978, *Women and Medicine*, Tavistock

Le Grand, Julian, 1982, *Strategy of Equality: Redistribution and the Social Services*, Allen and Unwin

Lemert, Edwin, 1967, *Human Deviance, Social Problems and Social Control*, Prentice Hall

Lerner, D., 1964, *The Passing of Traditional Society*, The Free Press

Lewis, Oscar, 1958, *La Vida: A Puerto Rican Family in the Culture of Poverty*, Panther

Lewis, Oscar, 1961, *The Children of Sanchez*, Random House

Lewis, W. A., 1954, *Economic Development with Unlimited Supplies of Labour*, Manchester School

Liebow, E., 1967, *Tally's Corner*, Little Boston

Lipietz, A., 1993, *Towards a New Economic Order: Postfordism, Ecology and Democracy*, Polity Press

Lipset, Seymour, 1963, *Political Man*, Mercury Books

Lipset, Seymour, 1964, 'The changing class structure of contemporary European politics', *Daedalus*, vol. 93

Lipset, Seymour *et al.*, 1956, *Union Democracy*, The Free Press

Lockwood, D., 1958, *The Black-Coated Worker*, Allen and Unwin

Lombroso, Cesare, 1876, *L'Uomo Delinquente*, Fratelli-Bocca

Lombroso, C. and Ferrero, W., 1895, *The Female Offender*, Fisher Unwin

Lukes, Steven, 1974, *Power: A Radical View*, Macmillan

Lynd, R. S., 1939, *Knowledge for What? The Place of Social Science in American Culture*, Princeton University Press

Lyotard, Jean-François, 1984, *The Postmodern Condition: A Report on Knowledge*, Manchester University Press

MacInnes, J., 1987, *Thatcherism at Work*, Open University Press

Mack, J. and Lansley, S., 1985, *Poor Britain*, Allen and Unwin

Maguire, M. and Pointing, V. (eds.), 1988, *Victims of Crime: A New Deal?*, Open University Press

Mallet, S., 1963, *The New Working Class*, Spokesman

Mann, Michael, 1973, *Consciousness and Action Among the Western Working Class*, Macmillan

Mann, Michael, 1986 and 1993, *The Sources of Social Power*, 2 vols., Cambridge University Press

Marcuse, H., 1964, *One Dimensional Man: Studies in the Ideology of Advanced Industrial Society*, Routledge and Kegan Paul

Mares, P. *et al.*, 1987, *Training in Multiracial Health Care*, National Extension College

Marmot, M. *et al.*, 1983, 'Immigrant mortality in England and Wales', *Population Trends*, 33

Marrus, M., 1974, *The Emergence of Leisure*, Meckler

Marshall, G. *et al.*, 1988, *Social Class in Modern Britain*, Hutchinson

Marshall, T. H., 1970, 'Review of *The Affluent Worker in the Class Structure*', *Economic Journal*, 80

Martin, David, 1969, *The Religious and the Secular*, Routledge and Kegan Paul

Martin, David, 1978, *A General Theory of Secularisation*, Blackwell

Martin, David, 1990, *Tongues of Fire: The Explosion of Protestantism in Latin America*, Blackwell

Martin, David *et al.*, 1988, *The Prevalence of Disability Among Adults*, HMSO

Marx, Karl, 1845, 'Theses on Feurbach' from T. Bottomore and M. Rubel, *Karl Marx: Selected Writings in Sociology and Social Philosophy* (Pelican, 1976)

Marx, Karl, 1845–6, *The German Ideology* (Lawrence and Wishart, 1965)

Marx, Karl, 1857/8, *The Grundrisse*, translated by Martin Nicolaus (Pelican, 1973)

Marx, Karl, 1859, 'Preface to a contribution to a critique of political economy' in Bottomore and Rubel, 1976

Marx, Karl, 1867, *Capital*, translated by S. Moore and E. Aveling (Penguin, 1976)

Marx, Karl and Engels, Friedrich, 1848, *The Communist Manifesto*, translated by S. Moore and edited by A. J. P. Taylor (Penguin, 1967)

Massey, D., 1984, *Spatial Divisions of Labour*, Macmillan

Matza, D., 1964, *Delinquence and Drift*, John Wiley and Sons

Mawby, R., 1980, 'Sex and crime: the results of a sef-report study', *British Journal of Sociology*, vol. 31, no. 52

Mayhew, P. and Hough, M., 1983 and 1985, *The British Crime Survey*, HMSO

Mayhew, P. *et al.*, 1989, *The 1988 British Crime Survey*, HMSO

Mayo, Elton, 1933, *The Human Problems of an Industrial Civilisation*, Macmillan

McClelland, D., 1961, *The Achieving Society*, Princeton University Press

McIlroy, J., 1988, *Trade Unions in Britain Today*, Manchester University Press

McKenzie, R. and Silver, A., 1968, *Angels in Marble*, Heinemann

McKeown, T., 1976, *The Modern Rise of the Population*, Edward Arnold

McLuhan, M. and Fiore, Q., 1967, *The Medium is the Message*, Penguin

McNaught, A., 1987, *Race and Health Policy*, Croom Helm

McRobbie, A. and Garber, J., 1976, 'Girls and subcultures: and exploration' in S. Hall and T. Jefferson (eds), *Resistance through Rituals*, Hutchinson

McRobbie, A. and McCabe, T., 1981, *Feminism for Girls: An Adventure Story*, Routledge and Kegan Paul

Mead, Margaret, 1928, *Coming of Age in Samoa: A Study of Adolescence and Sex in Primitive Societies* (Penguin,1961)

Merton, R., 1949, *Social Theory and Social Structure*, The Free Press

Merton, R., 1949a, *Bureaucratic Structure and Personality*, The Free Press

Michels, Robert, 1911, *Political Parties: A Sociological Study of the Oligarchical Tendencies of Modern Democracy*, The Free Press

Miles, I., 1984, *Unemployment, Time Use and the Context of Experience*, University of Sussex

Miles, R., 1982, *Racism and Migrant Labour*, Routledge and Kegan Paul

Miliband, Ralph, 1969, *The State in Capitalist Society* , Weidenfeld and Nicolson

Millar, J. and Glendinning, C., 1989, 'Gender and Poverty', *Journal of Social Policy*, vol. 18, no. 3

Miller, Walter, 1962, 'Lower-class culture as a generating milieu of gang delinquency' in M. Wolfgang et al., *The Sociology of Crime and Delinquency*, John Wiley and Sons

Mills, C. Wright, 1956, *The Power Elite*, Oxford University Press

Mills, C. Wright, 1959, *The Sociological Imagination*, Oxford University Press

Minford, Patrick, 1982, *Unemployment: Cause and Cure*, Basil Blackwell

Ministry of Education, 1963, *Half Our Future: A Report of the Central Advisory Council for Education*, HMSO

Mogey, J. M., 1956, *Family and Neighbourhood: Two Studies in Oxford*, Oxford University Press

Moores, Mike and Breslin, Tony, 1991, 'So what is good sociology? The view from the chief examiners', *Social Science Teacher*, vol. 20, no. 3

Mosca, G., 1896, *The Ruling Class* (McGraw Hill, 1939)

Murdock, G. P., 1949, *Social Structure*, Macmillan

Murdock, G., 1980, 'Class, power and the press: problems of conceptualisation and evidence' in H. Christian (ed.), *The Sociology of Journalism and the Press*, University of Keele

Murdock, G. and Golding, P., 1977, 'Capitalism, communications and class relations' in J. Curran et al., *Mass Communication and Society*, Edward Arnold

Myrdal, G., 1944, *An American Dilemma: The Negro Problem and American Democracy*, Harper and Brothers

Navarro, V., 1976, *Medicine under Capitalism*, Croom Helm

Nelken, D., 1983, *The Limits of Legal Process: A Study of Landlords, Law and Crime*, Academic Press

Newby, H., 1979, *Green and Pleasant Land: Social Change in Rural Britain*, Hutchinson

Newby, H., 1985, *Restructuring Capital: Recession and Reorganisation in Industrial Society*, Macmillan

Newby, H. and Bell, C., 1971, *Community Studies*, George Allen and Unwin

Niebuhr, H., 1929, *The Social Sources of Denominationalism*, Holt, Rinehart and Wilson

Nisbet, R., 1966, *The Sociological Tradition*, Heinemann

Nkrumah, Kwame, 1965, *Neo-colonialism: The Last Stage of Imperialism*, Nelson

Noble, David, 1984, *Forces of Production*, Knopf

Nordlinger, E., 1967, *The Working-Class Tories: Authority, Deference and Stable Democracy*, MacGibbon

Nyerere, Julius, 1973, *Freedom and Development*, Oxford University Press

Oakley, A., 1972, *Sex, Gender and Society*, Temple Smith

Oakley, A., 1974a, *Housewife*, Allen Lane

Oakley, A., 1974b, *The Sociology of Housework*, Martin Robertson

Oakley, A., 1981, *Subject Women*, Martin Robertson

O'Connor, J., 1973, *The Final Crisis of the State*, St Martin's Press

Opie, Peter and Iona, 1967, *The Lore and Language of Schoolchildren*, Clarendon Press

Orwell, George, 1945, *Animal Farm*, Martin Secker and Warburg

Pahl, Ray, 1965a, *Urbs in Rure*, Weidenfeld and Nicolson

Pahl, Ray, 1965b, 'Urbs in rure: the metropolitan fringe in Hertfordshire', *Geographical Papers*, LSE

Pahl, Ray, 1965c, 'Class and community in English commuter villages', *Sociological Review*, 6

Pahl, Ray, 1968, *Readings in Urban Sociology*, Pergamon Press

Pahl, Ray, 1975, *Whose City?*, Penguin

Pahl, Ray, 1984, *Divisions of Labour*, Basil Blackwell

Pareto, Vilfredo, 1978, *Socialist Systems*, first published in 1902, Librairie Droz

Park, R. E. and Burgess, E., 1921, *Introduction to the Science of Sociology*, University of Chicago Press

Park, R. E. and Burgess, E., 1925, *The City*, University of Chicago Press

Parker, Stanley, 1983, 'Work and Leisure' in E. Butterworth and D. Weir (eds.), *The Sociology of Leisure*, George Allen and Unwin

Parkin, Frank, 1971, *Class Inequality and Political Order*, MacGibbon and Kee

Parry, N. and J., 1976, *The Rise of the Medical Profession*, Croom Helm

Parsons, Talcott, 1951, *The Social System*, The Free Press

Parsons, Talcott, 1952, 'The superego and the theory of social systems', *Psychiatry*, 15

Parsons, Talcott, 1953, 'A revised analytical approach to the theory of stratification' in R. Bendix and S. Lipset (eds.), *Class, Status and Power*, The Free Press

Parsons, Talcott, 1959a, 'The social structure of the family' in R. Anshen (ed.), *The Family: Its Functions and Destiny*, Harper and Row

Parsons, Talcott, 1959b, 'The school class as a social system', *Harvard Educational Review*, Fall

Parsons, Talcott, 1959c, 'The principal structure of community' in Carl J. Friedrich (ed.), *Community*, Liberal Arts Press

Parsons, Talcott, 1960, *Structure and Process in Modern Societies*, The Free Press

Parsons, Talcott, 1965, 'Religious perspectives in sociology and social psychology' in Lessa, W. and Vogt, E., *Reader in Comparative Religion*, Harper and Row

Parsons, Talcott, 1969, *Politics and Social Structure*, The Free Press

Parsons, Talcott, 1969a, *Structure and Process in Modern Societies*, The Free Press

Parsons, Talcott and Shils, E., 1951, *Towards a General Theory of Action*, Harvard University Press

Parsons, Talcott and Bales, R., 1955, *Family, Socialisation and Interaction Process*, The Free Press

Parsons, Talcott et al., 1953, *Working Papers in the Theory of Action*, The Free Press

Passas, N., 1990, 'Anomie and corporate deviance', *Contemporary Crises*, 14

Payer, Cheryl, 1974, *The Debt Trap*, Harmondsworth

Pearce, Frank, 1976, *Crimes of the Powerful*, Pluto Press

Pearson, G., 1983, *Hooligans: A History of Respectable Fears*, Macmillan

Pen, J., 1971, *Income Distribution*, Allen Lane

Phillips, A., 1987, *Divided Loyalties*, Virago

Philo, Greg, 1990, *Seeing and Believing*, Routledge

Philo, Greg, 1991, 'Seeing is believing', *Social Studies Review*, May

Piaget, Jean, 1954, *The Construction of Reality in the Child*, Basic Books

Pollack, O., 1950, *The Criminality of Women*, University of Pennsylvania Press

Pollock, Linda, 1983, *Forgotten Children*, Cambridge University Press

Polsby, N., 1963, *Community Power and Political Theory*, Yale University Press

Polsky, N., 1969, *Hustlers, Beats and Others*, Penguin

Popper, Karl, 1963, *Conjectures and Refutations: The Growth of Scientific Knowledge*, Routledge and Kegan Paul

Postman, Neil, 1985, *The Disappearance of Childhood*, Comet

Poulantzas, Nikos, 1969, 'The problem of the capitalist state', *New Left Review*, vol. 58

Prahalad, G. and Hamal, G., 1990, 'The core competence of the corporation', *Harvard Business Review*, 90

Pryce, Ken, 1979, *Endless Pressure*, Bristol Classical Press

Purcell, J., 1982, 'Macho managers and the new industrial relations', *Employee Relations*, vol. 4, no. 1

Quinney, Richard, 1975, 'Crime control in capitalist society: a critical philosophy of legal order' in I. Tayor *et al.* (eds.), *Critical Criminology*, Routledge and Kegan Paul

Radcliffe-Brown, A. R., 1952, *Structure and Function in Primitive Society*, Cohen and West

Rae, M. *et al.*, 1983, *First Rights: A Guide to Legal Rights for Young People*, National Council for Civil Liberties

Rapoport, R. and R., 1976, *Dual Career Families Re-examined*, Martin Robertson

Rathwell, T. and Phillips, D., 1986, *Race, Disease and Health*, Croom Helm

Redfield, Robert, 1941, *The Folk Culture of Yucatan*, University of Chicago Press

Redfield, Robert, 1947, 'Folk society', *American Journal of Sociology*, 52

Rex, John, 1968, 'The sociology of a zone of transition' in R. E. Pahl (ed.), *Readings in Urban Sociology*, Pergamon Press

Rex, John and Moore, Robert, 1967, *Race, Community and Conflict*, Oxford University Press

Rex, J. and Tomlinson, S., 1979, *Colonial Immigrants in a British City*, Routledge and Kegan Paul

Richardson, J. and Jordan, G., 1979, *Governing under Pressure*, Martin Robertson

Robbins, D., 1963, *Higher Education* – report of the committee appointed by the prime minister under the chairmanship of Lord Robbins, 1961–3, HMSO

Roberts, H. (ed.), 1981, *Doing Feminist Research*, Routledge

Roberts, H., 1987, *Women and Social Classification*, Wheatsheaf

Roberts, K., 1974, 'The changing relationship between work and leisure' in I. Appleton (ed.), *Leisure Research and Policy*, Scottish Academic Press

Roberts, K., 1984, *School Leavers and their Prospects: Youth and the Labour Market in the 1980s*, Open University Press

Roberts, Ken *et al.*, 1977, *The Fragmentary Class Structure*, Heinemann

Rodney, Walter, 1972, *How Europe Underdeveloped Africa*, Tanzania Publishing House

Rose, H., 1982, 'Making science feminist' in E. Whitelegg *et al.*, (eds.), *The Changing Experience of Women*, Martin Robertson

Rose, R., 1984, *Do Parties Make a Difference?*, Macmillan

Rossi, P. and Blum, A., 1968, in D. P. Moynihan (ed.), *On Understanding Poverty*, Basic Books

Rostow, W. W., 1960, *The Stages of Economic Growth: A Non-Communist Manifesto*, Cambridge University Press

Rowntree, B. S. and Lavers, G. R., 1951, Poverty and The Welfare State, Longman

Rowntree, B. S., 1901, Poverty: A Study of Town Life, Macmillan

Royal Commission on Trade Unions and Employers' Associations (the Donovan commission), 1968, Report, Cmd 3623, HMSO

Rubery, J., 1980, 'Structured labour markets, worker organisation and low pay' in A. H. Amsden (ed.), The Economics of Women and Work, Penguin

Russell, J. C., 1948, British Medieval Population, Melbourne University Press

Rutter, Michael et al., 1979, Fifteen Thousand Hours, Open Books

Rutter, M. and Madge, N., 1976, Cycles of Deprivation, Heinemann

Sarlvik, B. and Crewe, I., 1983, Decade of Dealignment: The Conservative Victory of 1979 and Electoral Trends in the 1970s, Cambridge University Press

Sayers, Janet et al., (eds.), 1987, Engels Revisited, Tavistock

Sayles, L., 1958, The Behaviour of Industrial Work Groups, Wiley

Scarman, Lord, 1981, The Scarman Report: The Brixton disorders 10–12 April 1981, Cmd 8247, HMSO

Schumacher, E. F., 1973, Small is Beautiful, Harper and Row

Scott, J. and Homans, G., 1947, 'Reflections on the wildcat strikes', American Sociological Review, January

Scott, John, 1979, Corporations, Classes and Capitalism, Hutchinson

Scott, John, 1986, 'The debate on ownership and control', Social Studies Review, January

Scott, John, 1991, Who Rules Britain?, Polity Press

Scraton, Phil, 1985, The State of the Police, Pluto Press

Seabrook, Jeremy, 1984, The Leisure Society, Basil Blackwell

Seeley, J. et al. 1963, Crestwood Heights, Basic Books

Segal, L., 1983, What is to be Done about the Family?, Penguin

Seeman, M., 1959, 'On the meaning of alienation', American Sociological Review, 24

Selznick, P., 1949, The TVA and the Grassroots: A Study in the Sociology of Formal Organisation, California University Press

Shaiken, Harley, 1986, Work Transformed: Automation and Labor in the Computer Age, Lexington Books

Sharpe, Sue, 1976, Just Like a Girl: How Girls Learn to be Women, Penguin

Shaw, C. and McKay, H., 1942, Juvenile Delinquency and Urban Areas, University of Chicago Press

Shils, E., 1971,'Mass society and its culture' in B. Rosenberg and D. M. White (eds.), Mass Culture Revisited, Van Nostrand

Shiner, Larry, 1971, 'The concept of secularisation in empirical research' in K. Thompson and J. Tunstall, Sociological Perspectives, Penguin

Silverman, David, 1970, The Theory of Organisations, Heinemann

Simmel, Georg, 1903, 'The metropolis and mental life' in K. Wolff (ed.), The Sociology of Georg Simmel, The Free Press

Sinfield, A., 1981, What Unemployment Means, Martin Robertson

Sklair, L., 1973, Organised Knowledge, MacGibbon and Kee

Sklair, L., 1991, Sociology of the Global System, Harvester and Johns Hopkins University Press

Skocpol, T., 1979, States and Social Revolutions, Cambridge University Press

Smith, Adam, 1776, The Wealth of Nations (Everyman, 1991)

Smith, D., 1994, 'Race, crime and criminal justice' in M. Maguire et al., The Oxford Handbook of Criminology, Clarendon Press

Spelman, Elizabeth, 1988, Inessential Woman, The Women's Press

Stanworth, M., 1983, Gender and Schooling: A Study of Sexual Divisions in the Classroom, Hutchinson

Stanworth, M., 1984, 'Women and class analysis: a reply to Goldthorpe', *Sociology*, 18

Stern, J., 1983, 'Social mobility and the interpretation of social class mortality differentials', *Journal of Social Policy*, vol. 12, no. 1

Stewart, Michael, 1972, *Keynes and After*, Pelican

Straussman, P., 1985, *Information Payoff: The Transformation of Work in the Electronic Age*, Basic Books

Strinati, Dominic, 1992, 'Postmodernism and popular culture', *Sociology Review*, April

Sutherland, Edwin, 1949, *White Collar Crime*, Holt, Rinehart and Wilson

Sykes, G. and Matza, D., 1962, 'Techniques of neutralisation: a theory of delinquency' in M. Wolfgang *et al.* (eds.), *The Sociology of Crime and Delinquency*, John Wiley and Sons

Tapper, T. and Bowles, N., 1981, 'Working-class Tories: the search for theory', *Teaching Politics*, vol. 10, no. 2

Taylor, F. W., 1911, *The Principles of Scientific Management*, Harper

Taylor, John, 1979, *From Modernisation to Modes of Production*, Macmillan

Taylor, Steve, 1990, 'Beyond Durkheim: sociology and suicide', *Social Studies Review*, November

Thompson, P., 1983, *The Nature of Work: An Introduction to Debates on the Labour Process*, Macmillan

Thompson, P. and McHugh, D., 1990, *Work Organisations*, Macmillan

Thorns, D., 1973, *Suburbia*, Granada Publishing Limited

Tönnies, Ferdinand, 1887, *Community and Society*, Harper Row

Townsend, P. *et al.*, 1986, *Inequalities in Health in the Northern Region: An Interim Report*, Northern Region Health Authority

Townsend, Peter, 1979, *Poverty in the United Kingdom*, Penguin

Townsend, Peter *et al.*, 1987, *Poverty and Labour in London*, Low Pay Unit

Toynbee, P., 1978, *The Guardian*, 30.10.78

Troeltsch, E., 1931, *The Social Teaching of the Christian Churches*, Allen and Unwin

Trow, M., 1957, 'Participant observation and interviewing: a comparison', *Human Organisation*, vol. 16

Tudor-Hart, Julian, 1971, 'The inverse care law', *The Lancet*, 1

Tumin, M., 1953, 'Some principles of stratification: a critical analysis', *American Sociological Review*, 18

Tunstall, J., 1983, *The Media in Britain*, Constable

Tylor, E., 1871, *Primitive Culture*, Murray

Veit-Wilson, John, 1986, 'Paradigms of poverty: a rehabilitation of B. S. Rowntree', *Journal of Social Policy*, vol. 15, no. 1

Wadsworth, M., 1986, 'Serious illness in childhood and its association with later life achievement' in R. G. Wilkinson, *Class and Health: Research and Longitudinal Data*, Tavistock

Walby, S., 1986, *Patriarchy at Work: Patriarchal and Capitalist Relations in Employment*, Polity Press

Waldron, I., 1976, 'Why do women live longer than men?', *Social Science and Medicine*, 10

Walker, A. and Townsend, P. (eds.), 1981, *Disability in Britain*, Martin Robertson

Wallerstein, Immanuel, 1974, 1980 and 1989, *The Modern World System*, 3 vols., Academic Press

Wallerstein, Immanuel, 1979, *The Capitalist World Economy*, Cambridge University Press

Wallerstein, Immanuel, 1984, *The Politics of the World Economy*, Cambridge University Press

Wallis, R., 1984, *The Elementary Forms of the New Religious Life,* Routledge and Kegan Paul

Warren, Bill, 1980, *Imperialism, Pioneer of Capitalism,* Verso

Warwick, D. P., 1983, 'On methodological integration in social research' in M. Bulmer and D. P. Warwick (eds.), *Social Research in Developing Countries,* Macmillan

Watson, Catherine and Hayter, Theresa, 1985, *Aid: Rhetoric and Reality,* Pluto Press

Weber, Max, 1904–5, *The Protestant Ethic and the Spirit of Capitalism,* translated by Talcott Parsons (George Allen and Unwin,1930)

Weber, Max, 1922, *Economy and Society,* (Bedminster Press, 1968)

Weber, Max, 1922–3, 'Class, status, party' in H. Gerth and C. Wright Mills, *From Max Weber: Essays in Sociology,* Oxford University Press, 1946

Weber, Max, 1904, 'Objectivity' in *On the Methodology of the Social Sciences,* translated by Edward Shils and Henry Finch, The Free Press, 1949

Weber, Max, 1958, *The City,* translated by Don Martindale and Gertrud Neuwirth, The Free Press

Westergaard, J. and Resler, H., 1976, *Class in a Capitalist Society,* Penguin

Whale, J., 1977, *The Politics of the Media,* Fontana

Whitehead, Margaret, 1987, *The Health Divide: Inequalities in Health in the 1980s,* Health Education Council

Whitely, P., 1983, *The Labour Party in Crisis,* Methuen

Whyte, W. H., 1951, *Pattern for Industrial Peace,* Harper and Row

Whyte, W. H., 1956, *The Organisation Man,* Doubleday Anchor Books

Wilding, P. (ed.), 1986, *In Defence of the Welfare State,* Manchester University Press

Wilensky, H., 1963, 'The uneven distribution of leisure: the impact of economic growth on free time' in E. Smigel (ed.), *Work and Leisure,* College and University Press

Willis, P., 1977, *Learning to Labour: How Working Class Kids Get Working Class Jobs,* Saxon House

Willis, P., 1990, *Common Culture: Symbolic Work at Play in the Everyday Culture of the Young,* Open University Press

Willmott, P. and Young, M., 1960, *Family and Class in a London Suburb,* Routledge and Kegan Paul

Willmott, P. and Young, M., 1973, *The Symmetrical Family,* Routledge and Kegan Paul

Wilson, B., 1966, *Religion in Secular Society,* Watts

Wilson, B., 1977a, 'How religious are we?', *New Society,* 27.10.77

Wilson, B., 1977b, *Religion in Secular Society,* Watts

Wilson, B., 1982, *Religion in Sociological Perspective,* Oxford University Press

Wilson, James and Herrnstein, R., 1985, *Crime and Human Nature,* Simon Schuster

Wilson, W. J., 1987, *The Truly Disadvantaged,* University of Chicago Press

Wirth, Louis, 1938, 'Urbanism as a way of life', *American Journal of Sociology,* 44

Wolfgang, M. E., 1958, *Patterns of Homicide,* Wiley

Wolpe, AnnMarie, 1988, *Within School Walls: The Role of Discipline, Sexuality and the Curriculum,* Routledge

Woodward, J., 1958, *Management and Technology,* HMSO

Wootton, B., 1959, *Social Science and Social Pathology,* Allen and Unwin

Wright, E. O., 1985, *Classes,* Verso

Wrong, Dennis, 1961, 'The oversocialised conception of man in modern sociology', *American Sociological Review,* vol. 26

Yinger, M., 1957, *Religion, Society and the Individual,* Macmillan

Yinger, M., 1981, 'Toward a theory of assimilation and dissimilation', *Ethnic and Racial Studies,* vol. 4, no. 3

Young, Jock, 1988a, 'The tasks of a realist criminologist', Contemporary Criminology, 2

Young, Jock, 1988b, *Realist Criminology*, Sage

Young, Jock, 1994, 'Incessant chatter: recent paradigms in criminology' in M. Maguire et al., *The Oxford Handbook of Criminology*, Clarendon Press

Young, J., 1971, 'The role of the police as amplifiers of deviance, negotiators of reality and translators of fantasy' in S. Cohen (ed.), *Images of Deviance*, Penguin

Young, M. F. D. (ed.), 1971, *Knowledge and Control*, Collier-Macmillan

Young, M. and Wilmott, P., 1957, *Family and Kinship in East London*, RKP

Zeitlin, Maurice, 1974, 'Corporate ownership and control: the large corporation and the capitalist class', *American Journal of Sociology*, vol. 79, no. 5

Zeitlin, Maurice, 1989, *The Large Corporation and Contemporary Classes*, Polity Press

Zelizer, V., 1985, *Pricing the Priceless Child*, Basic Books

Zweig, F., 1952, *The British Worker*, Pelican

Glossary

absolute poverty
state of poverty in which a person lacks the minimum needs to keep them alive and healthy (*contrast* relative poverty)

accumulation
term used within Marx's theory to describe the process by which the capitalist class gain profit which accumulates and so forms the basis of their wealth and therefore their power

aetiology
the study of the causes of an event or phenomenon (e.g. crime or illness)

ageism
prejudice or discrimination against an individual on the basis of age, on the assumption that particular age-groups are superior or inferior

agenda setters
people who decide what subjects the mass media will report or bring to the public's attention

agrarian society (culture)
society (or culture) based on agriculture (*contrast* urban society)

alienation
often used to describe the sense of meaninglessness, powerlessness, isolation and self-estrangement many individuals feel at work or at home. Used by Marx to describe the way that capitalism dehumanises people as a result of their abilities, and the products of their abilities, being taken over by the bourgeoisie

anomie
term used by Durkheim to mean a situation where the norms and values of a society are unclear and people feel unsure about the rules that should guide their behaviour. People are in effect without norms

authority
power in a society or social group which is accepted as legitimate (fair or just)

automation
production of industrial goods by self-controlling machines, with minimal human supervision

autonomy
power to act with free will, to govern your own actions

blue-collar worker
manual worker, whether skilled, semi-skilled, or unskilled (*contrast* white-collar worker)

bourgeoisie
owners of the means of production in capitalism (the capitalists) (*contrast* proletariat)

bureaucracy
type of organisation that is based on agreed and established rules and procedures. It is organised hierarchically and staffed by full-time, salaried officials (bureaucrats)

capitalism
organisation of society in such a way that the wealth and means of production are privately owned by capitalists, commodities are produced for profit through a market mechanism, and workers are free to sell their labour to the highest bidder (*contrast* feudalism, socialism)

cartel
combination of firms formed for certain explicit purposes, often to keep prices up and to kill off competition

caste system
hierarchical, stratified system, ranking individuals in society according to prestige, often on religious grounds. The status of individuals is ascribed at birth, not achieved, and social mobility is highly limited, with no intermarriage between castes

causation
occurs when one variable factor (the cause) – an event or state of affairs – is thought to produce another (the effect) (*see also* aetiology)

child benefit
in the UK, a benefit paid by the State to mothers (and occasionally fathers). The amount a mother receives is related to the number of children. This is a universal benefit and is not based on need

citizen
member of a nation-state, or political community, with rights and duties resulting from that membership

civil rights
freedoms and rights, guaranteed by law to all citizens of a given nation-state or political community

clan
kinship group wider than a family, found mostly in traditional, pre-industrial societies

class
no clear agreement in sociology, but most definitions refer to a group of people in the same or similar socio-economic circumstances, usually defined by occupation or relationship to the means of production. The socio-economic differences between social groups result in differences in wealth, power and life-chances

class consciousness
degree of awareness by a class of a class system, of their common economic interests, and of their capacity for collective political or industrial action

coercion
rule exercised by force or the threat of force

colonisation
process of conquering and ruling countries that is undertaken by another country; mostly associated with the establishment of colonies by European states in Africa, Asia and Latin America, in previous centuries

communism

political theory, associated with Marx and Engels, relating to a society where the means of production are held in common and separate classes do not exist, creating an egalitarian society without class conflict. Up to 1989–91, used to refer to Eastern Europe and the Soviet Union; today, to China, Vietnam, Cuba and other similar states

compensatory education

additional educational help given to socially disadvantaged groups to enable them to have equal educational opportunities

comprador

intermediary of a country through whom a foreign firm will trade to gain access to, and control of, a sector of the economy of that country

conformity

behaviour that follows the established norms and values of society, often as a result of group pressure to accept these norms (*contrast* deviance)

congenital illness

medical condition present from birth

conglomerate

business corporation which consists of different companies producing or trading in a range of products or services

consensus

agreement that exists in society concerning the values by which people live their lives and by which society is organised, leading to social stability

conservatives

people who desire slow, evolutionary change in society or, in some instances, no change, in order to conserve traditional institutions, relationships and behaviour

contradictory class locations

positions in the class structure which combine characteristics of class positions immediately above and below them; mostly applied to routine white-collar, lower professional and managerial workers

core

countries which have a central position in the world economy, mostly the highly industrialised countries (e.g. the USA, Western Europe and Japan) (*contrast* periphery, semi-periphery)

corporations

larger business companies

corporatism

originally associated with the ideas of Mussolini and fascism in Italy in the 1920s, but more often now a view of business organisation, prevalent in the 1970s, based on a partnership between leaders of employers' organisations, trade union leaders and government

correlation

the degree of a regular, statistical relationship between at least two variables, which can be measured; the correlation can be either positive or negative

critical theory

approach to the social sciences developed by the Frankfurt Institute in the 1930s and 1940s. It is an interdisciplinary theory drawing on the early work of Marx and the late work of Freud. It aims to criticise, as well as understand, society and is therefore opposed to positivism

cult

small religious grouping similar to a sect, emphasising private, individual experience rather than group fellowship, with individuals only loosely affiliated, and lacking any permanent structure

culture

mainly used in sociology to describe the shared norms and values, as well as the shared language, knowledge and material goods, of a society. As noted in chapter 2, however, it has many other meanings

decoding

understanding the symbolic meaning in something

democracy

political system in which citizens are able to choose their government through elections. It is characterised by freedom of movement, freedom of speech and freedom of the media, and the separation of the judiciary from the legislature and executive (*see also* participatory democracy and representative democracy; *contrast* dictatorship, oligarchy, totalitarianism)

demography

study of population and population trends

denomination

institutionalised religious body, with a significant number of members, but with less influence than the established church.

dependency theory

argument that post-colonial countries have been made more and not less dependent on their former colonial power, and so lack the ability to control major aspects of their economy. This dependency results from the domination of the world economy by industrialised countries in general, not just by the former colonial powers

deskilling

process described by the Marxist, Braverman, whereby a job loses its skill and becomes more simplified and routinised (e.g. a chef becomes a fast food worker as a result of the introduction of new technology)

determinism

theory that people have no choice in their behaviour, as their behaviour is caused by social forces beyond their control (*contrast* free will)

deviance

behaviour which departs from social norms and values held by the majority in a social group; its definition varies across time and cultures (*contrast* conformity)

deviancy amplification

process by which mass media coverage and exaggeration creates more crime or deviance

dictatorship

political system of rule in which power is concentrated in the hands of one person, or a small ruling group, over whom citizens have little or no control (*contrast* democracy, oligarchy, totalitarianism)

division of labour

the way that roles in society (e.g. at work and in the home) are divided so that they become far more differentiated and specialised, creating economic interdependence. It is more complex in industrial societies, and there is now a global or new international division of labour (NIDL), where parts of a commodity are made across the globe before final assembly

DSS

the Department of Social Security, in the UK a government department responsible for providing maintenance for those in a position of economic or social need

dual labour market

labour market which is split into primary (or core) and secondary (or peripheral) sectors

economic base

the economy and economic institutions which produce goods and services. Often characterised as the 'engine' of any society, it is of key importance, usually influencing many other aspects of social life. Marxists argue that class relations are determined here (*contrast* superstructure)

ecumenical movement

movement attempting to achieve greater unity between various Christian denominations

educational priority areas (EPAs)

in the UK, areas of significant social problems (e.g. poverty, unemployment) in which schools were given extra resources to help children overcome the disadvantages arising from such problems

egalitarian society

society in which everyone is treated as being equal (*contrast* meritocracy)

elaborated code

pattern of speech thought to characterise the complex structure of middle-class language. The term is mainly associated with the work of Basil Bernstein (*contrast* restricted code)

élite

minority group at the apex of society or a social group who have power and influence over others

emancipation

act of setting free from oppression of some kind

embourgeoisement

theory that, as capitalism expands, the working class adopt the norms and values of the middle class as their wages and living standards improve

empiricism

empirical investigation is based on evidence collected in the physical or social world; empiricism claims that all knowledge is based on such evidence (*contrast* metaphysics)

endogamy

system or marriage in which individuals can only marry those from within the same kinship group (*contrast* exogamy)

entrepreneur

someone who takes risks in developing a new market in a capitalist economy

ethnicity

the properties of people who share a similar culture, particularly language, customs, religion and history, that is distinct from that of other groups in society. The existence of different ethnic groups is often associated with variations in power, wealth and life-chances (*contrast* race)

ethnocentricity

occurs when a cultural group uses its own value system to try to understand the culture of a different group, often resulting in the devaluing and misrepresentation of the 'other' culture

ethnography

the case-study method applied to the study of groups or communities, examining the rules by which social reality is constructed

ethnomethodology

sociological perspective that investigates the rules concerning how people create and sustain meanings in everyday life

evangelicalism

form of Christianity based on a fundamentalist belief in the Bible and on the need to actively preach the Gospel

executive

those people, such as civil servants, charged with the administration of laws (*contrast* judiciary, legislature)

exogamy

system of marriage in which individuals can only marry those from outside their kinship group (*contrast* endogamy)

extended family

a family is vertically extended if it contains at least three generations (e.g. grandparents, parents, children), usually living under the same roof. Cousins, uncles, aunts form a horizontally extended family. The nuclear family is at the core of any extended family (*see also* nuclear family)

false consciousness

Marxist term meaning that the workers fail to see the true nature of their exploitation, or their real interests, owing to the power of bourgeois ideology

family credit

in the UK, a benefit paid by the State to those families deemed to be on low pay. The idea is to encourage people to work by supplementing low incomes

feminism

theory, dating from the late eighteenth century, based on the observation that women are systematically disadvantaged in society, and that women have the right to equality with men in all spheres of life

feudalism

system of production based on the ownership of land. The key relationship is that between landlord and serf, who is effectively owned by the landlord and has no rights. Feudalism preceded capitalism in Western Europe (*contrast* capitalism, socialism)

First World

collective name given to the economically developed capitalist world in Europe, North America, parts of Asia and Australasia, particularly the countries belonging to the OECD (Organisation for Economic Co-operation and Development) (*contrast* Second World, Third World)

folk devils

concept developed by the interactionist sociologist Stan Cohen. It refers to groups in society who are identified as being different from the mainstream and then demonised as deviant and as posing an imagined or exaggerated threat to society

Fordism

system of mass production on assembly lines, developed by Henry Ford, undertaken in large factories, with work-tasks increasingly simplified

free will

theory that people have choice over their behaviour and are able to resist external influences (*contrast* determinism)

functionalism

sociological perspective which emphasises the functional importance of institutions in society, and their role in maintaining a value consensus which leads to continuity in that society

fundamentalism

belief in the need to keep to, or return to, the original meaning of religious texts, particularly associated today with interpretations of Christianity and Islam

gate-keeping

process by which the mass media refuse to cover those issues and values seen to be outside the mainstream consensus

gender

culturally learnt aspect of a person's sexual identity. People are biologically female or male, but their behaviour is either feminine or masculine as defined by the social expectations of their society. In this way, behavioural differences between men and women are culturally created

generalised other

social group within which we are socialised, where the individual takes in the values of a given group or society; associated with G H Mead

glass ceiling

invisible barrier which prevents people from breaking through to top jobs, frequently used in sociology in relation to female inequalities

global city

city which is an organising centre of the new global economy (e.g. London, New York, Tokyo)

globalisation

theory that the development of social, cultural and economic relationships on a world scale has created a single social order or world system, in which many aspects of an individual's social life are affected by organisations and developments located thousands of miles away (e.g. investment decisions, pollution, the mass media, production and cultural patterns)

hegemony

intellectual leadership, and ideological and political dominance. Concept used by Antonio Gramsci to explain the continued rule of the ruling class with the support of the working class. He believed that this leadership can and should be challenged, both politically and through the institutions of civil society

heterogeneous group

group that is mixed, rather than uniform, in composition (*contrast* homogeneous group)

hidden curriculum

the 'unstated agenda' involved in school organisation and teachers' attitudes which develops behaviour and beliefs that are not part of the formal timetable (e.g. beliefs about gender, ethnic or class differences), and which some sociologists argue forms the main way that schools socialise their pupils

hidden economy

informal economy where people do jobs for others and may get paid 'cash in hand'. Such people do not pay income tax or national insurance contributions and will not show up on government statistics as employed. Indeed, they may show up on the unemployment register as without work

historical materialism

theory that historical change is determined by material and economic factors, particularly changes in modes of production. This concept was applied by Marx to envisage social change being brought about in a scientific and informed way

homogeneous group

group that is uniform, rather than mixed, in composition (*contrast* heterogeneous group)

hypothesis

idea or guess about an event or phenomenon, which then has to be tested by conducting empirical research and collecting evidence to prove or disprove the original idea

ideal type

Weber's notion that abstract models (such as perfect competition or bureaucracy) could be used to make comparisons with the real world

ideological State apparatus

term used by the French Marxist Louis Althusser to describe those parts of the superstructure (such as religion, the media, the family or education) which maintain class control through consent rather than coercion

ideology

first used by Destutt de Tracey in the eighteenth century, the term meant the science of ideas. It has also come to be used in a pejorative sense to mean false or mistaken ideas imposed by one group on another to maintain their advantaged position in society, for example bourgeois, racial or patriarchal ideologies. These shared beliefs, seeming to justify the interests of dominant groups, are to be found in all societies where systematic inequalities exist between social groups, and are thus closely related to power. The term is now used with both meanings

imperialism

policy of making or maintaining an empire under the control of one country, formally or informally, particularly associated with the period of European colonisation of Africa and Asia in the nineteenth century and with economic and political control by great powers in the twentieth century

indigenous population

natural, home-based population of a community or state

indoctrination

instruction in a doctrine that gives little or no choice of alternative beliefs

induction

process of drawing general conclusions from the collection of particular facts or observations

industrial democracy

a way of organising a firm or industry whereby the employees have some participation or representation in some of the decision-making processes of that firm or industry (contrast workers' control)

intelligence

a particularly controversial term in sociology. Hans Eysenck defined intelligence as abstract reasoning ability, measurable through intelligence tests. It is often thought to be innate

interest groups

groups formed to advance their own interests, particularly in politics, by lobbying or pressurising members of the public and, especially, members of legislative and executive bodies (see also pressure groups)

intergenerational mobility

social mobility from one generation to the next; it can be vertical (up or down) or lateral within a social stratification hierarchy, and can be short-range or long-range (contrast intragenerational mobility)

interpretive sociology

another term for phenomenology, which emphasises the role played by actors in interpreting their social situation

intragenerational mobility

social mobility during an individual's working life; it can be vertical (up or down) or lateral within a social stratification hierarchy, and can be short-range or long-range (contrast intergenerational mobility)

judiciary

collective noun for judges and magistrates (contrast executive, legislature)

kinship

central to the study of anthropology, the study of kinship examines the relationship of biological connections, such as blood ties, marriage or adoption, to other forms of rights and obligations in society. In modern societies kinship involves few social obligations, but it plays a vital role in the social life of more traditional societies

labelling

the way that people place labels on others, often based on stereotypes. It is particularly associated with the study of education and deviance, with individuals becoming failures or deviants because of the label attached to their behaviour by those in authority

latent function

unintended action of a social institution (e.g. the way a religious ceremony can unite a group), a term used by functionalists (contrast manifest function)

legislature

body which makes formal laws in a society (e.g. parliament) (contrast executive, judiciary)

legitimacy

term used to describe the sanctioning by society of institutions, actions and ideas, and the belief that a particular political, social or economic order is just and valid. Social and political changes can produce legitimacy crises

less-developed country (LDC)

country with no or relatively little industrial production, usually in Africa, Asia or Latin America. Such countries are sometimes referred to as Third World or underdeveloped countries, to distinguish them from the industrialised First and Second World countries

liberation

setting free or releasing of a group from social injustice, subordination, prejudice or abuse

liberation theology

Christian doctrine, mixing elements of Marxism and Catholicism, which supports the poor in their struggles for equality and freedom; particularly associated with Latin America. It is disowned by the official Catholic Church

longitudinal research

research which is replicated over a period of time to find out how much change is taking place in a society or smaller group

macro-sociology

study of social systems, large social groups or organisations; usually associated with functionalist or conflict theory sociologists (contrast micro-sociology)

manifest function

intended action of a social institution (e.g. a religious ceremony as an act of collective worship), a term used by functionalists (contrast latent function)

marginalised group
group that is pushed onto the periphery, or edge, of society

Marxism
sociological perspective based on the writings of Karl Marx, in particular his division of society into economic base and superstructure, and the analysis of class conflict as the main source of social change

mass media
forms of communication designed for the consumption of mass audiences (e.g. newspapers, magazines, radio, television, cinema)

matriarchy
domination by women over men in all important aspects of society – economic, social, political and cultural. Such power and authority held by women is found in very few societies (*contrast* patriarchy)

means of production
means by which material production is organised in a society. It includes the key resources for providing society's goods (e.g. land, factories), the technological aspects (e.g. tools, techniques) *and* the social relations between the producers

meritocracy
society in which individuals achieve educational qualifications, and their consequent position in the stratification system, on the basis of merit, talent, skills, ability and achievement (*contrast* egalitarian society)

metaphysics
knowledge of the world beyond or prior to sensory experience (*contrast* empiricism)

micro-sociology
study of small-scale aspects of human behaviour, often of one-to-one interactions; usually associated with interpretivist sociologists (*contrast* macro-sociology)

middle class
non-manual workers, from professionals to routine clerical staff, often referred to as white-collar workers

military industrial complex
personal and institutional connections between business firms, the armed forces and government, based on common beliefs and interests in weapons production; originally used in relation to the USA

millenarianism
beliefs associated with certain types of religious movements, according to which disasters and cataclysmic changes will happen soon to usher in a new epoch or beginning

mode of production
specific forces and relations of production that determine the character of a historical period (e.g. feudalism, capitalism)

monocausality
theory that there is only one cause for any phenomenon

monogamy
situation in which a man and woman have only one partner at any one time. Serial monogamy describes a succession of monogamous relationships (*contrast* polygamy)

monopoly capitalism
Marxist term to describe the situation that occurs in mature capitalism where firms become larger due to take-over and can control the market, for example through cartels

moral panic
wave of public concern about a social activity or group, which becomes seen as a threat to the common values or interests of society as a result of exaggerated, stereotypical and sensationalised coverage by the mass media or politicians

morbidity rate
degree or incidence of illness and disease in a society or social group

mortality rate
degree or incidence of death in a society or social group

nation-state
particular type of state, especially associated with modern societies, in which a government has sovereign power over a specific territory, and where the population (or citizens) think of themselves as belonging to that nation; closely associated with the rise of nationalism

nationalism
set of political and cultural beliefs and symbols expressing a sense of identity for a particular national community, a community that does not necessarily conform to the boundaries of an existing nation-state. Taken to extremes, it results in aggression towards other nations and in hatred of foreigners

neo-imperialism
economic domination of some nations over others resulting from inequalities of economic exchange; usually the dominance of developed countries over less-developed countries, and often, but not exclusively, replacing the former direct political rule during imperialism or colonialism

newly industrialising country (NIC)
a less-developed country which, in recent times, has undergone extensive and rapid industrial expansion (e.g. South Korea, Hong Kong, Singapore)

norms
expected patterns of rules and social behaviour which specify appropriate conduct in different social contexts, either prescribing or forbidding this conduct; enforced by sanctions, either positive (rewards) or negative (punishment)

nuclear family
family group consisting of two generations (parents and at least one child) living in the same household. A tendency in modern societies is for the nuclear family to become privatised, i.e. becoming isolated and separated from wider kin and society, with members spending time together in home-centred activities (*see also* extended family)

objectivity
investigation of behaviour free from the personal opinion or prejudice of the investigator, associated with the natural sciences. Sociologists attempt to achieve objectivity by trying to reduce or eliminate bias in their interpretation of data, and making their findings open to critical assessment (*contrast* subjectivity)

oligarchy
rule by a small group of people (*contrast* democracy, dictatorship, totalitarianism)

organised crime
crime committed by criminal organisations which operate on normal business lines

paradigm
conceptual framework against which other theories are compared

participant observation
research method whereby the researcher joins and takes part in the activities of the group they are observing. Their identity may be disclosed to the other members of the group (overt) or may be undisclosed (covert); this is often referred to as fieldwork

participatory democracy
system of democracy in which all members of a society or social group participate directly and collectively in the decision-making processes, and in putting decisions into effect (*contrast* representative democracy)

particularistic values
values which judge people on the basis of ascribed status (e.g. parents thinking that their own children are unique and special) (*contrast* universalistic values)

partisan alignment
voting according to self-identification as a member of a class; where this identification begins to weaken, the term 'partisan realignment' is used

party
according to Weber, the political aspect of stratification, the other two aspects being economic (class) and social (status); operating via organised political parties

paternalism
power resting with the father or a situation where the effect is simulated, as in industry where management may take on the role of father, directing the workers as if they are children

patriarchy
domination by men over women in all aspects of society – economic, social, political and cultural. Most societies are patriarchal, though there are some exceptions. The women's movement has attempted to alter the existing patriarchal institutions in society (*contrast* matriarchy)

peasants
people producing food from the land (including small-scale owners of land and agricultural labourers) using traditional farming methods, particularly in feudal societies

peer group
friendship group, composed of individuals sharing similar age and social status, with whom an individual mixes socially

periphery
countries which play only a marginal role in the world economy, for example less-developed countries that are dependent on the developed, or core, industrial economies (*contrast* core, semi-periphery)

perspective
set of ideas, or viewpoint, which helps you to explain the world

phenomenology
see interpretative sociology

pluralism
ownership, power and influence diffused between a multiplicity of competing groups, for example in politics or the media. Pluralist theories of democracy are based on this view of a plural society containing many different groups

polarisation
Marxist term describing the process whereby the two major classes, capitalist and proletariat, are expected to split further apart – the rich capitalist class getting richer and the working class getting relatively poorer. The workers themselves may have a better lifestyle, but their collective position will become poorer in relation to the wealth of the capitalist class

polygamy
form of marriage in which an individual can have two or more partners (spouses) at the same time. The most frequent form of polygamy is a man with two or more wives, but there are a few societies in which polyandry exists (a woman having two or more husbands) (*contrast* monogamy)

positivism
view that the methods of natural science can be used with equal effect in social science, as they share a common logical framework

post-feminism
assumption that both the theory and practice of feminism have ceased to be useful as most of women's demands have been met. The term 'woman' is seen as having no single meaning as women's identity has become increasingly fragmented (e.g. black women, lesbian women, working-class women). There is agreement with post-modernism that large-scale theorising is no longer valid

post-Fordism
argument that the era of mass production has ended as a consequence of deregulated capitalism, which now prefers flexible production of small, specialised batches of items by small groups of unorganised, often temporary, employees

post-industrialism
theory that suggests modern society is in transition, no longer being primarily based on manufacturing but moving into a phase of development beyond the industrial production era, where, for instance, knowledge, information and services will be of prime importance

post-modernism
theory that modern social development is more than just the end of the era of industrialism, but rather a complete break with the concept of 'modernity' (institutions and modes of life based on the ideas of a shape to history, the concept of continuing progress etc.). Post-modernity instead sees the 'end of history' (with no overall concepts of history making any sense), rejects the idea of 'progress' (whether in history, science or society as a whole), and sees the creation of a highly pluralistic society with individuals possessing a multiplicity of identities

post-structuralism
theory that rejects the idea of a unified sociological paradigm, and is critical of all theories because they all contain the subjective element of the observer. Consequently, sociology (and other sciences) must accept a wide variety of perspectives as inevitable

power
ability of individuals or social groups to exert their will over others, and to ensure decisions taken reflect their own interests; hence societies often contain conflicts over power, and unequal access to resources

pressure groups
groups formed to put pressure on powerful organisations and those in power to implement the policies they favour. They may be sectional, promoting a sector (e.g. the elderly), or promotional, representing a cause (e.g. the abolition of smoking). Pressure groups have been increasingly studied with the development of pluralist theory (*see also* interest groups)

primary labour market
area of the economy with secure, well-paid, usually full-time, jobs (*contrast* secondary labour market)

primary sector
part of a modern society's economy based on the gathering or extraction of natural or raw materials (e.g. farming, mining, fishing) (*contrast* secondary sector, tertiary sector)

private health care
health-care services which are only available to those who are able to pay the full cost of them

progressive taxation
form of taxation where the rate of taxation increases with income, so that the highest earners pay the highest rate (*contrast* regressive taxation)

proletariat
subject class in capitalism. This group (the industrial working class) are exploited by the bourgeoisie and are defined as having only their labour power to sell to the highest bidder (*contrast* bourgeoisie; *see also* working class)

psephology
sociological and statistical study of voting behaviour and trends

qualitative research
research methods that replace data, such as statistics, with a depth study of people's meanings and understandings that is non-statistical and therefore not capable of generalisation (*contrast* quantitative research)

quantitative research
use of methods that generate statistical data that can be compared and contrasted (*contrast* qualitative research)

race
category which includes a large number of individuals having physical or biological characteristics different from other human groups or categories; now felt to be a scientifically dubious and politically dangerous concept (*contrast* ethnicity)

racism
belief and/or behaviour based on the assumption that a social group is inferior/superior on the grounds of racial or ethnic origin (defined by reference to certain inherited physical or biological characteristics). Often used to justify political and material inequalities

rational thinking
way of thought based on scientific thinking and logic

rational–legal authority
type of authority structure based on an agreed set of rules and procedures, which are seen as fair and impartial

rationalisation
according to Weber, the process by which all parts of society become increasingly subject to precise calculation, measurement, organisation and control

regressive taxation
form of taxation which takes a decreasing proportion of income as the amount earned rises (*contrast* progressive taxation)

relations of production
social relationships that characterise a particular mode of production and involve ownership/non-ownership of the means of production (e.g. between peasants and landlords in feudalism, or bourgeoisie and proletariat in capitalism)

relative poverty
poverty that is seen in relation to the standard of living of the majority of people in any one society at any one time (*contrast* absolute poverty)

representative democracy
system of democracy in which all members of a social group participate indirectly and individually in the decision-making processes by electing political leaders to represent their views and interests (*contrast* participatory democracy)

reserve army of labour
workers that can be moved in and out of the labour force. In the case of women, they may be encouraged or coerced to become carers and housewives at home, where they form a reserve army of labour until required for paid employment. Also used in relation to ethnic minorities and immigrants

restricted code
according to Bernstein, the language spoken by working-class people, in which meaning is dependent on context, is often implicit, and in which sentence structure is not developed (*contrast* elaborated code)

ruling class
Marxist term describing the group who own the means of production and exploit the subordinate classes. In a capitalist society this is the bourgeoisie

sampling
selection, in a scientific and systematic way, of a representative group of individuals or cases from a larger survey population; in sociology, the sample is often given a questionnaire, or is interviewed

scape-goating
blaming an individual or social group for a problem or situation which they are not responsible for

Second World
almost defunct term, used to describe the industrialised, former communist Soviet Union and the Soviet-aligned or communist countries of the world. (*contrast* First World, Third World)

secondary labour market
area of the economy with insecure, low-paid, usually part-time jobs, with poor conditions of work (*contrast* primary labour market)

secondary sector
the part of a modern society's economy based on the production of manufactured goods (*contrast* primary sector, tertiary sector)

sect
religious group or movement which has broken away from a more orthodox mainstream religious denomination, or represents an entirely new religious formation

secularisation
term generally used to describe the process by which a society loses its religious orientation and values, with religion thus losing its social significance and influence. This is thought to be true of modern societies, but it is difficult to quantify

self-fulfilling prophecy
situation in which people act in accordance with predictions made by people in authority about their likely behaviour or performance; associated with labelling theory in the study of education and deviance

semi-periphery
term used to describe a country which supplies sources of labour and/or raw materials to the core industrial economies of the world, but which is not itself fully industrialised, or is in the process of being industrialised (*contrast* core, periphery)

semiotics
study of how non-verbal phenomena can have important cultural meanings (e.g. styles of clothing)

sexism
belief and/or behaviour based on the assumption that a gender group as a whole is inferior/superior on the grounds of differences in capacities and abilities. As with racism, often used to justify inequalities in society

social action
interaction of people, or actors, with each other in social situations

social construction
term derived from action theory describing the process by which social roles are produced through interaction and negotiation between actors

social facts
term used by Emile Durkheim to describe the external phenomena constraining an individual's behaviour, for example formal laws

social mobility
movement of individuals or groups in a social hierarchy of stratification. Movement between social positions can be vertical (up or down) or horizontal (lateral) (*see also* intergenerational mobility, intragenerational mobility)

social self
combination of the inner self with the reflected self, emerging through interaction with others. According to G H Mead, this combination is the basis of self-consciousness in human individuals, the individual achieving self-consciousness by becoming aware of their social identity

social stratification
division of society into a hierarchy of unequal social groups who have differential access to material goods and power (e.g. groups defined by class, gender, age and ethnicity)

socialisation

social process by which people learn norms and values and a distinct sense of self; mainly takes place during childhood, but continues throughout life via various agencies of society (e.g. educational system, mass media)

socialism

political philosophy which stresses the co-operative nature of modern industrial production, and the need to achieve an egalitarian community. For Marxists, it is a transitionary phase on the path to communism, where the means of production are socially owned and production is planned (*contrast* capitalism, feudalism)

sovereignty

undisputed, or claimed, political rule of a state over a given territory

State

political apparatus of any society (including the legislature, judiciary, executive, police and armed forces) ruling over a given territory, and with authority backed by law and force. Virtually absent in traditional hunting and food-gathering societies

stereotype

fixed, general, over-simplified image of what an individual or group is like, allowing for few differences between members of the same group, and often stated in an over-simplified or even erroneous way

structuralism

theoretical approach, originating in the study of language (Ferdinand de Saussure), which concentrates on attempting to identify and analyse structures in social and cultural systems

subculture

culture within a culture, with some norms and values exclusive to it and distinct from those of the majority in a society. Though a subgroup's culture will be different in many ways from the main culture, there will also be some aspects of culture that they share

subjectivity

investigation of behaviour which involves the researcher allowing their own experiences and opinions to affect their research (*contrast* objectivity)

subordination

the keeping of an individual or group in an exploited or disadvantaged situation

suburbanisation

development of suburbs, or areas of housing, outside the inner-city area

superstructure

system of structures and ideas that are formed to fit in with the needs of the economy, and to ensure the continuity of a given society (*contrast* economic base)

surplus value

in Marxist theory, the value of an individual's labour power which is 'left over' when an employer has repaid the costs involved in employing the worker, i.e. the profit that is made by paying an individual for fewer hours than the economic value of the hours actually worked

symbolic interactionism

theoretical approach and sociological perspective, developed by G.H. Mead, that emphasises motives and meaning for individuals. It focuses on the importance of symbols for people, particularly language, as the core elements of all human interaction

symmetrical family

family in which the conjugal roles of husband and wife have become more alike and equal

Taylorism

practice of the ideas of F.W. Taylor and his theory of scientific management, whereby the labour process is broken up into its simplest parts (involving simple co-ordination operations in industry), and management controls the pace of work

technological determinism

idea that technological developments direct, in a causal way, developments in industry, the economy and the wider society

tertiary sector

the part of a modern society's economy based on the provision of services (*contrast* primary sector, secondary sector)

time–space convergence

process by which distances become 'shortened' as a result of improvements in transport and communication systems, especially as an aspect of globalisation

Third World

former colonial countries of Africa, Asia, Central and South America and Australasia, based mainly in the southern hemisphere. They are characterised as being less developed than countries of the First World or Second World, with industrial production either virtually non-existent, or only developed to a limited degree. Usually referred to now as developing, or less-developed countries (LDCs); the majority of the world's population live in such countries (*contrast* First World, Second World)

totalitarianism

form of government in which everything is under the political control of the State, and opposition is not tolerated; ordinary people lack any control over the decisions of government, which is in the hands of a small group of people, or even an individual (*contrast* democracy, dictatorship, oligarchy)

totemism

system of religious belief which ascribes special and holy significance to particular objects, animals or plants

trade union

employees' organisation formed to protect pay, conditions and rights at work

transitional classes

Marxist term used to describe classes from one type of society which have not yet disappeared from a new type of society (e.g. peasants still existing in a capitalist economy)

transnational corporations (TNCs)

business corporations based in two or more countries; these can be divided into ethnocentric TNCs (largely administered from the headquarters of the parent company), geocentric TNCs (being administered globally rather than from any particular country), or polycentric TNCs (administered from two or more centres in different countries)

underclass

lowest social class, beneath and detached from the working class. This term is rejected by many Marxists, who see this group as merely the most exploited section of the working class. Usually used in relation to ethnic minorities, immigrants, the long-term poor and unemployed, and female single parents

unemployment benefit

in the UK, benefit paid by the State to people who are out of work and qualify for payment of the benefit

universalistic values

values which base the judgement of individuals on meritocratic criteria (e.g. you get a job on the basis of qualifications and suitability) (*contrast* particularistic values)

upper class

social class based on inherited wealth and/or the ownership of large businesses and/or holdings of stocks and shares

urban society (culture)

society (or culture) based on industry, in which towns and cities predominate (*contrast* agrarian society)

urbanisation

development of towns and cities to become major centres of population as people move from rural to urban areas. De-urbanisation is the movement of populations from urban to rural areas

values

beliefs and goals held to be important in a society

victimless crime

activity which is defined as criminal, but which only involves an individual (e.g. drug-taking) or has no obvious victim (e.g. bribery, illegal gambling)

wealth

money, and/or property and other fixed assets, held by an individual or social group, which can be sold for the benefit of the owner(s)

Welfare State

arm of the State that deals with the welfare of people through providing education, health care, housing, and support in times of want (such as unemployment). It has been described as the commitment by the State to care for its citizens 'from the cradle to the grave'

white-collar crime

criminal activity committed by those in white-collar or professional jobs, often while performing their job

white-collar worker

non-manual worker, though this term is increasingly used to describe those whose work is non-professional and non-managerial (e.g. clerical or other office work) (*contrast* blue-collar worker)

work

activity by which humans produce from the natural world in order to survive. In traditional societies, money payments for such activities are rare, but in modern societies, such production of goods or services usually receives a wage or salary; however, that performed (mostly by women) in the home (housework) remains unpaid

workers' control

a way of organising a firm whereby the employees make all the major business decisions affecting that firm (*contrast* industrial democracy)

working class

social class comprising those workers who earn their income through manual labour, often referred to as blue-collar workers. In Marxist theory, comprises all people who sell their labour (the proletariat), predominantly blue-collar workers in Marx's lifetime (*see also* proletariat)

World Systems Theory

theoretical approach, particularly associated with I. Wallerstein, which analyses the development of societies in relation to a global economic system; it has much in common with globalisation theories in general

Index

Where there is more than one location reference for a heading, any major reference is printed in **bold**. Glossary references are indicated by 'G'.